HEY THERE, GANG! DEADPOOL HERE--EMPHASIS ON THE **DEAD!** BUT NONE OF THAT REALLY MATTERS HERE, BECAUSE THIS BOOK ISN'T ALL ABOUT ME (HARD TO BELIEVE, I KNOW), IT'S ABOUT MY LOVELY WIFE--

Mrs. DEADPOOL
AND THE
HOWLING COMMANDOS

WRITTEN BY
GERRY DUGGAN

WITH ART BY
SALVA ESPIN

COLORED BY
VAL STAPLES
LETTERED BY
VC'S JOE SABINO
AND FEATURING
COVER ART FROM
**REILLY BROWN &
JIM CHARALAMPIDIS**

EDITED BY
JORDAN D. WHITE
WITH ASSISTANT EDITOR
HEATHER ANTOS

I, DEADPOOL, WAS BRILLIANTLY CREATED BY ROB LIEFELD & FABIAN NICIEZA, AND THOSE HOWLING COMMANDOS WERE CREATED BY STAN LEE & JACK KIRBY.

GHOST DEADPOOL BY
IRENE LEE

COLLECTION EDITOR: JENNIFER GRUNWALD
ASSOCIATE EDITOR: SARAH BRUNSTAD
ASSOCIATE MANAGING EDITOR: ALEX STARBUCK
EDITOR, SPECIAL PROJECTS: MARK D. BEAZLEY
VP, PRODUCTION & SPECIAL PROJECTS: JEFF YOUNGQUIST
SVP PRINT, SALES & MARKETING: DAVID GABRIEL
BOOK DESIGNER: ADAM DEL RE

EDITOR IN CHIEF: AXEL ALONSO
CHIEF CREATIVE OFFICER: JOE QUESADA
PUBLISHER: DAN BUCKLEY
EXECUTIVE PRODUCER: ALAN FINE

MRS. DEADPOOL AND THE HOWLING COMMANDOS. Contains material originally published in magazine form as MRS. DEADPOOL AND THE HOWLING COMMANDOS #1-4 and WEREWOLF BY NIGHT #1. First printing 2016. ISBN# 978-0-7851-9880-2. Published by MARVEL WORLDWIDE, INC., a subsidiary of MARVEL ENTERTAINMENT, LLC. OFFICE OF PUBLICATION: 135 West 50th Street, New York, NY 10020. Copyright © 2016 MARVEL. No similarity between any of the names, characters, persons, and/or institutions in this magazine with those of any living or dead person or institution is intended, and any such similarity which may exist is purely coincidental. Printed in Canada. ALAN FINE, President, Marvel Entertainment; DAN BUCKLEY, President, TV, Publishing & Brand Management; JOE QUESADA, Chief Creative Officer; TOM BREVOORT, SVP of Publishing; DAVID BOGART, SVP of Business Affairs & Operations, Publishing & Partnership; C.B. CEBULSKI, VP of Brand Management & Development, Asia; DAVID GABRIEL, SVP of Sales & Marketing, Publishing; JEFF YOUNGQUIST, VP of Production & Special Projects; DAN CARR, Executive Director of Publishing Technology; ALEX MORALES, Director of Publishing Operations; SUSAN CRESPI, Production Manager; STAN LEE, Chairman Emeritus. For information regarding advertising in Marvel Comics or on Marvel.com, please contact Vit DeBellis, Integrated Sales Manager, at vdebellis@marvel.com. For Marvel subscription inquiries, please call 888-511-5480. Manufactured between 2/19/2016 and 3/28/2016 by SOLISCO PRINTERS, SCOTT, QC, CANADA.

10 9 8 7 6 5 4 3 2 1

MRS. DEADPOOL AND THE HOWLING COMMANDOS #1 VARIANT BY
ADAM WARREN & GURU-eFX

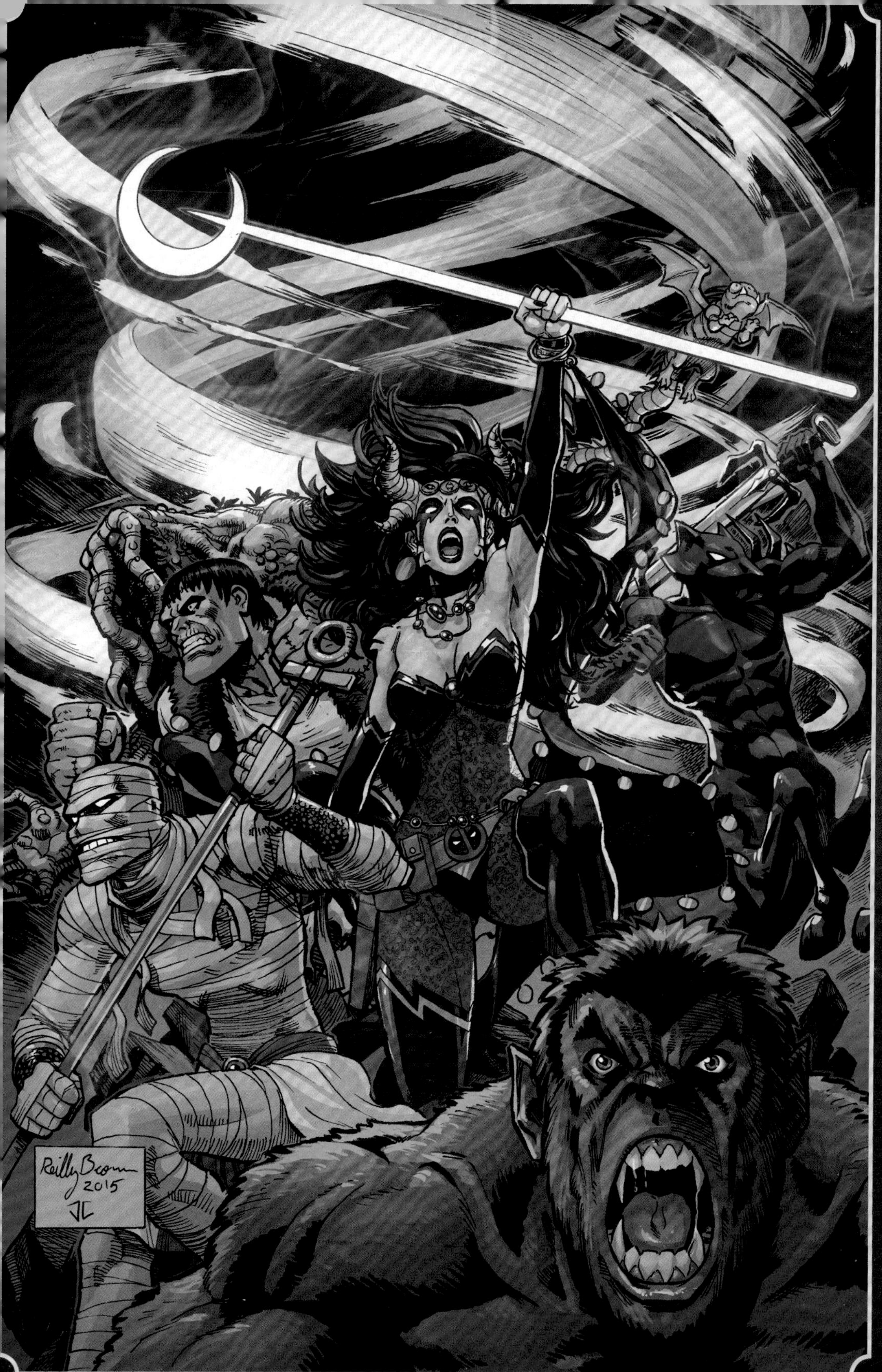
Reilly Brown
2015
JC

SECRET WARS

THE MULTIVERSE WAS DESTROYED!

·

THE HEROES OF EARTH-616 AND EARTH-1610
WERE POWERLESS TO SAVE IT!

·

NOW, ALL THAT REMAINS...IS **BATTLEWORLD**!

·

A MASSIVE, PATCHWORK PLANET COMPOSED OF THE FRAGMENTS OF
WORLDS THAT NO LONGER EXIST, MAINTAINED BY THE IRON WILL OF ITS
GOD AND MASTER, VICTOR VON DOOM!

·

EACH REGION IS A DOMAIN UNTO ITSELF!

R.I.P.
WADE WILSON
A.K.A. DEADPOOL

Blah, blah, blah....
more importantly
DEADPOOL DIED!

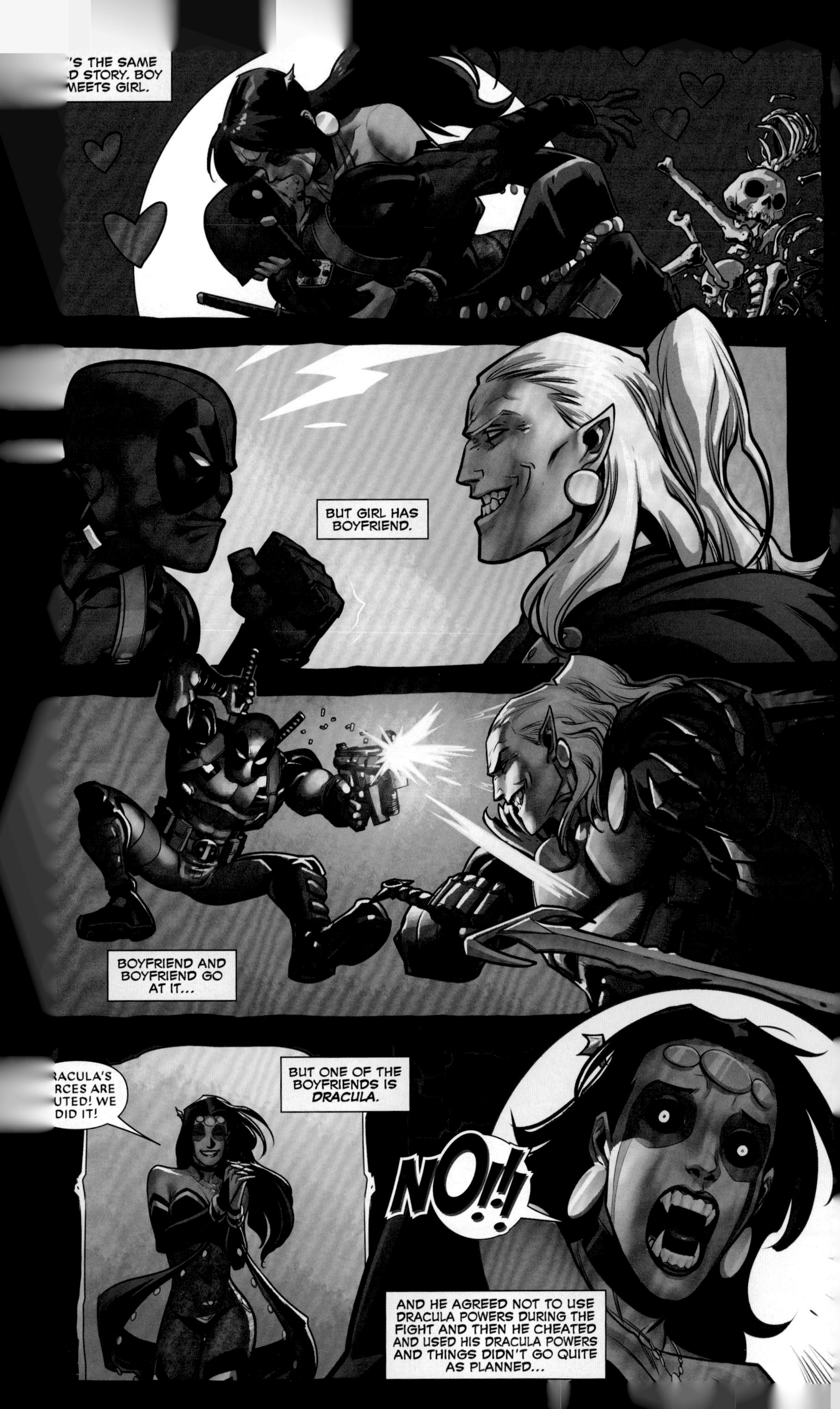
'S THE SAME D STORY. BOY MEETS GIRL.
BUT GIRL HAS BOYFRIEND.
BOYFRIEND AND BOYFRIEND GO AT IT...
RACULA'S RCES ARE UTED! WE DID IT!
BUT ONE OF THE BOYFRIENDS IS *DRACULA*.
NO!!
AND HE AGREED NOT TO USE DRACULA POWERS DURING THE FIGHT AND THEN HE CHEATED AND USED HIS DRACULA POWERS AND THINGS DIDN'T GO QUITE AS PLANNED...

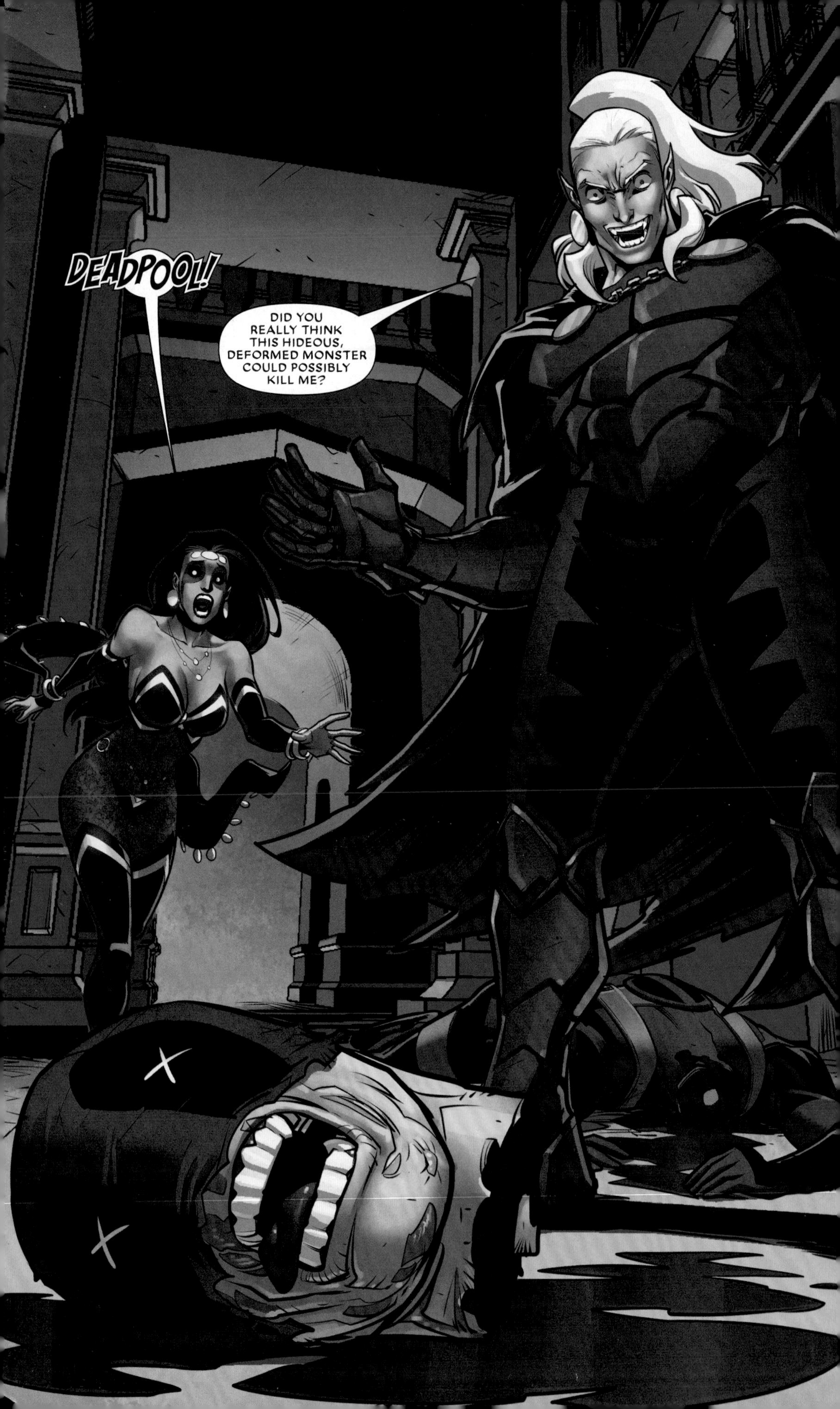
DEADPOOL!
DID YOU REALLY THINK THIS HIDEOUS, DEFORMED MONSTER COULD POSSIBLY KILL ME?

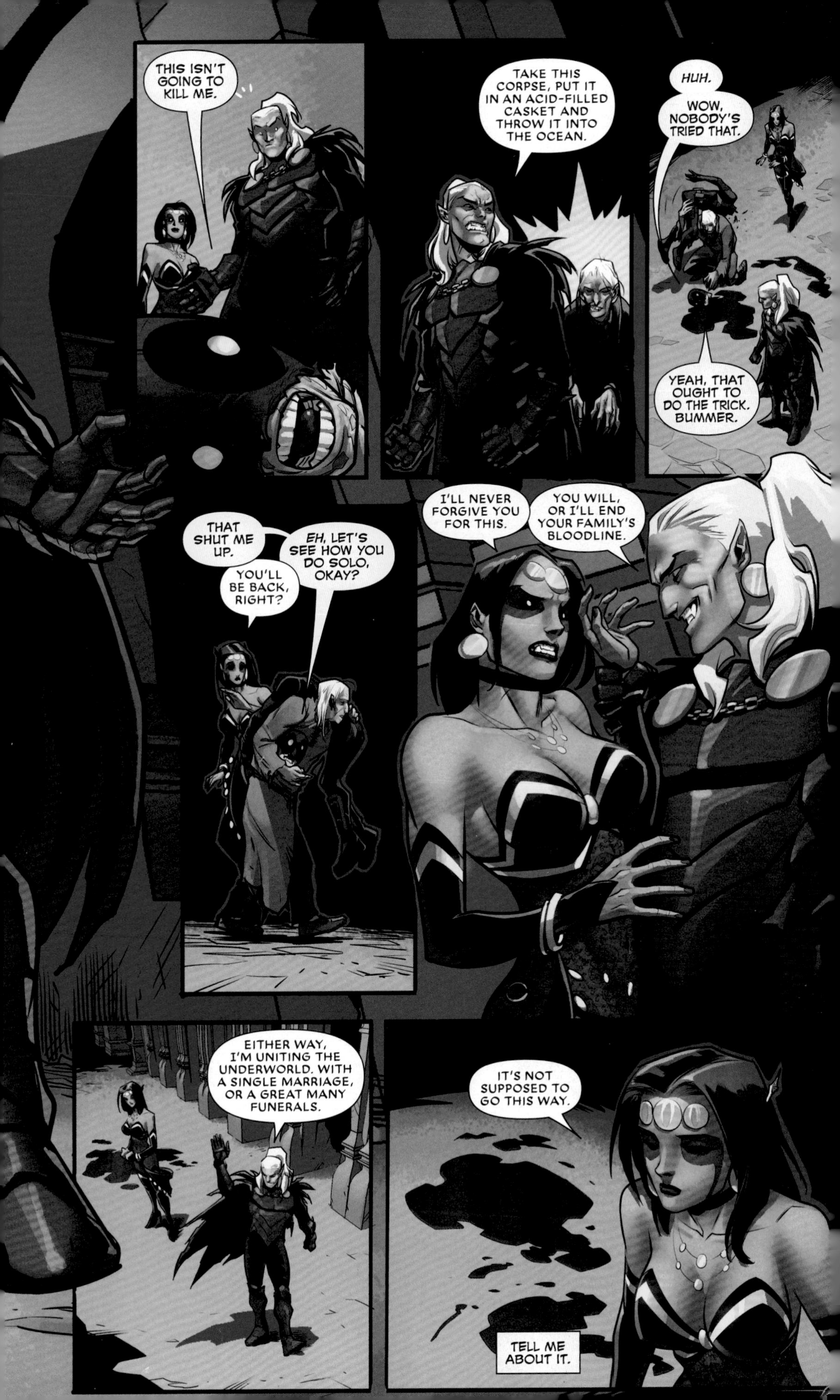

THIS ISN'T GOING TO KILL ME.
TAKE THIS CORPSE, PUT IT IN AN ACID-FILLED CASKET AND THROW IT INTO THE OCEAN.
HUH.
WOW, NOBODY'S TRIED THAT.
YEAH, THAT OUGHT TO DO THE TRICK. BUMMER.
THAT SHUT ME UP.
YOU'LL BE BACK, RIGHT?
EH, LET'S SEE HOW YOU DO SOLO, OKAY?
I'LL NEVER FORGIVE YOU FOR THIS.
YOU WILL, OR I'LL END YOUR FAMILY'S BLOODLINE.
EITHER WAY, I'M UNITING THE UNDERWORLD. WITH A SINGLE MARRIAGE, OR A GREAT MANY FUNERALS.
IT'S NOT SUPPOSED TO GO THIS WAY.
TELL ME ABOUT IT.

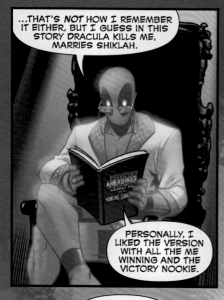

...THAT'S *NOT* HOW I REMEMBER IT EITHER, BUT I GUESS IN THIS STORY DRACULA KILLS ME, MARRIES SHIKLAH.

PERSONALLY, I LIKED THE VERSION WITH ALL THE ME WINNING AND THE VICTORY NOOKIE.

ANYWAY, THAT WASN'T THE END OF THIS BANANAS STORY.

'CAUSE MY WIFE GOT INTO SOME WEIRD STUFF ON *BATTLEWORLD.*

GUESS WE'RE GONNA SEE WHAT MY OLD LADY DOES WHEN I'M NOT AROUND.

HERE'S 2015'S CLASSIC "MRS. DEADPOOL AND THE HOWLING COMMANDOS."

I'LL SEE YOU AT THE END OF YOUR COMIC BOOK, OR IF YOU'RE ONE OF THOSE PEOPLE IN A HAT AND BEARD, "*GRAPHIC NOVEL.*"

GERRY DUGGAN
WRITER

SALVA ESPIN
ARTIST

VAL STAPLES
COLORIST

VC'S JOE SABINO
LETTERER

HEATHER ANTOS
ASST. EDITOR

JORDAN D. WHITE
EDITOR

AXEL ALONSO
EDITOR IN CHIEF

JOE QUESADA
CHIEF CREATIVE OFFICER

DAN BUCKLEY
PUBLISHER

ALAN FINE
EXECUTIVE PRODUCER

THIS SUCKS. I'VE DIED TWICE IN, LIKE, TWO MONTHS.

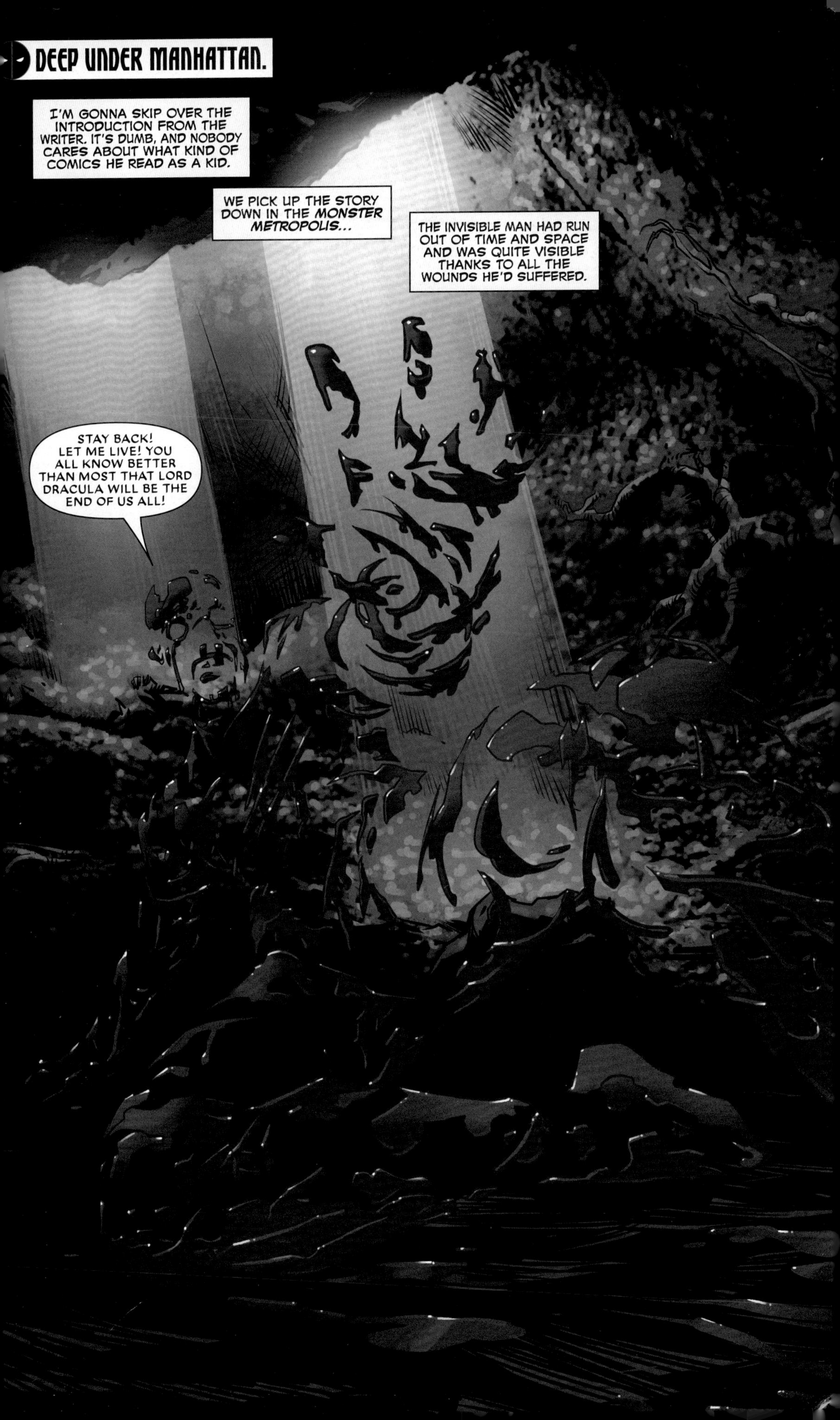
DEEP UNDER MANHATTAN.
I'M GONNA SKIP OVER THE INTRODUCTION FROM THE WRITER. IT'S DUMB, AND NOBODY CARES ABOUT WHAT KIND OF COMICS HE READ AS A KID.
WE PICK UP THE STORY DOWN IN THE *MONSTER METROPOLIS...*
THE INVISIBLE MAN HAD RUN OUT OF TIME AND SPACE AND WAS QUITE VISIBLE THANKS TO ALL THE WOUNDS HE'D SUFFERED.
STAY BACK! LET ME LIVE! YOU ALL KNOW BETTER THAN MOST THAT LORD DRACULA WILL BE THE END OF US ALL!

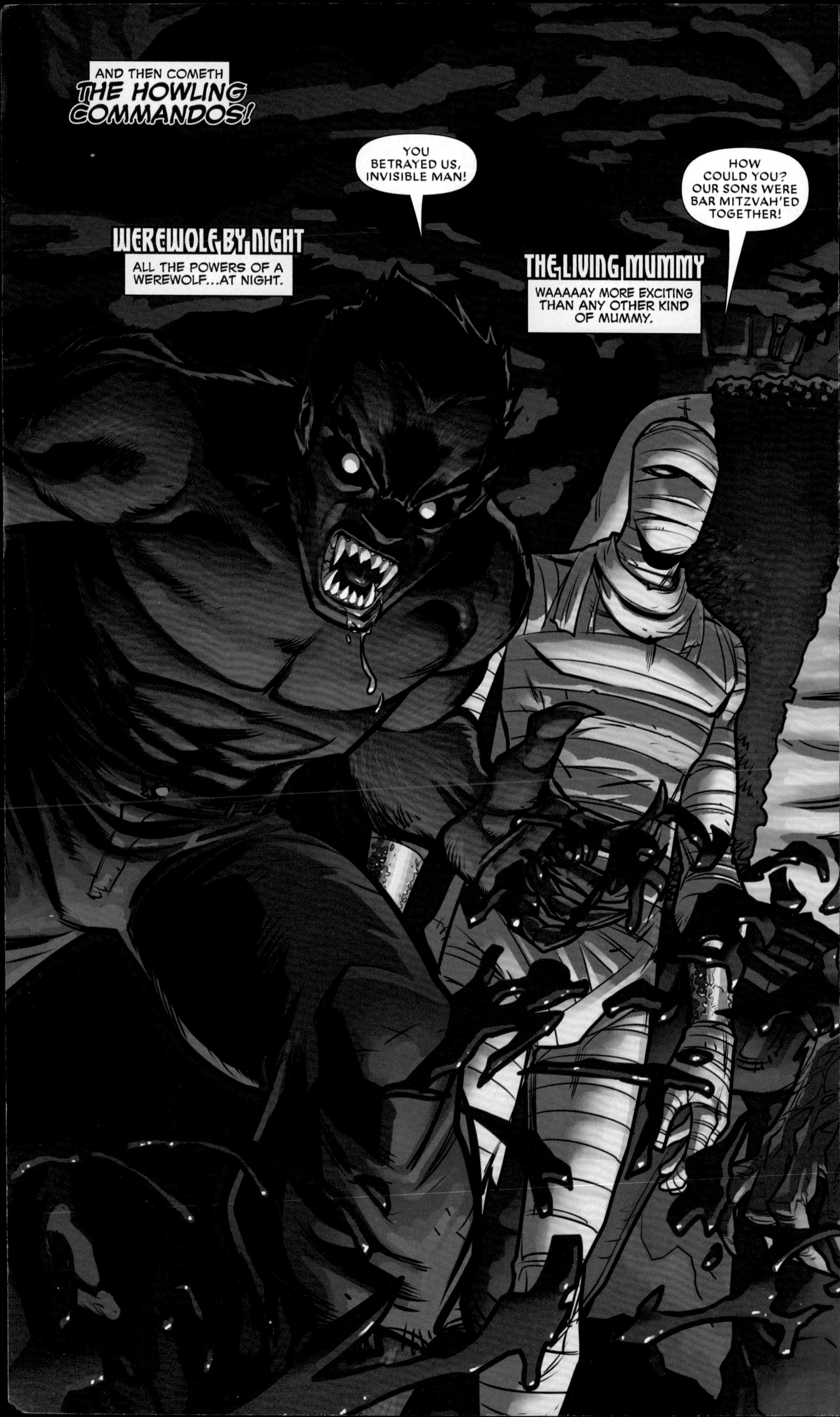
AND THEN COMETH THE HOWLING COMMANDOS!
YOU BETRAYED US, INVISIBLE MAN!
HOW COULD YOU? OUR SONS WERE BAR MITZVAH'ED TOGETHER!
WEREWOLF BY NIGHT
ALL THE POWERS OF A WEREWOLF...AT NIGHT.
THE LIVING MUMMY
WAAAAAY MORE EXCITING THAN ANY OTHER KIND OF MUMMY.

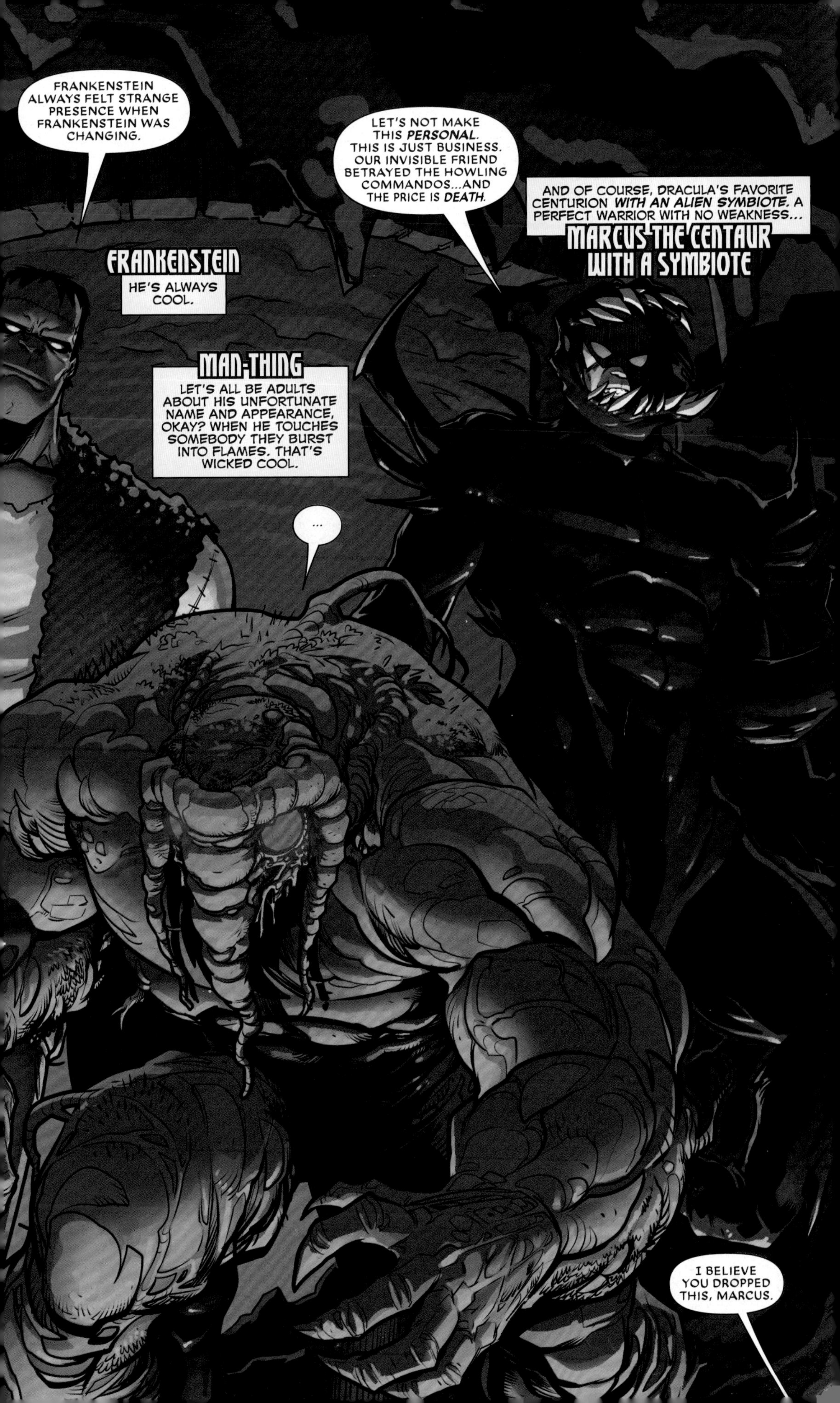

FRANKENSTEIN ALWAYS FELT STRANGE PRESENCE WHEN FRANKENSTEIN WAS CHANGING.
LET'S NOT MAKE THIS PERSONAL. THIS IS JUST BUSINESS. OUR INVISIBLE FRIEND BETRAYED THE HOWLING COMMANDOS...AND THE PRICE IS DEATH.
AND OF COURSE, DRACULA'S FAVORITE CENTURION WITH AN ALIEN SYMBIOTE. A PERFECT WARRIOR WITH NO WEAKNESS...
MARCUS THE CENTAUR WITH A SYMBIOTE
FRANKENSTEIN
HE'S ALWAYS COOL.
MAN-THING
LET'S ALL BE ADULTS ABOUT HIS UNFORTUNATE NAME AND APPEARANCE, OKAY? WHEN HE TOUCHES SOMEBODY THEY BURST INTO FLAMES. THAT'S WICKED COOL.
...
I BELIEVE YOU DROPPED THIS, MARCUS.

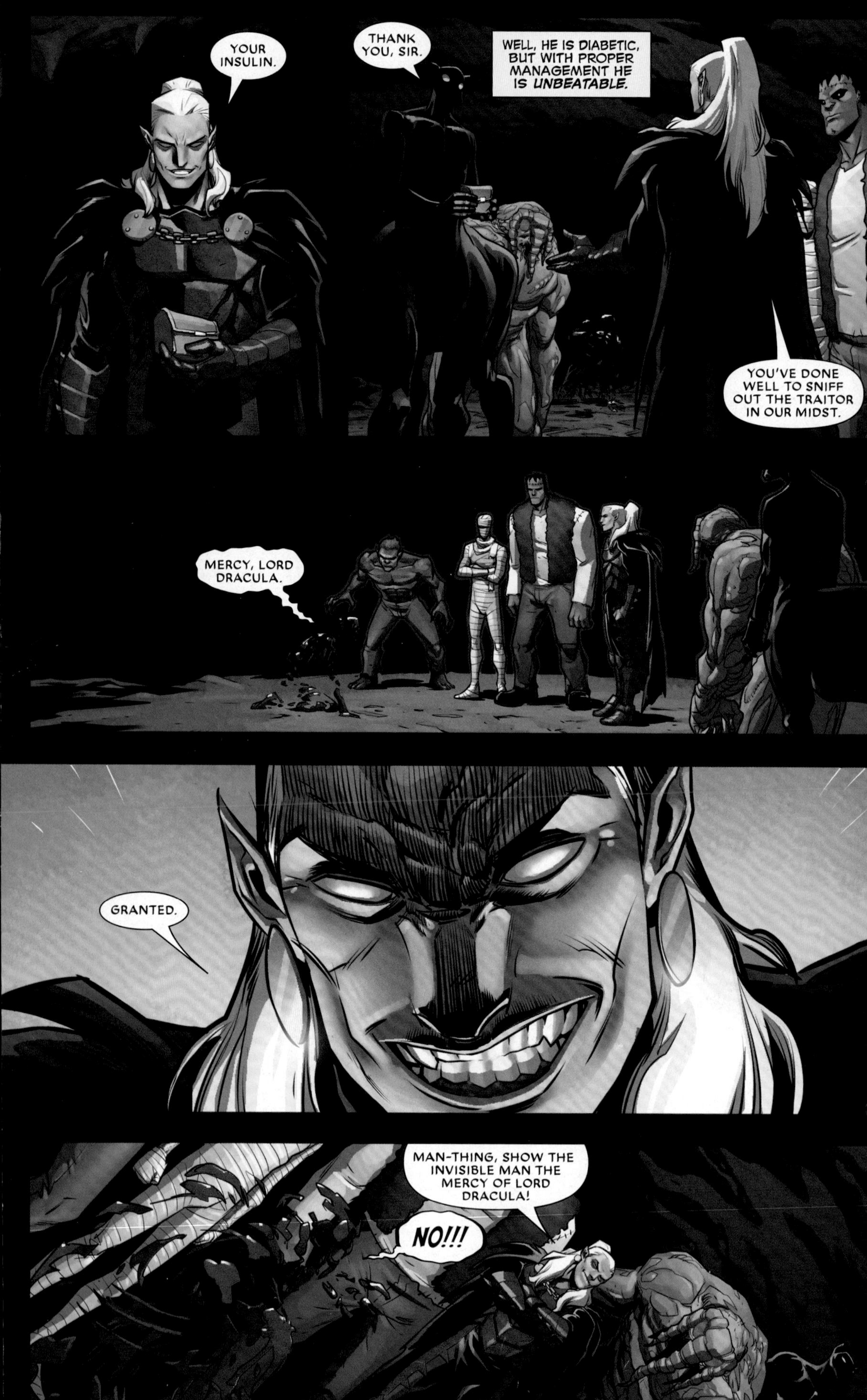
YOUR INSULIN.
THANK YOU, SIR.
WELL, HE IS DIABETIC, BUT WITH PROPER MANAGEMENT HE IS *UNBEATABLE.*
YOU'VE DONE WELL TO SNIFF OUT THE TRAITOR IN OUR MIDST.
MERCY, LORD DRACULA.
GRANTED.
MAN-THING, SHOW THE INVISIBLE MAN THE MERCY OF LORD DRACULA!
NO!!!

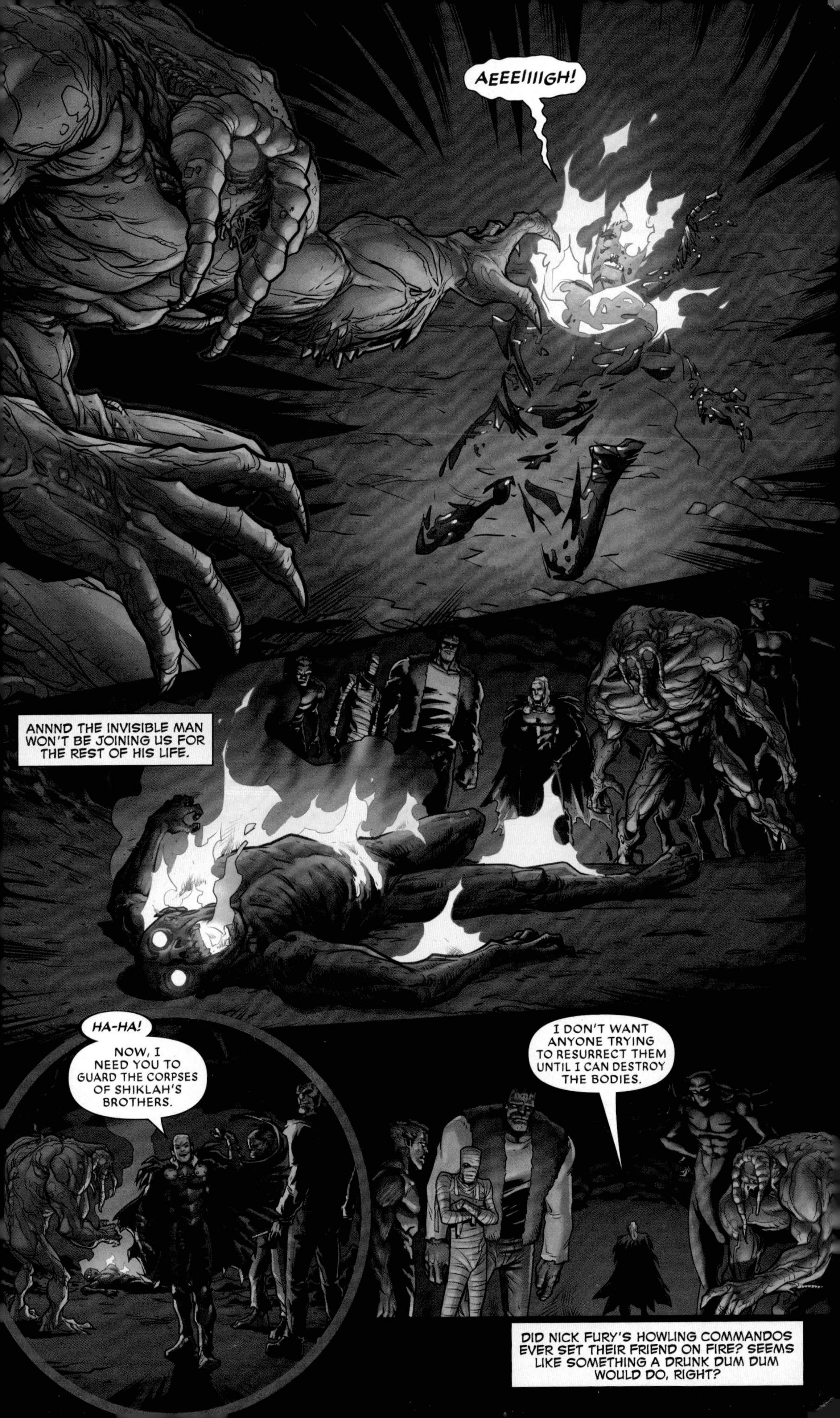
AEEE!!!!IGH!
ANNND THE INVISIBLE MAN WON'T BE JOINING US FOR THE REST OF HIS LIFE.
HA-HA!
NOW, I NEED YOU TO GUARD THE CORPSES OF SHIKLAH'S BROTHERS.
I DON'T WANT ANYONE TRYING TO RESURRECT THEM UNTIL I CAN DESTROY THE BODIES.
DID NICK FURY'S HOWLING COMMANDOS EVER SET THEIR FRIEND ON FIRE? SEEMS LIKE SOMETHING A DRUNK DUM DUM WOULD DO, RIGHT?

WHAT DO YOU MEAN I CANNOT PREPARE MY BROTHERS FOR BURIAL?

BOSS SAID "*GUARD BODIES*," WE GUARD BODIES.

I SEE.

WHAM

STAND DOWN, LADY SHIKLAH!

YOUR BROTHERS BETRAYED LORD DRACULA--BUT YOU HAVE TO BE PATIENT!

LISTEN, GUYS, THE BOSS AIN'T GONNA LIKE US BUTTING HEADS WITH HIS LADY.

LET'S TONE IT DOWN.

BO-O-OYS!

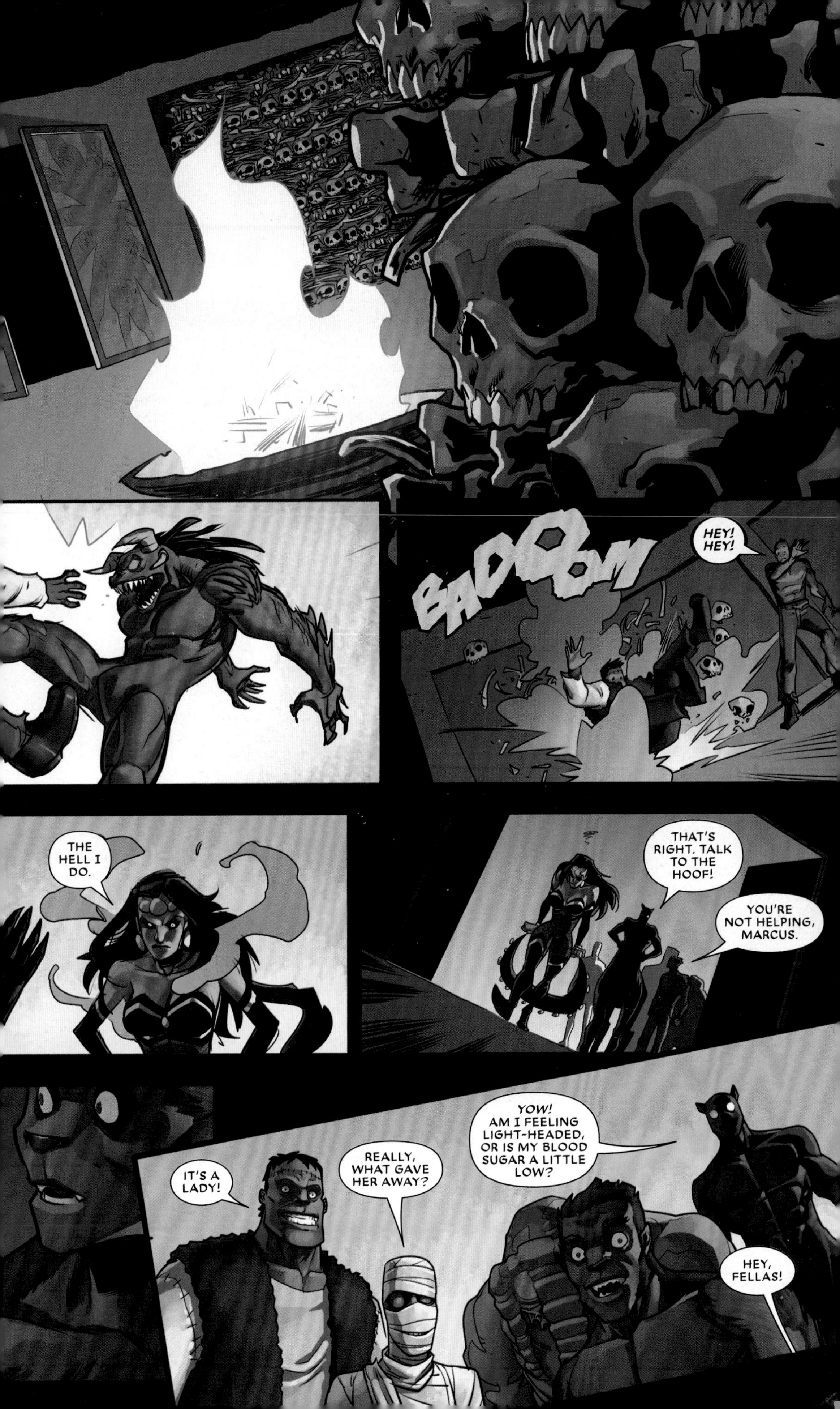
BADOOM
HEY! HEY!
THE HELL I DO.
THAT'S RIGHT. TALK TO THE HOOF!
YOU'RE NOT HELPING, MARCUS.
IT'S A LADY!
REALLY, WHAT GAVE HER AWAY?
YOW! AM I FEELING LIGHT-HEADED, OR IS MY BLOOD SUGAR A LITTLE LOW?
HEY, FELLAS!

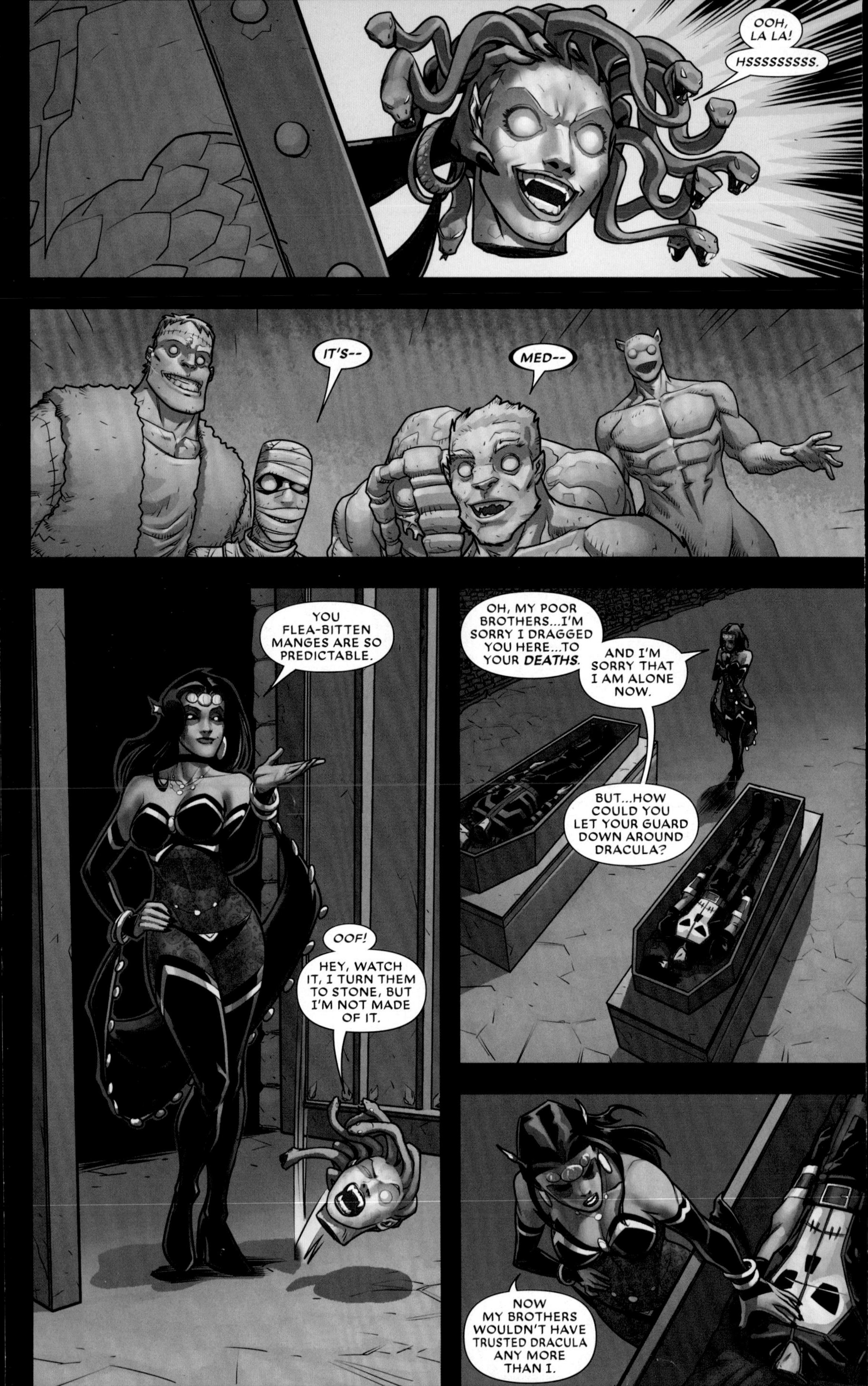
OOH, LA LA!
HSSSSSSSSS.
IT'S--
MED--
YOU FLEA-BITTEN MANGES ARE SO PREDICTABLE.
OOF!
HEY, WATCH IT, I TURN THEM TO STONE, BUT I'M NOT MADE OF IT.
OH, MY POOR BROTHERS...I'M SORRY I DRAGGED YOU HERE...TO YOUR DEATHS.
AND I'M SORRY THAT I AM ALONE NOW.
BUT...HOW COULD YOU LET YOUR GUARD DOWN AROUND DRACULA?
NOW MY BROTHERS WOULDN'T HAVE TRUSTED DRACULA ANY MORE THAN I.

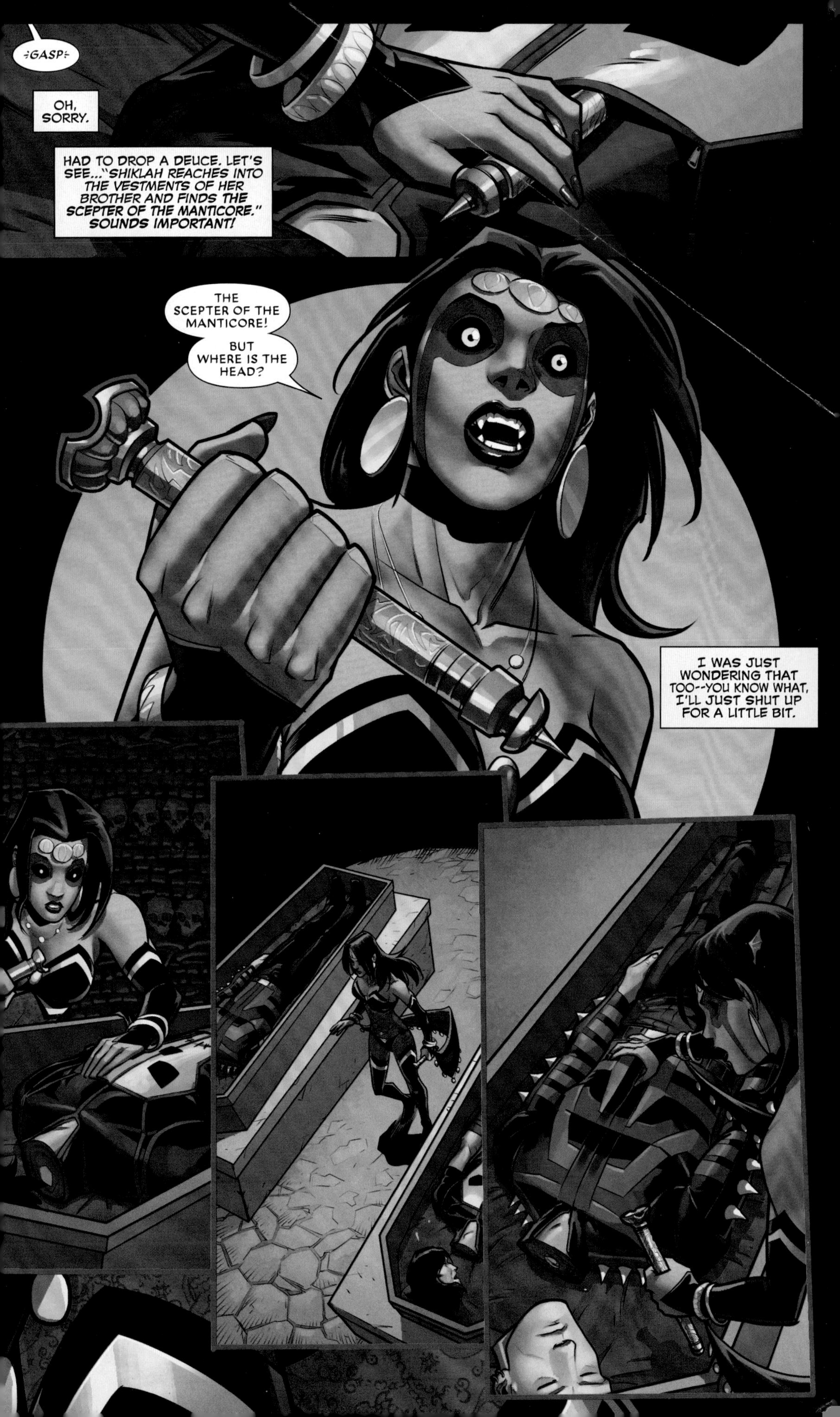

GASP
OH, SORRY.
HAD TO DROP A DEUCE. LET'S SEE..."SHIKLAH REACHES INTO THE VESTMENTS OF HER BROTHER AND FINDS THE SCEPTER OF THE MANTICORE." SOUNDS IMPORTANT!
THE SCEPTER OF THE MANTICORE!
BUT WHERE IS THE HEAD?
I WAS JUST WONDERING THAT TOO--YOU KNOW WHAT, I'LL JUST SHUT UP FOR A LITTLE BIT.

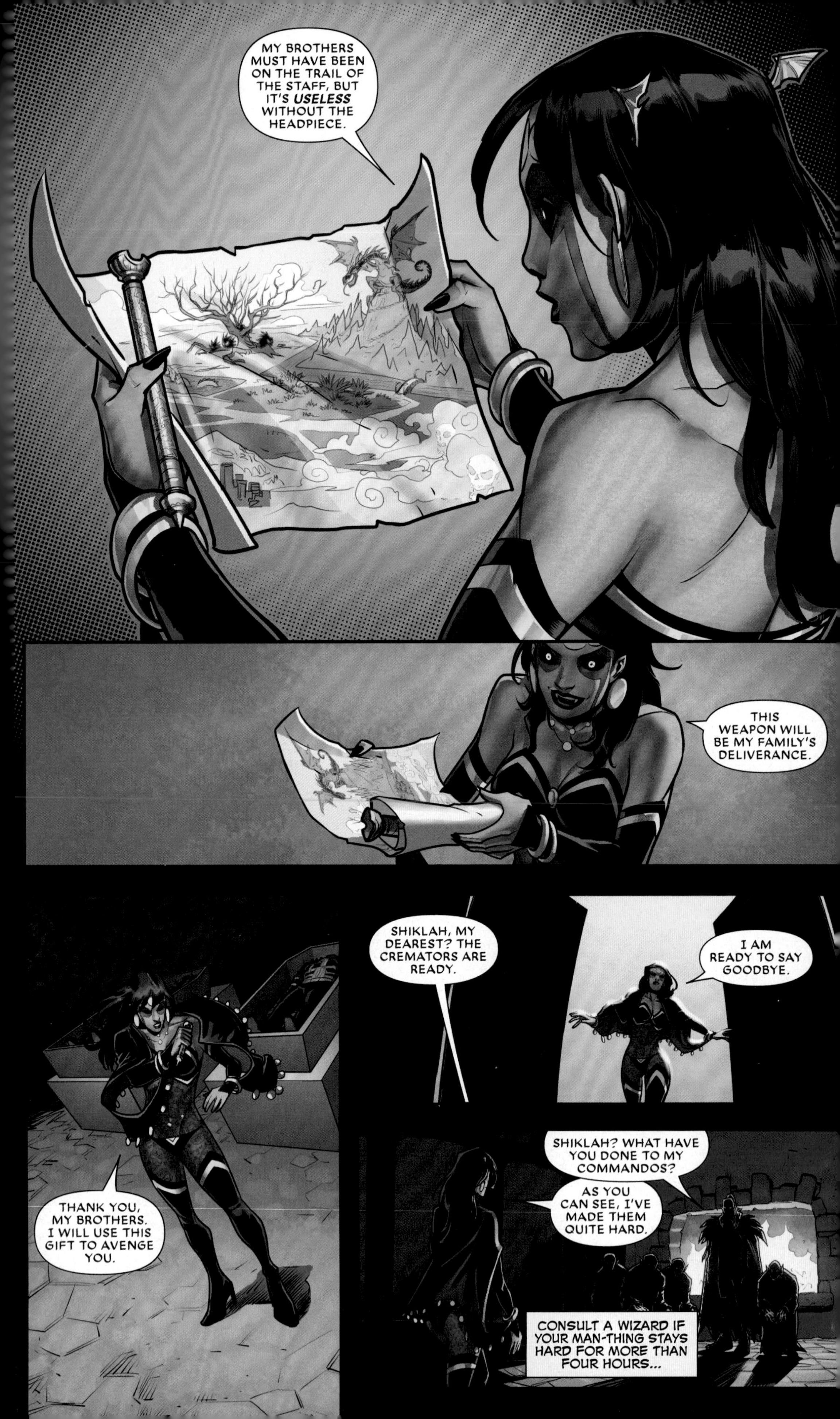

MY BROTHERS MUST HAVE BEEN ON THE TRAIL OF THE STAFF, BUT IT'S ***USELESS*** WITHOUT THE HEADPIECE.
THIS WEAPON WILL BE MY FAMILY'S DELIVERANCE.
THANK YOU, MY BROTHERS. I WILL USE THIS GIFT TO AVENGE YOU.
SHIKLAH, MY DEAREST? THE CREMATORS ARE READY.
I AM READY TO SAY GOODBYE.
SHIKLAH? WHAT HAVE YOU DONE TO MY COMMANDOS?
AS YOU CAN SEE, I'VE MADE THEM QUITE HARD.
CONSULT A WIZARD IF YOUR MAN-THING STAYS HARD FOR MORE THAN FOUR HOURS...

FREE THEM FROM MEDUSA'S GRASP AND PUT HER WRETCHED HEAD BACK IN THE CABINET!

NOW WITH THIS UGLINESS BEHIND US, WE CAN BE JOINED AS ONE.

I'M AFRAID I HAVE ONE MORE SACRED DUTY TO ATTEND TO.

I MUST DELIVER MY BROTHERS' ASHES ACROSS THE RIVER STYX, OR THEIR SOULS WILL HAUNT AND CURSE US BOTH.

VERY WELL. SEVEN DAYS!

COME NOW, THIS IS--

IT WILL ONLY TAKE ME A *FEW* DAYS.

OR THERE'S ROOM FOR ANOTHER CASKET IN THE CREMATORIUM IF YOU'RE CONSIDERING REFUSING THIS HUMBLE REQUEST BEFORE OUR WEDDING.

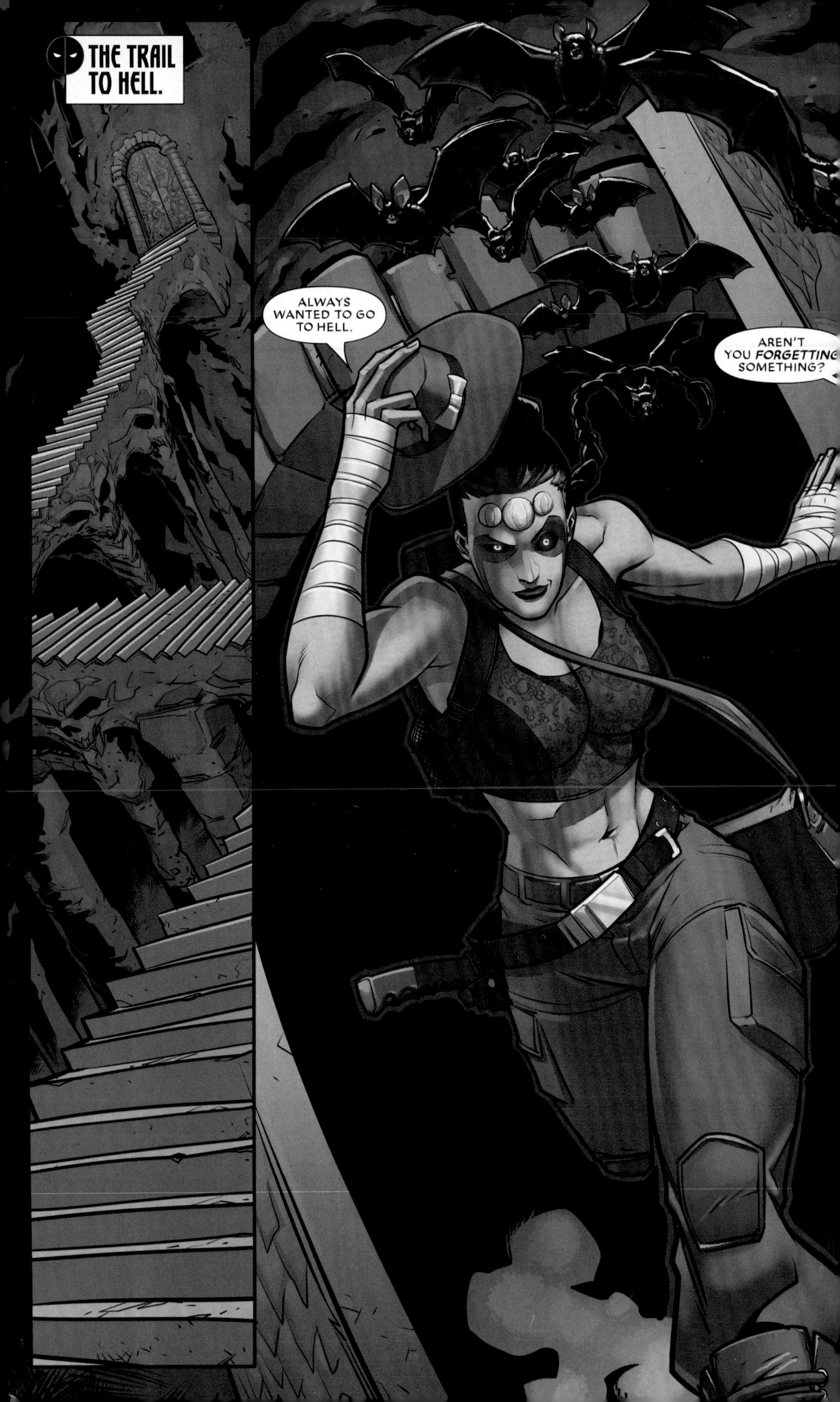
THE TRAIL TO HELL.
ALWAYS WANTED TO GO TO HELL.
AREN'T YOU FORGETTING SOMETHING?

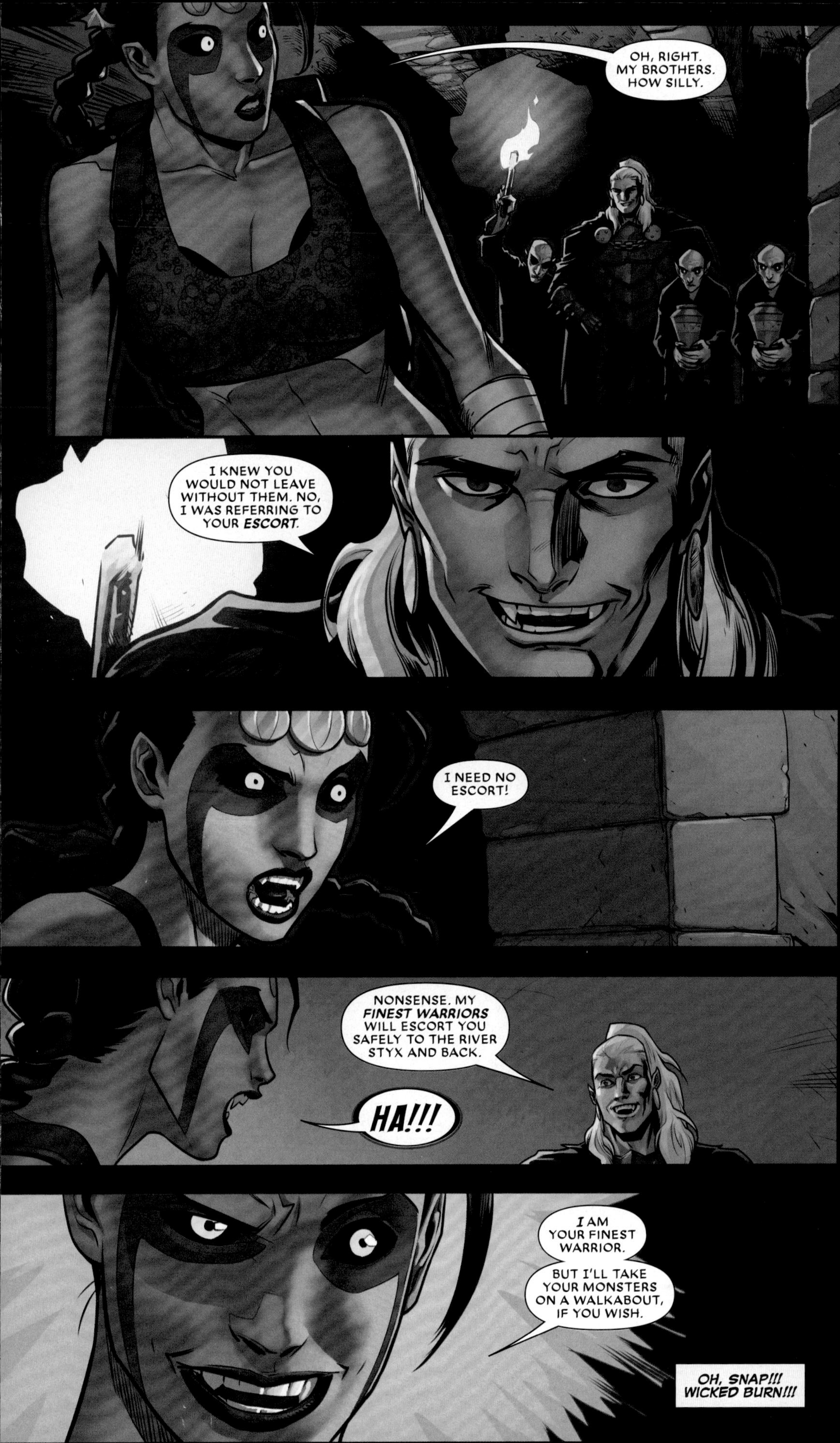
OH, RIGHT. MY BROTHERS. HOW SILLY.
I KNEW YOU WOULD NOT LEAVE WITHOUT THEM. NO, I WAS REFERRING TO YOUR ESCORT.
I NEED NO ESCORT!
NONSENSE. MY FINEST WARRIORS WILL ESCORT YOU SAFELY TO THE RIVER STYX AND BACK.
HA!!!
I AM YOUR FINEST WARRIOR.
BUT I'LL TAKE YOUR MONSTERS ON A WALKABOUT, IF YOU WISH.
OH, SNAP!!! WICKED BURN!!!

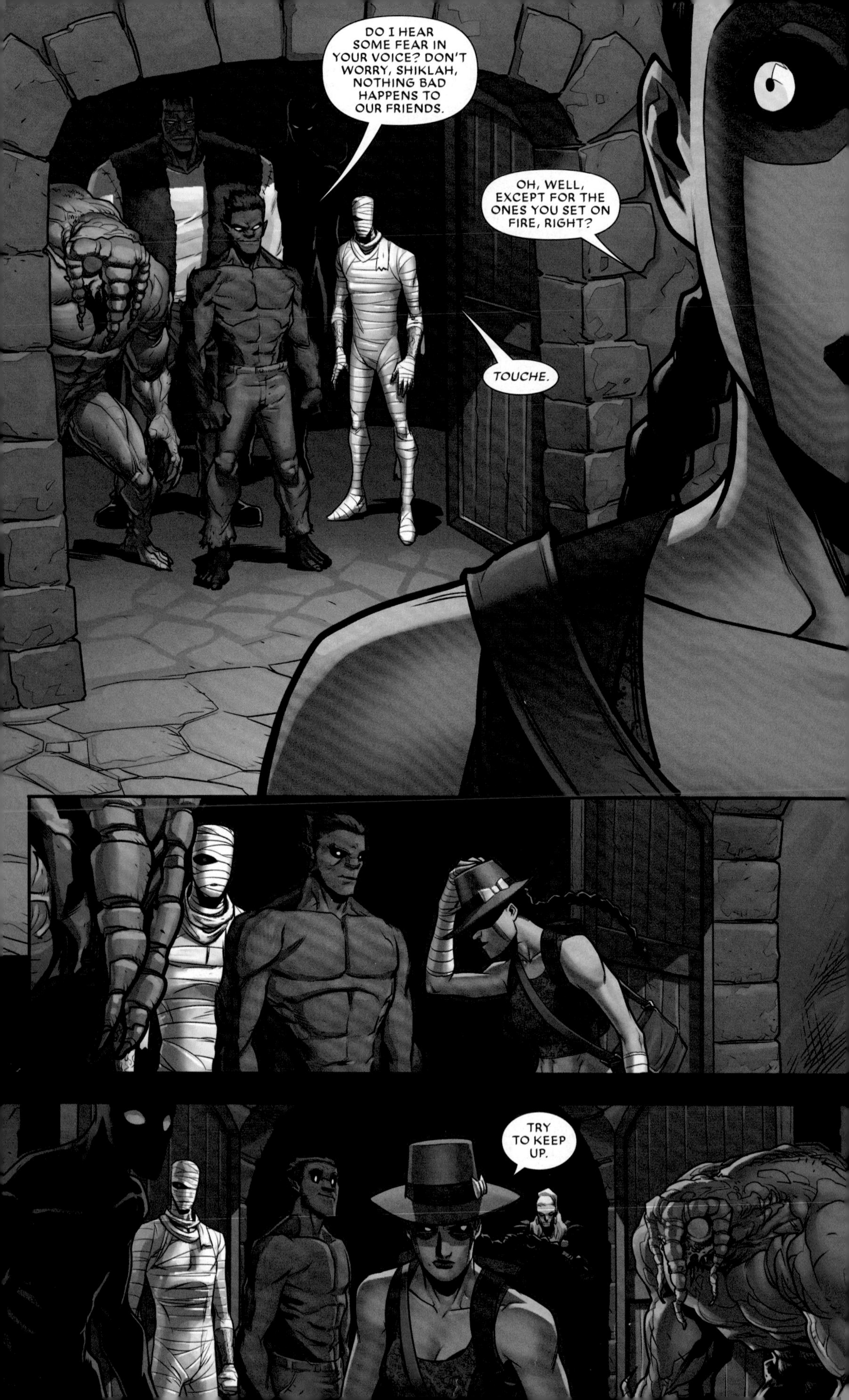
DO I HEAR SOME FEAR IN YOUR VOICE? DON'T WORRY, SHIKLAH, NOTHING BAD HAPPENS TO OUR FRIENDS.
OH, WELL, EXCEPT FOR THE ONES YOU SET ON FIRE, RIGHT?
TOUCHE.
TRY TO KEEP UP.

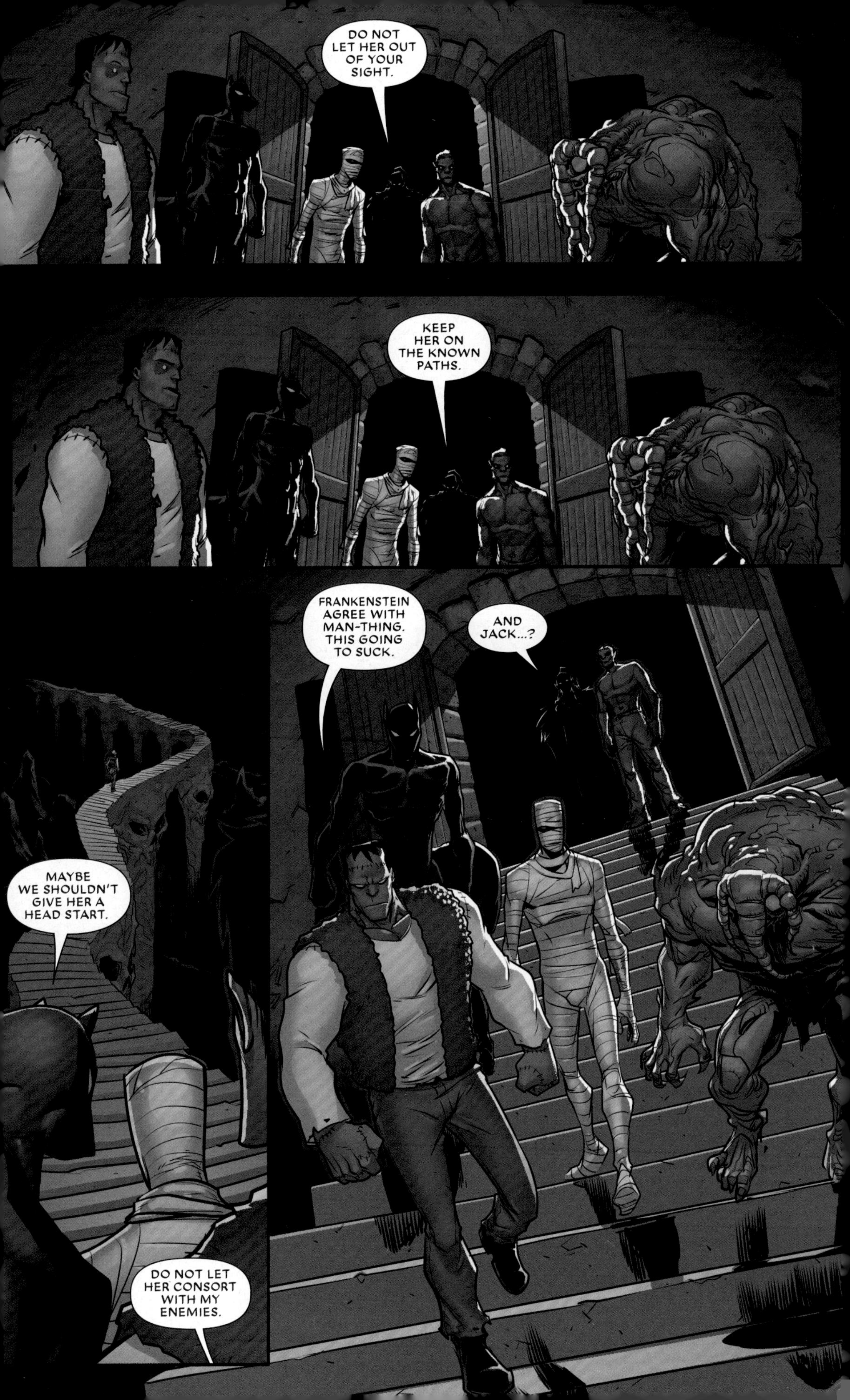
DO NOT LET HER OUT OF YOUR SIGHT.
KEEP HER ON THE KNOWN PATHS.
FRANKENSTEIN AGREE WITH MAN-THING. THIS GOING TO SUCK.
AND JACK...?
MAYBE WE SHOULDN'T GIVE HER A HEAD START.
DO NOT LET HER CONSORT WITH MY ENEMIES.

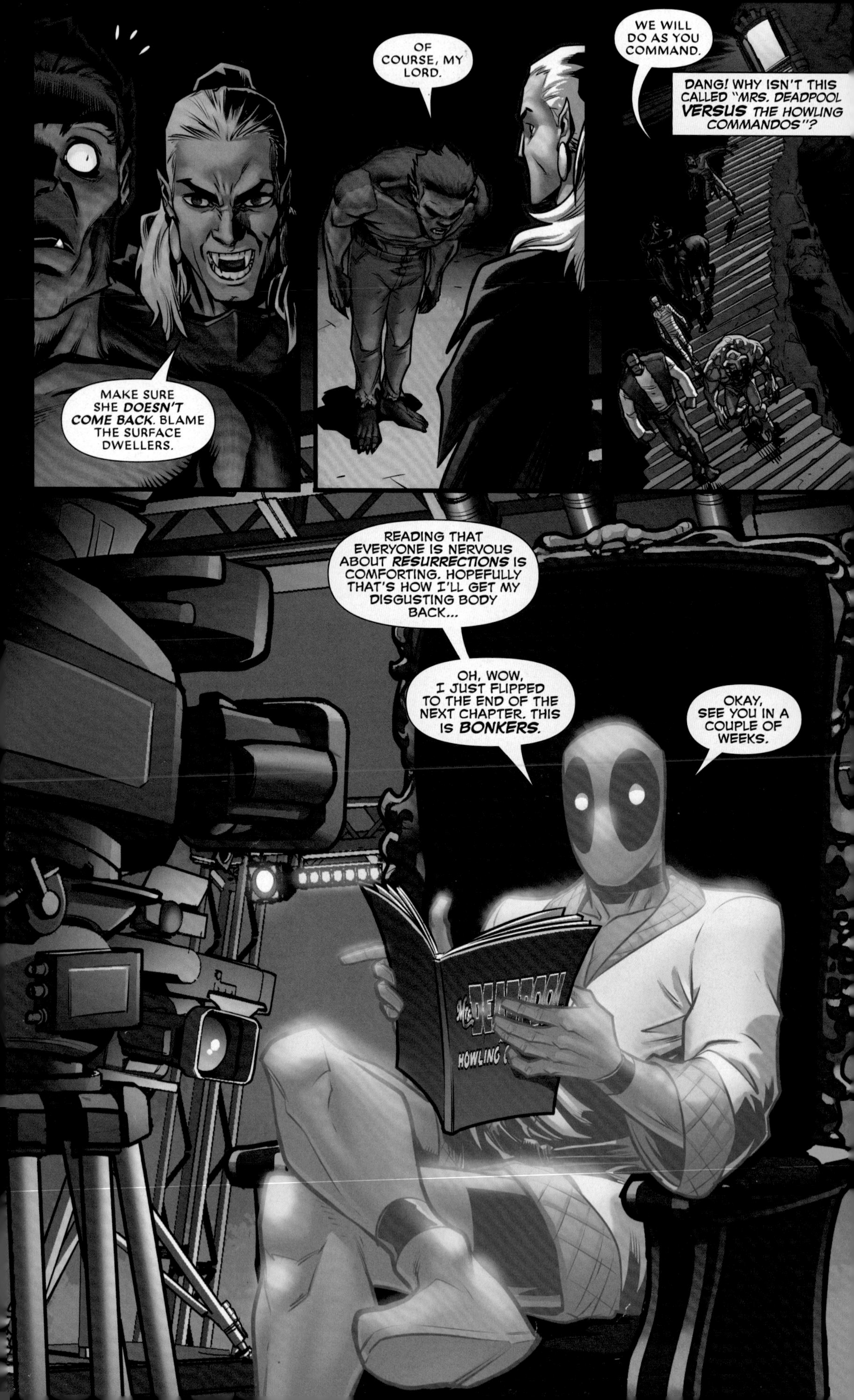
MAKE SURE SHE DOESN'T COME BACK. BLAME THE SURFACE DWELLERS.
OF COURSE, MY LORD.
WE WILL DO AS YOU COMMAND.
DANG! WHY ISN'T THIS CALLED "MRS. DEADPOOL VERSUS THE HOWLING COMMANDOS"?
READING THAT EVERYONE IS NERVOUS ABOUT RESURRECTIONS IS COMFORTING. HOPEFULLY THAT'S HOW I'LL GET MY DISGUSTING BODY BACK...
OH, WOW, I JUST FLIPPED TO THE END OF THE NEXT CHAPTER. THIS IS BONKERS.
OKAY, SEE YOU IN A COUPLE OF WEEKS.

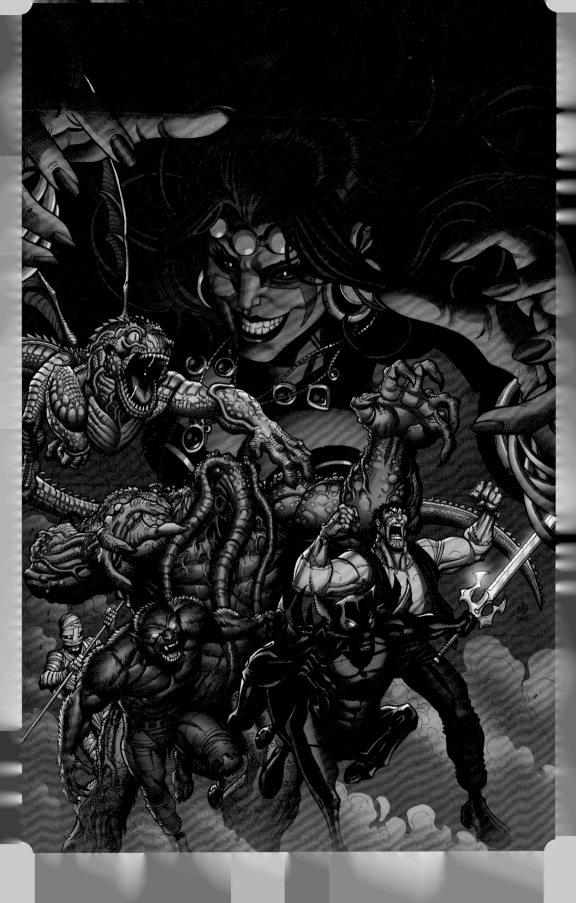

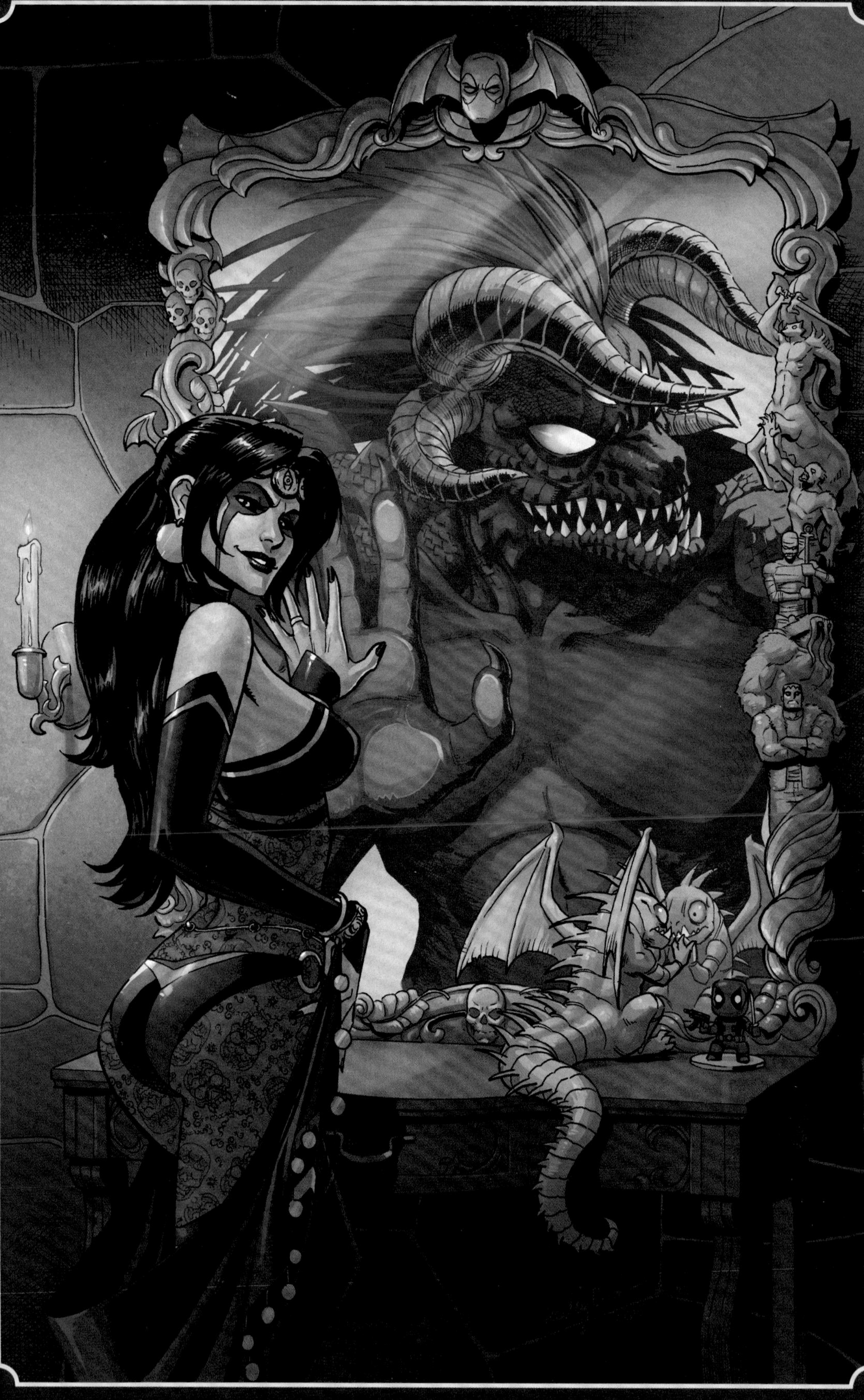

2

JEEZ, THIS IS A HELL OF A READ.

WHY AREN'T MORE PEOPLE TALKING ABOUT HOW GOOD THIS IS?

OH, HELLO AGAIN.

WHERE WERE WE IN THE TALE OF MRS. DEADPOOL AND THE HOWLING COMMANDOS?

DID SHIKLAH KILL DRACULA YET? HMM, NO-- OKAY, SPOILER ALERT, BY THE WAY.

"THE ASSEMBLAGE DELVED DEEPER UNDER THE MONSTER METROPOLIS WITH SHIKLAH IN FRONT, AND MAN-THING IN THE REAR."

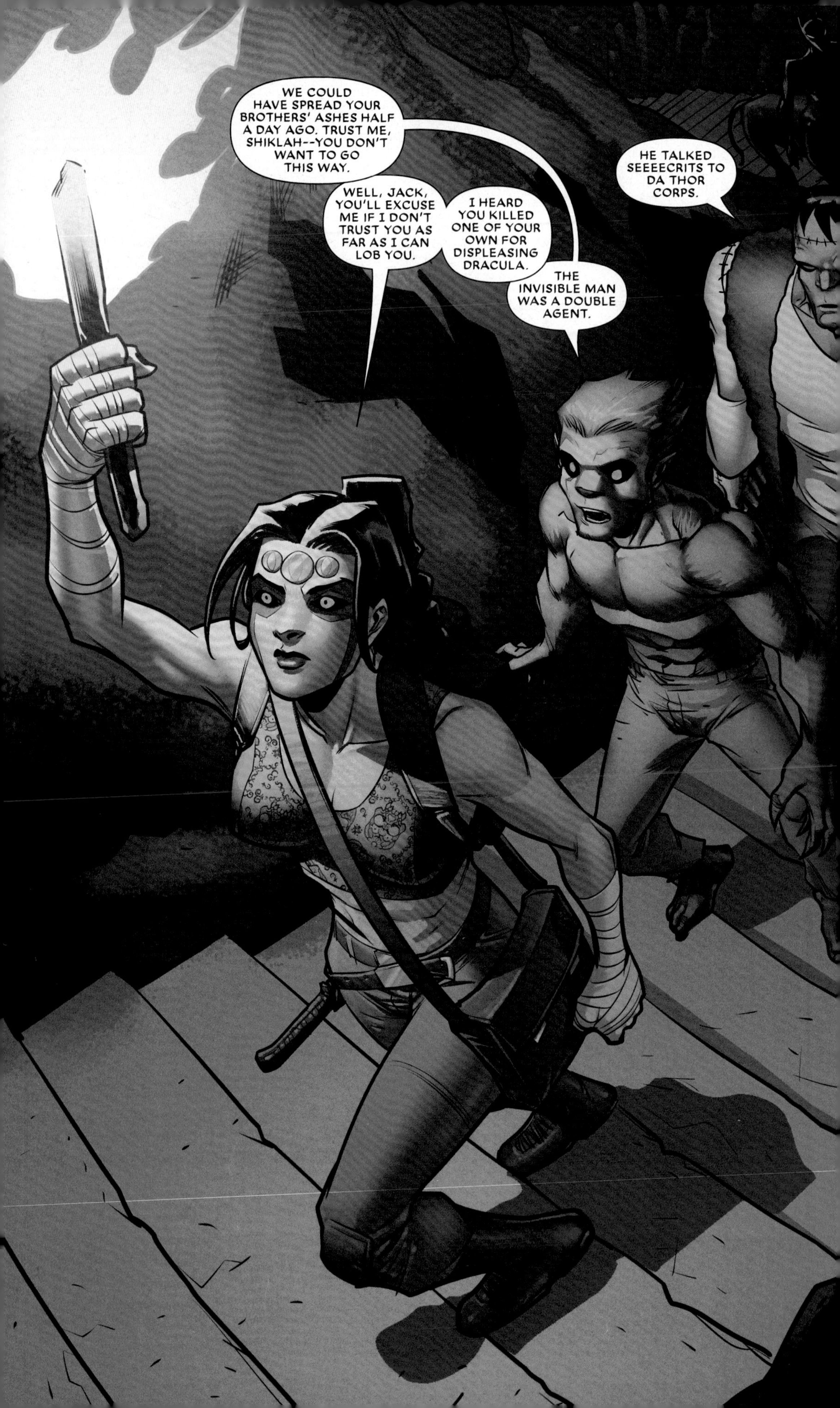

WE COULD HAVE SPREAD YOUR BROTHERS' ASHES HALF A DAY AGO. TRUST ME, SHIKLAH--YOU DON'T WANT TO GO THIS WAY.
WELL, JACK, YOU'LL EXCUSE ME IF I DON'T TRUST YOU AS FAR AS I CAN LOB YOU.
I HEARD YOU KILLED ONE OF YOUR OWN FOR DISPLEASING DRACULA.
THE INVISIBLE MAN WAS A DOUBLE AGENT.
HE TALKED SEEEECRITS TO DA THOR CORPS.

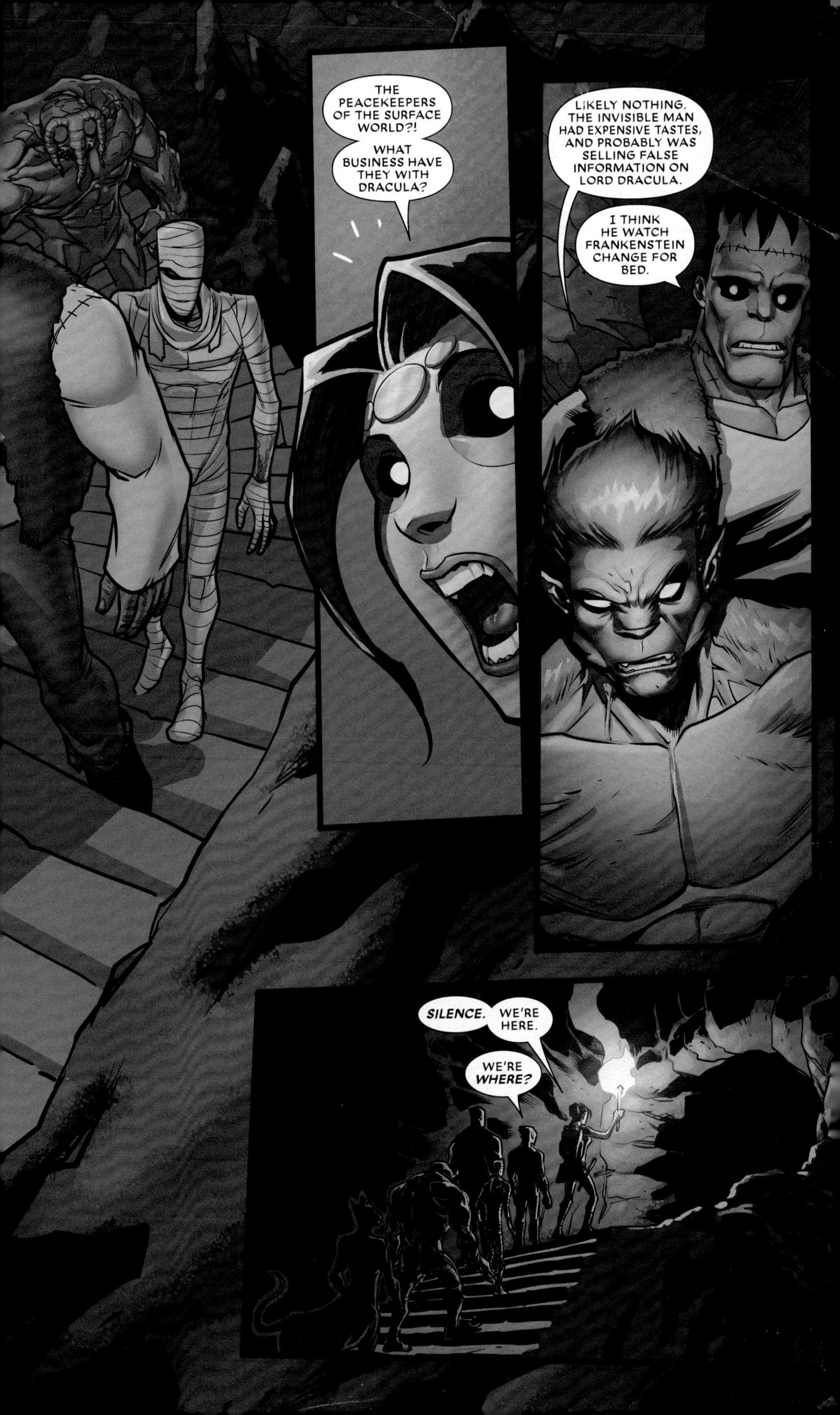
THE PEACEKEEPERS OF THE SURFACE WORLD?!
WHAT BUSINESS HAVE THEY WITH DRACULA?
LIKELY NOTHING. THE INVISIBLE MAN HAD EXPENSIVE TASTES, AND PROBABLY WAS SELLING FALSE INFORMATION ON LORD DRACULA.
I THINK HE WATCH FRANKENSTEIN CHANGE FOR BED.
SILENCE.
WE'RE HERE.
WE'RE WHERE?

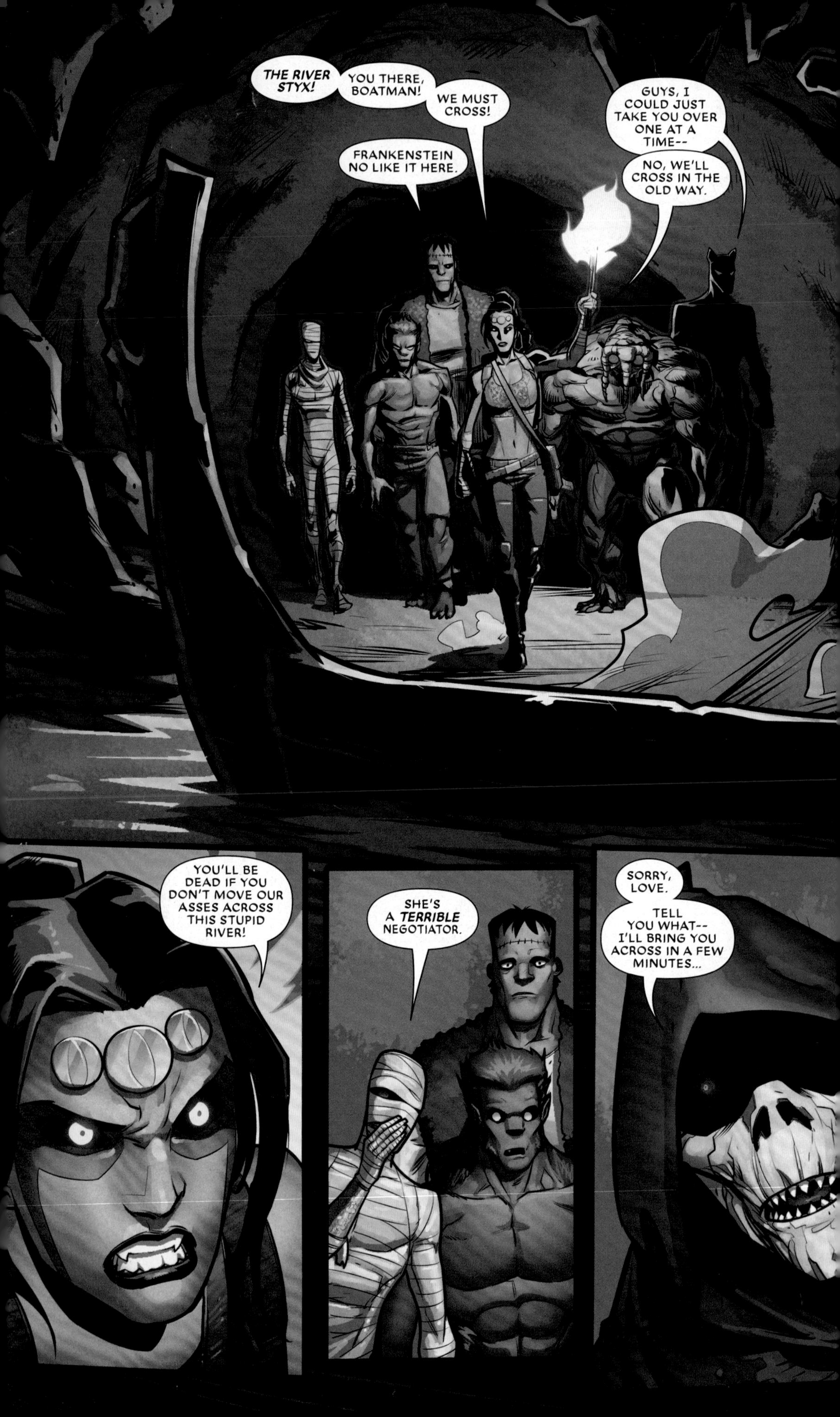
THE RIVER STYX!
YOU THERE, BOATMAN!
WE MUST CROSS!
FRANKENSTEIN NO LIKE IT HERE.
GUYS, I COULD JUST TAKE YOU OVER ONE AT A TIME--
NO, WE'LL CROSS IN THE OLD WAY.
YOU'LL BE DEAD IF YOU DON'T MOVE OUR ASSES ACROSS THIS STUPID RIVER!
SHE'S A *TERRIBLE* NEGOTIATOR.
SORRY, LOVE.
TELL YOU WHAT-- I'LL BRING YOU ACROSS IN A FEW MINUTES...

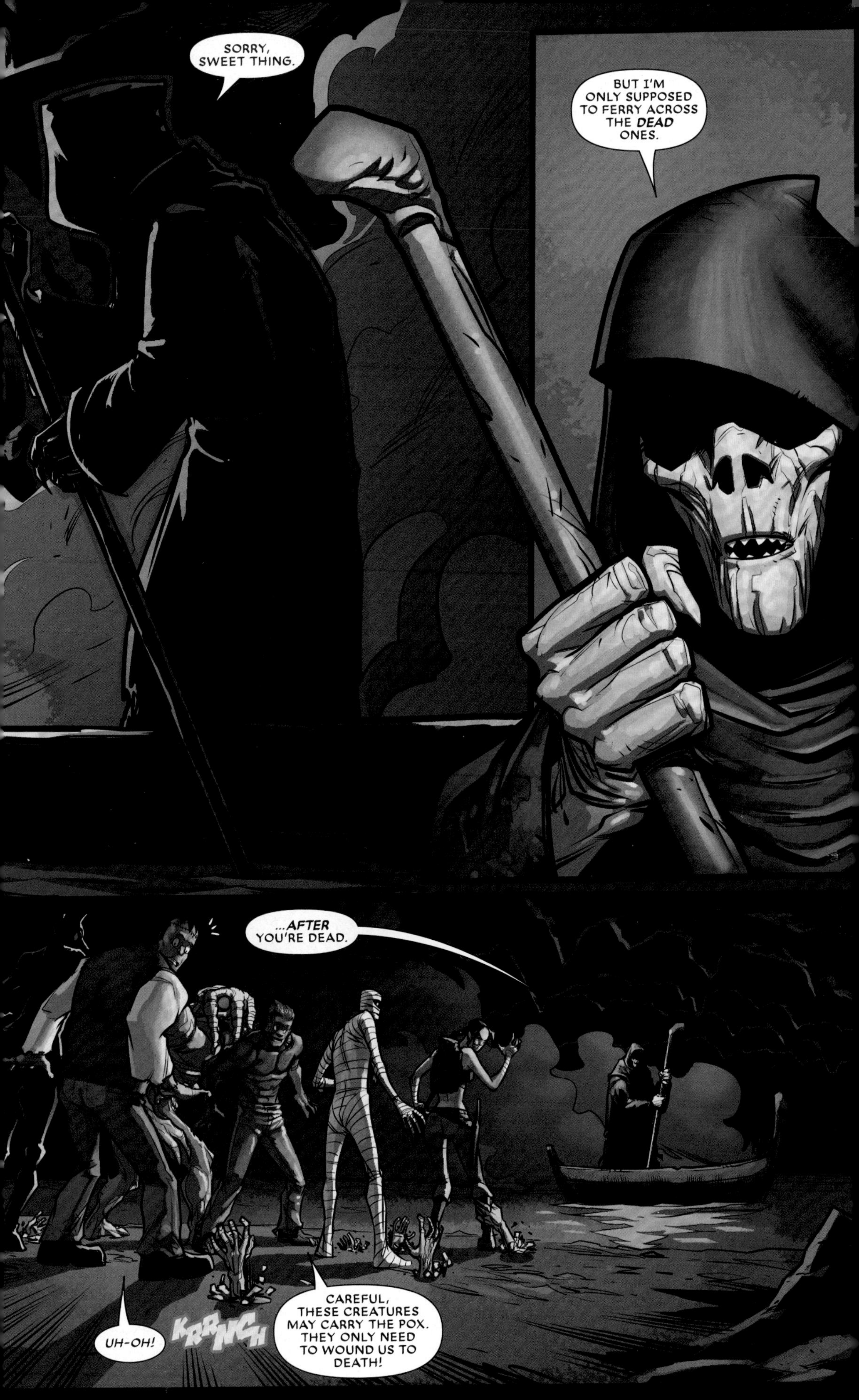
SORRY, SWEET THING.
BUT I'M ONLY SUPPOSED TO FERRY ACROSS THE *DEAD* ONES.
...*AFTER* YOU'RE DEAD.
UH-OH!
KRRNCH
CAREFUL, THESE CREATURES MAY CARRY THE POX. THEY ONLY NEED TO WOUND US TO DEATH!

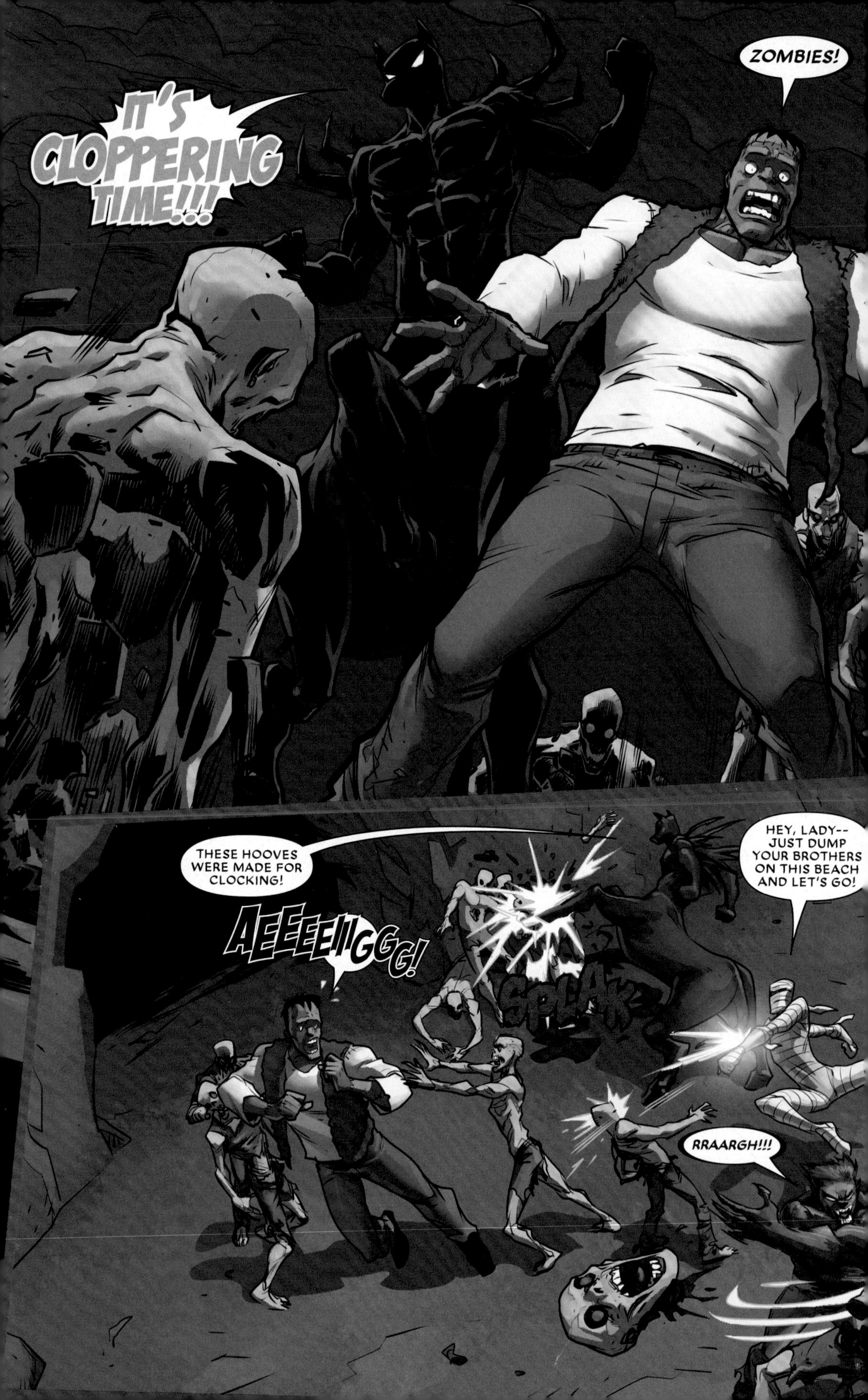
IT'S CLOPPERING TIME!!!
ZOMBIES!
THESE HOOVES WERE MADE FOR CLOCKING!
AEEEEIIIGGG!
SPLAK
HEY, LADY-- JUST DUMP YOUR BROTHERS ON THIS BEACH AND LET'S GO!
RRAARGH!!!

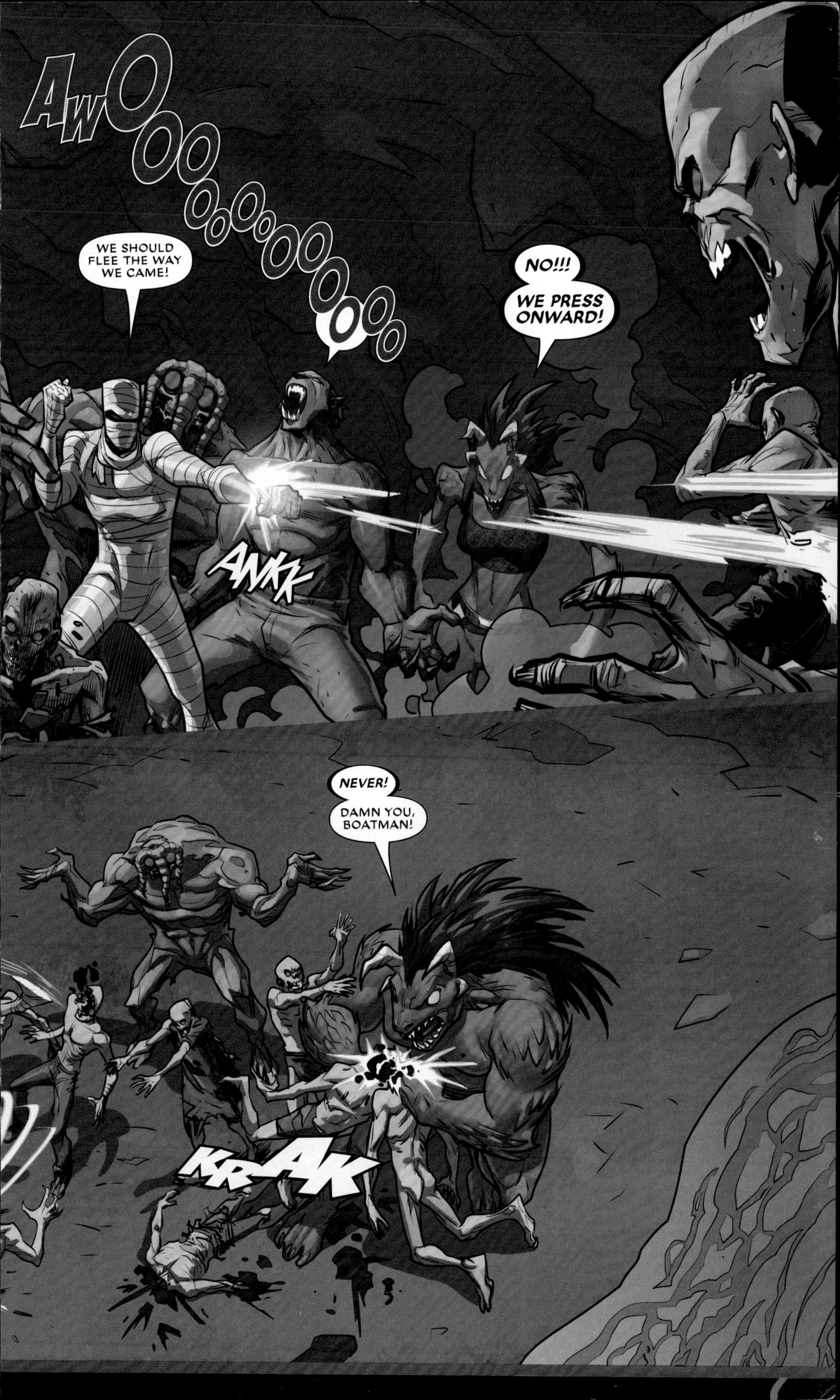
AWOOOOoOoOOOOOOoo
WE SHOULD FLEE THE WAY WE CAME!
NO!!! WE PRESS ONWARD!
ANKK
NEVER! DAMN YOU, BOATMAN!
KRAK

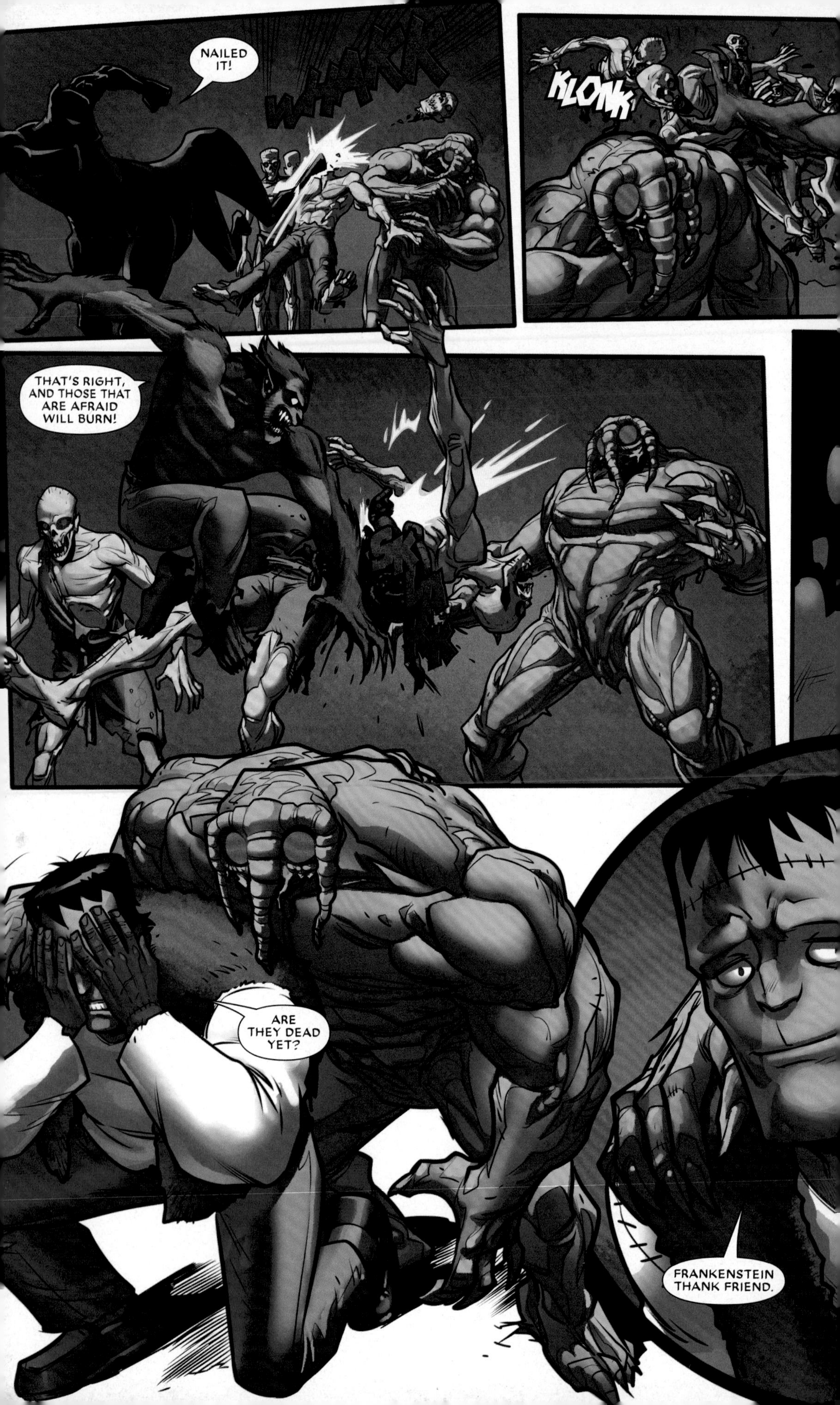
NAILED IT!
WHAKK
KLONK
THAT'S RIGHT, AND THOSE THAT ARE AFRAID WILL BURN!
ARE THEY DEAD YET?
FRANKENSTEIN THANK FRIEND.

MAN-THING? HE'S VERY POWERFUL, BUT HE'S ALSO SENSITIVE TO EMOTIONS.

WHAT DOES YOUR GREEN FRIEND DO BESIDES LUMBER ABOUT AND GET IN MY WAY?

FWASH

FRANKENSTEIN NO LIKE ZOMBIES!

AEEEIII!

BAD FRIEND! BAD!

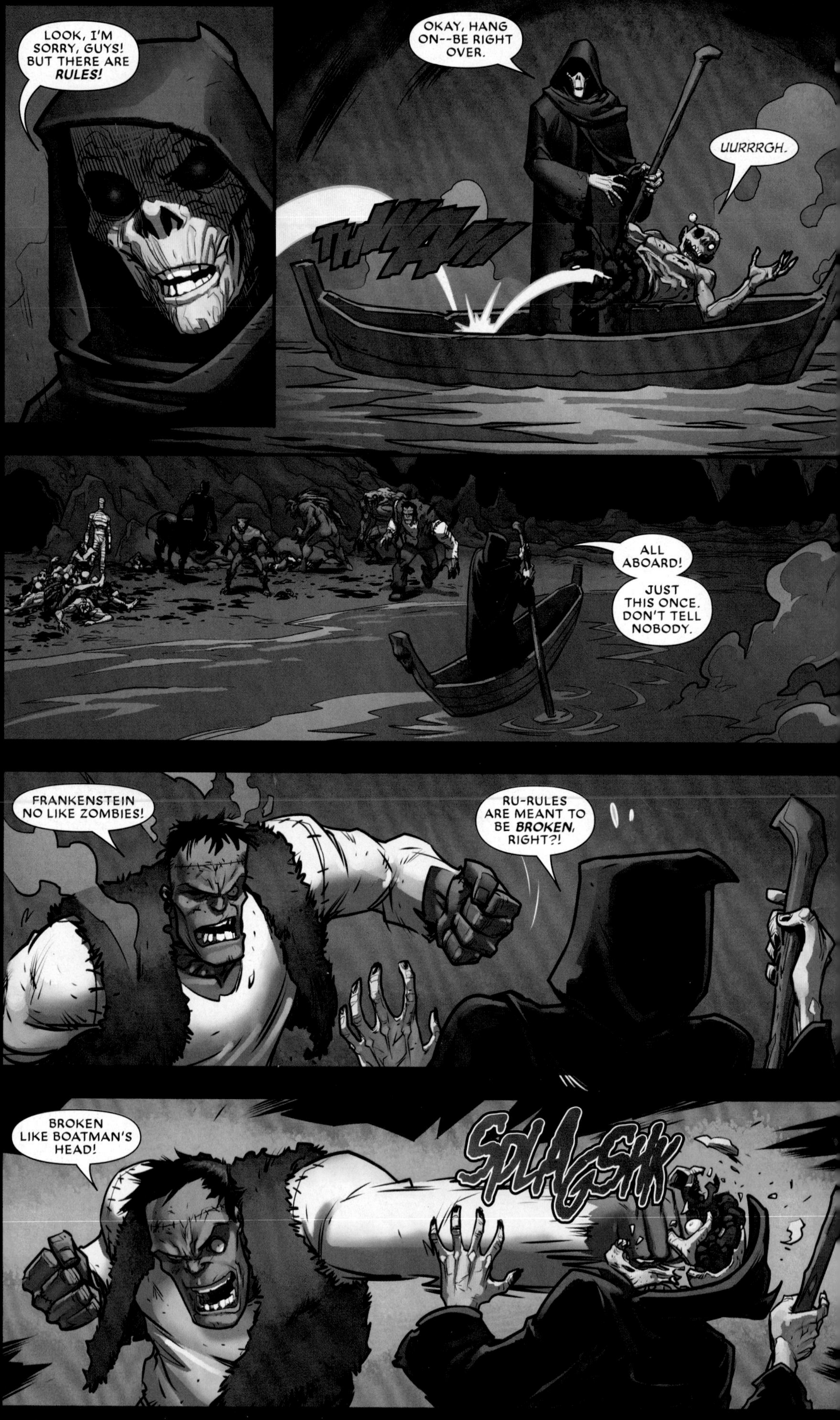
LOOK, I'M SORRY, GUYS! BUT THERE ARE *RULES!*
OKAY, HANG ON--BE RIGHT OVER.
UURRRGH.
THWAW
ALL ABOARD!
JUST THIS ONCE. DON'T TELL NOBODY.
FRANKENSTEIN NO LIKE ZOMBIES!
RU-RULES ARE MEANT TO BE *BROKEN,* RIGHT?!
BROKEN LIKE BOATMAN'S HEAD!
SPLAGSHK

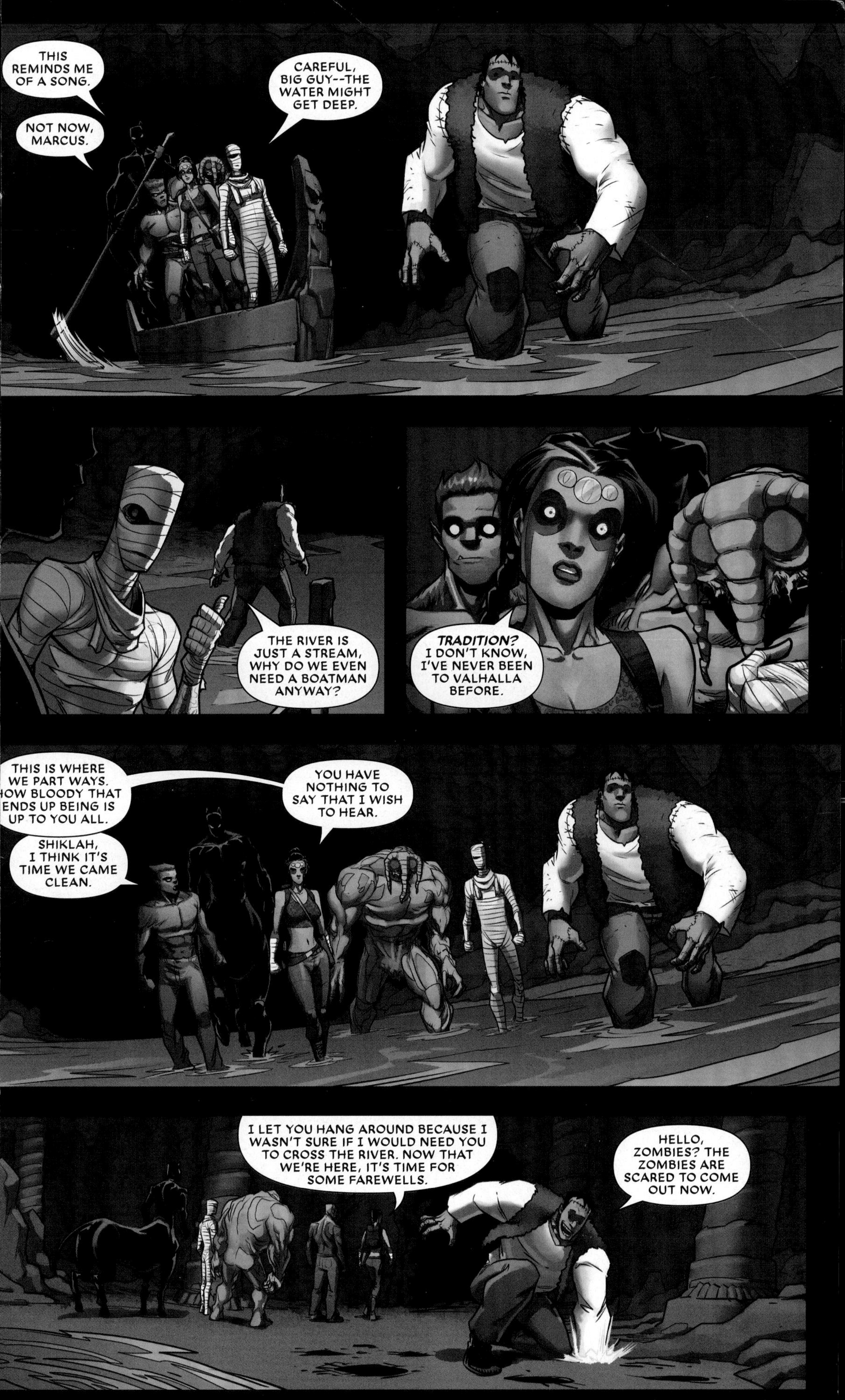
THIS REMINDS ME OF A SONG.
NOT NOW, MARCUS.
CAREFUL, BIG GUY--THE WATER MIGHT GET DEEP.
THE RIVER IS JUST A STREAM, WHY DO WE EVEN NEED A BOATMAN ANYWAY?
TRADITION? I DON'T KNOW, I'VE NEVER BEEN TO VALHALLA BEFORE.
THIS IS WHERE WE PART WAYS. OW BLOODY THAT ENDS UP BEING IS UP TO YOU ALL.
YOU HAVE NOTHING TO SAY THAT I WISH TO HEAR.
SHIKLAH, I THINK IT'S TIME WE CAME CLEAN.
I LET YOU HANG AROUND BECAUSE I WASN'T SURE IF I WOULD NEED YOU TO CROSS THE RIVER. NOW THAT WE'RE HERE, IT'S TIME FOR SOME FAREWELLS.
HELLO, ZOMBIES? THE ZOMBIES ARE SCARED TO COME OUT NOW.

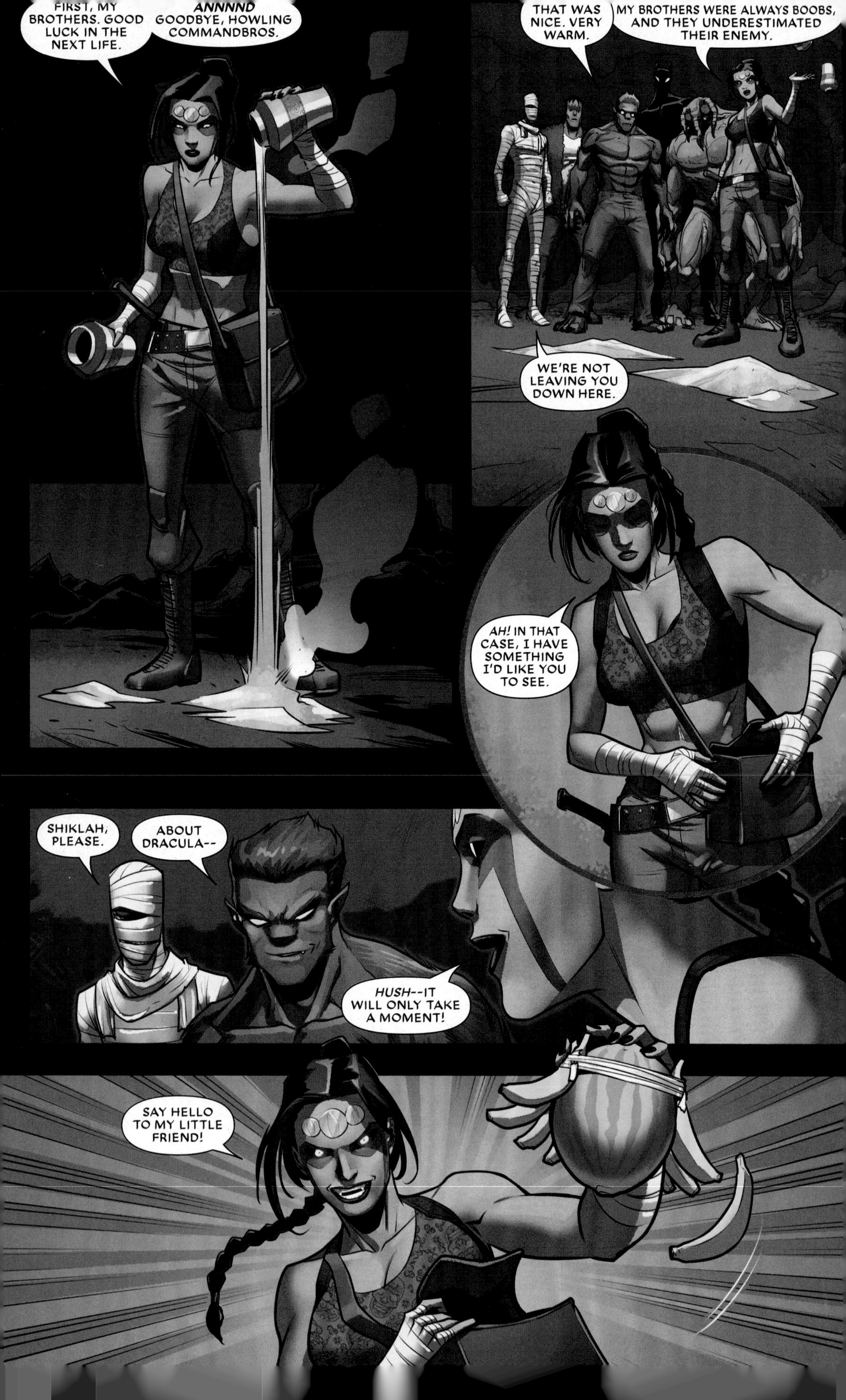
FIRST, MY BROTHERS. GOOD LUCK IN THE NEXT LIFE.
ANNNND GOODBYE, HOWLING COMMANDBROS.
THAT WAS NICE. VERY WARM.
MY BROTHERS WERE ALWAYS BOOBS, AND THEY UNDERESTIMATED THEIR ENEMY.
WE'RE NOT LEAVING YOU DOWN HERE.
AH! IN THAT CASE, I HAVE SOMETHING I'D LIKE YOU TO SEE.
SHIKLAH, PLEASE.
ABOUT DRACULA--
HUSH--IT WILL ONLY TAKE A MOMENT!
SAY HELLO TO MY LITTLE FRIEND!

AH. I SEE ONE OF YOU IS QUITE AN ADEPT PICKPOCKET.

I LEARNED FROM THE BEST CRIMINALS IN ANCIENT PHARBAETUS.

THAT WAS PERFECTLY GOOD FRUIT. IT LOOKS DELICIOUS.

IT'S JUST THE RIGHT KIND OF NATURAL SUGAR THAT CAN CONTROL MY DIABETES.

I TRUST YOU LEFT MY FRIEND MEDUSA WHERE SHE CAN BE RETRIEVED?

FAP

LET'S JUST SAY MY WRAP IS ROOMIER THAN IT APPEARS.

WAIT, WHAT?

ENOUGH! ARE WE ALL GOING TO PRETEND THAT DRACULA HASN'T ORDERED YOU TO KILL ME?

INDEED HE DID, BUT WE HAVE NO DESIRE TO DO SO.

I'M JUST SAYING: IF MY BLOOD SUGAR CRASHES DURING A FIGHT, IT WOULD PLACE US AT A SERIOUS DISADVANTAGE.

FINE, IF YOU WON'T GO HOME TO YOUR MASTER, THEN YOU MIGHT AS WELL HELP.

FRANKENSTEIN'S MONSTER, MORE ZOMBIES ARE COMING SO--TAKE DOWN THIS WALL.

STUPID WALL, GET OUT OF FRANKENSTEIN'S WAY!

WHY ARE YOU LEADING US DEEPER INTO THE LAND OF THE DEAD?

WE'RE TAKING A SHORT-CUT.

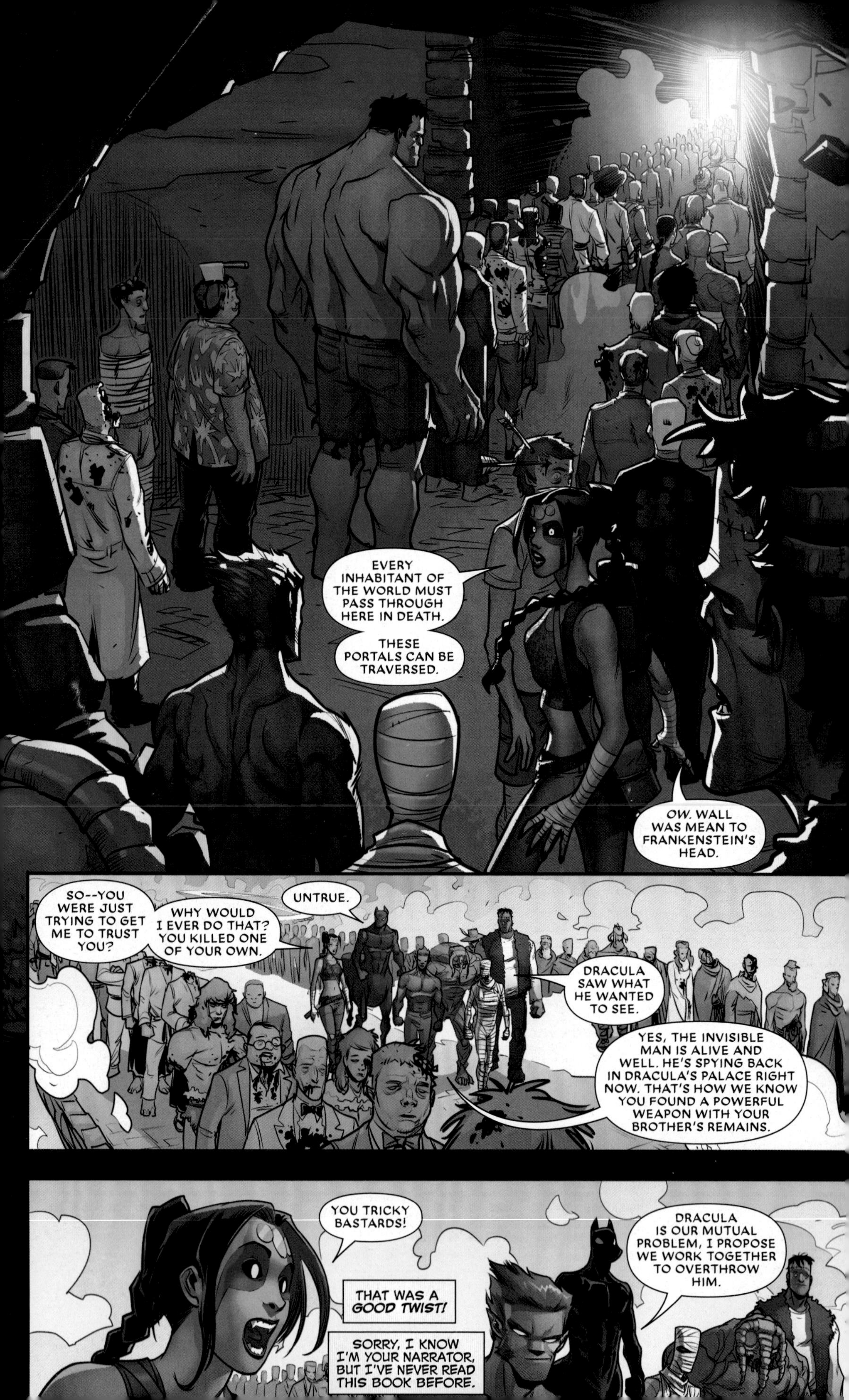

EVERY INHABITANT OF THE WORLD MUST PASS THROUGH HERE IN DEATH.
THESE PORTALS CAN BE TRAVERSED.
OW. WALL WAS MEAN TO FRANKENSTEIN'S HEAD.
SO--YOU WERE JUST TRYING TO GET ME TO TRUST YOU?
WHY WOULD I EVER DO THAT? YOU KILLED ONE OF YOUR OWN.
UNTRUE.
DRACULA SAW WHAT HE WANTED TO SEE.
YES, THE INVISIBLE MAN IS ALIVE AND WELL. HE'S SPYING BACK IN DRACULA'S PALACE RIGHT NOW. THAT'S HOW WE KNOW YOU FOUND A POWERFUL WEAPON WITH YOUR BROTHER'S REMAINS.
YOU TRICKY BASTARDS!
THAT WAS A *GOOD TWIST!*
SORRY, I KNOW I'M YOUR NARRATOR, BUT I'VE NEVER READ THIS BOOK BEFORE.
DRACULA IS OUR MUTUAL PROBLEM, I PROPOSE WE WORK TOGETHER TO OVERTHROW HIM.

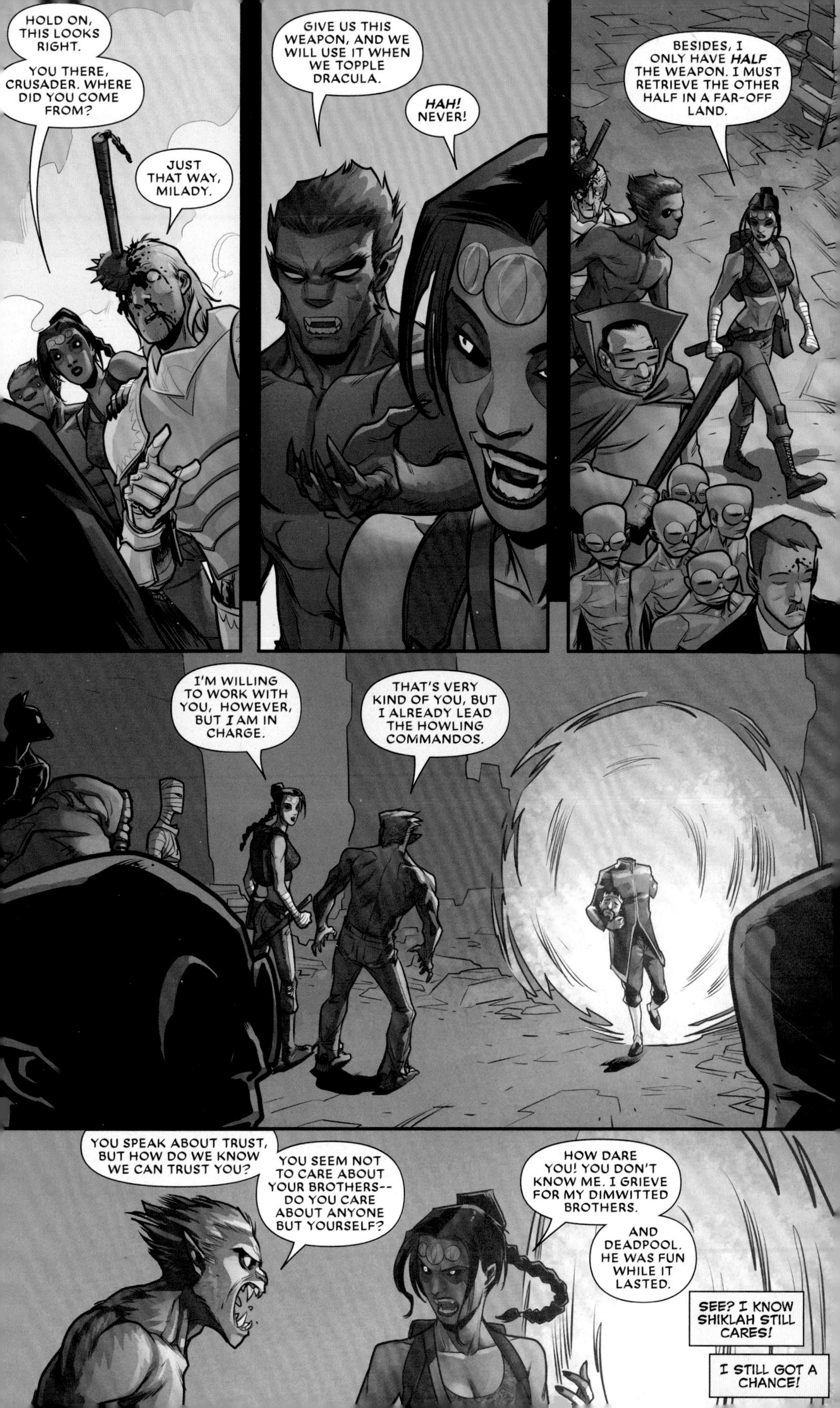
HOLD ON, THIS LOOKS RIGHT.
YOU THERE, CRUSADER. WHERE DID YOU COME FROM?
JUST THAT WAY, MILADY.
GIVE US THIS WEAPON, AND WE WILL USE IT WHEN WE TOPPLE DRACULA.
HAH! NEVER!
BESIDES, I ONLY HAVE HALF THE WEAPON. I MUST RETRIEVE THE OTHER HALF IN A FAR-OFF LAND.
I'M WILLING TO WORK WITH YOU, HOWEVER, BUT I AM IN CHARGE.
THAT'S VERY KIND OF YOU, BUT I ALREADY LEAD THE HOWLING COMMANDOS.
YOU SPEAK ABOUT TRUST, BUT HOW DO WE KNOW WE CAN TRUST YOU?
YOU SEEM NOT TO CARE ABOUT YOUR BROTHERS-- DO YOU CARE ABOUT ANYONE BUT YOURSELF?
HOW DARE YOU! YOU DON'T KNOW ME. I GRIEVE FOR MY DIMWITTED BROTHERS.
AND DEADPOOL. HE WAS FUN WHILE IT LASTED.
SEE? I KNOW SHIKLAH STILL CARES!
I STILL GOT A CHANCE!

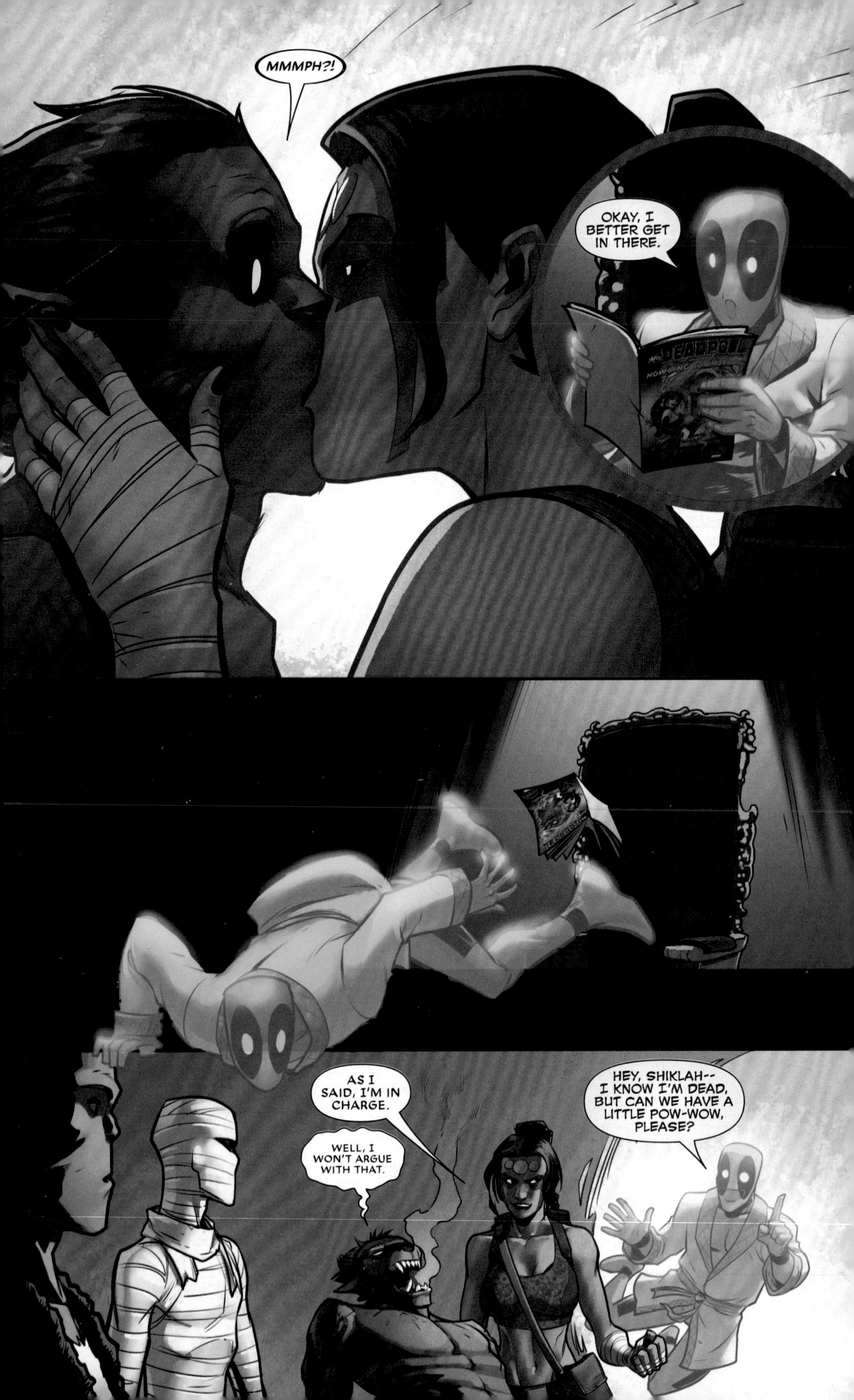
MMMPH?!
OKAY, I BETTER GET IN THERE.
DEADPOOL
AS I SAID, I'M IN CHARGE.
WELL, I WON'T ARGUE WITH THAT.
HEY, SHIKLAH-- I KNOW I'M DEAD, BUT CAN WE HAVE A LITTLE POW-WOW, PLEASE?

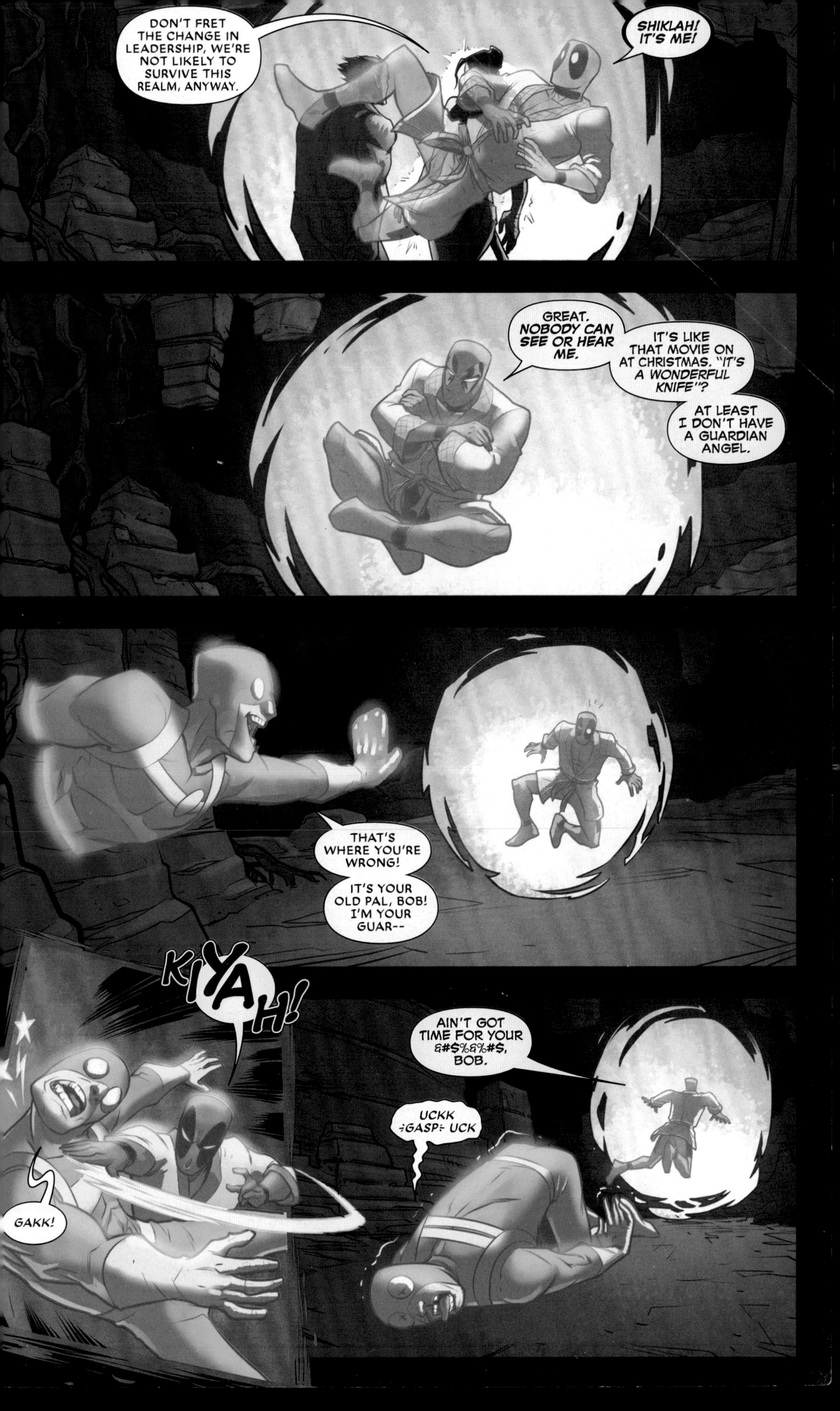
DON'T FRET THE CHANGE IN LEADERSHIP, WE'RE NOT LIKELY TO SURVIVE THIS REALM, ANYWAY.
SHIKLAH! IT'S ME!
GREAT. NOBODY CAN SEE OR HEAR ME.
IT'S LIKE THAT MOVIE ON AT CHRISTMAS. "IT'S A WONDERFUL KNIFE"?
AT LEAST I DON'T HAVE A GUARDIAN ANGEL.
THAT'S WHERE YOU'RE WRONG!
IT'S YOUR OLD PAL, BOB! I'M YOUR GUAR--
KIYAH!
GAKK!
AIN'T GOT TIME FOR YOUR &#$%&%#$, BOB.
UCKK ÷GASP÷ UCK

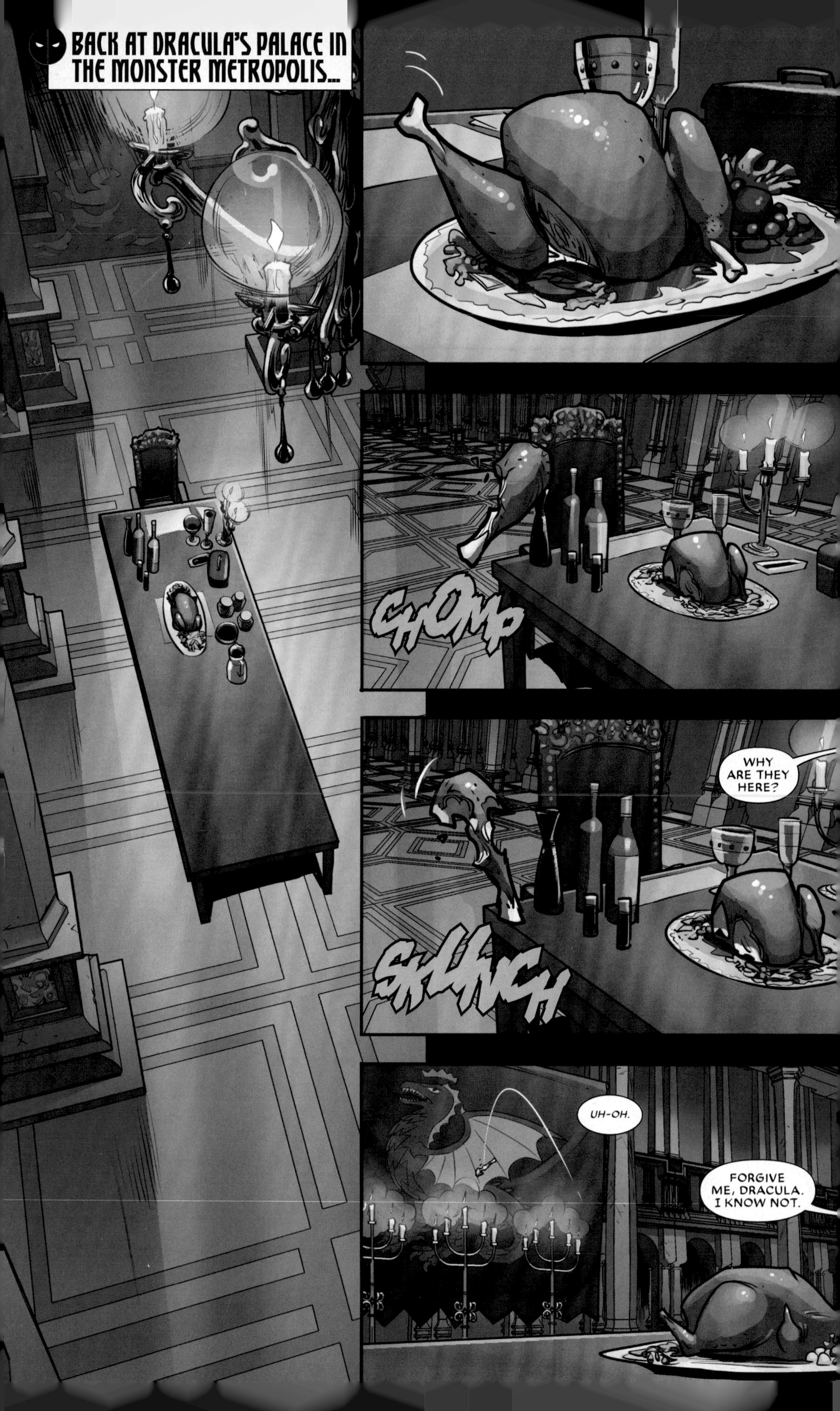
BACK AT DRACULA'S PALACE IN THE MONSTER METROPOLIS...
CHOMP
SKLUNCH
WHY ARE THEY HERE?
UH-OH.
FORGIVE ME, DRACULA. I KNOW NOT.

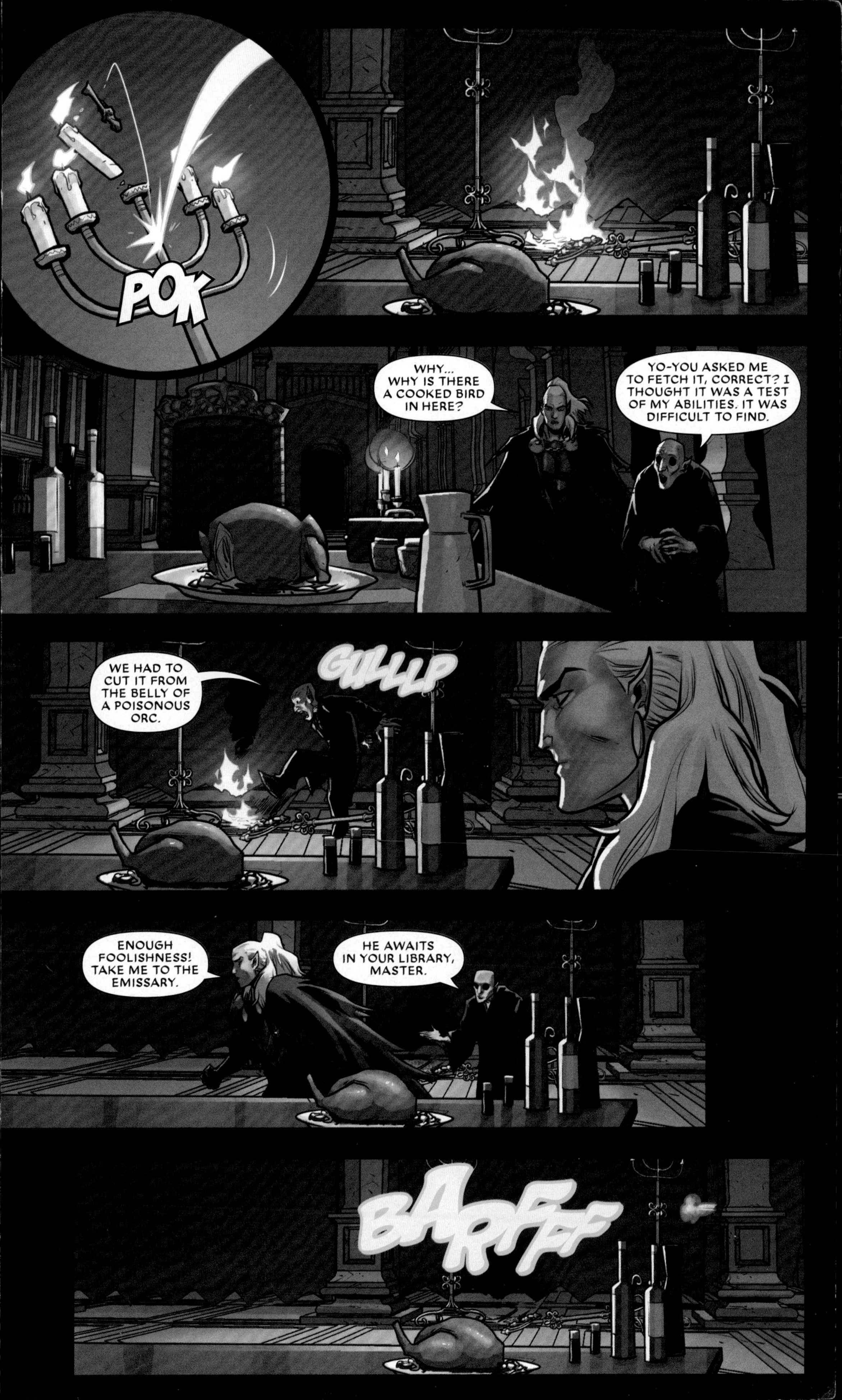
POK
WHY... WHY IS THERE A COOKED BIRD IN HERE?
YO-YOU ASKED ME TO FETCH IT, CORRECT? I THOUGHT IT WAS A TEST OF MY ABILITIES. IT WAS DIFFICULT TO FIND.
WE HAD TO CUT IT FROM THE BELLY OF A POISONOUS ORC.
GULLLP
ENOUGH FOOLISHNESS! TAKE ME TO THE EMISSARY.
HE AWAITS IN YOUR LIBRARY, MASTER.
BARFFF

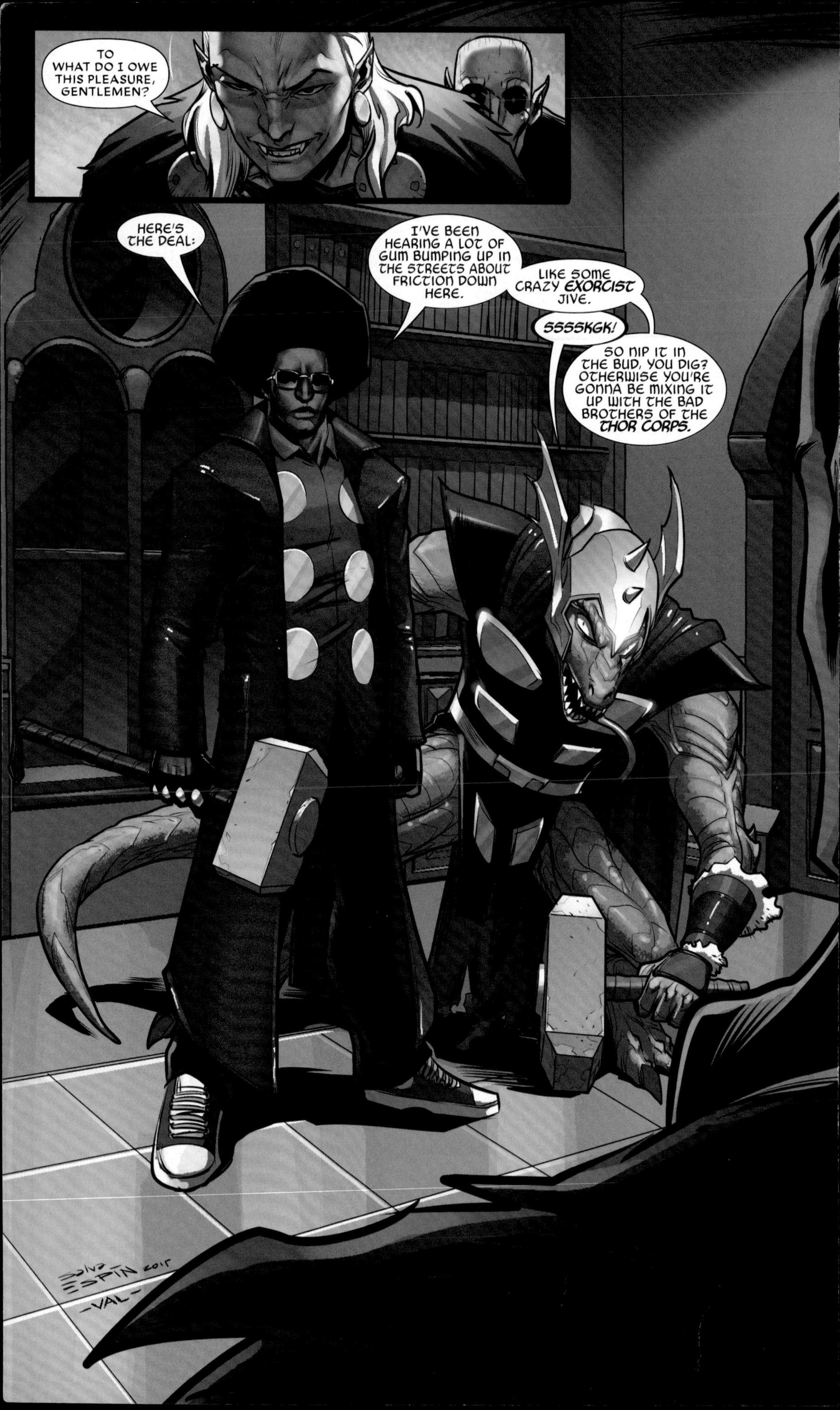
TO WHAT DO I OWE THIS PLEASURE, GENTLEMEN?
HERE'S THE DEAL:
I'VE BEEN HEARING A LOT OF GUM BUMPING UP IN THE STREETS ABOUT FRICTION DOWN HERE.
LIKE SOME CRAZY EXORCIST JIVE.
SSSSKGK!
SO NIP IT IN THE BUD, YOU DIG? OTHERWISE YOU'RE GONNA BE MIXING IT UP WITH THE BAD BROTHERS OF THE THOR CORPS.
SALVA ESPIN 2015
-VAL-

MRS. DEADPOOL AND THE HOWLING COMMANDOS #1 VARIANT BY
GIUSEPPE CAMUNCOLI & MARTE GRACIA

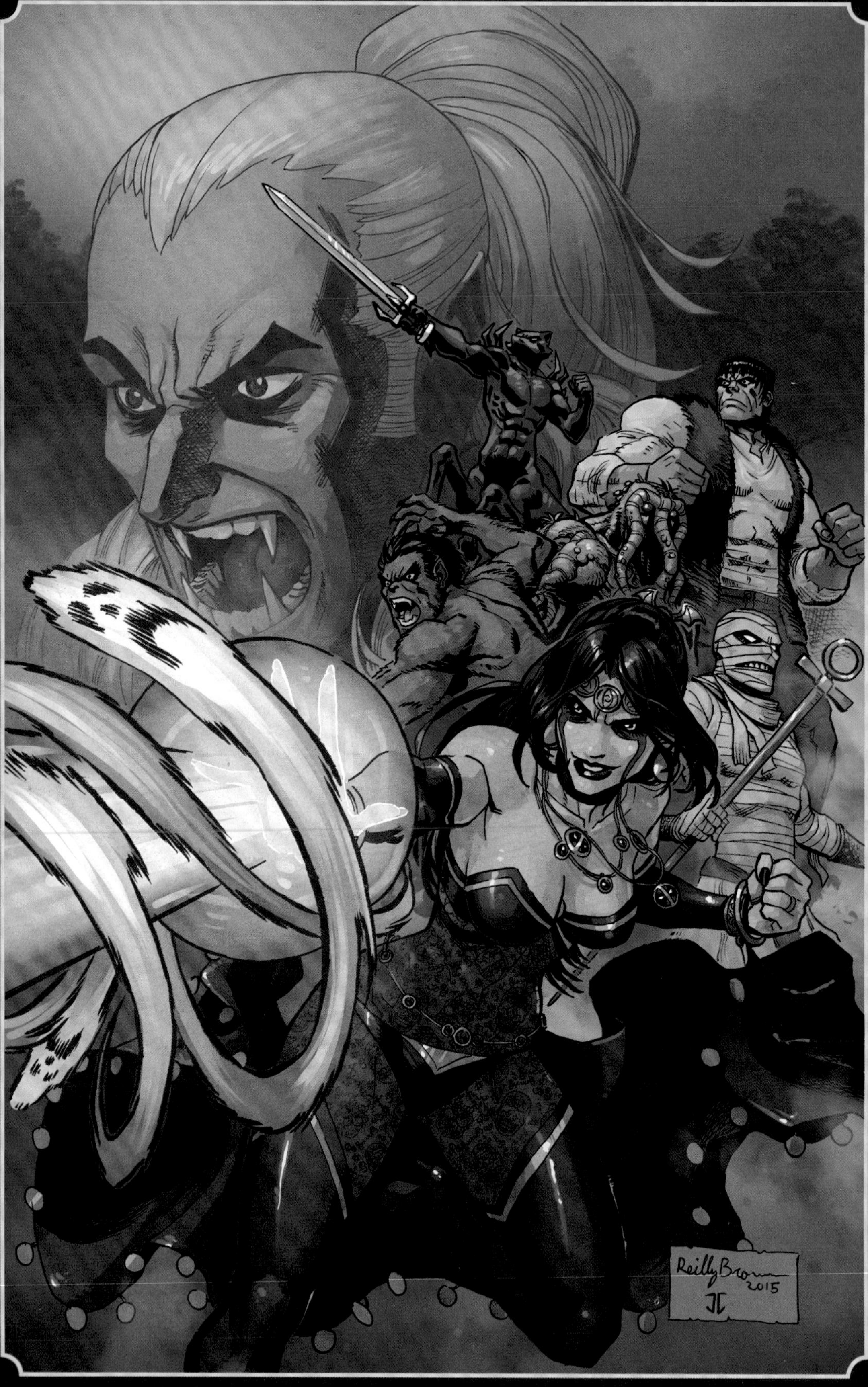
Reilly Brown
2015
JC

3

HEY, DEADPOOL HERE. WHILE YOU'VE BEEN GONE MY WAIFU AND HER "HAPPY HALLOWEENERS" MARCHED AROUND SOME JUNGLE LOOKING FOR AN OLD BUILDING.

FRANKENSTEIN'S SHOES HURT.

QUITE. PARDON, BUT IS IT IMPOLITE TO ASK HOW MUCH FURTHER?

WITHOUT MUCH LUCK...UNTIL NOW.

DEATH SMELLS.

ARE YOU HAVING ANOTHER STROKE?

WE'RE HERE.

FRANKENSTEIN'S MONSTER SMELLS THE ROT FROM BELOW.

BEHOLD, WEIRDWORLD.

BY BROTHER HO-TEP!

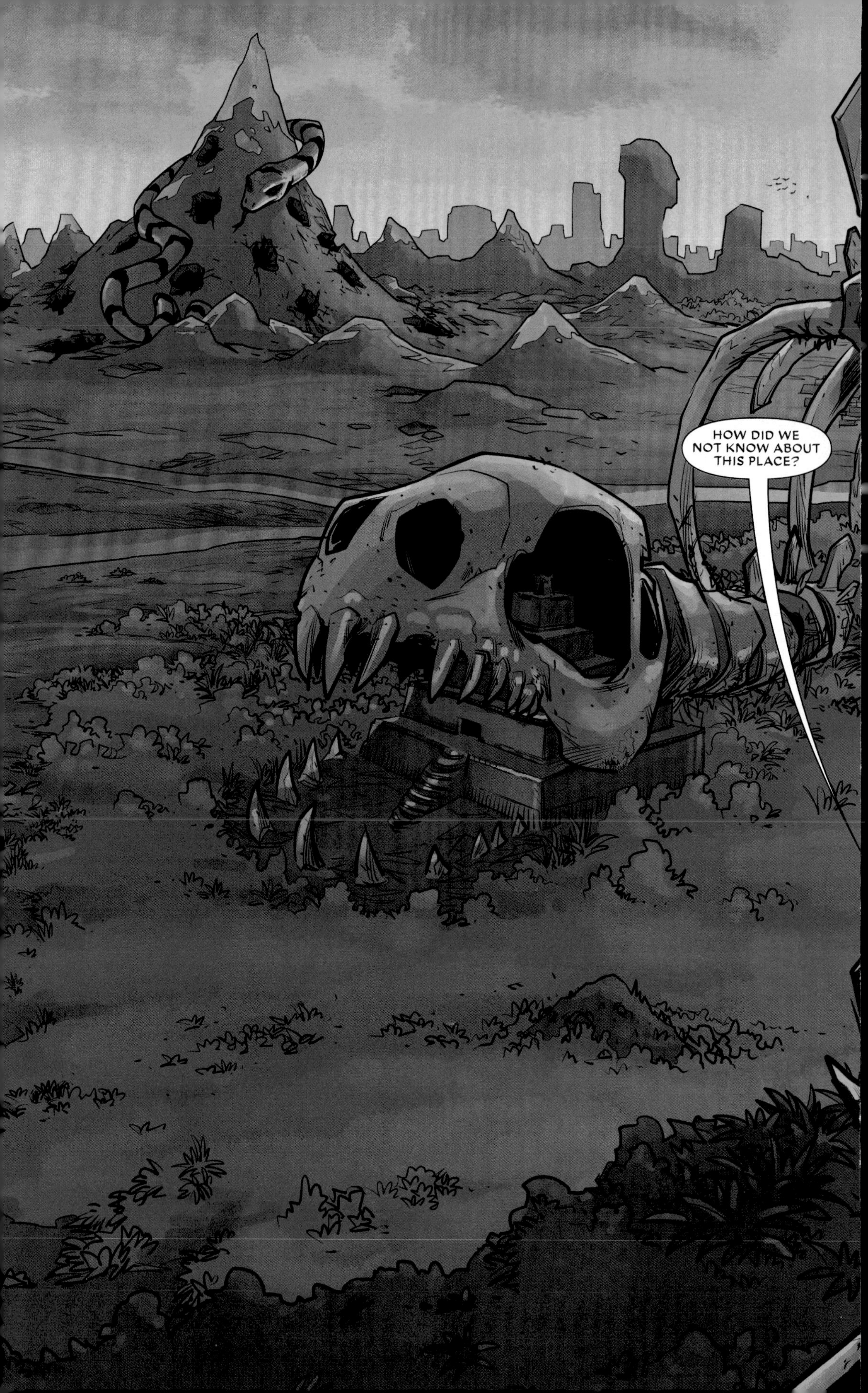
HOW DID WE NOT KNOW ABOUT THIS PLACE?

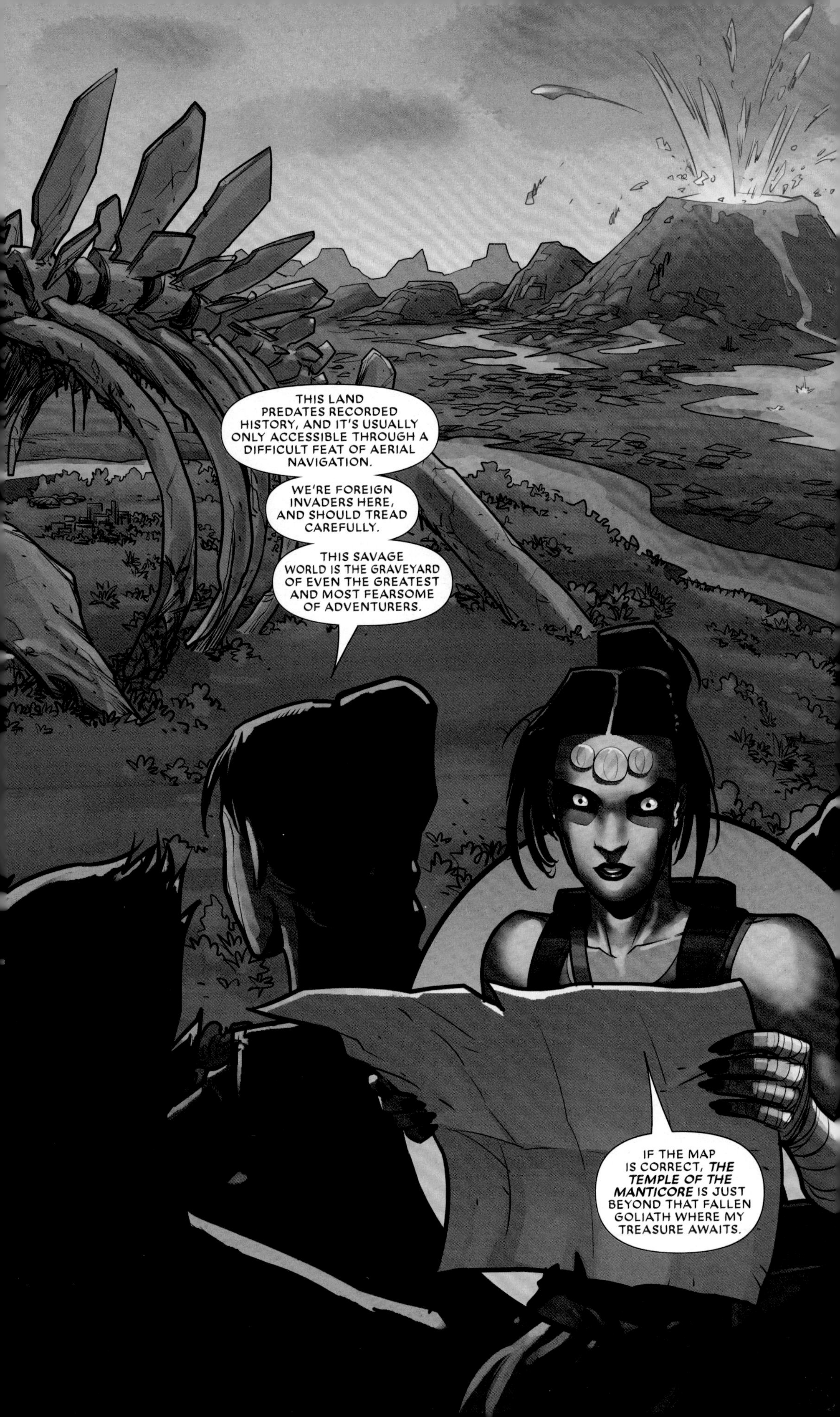
THIS LAND PREDATES RECORDED HISTORY, AND IT'S USUALLY ONLY ACCESSIBLE THROUGH A DIFFICULT FEAT OF AERIAL NAVIGATION.
WE'RE FOREIGN INVADERS HERE, AND SHOULD TREAD CAREFULLY.
THIS SAVAGE WORLD IS THE GRAVEYARD OF EVEN THE GREATEST AND MOST FEARSOME OF ADVENTURERS.
IF THE MAP IS CORRECT, *THE TEMPLE OF THE MANTICORE* IS JUST BEYOND THAT FALLEN GOLIATH WHERE MY TREASURE AWAITS.

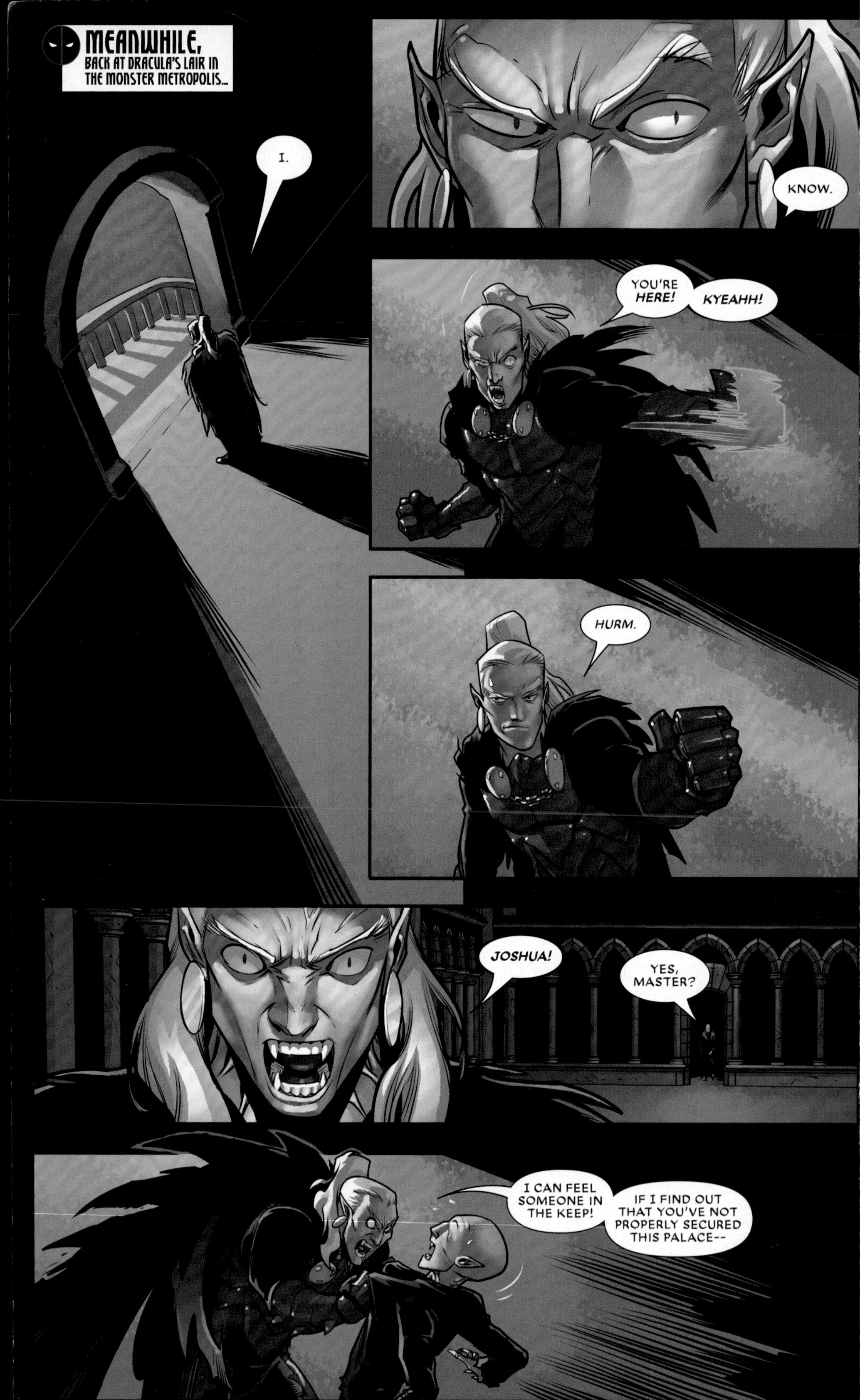
MEANWHILE,
BACK AT DRACULA'S LAIR IN THE MONSTER METROPOLIS...
I.
KNOW.
YOU'RE HERE!
KYEAHH!
HURM.
JOSHUA!
YES, MASTER?
I CAN FEEL SOMEONE IN THE KEEP!
IF I FIND OUT THAT YOU'VE NOT PROPERLY SECURED THIS PALACE--

N-NO.

I'LL EAT YOU WHILE YOU'RE ALIVE!

ARE YOU CRYING?!

IS THERE AN INVISIBLE MAN IN THE PLACE?

TELL ME THE TRUTH OR I'LL GUT YOU RIGHT NOW!

AAARGH!

I CAN SMELL HIM!

N-NNO. HE'S DEAD!

HE HAD BETTER BE.

GET OUT!

HAVE I BEEN BETRAYED BY THE HOWLING COMMANDOS?!

KYEAHH!

"I DON'T WANT TO USE THE *L WORD*, BUT, ARE WE...*LOST*?"

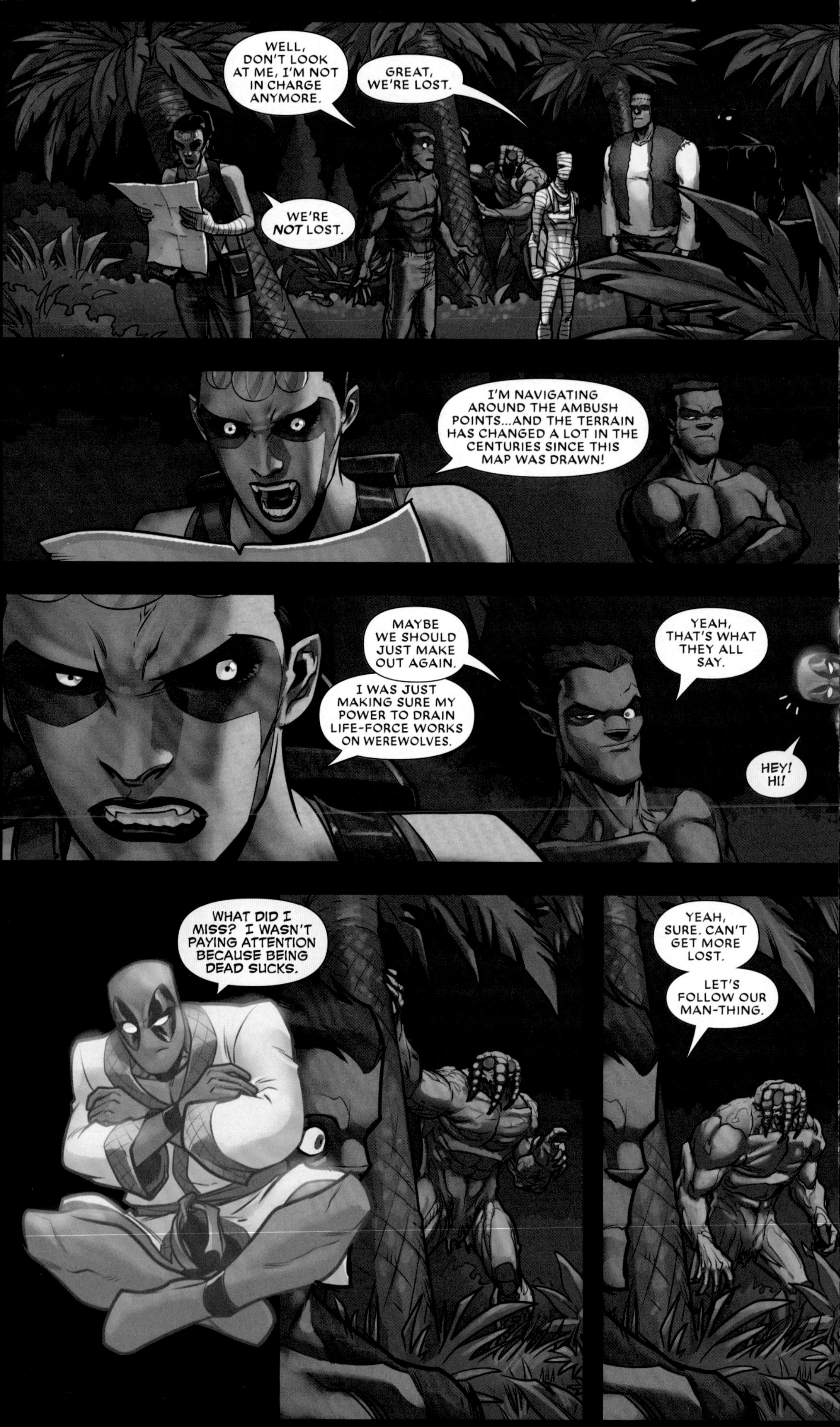
WELL, DON'T LOOK AT ME, I'M NOT IN CHARGE ANYMORE.
GREAT, WE'RE LOST.
WE'RE NOT LOST.
I'M NAVIGATING AROUND THE AMBUSH POINTS...AND THE TERRAIN HAS CHANGED A LOT IN THE CENTURIES SINCE THIS MAP WAS DRAWN!
MAYBE WE SHOULD JUST MAKE OUT AGAIN.
I WAS JUST MAKING SURE MY POWER TO DRAIN LIFE-FORCE WORKS ON WEREWOLVES.
YEAH, THAT'S WHAT THEY ALL SAY.
HEY! HI!
WHAT DID I MISS? I WASN'T PAYING ATTENTION BECAUSE BEING DEAD SUCKS.
YEAH, SURE. CAN'T GET MORE LOST.
LET'S FOLLOW OUR MAN-THING.

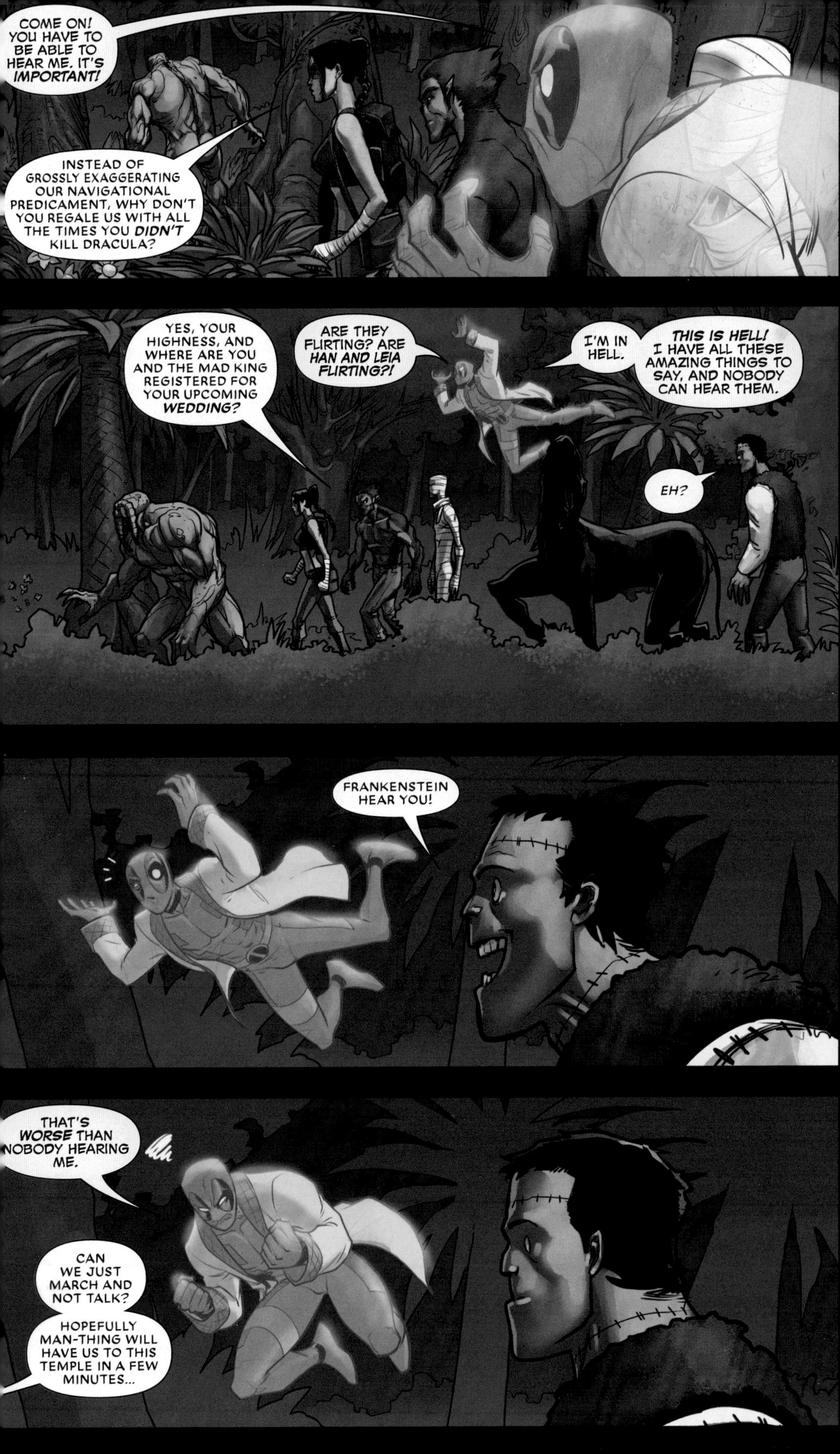
COME ON! YOU HAVE TO BE ABLE TO HEAR ME. IT'S IMPORTANT!
INSTEAD OF GROSSLY EXAGGERATING OUR NAVIGATIONAL PREDICAMENT, WHY DON'T YOU REGALE US WITH ALL THE TIMES YOU DIDN'T KILL DRACULA?
YES, YOUR HIGHNESS, AND WHERE ARE YOU AND THE MAD KING REGISTERED FOR YOUR UPCOMING WEDDING?
ARE THEY FLIRTING? ARE HAN AND LEIA FLIRTING?!
I'M IN HELL.
THIS IS HELL! I HAVE ALL THESE AMAZING THINGS TO SAY, AND NOBODY CAN HEAR THEM.
EH?
FRANKENSTEIN HEAR YOU!
THAT'S WORSE THAN NOBODY HEARING ME.
CAN WE JUST MARCH AND NOT TALK?
HOPEFULLY MAN-THING WILL HAVE US TO THIS TEMPLE IN A FEW MINUTES...

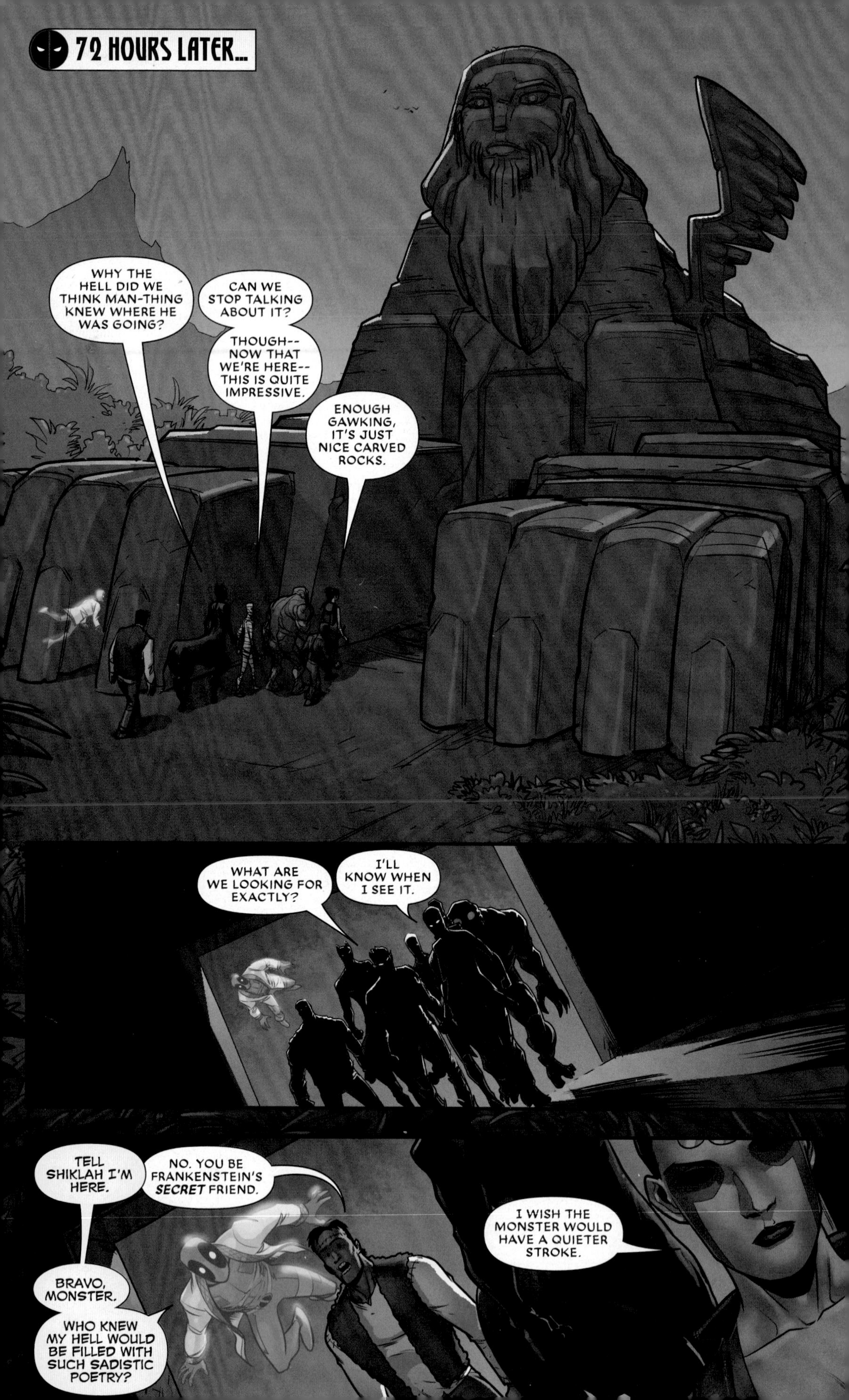
72 HOURS LATER...
WHY THE HELL DID WE THINK MAN-THING KNEW WHERE HE WAS GOING?
CAN WE STOP TALKING ABOUT IT?
THOUGH-- NOW THAT WE'RE HERE-- THIS IS QUITE IMPRESSIVE.
ENOUGH GAWKING, IT'S JUST NICE CARVED ROCKS.
WHAT ARE WE LOOKING FOR EXACTLY?
I'LL KNOW WHEN I SEE IT.
TELL SHIKLAH I'M HERE.
NO. YOU BE FRANKENSTEIN'S *SECRET* FRIEND.
BRAVO, MONSTER.
WHO KNEW MY HELL WOULD BE FILLED WITH SUCH SADISTIC POETRY?
I WISH THE MONSTER WOULD HAVE A QUIETER STROKE.

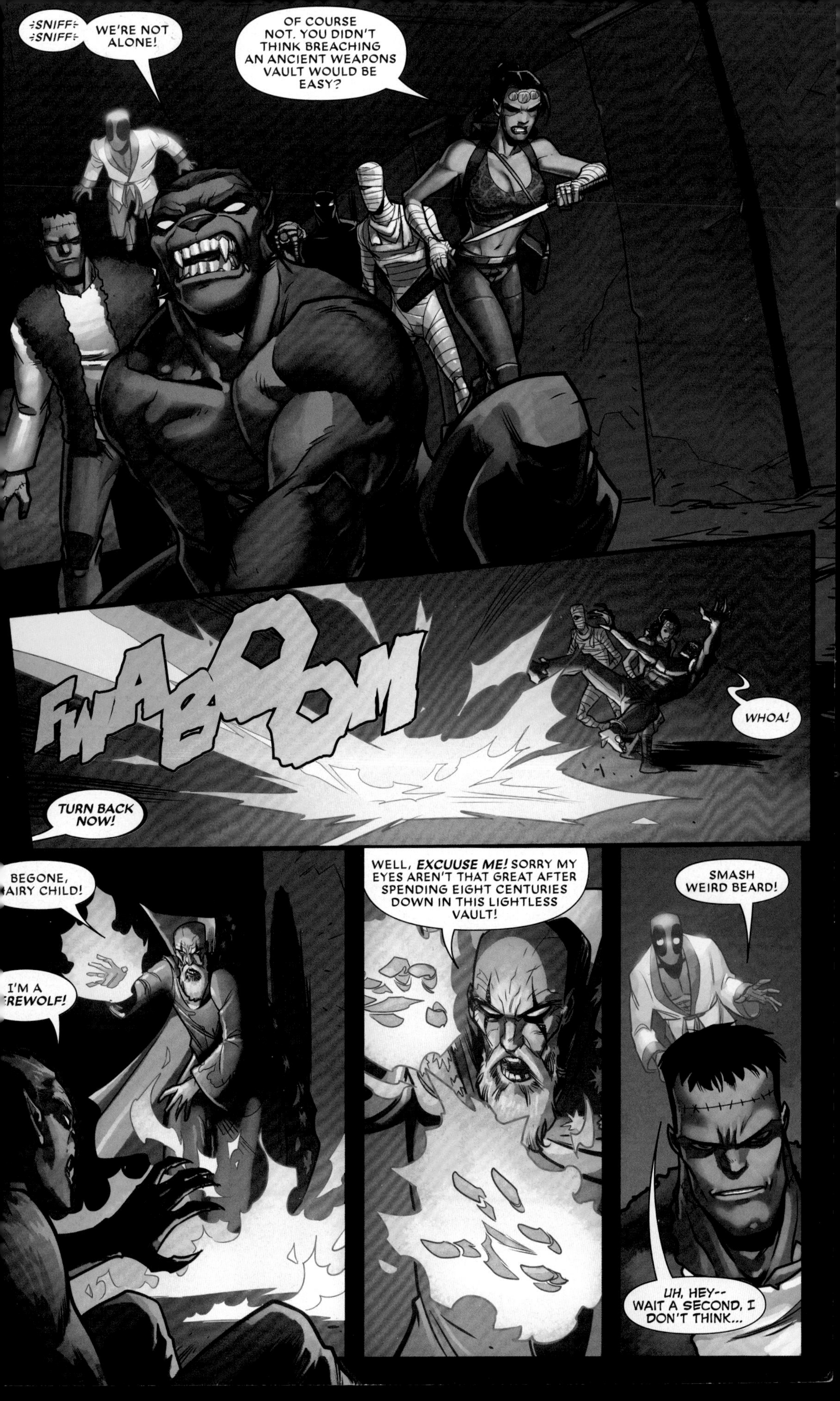

SNIFF SNIFF
WE'RE NOT ALONE!
OF COURSE NOT. YOU DIDN'T THINK BREACHING AN ANCIENT WEAPONS VAULT WOULD BE EASY?
FWABOOM
WHOA!
TURN BACK NOW!
BEGONE, AIRY CHILD!
I'M A EREWOLF!
WELL, EXCUUSE ME! SORRY MY EYES AREN'T THAT GREAT AFTER SPENDING EIGHT CENTURIES DOWN IN THIS LIGHTLESS VAULT!
SMASH WEIRD BEARD!
UH, HEY-- WAIT A SECOND, I DON'T THINK...

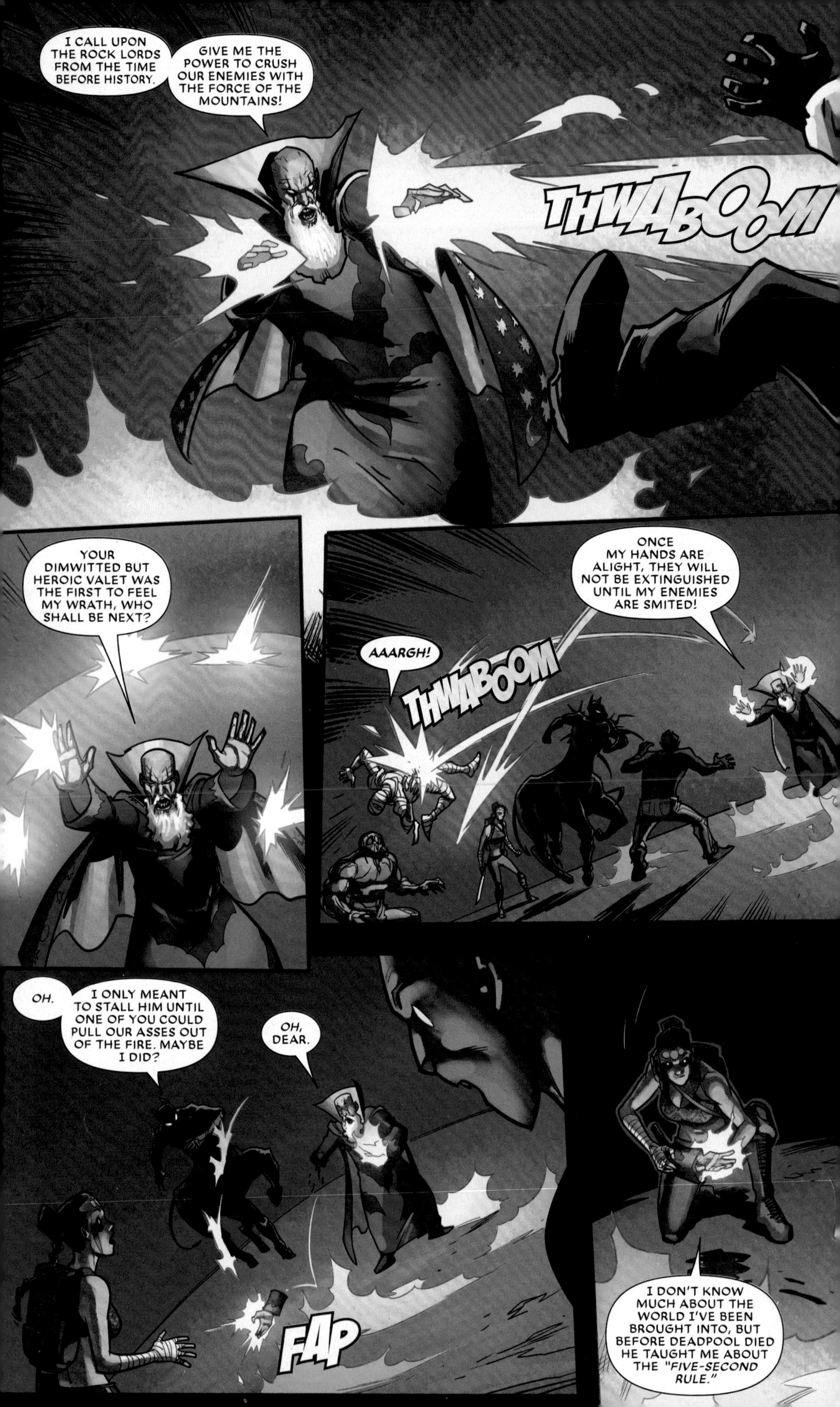
I CALL UPON THE ROCK LORDS FROM THE TIME BEFORE HISTORY.
GIVE ME THE POWER TO CRUSH OUR ENEMIES WITH THE FORCE OF THE MOUNTAINS!
THWABOOOM
YOUR DIMWITTED BUT HEROIC VALET WAS THE FIRST TO FEEL MY WRATH, WHO SHALL BE NEXT?
ONCE MY HANDS ARE ALIGHT, THEY WILL NOT BE EXTINGUISHED UNTIL MY ENEMIES ARE SMITED!
AAARGH!
THWABOOM
OH.
I ONLY MEANT TO STALL HIM UNTIL ONE OF YOU COULD PULL OUR ASSES OUT OF THE FIRE. MAYBE I DID?
OH, DEAR.
FAP
I DON'T KNOW MUCH ABOUT THE WORLD I'VE BEEN BROUGHT INTO, BUT BEFORE DEADPOOL DIED HE TAUGHT ME ABOUT THE *"FIVE-SECOND RULE."*

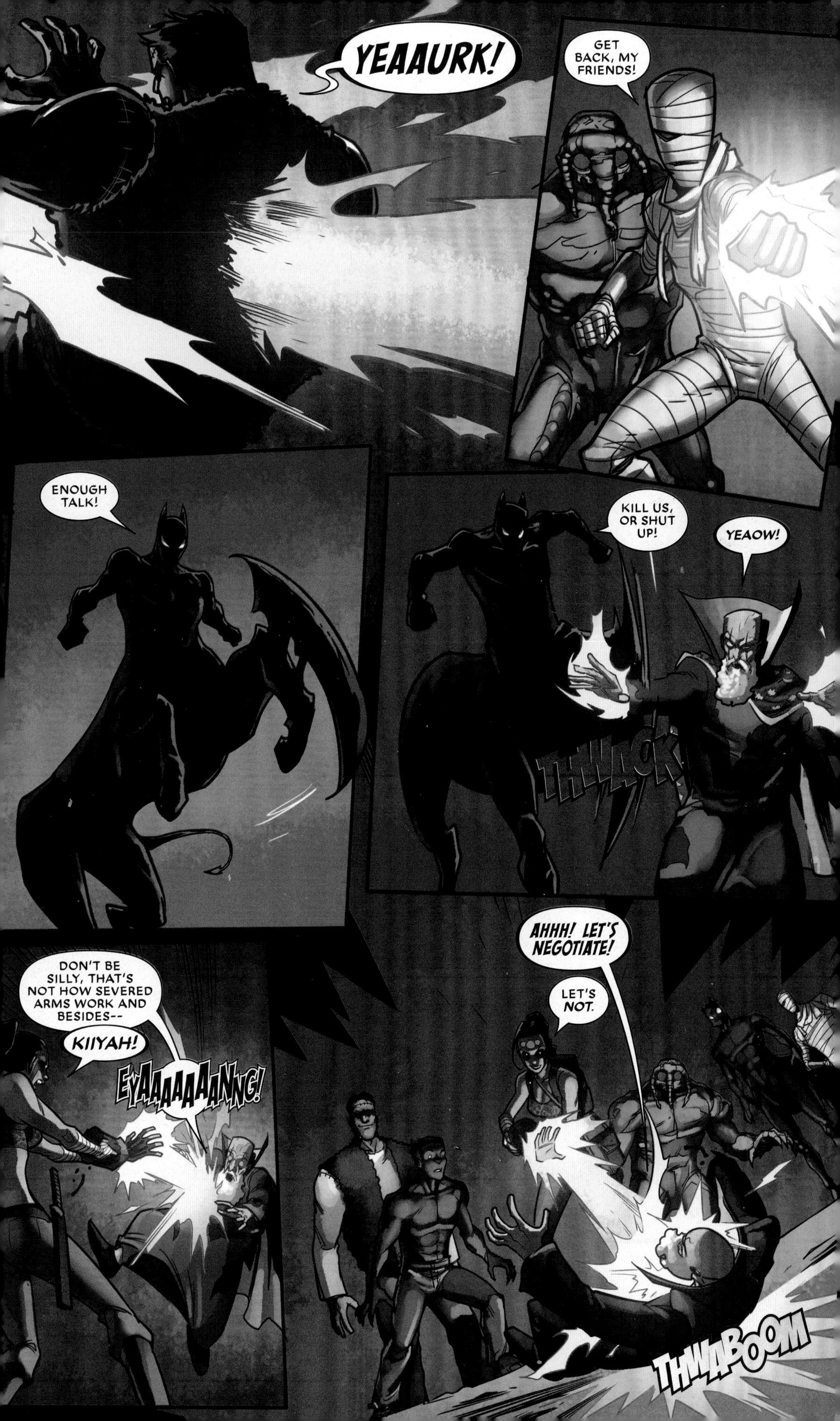
YEAAURK!
GET BACK, MY FRIENDS!
ENOUGH TALK!
KILL US, OR SHUT UP!
YEAOW!
THWACK!
DON'T BE SILLY, THAT'S NOT HOW SEVERED ARMS WORK AND BESIDES--
KIIYAH!
EYAAAAAAANNG!
AHHH! LET'S NEGOTIATE!
LET'S NOT.
THWABOOM

FRANKENSTEIN KEEP HIS DRESS.

ARE WE SURE THIS IS NECESSARY?

I KNOW DRACULA IS A MONSTER, BUT WE'RE ALL LIVING IN A GLASS HOUSE ON THAT ONE.

HE WILL EAT US ALL.

SHOW SOME BACKBONE.

NOW I KNOW WHY THEY CALL YOU "THE MEWLING COMMANDOS."

HAH!

IT'S EMPTY! WE CAME ALL THIS WAY FOR NOTHING.

WHAT A WASTE.

STEP ASIDE.

FRANKENSTEIN. PUSH.

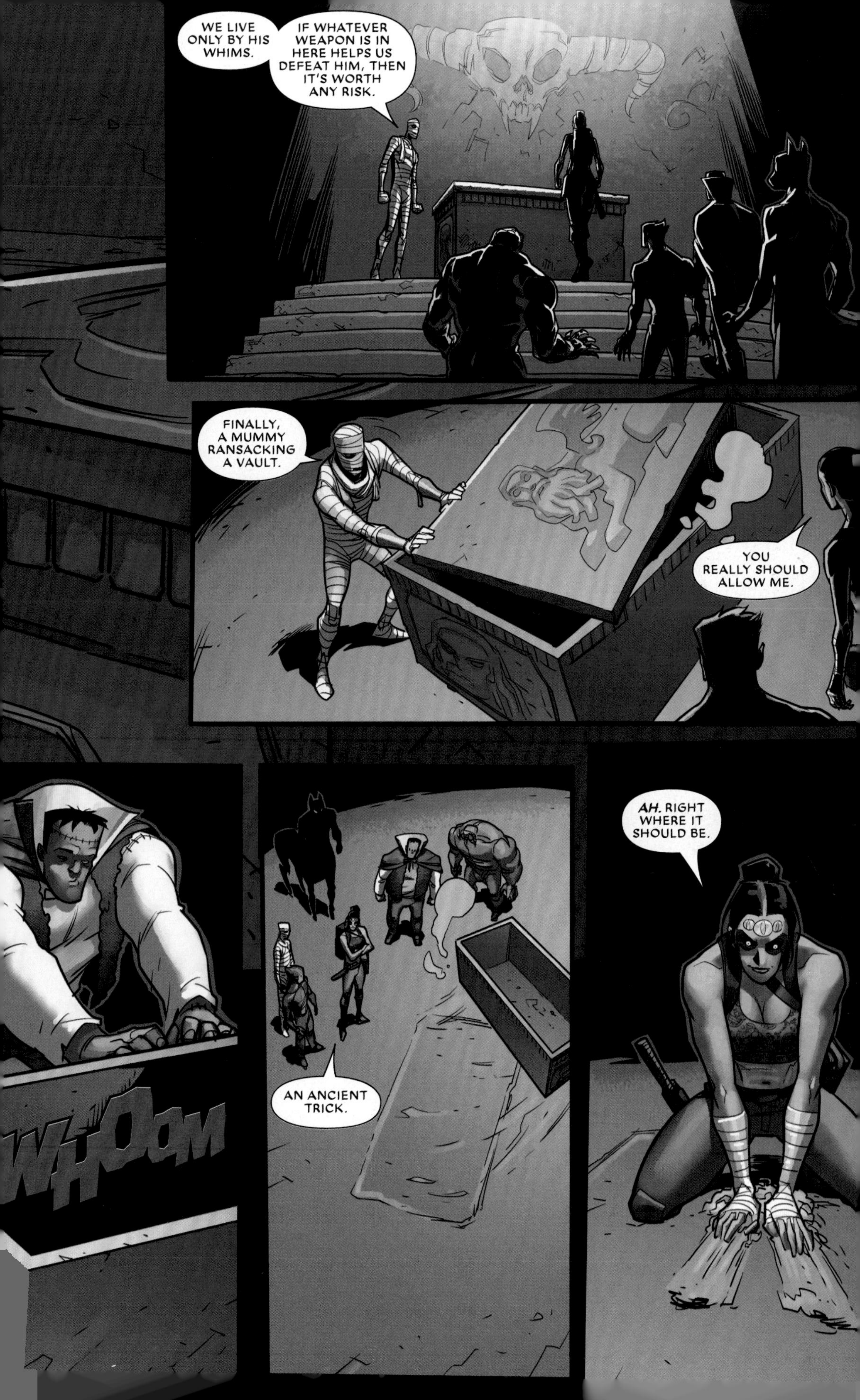
WE LIVE ONLY BY HIS WHIMS.
IF WHATEVER WEAPON IS IN HERE HELPS US DEFEAT HIM, THEN IT'S WORTH ANY RISK.
FINALLY, A MUMMY RANSACKING A VAULT.
YOU REALLY SHOULD ALLOW ME.
WHOOM
AN ANCIENT TRICK.
AH. RIGHT WHERE IT SHOULD BE.

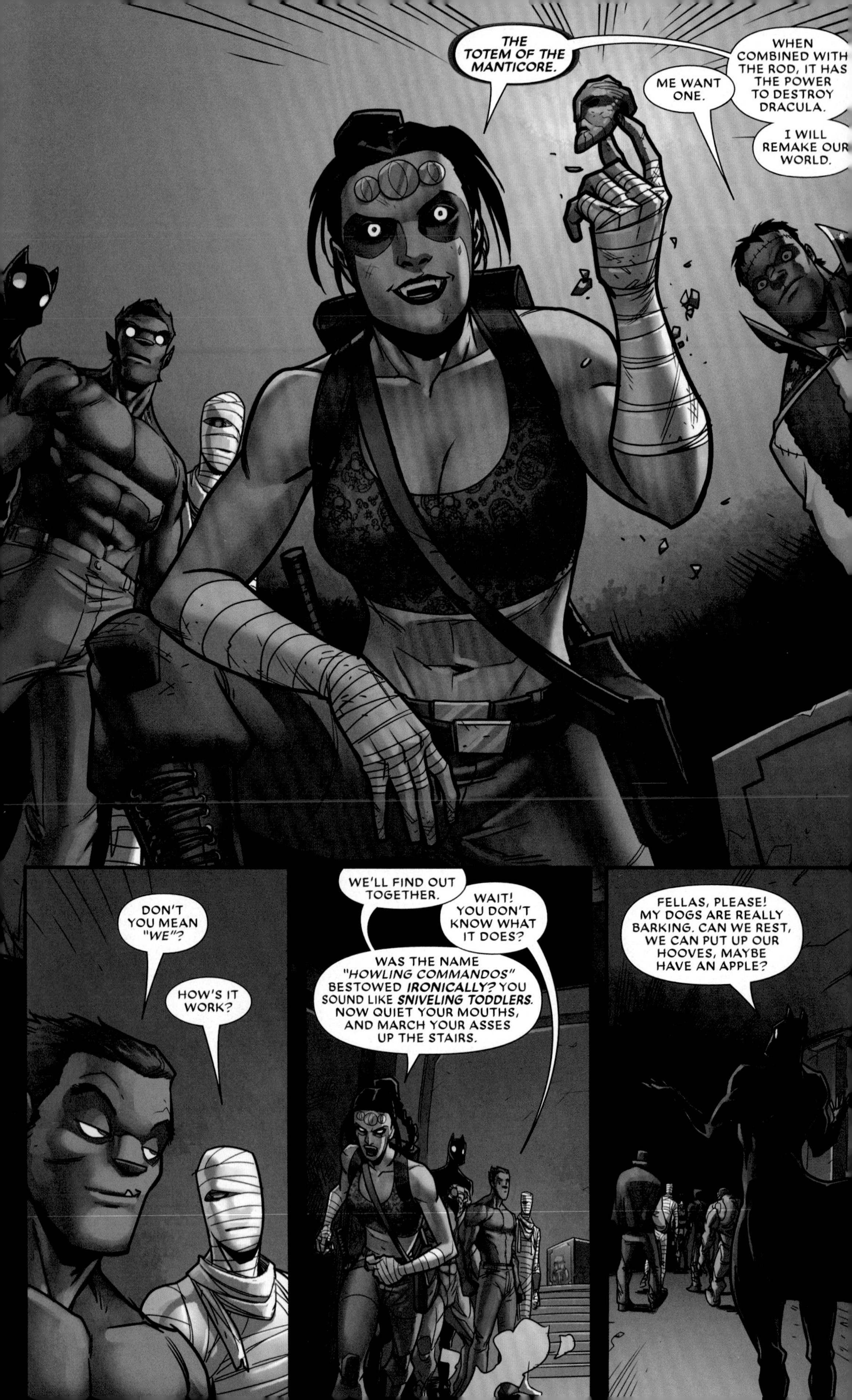
THE TOTEM OF THE MANTICORE.
WHEN COMBINED WITH THE ROD, IT HAS THE POWER TO DESTROY DRACULA.
I WILL REMAKE OUR WORLD.
ME WANT ONE.
DON'T YOU MEAN "WE"?
HOW'S IT WORK?
WE'LL FIND OUT TOGETHER.
WAIT! YOU DON'T KNOW WHAT IT DOES?
WAS THE NAME "HOWLING COMMANDOS" BESTOWED IRONICALLY? YOU SOUND LIKE SNIVELING TODDLERS. NOW QUIET YOUR MOUTHS, AND MARCH YOUR ASSES UP THE STAIRS.
FELLAS, PLEASE! MY DOGS ARE REALLY BARKING. CAN WE REST, WE CAN PUT UP OUR HOOVES, MAYBE HAVE AN APPLE?

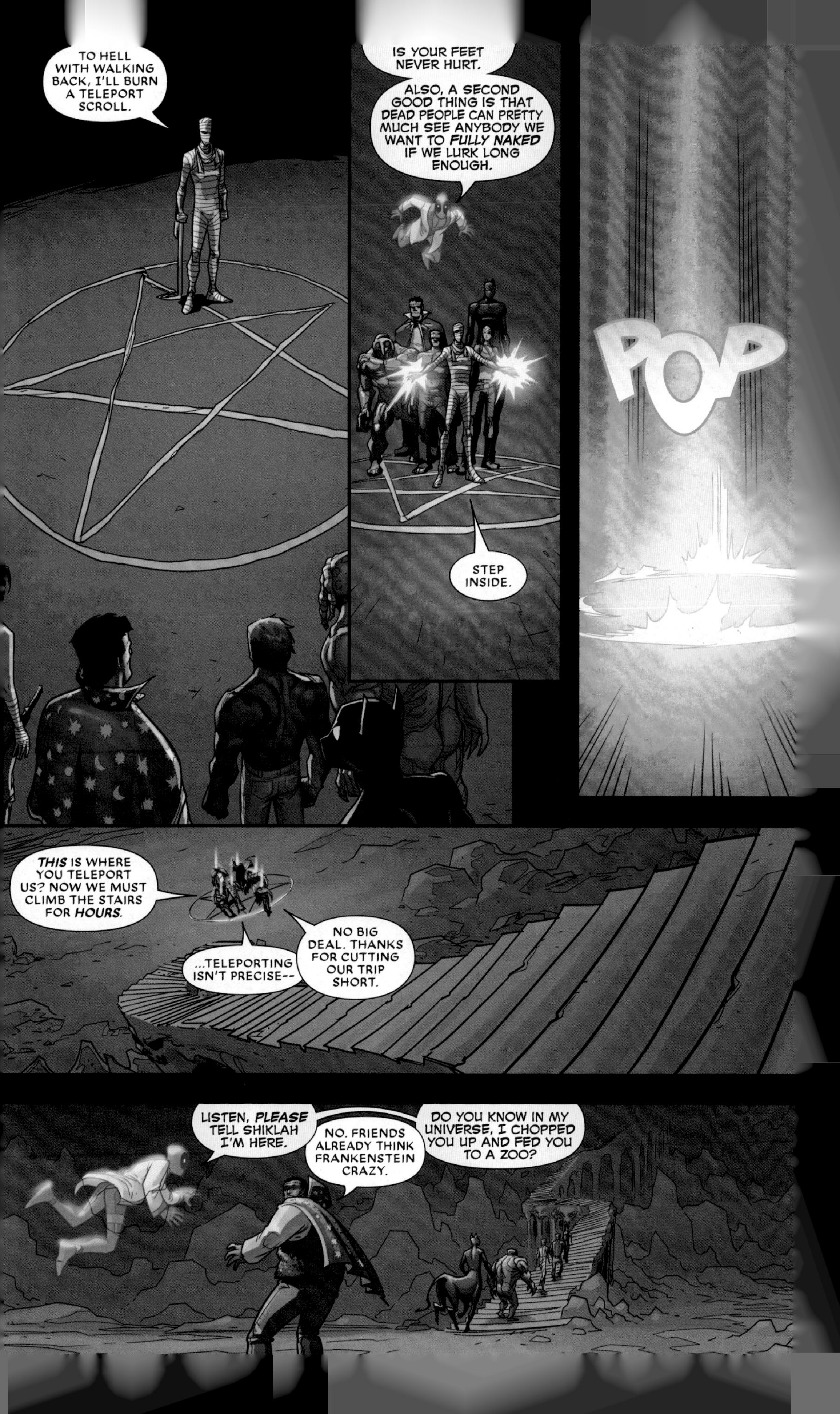
TO HELL WITH WALKING BACK, I'LL BURN A TELEPORT SCROLL.
IS YOUR FEET NEVER HURT.
ALSO, A SECOND GOOD THING IS THAT DEAD PEOPLE CAN PRETTY MUCH SEE ANYBODY WE WANT TO FULLY NAKED IF WE LURK LONG ENOUGH.
STEP INSIDE.
POP
THIS IS WHERE YOU TELEPORT US? NOW WE MUST CLIMB THE STAIRS FOR HOURS.
...TELEPORTING ISN'T PRECISE--
NO BIG DEAL. THANKS FOR CUTTING OUR TRIP SHORT.
LISTEN, PLEASE TELL SHIKLAH I'M HERE.
NO. FRIENDS ALREADY THINK FRANKENSTEIN CRAZY.
DO YOU KNOW IN MY UNIVERSE, I CHOPPED YOU UP AND FED YOU TO A ZOO?

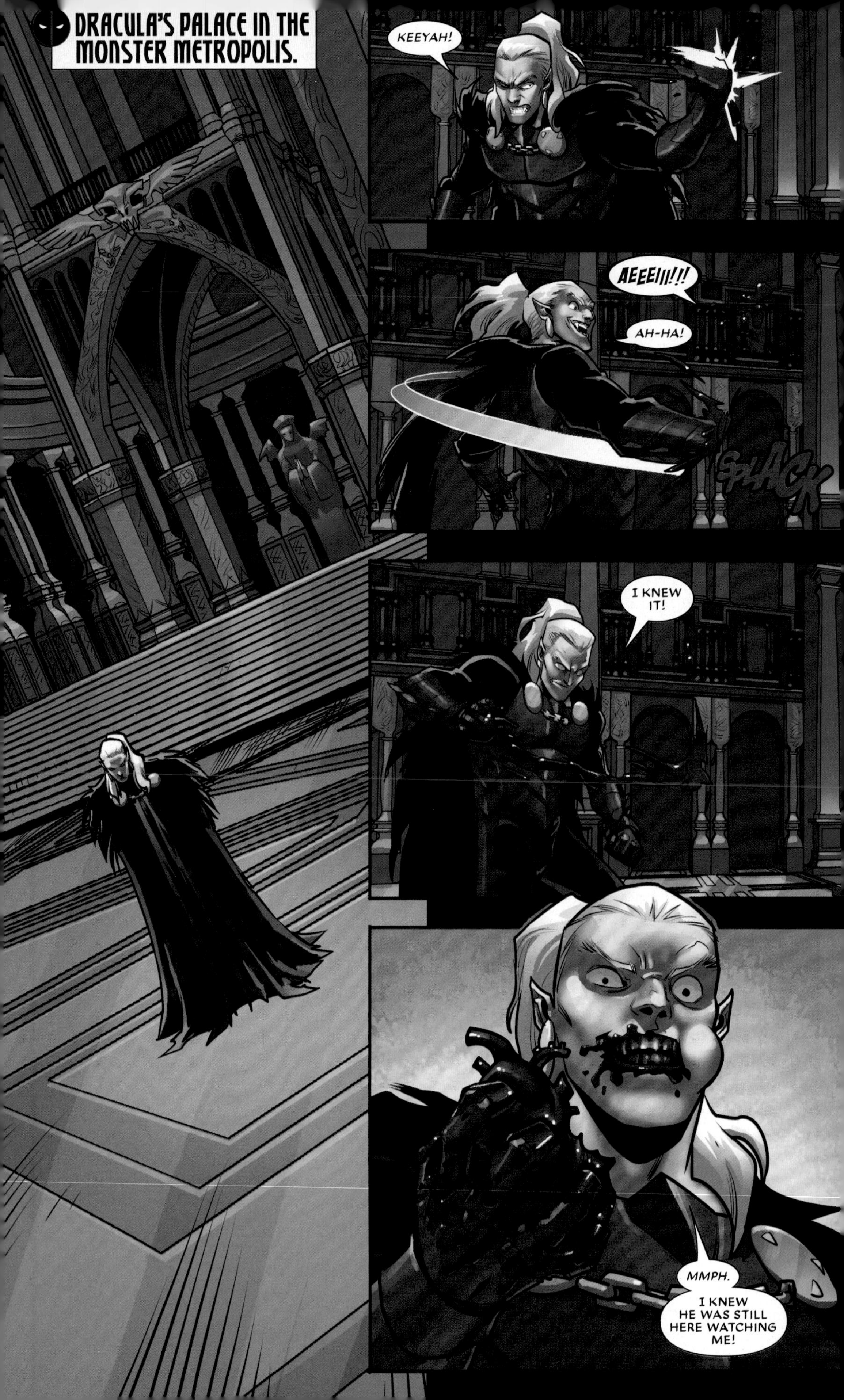
DRACULA'S PALACE IN THE MONSTER METROPOLIS.
KEEYAH!
AEEIIII!!!
AH-HA!
SPLACK
I KNEW IT!
MMPH.
I KNEW HE WAS STILL HERE WATCHING ME!

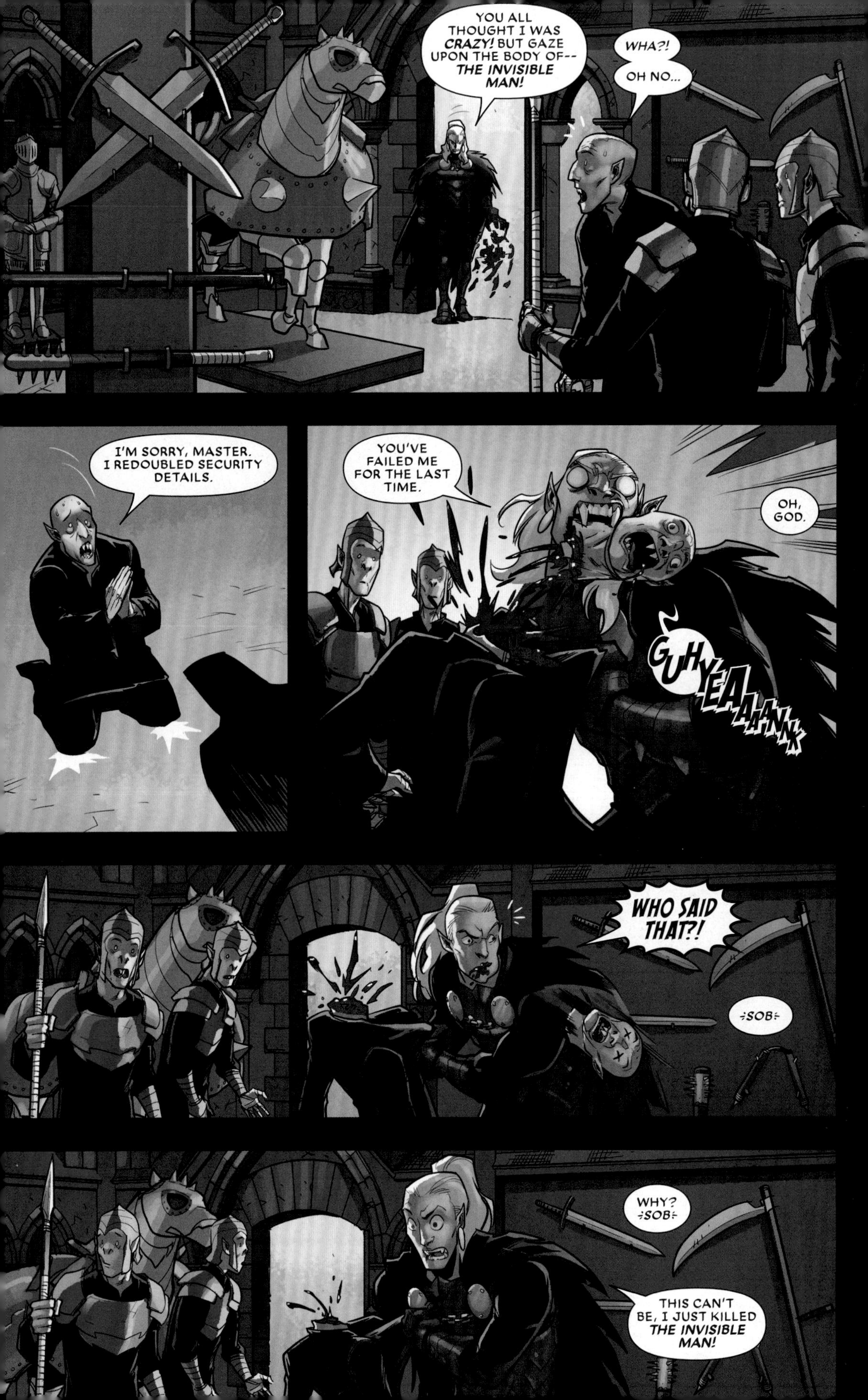
YOU ALL THOUGHT I WAS CRAZY! BUT GAZE UPON THE BODY OF-- THE INVISIBLE MAN!
WHA?!
OH NO...
I'M SORRY, MASTER. I REDOUBLED SECURITY DETAILS.
YOU'VE FAILED ME FOR THE LAST TIME.
OH, GOD.
GUHYEAAAANNK
WHO SAID THAT?!
-SOB-
WHY? -SOB-
THIS CAN'T BE, I JUST KILLED THE INVISIBLE MAN!

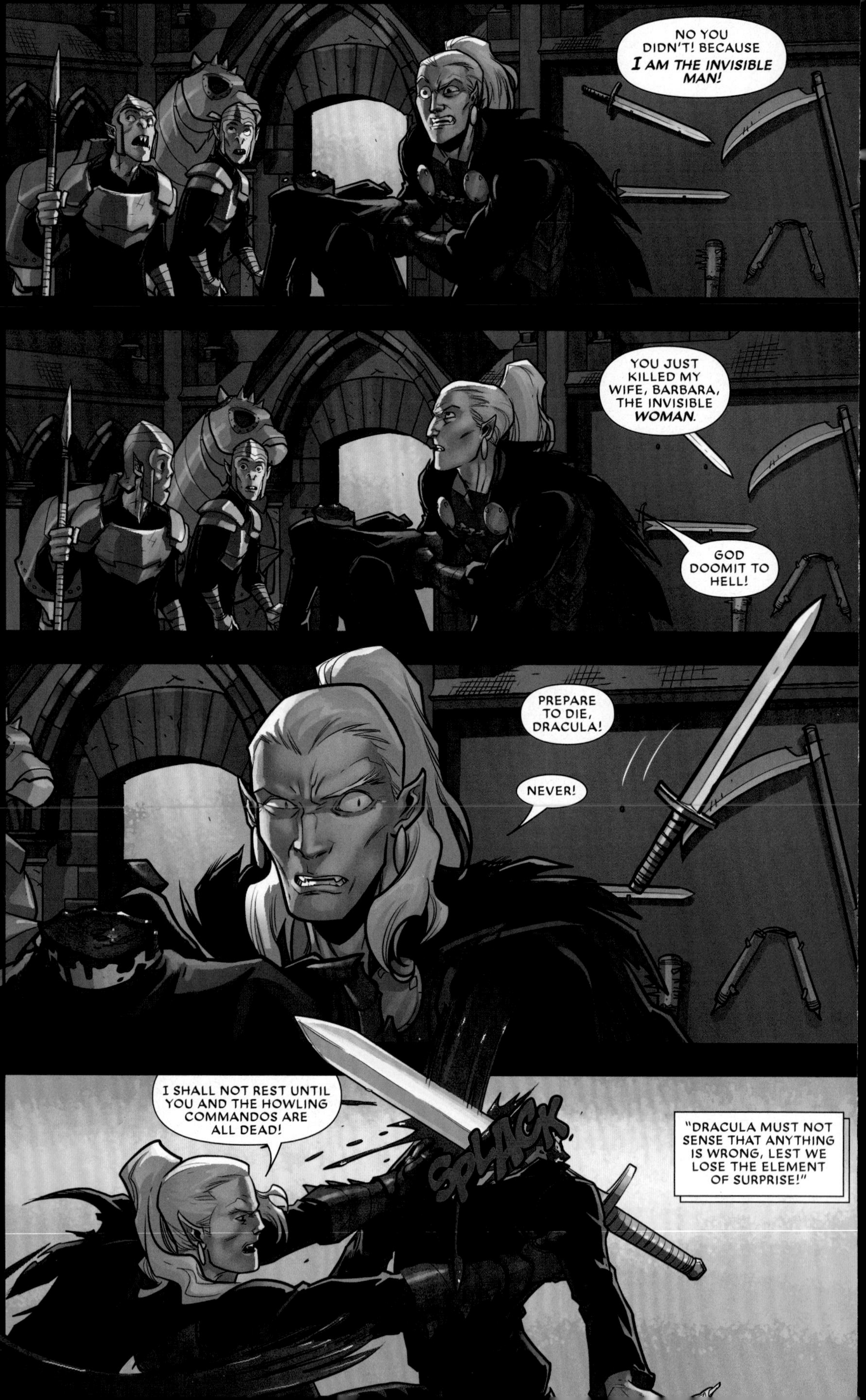
NO YOU DIDN'T! BECAUSE *I AM THE INVISIBLE MAN!*
YOU JUST KILLED MY WIFE, BARBARA, THE INVISIBLE *WOMAN*.
GOD DOOMIT TO HELL!
PREPARE TO DIE, DRACULA!
NEVER!
I SHALL NOT REST UNTIL YOU AND THE HOWLING COMMANDOS ARE ALL DEAD!
SPLACK
"DRACULA MUST NOT SENSE THAT ANYTHING IS WRONG, LEST WE LOSE THE ELEMENT OF SURPRISE!"

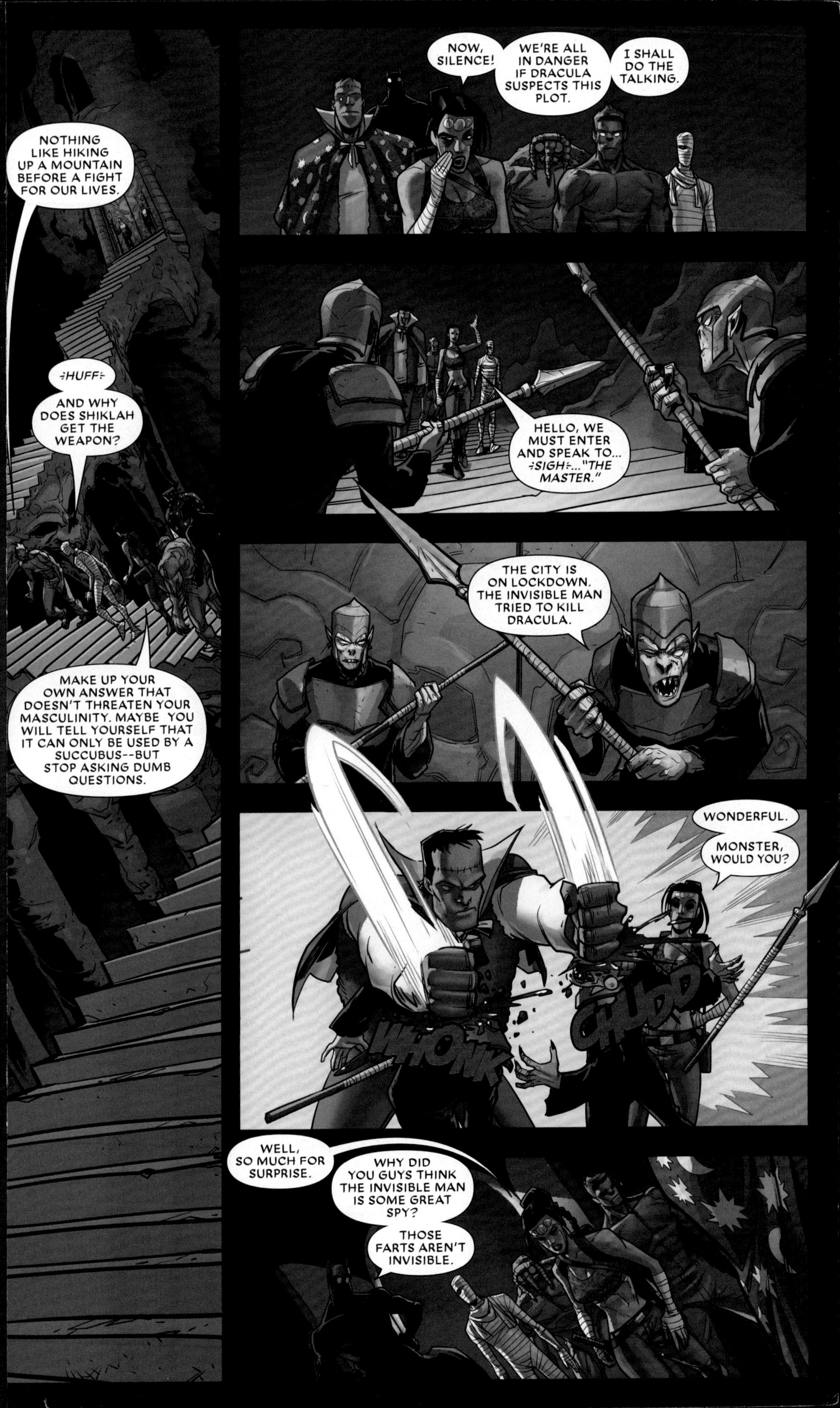
NOTHING LIKE HIKING UP A MOUNTAIN BEFORE A FIGHT FOR OUR LIVES.
=HUFF=
AND WHY DOES SHIKLAH GET THE WEAPON?
MAKE UP YOUR OWN ANSWER THAT DOESN'T THREATEN YOUR MASCULINITY. MAYBE YOU WILL TELL YOURSELF THAT IT CAN ONLY BE USED BY A SUCCUBUS--BUT STOP ASKING DUMB QUESTIONS.
NOW, SILENCE!
WE'RE ALL IN DANGER IF DRACULA SUSPECTS THIS PLOT.
I SHALL DO THE TALKING.
HELLO, WE MUST ENTER AND SPEAK TO... =SIGH=..."THE MASTER."
THE CITY IS ON LOCKDOWN. THE INVISIBLE MAN TRIED TO KILL DRACULA.
WONDERFUL.
MONSTER, WOULD YOU?
WHONK
CHUDD
WELL, SO MUCH FOR SURPRISE.
WHY DID YOU GUYS THINK THE INVISIBLE MAN IS SOME GREAT SPY?
THOSE FARTS AREN'T INVISIBLE.

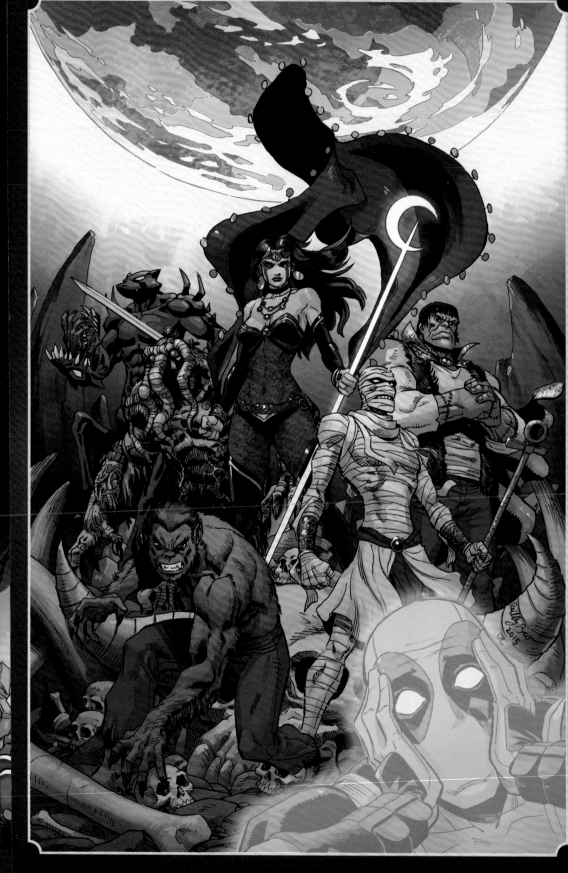

ZSZSGRAAKK!

YEAH, I HEAR THAT.

LOOKS LIKE WE'RE GOING TO GO KICK SOME MONSTER TAIL.

SKRRAKK!

EASE UP. NOTHING PERSONAL.

RUN FOR YOUR LIFE!

DAMN. I THOUGHT WE STRAIGHTENED THESE CELLAR-DWELLIN' SUCKERS OUT.

HEY, CAN YOU FELLAS HEAR ME?

SE HABLA MORT???

NO?

DAMN. THERE'S KIND OF A DOMESTIC DISPUTE JUMPING OFF DOWNSTAIRS THAT COULD USE SOME HAMMER TIME FROM THE THOR CORPS.

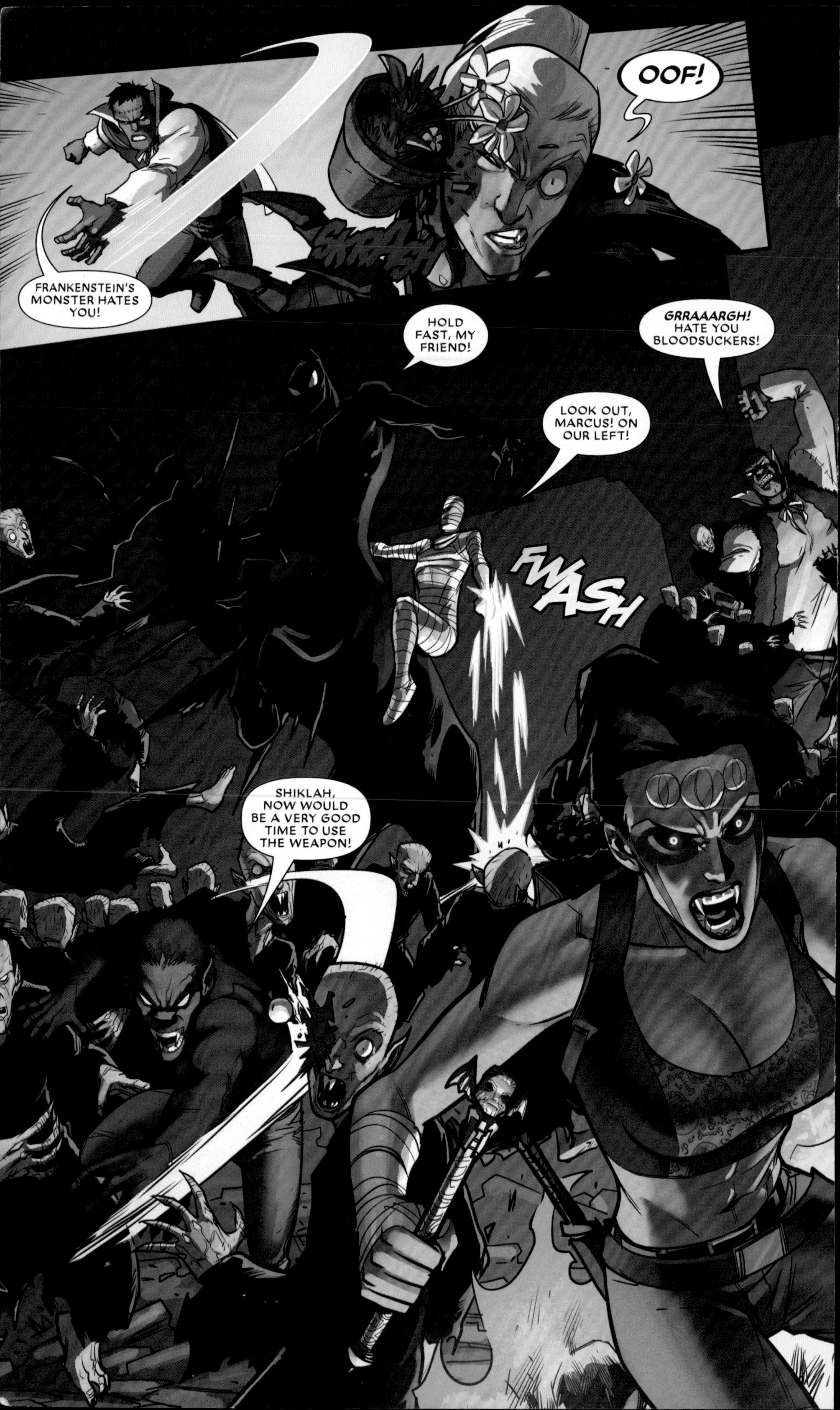

OOF!
SKRAASH
FRANKENSTEIN'S MONSTER HATES YOU!
HOLD FAST, MY FRIEND!
GRRAAARGH! HATE YOU BLOODSUCKERS!
LOOK OUT, MARCUS! ON OUR LEFT!
FWASH
SHIKLAH, NOW WOULD BE A VERY GOOD TIME TO USE THE WEAPON!

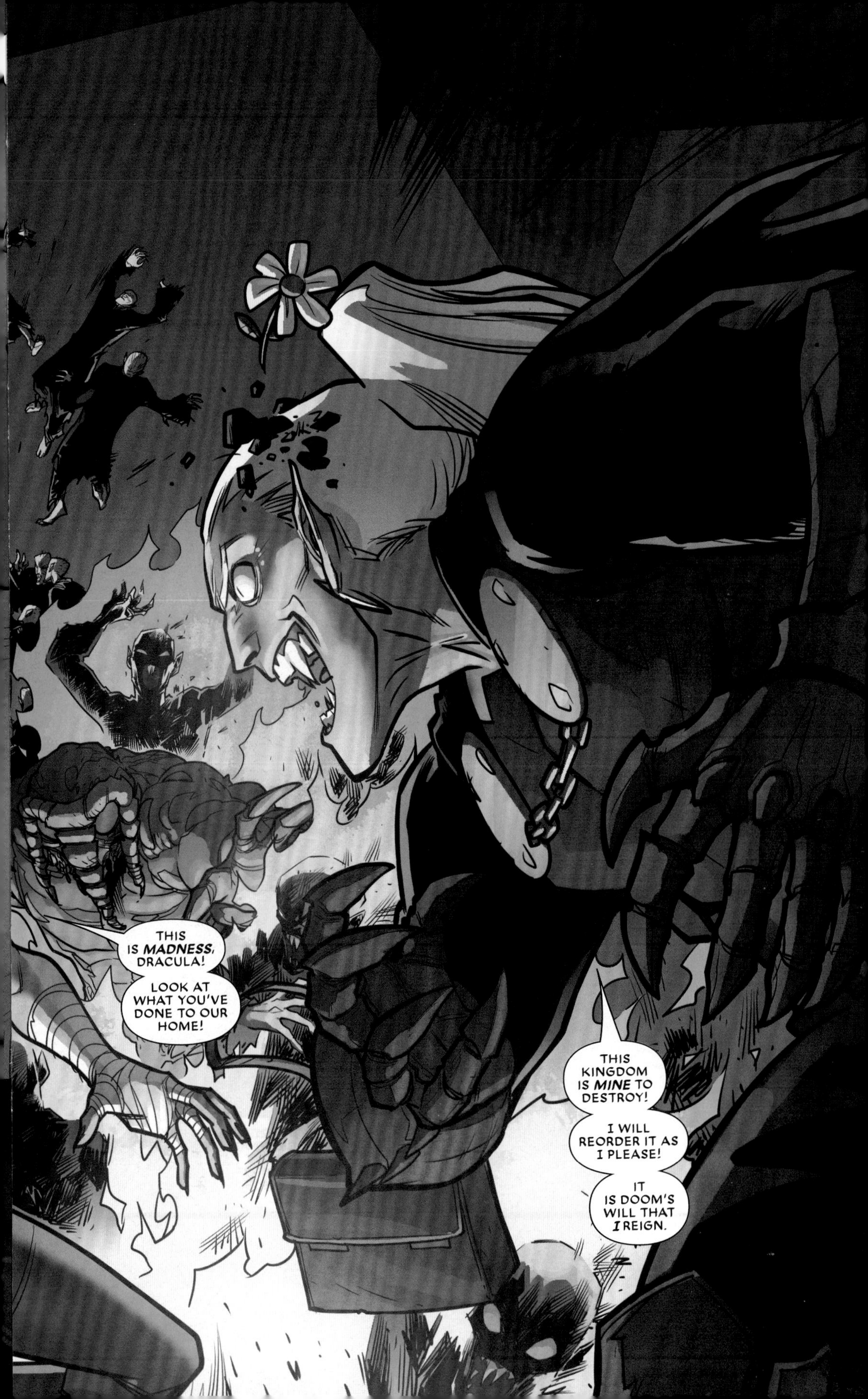
THIS IS *MADNESS*, DRACULA!
LOOK AT WHAT YOU'VE DONE TO OUR HOME!
THIS KINGDOM IS *MINE* TO DESTROY!
I WILL REORDER IT AS I PLEASE!
IT IS DOOM'S WILL THAT *I* REIGN.

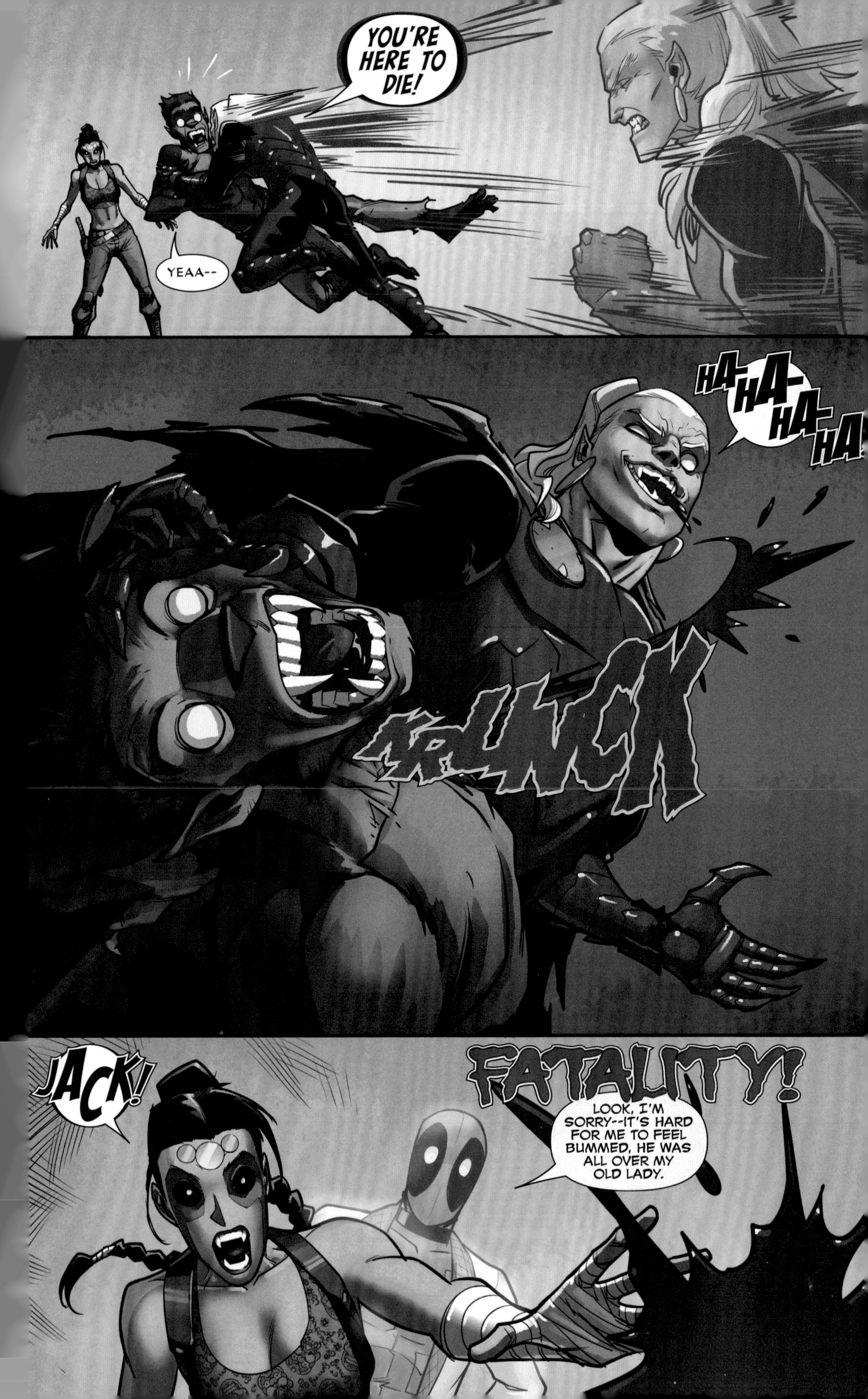
YOU'RE HERE TO DIE!
YEAA--
HA-HA-HA-HA!
KRUNCK
JACK!
FATALITY!
LOOK, I'M SORRY--IT'S HARD FOR ME TO FEEL BUMMED, HE WAS ALL OVER MY OLD LADY.

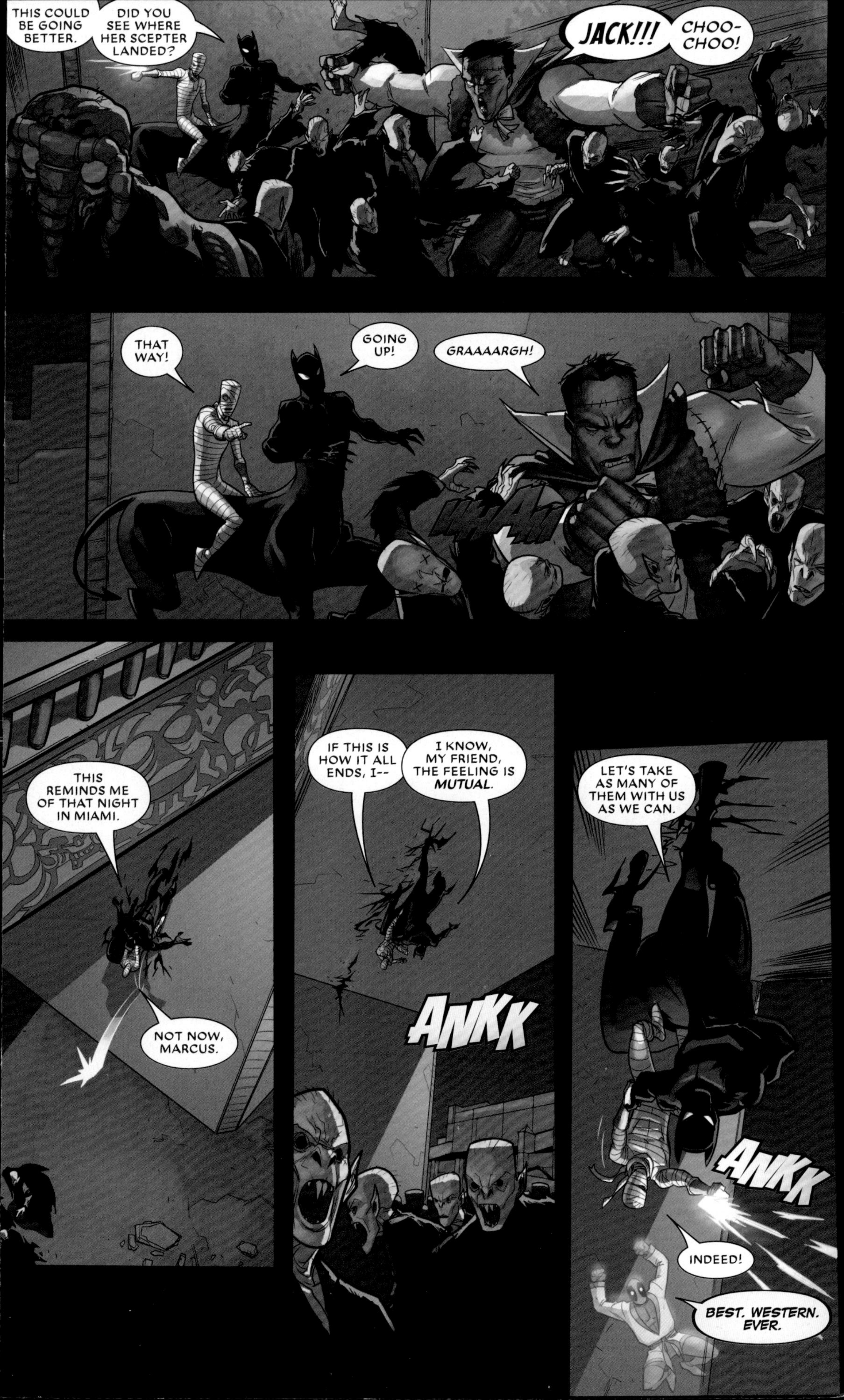
THIS COULD BE GOING BETTER.
DID YOU SEE WHERE HER SCEPTER LANDED?
JACK!!!
CHOO-CHOO!
THAT WAY!
GOING UP!
GRAAAARGH!
THIS REMINDS ME OF THAT NIGHT IN MIAMI.
NOT NOW, MARCUS.
IF THIS IS HOW IT ALL ENDS, I--
I KNOW, MY FRIEND, THE FEELING IS MUTUAL.
ANKK
LET'S TAKE AS MANY OF THEM WITH US AS WE CAN.
ANKK
INDEED!
BEST. WESTERN. EVER.

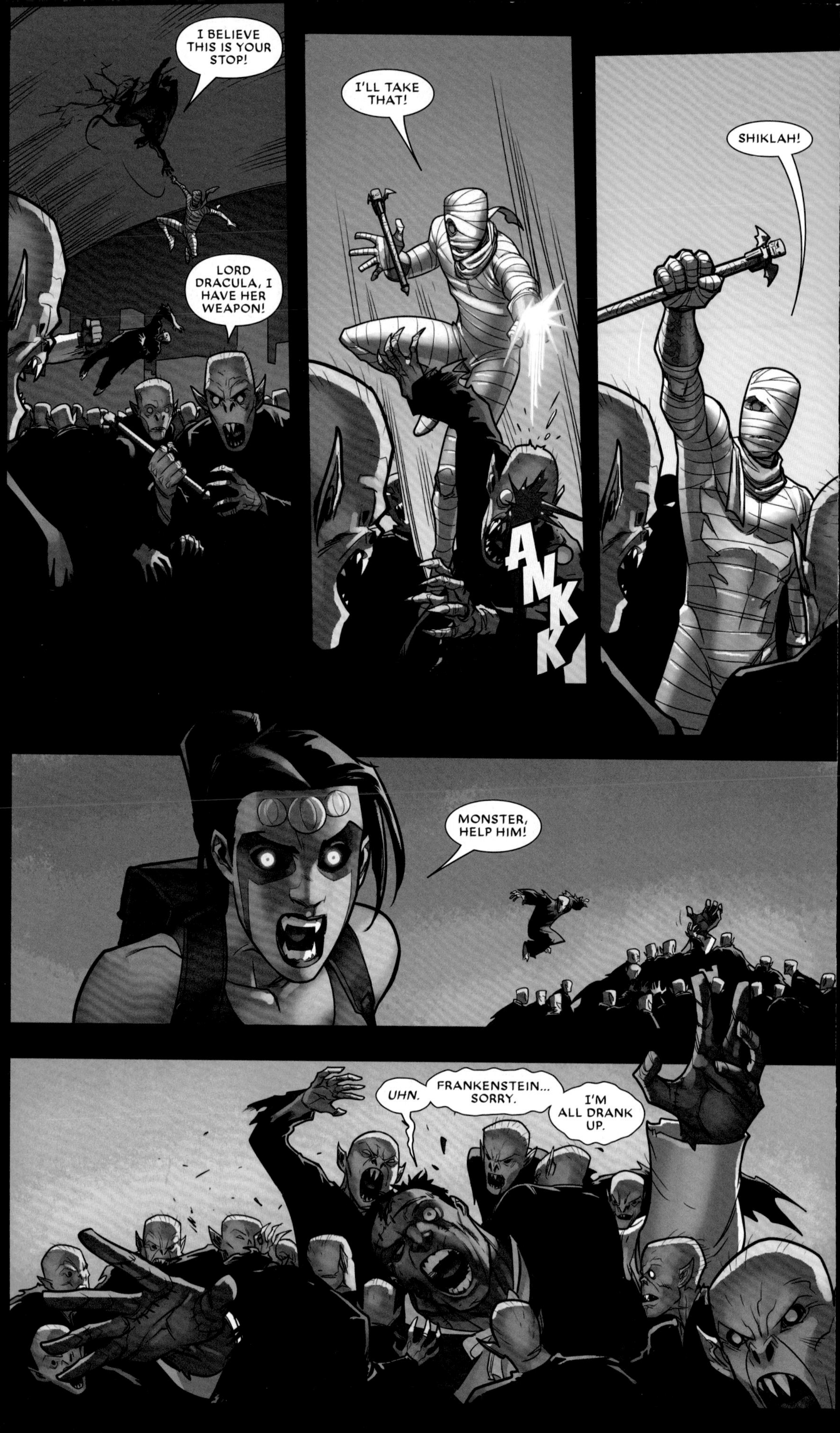
I BELIEVE THIS IS YOUR STOP!
LORD DRACULA, I HAVE HER WEAPON!
I'LL TAKE THAT!
ANKK
SHIKLAH!
MONSTER, HELP HIM!
UHN.
FRANKENSTEIN... SORRY.
I'M ALL DRANK UP.

YEAAGH!

N'KANTU!!!

NO!!!

JOIN HIM--IN DEATH.

I GOT IT!

HERE, MASTER.

WELL DONE.

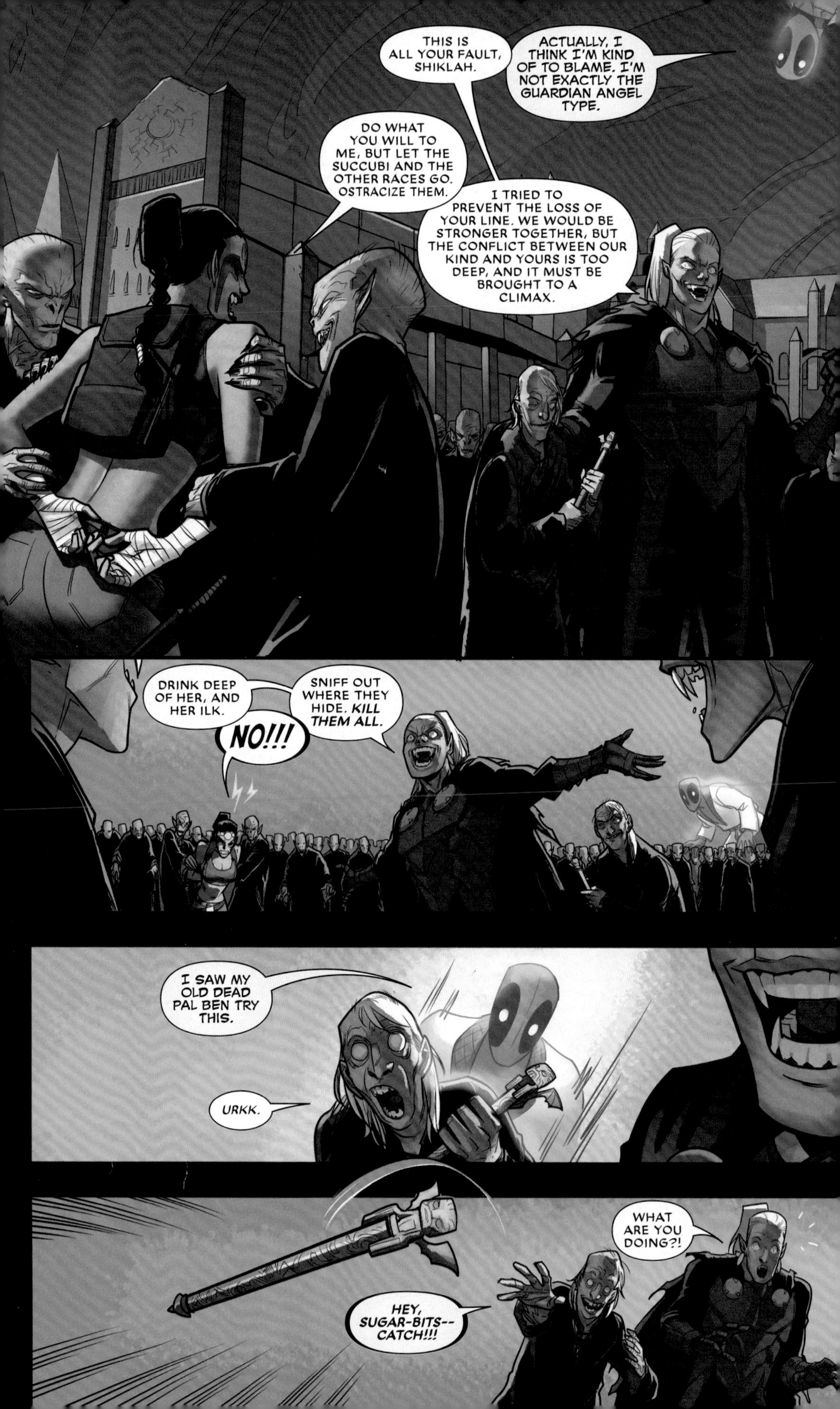
THIS IS ALL YOUR FAULT, SHIKLAH.
ACTUALLY, I THINK I'M KIND OF TO BLAME. I'M NOT EXACTLY THE GUARDIAN ANGEL TYPE.
DO WHAT YOU WILL TO ME, BUT LET THE SUCCUBI AND THE OTHER RACES GO. OSTRACIZE THEM.
I TRIED TO PREVENT THE LOSS OF YOUR LINE. WE WOULD BE STRONGER TOGETHER, BUT THE CONFLICT BETWEEN OUR KIND AND YOURS IS TOO DEEP, AND IT MUST BE BROUGHT TO A CLIMAX.
DRINK DEEP OF HER, AND HER ILK.
SNIFF OUT WHERE THEY HIDE. KILL THEM ALL.
NO!!!
I SAW MY OLD DEAD PAL BEN TRY THIS.
URKK.
WHAT ARE YOU DOING?!
HEY, SUGAR-BITS-- CATCH!!!

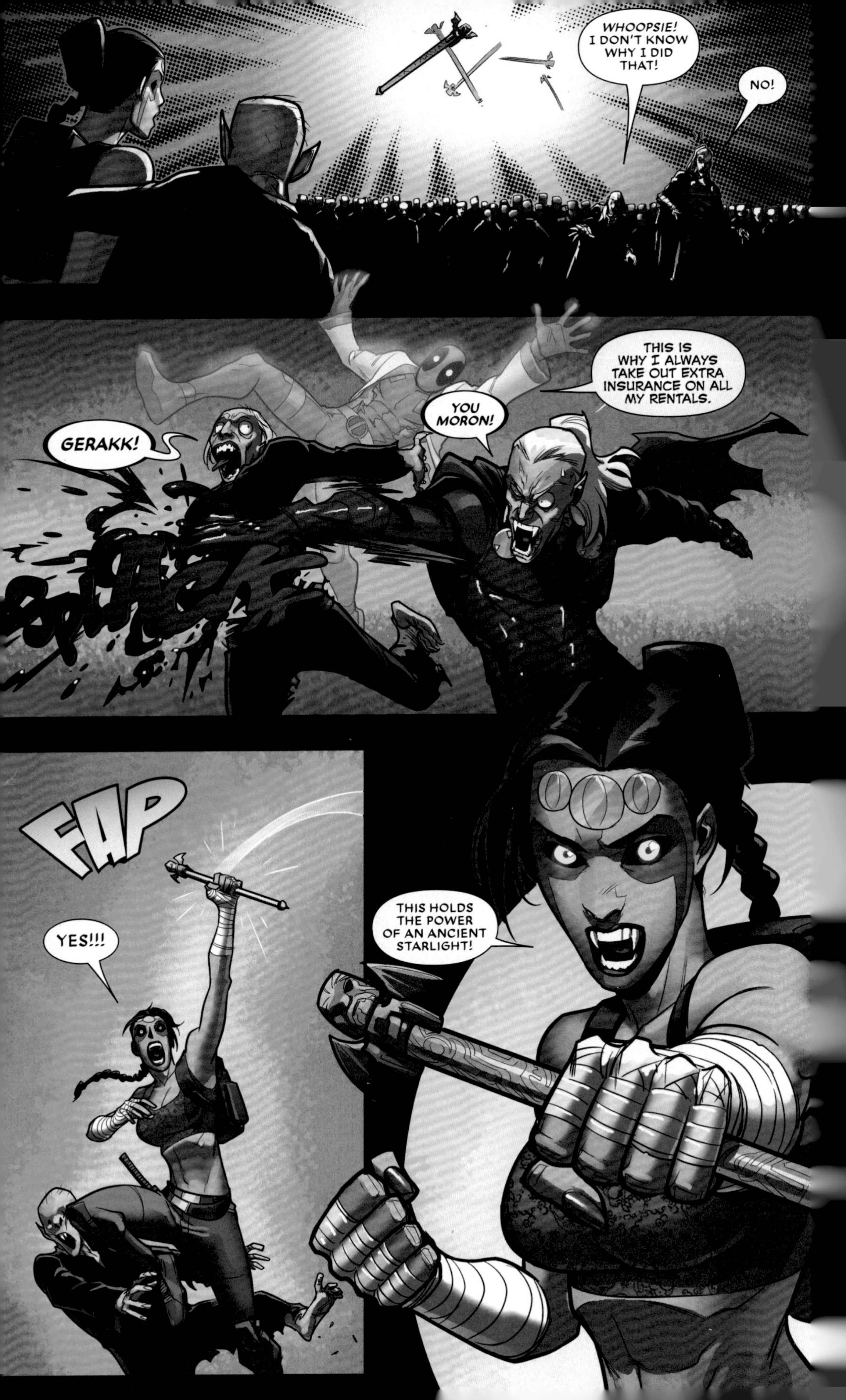
WHOOPSIE! I DON'T KNOW WHY I DID THAT!
NO!
THIS IS WHY I ALWAYS TAKE OUT EXTRA INSURANCE ON ALL MY RENTALS.
YOU MORON!
GERAKK!
FAP
YES!!!
THIS HOLDS THE POWER OF AN ANCIENT STARLIGHT!

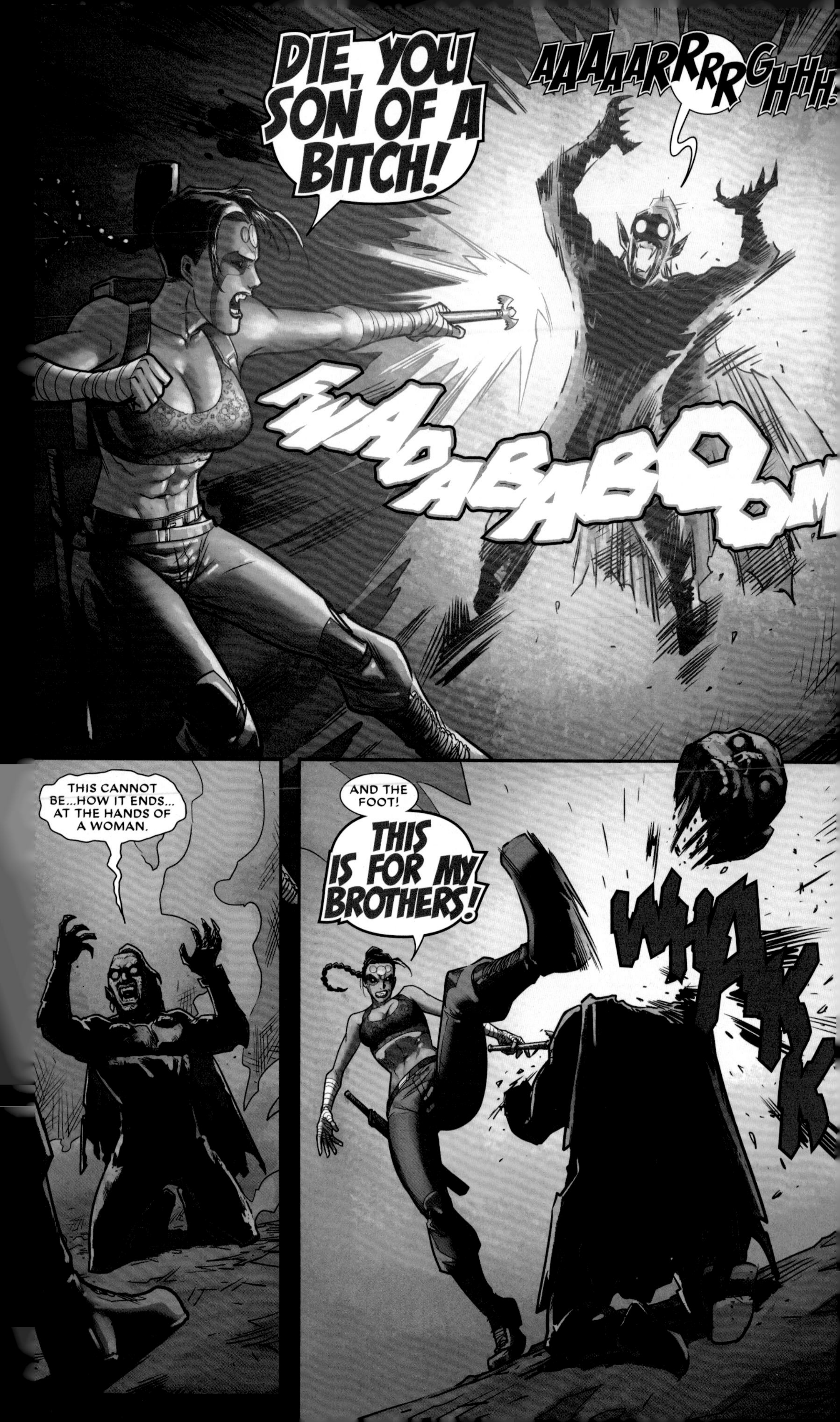
DIE, YOU SON OF A BITCH!
AAAAARRRRRGHHH!
FWADABABOOM
THIS CANNOT BE...HOW IT ENDS... AT THE HANDS OF A WOMAN.
AND THE FOOT!
THIS IS FOR MY BROTHERS!
WHAKK

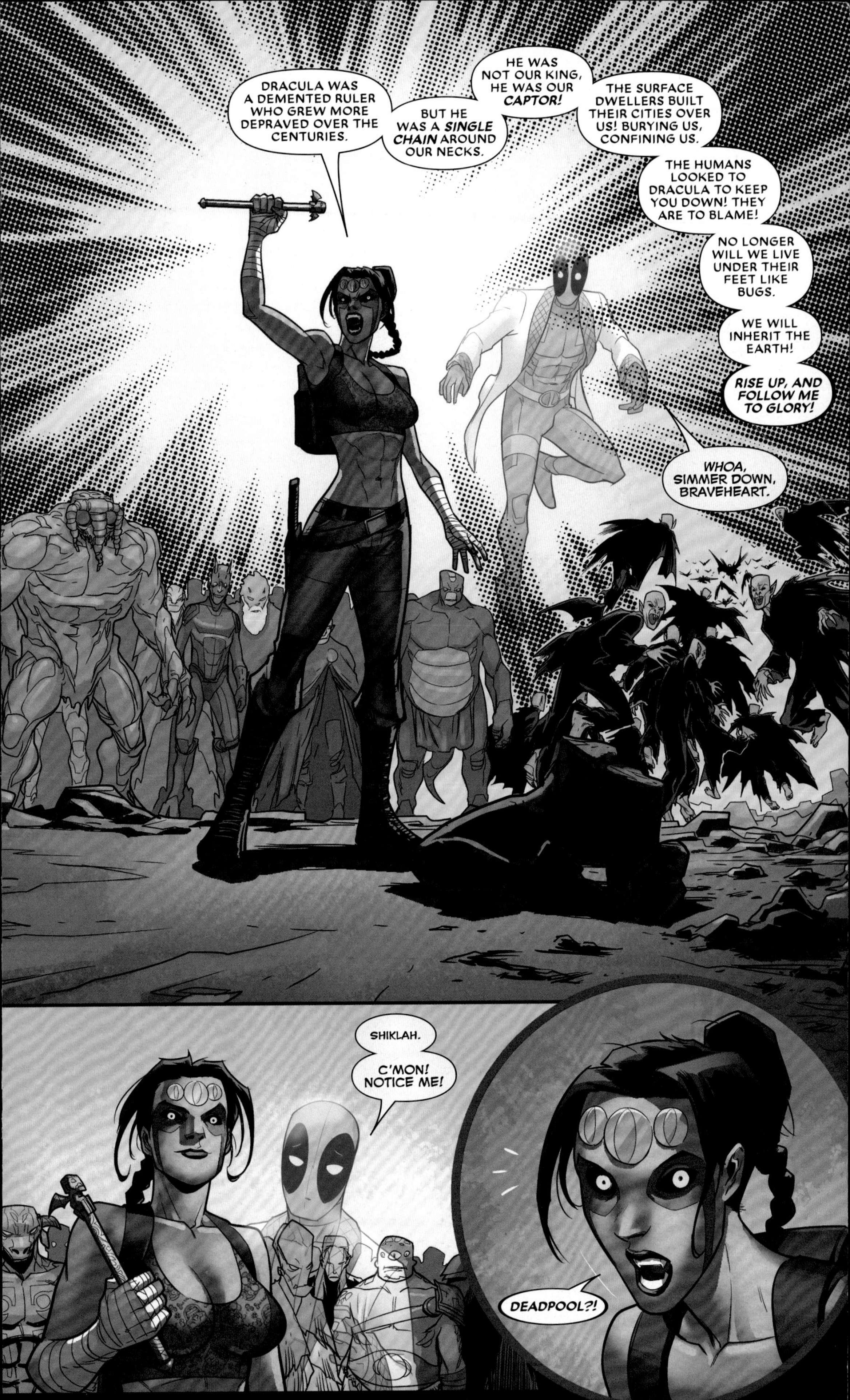
DRACULA WAS A DEMENTED RULER WHO GREW MORE DEPRAVED OVER THE CENTURIES.
BUT HE WAS A *SINGLE CHAIN* AROUND OUR NECKS.
HE WAS NOT OUR KING, HE WAS OUR *CAPTOR!*
THE SURFACE DWELLERS BUILT THEIR CITIES OVER US! BURYING US, CONFINING US.
THE HUMANS LOOKED TO DRACULA TO KEEP YOU DOWN! THEY ARE TO BLAME!
NO LONGER WILL WE LIVE UNDER THEIR FEET LIKE BUGS.
WE WILL INHERIT THE EARTH!
RISE UP, AND FOLLOW ME TO GLORY!
WHOA, SIMMER DOWN, BRAVEHEART.
SHIKLAH.
C'MON! NOTICE ME!
DEADPOOL?!

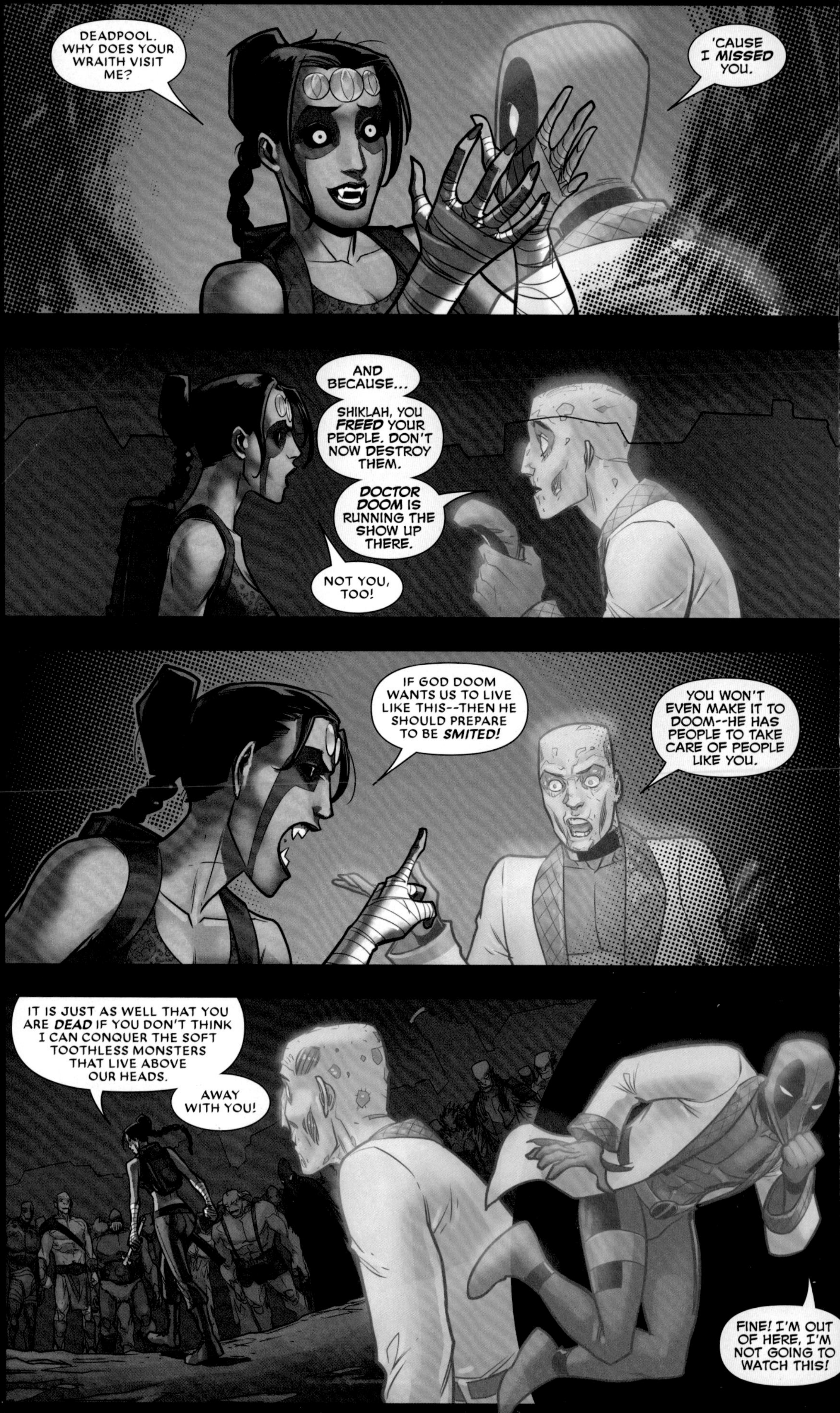
DEADPOOL. WHY DOES YOUR WRAITH VISIT ME?
'CAUSE I *MISSED* YOU.
AND BECAUSE...
SHIKLAH, YOU *FREED* YOUR PEOPLE. DON'T NOW DESTROY THEM.
DOCTOR DOOM IS RUNNING THE SHOW UP THERE.
NOT YOU, TOO!
IF GOD DOOM WANTS US TO LIVE LIKE THIS--THEN HE SHOULD PREPARE TO BE *SMITED!*
YOU WON'T EVEN MAKE IT TO DOOM--HE HAS PEOPLE TO TAKE CARE OF PEOPLE LIKE YOU.
IT IS JUST AS WELL THAT YOU ARE *DEAD* IF YOU DON'T THINK I CAN CONQUER THE SOFT TOOTHLESS MONSTERS THAT LIVE ABOVE OUR HEADS.
AWAY WITH YOU!
FINE! I'M OUT OF HERE, I'M NOT GOING TO WATCH THIS!

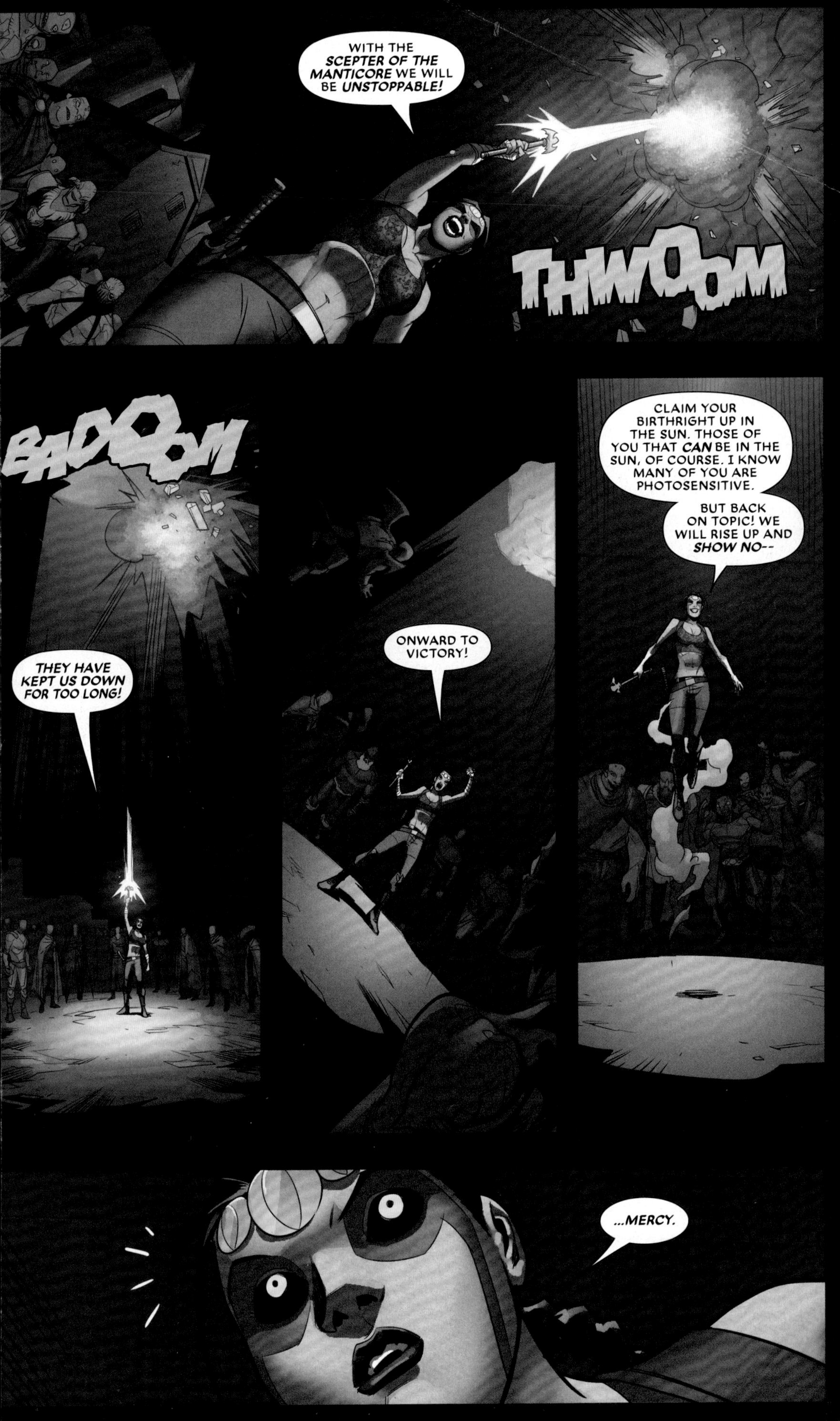
WITH THE SCEPTER OF THE MANTICORE WE WILL BE UNSTOPPABLE!
THWOOOM
BADOOOM
THEY HAVE KEPT US DOWN FOR TOO LONG!
ONWARD TO VICTORY!
CLAIM YOUR BIRTHRIGHT UP IN THE SUN. THOSE OF YOU THAT CAN BE IN THE SUN, OF COURSE. I KNOW MANY OF YOU ARE PHOTOSENSITIVE.
BUT BACK ON TOPIC! WE WILL RISE UP AND SHOW NO--
...MERCY.

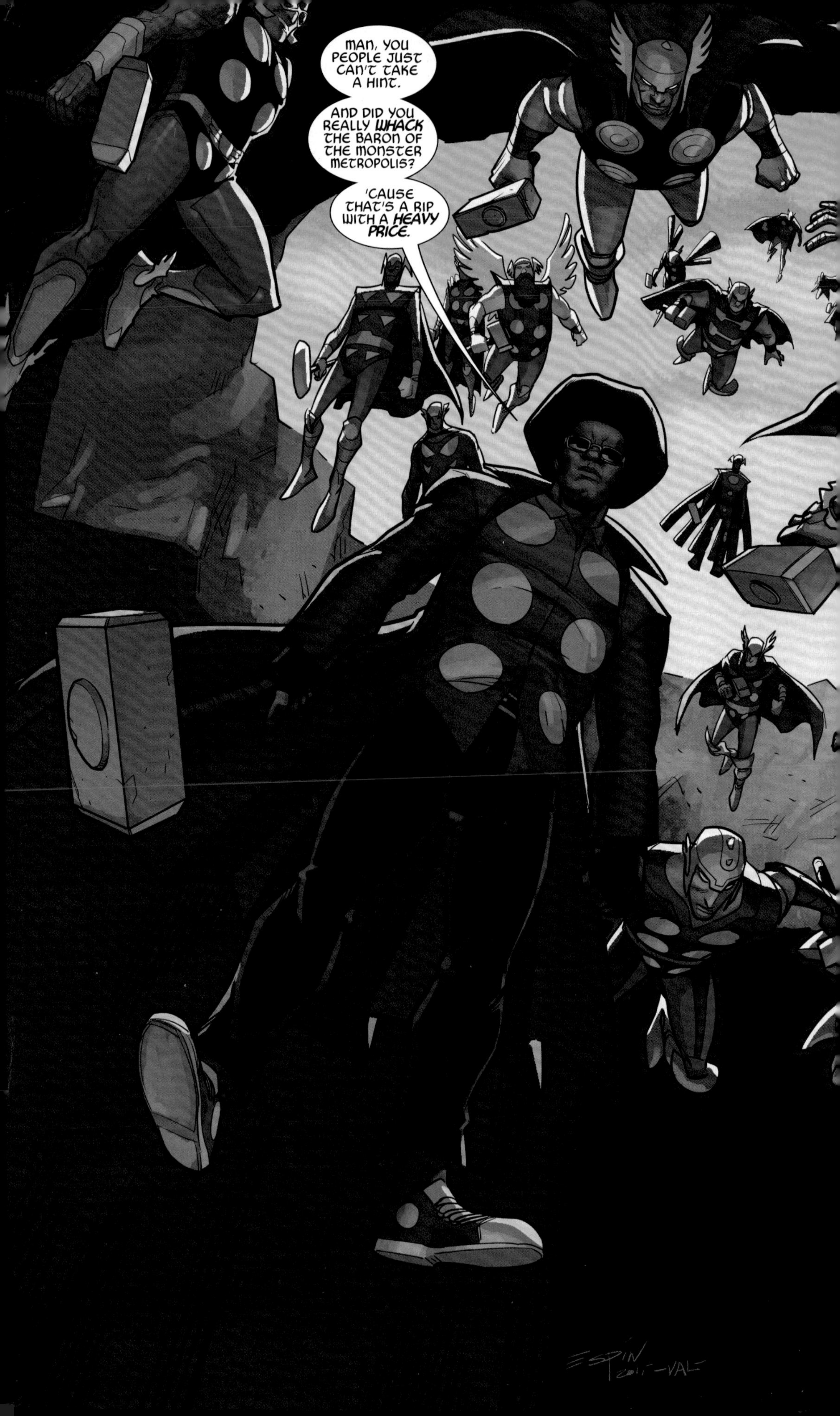
MAN, YOU PEOPLE JUST CAN'T TAKE A HINT.
AND DID YOU REALLY WHACK THE BARON OF THE MONSTER METROPOLIS?
'CAUSE THAT'S A RIP WITH A HEAVY PRICE.
ESPIN 2011 -VAL-

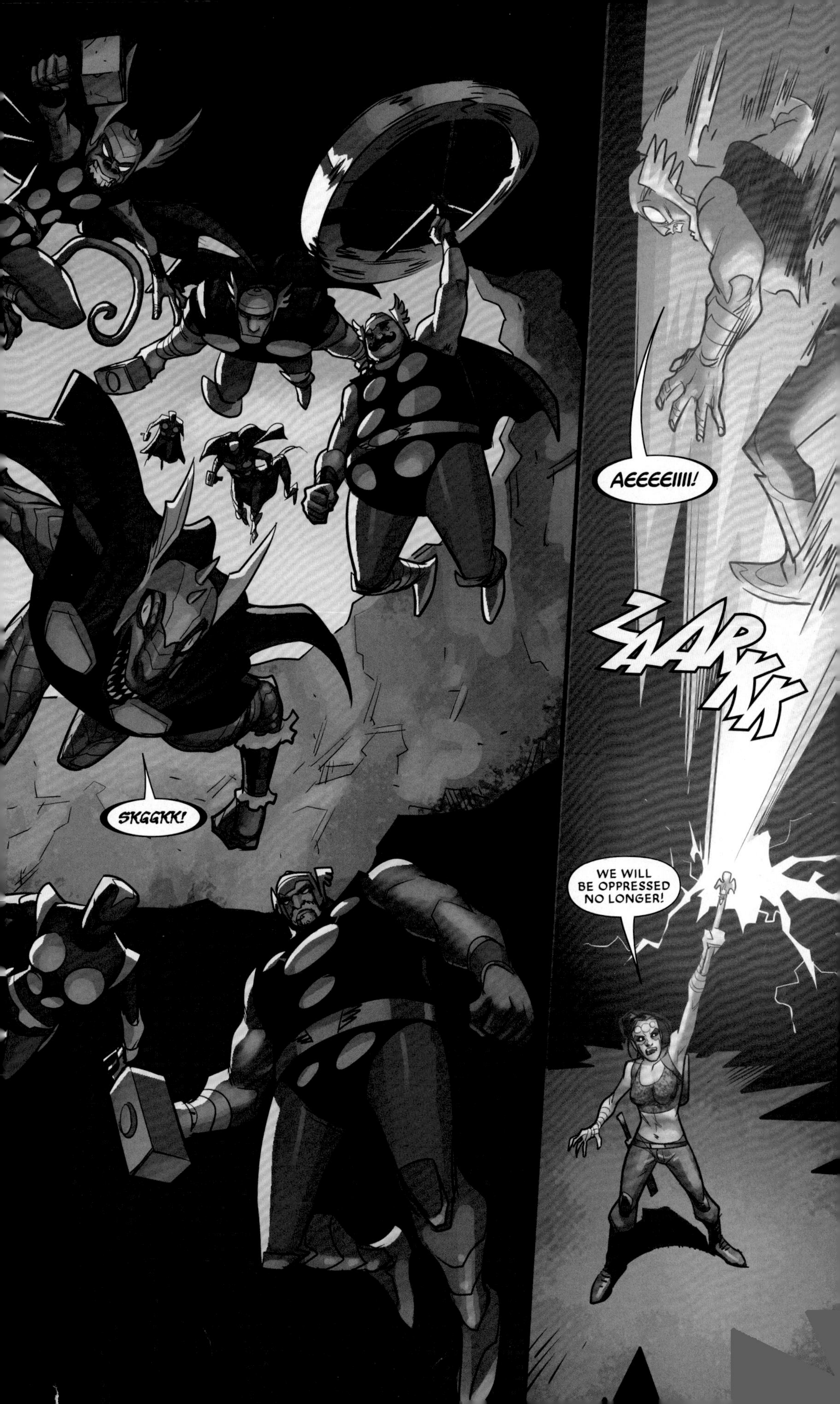
SKGGKK!
AEEEEIIII!
ZZARKK
WE WILL BE OPPRESSED NO LONGER!

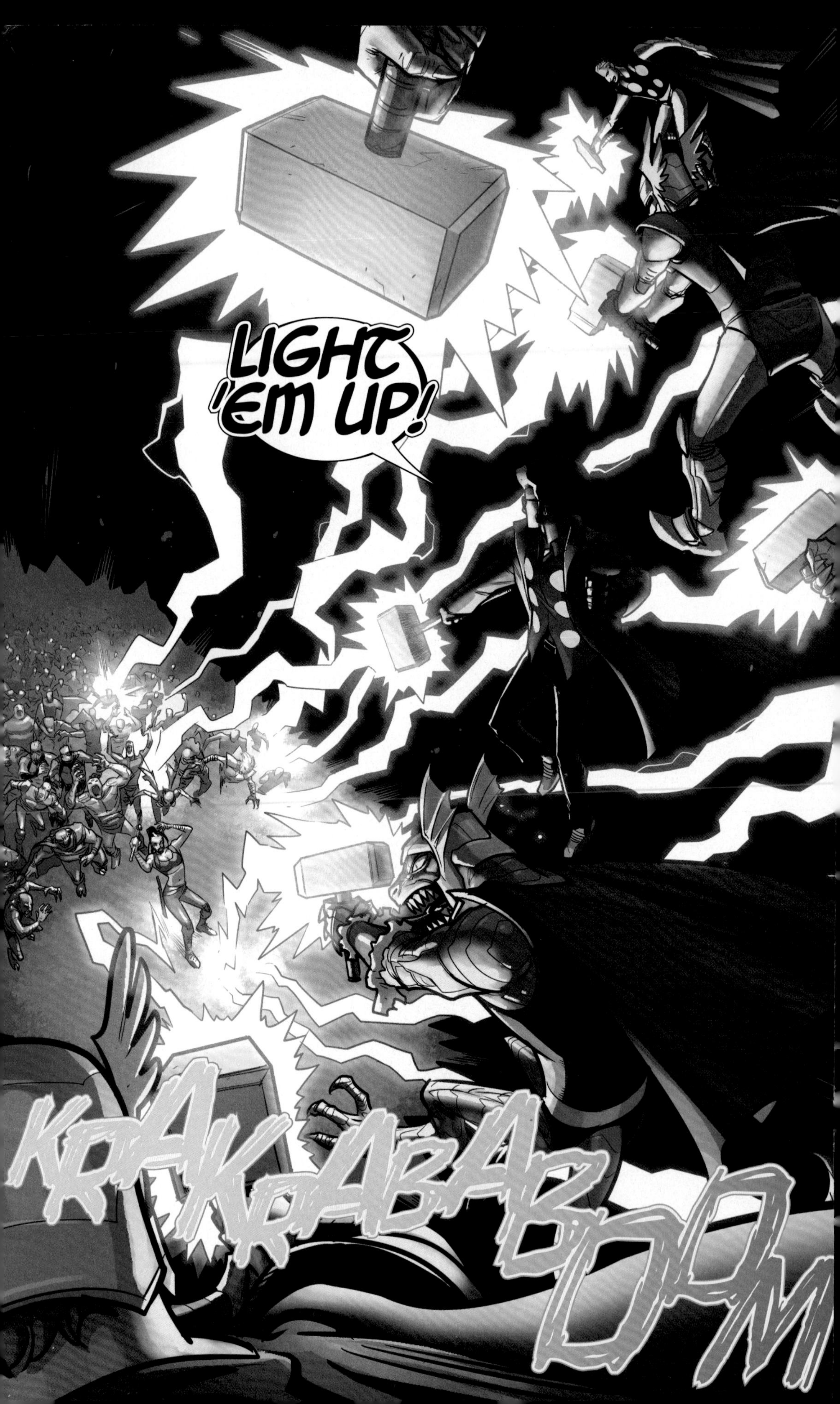
LIGHT 'EM UP!
KRAKKRABABOOM

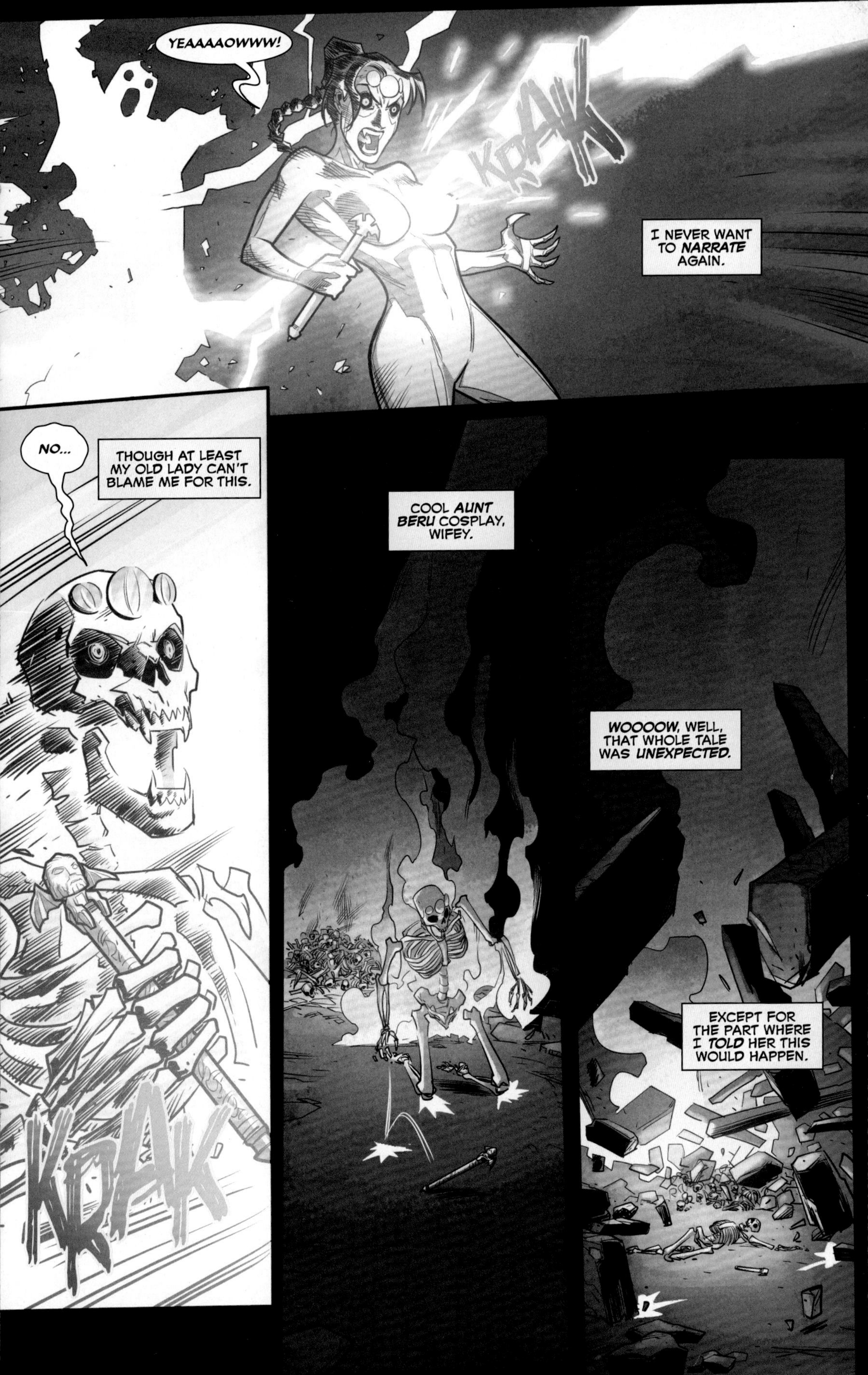

YEAAAAOWWW!
KRAK
I NEVER WANT TO NARRATE AGAIN.
NO...
THOUGH AT LEAST MY OLD LADY CAN'T BLAME ME FOR THIS.
KRAK
COOL AUNT BERU COSPLAY, WIFEY.
WOOOOW, WELL, THAT WHOLE TALE WAS UNEXPECTED.
EXCEPT FOR THE PART WHERE I TOLD HER THIS WOULD HAPPEN.

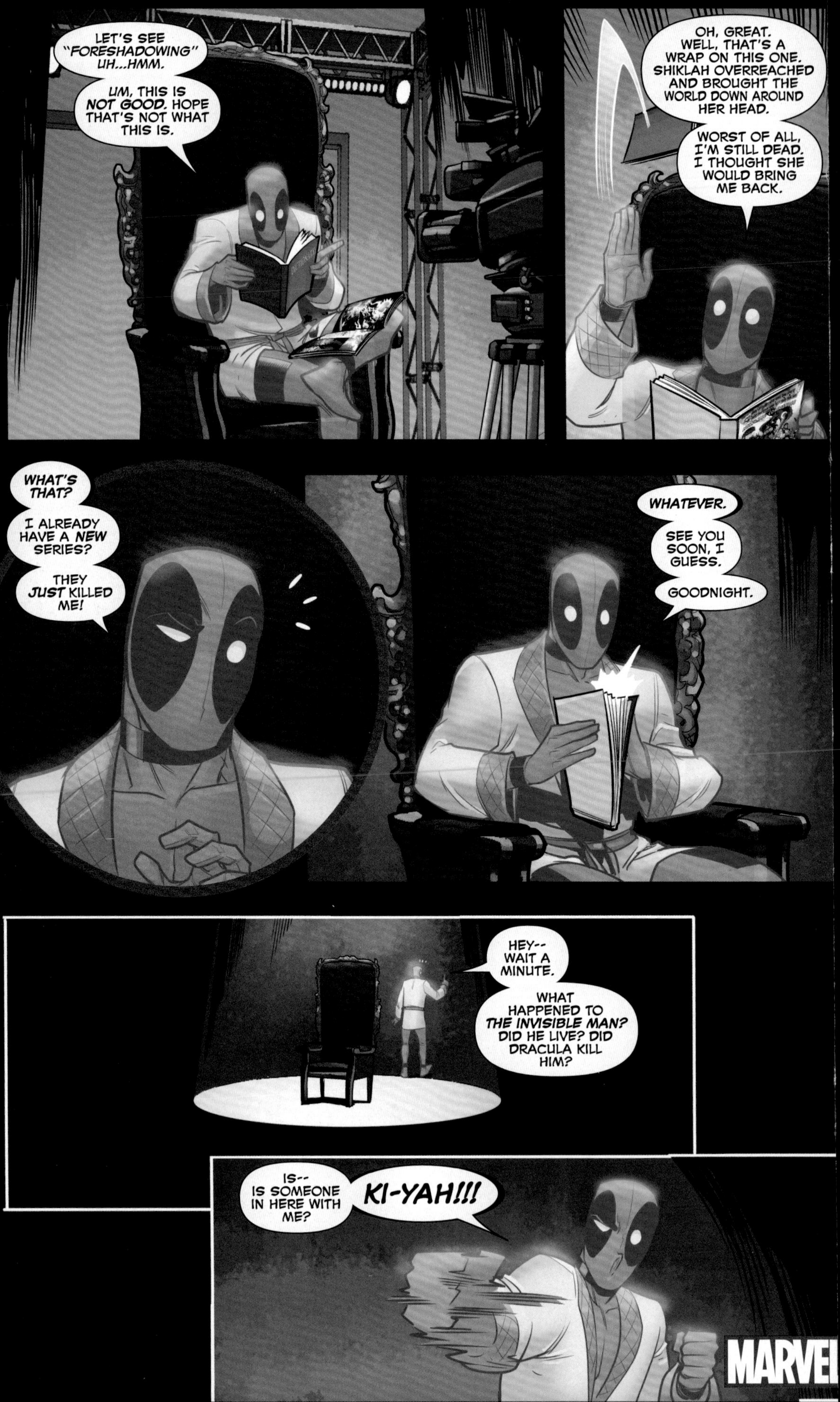
LET'S SEE "FORESHADOWING" UH...HMM.
UM, THIS IS NOT GOOD. HOPE THAT'S NOT WHAT THIS IS.
OH, GREAT. WELL, THAT'S A WRAP ON THIS ONE. SHIKLAH OVERREACHED AND BROUGHT THE WORLD DOWN AROUND HER HEAD.
WORST OF ALL, I'M STILL DEAD. I THOUGHT SHE WOULD BRING ME BACK.
WHAT'S THAT?
I ALREADY HAVE A NEW SERIES?
THEY JUST KILLED ME!
WHATEVER.
SEE YOU SOON, I GUESS.
GOODNIGHT.
HEY-- WAIT A MINUTE.
WHAT HAPPENED TO THE INVISIBLE MAN? DID HE LIVE? DID DRACULA KILL HIM?
IS-- IS SOMEONE IN HERE WITH ME?
KI-YAH!!!
MARVEL

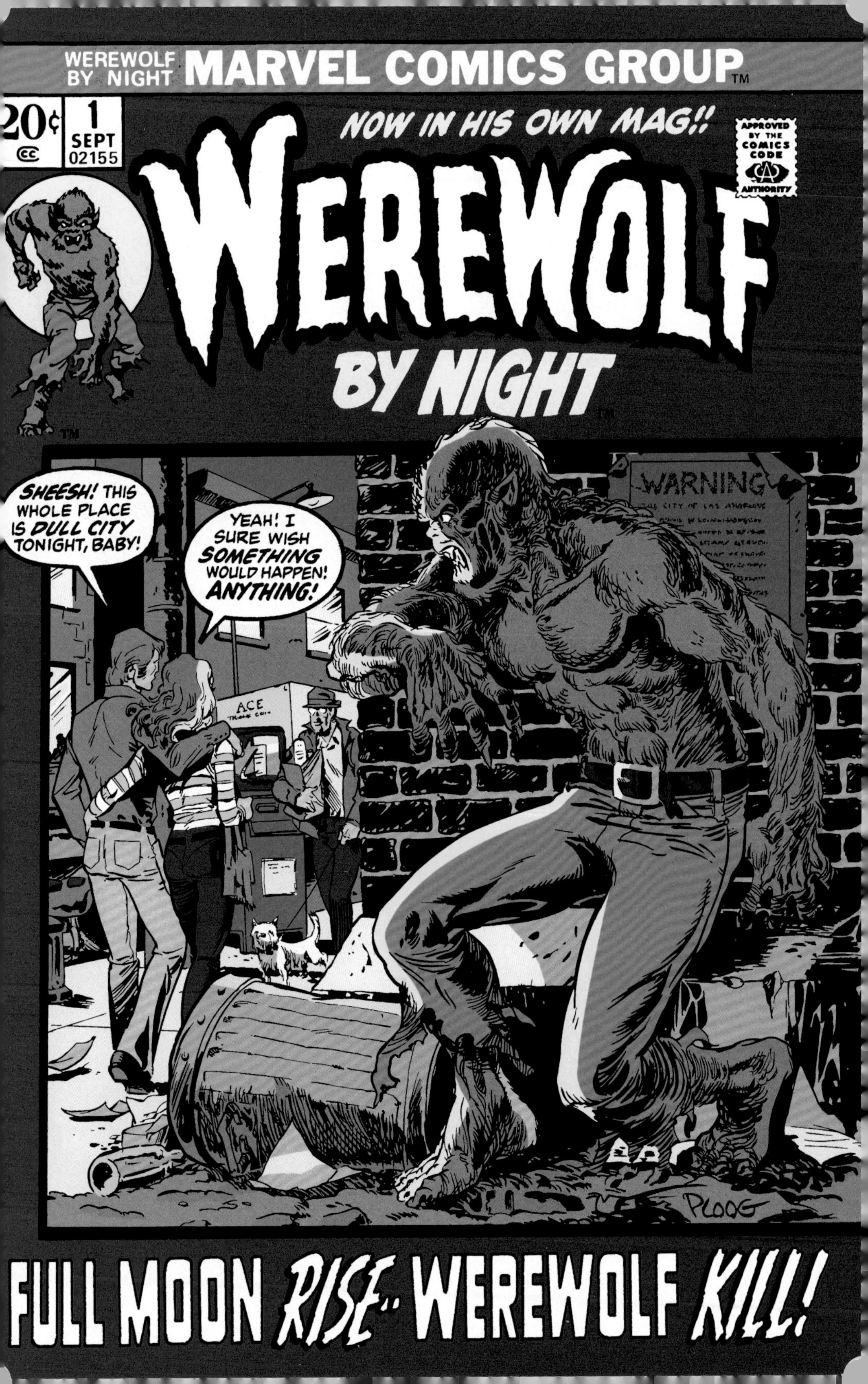
WEREWOLF BY NIGHT
MARVEL COMICS GROUP
20¢
1 SEPT 02155
NOW IN HIS OWN MAG!!
APPROVED BY THE COMICS CODE AUTHORITY
WEREWOLF
BY NIGHT
SHEESH! THIS WHOLE PLACE IS DULL CITY TONIGHT, BABY!
YEAH! I SURE WISH SOMETHING WOULD HAPPEN! ANYTHING!
WARNING
ACE
PLOOG
FULL MOON RISE.. WEREWOLF KILL!

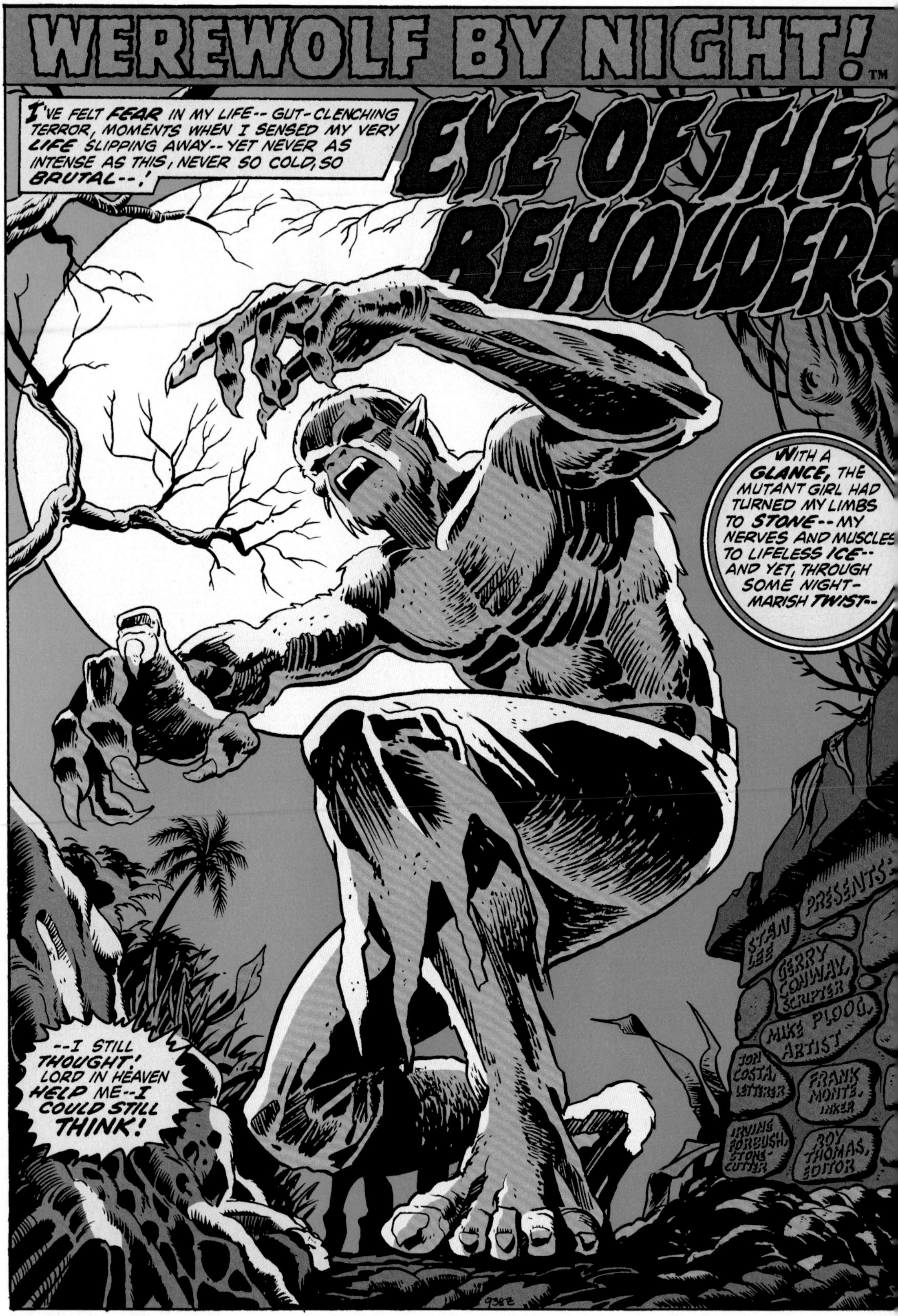
WEREWOLF BY NIGHT! ™
I'VE FELT FEAR IN MY LIFE-- GUT-CLENCHING TERROR, MOMENTS WHEN I SENSED MY VERY LIFE SLIPPING AWAY--YET NEVER AS INTENSE AS THIS; NEVER SO COLD, SO BRUTAL--!
EYE OF THE BEHOLDER!
WITH A GLANCE, THE MUTANT GIRL HAD TURNED MY LIMBS TO STONE--MY NERVES AND MUSCLES TO LIFELESS ICE--AND YET, THROUGH SOME NIGHT-MARISH TWIST--
--I STILL THOUGHT! LORD IN HEAVEN HELP ME--I COULD STILL THINK!
STAN LEE PRESENTS:
GERRY CONWAY, SCRIPTER
MIKE PLOOG, ARTIST
JON COSTA, LETTERER
FRANK MONTE, INKER
IRVING FORBUSH, STONE-CUTTER
ROY THOMAS, EDITOR

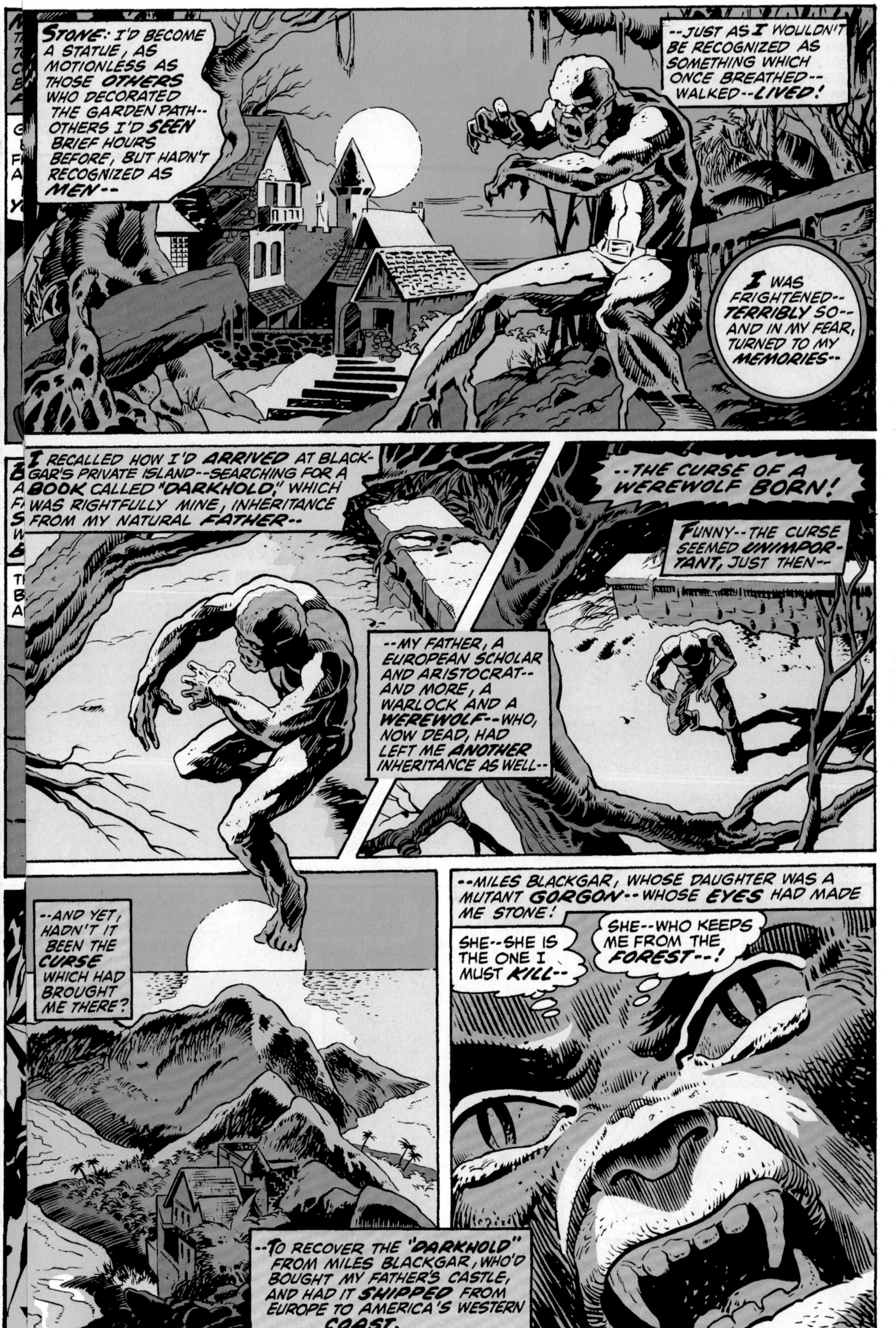
STONE: I'D BECOME A STATUE, AS MOTIONLESS AS THOSE OTHERS WHO DECORATED THE GARDEN PATH-- OTHERS I'D SEEN BRIEF HOURS BEFORE, BUT HADN'T RECOGNIZED AS MEN--
--JUST AS I WOULDN'T BE RECOGNIZED AS SOMETHING WHICH ONCE BREATHED-- WALKED--LIVED!
I WAS FRIGHTENED-- TERRIBLY SO-- AND IN MY FEAR, TURNED TO MY MEMORIES--
I RECALLED HOW I'D ARRIVED AT BLACKGAR'S PRIVATE ISLAND--SEARCHING FOR A BOOK CALLED "DARKHOLD," WHICH WAS RIGHTFULLY MINE, INHERITANCE FROM MY NATURAL FATHER--
--MY FATHER, A EUROPEAN SCHOLAR AND ARISTOCRAT-- AND MORE, A WARLOCK AND A WEREWOLF--WHO, NOW DEAD, HAD LEFT ME ANOTHER INHERITANCE AS WELL--
--THE CURSE OF A WEREWOLF BORN!
FUNNY--THE CURSE SEEMED UNIMPORTANT, JUST THEN--
--AND YET, HADN'T IT BEEN THE CURSE WHICH HAD BROUGHT ME THERE?
--TO RECOVER THE "DARKHOLD" FROM MILES BLACKGAR, WHO'D BOUGHT MY FATHER'S CASTLE, AND HAD IT SHIPPED FROM EUROPE TO AMERICA'S WESTERN COAST.
--MILES BLACKGAR, WHOSE DAUGHTER WAS A MUTANT GORGON--WHOSE EYES HAD MADE ME STONE!
SHE--SHE IS THE ONE I MUST KILL--
SHE--WHO KEEPS ME FROM THE FOREST--!

NO, JACK,..NOTHING'S WRONG, NO...FATHER... STEP-FATHER ISN'T HERE JUST NOW... WE CAN TALK.

2394 VENICE BOULEVARD? YES, I'VE GOT IT, JACK.

I'LL BE THERE IN HALF AN HOUR.

I HUNG UP--AND AS I GLANCED AT COWAN, SOMETHING NAGGED AT THE BACK OF MY MIND. I COULDN'T FIGURE IT-- THE WAY SHE TALKED; IT WASN'T LIKE LISSA--!

...I ONLY WISH I KNEW.

SHE'S COMIN' OVER?

DO YOU THINK THAT'S WISE?

I WISH I KNEW, FRIEND...

PERHAPS IF I'D KNOWN THEN WHAT I KNOW NOW, I'D HAVE DONE THINGS DIFFERENTLY--BUT HOW COULD I HAVE GUESSED THE SCENE IN OUR WESTWOOD HOME? HOW?

DAD, ARE YOU SURE, WE--

NONE OF THAT, YOUNG LADY.

MISS BLACKGAR HAS MADE EVERYTHING QUITE CLEAR.

PRECISELY, MR. RUSSELL. WE ONLY WISH TO SPEAK WITH YOUR...AH...SON.

AND REGAIN CERTAIN PROPERTIES WE THINK HE MAY HAVE TAKEN.

YOU MEAN STOLEN.

THAT'S A HARSH WORD, MR. RUSSELL... AND YET, IF HE DID TAKE THE BOOK WE SEEK...

...NATURALLY, WE WILL NOT SEEK TO PROSECUTE IF YOUR SON WILL RETURN IT.

HE WILL, MISS BLACKGAR ...I PROMISE YOU.

JACK'S GOTTEN A LITTLE BIG FOR HIMSELF, LATELY...

IT'S TIME HE WAS TAUGHT A LESSON IN SELF-CONTROL!

LISSA-- YOU'RE GOING WITH THEM!

BUCK HAD WORKED HIS WAY THROUGH THREE-QUARTERS OF A PAGE--AND MY MIND WAS WHIRLING WITH THE IMPLICATIONS OF MY FATHER'S DIARY--WHEN--

WHAT IN THE NAME OF A PURPLE HEAVEN--?

WHUMP

CORN FLAKES

BUCK-- LOOK OUT!

COWAN DIDN'T LISTEN--WITH AN ANGRY SHOUT, HE LUNGED AT THE CHARGING FREAK--AND FELL TO AN OFF-HAND BLOW--

BTAK

UNNNHHH!

I WAS ON MY FEET IN AN INSTANT--PAUSING ONLY A MOMENT BY THE TABLE--AND THEN--

CHUNK!

THAT'S ENOUGH, JACK--

I SAID--THAT'S ENOUGH!

MARLENE!

YOU REMEMBER ME, JACK...I'M FLATTERED. WE THOUGHT YOU'D FORGOTTEN US, WHEN YOU LEFT SO... ABRUPTLY.

FATHER, YOU REMEMBER JACK RUSSELL...THE BOY WHO TRIED TO KILL YOU?

YOU'LL HAVE TO FORGIVE HIM, JACK. HE HASN'T BEEN THE SAME SINCE HIS NASTY FALL.

HIS SPINE'S CRUSHED--HE'S PARALYZED FROM THE WAIST DOWN.

NOW--BE QUITE MOTIONLESS--UNLESS YOU WANT YOUR SISTER TO BE AS HELPLESS AS MY FATHER.

JACK--PLEASE FORGIVE ME.

DAD-- FORCED ME--!

I STARTED TO *ANSWER* HER-- BUT BEFORE I COULD SPEAK, THE FREAK HAD CAUGHT ME FROM *BEHIND*--

FILIAL DEVOTION IS AN *ODD* THING, JACK--

BEFORE HIS--ACCIDENT --I *DESPISED* MY FATHER--

--BLAMING *HIM* FOR MY MUTANT EYES--

--YET NOW, I WANT ONLY TO *AID* HIM--

BY FINDING THE BOOK CALLED THE *DARKHOLD*--

--AND USING IT TO *RESTORE* HIS NOW-CRIPPLED FORM!

WHY, STRUG... HE SEEMS TO HAVE GONE TO *SLEEP*.

THOSE WERE THE LAST WORDS I HEARD...

I AWOKE *HOURS* LATER. OUTSIDE THE PATIO DOORS, THE SKY WAS TURNING A DUSKY *PURPLE*...

IT WAS ALMOST EVENING...ALMOST *NIGHT*!

NOTHING! STRUG, ARE YOU SURE YOU'VE SEARCHED *EVERY-WHERE*?

STRUG *LOOKED*.

ONLY SCENT... LIKE *BEFORE*.

YES... LIKE BEFORE.

SHE SIGHED AND SHOOK HER HEAD. THE LAST RAYS OF SUNLIGHT *GLINTED* ON HER GLASSES --AND I KNEW I HAD TO ESCAPE, BEFORE THE *TRANSFORMATION* OCCURED--! BUT AS I STARTED TO MY FEET, THE MAN WHO ONCE HAD BEEN *MILES BLACKGAR* TWISTED IN HIS CHAIR--AND *BLINKED* AT ME--

UNNNNNNN-NNNHH!

HE *SEES* ME--I'VE GOTTA MAKE MY MOVE--

UUNNNNNNNNHH!

--NOW!

MY HEART WAS RACING --THE ROOM WAS FLOODED IN DARKNESS--

ALREADY, I FELT IT BEGINNING--

THE CHANGE--*BOILING* INSIDE ME--I PUSHED PAST MARLENE, BOLTED FOR THE *DOORS*--

THAK!

JACK-- WHAT ARE YOU *DOING*, BOY?

UNTIE US, JACK-- JACK!

WHAT IS IT? WHAT'S *WRONG* WITH YOU?

CAN'T STOP-- GOTTA KEEP *MOVING!*

DON'T YOU EVEN *HEAR* US--?

LISSA BROKE OFF--AND SOME-THING ABOUT HER BREATHING MADE ME *TURN.* HER EYES WERE FILLING, HER MOUTH *TREMBLING*--

LISSA, I--

IT WAS *USELESS.* HOW COULD I EXPLAIN? I COULDN'T WASTE A SECOND--IF I STAYED, HER VERY *LIFE* WAS IN DANGER--

BUT, IF I RAN--?

PLEASE, JACK-- DON'T *LEAVE* ME--

I--I--

I'VE *GOT* TO, LISSA--

HEAVEN HELP ME, I'VE GOT TO!

RUN, JACK--*RUN,* BEFORE THE *MOONLIGHT* COMES--

--BEFORE EVERYTHING YOU ARE--OR *THINK* YOU ARE--

--*VANISHES*--AND *DIES!*

TINKER BELL

BUS STOP

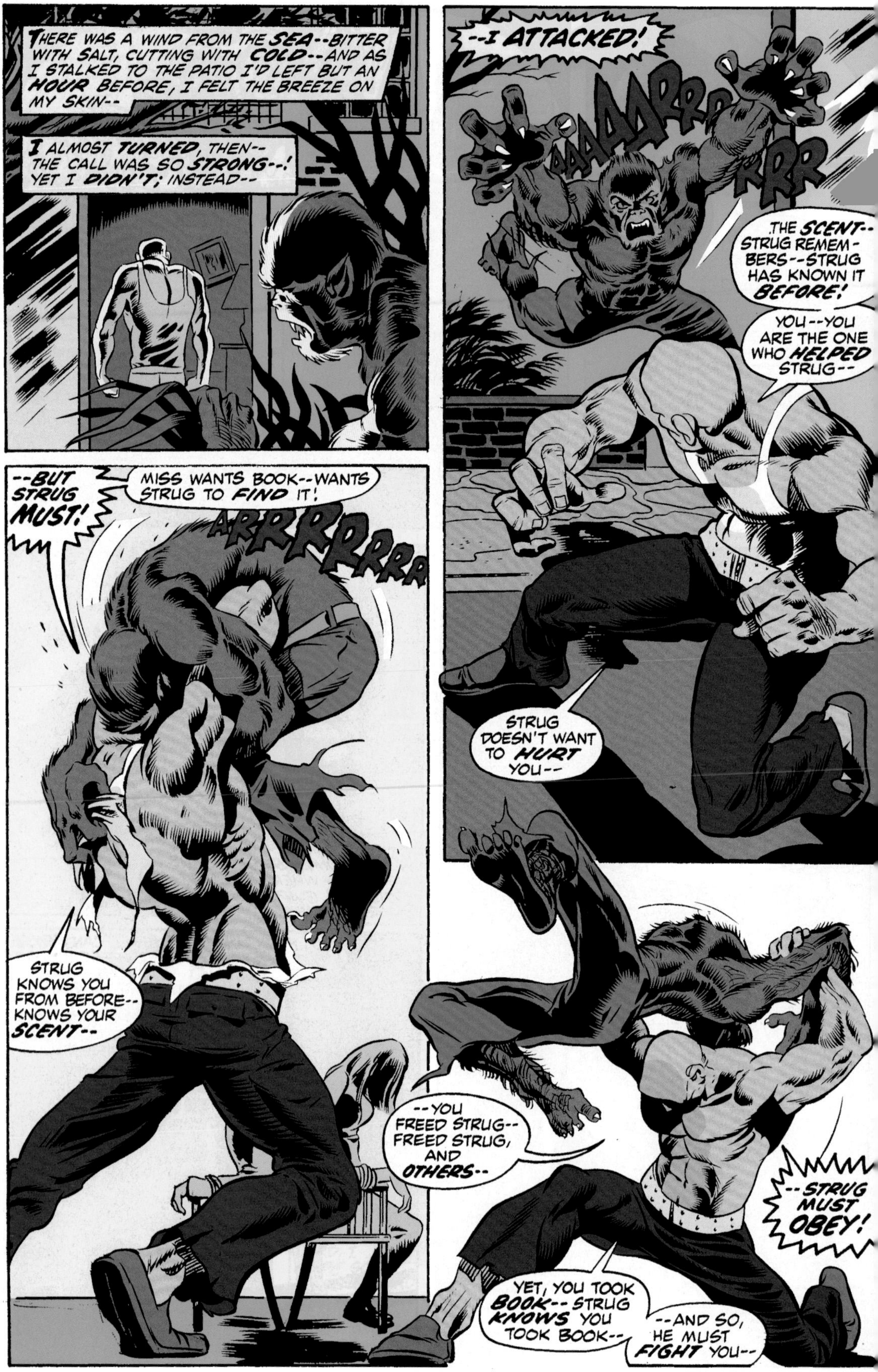

THERE WAS A WIND FROM THE SEA--BITTER WITH SALT, CUTTING WITH COLD--AND AS I STALKED TO THE PATIO I'D LEFT BUT AN HOUR BEFORE, I FELT THE BREEZE ON MY SKIN--
I ALMOST TURNED, THEN-- THE CALL WAS SO STRONG--! YET I DIDN'T; INSTEAD--
--I ATTACKED!
AAAAARRRRRRR
THE SCENT-- STRUG REMEMBERS--STRUG HAS KNOWN IT BEFORE!
YOU--YOU ARE THE ONE WHO HELPED STRUG--
STRUG DOESN'T WANT TO HURT YOU--
--BUT STRUG MUST!
MISS WANTS BOOK--WANTS STRUG TO FIND IT!
ARRRRRRRR
STRUG KNOWS YOU FROM BEFORE-- KNOWS YOUR SCENT--
--YOU FREED STRUG-- FREED STRUG, AND OTHERS--
--STRUG MUST OBEY!
YET, YOU TOOK BOOK-- STRUG KNOWS YOU TOOK BOOK--
--AND SO, HE MUST FIGHT YOU--

HIS VOICE CAUGHT, *BROKE*--FOR A MOMENT, HIS GRIP LOOSENED, AND I STRUGGLED FOR FREEDOM; WITH A GRUNT, HE *SHIFTED HIS HOLD*--

STRUG'S SORRY-- HE DOESN'T *WANT* TO HURT YOU!

BUT WHAT STRUG WANTS DOESN'T *MATTER*-- HE MUST OBEY MISS--HE *MUST!*

CATCHING THE LANTERN CHANDELIER, I SWUNG *UPWARD*--CLEARED THE BALCONY AND *WHIRLED*--

AAAARRRRRR

WHAT WAS LEFT OF MY HUMANITY FELT *PITY* FOR THE MUTATED CREATURE CALLED STRUG... YET THAT EMOTION DIED AT BIRTH, LEAVING ONLY ANGER... BURNING *RAGE!*

AARRRRRRR

NOW, STRUG-- KILL HIM *NOW!*

STRUG--SO *MINDLESS*...

WHY DID I SPARE *HIM*, AND NOT ONE OF THE *OTHERS?*

ALL OF THEM, *STONE*--

--AND ONLY *STRUG* TO AID US NOW!

STRUG *FIGHTS* HIM, MISS--

STRUG WILL *WIN*--HE WILL, MISS-- HE *WILL!*

PERHAPS HE *WOULD* HAVE-- BUT THEY NEVER GAVE HIM THE CHANCE. DIMLY, I COULD HEAR THE OLD MAN *SNARLING*, WORDLESSLY COMMANDING HIS DAUGHTER--

--AND EQUALLY WORDLESS, SHE *FIRED*!

KRAK!

DIDN'T NEED TO *SHOOT*-- STRUG WOULD HAVE STOPPED HIM, STRUG WOULD HAVE DONE WHAT YOU *ASKED*!

HASN'T STRUG *ALWAYS* DONE WHAT MISS ASKED?

EVEN WHEN IT *HURT* HIM, STRUG *TRIED*--

EVEN AGAINST *HIM*-- AGAINST THE ONE WHO *FREED* STRUG.

STRUG *TRIED*, DIDN'T HE?

HASN'T STRUG ALWAYS--

--ALWAYS--

--TRIED?

OH MY GOD.

STARING AT ME, SHE SHIVERED, AND HER VOICE--A WHISPER--FADED. SHE LOOKED AT HER FATHER, FOUND THE ANSWER SHE NEEDED IN HIS EYES, HER HANDS WENT TO HER GLASSES...

THIS FAILED ONCE BEFORE, JACK--I DON'T KNOW HOW, AND IT DOESN'T MATTER.

THIS TIME, YOU WON'T ESCAPE--

--THIS TIME, JACK RUSSELL--YOU'LL DIE!

I DUCKED BACK, A GROWL RUMBLING UP FROM MY THROAT--

AAARRRRR

I FELT THE STING OF HER VISION ON MY SKIN--

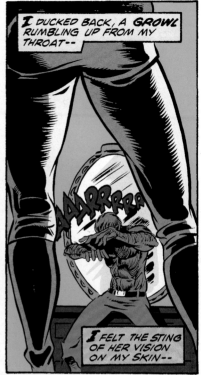

--AND THEN THE STING VANISHED, AND I HEARD TWO OF THEM SCREAM!

OH MY LORD--NO! THE MIRROR! THE MIRROR!

AIEEEEEE

THEN HER VOICE WAS SILENCED, AND SOMEHOW, MY BESTIAL BRAIN KNEW THEY'D TROUBLE ME NO MORE--

FOR BOTH OF THEM, FATHER AND MUTATED DAUGHTER... THE AGONY OF LIFE WAS OVER... THE NIGHTMARE OF HELL WAS JUST BEGUN!

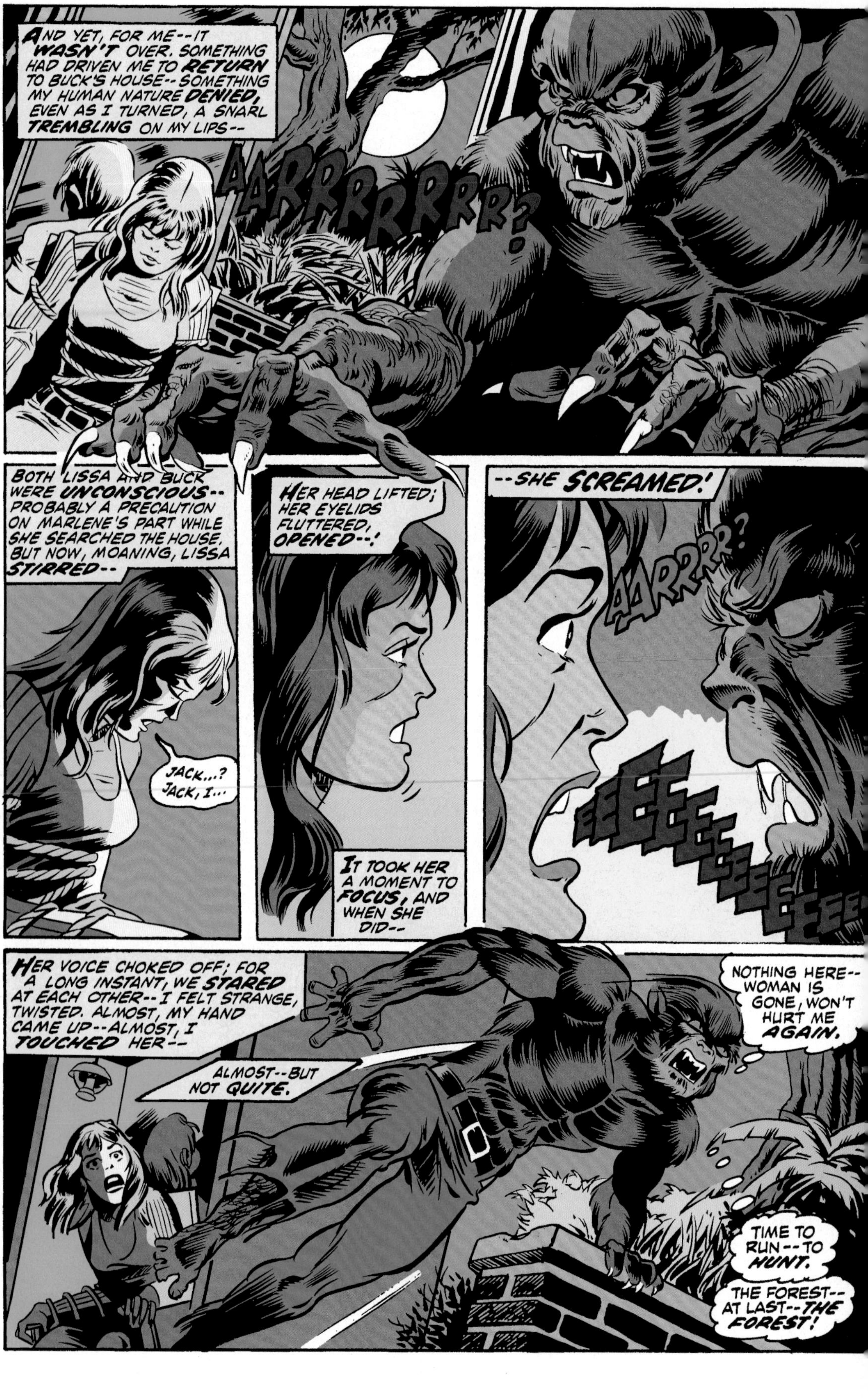
AND YET, FOR ME--IT WASN'T OVER. SOMETHING HAD DRIVEN ME TO RETURN TO BUCK'S HOUSE--SOMETHING MY HUMAN NATURE DENIED, EVEN AS I TURNED, A SNARL TREMBLING ON MY LIPS--
AARRRRRRRRR?
BOTH LISSA AND BUCK WERE UNCONSCIOUS--PROBABLY A PRECAUTION ON MARLENE'S PART WHILE SHE SEARCHED THE HOUSE, BUT NOW, MOANING, LISSA STIRRED--
JACK...? JACK, I...
HER HEAD LIFTED; HER EYELIDS FLUTTERED, OPENED--!
IT TOOK HER A MOMENT TO FOCUS, AND WHEN SHE DID--
--SHE SCREAMED!
AARRRR?
EEEEEEEEEEEEEE
HER VOICE CHOKED OFF; FOR A LONG INSTANT, WE STARED AT EACH OTHER--I FELT STRANGE, TWISTED. ALMOST, MY HAND CAME UP--ALMOST, I TOUCHED HER--
ALMOST--BUT NOT QUITE.
NOTHING HERE--WOMAN IS GONE, WON'T HURT ME AGAIN.
TIME TO RUN--TO HUNT.
THE FOREST--AT LAST--THE FOREST!

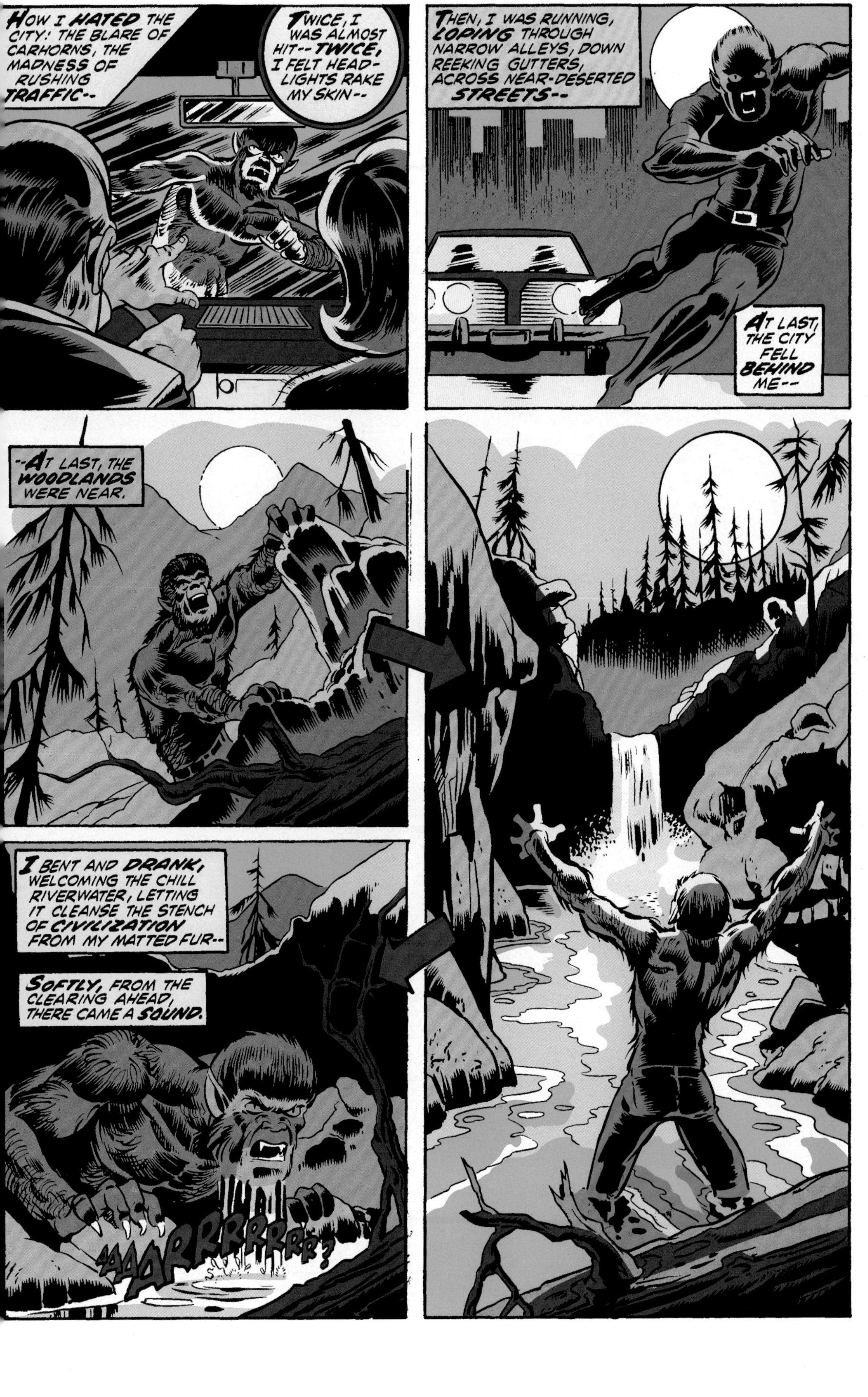
HOW I HATED THE CITY: THE BLARE OF CARHORNS, THE MADNESS OF RUSHING TRAFFIC--
TWICE, I WAS ALMOST HIT-- TWICE, I FELT HEAD-LIGHTS RAKE MY SKIN--
THEN, I WAS RUNNING, LOPING THROUGH NARROW ALLEYS, DOWN REEKING GUTTERS, ACROSS NEAR-DESERTED STREETS--
AT LAST, THE CITY FELL BEHIND ME--
--AT LAST, THE WOODLANDS WERE NEAR.
I BENT AND DRANK, WELCOMING THE CHILL RIVERWATER, LETTING IT CLEANSE THE STENCH OF CIVILIZATION FROM MY MATTED FUR--
SOFTLY, FROM THE CLEARING AHEAD, THERE CAME A SOUND.
AAAARRRRRRRR?

RISING TO MY FEET, I MOVED FORWARD, THROUGH A VEIL OF GREEN LEAVES. THE SOUND STOPPED--I ENTERED THE CLEARING; THERE, EYES GLEAMING SOFT CRIMSON IN THE MOONLIGHT, A LIGHT MIST DRIFTING FROM ITS NOSTRILS, WAS A BUCK--

OUR EYES MET...AND IN THAT MOMENT, WE KNEW...

IT WAS DONE QUICKLY.

AFTERWARDS, I RACED THROUGH THE FOREST DARKNESS--MY HEART POUNDING, MY BREATH COMING IN SHORT, VIOLENT GASPS--

ARROOOOO...

I CAME TO A BARREN HILLSIDE, A PLACE I'D SEEN IN MY TROUBLED DREAMS--AND UNDER A SETTING MOON, IN THE COMPANY OF A SLEEK GREY WOLF--I HOWLED.

AND IN THE MORNING... I STARTED HOME.

...NOR COULD I HELP WONDERING--HOW MUCH OF MYSELF HAD I LEFT IN THAT EMERALD HEAVEN--THAT EMERALD HELL?

WOULD I EVER KNOW? AND IF I COULD--WOULD I WANT TO?

I ARRIVED AT BUCK'S SOON AFTER *NOON*; HE AND LISSA WERE FREE:

--MUST'VE BLACKED OUT WHEN THAT FREAK *GRABBED* ME, BUCK.

UP UNTIL AN *HOUR* AGO-- IT'S ALL A *BLANK!*

SURE, KID-- NO *PROBLEM.*

--SEEMS WE *ALL* MISSED THE ACTION LAST NIGHT, *RIGHT,* MISSY?

ASK *LISSA,* JACK--SHE'S GOT A WILD TALE TO TELL--

--AND IN *SOME* WAYS, IT ALMOST--ONLY *ALMOST*--MAKES SENSE.

I'I'D RATHER NOT *TALK* ABOUT IT, BUCK.

PERHAPS I NEED SOME TIME TO *THINK*... TO FIGURE THINGS *OUT.*

BUT, JACK... WHAT ABOUT FATHER'S *BOOK?*

YEAH, JACK...I TOLD HER 'BOUT IT, AND WE SEARCHED FOR *HOURS*...

...BUT YOU NEVER THOUGHT TO LOOK IN *HERE?*

KID, SOME-TIMES YOU *ASTOUND* ME,

COME *ON,* BUCK.WE'LL BE LATE FOR YOUR *OPENING.*

CORN FLAKES

HIS *WHAT?*

BUCK LAUGHED, AND LISSA SMILED--BUT *NEITHER* OF THEM WOULD EXPLAIN ANY FURTHER; IT WASN'T UNTIL WE DROVE UP IN FRONT OF THE SANTA MONICA ART MUSEUM THAT I BEGAN TO UNDER-STAND...

ART MUSEUM PARKING

COST ME A SPRAINED BACK, KID--BUT IT'S *WORTH* IT.

THEY'RE *OPENING* UP ABOUT NOW--SHOULD BE *QUITE* INTERESTING.

BUCK, YOU *DIDN'T--?*

YEAH, WE DID--THIS *MORNING.*

THEY WERE TWO OF THE MOST *LIFE-LIKE* STATUES I'D EVER SEEN.

DO NOT TOUCH THE EXHIBITS

THE END?

MRS. DEADPOOL AND THE
HOWLING COMMANDOS #3-4
VARIANTS BY GIUSEPPE CAMUNCOLI
& MARTE GRACIA

Made in the USA
Middletown, DE
29 May 2020

96266127R00179

The Picture Language of Folktales

Friedel Lenz

Original German Title: Bildsprache der Märchen

The German original is copyrighted in 1971

by Urachhaus, Stuttgart

Translation and introduction by Clopper Almon

The appendix, "A Brief Symbol Overview", has not been translated,

nor has the publisher's introduction.

Contents

4

Prefaces

The Shattered Jewel

All folktales have in common that they are the remains of a faith going back to the earliest times, a faith, a religion that speaks of supersensible things in pictures. These pictures are like fragments of a shattered jewel that lie strewn on the ground overgrown with grass and flowers. Only the sharpest eye can discover them. Their meaning is long lost but can still be felt and gives the folktales their substance. At the same time, these stories satisfy the natural longing for the Wonderful. But never are the folktales just the play of colors of a content-free fantasy.

– Wilhelm Grimm

5

Translator's Introduction

In this book, Friedel Lenz intersperses her commentary on 25 of the Grimm folktales with a telling of the tale. The commentary is based on the anthroposophy of Rudolf Steiner, and without some basic knowledge of it such as found in Steiner's *Theosophy* and *Cosmic Memory* or his comprehensive *Esoteric Science* (also called *Occult Science*) the commentary may seem puzzling. With that basic knowledge, however, her interpretation is wondrously illuminating.

The Grimm stories and other genuine folktales are, as Wilhelm Grimm says in the passage quoted above, fragments of an ancient faith. They are probably the most profound literature we possess. We tell them to children because they speak to the deepest reaches of the child's soul. Friedel Lenz helps even educated modern adults understand them.

The explanations should be especially helpful to teachers in Waldorf kindergartens and first grades. The explanations are not, of course, to be told to the children. They understand without explanation. A kindergarten teacher of many years experience told me that when she first began to use the Grimm folktales in her classes, the children would sometimes ask, "Is the story true?" But when she herself became fully convinced of the deep truth of the stories, the children stopped asking. It is my hope that this translation of the text of Friedel Lenz will help teachers to tell the stories so that the children will feel no need to ask if they are true.

The life story of Friedel Lenz is as remarkable as her book. Born Friedel Ganz in 1897 in Heigenbrücken near Aschaffenburg

in Bavaria, she was the daughter of a teacher and attended a private girls school and later completed a teachers seminar. She belonged to the Wandervogel back-to-nature youth movement and led the Aschaffenburg group. With it she met the Erlangen group, which unlike many other groups, was not nationalistic, but rather took its ideals from the German classics and romantics, especially the philosophy of Schelling. In 1919, she took part in a festival of the Bavarian Wandervogel in the Spielberg castle atop a hill near Brno. There she met her future husband, Eduard Lenz. Together they became acquainted with the brand-new Waldorf school movement and with Rudolf Steiner. Friedel and Eduard were married in 1920 and in 1922 together studied at the Waldorf teacher training program in Stuttgart. Eduard was soon one of the founders of the Christian Community, became a priest, and later Lenker. In 1925, Eduard was sent to Prague to found the Christian Community there. Friedel went with him and learned both Czech and Russian, which years later enabled her to translate Russian folktales. In 1934, they moved to Dresden.

Eduard played a major role in negotiating with the Nazi government to avoid closure of the Christian Community, but was in the end unsuccessful. It was closed, and he was drafted into the army and sent to the Russian front. There he was taken prisoner and sent to work in a coal mine in Siberia. At the end of the war, in November 1945, he was put on a train in a cattle car to be taken back to Germany, but he died on the train. His body was put off near Omsk and left there. Friedel and the four children had remained in Dresden, where the two daughters were killed in the February 1945 bombing of the city by the British and Americans. Friedel and the two sons survived. One of the sons, Johannes, born

in 1927, became a priest in the Christian Community and eventually "Oberlenker".

Thus, in early 1946 Friedel realized that she must make a new life for herself. She had always been fascinated by the sagas and folktales and now saw her calling to make them known and understood. A further motivation was that at that time there was strong sentiment against the sagas and tales by those who thought they shared in the blame for the horrors of Nazism and the war. She wanted to come to their defense and show that they speak of the highest in Man, the opposite of what led to the war.

She moved for a while to Bremen, was active in the Anthroposophical Society there, and in 1947 gave her first talk on folktales. Soon she was lecturing on the subject widely throughout Germany and Switzerland. She loved to tell the tales to children and did so in kindergartens and on playgrounds. In Hanover, at the big "Housewife Fair," they built a special "Märchenpavillion" for her.

Friedel Lenz dealt with European folktales from Russia to Ireland, but she did not interpret non-European tales, of which there are many. This limitation was not because she did not value the non-European tales, but rather out of respect for them. She felt that to interpret a folktale properly one had to know the whole cultural heritage of the people in which it was found. She recognized that she herself simply did not have the background necessary to interpret non-European tales.

Her reputation as lecturer and teller of tales and sagas spread internationally. She was invited to Switzerland, England, Austria, the Netherlands, and Sweden. At the end of her life, she was living

in Munich and working on this book up to her very last days. She died in 1970.

There are several other books about folktales by writers influenced by anthroposophy. *The Wisdom of Fairy Tales* by Rudolf Meyer is a classic. Meyer, with profound erudition, discusses themes appearing in many stories, but does not work through individual stories in detail, as Lenz does. It is thus more difficult for a teacher to use in preparing to tell a particular tale. Rudolf Geiger's *Mit Märchensöhnen Unterwegs* is more like Lenz with interpretation of twelve individual stories, with no overlap with the ones covered in this book. There is also *The World of Fairy Tales: A path to the essence of the young child through fairy tales* by Daniel Udo de Haes.

Translation is sometimes easy and sometimes well-nigh impossible. The tales themselves do not often present major problems of translation, and I have used, with minor changes, anonymous translations found either in books printed before 1923 or on the Internet (especially www.grimmstories.com) with no indication of translator or copyright. The text of Friedel Lenz is another story. In the first place, she delights in the idioms and colorful expressions of German that often have no close equivalent in English. I have had recourse to a native German speaker to understand some of these and to footnotes to explain them. (All footnotes are by me unless otherwise indicated.) The rather literal kind of translation that usually works well enough for the tales would, applied to her text, often result in utterly incomprehensible English. I have translated literally where the result was understandable. But I have often had to stop and re-think a whole paragraph and then search for some way to express her thoughts in my own words. I hope the result is true to her meaning, but it is

sometimes far, far from literal. Anyone who knows a little German should enjoy the treat of reading this book in the original.

Today one is of course expected to produce "gender neutral" English. This is not easy when translating from German, for English lacks a good translation of *Mensch* which is unambiguously common gender and includes both men and women, although grammatically masculine and using the masculine pronouns. Using "human" for the common gender is unfortunate, for it is related to *humus* and refers to the part of us that is a clod, whereas *man* is etymologically a thinking being. "Person" is a poor substitute, for it is from Latin *persona,* a mask, almost the opposite of a *Mensch.* Perhaps the worst solution is to randomly alternate between "man" and "woman", between "he" and "she". This practice rightfully offends a group of true feminists who regard the feminine as special, refined, elevated and by no means to be used to include common, ordinary males. Sometimes I have used the impersonal "one". In the plural, *people* often works. When cornered, I have used Man with a capital M to translate Mensch, and have used masculine pronouns with it.[1]

And finally, there is the problem of how to translate the German word for these stories: *Märchen.* It is the diminutive of *Mär*, which currently means *news, tidings, report, story.* The Niebelungenlied, put into writing about 1200 but drawing on oral

---

1 English has a number of animal triplets with masculine, feminine, and common gender words, for example: rooster, hen, chicken; stag, doe, deer; stallion, mare, horse. But for we ourselves we have only two words, so the triplet is: man, woman, man. Some women now object that using "man" for the common gender is unacceptable. I think the problem is using "man" for the masculine and have proposed: yoman, woman, man, and for the pronouns of the common gender, just drop the initial t off the plural forms. This is a neat solution, but seems to satisfy only me.

heroic traditions going back to the 5th or 6th century, refers to these traditions as *mären*, It begins

> Uns ist in alten mæren wunders vil geseit
> To us in old *mæren* wonders many are told

Thus a *Mär* can be a heroic tradition, an epic, such as found in the *Niebelungenlied.* And a *Märchen* is a little *Mär.*

Unfortunately, there does not seem to be a close English equivalent. In English they are sometimes called fairy stories, but that is quite misleading for not only do they only rarely involve fairies but also the term suggests a light, fanciful, Ariel-like quality which is often quite foreign to the earthy *Märchen.* It also suggests to many people something that is not true.

I have called them *tales* or *folktales* because *folk* points to their transmission in oral traditions and *tale* points to the Germanic roots of the Grimm tales, is intimately connected with *telling,* and somewhat mysteriously, with counting. The English words *tell* and *tale* are both related etymologically to German *Zahl* (number) and *zahlen* (count) and *erzählen* (to tell). Remember the *teller* at the bank, so called because he *counts.* The Russian word for the tales is сказка (pronounced skazka) related to сказать, *to say,* again emphasizing something *told.* The French word for the tales is *contes,* related to *count* and thus again to number. To *tell* the tale is to *recount* it. I suspect that the telling of these tales was once, like the Kalevala or the Greek epics, metrical and thus involved counting and number. All that gets somehow summed up in *tale.*[2]

---

2   Some argue that whereas fairy stories involve magic and enchantment, "a folktale derives its story from real-life phenomena" and then give as examples of folktales Chicken Little and Henny Penny, as if chickens that talk, plant wheat, bake bread or rush off to tell the king something are "real-life phenomena." In other words, by this definition there are few if any

Introduction

How did mankind come to speak in picture language? And what supersensible things are expressed in the folktales?

Modern research on the folktales considers them the reality dreams (Wahreträume) of humanity. In dreaming one does not think. Pictures in colorful variety stream through the soul. Today these pictures are for the most part chaotic reflections of daily events, often colored by wishes or fears. But a different type of dream points to deeper connections. We can, for example, dream that the house we are in begins to burn. We flee from the fire and awaken – with a fever. The body has represented itself as the house; and the fever, as the fire. People close to death often dream that they must move out of their house. Children, on the other hand, dream that they are seeking a house. Or we have become lost in a forest and cannot find a path, or cliffs and mountains rise before us and we can find no way past them. We recognize that these dreams are not the usual chaotic reflections of daily events, rather they reflect situations in which we find ourselves with no way out. A third type of dream is seldom experienced today, but it does still occurs, especially at times of great shocks to the soul. It is the destiny dream, the prophetic reality dream in which the inner human speaks. Here we are on the plane of the exact true image, on the plane of the picture-creating consciousness out of which the folktales arise.

At an earlier stage of human evolution, all peoples had this consciousness. Today, the nighttime dreams while sleeping are but

---

"folktales." The term is too good to waste on an almost empty set. But if *folktales* is not allowed, then I would call the *Märchen* "wisdom tales" for, as this book shows, they are based in profound wisdom.

a last remnant. Originally, mankind lived in a sea of dreamy pictures even in the daytime, though later mainly at night. He saw not only – like modern Man – the external world of graspable objects with his bodily eyes; he saw also beings without bodies working and creating in these pictures. As his still unequally malleable being came into contact with these other beings, he reproduced them in himself; the inner being of these other beings expressed itself in inner true-to-life pictures. This clairvoyance lived in him like a natural force. This was the mythological age. Out of the experience of the divine world above, Man received his majestic imaginations about the origins of the world and of mankind – the **myths**.

Divine powers were innerly visible to him. He grasped the guiding spirit of his people, not abstractly as we do, but vividly and as a working being. So, for example, the German folk spirit, which could not yet express itself in a united people but appeared today in one tribe and tomorrow in another was imaginatively experienced as the Wanderer, as Odin is often called. In this way there was revealed to Man the destiny and development of the peoples of the earth, both of the one to which he belonged and of those with which he was involved. Out of these pictures came the great heroic **sagas.**

Out of Man's experience of his own being and his own destiny, a third form of story was created: the **folktale.**

Folktales show the Inner Destiny and Development of the Individual Human Being in Pictures.

In the age when the myths originated, Man saw in dreamy imaginations true pictures of spiritual beings and events. With the development of thinking, these pictures were expressed in words and told. The earliest tellers were, in the feminine age of mankind, women, the preservers and protectors of all that gave the tribe coherence and permanence, They were seeresses and priestesses, as Tacitus reports of the great seeress Veleda[3], a late example.

In the later masculine age it was the task of the bards and rhapsodes – sent out from the mystery centers of the druids in Celtic lands and from courts of kings in Germanic lands – to tell the mythos, heroic sagas, and *mären*.

At the center of our Germanic mythology stands that great change of consciousness for which Karl Josef Simrock in the 19th century introduced the picture-word "Twilight of the Gods" Götterdämmerung). The clairvoyant view of a divine over-world faded, and the independent connection of ordinary people to the spiritual world came to an end. Simultaneously, there awoke in western peoples the independent personality, the I. This great event affected the destiny of western humanity and of each individual. The folktales which the Grimm brothers have untiringly collected reflect in their essence this change of consciousness. A realm must be left behind, a kingdom given up; poverty and trials begin. Finally, through one's own strength a new kingdom is earned. We recognize the ways of personality development, of individualization. The tales show the dangers that lurk along the way, the tasks and the tests which must be mastered, as well as the

---

3   Tacitus, *Germania* 8.2. Veleda lived in the first century A.D.

stages reached. The highest stage is the Christ-permeated Man. That becomes clear not from the use of the name of the Christ but from the content. As St. John says,[4] "He has made us kings"

The capacity for forming images was widespread and many tales may have originated here or there. But our most important tales show such a deep knowledge of the human being, a guidance so free of gaps to inner development towards goals both near at hand and far into the future that we must recognize the leadership of great teachers. We know no names, but careful observation of the way the pictures are formed and the symbols used enables us to recognize certain centers.

Folktales are Conscious Instruction and the Great Educational Material of the Peoples of the World

Up until the 9th century Man was considered in the West as a threefold being of body, soul and spirit. The creators of the folktales continued to honor this threefold structure which had been conceptually formulated by Aristotle despite the fact that a two-fold structure of just body and soul had become the dogma of the church. It can be an important key to observe this aspect of the folktales. The spirit in Man, his eternal entelechy, his I, appears in a masculine image and all forces related to him are masculine. The soul appears in the picture language of all peoples as feminine and all soul properties as feminine images. The body as the sheltering surrounding appears as house, castle, hut, or tower.

Every folktale is a small drama played out on our internal stage. Its human figures are personifications of soul and spiritual forces; drives and instincts on the other hand appear in this connection as animals. The action takes its pictures, to be sure,

---

4   Rev. 1:6

15

from the objects of the outer world but is to be understood as absolutely internal happenings. Each landscape is an inner theater.

Today we must ever anew work to understand the folktales, for modern man no longer automatically understands their picture language. To be sure, our speech is full of pictorial expressions. Most words come from pictures. Speech is pictures run together. But intellectual thinking no longer sees the picture. To recognize the picture in words is a further useful key.

Why are Folktales Important for the Spiritual Development of Children?

A key to the significance of the folktales and their inclusion in the education of children is given by passage by a younger contemporary of Goethe. "The history of each person's attainment of complete individual development is also the history of his genus." (Karl Ferdinand Wieck (1787 – 1864))

The development which the whole of mankind has gone through is repeated in each individual. The early ages of mankind are reflected in the child; each child repeats the mythological age. The child is no abstract thinker, but a former of soul-rich pictures, as the play of all children demonstrates. And there is an important second law: the consciousness of Man constantly changes. And education must respect this change of consciousness.

After the mythical age comes the development of thinking. Man lived both in dreamy-clairvoyant visions and in also in thinking. The stories speak now in pictures and thoughts. Outer events are expressed in ordinary language; inner experiences, in pictures. This epoch repeats itself in the child as the picture-thought-stage beginning in about the eighth year. To this age belong

sagas and legends, both the heroic sagas of the child's own folk and of other peoples. A great document of this epoch is the Old Testament which speaks in two languages.

With the beginning of puberty the true thinking stage is reached. At this age, the composed tales, such as those of Hans Christian Andersen, first become appropriate. They come from a wholly different realm; they are products of understanding and fantasy. The composed tales are literature; the genuine folktales are pictures of soul and spiritual realities: imaginations.

The explanations offered in this book, it should go without saying, are not for the child. In childhood, the soul should not be led from the picture to intellectual understanding. But parents, kindergarten teachers, and first grade teachers can be more responsible in the choice of stories and more convincing in their telling if they know the sense and meaning of this venerable heritage.

The interpretations brought together in this volume are taken from lectures held in various cities and different countries. Each one is intended to be complete in itself, so some repetitions were unavoidable.

Tales of Destiny

Good and Evil are in the World

Both try to claim the soul

But Good wins.

Briar Rose

Grimm 50

(Sleeping Beauty)

Before times there was a king and a queen who everyday said, "Ah, if we but had a child!" but they had no child. And then it happened that one day, as the queen sat in her bath, a frog crawled out of the water onto the land and said to her, "Your wish will be fulfilled; before a year has passed you will bring a daughter into the world."

"Before times" (*vor Zeiten*) – so begins the tale – and one must take it quite literally – before the historical time that we so easily grasp, in the mythological age – Man was a potent being, gifted with great power, a crowned king. And his soul was a queen. For him the sense world and the spiritual world were still a unity. In the sense of Novalis, the world was still in the world. The day was filled with true images, with imaginations. In these images, nature and the world manifested themselves to mankind; the external objects of the sense world were of less importance. Human consciousness was in a state of natural clairvoyance completely opposite to our present consciousness. Mankind was in contact with spiritual beings.

Man of the mythological age yearned with his soul – the queen – for a transformation of consciousness. A different kind of soul should come to life. The Golden Age of mankind – of which the Greek poet Hesiod and the Roman poet Ovid wrote – must pass away, for in mankind there rules the law of the transformation of consciousness.

An instinct foretold that a new kind of soul – a daughter – should come. The image for this instinct is the frog that "crawled out of the water onto the land." Just as the ever-moving soul world of the mythological age with its depths and shallows, its undulating feelings and pictures is like water – and all myths use for it the picture-word water – so is the world of hard facts into which mankind gradually came like land. Mankind then grasped the sense world. The firm, material replaced the mobile; the constant replaced the fluctuating. Compare dreams, which for every subtle inner feeling find endless new pictures, with our present day object consciousness that counts, measures and weighs and expects certain, dependable results – and you understand the pictures "Water" and "Land."

The frog, living first in water and then on land, through long metamorphosis, changes from a gill-breather in water to a lung-breather in air. It is very sensitive to weather changes and thus is regarded as a weather prophet. In the story, it symbolizes the capacity to grasp a change in the spiritual atmosphere and therefore to be a weather prophet in an extended sense. This symbol also points to the lability of an inner double consciousness.

What the frog had foretold happened, and the queen bore a daughter who was so beautiful that the king for joy didn't know what to do. He put on a great feast. He invited to it not only his relatives, friends and acquaintances but also the wise women so that they would be sweet and well-disposed to the child. There were thirteen wise women in his realm, but as he had only twelve golden plates from which they should eat, one must remain at home.

Man still knew himself protected and cared for in the cosmos. Macrocosmic forces came to him from the twelve-fold zodiac and

he had sufficient wisdom that he could take them up and nourish himself from them: he had twelve golden plates. The forces that weave between the cosmos and the earth appear – as experienced by the soul – in the image of the wise women or fairies. Goethe openly alludes to such forces when, in the scene in Faust's study, he has Faust say, "If heavenly forces move up and down and pass to one another the golden bucket ...." Our tale says there were thirteen wise women in the king's realm. Who was the thirteenth?

For our forebears, the council of the gods had twelve members while a thirteenth – Loki or Lodur, the northern Lucifer, the bringer of the end – stood in a certain opposition to them. In the heavens, beside the twelve-fold zodiac there is a *thirteenth force, the sun.* And it is just this thirteenth that makes Man a day being awake for the sense world. But in the mythological age, night had the greater significance, for it was the time of a different wakefulness, a wakefulness to pictorial visions. In his *Hymn to Night*, Novalis called them the "manifestations of a fruitful womb."[5] Even today, language recalls the importance of nocturnal experiences. English uses the expressions "a senight" and "a fortnight" for a period of seven or fourteen "days". We use months in expressing dates, but months are related to the moon, which we notice mainly at night.

Just as, in the story the effect of the twelve-fold zodiac on every human being is shown through the twelve invited wise women, so also in the background appears the thirteenth cosmic force. Our forefathers knew that with Loki, the thirteenth of the Asen, a new consciousness was appearing. Mankind was cutting

---

5. "die Nacht ward der Offenbarungen fruchtbarer Schoß," Night became the fruitful womb of manifestations.

loose from an other-worldly inner life and was turning to the outer sense world. The creation story of Genesis describes precisely this transformation of consciousness. Lucifer is the fallen angel who awakens Man's awareness of his independence and of his similarity to God but thereby sets him in opposition to the divine and makes him responsible for distinguishing between good and evil. In the microcosmic Man there awakens the I, the thirteenth force. Mankind has as yet no way of grasping this thirteenth force, no knowledge with which to understand it, much less the wisdom to deal with it. He has no golden plate for it. Even today many people feel slightly uncomfortable with the number thirteen. It is as if the ancient uncertainty about how to deal with the free I seeps up from deep within our unconscious memory. So the thirteenth fairy at first appears as the representative of Evil – until she is understood as a bringer of a new conscious Good.

The feast was celebrated with all due splendor, and as it was coming to an end the wise women bestowed on the child their wondrous gifts. One gave Virtue, another Beauty, the third Wealth, and so on with all that can be wished for in the world. But when the eleventh had given her blessing, the thirteenth suddenly entered. She wanted to avenge herself for not having been invited, and without greeting anyone or even looking at them, she cried with a loud voice, "In her fifteenth year the king's daughter shall prick a finger on a spindle and fall dead." And without speaking one more word, she turned and left the room. All were shocked, but then the twelfth, still had her wish to bestow. She could not remove the evil wish but could only soften it, so she said, "It will be no death, but a hundred-year-long deep sleep into which the king's daughter shall fall."

The thirteenth wise woman was not invited to the birth celebration. In those early times, souls living with a constant

awareness of the cosmic connections would have no idea how to deal with her. A soul could recognize that it was protected and influenced by, for example, the constellation Aquarius or Pisces or Libra and so on, but it had no feeling for the thirteenth force, the awakening Personality. Its coming appears as a curse: death through a prick from a spindle. But the final gift of the Twelve changes the death to a hundred-year sleep which becomes a transformation. Now spinning and thinking are deeply related, as our speech shows. We *spin* thoughts or *spin* a *yarn* or we follow the *thread* of an argument, or we loose the thread. Just as a thread is developed from a mass of wool or flax so does thinking develop a clear, logical thread of thought from a mass of hazy impressions. But thinking also risks soul death, loss of awareness of the world of soul and spirit. Each human life repeats the process that mankind as a whole once went through, and this stage comes at about the age 15, after the completion of the first two seven-year periods. (This is very freely translated with some additions.)

The age of thinking can be delayed – spindles burned – and a dreamy consciousness – eating from golden plates – preserved for some time, but ultimately the golden age comes to an end. Out of childhood, each human being, repeating the history of mankind, strides forward to maturity.

The king, who would protect his dear child from misfortune, ordered that all spindles in the whole kingdom should be burned. On the maiden all of the gifts of the wise women were completely fulfilled, so that anyone who saw her had to love her.

Now it happened that on the day she turned fifteen, the king and queen were not at home and the maiden was totally alone in the castle. She went all around looking into rooms and chambers and at

last came to an old tower. She climbed up the narrow winding staircase and came to a little door. In the lock was a rusty key, and as she turned it, the door sprang open and there in a little room sat an old woman diligently spinning her flax. "Good day to you, little old mother," said the princess, "What are you doing there?" "I am spinning," said the old woman, and nodded her head. "And what is that thing that is jumping about so merrily?" said the maiden, and took the spindle and wanted to spin too. But scarcely had she touched the spindle than the magic spell went into effect, and she pricked her finger.

When the princess turned fifteen, the king and queen were away. The fatherly spiritual support and the motherly soul protection ceased. The young personality stood by itself. The house of the body, in childhood still unknown, vast and unbounded as a castle, is now thoroughly explored. But as it is explored and consciously experienced, it becomes narrower and narrower. We come to know its limitations. It becomes a tower. But the tower is not only the picture of the narrowing which leads to self knowledge. It is also the picture of self-sufficiency, of structural stability within itself. In the tower of the body, the princess climbs up to the little room at the top. There sits the old woman and spins. Unconsciously but irrepressibly, along with childhood dreams there now arise once hidden thoughts. The princess takes the spindle. Conscious, self-aware thinking begins. But the yearning for self-aware thinking stands under the curse of the Thirteenth. It is Loki-like, Lucifer-influenced egocentric thinking. Just as Loki stood in opposition to the twelve Asen and brought to an end an old world order, so in western mankind a world comes to an end. A dreamlike dedication to the cosmos disappears and the self-aware world of the I awakens; the Twilight of the Gods begins. Man separates himself

from the world of higher beings and becomes a citizen of the earthly, object world, which must be mastered by thought.

Becoming awake for this lower world, however, means at first falling asleep for the higher, spiritual world. Ancient sagas of the heroic age tell of Brunhilde, a daughter of gods, who was stuck by a thorn (Schlafdorn) and fell into sleep until her awakener came. In the fifteen-year-old child, this process means an increased self-awareness and egoism. "Only what I can grasp with my own thoughts can be my standard. Only my own conception of the world counts for me." Caught in this sharp change of consciousness, the young person often withdraws into himself or herself. Busy creating his or her own view of the world (Weltanschauung), the adolescent is often defensive, even aggressive, but inwardly lonesome. The story tells us: around the tower grew impenetrable thorns. External, loving, life-giving forces are shut out – father and mother, the court and even nature go to sleep. From the little room at the top of the tower spreads the enchantment.

The instant she felt the prick she fell upon the bed which was standing near, and lay still in a deep sleep which spread over the whole castle. The King and Queen, who had just come home and had stepped into the hall, went to sleep, and all their courtiers with them. The horses went to sleep in the stable, the dogs in the yard, the doves on the roof, the flies on the wall; yes, even the fire flickering on the hearth grew still and went to sleep, and the roast meat stopped crackling; the cook, who was pulling the scullion's hair because he had made some mistake, let him go and went to sleep. The wind dropped, and on the trees in front of the castle not a leaf stirred. But round the castle a hedge of briar roses began to grow up; every year it grew higher, till at last it surrounded the whole castle so that nothing could be seen of it, not even the flags on the roof.

But there was a legend in the land about the lovely sleeping Briar Rose, as the King's daughter was called, and from time to time princes came and tried to force a way through the hedge into the castle. They found it impossible, for the thorns, as though they had hands, held them fast, and the princes remained caught in them without being able to free themselves, and so died a miserable death. After many, many years a Prince came again to the country and heard an old man tell of the castle which stood behind the briar hedge, in which a most beautiful maiden called Briar Rose had been asleep for the last hundred years, and with her slept the King, Queen, and all her courtiers. He knew also, from his grandfather, that many princes had already come and sought to pierce through the briar hedge, and had remained caught in it and died a sad death. Then the young Prince said, " I am not afraid; I am determined to go and look upon the lovely Briar Rose." The good old man did all in his power to dissuade him, but the Prince would not listen to his words.

The time in which Man is both a stranger to himself and caught within himself and cannot find the right contact to the surrounding world has its limits both for the individual and for humanity. There were always spiritual heroes who would awaken Brunhilde-BriarRose, but the hundred years must first be fulfilled. When the time is fulfilled, the Awakener comes. In our story, he comes in the sign of the rose and awakens by a kiss – through love. We must pay attention to the symbol of the rose, so essential in the Middle Ages.

The rose roots itself deeply and firmly in the earth. Out of wood and thorns grows the beautiful blossom with its always health-bringing aroma and its intense red. The fruits of the rose neither rise up nor hang down (like the apple) and thus represent

the weighted middle. The blossom is built on the number five, a significant sign. The human being is at first fourfold, consisting of body, life, soul and spirit. The higher I, capable of love, must be developed, the fifth member. One who can say yes to earthly life and root himself firmly in it, who takes on challenges and difficulties, to grow through them, who like the rose, overcomes everything hardening and wounding, who brings to fruition selfless love as the flower of existence, who so cleanses his soul of base passions that he is as innocent as a plant is innocent, he can take the rose as symbol. There were streams in the cultivation of the Christian life that took the rose as symbol. In Gothic cathedrals, where the ribs of the vaulting come together, the five-petaled rose often appears on the keystone. The painters of the Madonna knew well why they put a rose by her or surrounded her with roses.

Now, however, the hundred years were just ended, and the day had come when Briar Rose was to awaken. When the Prince approached the briar hedge it was in blossom, and was covered with beautiful large flowers which made way for him of their own accord and let him pass unharmed, and then closed up again into a hedge behind him. In the courtyard he saw the horses and brindled hounds lying asleep, on the roof sat the doves with their heads under their wings; and when he went into the house the flies were asleep on the walls, and near the throne lay the King and Queen; in the kitchen was the cook, with his hand raised as though about to strike the scullion, and the maid sat with the black fowl in her lap which she was about to pluck. He went on further, and all was so still that he could hear his own breathing. At last he reached the tower, and opened the door into the little room where Briar Rose was asleep. There she lay, looking so beautiful that he could not take his eyes off her; he bent down and gave her a kiss. As he touched her, Briar

*Rose opened her eyes and looked lovingly at him. Then they went
down together; and the King awoke, and the Queen, and all the
courtiers, and looked at each other with astonished eyes. The horses
in the stable stood up and shook themselves, the hounds leaped
about and wagged their tails, the doves on the roof lifted their heads
from under their wings, looked round, and flew into the fields; the
flies on the walls began to crawl again, the fire in the kitchen roused
itself and blazed up and cooked the food, the meat began to crackle,
and the cook boxed the scullion''s ears so soundly that he screamed
aloud, while the maid finished plucking the fowl. Then the wedding
of the Prince and Briar Rose was celebrated with all splendor, and
they lived happily until their end.*

The story does not say from where the prince comes. He is the
image of the higher, Christianized I. With the ancient, pre-
Christian image of the maiden awaiting the Awakener, the story
began. With the Christian symbol of the bridegroom who comes in
the sign of the rose it closes.

Briar Rose is a tale of fate. Without personal guilt the maiden
undergoes the fate of all mankind. But also without personal merit,
through Grace, comes redemption.

Snow White[6]

Grimm 53

(Sneewittchen)

*T' was the middle of winter, and the snowflakes were falling
from the sky like feathers. Now, a queen sat sewing at a window
framed in black ebony, and as she sewed she looked out upon the
snow. Suddenly she pricked her finger and three drops of blood fell
on to the snow. And the red looked so lovely on the white that she
thought to herself, "If only I had a child as white as snow and as red
as blood, and as black as ebony wood of the window frame!" Soon
after, she had a daughter, whose hair was black as ebony, while her
cheeks were red as blood, and her skin as white as snow; so she was
called Snow White. But when the child was born the queen died.*

The Snow White tale begins where in the Briar Rose story the
princess pricks her finger on the spindle and falls asleep. Here again
the human soul (the queen) yearns for a transformation of
consciousness. This time should the daughter for whom she longs
should be a child as *as white as snow and as red as blood and as
black as ebony wood.* This theme arises at the three most important
points of the story.

---

6   The publisher's introductory note tells us that Friedel Lenz was working on
     this book during the last days of her life and finished everything except the
     Snow White section, which was then written by some of her friends on the
     basis of remembered lectures and conversations. But it is not precisely her
     wording, and at several places I have explained the ideas in my own way
     rather than translate the text.

What sphere of the human being can be imaged in the picture, "so white as snow" that forms crystals and little stars and comes from heaven? The picture points to "crystal clear" *Thinking*. And in the picture "so red as blood" is it not the sphere of the heart and *Feeling* that is indicated? A third realm exists in each human being in which he devotes himself to service, self-sacrifice, and earthly work. And in this area the Will must be strong as the black ebony wood. The story speaks of black hair, and it may be recalled that black-haired people often have much iron in their blood, while iron deficiency may lead to hair loss. An iron Will completes the threefold being.

A year later the King took another wife. She was a handsome woman, but proud and overbearing, and could not endure that any one should surpass her in beauty. She had a magic looking-glass, and when she stood before it and looked at herself she used to say

> *Mirror, Mirror on the wall,*
> *Who is fairest of us all ?*

then the Glass answered,

> *Queen, thou'rt fairest of them all.*

Then she was content, for she knew that the looking-glass spoke the truth.

But Snow White grew up and became more and more beautiful, so that when she was seven years old she was as beautiful as the day, and far surpassed the Queen. Once, when she asked her glass,

> *Mirror, Mirror on the wall,*
> *Who is fairest of us all?*

it answered

> *Queen, thou art fairest here, I hold,*
> *But Snow White's fairer a thousandfold.*

Then the Queen was horror-struck, and turned green and yellow with jealousy. From the hour that she saw Snow White her heart sank, and she hated the little girl. The pride and envy of her heart grew like a weed, so that she had no rest day nor night. At last she called a huntsman, and said: "Take the child out into the wood; I wish not set eyes on her again; you must kill her and bring me her lungs and liver as proof."

The huntsman obeyed, and took Snow White out into the forest, but when he drew his hunting-knife and was preparing to plunge it into her innocent heart, she began to cry: "Alas! dear Huntsman, spare my life, and I will run away into the wild forest and never come back again." And because of her beauty the Huntsman had pity on her and said, "Well, run away, poor child." Wild beasts will soon devour you, he thought, but still he felt as though a weight were lifted from his heart because he had not been obliged to kill her. And as just at that moment a young fawn came leaping by, he pierced it and took the lungs and liver as proof to the Queen. The cook was ordered to serve them up in pickle, and the wicked queen ate them thinking that they were Snow White's.

In the story of Briar Rose, the thirteenth fairy was indeed evil, but it was precisely she who advanced the human soul. The same is true of the wicked stepmother, who drives Snow White out of the royal spiritual home into earthly life, into her own body – the dwarfs' house. Every human being knows only too well that being within him that tempts to egoism and jealousy.

The stepmother knows the great mirror, that world eye that perceives all. It reflects all and tells us the truth about everything. "To hold the mirror to someone" is a German expression meaning to enable someone to see himself as others see him. But naturally

we can also mirror ourselves. Before birth, after death, and every night the human soul stands spiritually before such a mirror.

The Snow White story is all about Beauty. "Who is the most beautiful in all the land?" This question is repeated seven times. When they see Snow White in the bed, they exclaim, "Oh God, oh God! How *beautiful* is the child."

Snow White is seven years old. In the course of the first seven years of life, each human being uses his or her formative forces to transform the inherited body into his or her own human body. (After this transformation, these forces are freed from their work on the body and can be applied to school learning. The same process – on a vastly different time scale – has occurred in human evolution.) The formative forces that are now released – still pure and innocent – are "the most beautiful in the whole land." The human being has these growing and forming forces in common with the plant world. In it, unconscious beauty is most evident. The Snow White story tells how in earthly experience these forces are in three ways "poisoned." One who accompanies children from the seventh to the fourteenth year of their development can directly perceive how in their feeling life they must deal with selfishness, in their thinking with rationalism, and in willing with earth drives – according to the development of earthly humanity.

Briar Rose, Snow White, and Little Red Cap present a trilogy in the realm of fundamental folktales. All three tell of the fate and descent of Man out of spiritual home into the earthly realm. Briar Rose remains in the spindle-realm, in the little room at the top of the tower. Snow White lives in an earthly house but closely connected to beings of nature represented by the dwarfs. Little Red Cap is the first to step from the twilight of the forest into the bright

meadow and into sunshine of fully waking consciousness and lives, deceived by the wolf, completely in bright and shiny sense impressions. The Snow White story, the middle of the three, lies in the sphere between "so white as snow" and "so black as ebony." It was the destiny of the human soul to move from awareness of the twelve-fold cosmic forces of the zodiac, through the seven-fold world of the planets, to the intrepid earthly Little Red Cap. All three speak of the darkening of consciousness – otherwise our story would not be called Snow White. The sleep in the tower room, the glass coffin on the mountain, the dark stomach of the wolf show in pictures the progressive darkening.

Now the poor child was alone in the great wood, with no living soul near, and she was so frightened that she knew not what to do. Then she began to run, and ran over the sharp stones and through the brambles, while the animals passed her by without harming her.

Hard it is to find the earthly body, the dwarf's house, and to enter it. The sharp stones and thorns bring pain. Anxiety beset the human soul, and in every child this anxiety still lives. The forest, the realm of the growing formative forces, is still innocent in this age. Wild animals live there, but they do not harm the seven-year old child.

She ran as far as her feet could carry her till it was nearly evening, when she saw a little house and went in to rest. Inside, everything was small, but as precious and pure as could be. A small table covered with a white cloth stood ready with seven small plates, and by every plate was a spoon, knife, fork, and cup. Seven little beds were ranged against the walls, covered with snow-white coverlets. As Snow White was very hungry and thirsty she ate a little bread and vegetable from each plate, and drank a little wine from

each cup, for she did not want to eat up the whole of one portion. Then, being very tired, she lay down in one of the beds. She tried them all but none suited her; one was too short, another too long, all except the seventh, which was just right. She remained in it, said her prayers, and fell asleep.

When it was quite dark the masters of the house came in. They were seven dwarfs, who used to dig in the mountains for ore. They kindled their lights, and as soon as they could see they noticed that some one had been there, for nothing was in the order in which they had left it.

The first said, " Who has been sitting in my chair? " The second said, " Who has been eating off my plate? " The third said, " Who has been nibbling my bread? " The fourth said, " Who has been eating my vegetables?" The fifth said, " Who has been using my fork?" The sixth said, " Who has been cutting with my knife? " The seventh said, " Who has been drinking out of my cup ? '

Then the first looked and saw a slight impression on his bed, and said, "Who has been treading on my bed?" The others came running up and said, " And mine, and mine." But the seventh, when he looked into his bed, saw Snow White, who lay there asleep. He called the others, who came up and cried out with astonishment, as they held their lights and gazed at Snow White. "Oh God, oh God" they cried out, "How beautiful is the child." They were so delighted that they did not wake her up but left her asleep in bed. And the seventh Dwarf slept with his comrades, an hour with each all through the night.

In the Briar Rose story, there were twelve good fairies and twelve golden plates. Snow White is a story of the number seven. (In Little Red Cap, the story of the earthly child, there is no longer

a number theme.) Not just the seven dwarfs but seven plates, seven forks, seven knives, seven questions when the dwarfs come home, seven tasks that they give to Snow White, and seven times the queen queries the mirror. Twelve is the number of space – think of the signs of the zodiac – while seven is the number of time.

We are told – and it is worth thinking about – that the dwarfs are only at home at night; during the day they work in the mountain. At night the human the human soul "out of the house" – that is, the astral body leaves the physical and etheric during sleep. During the day, the soul is in the body. With the dwarfs it is the other way around. They are not human. But one thing is certain, as the next part of the story tells, namely that the dwarfs live from the nourishment that Snow White prepares for them. That fact points to many secrets of the interaction of visible and invisible effects in the human body. The elementary beings live from what the human soul during the day prepares in their houses!

The seventh bed fits Snow White. What is special about seven?[7] In "The Wolf and the Seven Kids", the seventh kid hides in the grandfather clock that ticks so regularly as the human heart beats. One who would meditate on the meaning of the seventh bed may find a hint in the direction of the question of the seventh dwarf, "Who has drunk from my cup?"

Rudolf Steiner describes how the elementary beings can perceive and recognize humans by their physiognomy and gesture.

---

7   The text attempts no explicit answer to this question but only offers suggestions for meditation. Students of Rudolf Steiner's *Theosophy* or of his *Occult Science* (also translated as *Esoteric Science*) will think immediately of the seven-fold structure of the human being and of the seven-year growth phases, so that seven is especially the human number. The external connection of 12 with the zodiac is that it takes the planet Jupiter 12 years (more precisely, 11.85 years) to pass through the whole of the zodiac.

He describes how the physiognomy and gesture of humans go into the interior of nature and can be perceived especially by the gnomes and undines. Because the child, with its inherited body up to the seventh year, has not fully developed its own gesture and physiognomy, the dwarfs cannot at first perceive it. But then it appears to them already in a certain completion: "Oh God, oh God, How beautiful is the child!" they cry. For them the human child is a mystery, and they are thankful to humans who can tell them of small children. And for their part, they tell us the folktales as reciprocal gift.

In the dwarf's house, *"everything was small, but as precious and pure as could be."* This could be said of the earthly human body because it was felt that this body is a small image of the great world of the heavens.

Snow White is seven years old when she comes to the dwarf's house. Here again a comparison is interesting. Briar Rose was 15 when she pricked her finger on the spindle. Little Red Cap is just a "sweet little maiden" (*Dirne*).

When morning came Snow White woke up, and when she saw the seven dwarfs she was frightened. But they were very kind and asked her name.

"I am called Snow White," she answered.

"How did you get into our house ?" they asked. Then she told them how her stepmother had wished to get rid of her, how the huntsman had spared her life, and how she had run all day till she had found the house. Then the dwarfs said, " Will you look after our household, cook, make the beds, wash, sew and knit, and keep

everything neat and clean? If so you shall stay with us and want for nothing."

"Yes," said Snow White, "with all my heart," and she stayed with them.

The answer could have been phrased differently, but it is noteworthy that it was "Yes, with all my heart." ("Ja, vom Hertzen gern.").

She kept the house in order. In the morning they went to the mountain and searched for copper and gold, and in the evening they came back and then their meal had to be ready. All day the maiden was alone, and the good Dwarfs warned her and said, "Beware of your stepmother, who will soon learn that you are here. Don't let any one in."

But the Queen, having, as she imagined, eaten Snow White"s liver and lungs, and feeling certain that she was the fairest of all, stepped in front of her glass, and asked—

> *Mirror, Mirror on the wall,*
> *Who is fairest of us all?*

the Glass answered as usual

> *Queen, thou art fairest here, I hold,*
> *But Snow White over the fells,*
> *Who with the seven Dwarfs dwells,*
> *Is fairer still a thousandfold.*

She was dismayed, for she knew that the glass told no lies, and she saw that the hunter had deceived her and that Snow White still lived. Accordingly she began to wonder afresh how she might compass her death; for as long as she was not the fairest in the land her jealous heart left her no rest. At last she thought of a plan. She

dyed her face and dressed up like an old candle maker, so that she was quite unrecognizable. In this guise she crossed over the seven mountains to the home of the seven Dwarfs and called out, "Wares for sale." Snow White peeped out of the window and said, "Good-day, mother, what have you got to sell?" "Good wares, fine wares," she answered, "laces of every color," and she held out one which was made of gay plaited silk. "I may let the honest woman in," thought Snow White, and she unbolted the door and bought the pretty lace. "Child," said the Old Woman, "what a sight you are, I will lace you properly for once." Snow White made no objection, and placed herself before the Old Woman to let her lace her with the new lace. But the Old Woman laced so quickly and tightly that she took away Snow White's breath and she fell down as though dead. " Now I am the fairest," she said to herself, and hurried away.

Not long after the seven Dwarfs came home, and were horror-struck when they saw their dear little Snow White lying on the floor without stirring, like one dead. When they saw she was laced too tight they cut the lace, whereupon she began to breathe and soon came back to life again. When the Dwarfs heard what had happened, they said that the old candlemaker was no other than the wicked Queen. "Take care not to let any one in when we are not here," they said.

Snow White and the stepmother live in different worlds separated by seven high mountains. The queen disguises herself, and the human soul fails to recognize her, for indeed, she is unrecognizable.

The thirteenth fairy in Briar Rose – later the old woman in the tower room – *just waited* for the human soul to climb the tower and prick herself on the spindle, whereby part of her forces sink into

sleep. In human history, it took millennia before the human body was so hardened that the soul, which in former times experienced much more strongly the cosmos, could enter the tower room and there be shut in. Only then begins this last phase of the entry of the human soul into body, the falling asleep to any knowledge of the royal homeland. But note, the thirteenth *just waits*. Not so in the Snow White story. The opposing forces take stronger measures.

The wicked stepmother, disguised as a candlemaker, trudges over seven mountains to the seven dwarfs. Three times she disguises herself. Once as the candlemaker, then "as another old woman", and then as an old peasant woman. The candle maker shows Snow White things that look pretty, bright colored, glittering silk laces. Now music and color, and the beautiful in general – which is everywhere in this story – though perceived, to be sure, by the eye and ear, also subtly affect the breathing. In them also lives the illusion, deceit, seduction to which the human being is so subject. In breathing, the human being is connected to the wide world. So the first attack of Evil on the human soul must be to cut off its feeling life from the world around it, to make it egocentric. The Snow White story lives especially in the middle sphere that is "so red as blood" so it precisely here in the middle realm that the wicked queen begins her work. She stops the child's breathing. But the dwarfs can still help, for only a part of the human soul is in the power of the queen.

Now the wicked Queen, as soon as she got home, went to the glass and asked—

> *Mirror, Mirror on the wall,*
> *Who is fairest of us all?*

and it answered as usual

Queen, thou art fairest here, I hold,
But Snow White over the fells,
Who with the seven Dwarfs dwells,
Is fairer still a thousandfold.

When she heard it all her blood flew to her heart, so enraged was she, for she knew that Snow White had come back to life again. Then she thought to herself, "I must plan something which will put an end to her." By means of witchcraft, in which she was skilled, she made a. poisoned comb. Next she disguised herself and took the form of a different Old Woman. She crossed the mountains and came to the home of the seven Dwarfs, and knocked at the door calling out, "Good wares to sell."

Snow White looked out of the window and said, "Go away, I must not let any one in." "At least you may look," answered the Old Woman, and she took the poisoned comb and held it up.

The child was so pleased with it that she let herself be beguiled, and opened the door. When she had made a bargain the Old Woman said, "Now I will comb your hair properly for once." Poor Snow White, suspecting no evil, let the Old Women have her way, but scarcely was the poisoned comb fixed in her hair than the poison took effect, and the maiden fell down unconscious. "You paragon of beauty," said the wicked woman, "now it is all over with you," and she went away.

Happily it was near the time when the seven Dwarfs came home. When they saw Snow White lying on the ground as though dead, they immediately suspected her stepmother, and searched till they found the poisoned comb. No sooner had they removed it than Snow White came to herself again and related what had happened.

They warned her again to be on her guard, and to open the door to no one.

The poisoned comb is reminiscent of the spindle prick in Briar Rose. One combed with the poisoned comb can no longer have thinking "as white as snow" and becomes incapable of being aware of the invisible nature beings. But once again the dwarfs could help.[8]

When she got home the Queen stood before her glass and said

> *Mirror, Mirror on the wall,*
> *Who is fairest of us all?"*
and it answered as usual
> *Queen, thou art fairest here, I hold,*
> *But Snow White over the fells,*
> *Who with the seven Dwarfs dwells,*
> *Is fairer still a thousandfold.*

When she heard the glass speak these words she trembled and quivered with rage, "Snow White shall die," she said, " even if it cost me my own life." Thereupon she went into a secret room, which no one ever entered but herself, and made a poisonous apple. Outwardly it was beautiful to look upon, with rosy cheeks, and every one who saw it longed for it, but whoever ate of it was certain to die. When the apple was ready she dyed her face and dressed herself like an old peasant woman and so crossed the seven hills to the Dwarfs" home. There she knocked.

---

8   There follows here a discussion of how the mirror could ever have said that the wicked queen was the most beautiful in the whole land, as it does the first time and the last time it is asked. I find the discussion a bit confused and out of place and have omitted it.

Snow White put her head out of the window and said, "I must not let any one in, the seven Dwarfs have forbidden me." "It is all the same to me," said the peasant woman. "I shall soon get rid of my apples. There, I will give you one."

"No; I must not take anything."

"Are you afraid of poison?" said the woman. "See, I will cut the apple in half; you eat the red side and I will eat the other." Now the apple was so cunningly painted that the red half alone was poisoned. Snow White longed for the apple, and when she saw the peasant woman eating she could hold out no longer, stretched out her hand and took the poisoned half. Scarcely had she put a bit into her mouth than she fell dead to the ground.

The Queen looked with a fiendish glance, and laughed aloud and said, "White as snow, red as blood, and black as ebony, this time the Dwarfs cannot wake you up again." And when she got home and asked the looking-glass

Mirror, Mirror on the wall,
Who is fairest of us all?

it answered at last
Queen, thou 'rt fairest of them all.

Then her jealous heart was at rest, as much at rest as a jealous heart can be.

Here for the second time sound the words, this time spoken by the stepmother, that describe the ideal human, "So white as snow, so red as blood, so black as ebony wood." The tale tells of the three great constrictions of the human being from the cosmic consciousness to the completely earthly that is dead to anything of a spiritual nature. It is a road the whole of humanity has traveled over

millennia and which every human life traverses between the seventh and fifteen year, between the ages of Snow White and Briar Rose. Feeling is associated with the chest, thinking with the head, and willing with the digestive tract. (When we want to say that a strong will is need for something, we may say, "It takes guts.") The laces, the comb, and the apple were aimed at each in turn with the intent to kill Snow White, that is, to separate forever humanity from its spiritual home. The intensity of the separation increases from sleeping in Briar Rose, to poisoning in Snow White, to devouring by the wolf in Little Red Cap.

The creators of the folktales picked their images with great precision. Here, in poisoning with a fruit, the apple is the perfect choice. It is in the rose family, but unlike the fruits of most members of that family, it is juicy. In most other members of the family, as the ovaries swell and ripen, they also dry out. In plants with juicy fruits something exceptional and quite wonderful happens. The ovary, this being of light and warmth sinks itself deep into the receptacle to gain access to the stem where water and root forces work from below upwards. (In botany, this called and "inferior" ovary and the fruit that is then formed, mostly from the receptacle – rather than the ovary – is called an "accessory" fruit. Apples, pears, bananas, and strawberries are common accessory fruits.) Thus the apple, as representative of juicy fruits, besides its relation to light and warmth that all fruits have, has also an special connection to the earthy element. – Of course the apple reminds us of the Genesis story of temptation and fall; and there also it is a story of descent into the earthly. Just hold an apple in your hand and you can feel that it is both heavenly and earthly. In former times, when mankind had a more dreamlike conscious than today, such connections were more readily felt.

Now the dwarfs cannot help, for no part of Snow White has not been poisoned, nothing has remained healthy. With irony the queen says, "White as snow, red as blood, and black as ebony" for she knows no part of it is now true.

The dwarfs, when they came at evening, found Snow White lying on the ground and not a breath escaped her lips, and she was quite dead. They lifted her up and looked to see whether any poison was to be found, unlaced her dress, combed her hair, washed her with wine and water, but it was no use ; their dear child was dead. They laid her on a bier, and all seven sat down and bewailed her and lamented over her for three whole days. Then they prepared to bury her, but she looked so fresh and living, and still had such beautiful rosy cheeks, that they said, "We cannot bury her in the dark earth." And so they had a transparent glass coffin made, so that she could be seen from every side, laid her inside and wrote on it in letters of gold her name and how she was a king"s daughter. Then they set the coffin out on the mountain, and one of them always stayed by and watched it.

And the birds came too and mourned for Snow White, first an owl, then a raven, and lastly a dove.

Now Snow White lay a long, long time in her coffin and decayed not but looked as though she were asleep, for she was still so white as snow, so red as blood, and black-haired as ebony wood.

Here those words are said for the third time. This image, Snow White in the glass coffin on the mountain top is the most powerful in this story. Is it not the true picture of the human soul in today's world? She is dead to the elementary beings. They can still see the human soul and bewail the loss. They weep for three days, then

write in gold letters on the coffin the wisdom forgotten by humans, that Snow White is a king's daughter.

But the human soul, though dead to the elementary beings, was still living, for Snow White did not decay. From glass and quartz, like the coffin, are made the instruments like glasses, microscopes, telescopes, and spectroscopes with which we humans try to probe ever deeper through our senses into the outer world – while in fact we lie sleeping in the glass coffin. But the dwarfs are always with the human soul, guarding the mountain and waiting. All of nature, here represented by the owl, the raven, and the dove – the sighing creatures, as Paul says[9] – watches over the coffin and awaits the awakening of the human soul.

All folktales simultaneously look back and foretell the future. They thus give us courage for our life adventure. For just when all seems lost, the savior of the human soul, which can no longer help itself, is closest. "When the time was fulfilled" as it says in the Bible, the great helper of the human soul enters the stream of events in time. Just as in Briar Rose, "when the hundred years had passed" then and only then can the king's son come.

---

9   I am unable to identify a passage to which these words would seem to refer. Paul indeed speaks of sighing; "Likewise the Spirit helps us in our weakness; for we do not know how to pray as we ought, but that very Spirit intercedes with sighs too deep for words." (Romans 8:26). There is an interesting book by G. Ronald Murphy SJ, *The Owl, the Raven, and the Dove– the Religious Meaning of the Grimms' Magic Fairy Tales.* Murphy has studied the Grimms, especially Wilhelm, very deeply, traveling to their home town, reading Wilhelm's copy of various books with his marginal notes. He tells us that they believed that the stories they collected were remnants of religions. He does not explain his choice of title but from one hint, I believe that the Owl refers to religious traditions of the "wise women" while the Raven, a strong and brave bird, refers to the heroic tradition exemplified in the hunter in Little Red Cap, and the Dove refers to the Christian tradition. All the traditions come to honor and protect Snow White.

It happened that a king's son was wandering in the wood, and came to the home of the seven Dwarfs there to spend the night. He saw the coffin on the mountain and lovely Snow White inside, and read what was written in golden letters. Then he said to the Dwarfs, "Let me have the coffin; I will give you whatever you like for it." But they said, "We will not give it up for all the gold of the world."

Then he said, "Then give it to me as a gift, for I cannot live without Snow White to gaze upon; and I will honor and reverence it as my dearest treasure."

When he had said these words the good Dwarfs pitied him and gave him the coffin. The Prince bade his servants carry it on their shoulders.

When the hundred years had passed, the thorns became roses. With the force of love, with a kiss, Briar Rose was awakened. But Snow White, still in the glass coffin and seemingly dead, is carried by the king's servants from the mountain of clear-thinking consciousness. And what helps here?

Now it happened that they stumbled over some brushwood, and the shock dislodged the piece of apple from Snow White's throat. In a short time she opened her eyes, lifted the lid of the coffin, sat up and came back to life again completely.

"O Heaven, where am I?" she asked.

The Prince, full of joy, said, "You are with me," and he related what had happened, and then said, "I love you better than all the world; come with me to my father"s castle and be my wife." Snow White agreed and went with him, and their wedding was celebrated with great magnificence.

The prince comes into the dwarfs' house "there to spend the night." It is at night that the prince first comes close to the human soul. In the soul world of the story of Snow White, who is "so red as blood", the only exchange is giving. To this prince the dwarfs can give (but not sell) the beloved, long-protected coffin with their Snow White inside. In each folktale, with ever new and manifold images, it is told how the human soul and the human spirit seek and approach one another. Here the prince is simultaneously the leader of all human spirits and he says to the soul, "I love you better than all the world. Come with me into my father's castle."

The servants carrying Snow White "stumble." What does that mean? Snow White in the coffin must experience a shock, and only the shock through fate and "the servants of the king" has the power to awaken the human soul, whose thinking and understanding is in the coffin. And now Snow White must do her part. The piece of apple that lamed her will forces is out. Now must Snow White open her eyes, lift the lid of the coffin, and sit up straight. And only when the human soul has done these things can the wedding be celebrated.

Here there is missing, as sometimes happens in the Grimm's telling of a story, a nuance. The fragments of these stories were rescued and assembled and written down by the Grimms at the last moment before they would have otherwise disappeared and been lost forever. Previously they were transmitted from generation to generation by word of mouth. Often one telling found by the Grimms would would have a detail missing in all other tellings. It is thus not unlikely that some detail that belonged in the original conception was missing in all the versions found by the Grimms. Can it be that the dwarfs, who so long had protected Snow White and the coffin, should now stay at home? No, the dwarfs surely went

to the wedding of the human soul with the King's Son. They also entered into His kingdom. Once the human soul is "awake," the elementary beings can once again participate in the spiritual life of the human soul.

In Little Red Cap, no king's son comes as savior but a hunter who is outstanding for strength and marksmanship. He boldly takes the scissors, an image of sharpened powers of judgment of a new, transformed thinking, to free Little Red Cap from darkness. Little Red Cap is completely submerged in the sense world. She wanders from the way and gives the wolf the possibility to overcome the old clairvoyance, the grandmother, and then Little Red Cap herself.

Only from the comparison of the three stories, as has been indicated here at some points, does it become clear exactly what is happening in each of them separately. Rudolf Steiner recommended that these three stories be read together. What then emerges from the individual pictures agrees with his indication that Briar Rose tells in pictures of the development of the sentient soul; Snow White, of the intellectual soul; and Little Red Cap, of the consciousness soul. In Briar Rose, the old king and the whole court are redeemed along with the girl. In Snow White, (if our emendation is accepted) the elementary beings as well as the human beings are redeemed. Only in Little Red Cap is it indicated that the soul's forces of perception are lifted to a new level.

Snow White's wicked stepmother was invited to the feast; and when she had put on her fine clothes she stepped to her glass and asked

> *Mirror, Mirror on the wall,*
> *Who is fairest of us all?*

The glass answered

> *Queen, thou art fairest here, I hold,*
> *The young Queen fairer is a thousandfold.*

The mirror knows of the progress in the history of consciousness of the beauty of the young new queen, the transformed human soul.

> *Then the wicked woman uttered a curse, and was so terribly frightened that she didn't know what to do. Yet she had no rest; she felt obliged to go and see the young queen. And when she came in she recognized Snow White, and stood stock still with fear and terror. But iron slippers were heated over the fire, and were soon brought in with tongs and put before her. And she had to step into the red-hot shoes and dance till she fell down dead.*

Every folktale is a part of the drama of the development of the total soul forces of the human being. In the human being lives also the wicked queen filled with vanity, jealousy, and deception. These soul forces must be overcome, so that higher development and marriage of the purified soul with the king's son can take place. The "burning ambition" and "glowing hatred" must be destroyed by the soul itself in a fire of purification.

When the story is told to a child by an adult who understands the picture language, the violent images arouse no anxiety in the child. Rather – how often is it experienced! – the child feels a deep satisfaction in the victory of the Good and the overcoming of Evil. If we have lived deeply into these pictures, we can in all truthfulness say to the young person: We live in the most significant turning point of world history. We are at the point where Briar Rose is awakened, where Snow White lifts the lid of the coffin, where the hunter cuts open the belly of the wolf. The descent has taken place of its own accord. On the way back to the spiritual

world, every human soul must do its part to help. The folktales foretell the need for totally new ways into the future.

The very special message of the Snow White story is the certainty that the elementary beings who have served humanity through the ages – suffering and waiting – shall again participate in the spiritual life of mankind.

Little Red Cap[10]

(Little Red Riding Hood)

Grimm 26

The Little Red Cap story is similar in its drama to the Wolf and the Seven Kids. But here the events occur not in the instinctive sphere but in the soul itself.

There was once a sweet little maid, much beloved by everybody, but most of all by her grandmother, who never knew how to make enough of her. Once she sent her a little cap of red velvet, and as it

---

10   In German, the name of our story and its heroine is *Rot Käppchen.* *Käppchen* is the diminutive of *Kappe,* which is simply "cap". So the German-to-English translation is simply Little Red Cap. To the German speaker, it would never occur to picture anything like a "riding hood" which Merriam Webster defines as "an enveloping hood or hooded cloak worn for riding and as an outdoor wrap by women and children." Friedel Lenz in our text strongly connects the word *Käppchen* with a cap or hat, so to match her commentary, we must use Little Red Cap as the girl's name.

Where then did *Riding Hood* come from in the first place? I have no doubt but that the story first became known in English through translation from the French of Charles Perrault. Perrault's small collection was published in 1697, over a century before the first Grimm edition. In it, the story's name was "Le petit chaperon rouge." In a modern French dictionary, the first meaning (marked *ancien*) of "chaperon" is a "a *capuchon* covering the head and shoulders." And what is a *capuchon*? "An ample bonnet that can be thrown back over the shoulders." In other words, a *hood.* Thus, *hood* fits the French but not the German. The second meaning of "chaperon," incidentally, is "an elderly woman (presumably wearing such a bonnet) who accompanies a young woman." *Capuchon* comes from the Latin *cappa,* meaning a hood, a *cappuccio* in Italian, a word adopted as their name by an order of brown-robed monks, who willy nilly passed on their name to a mixture of coffee and milk the color of their habit.

was very becoming to her, and she always wore it, people called her Little Red Cap.

Inexperienced, naive, innocent and beloved by all is the human soul at the outset of its journey. The little red cap from the grandmother is her most striking and important possession. "I'll take that on my cap" is a German picturesque expression meaning "I'll take full responsibility for that." Not the outer hat or cap but an inner one is meant when we say "Da geht mir der Hut hoch" (literally "There my hat goes high" meaning "That's outrageous" or "There I become angry.") What is the inner cap? It is our brain-based thinking. Indeed, the brain sits like a cap on the head. And just as it covers us and closes us off from above, so also our brain thinking marks a certain limitation. Our whole personal inner world lives in this thinking. But this personal world also cuts us off from a spiritual over-world. We can, to be sure, through thinking come again into connection with this over-world, but not if we remain, like Little Red Cap, naive and inexperienced. For then we experience only our own subjective perception of the world. Earlier mankind gained knowledge through clairvoyant pictures – even into classical antiquity Man saw such spirits as the Erinyes or Furies holding a man responsible for his actions. Modern Man must through thought work out in his conscience the consequences of his actions and "take them onto his cap."

When the tale wants to indicate that blood works into this brain-thinking, it speaks of the red cap. As both a positive and as a negative image the red cap appears in various European folktales. The passionate nature lives in the blood; "I see red" means "I am angry." But our I is dependent on our blood. Healthy red blood enables us to be awake; without it, we become weak and apathetic. In both liturgy and custom, the color of the cap indicates the kind

of thinking going on under it. A white cap indicates that the thinking under it is – or should be – directed to the immaterial, other worldly – as with the bishops mitre or the headcoverings in the cloister. A black cap indicates the opposite, that the thinking is about the earthly. In the Christian Community, when the priest is saying the service he is bare-headed; during the sermon, when he is expressing his own thoughts, he wears a black cap. A judge, in pronouncing judgment, puts on a black cap, for he must arrive at the judgment through his own insight and take responsibility for it "onto his own cap." The custom of taking off one's hat before respected people has the same origin and signifies, "I am open to your thoughts and being."

The grandmother has given the child the cap. The grandmother represents the ancient, semi-clairvoyant consciousness that preceded and laid the foundation for the I consciousness of personal, brain-based thinking. She herself does not have this new consiousness. She is "weak and ill." A new, arising consciousness and an old, ending consciousness stand next to one another. The I-based, thinking soul is appearing, and everyone welcomes this event.

One day her mother said to her, "Come, Little Red Cap, here are some cakes and a flask of wine for you to take to grandmother; she is weak and ill, and they will do her good. Make haste and start before it grows hot, and walk properly and nicely, and don't run, or you might fall and break the flask of wine, and there would be none left for grandmother. And when you go into her room, don't forget to say good morning, instead of staring about you." "I will be sure to take care," said Little Red Cap to her mother, and gave her hand upon it.

The old consciousness needs the loving thoughts and care of remembrance. Bread and wine, are holy gifts. The motherly soul created them; the child-like soul must take them. Just how childly the soul still is the tale tells in few words. Does not every Little Red Cap wander from the way and follow her own head? Politeness to others must always be practiced lest she become too self-centered. But curiousity runs away with her, and it seems she must explore every corner of her world.

Here we have described for us the soul as yet inexperienced in thinking, still naive in her knowing. So was it for all humanity when intellectual thinking began, and so is it in every human soul at about the time a child starts to go to school. This point in time brings on a crisis.

Now the grandmother lived away in the wood, half an hour's walk from the village; and when Little Red Cap had reached the wood, she met the wolf; but as she did not know what a bad sort of animal he was, she did not feel frightened.

"Good day, Little Red Cap," said he. "Thank you kindly, wolf," answered she. "Where are you going so early, Little Red Cap?" "To my grandmother's." "What are you carrying under your apron?" "Cakes and wine; we baked yesterday; and my grandmother is very weak and ill, so they will do her good, and strengthen her." "Where does your grandmother live, Little Red Cap?" "A quarter of an hour's walk from here; her house stands beneath the three oak trees, by the house are hazel bushes, that you will certainly know," said Little Red Cap.

The wolf thought to himself, "That tender young thing would be a delicious morsel, and would taste better than the old one; I must manage somehow to get both of them."

54

In *Briar Rose* we met that evil power that our ancestors called Loki and the Bible called Lucifer. Here we encounter the power called in the Bible Satan. Generally today these two powers are often not clearly distinguished but both call simply Devil. But the folktales distinguish spiritual relations very exactly. This being, represented by the wolf, is the known but not seen-through power of deception and falsehood that darkens Truth for mankind and makes us believe that only the sense world is true and real, and thereby delivers us up to a one-sided materialism. This power hides as an "innocent" animal, the wolf. The Persians called this power Ahriman; our Germanic ancestors called it Fenris wolf. Germanic myths foretell that it will bring about the Twilight of the Gods. But when a divine world is darkened and no more seen, then individual souls also experience the darkening. Little Red Cap shows us an inner human crisis brought on by the workings of the Wolf forces. The greatest danger relative to Evil is the naiveté that does not recognize it. Little Red Cap "did not know what a bad sort of animal" the wolf was. Worse still, she betrays to him the way to the grandmother's house and how to recognize it. That is, she exposes a precious heritage to the wolf-forces.

Before the Germans, the Celts ruled Middle Europe. They had a highly educated priesthood, the Druids. (In Greek, δρυς (drus) means oak.) Before the house of a Druid there stood as a marker three oaks. These Druids were the great defenders of a cosmic knowledge against the darkening of spiritual awareness. They recognized the wolf. The hazel bush is a kind of Tree of Life in Celtic tradition. There where the Druid traditions rule, under the three great oak trees, there is also a center of life forces (the hazel-nut hedge). "That you will certainly know," says Little Red Cap. So speaks total naiveté.

Then he walked by Little Red Cap a little while, and said, "Little Red Cap, just look at the pretty flowers that are growing all round you; and I don't think you are listening to the song of the birds; you are posting along just as if you were going to school, and it is so delightful out here in the wood." Little Red Cap opened her eyes, and when she saw the sunbeams darting here and there through the trees, and lovely flowers everywhere, she thought to herself, "If I were to take a fresh nosegay to my grandmother she would be very pleased, and it is so early in the day that I shall reach her in plenty of time"; and so she ran about in the wood, looking for flowers. And as she picked one she saw a still prettier one a little farther off, and so she went farther and farther into the wood.

"Little Red Cap opened her eyes": "Then were their eyes opened" it says in the Bible just after the temptation by the serpent. Attention was turned from the inner soul world to the outer world of the senses. The soul rushes from one sense impression to another, from one sensual delight to another. They are gathered like flowers to a bouquet.

But the wolf went straight to the grandmother's house and knocked at the door. "Who is there?" cried the grandmother. "Little Red Cap," he answered, "and I have brought you some cake and wine. Please open the door." "Lift the latch," cried the grandmother; "I am too feeble to get up." So the wolf lifted the latch, and the door flew open, and he fell on the grandmother and ate her up without saying one word. Then he drew on her clothes, put on her cap, lay down in her bed, and drew the curtains.

Little Red Cap was all this time running about among the flowers, and when she had gathered as many as she could hold, she remembered her grandmother, and set off to go to her. She was

surprised to find the door standing open, and when she came inside she felt very strange, and thought to herself, "Oh dear, how uncomfortable I feel, and I was so glad this morning to go to my grandmother!" And when she said, "Good morning," there was no answer. Then she went up to the bed and drew back the curtains; there lay the grandmother with her cap pulled over her eyes, so that she looked very odd.

"O grandmother, what large ears you have!" "The better to hear with." "O grandmother, what great eyes you have!" "The better to see with." "O grandmother, what large hands you have!" "The better to take hold of you with." "But, grandmother, what a terrible large mouth you have!" "The better to devour you!" And no sooner had the wolf said it than he made one bound from the bed, and swallowed up poor Little Red Cap.

While the soul is totally given over to the sense world – not bad were it not done on the advice of the wolf – the old instinctive wisdom, the grandmother, falls prey to darkening fate. Just as venerable customs and ancient uses were lost, and traditions going back hundreds of years were forgotten and even despised as modern thinking unfolded, so in the individual soul there disappeared instinctive caution and wary thoughts that had long prevailed. Man delivered himself without the slightest qualm to those life-limiting and life-destroying forces that our ancestors call the Wolf. Here he slips – not into a sheepskin – but into the clothes of the grandmother, that is, he so "clothes" himself in traditional wisdom that Inexperience believes she is hearing the voice of ancient wisdom, when in fact it is the voice of the great Liar. Selfishness and greed grab the human soul, and swallow it whole into the realm of darkness.

Then the wolf, having satisfied his hunger, lay down again in the bed, went to sleep, and began to snore loudly. The huntsman heard him as he was passing by the house, and thought, "How the old woman snores; I had better see if there is anything the matter with her." Then he went into the room, and walked up to the bed, and saw the wolf lying there. "At last I find you, you old sinner!" said he; "I have been looking for you a long time." And he made up his mind that the wolf had swallowed the grandmother whole, and that she might yet be saved. So he did not fire, but took a pair of shears and began to slit up the wolf's body. When he made a few snips Little Red Cap appeared, and after a few more snips she jumped out and cried, "Oh dear, how frightened I have been! It is so dark inside the wolf." And then out came the old grandmother, still living and breathing. But Little Red Cap went and quickly fetched some large stones, with which she filled the wolf's body, so that when he waked up, and was going to rush away, the stones were so heavy that he sank down and fell dead.

In the Germanic myths, Vidar, the silent one of the Asen, who after long waiting – for the Wolf must have his time – will shove his foot protected by a great, magical shoe into the mouth of Fenris Wolf, and holding the lower jaw down by this foot, grab the upper jaw and, after long struggle, tear the wolf apart. The myth speaks of a great spiritual struggle of Mankind; the folktale tells of a related personal inner event. It is, as Wilhelm Grimm said, but a fragment of a great jewel now shattered. (See the Introduction.)

Here appears the hunter who symbolizes the force that "takes aim" at the wild drives and destroys them. The shears, which consist of a pair of knives, are a symbol of a doubly sharpened power of judgment. Only this power of judgment can free the soul.

"It is so dark inside the wolf," says Little Red Cap, of the time between the fall in consciousness and the redemption.

From his own deadly materialism (the stones) must the Wolf perish.

They were all three very pleased. The huntsman took off the wolf's skin, and carried it home. The grandmother ate the cakes, and drank the wine, and held up her head again, and Little Red Cap said to herself that she would never more stray about in the wood alone, but would mind what her mother told her.

The Wolf and the Seven Kids
Grimm 5

There was once an old Nanny-goat who had seven kids, and she was just as fond of them as a mother of her children. One day she was going into the woods to fetch some food for them, so she called them all to her and said, "My dear children, I am going out into the woods. Beware of the Wolf! If once he gets into the house, he will eat you up, skin, and hair, and all. The rascal often disguises himself, but you will know him by his rough voice and his black feet." The kids said, "Oh, we will be very careful, dear mother. You can go without worrying about us." The old Goat bleated and went her way confidently.

Animals are beings without spiritual insight and knowledge. They live out of their natural drives and instincts. To be sure, higher animals in some sense have souls, but it is a carnal soul [*Triebseele*], not a spiritual soul. Humans also have such instinctive forces, and they appear in dreams and folktales as animal images. Our tale tells in such simple pictures what can and so often does happen in our instinctive nature that it is one of the first and most important for our children to hear.

The wolf is a predator who lives from living flesh that he procures with sly deception. Our most ancient forebears found in the wolf the image of that dark force that threatens and destroys our inner life. For them, that inner life was, above all else, the knowledge that in truth there exists a divine, spiritual world. They experienced this world through clairvoyant inner vision. When in the course of the evolution of consciousness this vision became

dimmed and darkness swallowed up the knowledge of the Truth, they called this process the work of Fenris Wolf. And as within Man deception, untruth, and lie awoke and made the sense world appear as the only one true and worth striving to master, as egoism and greedy self-seeking took hold of Man, there appeared in the folk wisdom a warning image: the Wolf swallows the human.

The goat is the symbol of curiosity, as appears in common speech when we say our are children "curious as goats" or even call them "kids" as in America. (Just watch a goat in a new situation.) A child can seem made of curiosity as it comes to know the world into which it has been born. Indeed, one can say that primal curiosity (*Ur-Neugierde*) lives in the child. Sometimes, of course, these drives to learn about the world appear to the adult as immature, naive, ill-advised, and even reckless. Are we not like the old mother goat with her young kids?

Before long, some one knocked at the door, and cried, "Open the door, dear children. Your mother has come back and brought something for each of you." But the kids knew quite well by the voice that it was the Wolf. "We won't open the door," they cried. "You are not our mother. She has a soft gentle voice; but yours is rough, and we are quite sure that you are the Wolf."

So he went away to a shop and bought a lump of chalk, which he ate, and it made his voice quite soft. He went back, knocked at the door again, and cried, "Open the door, dear children. Your mother has come back and brought something for each of you." But the Wolf had put one of his paws on the window sill, where the kids saw it, and cried "We won't open the door. Our mother has not got a black foot as you have; you are the Wolf."

Then the Wolf ran to a baker, and said, "I have bruised my foot; please put some dough on it." And when the baker had put some dough on his foot, he ran to the miller and said, "Strew some flour on my foot." The miller thought, "The old Wolf is going to take somebody in," and refused. But the Wolf said, "If you don't do it, I will eat you up." So the miller was frightened, and whitened his paws. People are like that, you know.

The seven kids represent our seven-fold instinctual nature which is connected with our seven principal organs: brain, lung, kidney, heart, gall-bladder, liver and spleen. They are the bearers and support of our sense life. A healthy person, of course, is not aware of this, but a sick person can become very aware of it. "To search the heart and reins (kidney)" it says in the Bible, (for example, Revelation 2:23) but that does not mean the physical organ but the soul realm that underlies it. One can ask a question just from the head, but one can also ask a question with all the earnestness of the soul. The German language has a number of expressions relating feelings to the organs. For example, "Something ran over his liver", "A louse crawled over his liver," In English, we say, "it galls me." The heart asks out of love and for love. In children, the drive to question is very strong, but it can easily fall prey to the forces of darkness.

Now the wretch went for the third time to the door, and knocked, and said "Open the door, children. Your dear mother has come home, and has brought something for each of you out of the wood." The kids cried, "Show us your feet first, that we may be sure you are our mother." He put his paws on the window sill, and when they saw that they were white, they believed all he said, and opened the door.

Alas! It was the Wolf who walked in. They were terrified, and tried to hide themselves. One ran under the table, the second jumped into bed, the third into the oven, the fourth ran into the kitchen, the fifth got into the cupboard, the sixth into the wash-tub, and the seventh hid in the tall clock-case. But the Wolf found them all but one, and made short work of them. He swallowed one after the other, except the youngest one in the clock-case, whom he did not find. When he had satisfied his appetite, he took himself off, and lay down in a meadow outside, where he soon fell asleep.

Not long after the old Nanny-goat came back from the woods. Oh what a terrible sight met her eyes! The house door was wide open, table, chairs, and benches were over-turned, the washing bowl was smashed to atoms, the covers and pillows torn from the bed. She searched all over the house for her children, but nowhere were they to be found. She called them by name, one by one, but no one answered.
At last, when she came to the youngest, a tiny voice cried: "I am here, dear mother, hidden in the clock-case." She brought him out, and he told her that the Wolf had come and devoured all the others. You may imagine how she wept over her children.

Materialism threatens as the devouring force. An inner soul world of Innocence and Trust is in danger of being caught by that deception that only the sense world, into which we so happily grow, is the only only true world. Each of us is a child of his time and civilization and must accept conventions and half-truths, and experience delusion and lies. And though there are instinctive warnings (the mother goat), the Wolf-power is strong and overcomes the innocent instincts. Only the youngest kid in the clock case escapes. Only that force that hides in the beating heart is not seized. For in the heart, each one of us has, despite all

temptations, an instinct for the Good that cannot be deceived. And this innocent but knowing instinct helps us to track down Evil.

At last, in her grief, she went out, and the youngest kid ran by her side. When they went into the meadow, there lay the Wolf under a tree, making the branches shake with his snores. They examined him from every side, and they could plainly see movements within his distended body.

"Ah, heavens!" thought the Goat, "is it possible that my poor children whom he ate for his supper, should be still alive?" She sent the kid running to the house to fetch scissors, needles, and thread. Then she cut a hole in the monster's side, and, hardly had she begun, when a kid popped out its head, and as soon as the hole was big enough, all six jumped out, one after the other, all alive, and without having suffered the least injury, for, in his greed, the monster had swallowed them whole. You may imagine the mother's joy. She hugged them, and skipped about like a tailor on his wedding day. At last she said, "Go and fetch some big stones, children, and we will fill up the brute's body while he is asleep." Then the seven kids brought a lot of stones, as fast as they could carry them, and stuffed the Wolf with them till he could hold no more. The old mother quickly sewed him up, without his having noticed anything, or even moved. At last, when the Wolf had had his sleep out, he got up, and, as the stones made him feel very thirsty, he wanted to go to a spring to drink. But as soon as he moved the stones began to roll about and rattle inside him. Then he cried

What 's the rumbling and tumbling
That sets my stomach grumbling?
I thought 'twas six kids, flesh and bones,
Now find it's nought but rolling stones.

When he reached the spring, and stooped over the water to drink, the heavy stones dragged him down, and he was drowned miserably.

When the seven kids saw what had happened, they came running up, and cried aloud, "The Wolf is dead, the Wolf is dead!" and they and their mother eapered and danced round the spring in their joy.

All that had become darkened (swallowed by the Wolfe) again shines forth with the help of the loving force of the heart (the kid in clock-case).

The kids fill the belly of the Wolf with stones. The stone is the picture of the greatest hardening, of dead matter. Wolf-like in its insatiable greed, Materialism falls prey to a fatal hardening. And this hardening is the reason why the water of thr spring, the very image of life-bring creative forces, cannot quench the thirst of the Wolf, but brings on its death.

Our folktale is tale of Fate, and one of the first that we tell children. In it, we encounter the loss of the innocence and security of paradise and dealing with evil, but also the ultimate victory over evil. The children to whom it is told experience unconsciously the Fall and Redemption.

Hansel and Gretel

Grimm 15

Near a great forest there lived a poor woodcutter and his wife, and his two children; the boy's name was Hansel[11] and the girl's Gretel. They had very little to bite or to sup, and once, when there was great dearth in the land, the man could not even gain the daily bread. As he lay in bed one night thinking of this, and turning and tossing, he sighed heavily, and said to his wife, "What will become of us? we cannot even feed our children; there is nothing left for ourselves."

"I will tell you what, husband," answered the wife; "we will take the children early in the morning into the forest, where it is thickest; we will make them a fire, and we will give each of them a piece of bread, then we will go to our work and leave them alone; they will never find the way home again, and we shall be quit of them."

"No, wife," said the man, "I cannot do that; I cannot find in my heart to take my children into the forest and to leave them there alone; the wild animals would soon come and devour them." - "O you fool," said she, "then we will all four starve; you had better get the coffins ready," and she left him no peace until he consented. "But I really pity the poor children," said the man.

All true wisdom is always growing, like the green twigs of a tree. It strives towards heaven like the tree strives up. Goethe says, "Gray, my friend, is all theory and green the golden tree of life."[12]

---

11   In German the boy's name is written Hänsel; the two dots over the *a* indicate that it should be pronounced something like Hensel. It is a diminutive of Johannes, John.

When one turns to abstract thinking, this tree withers. No longer does he follow his living observations, always making room for experiences and turning them into insight; rather he remains stuck in gray theory. He cuts this tree of life, for he can no longer comprehend the Living Whole. He can understand only fragmentary pieces. He analyses and classifies. His thoughts are exact but no longer full of force and vigor.[13] He "splits" the concepts and "makes kindling" of them, as the idiom so vividly expresses[14] and often enough finds himself "on the logging road."[15] The tale calls such a man "a poor woodcutter" for he must deal with what was once living but has hardened into wood. To be sure, wood cutting is totally necessary and useful, and the picture is often used in a positive sense. The modern thinker must absolutely also be a "wood cutter." But here unfolds the drama of one who is totally only a poor wood cutter.

He has lost his warm, loving soul being – his wife and mother of the children. It has died and now there rules inside him the hard, materialistic soul. It is the evil step-mother to the children. The young, happy and hopeful forces striving for life are half starved and must suffer under the harshness of the soul. The children are, indeed, the best of the father's own soul. Gretel is Feeling born of true soulfulness, and Hansel is Will growing stronger. Feeling and Will are bound together like sister and brother. But we must be careful not to let the woodchopper in us regard these two as abstract forces. They are living forces in each human being. Every

---

12 Actually, Goethe has Mephistopheles say this to Faust, so it may be the opposite of what Goethe himself thought.
13 "Saft und Kraft" – literally "juice and force" or "sap and force".
14 "macht Kleinholz" – literally "make kindling" has the idiomatic meaning of to utterly destroy, to "trash" something.
15 "auf dem Holzweg" – literally "on the logging road" has the idiomatic meaning of "on the wrong track."

one of us has both old, inherited abilities and new, developing ones. We always stand between yesterday and tomorrow.

The woodchopper hungers and with him the children. They have no more bread. In the most complete of all prayers we ask for our daily bread. It is the most important nourishment for our body. What is as important to our inner being as bread is to our body? When Christ says, "I am the Bread of Life,"[16] he uses the word with its greatest symbolic force, for He is the creator and savior who must be recognized. Spiritual knowledge is the most important nourishment. It is Bread.

So Hansel and Gretel sat by the fire, and at noon they each ate their pieces of bread. They thought their father was in the wood all the time, as they seemed to hear the strokes of the ax: but really it was only a dry branch hanging to a withered tree that the wind moved to and fro. So when they had stayed there a long time their eyelids closed with weariness, and they fell fast asleep.

When at last they woke it was night, and Gretel began to cry, and said, "How shall we ever get out of this wood?" But Hansel comforted her, saying, "Wait a little while longer, until the moon rises, and then we can easily find the way home." And when the full moon got up Hansel took his little sister by the hand, and followed the way where the flint stones shone like silver, and showed them the road. They walked on the whole night through, and at the break of day they came to their father's house. They knocked at the door, and when the wife opened it and saw that it was Hansel and Gretel she said, "You naughty children, why did you sleep so long in the wood? we thought you were never coming home again!" But the father was

---

16   John 6:35,

glad, for it had gone to his heart to leave them both in the woods alone.

Not very long after that there was again great scarcity in those parts, and the children heard their mother say at night in bed to their father, "Everything is finished up; we have only half a loaf, and after that the tale comes to an end. The children must be off; we will take them farther into the wood this time, so that they shall not be able to find the way back again; there is no other way to manage." The man felt sad at heart, and he thought, "It would better to share one's last morsel with one's children." But the wife would listen to nothing that he said, but scolded and reproached him. He who says A must say B too, and when a man has given in once he has to do it a second time.

But the children were not asleep, and had heard all the talk. When the parents had gone to sleep Hansel got up to go out and get more flint stones, as he did before, but the wife had locked the door, and Hansel could not get out; but he comforted his little sister, and said, "Don't cry, Gretel, and go to sleep quietly, and God will help us." Early the next morning the wife came and pulled the children out of bed. She gave them each a little piece of "bread -less than before; and on the way to the wood Hansel crumbled the bread in his pocket, and often stopped to throw a crumb on the ground. "Hansel, what are you stopping behind and staring for?" said the father.

"I am looking at my little pigeon sitting on the roof, to say good-bye to me," answered Hansel. "You fool," said the wife, "that is no pigeon, but the morning sun shining on the chimney pots." Hansel went on as before, and strewed bread crumbs all along the road. The woman led the children far into the wood, where they had

*never been before in all their lives. And again there was a large fire
made, and the mother said, "Sit still there, you children, and when
you are tired you can go to sleep; we are going into the forest to cut
wood, and in the evening, when we are ready to go home we will
come and fetch you."*

*So when noon came Gretel shared her bread with Hansel, who
had strewed his along the road. Then they went to sleep, and the
evening passed, and no one came for the poor children. When they
awoke it was dark night, and Hansel comforted his little sister, and
said, "Wait a little, Gretel, until the moon gets up, then we shall be
able to see the way home by the crumbs of bread that I have
scattered along it."*

*So when the moon rose they got up, but they could find no
crumbs of bread, for the birds of the woods and of the fields had
come and picked them up. Hansel thought they might find the way
all the same, but they could not. They went on all that night, and the
next day from the morning until the evening, but they could not find
the way out of the wood, and they were very hungry, for they had
nothing to eat but the few berries they could pick up. And when they
were so tired that they could no longer drag themselves along, they
lay down under a tree and fell asleep.*

*It was now the third morning since they had left their father's
house. They were always trying to get back to it, but instead of that
they only found themselves farther in the wood, and if help had not
soon come they would have been starved.*

*About noon they saw a pretty snow-white bird sitting on a
bough, and singing so sweetly that they stopped to listen. And when
he had finished the bird spread his wings and flew before them, and
they followed after him until they came to a little house, and the bird*

perched on the roof, and when they came nearer they saw that the house was built of bread, and roofed with cakes; and the window was of transparent sugar.

Three days – a significant time in the development of the tale – Hansel and Gretel are on their way in confusion and need. Under the thick romanticism of this story we can recognize the strict cannon of an event in the mysteries. On the third day, knowledge must have ripened, a manifestation must occur, a decision must be made. It says: after the third morning, at noon, they see a beautiful snow-white bird and follow it.

This snow-white bird that sings so beautifully, what a propitious sign it would have been at a different time! But it appeared at noon.

We know that both man and animal experience a special lethargy as the sun reaches its highpoint. Modern man has largely freed himself from this experience, but in earlier times it was so strong that peasants would avoid being outside in the fields at noon. In folk sagas many such experiences are reflected such as encountering the Noonday Witch[17] who with her sickle splits consciousness or meeting a sphinx-like monster who torments with questions. It is the hour when we are most susceptible to illusion and unclear thinking. That is why many will avoid signing a contract at noon. The folk wisdom says: It is the hour of Lucifer. The midday ringing of bells was to keep humans conscious and to drive away the misleading spirits. Had the white bird appeared in the morning with the fresh dew on the grass or in evening hour of reflection, it would be the symbol of enlightening inspiration of the

---

17 See "Lady Midday" in the English Wikipedia or "Mittagsfrau" in the German.

thought sphere. But at noon, its voice is misleading temptation. It flies before the children and leads them to the witch's house. It is a house of bread, but it is witch bread.

"We will have some of this," said Hansel, "and make a fine meal. I will eat a piece of the roof, Gretel, and you can have some of the window-that will taste sweet." So Hansel reached up and broke off a bit of the roof, just to see how it tasted, and Gretel stood by the window and gnawed at it. Then they heard a thin voice call out from inside,

> *"Nibble, nibble, like a mouse,*
> *Who is nibbling at my house?"*

And the children answered,

> *"The wind so mild*
> *The heavenly child."*

And they went on eating, never disturbing themselves. Hansel, who found that the roof tasted very nice, took down a great piece of it, and Gretel pulled out a large round window-pane, and sat her down and began upon it.

Then the door opened, and an aged woman came out, leaning upon a crutch. Hansel and Gretel felt very frightened, and let fall what they had in their hands. The old woman, however, nodded her head, and said, "Ah, my dear children, how come you here? you must come indoors and stay with me, you will be no trouble." So she took them each by the hand, and led them into her little house. And there they found a good meal laid out, of milk and pancakes, with sugar, apples, and nuts. After that she showed them two little white beds, and Hansel and Gretel laid themselves down on them, and thought they were in heaven.

72

The German word for witch, *Hexe*, comes from the Old High German *hagazussa*. This *hagasussa* was once a wise woman living in a grove, a prophetic seeress, and even earlier, a clairvoyant protectress and priestess of the clan. In the course of time, the capacity for clairvoyant leadership faded and demonic influences became active. True magic became lower magic, and the once holy original wisdom was falsified. The hagazussa became the exact opposite of what she had once been. Today the witch represents that tempting power that offers an atavistic pseudowisdom that only deceives and deludes. Naive, inexperienced people are in danger of falling prey to the temptation. The Occult attracts them. They believe they are finding tested, traditional truths or training that leads to true knowledge only to fall prey to delusion. What was right for one age and for one stage of development can at a later time become just the opposite. Methods that were right centuries and millennia ago, cannot be right for modern mankind. This story warns against such atavistic doctrines and methods.

The witch is an old, old woman with red eyes that cannot see far. She does not take in the sense world clearly. But, as it says in the next paragraph, "she has a good nose, like the beasts." That means she does not grasp the spirit by thinking. She beckons the children to her: she reaches for the innocent, guileless childhood forces in mankind to which she offers the sweet bread of a magically bewitching delusion. "They thought they were in heaven."

The old woman, although her behavior was so kind, was a wicked witch, who lay in wait for children, and had built the little house on purpose to entice them. When they were once inside she used to kill them, cook them, and eat them, and then it was a feast day with her. The witch's eyes were red, and she could not see very far, but she had a good nose, like the beasts, and knew very well

when human creatures were near. When she knew that Hansel and Gretel were coming, she gave a spiteful laugh, and said triumphantly, "I have them, and they shall not escape me!"

Early in the morning, before the children were awake, she got up to look at them, and as they lay sleeping so peacefully with round rosy cheeks, she said to herself, "What a fine feast I shall have!" Then she grasped Hansel with her withered hand, and led him into a little stable, and shut him up behind a grating; and call and scream as he might, it was no good. Then she went back to Gretel and shook her, crying, "Get up, lazy bones; fetch water, and cook something nice for your brother; he is outside in the stable, and must be fattened up. And when he is fat enough I will eat him." Gretel began to weep bitterly, but it was of no use, she had to do what the wicked witch bade her. And so the best kind of victuals was cooked for poor Hansel, while Gretel got nothing but crab-shells.

Each morning the old woman visited the little stable, and cried, "Hansel, stretch out your finger, that I may tell if you will soon be fat enough." Hansel, however, used to hold out a little bone, and the old woman, who had weak eyes, could not see what it was, and supposing it to be Hansel's finger, wondered very much that it was not getting fatter.

When four weeks had passed and Hansel seemed to remain so thin, she lost patience and could wait no longer. "Now then, Gretel," cried she to the little girl; "be quick and draw water; be Hansel fat or be he lean, tomorrow I must kill and cook him." Oh what a grief for the poor little sister to have to fetch water, and how the tears flowed down over her cheeks! "Dear God, pray help us!" cried she; "if we had been devoured by wild beasts in the wood at least we should

74

have died together." – "Spare me your lamentations," said the old woman; "they are of no avail."

Hansel is locked in the little stable: the Will is blocked and has lost its freedom of action. Feeling can no longer follow its own impulses; Gretel must serve Evil. Cooking and roasting have to do with fire. Notice the images of our language. We must warm to a task; our enthusiasm must catch fire. How beautiful is the fire of a noble inspiration, the holy glow of inextinguishable love. But there is another fire, the fire ignited from demonized illusion, burning desires, and the heat of lower passions that unfailingly flares up if the will is lamed and the naive, unsuspecting soul fallen prey to occult delusion. In this fire the child-nature of Man can burn and finally be consumed by Evil.

Early next morning Gretel had to get up, make the fire, and fill the kettle. "First we will do the baking," said the old woman; "I have heated the oven already, and kneaded the dough." She pushed poor Gretel towards the oven, out of which the flames were already shining.

"Creep in," said the witch, "and see if it is properly hot, so that the bread may be baked." And with Gretel once in, she meant to shut the door upon her and let her be baked, and then she would have eaten her. But Gretel perceived her intention, and said, "I don't know how to do it: how shall I get in?"

"Stupid goose," said the old woman, "the opening is big enough, do you see? I could get in myself!" and she stooped down and put her head in the oven's mouth. Then Gretel gave her a push, so that she went in farther, and she shut the iron door upon her, and put up the bar. Oh how frightfully she howled! but Gretel ran away, and left the wicked witch to burn miserably.

Though the witch succeeded in making the masculine will forces fully passive, the feminine feeling forces were not overcome and bring help. Gretel delivers evil to its own element; the fire of illusion, desire, and lower passion becomes the fire of purification. For Evil destroys itself when courage and bravery go to work. Then the Will wins back its freedom of action.

Gretel went straight to Hansel, opened the stable-door, and cried, "Hansel, we are free! the old witch is dead!" Then out flew Hansel like a bird from its cage as soon as the door is opened. How they both rejoiced! How they fell each on the other's neck! and danced about, and kissed each other! And as they had nothing more to fear they went over all the old witch's house, and in every corner there stood chests of pearls and precious stones. "This is something better than flint stones," said Hansel, as he filled his pockets, and Gretel, thinking she also would like to carry something home with her, filled her apron full.

Just as every negative experience undergone, every overcoming of evil can lead to positive insights that make one rich in soul, so Hansel and Gretel find treasure in the house of the witch. The pearls born of water and the precious stones born of earth point to two planes of being which the witch had plundered. In the brave human who stands against evil, these planes are enriched by the treasures won. For the witch is but a part of "that power that always wishes to do evil and always does good." [18]

---

18 In Goethe's *Faust*, Part I, Mephistopheles introduces himself to Faust as "*Ein Teil von jener Kraft, die stets das Böse will und stets das Gute schafft*" A part of that power which always wishes to do evil and always does good. (lines 1335–6).

Of the pearls and precious stones, one might say more simply that they are treasures that the human spirit can acquire only in the physical world but can be carried over into the spiritual world.

Now, away we go," said Hansel, "if we only can get out of the witch's wood." When they had journeyed a few hours they came to a great piece of water. "We can never get across this," said Hansel, "I see no stepping-stones and no bridge."

"And there is no boat either," said Gretel; "but here comes a white duck; if I ask her she will help us over." So she cried,

"Duck, duck, here we stand,
Hansel and Gretel, on the land,
Stepping-stones and bridge we lack,
Carry us over on your nice back."

And the duck came accordingly, and Hansel got upon her and told his sister to come too. "No," answered Gretel, "that would be too hard upon the duck; we can go separately, one after the other." And the good animal did just that. After they were both over, they went on happily, until they came to the wood, and the way grew more and more familiar, till at last they saw in the distance their father's house.

The children reach the great open water. One must experience this as opposite to the confusion of the forest, to anxiety and fear of death. They have now won a broad vision, a clear view of the soul world. The white duck that carries the children over the water, does it not show the most beautiful capacity which the soul has won by its suffering? For it is Gretel who calls and commands the duck. An instinctive certainty has been won, and they do not hesitate to set out upon the waves of the deep. The feeling soul, that previously could have so easily have lost confidence on the unstable back of a duck now has no fear of sinking or going under.

The white duck is more common in the symbolic language of the East than in that of the West. In Indian temples the white duck appears along with the swan. In the Russian folktale of Elena the Beautiful, she demands of the hero the gift of a white duckling and we recognize the desired virtue: steadfastness of soul in the fluctuating water-world of our feelings. Unfortunately, in many editions of the Grimm stories the images of the water and the duck are left out. They are as, we have seen, the crowning event and fruition of the whole story.

Then they ran till they came up to it, rushed in at the door, and fell on their father's neck. The man had not had a quiet hour since he left his children in the wood; but the wife was dead. And when Gretel opened her apron the pearls and precious stones were scattered all over the room, and Hansel took one handful after another out of his pocket. Then was all care at an end, and they lived in great joy together. My tale is done, there runs a mouse, whosoever catches it, may make himself a big fur cap out of it.

All the actions in a folktale are events in the human soul. The father is, along with Hansel and Gretel. part of that soul. So the hardening that had so evilly influenced him, must now have been overcome; the step-mother is dead. And the riches that have been won by one part of the soul are shared by all of it. The old I no longer needs to be a woodcutter. Henceforth the whole Man endowed with new soul forces will "know the ever greening tree of golden wisdom."

Sweet Porridge

Grimm 103

Porridge made from grain was the first cooked food of humans[19], and the porridge pot was the symbol of this nourishment. In ancient India, the sun and the moon were called the heavenly porridge pot, for they held the macrocosmic forces. They were regarded as the heavenly vessels which gave to mankind cosmic nourishment. Humans could *fassen* (take) and *er-fassen* (comprehend) this nourishment. The sun makes day-awake, thinking beings of us; the moon works into the life rhythms, into growth and reproduction. Man of earlier epochs experienced these forces by his clairvoyant feeling and seeing and nourished himself in soul and spirit through them.

In the course of human development, the sun and moon came to be experienced only physically, no longer as strength-giving heavenly vessels. The soul became "poor", but Man is nonetheless the microcosmos in the macrocosmos, he is in his small world the image and reflection of the great world. The effects of the heavenly porridge pot are still there. We must only become aware of them.

---

19. This statement needs qualification. Cooking porridge requires a pot, and the first evidence of pots is in China and goes back only about 20,000 years. That these early pots were used for cooking is indicated by signs of being in fire on their outsides. There is, however, evidence of Homo Erectus having cooked meat, presumably on a spit, 1.5 million years ago. If we change the text to read, "Porridge is the first grain-based cooked food," it would probably be correct. The text of the tale specifies millet porridge, and the porridge in those first pots may well have been millet. Millet does not need to be ground to make good porridge, and there is evidence of its use in China back into the third millennia B.C. It may well go back much farther. (For a scholarly study of millet in Asia, see Naomi F. Miller, et. al., "Millet cultivation across Eurasia: Origins, spread, and the influence of seasonal climate" on the Internet.

Then we detect these forces as a perpetual source of spiritual nourishment within ourselves.

The tale tells all this in its own way.

There was once a poor, pious little girl who lived alone with her mother, and they had nothing more to eat. So the child set out into the forest, and there she met an old woman who already knew of her plight, and gave her a little pot, which when she said to it, "Little pot, cook" would cook good, sweet millet porridge, and when she said, "Little pot, stop" it would stop cooking. cook. The girl brought the pot home to her mother, and now they were freed from their poverty and from their hunger, and ate sweet porridge as often as they wished.

In the soul, poverty prevails. What is ancestral, well-established and conservative (the mother) hungers and also what is young, forward-striving and childlike (the daughter) suffers. But the daughter seeks help. She sets out. She is pious and good. Piety can create help, and Goodness can lead to a transformation of one's own being. There is a realm in Man where there is abundance. It is the vegetative world of luxuriant life and growth forces. It appears in dreams and folktales as the forest. Unsuspected revitalization can come from there. Our tale points to this fact. There old, long forgotten ideas and experience find new certainty. The ancestress, the old advice-giving woman, speaks. She points to the magical power of the word, to the Will in the word, and the nourishment that flows from it. She also gives the girl a new capacity for understanding – the pot.[20] And so the Child in Man can once again

20 The text connects the words for *pot* and *understanding* in an untranslatable way. The verb *fassen* basically means *to hold, take, contain* but has the extended meaning of *to understand*. A *Gefäß* is something that holds something, here the pot. The word *Vermögen* means ability, capacity. The

make the cosmic nourishment. But not only that, it can both stimulate and quiet down the process.

Once when the girl had gone out, the mother said, "Little pot, cook." And it cooked and she ate until she was satisfied, and then she wanted the pot to stop cooking, but did not know the word. So it went on cooking, and the porridge rose over the rim and filled the kitchen and then the whole house, and then a second house, and then the whole street, as if it wanted to satisfy the whole world. There was great panic, but no one knew how to stop it. At last when only one house remained, the child came home and just said, "Little pot, stop" and it stopped cooking, but anyone who wanted to get back into the town had to eat their way back!

The tale show us that the not all of the soul being has gone through the development but only the young, seeking and pious part that had "set out into the forest." The mother did not go into the forest. She is that aspect of the whole that has passively remained where she was. She can bring about inner filling, but she cannot control it, so she falls prey to intemperance.

This tale is often told quite incorrectly, namely that the girl set the pot to cooking but then forgot how to stop it and it cooked until the mother came home. But that is backwards and quite wrong.

So short and unpretentious as this tale is, it is the hymn of highest praise of the Child in Man. Can we possibly tell our children anything more comforting? Can we in any way better convey to them certainty the continuing nourishment of the soul so long as it childlike and pious? Of course, one must never explain to a child the picture language of the tale. In childhood, the pictures

---

text says that the old woman gives the girl a new "**Fass**ungs-Vermögen, das Ge-**fäß**"

speak for themselves. When children take them into their souls, they will not fail to work just as nourishingly as the sweet porridge of our story.

Tales with Man as Co-Actor

Development and Paths

Little Brother and Little Sister

(Brüderchen und Schwesterchen)

Grimm 11

Not only in the outer world do siblings live together, share joy
and sorrow, and fulfill their destiny. Also in the inner world there
are such "siblings" forces of our being that work together in
forming the growing human. When they are of a more feeling
nature, we may call them feminine; and when they are of a more
willful-spiritual nature, masculine. When a tale tells of Little
brother and Little sister, both children, we know that it deals with
young, immature will forces in union with a still developing, naive
soul. And if they are "orphans" and have a "wicked step-mother",
then we may suspect that the drama of maturation will not be
without problems. For where the "father" is dead, experienced
guidance in the realm of the spirit is lacking, and where the
"mother" is dead the motherly ground of the soul can offer no
further protection. The hardened, materialist soul – the step-mother
– rules. She seeks control over the whole human being, punishes
the good and is inclined to the evil. And the forces striving for the
good and the true must free themselves from her, become
independent, and enter upon their own way of development. So the
tale says:

*The brother took his sister's hand and said to her, "Since our
mother died we have had no good days; our stepmother beats us
every day, and if we go near her she kicks us away; we have
nothing to eat but hard crusts of bread left over; the dog under the
table fares better," he gets a good piece every now and then. If our
mother only knew, how she would pity us! Come, let us go together*

out into the wide world!" So they went, and journeyed the whole day through fields and meadows and stony places, and if it rained the sister said, "The skies and we are weeping together." In the evening they came to a great forest, and they were so weary with hunger and their long journey, that they got into a hollow tree and fell asleep.

The forest (*Wald* or *Waldung*) was in olden times the territory that lay beyond the town's rampart, its protective "Wall" of mounded earth which surrounded and protected the farmsteads of our forebears. The *Waldung* was unprotected land and full of dangers. In it, one had to find the way and could easily loose it and go astray. Wild animals threatened to attack one, as did also robbers and other riffraff. But also there lived in it the seeress and the pious hermit. The abundance of the nature forces weaving there to and fro awakens and strengthens and heals. The twilight-like darkness, the mysterious soughing of the trees can make one shudder with premonitions. And so the forest becomes the symbol for that inner seeking and erring, for feeling that there is no way out, but also for the oppressive abundance that everyone must go through who seeks an inner goal.

In the Grail legend, the castle of the Grail was surrounded by a forest sixty miles wide. Dante, at the beginning of the Divine Comedy, finds himself in a "dark forest" (*selva oscura*), the sphere of secrets which must be passed through. When children are plagued by dreams of being lost in a forest, it is a sign that they need more guidance, and one should tell them folktales and occupy their spirit, for they are pressured by their own vitality and can find no way out.

The tale goes on:

The next morning, when they awoke, the sun stood high in heaven, and shone brightly through the leaves. Then said the brother, "Sister, I am thirsty; if I only knew where to find a spring, that I might go and drink! I almost think that I hear one rushing."

So the brother got up and led his sister by the hand, and they went to seek the spring. But their wicked stepmother was a witch, and had known quite well that the two children had run away, and had sneaked after them, as only witches can, and had laid a spell on all the springs in the forest.

So when they found a little spring flowing smoothly over its pebbles, the brother was going to drink of it; but the sister heard how it said in its rushing, "He a tiger will be who drinks of me, Who drinks of me a tiger will be!"

Then the sister cried, "Pray, dear brother, do not drink, or you will become a wild beast, and will tear me in pieces."

So the brother refrained from drinking, though his thirst was great, and he said he would wait till he came to the next spring. When they came to a second spring the sister heard it say, "He a wolf will be who drinks of me, Who drinks of me a wolf will be!"

Then the sister cried, "Pray, dear brother, do not drink, or you will be turned into a wolf, and will eat me up!"

So the brother refrained from drinking, and said, "I will wait until we come to the next spring, and then I must drink, whatever you say; my thirst is so great."

And when they came to the third spring the sister heard how in its rushing it said, "Who drinks of me a fawn will be, He a fawn will be who drinks of me!"

Then the sister said, "O my brother, I pray drink not, or you will be turned into a fawn, and run away far from me."

But he had already kneeled by the side of the spring and stooped and drunk of the water, and as the first drops passed his lips he became a fawn.

Outgrowing childhood means continually awakening. In its earliest ages, human consciousness is caught in sleep and dreams. But day, the wide-awake thinking experience becomes ever more important. The tale says, "the sun stood high in heaven." All of mankind once went through this process of awakening, and it is repeated in each child. But because the age of the dreamlike consciousness with its wisdom has passed, and we must now go our way guided by thinking, there awakens in the will life desire – thirst awakens. One wants to find "springs," to become creative[21] and to "dip" into a new element. The thirst for existence burns in the Will life.

Sneaking secretly, as witches sneak, the step-mother has crept into the forest and bewitched all the springs. Without forethought and impetuously the Will pushes ahead; the inner feeling life can scarcely tame it. Only the soul hears the warning "He who drinks of me a tiger will be." We know the expression, "I'm torn apart." German is even more vivid[22]: "I feel cut to pieces, ripped open, and lacerated." The tale tells vividly of the danger into which the soul is thrust by the impetuous Will: "Pray, dear brother, do not drink, or you will become a wild beast, and will tear me in pieces." The Will

---

21 The German word for *creative* is *schöpferisch*. But the verb *schöpfen* means both "to create" and "to ladle up, to scoop up water with a dipper". The text says, one wants to become "*schöpferisch*". In other words, the brother's desire to drink is picture language for a desire to be creative.

22 "… ich fühle mich wie zerstückt, ich bin zerrissen, wie zerfetzt."

would fall into danger if the cautiousness of the soul did not preserve it. In the tale, it is a young, unformed and still naive will force that is yet to be formed and disciplined.

When the ancient Greeks gave to their god Dionysos the panther and later the tiger as symbol – and when they dressed the god Bacchus in a tiger skin and had his chariot pulled by tigers – they wanted to stress the positive side of this process. Becoming aware of one's own I was to them an experience like drunkenness. One readily recognizes the child almost drunk with the awakening of the I. One who makes everything his concern, even the quite trivial, who becomes excited over every new idea will inevitably be torn apart. In other words, the Will is no longer able to pull itself together and to contemplate itself. It then tears the soul apart.

The wolf represents a very different danger. The sister says, "Dear brother, do not drink, or you will be turned into a wolf, and will eat me up!" Again the language of the tale paints absolutely exactly. To "eat up" means to devour. The wolf is the symbol of that "devouring" power that makes Man prey to materialistic lies and deception by the senses. The ancient Germans called this power Fenris Wolf; the Bible calls it Satan. Just as the first accursed spring caused a Luciferic excessive growth of the Will forces – so that we can no longer concentrate – so the second accursed spring causes a laming of the Will, a passive losing of oneself in egotistical greed, untruth, and delusion.

From these two dangers the soul can still protect the Will, but not from the third – here it bucks.[23] When, in a folktale, a human is turned into an animal it means sinking into an animal condition.

23 Another play on words. The German is *"er verbockt."* Idiomatically translated, "he messes up." But the root is *Bock*, cognate of English *buck*, and is used for the male goat, sheep, or deer.

The human Will is insightful, patient, open to spiritual knowledge and capable of development. But now it becomes compulsively dumb and unteachable. The buck will butt his way through a wall. If, in our story, the Will becomes a buck deer, the accent must be placed on *deer*. That is, he roams and rambles, becomes fleeting and unstable, is never quite himself, and nibbles and tastes all around. Humans who do not rule their will seek all around for stimulus to their spirit but do not pause to research in depth and take responsibility. They are, in other words, very like deer. Russian tales use for them the image of the ram. Thus the various types of distortions of the human Will are drastically characterized by animals.

And the sister wept over her poor lost brother, and the fawn wept also, and stayed sadly beside her. At last the maiden said, "Be comforted, dear fawn, indeed I will never leave you." Then she untied her golden garter and bound it round the fawn's neck, and went and gathered rushes to make a soft cord, which she fastened to him; and then she led him on, and they went deeper into the forest. And when they had gone a long long way, they came at last to a little house, and the maiden looked inside, and as it was empty she thought, "We might as well live here." And she fetched leaves and moss to make a soft bed for the fawn, and every morning she went out and gathered roots and berries and nuts for herself, and fresh grass for the fawn, who ate out of her hand with joy, frolicking round her. At night, when the sister was tired, and had said her prayers, she laid her head on the fawn's back, which served her for a pillow, and softly fell asleep. And if only the brother could have got back his own shape again, it would have been a charming life.

Our tale shows in a wonderful way how the soul seeks to restrain the roving will. She puts on the fawn the golden girdle and

makes a cord of rushes and leads it. The golden garter may have brought a secret smile to many who knew something of the interpretations formerly given to symbols in the tales. But there is more to it than meets the eye. In the year 1348 King Edward III founded the Order of the Garter. The story goes that at a ball given by the king, the Countess of Salisbury lost her garter. The king picked it up and cried, "Honi soit qui mal y pense!" – "Shame on him who thinks ill of it!" He then established the Order of the Garter, the highest in England. But it was not just an ordinary lady's garter that brought this exclamation from the king and the significant result. The garter was the secret sign of a lodge of esoteric knowledge at the Arthurian Roundtable. So the golden garter says, One who possesses the wisdom of an esoteric knowledge can use it to bridle and lead his impetuous Will.

When, in a tale or in a dream, a house is found and occupied, it means that the house of the body is more intensely perceived and one comes more "to oneself." One becomes " domesticated". Soul and Will now "house" intimately together. "In the evening" when the sister has said her prayers she lays her head on the soft back of the fawn and falls asleep. Can there be a more a more telling picture of this inner duality of the outward striving Will come to rest in the hut of the Soul? The scene has been painted by Hermann Kaulbach; it would be a good model for the rooms of our children where today all too often caricatures and Mickey Mouse hold sway.

But the Soul knows well that during the day it must give the Will freedom. It cannot prove itself if always tied and bridled. It must actively take hold of the outer sense world, romp about in it, and then in the evening come back to peaceful stillness. One cannot achieve independence if the Will is not released to experience its freedom. And danger!

So they lived a long while in the wilderness alone. Now it happened that the King of that country held a great hunt in the forest. The blowing of the horns, the barking of the dogs, and the lusty shouts of the huntsmen sounded through the wood, and the fawn heard them and was eager to be among them.

"Oh," said he to his sister," do let me go to the hunt; I cannot stay behind any longer," and begged so long that at last she consented.

"But mind," said she to him," come back to me at night. I must lock my door against the wild hunters, so, in order that I may know you, you must knock and say, ' Little sister, let me in,' and unless I hear that I shall not unlock the door." Then the fawn sprang out, and felt glad and merry in the open air. The King and his huntsmen saw the beautiful animal, and began at once to pursue him, but they could not come within reach of him, for when they thought they were certain of him he sprang away over the bushes and disappeared. As soon as it was dark he went back to the little house, knocked at the door, and said, "Little sister, let me in." Then the door was opened to him, and he went in, and rested the whole night long on his soft bed.

The next morning the hunt began anew, and when the fawn heard the hunting-horns and the tally-ho of the huntsmen he could rest no longer, and said, "Little sister, let me out, I must go"

The sister opened the door and said, "Now, mind you must come back at night and say the same words." When the King and his hunters saw the fawn with the golden collar again, they chased him closely, but he was too nimble and swift for them. This lasted the whole day, and at last the hunters surrounded him, and one of them wounded his foot a little, so that he was obliged to limp and to go

slowly. Then a hunter slipped after him to the little house, and heard how he called out," Little sister, let me in," and saw the door open and shut again after him directly., The hunter noticed all this carefully, went to the King, and told him all he had seen and heard. Then said the King, "To-morrow we will hunt again."

But the sister was very terrified when she saw that her fawn was wounded. She washed his foot, laid cooling leaves round it, and said," Lie down on your bed, dear fawn, and rest, that you may be soon well." The wound was very slight, so that the fawn felt nothing of it the next morning. And when he heard the noise of the hunting outside, he said, "I cannot stay in, I must go after them; I shall not be taken easily again!"

The sister began to weep, and said, "I know you will be killed, and I left alone here in the forest, and forsaken of everybody. I cannot let you go!"

"Then I shall die here with longing," answered the fawn;" when I hear the sound of the horn I feel as if I should leap out of my skin."

Then the sister, seeing there was no help for it, unlocked the door with a heavy heart, and the fawn bounded away into the forest, well and merry.

When the King saw him, he said to his hunters, "Now, follow him up all day long till the night comes, and see that you do him no hurt." So as soon as the sun had gone down, the King said to the huntsmen:" Now, come and show me the little house in the wood." And when he got to the door he knocked at it, and cried, "Little sister, let me in!"

Deep in the background of the total human being lives the real force of being, the true I. As the ruling, leading being it appears in the story as the King, but – as we shall see – this I grows in self-aware worth and dignity. In life, the soul must often travel long and difficult ways before it meets this King and finds its kingdom, that is, becomes what it should be. When it has broken free from the restricting forces – here the stepmother – it finds itself on this way. Development of the I is a double process; while the soul is still bound to desires (the sister to the faun) is ripening toward the higher I, it – the king – approaches them. If here, on the difficult way to freedom, the soul must at first loose the "humanity" of the will, yet it has through tying and leading (golden band and rush cord) and through concentrated internalizing (living in the little house) done everything humanly possible with measure and composure. Thereby it comes closer to its objective; the King enters the forest.

The folktales often picture the I of modern Man as the hunter and so point to one of the primal activities of the I. It is constantly active; it wants to learn and to gain insights and "hunt down" knowledge. We know the hunt for money, success, and luck. The more noble the hunter, the more noble the hunt. The noble hunter takes aim at bad drives and instincts to kill them, but good natural drives are tamed, and lifted up to more noble service. In picture language, the King is on the hunt; he hunts and hunts down. The knowledge-seeking I, going after all the forces in the human being, calls to the Will – long bound and internalized – to freedom. The hunting horns sound, and the young buck must go out.

On the first day the king and his hunters see the animal with the golden head band and go after him. On the second day, they

track him. On the third day, the king finds the hut in the woods and asks to be let in.

One can say: The ennobled Will instinct, which has bravely put itself to the test of the hunt, can keep its freedom. It now leads directly to the soul – the sister. The Will forms the bridge between the I and the soul.

Then the door opened, and the King went in, and there stood a maiden more beautiful than any he had seen before. The maiden shrieked out when she saw, instead of the fawn, a man standing there with a gold crown on his head. But the King looked kindly on her, took her by the hand, and said, "Will you go with me to my castle, and be my dear wife?"

"Oh yes," answered the maiden, "but the fawn must come too. I could not leave him." And the King said, "He shall remain with you as long as you live, and shall lack nothing." Then the fawn came bounding in, and the sister tied the cord of rushes to him, and led him by her own hand out of the little forest house.

Beautiful becomes the soul that has so long controlled her Will life and faithfully waited with daily prayer until human insight has ripened. This independence, freedom and beauty, won in the poverty of homelessness did not previously exist. Only the modern soul can win it, must win it. Therefore the tale says: *there stood a maiden more beautiful than any he had seen before.* – "Will you be *my dear wife?*" "Will you, dear soul, become completely one with me?" This becoming one was called, in the language of the Middle Ages, the royal wedding and also the mystical wedding. Soul and spirit become an inseparable unity. But the Will remains compulsive; in the background there still live those limiting forces from which the soul has freed herself but are not yet overcome.

The King put the beautiful maiden on his horse, and carried her to his castle, where the wedding was held with great pomp; so she became lady Queen, and they lived together happily for a long while; the fawn was well tended and cherished, and he gambolled about the castle garden. Now the wicked stepmother, whose fault it was that the children were driven out into the world, never dreamed but that the sister had been eaten up by wild beasts in the forest, and that the brother, in the likeness of a fawn, had been slain by the hunters. But when she heard that they were so happy, and that things had gone so well with them, jealousy and envy arose in her heart, and left her no peace, and her chief thought was how to bring misfortune upon them. Her own daughter, who was as ugly as the night, and had only one eye, complained to her, and said, "I never had the chance of being a Queen." "Never mind," said the old woman, to satisfy her; "when the time comes, I shall be at hand."

Now we get a clearer idea of the old woman from her daughter. With this one-eyed creature will we become better acquainted in the story "One Eye, Two Eye, and Three Eye." The name points to an ancient power of sight that long ago became decadent. Present-day humans must look into the sense world, think, decide and be a wide-awake day-persons. They must not depend on old clairvoyance. The one-eyed daughter is "ugly as the night." She therefore represents the distortion of what was once a clairvoyant dream consciousness, called in the tale The Night. Where materialism (the step-mother) works in conjunction with atavistic clairvoyance (the one-eyed daughter) is the I-conscious development of the soul much endangered. When are such retarding forces most likely to attack? The tale says:

When the time had come, the Queen brought a beautiful baby-boy into the world, and that day the King was out hunting. The old witch took the shape of the bedchamber woman, and went into the room where the Queen lay, and said to her, "Come, the bath is ready; it will give you refreshment and new strength. Quick, or it will be cold." Her daughter was within call, so they carried the sick Queen into the bath-room, and left her there. And in the bath-room they had made a great fire, so as to suffocate the beautiful young Queen.

We know the words *überzeugen* and spiritually *befruchten*[24]. In the soul fertilized by the creative spirit is the germ of a new, future-bearing being matured and brought into the world. In this child of a king lives the eternal I born out of the soul struggling to be free. Everything tender and higher that is born of the working together of spirit and soul must be protected in concentrated stillness until it can grow to greater strength. And just as in the outer world the husband should stand by his wife when the difficult moment of childbirth comes, so in the inner world the inner awakening should be attended with attention and devotion, but: the King is out hunting. That is to say, the human spirit is so active, so zealously striving to gain new experience and knowledge that it pays attention only to its own impulses. The modern poet Juan Ramón Jiménez warns against this danger:

¡No corras. Ve despacio,	Don't run. Go slowly
que donde tienes que ir	for where you must go
es a ti solo!	is to yourself!

---

24 *Überzeugen* is the standard German word for *convince*; *über* means *over* and *zeugen* is both *testify* and *beget*. *Befruchten* with the root *Frucht*, fruit, means to *fertilize, inseminate*.

¡Ve despacio, no corras,	Go slowly, don't run,
que el niño de tu yo,	for the child of your I,
recién nacido eterno,	just born eternal
no te puede seguir!	cannot follow you!
Si vas deprisa,	If you hurry
el tiempo volará ante ti,	time will fly before you,
como una	like an
mariposilla esquiva.	elusive butterfly.
Si vas despacio,	If you go slowly,
el tiempo irá detras de ti,	time will go behind you
como un buey manso.	like a gentle ox.

Juan Ramón Jiménez, *Eternidades,* poema XXXVI, 1918.

The newborn eternal I in us needs protection. An inner cleaning must follow every creative act, and so in the tale the bath follows the birth. When the eternal I is born this cleaning must also be a purification. A holy inspiration must ignite the fire of the Will and spark the warmth of an unearthly love. But where the evil forces are at work, it becomes the flames of Hell and suffocates the soul.

When that was managed, the old woman took her daughter, put a cap on her, and laid her in the bed in the Queen's place, gave her also the Queen's form and countenance, only she could not restore the lost eye.

Here we must note that the Grimms' text, where it says "restore the lost eye" does not transmit the original folktale quite

the picture of cherishing and caring in the soul. Development takes time.

Then she told the King the snare that the wicked witch and her daughter had laid for her. The King had them both brought to judgment, and sentence was passed upon them. The daughter was sent away into the wood, where she was devoured by the wild beasts, and the witch was burned, and ended miserably. And as soon as her body was in ashes the spell was removed from the fawn, and he took human shape again; and then the sister and brother lived happily together until their end.

When the ruling power of the I itself calls to judgment, then what is directed backward in the soul (the one-eyed daughter) cannot hold out. It is torn apart by the force of drives. Ultimate purification destroys also the witch-like evil, and thereby the Will is freed from the spell of bestiality. The selfless patience of the soul has led it to freedom.

One-eye, Two-eye, Three-eye

Grimm 130

Our tale's title should be "One-Eye, Three-Eye, Two-Eye" if it is to be more than just an enumeration, for Two-Eye is clearly to be thought of as the youngest, despite the assertion in Grimms' text that Three-Eye is youngest. The development of the tale will show this.

There was once a woman who had three daughters, the eldest of whom was called One-eye, because she had only one eye in the middle of her forehead, and the second, Two-eye, because she had two eyes like other folks, and the youngest, Three-eye, because she had three eyes; and her third eye was also in the center of her forehead.

The Germanic myths tell of the loss of the original one-eyed one. Odin wanted to drink from the spring of the dwarf Mimir, wherein wisdom and understanding were hidden. Mimir would not let him drink until he gave his eye as a pledge. In the *Völuspa*, the *Song of the Seeress*, it says

Well I know, Odin, where your eye rests:
In the famous spring of Mimir.
Mimir drinks mead every morning from Odin's pledge.
Do you know what that means?

Baldur, the Light, beloved by all, the god who lived in Breidablick – Breidablick means "Wide View" – was killed by the blind Hödur. Baldur embodies the capacity of that blessed time when Man was still a seer. This divine capacity faded; the blind Hödur came to rule. Odin wanted to know the future. To do so, he

had to go through what Baldur's death brought mankind: he must give up clairvoyance. The folk spirit, incarnated in Odin, must go through in advance the fate of its people. It says, therefore, not that Odin sacrificed *an* eye, but *his* eye.[25]

For the Greek age, Homer described in the picture-rich language of antiquity the wanderings of Odysseus. He is the clever and cunning personification of the Greek intellectual soul which must find its way over the bottomless depths of the soul world (the sea) to the firm land of clear thought. He encounters the one-eyed giant Polyphemos, the cyclops who lives in a cave in the rock. Think of *cyclops* as composed of *cycle* and *optic*; the one-eyed cyclops "sees all around" and represents ancient clairvoyant consciousness. Odysseus gauges out the one eye with a burning shaft. Greek thinking conquers atavistic clairvoyance, which sometimes appears as a sort of natural force that must be overcome. Man of the age of the intellectual soul must fight against these remnants.

Every child repeats in a certain sense the earlier stages of humanity's evolution, and so repeats this one-eye stage when the child is predominantly a sleep and dream being.

In tribes as yet untouched by modern civilization occasionally there appears an individual of the One-eye type, a naturally clairvoyant person who lives in a dreamy consciousness. Much more common is the Three-eye type, especially outside areas of western culture. This type is indeed awake to the sense world and has to some extent developed object consciousness, but the old clairvoyant capacities are still present, so that it does not go on to

---

25 It is not clear to what source the author is referring here. Generally Odin is depicted as having had two eyes, one of which is missing.

logical thinking. Only in modern Man, especially in western civilization, is the two-eyed type practically universal. He lives in the sense world, builds his perceptions from sense impressions, forms them into concepts and ideas, and in his I, grasps the world by thinking. The transition from the One-eye and Three-eye means, at first, a certain impoverishment. The mythological age foresaw the coming time of the "Twilight of the Gods" as a necessary transitional phase which would in due time lead to a new Age of Light. The myth says: when all beings weep, Baldur returns.

Old, out-dated, atavistic abilities can still be present in individual humans. They can even predominate and make trouble for the soul in its development. The ways of the past and of the future are in conflict. Our tale describes such a situation. It must be understood both in terms of the whole of humanity and in terms of the individual human.

However, as Two-eye saw just as other human beings did, her sisters and her mother could not endure her. They said to her, "Thou, with thy two eyes, art no better than the common people; thou dost not belong to us!" They pushed her about, and threw old clothes to her, and gave her nothing to eat but what they left, and did everything that they could to make her unhappy.

It came to pass that Two-eye had to go out into the fields and tend the goat, but she was still quite hungry, because her sisters had given her so little to eat. So she sat down on a ridge and began to weep, and so bitterly that two streams ran down from her eyes.

Three fundamental forces live in the human soul: feeling, thinking, and willing. In the picture language of the folktale, they are the three daughters of one mother. In this particular tale, in the mother the past is stressed. In the human, feeling (One-eye)

103

develops first and lives completely out of clairvoyant experience. The thinking of the intellect (Three-eye) already lives in the sense world, but the spiritual is not yet grasped by thought, but only dreamily conceived. Only the third daughter (Two-eye) lives fully in the sense world; the Will is directed essentially to the exploration of the outer world. While the mother and the two other sisters still have dreamy-clairvoyant experiences which nourish and satisfy them, the soul that has become free from those experiences hungers. Consequently, her radiance diminishes; her aura fades – her clothes are bad.

And once when she looked up in her grief, a woman was standing beside her, who said, "Why art thou weeping, little Two-eye?" Two-eye answered, "Have I not reason to weep, when I have two eyes like other people, and my sisters and mother hate me for it, and push me from one corner to another, throw old clothes at me, and give me nothing to eat but the scraps they leave? Today they have given me so little that I am still quite hungry." Then the wise woman said, "Wipe away thy tears, Two-eye, and I will tell thee something to stop thee ever suffering from hunger again; just say to thy goat,

> *"Bleat, my little goat, bleat,*
> *Cover the table with something to eat,"*

and then a clean well-spread little table will stand before thee, with the most delicious food upon it of which thou mayst eat as much as thou art inclined for, and when thou hast had enough, and hast no more need of the little table, just say,

> *"Bleat, bleat, my little goat, I pray,*
> *And take the table quite away,"*

and then it will vanish again from thy sight." Hereupon the wise woman departed. But Two-eye thought, "I must instantly make a trial, and see if what she said is true, for I am far too hungry," and she said,

> *"Bleat, my little goat, bleat,*
> *Cover the table with something to eat,"*

and scarcely had she spoken the words than a little table, covered with a white cloth, was standing there, and on it was a plate with a knife and fork, and a silver spoon; and the most delicious food was there also, warm and smoking as if it had just come out of the kitchen. Then Two-eye said the shortest prayer she knew, "Lord God, be with us always, Amen," and helped herself to some food, and enjoyed it. And when she was satisfied, she said, as the wise woman had taught her,

> *"Bleat, bleat, my little goat, I pray,*
> *And take the table quite away,"*

and immediately the little table and everything on it was gone again. "That is a delightful way of keeping house!" thought Two-eye, and was quite glad and happy.

When the Two-eye soul accepted the loss of her spiritual radiance – the poor clothes with apparent equanimity, no help came. But when she feels pain and cries, then comes change. When all beings cry, says the Germanic myth, Baldur returns. All encompassing pain from an all encompassing loss restores clairvoyance, world-clairvoyance. Pain creates transformation. While Two-eye cries, the old woman who gives advice appears. All of us know her and know also how often we have not followed her advice and later said "Had I but followed my hunch (*Ahnung*)!" *Ahnung* (hunch, suspicion, presentiment, foreboding) and *Ahne*

105

(ancestor) are closely related in their origins. Knowledge arises out of sorrow and distress and gives wise advice: "Just say to your goat 'Bleat, my little goat, bleat. Cover the table with something to eat,'[26] and then a clean well-spread little table will stand before thee with the most delicious food upon it."

No other animal is so inquisitive, so curious as a goat, looking into every corner, following every fence, nibbling on every grass and twig. So it becomes the symbol for curiosity and the desire for knowledge.

"To take the goat into the fields" means to use one's natural desire for knowledge and therefore to take the sense world into one's self. Now Two-eye takes the goat into the fields, but she is still hungry, for she nourishes herself only from what her mother and sisters have left over, from meager crumbs of ancient wisdom. But the modern soul cannot live on that, and as yet it has nothing new. It realizes: I must not be content with the paltry remains of the past which do not nourish me. I must be active and create for myself new spiritual nourishment. That I must do with the aid of that open-to-the-world drive called curiosity. I must make curiosity yield results that speak to me and teach me. When curiosity has led me to observe the outer world so thoroughly and so lovingly that everything I see – stone and star, plant and animal, the earth itself and its highest, Man – I experience as a wonder and can internally recreate it, then will I have the internal nourishment I seek. Then is the table set.

In the evening, when she went home with her goat, she found a small earthenware dish with some food, which her sisters had set ready for her, but she did not touch it. Next day she again went out

---

26 "Zicklein meck, Tischlein deck."

with her goat, and left the few bits of broken bread which had been handed to her, lying untouched. The first and second time that she did this, her sisters did not remark it at all, but as it happened every time, they did observe it, and said, "There is something wrong about Two-eye, she always leaves her food untasted, and she used to eat up everything that was given her; she must have discovered other ways of getting food." In order that they might learn the truth, they resolved to send One-eye with Two-eye when she went to drive her goat to the pasture, to observe what Two-eye did when she was there, and whether any one brought her anything to eat and drink. So when Two-eye set out the next time, One-eye went to her and said, "I will go with you to the pasture, and see that the goat is well taken care of, and driven where there is food." But Two-eye knew what was in One-eye's mind, and drove the goat into high grass and said, "Come, One-eye, we will sit down, and I will sing something to you." One-eye sat down and was tired with the unaccustomed walk and the heat of the sun, and Two-eye sang constantly,

> "One eye, wakest thou?
> One eye, sleepest thou?"

until One-eye shut her one eye, and fell asleep, and as soon as Two-eye saw that One-eye was fast asleep, and could discover nothing, she said,

> "Bleat, my little goat, bleat,
> Cover the table with something to eat,"

and seated herself at her table, and ate and drank until she was satisfied, and then she again said,

> "Bleat, bleat, my little goat, I pray,
> And take the table quite away,"

and in an instant all was gone. Two-eye now awakened One-eye, and said, "One-eye, you want to take care of the goat, and go to sleep while you are doing it, and in the meantime the goat might run all over the world. Come, let us go home again." So they went home, and again Two-eye let her little dish stand untouched, and One-eye could not tell her mother why she would not eat it, and to excuse herself said, "I fell asleep when I was out."

One-eye cannot perceive this wonder at all; she sleeps when the goat grazes. One stuck at this level can never know the satisfaction that the active use of the senses can give. Observed as an inner drama: So long as the sentient soul is a day-dreamer, it cannot participate in joy and satisfaction that an actively seeking soul can experience.

Next day the mother said to Three-eye, "This time thou shalt go and observe if Two-eye eats anything when she is out, and if any one fetches her food and drink, for she must eat and drink in secret." So Three-eye went to Two-eye, and said, "I will go with you and see if the goat is taken proper care of, and driven where there is food." But Two-eye knew what was in Three-eye' mind, and drove the goat into high grass and said, "We will sit down, and I will sing something to you, Three-eye." Three-eye sat down and was tired with the walk and with the heat of the sun, and Two-eye began the same song as before, and sang,

"Three-eye, are you waking?"

but then, instead of singing,

"Three-eye, are you sleeping?"

as she ought to have done, she thoughtlessly sang,

"Two-eye, are you sleeping?"

and sang all the time,

"Three-eye, are you waking?
Two-eye, are you sleeping?"

Then two of the eyes which Three-eye had, shut and fell asleep,
but the third, as it had not been named in the song, did not sleep. It
is true that Three-eye shut it, but only in her cunning, to pretend it
was asleep too, but it blinked, and could see everything very well.
And when Two-eye thought that Three-eye was fast asleep, she used
her little charm,

"Bleat, my little goat, bleat,
Cover the table with something to eat,"

and ate and drank as much as her heart desired, and then ordered
the table to go away again,

"Bleat, bleat, my little goat, I pray,
And take the table quite away,"

and Three-eye had seen everything. Then Two-eye came to her,
waked her and said, "Have you been asleep, Three-eye? You are a
good care-taker! Come, we will go home." And when they got home,
Two-eye again did not eat, and Three-eye said to the mother, "Now,
I know why that high-minded thing there does not eat. When she is
out, she says to the goat,

"Bleat, my little goat, bleat,
Cover the table with something to eat,"

and then a little table appears before her covered with the best of
food, much better than any we have here, and when she has eaten
all she wants, she says,

"Bleat, bleat, my little goat, I pray,

And take the table quite away,"

*and all disappears. I watched everything closely. She put two of my
eyes to sleep by using a certain form of words, but luckily the one in
my forehead kept awake." Then the envious mother cried, "Dost thou
want to fare better than we do? The desire shall pass away," and
she fetched a butcher knife, and thrust it into the heart of the goat,
which fell down dead.*

The experience of the Three-eye soul is quite different from
that of the One-eye soul. The Three-eye soul has already developed
object consciousness and lives and thinks in the sense world, but
beyond this is still clairvoyant. Because she sees on both planes she
can grasp what nourishes Two-eye and recognize the "Cover-the-
table-with-something-to-eat" process. Because she is predominantly
backwards directed, she rejects future science and becomes
arrogant and traitorish. Through her the Old in Man, the mother, is
aroused to action in opposition and in her hatred kills the innocent
longing for knowledge – the goat. Knife-sharp criticism, cutting
judgments, destructive scorn and mockery become the butcher
knife that kills the goat.

*When Two-eye saw that, she went out full of trouble, seated
herself on the ridge of grass at the edge of the field, and wept bitter
tears. Suddenly the wise woman once more stood by her side, and
said, "Two-eye, why art thou weeping?" - "Have I not reason to
weep?" she answered. "The goat which covered the table for me
every day when I spoke your charm, has been killed by my mother,
and now I shall again have to bear hunger and want." The wise
woman said, "Two-eye, I will give thee a piece of good advice; ask
thy sisters to give thee the entrails of the slaughtered goat, and bury
them in the ground in front of the house, and thy fortune will be*

made." Then she vanished, and Two-eye went home and said to her
sisters, "Dear sisters, do give me some part of my goat; I don't wish
for what is good, but give me the entrails." Then they laughed and
said, "If that's all you want, you can have it." So Two-eye took the
entrails and buried them quietly in the evening, in front of the house-
door, as the wise woman had counseled her to do.

Two-eye has reached a difficult crisis. The naive, trusting drive
for knowledge has been killed, and hunger again threatens. But
from pain prophetic wisdom is born. The old woman advises that
the entrails of the goat should be buried in front of the house door.

For "buried" one can also say "sunken". The dead are sunken
into the ground. But we also say "sunken deep in thought" when we
meditate. To bury the entrails of the goat means to deepen the
inner content of the drive for knowledge, to sink it completely into
the earthly in order that it may become newly resurrected and bring
forth fruit. While the feeling and thinking of the other part (the
mother and sisters) were averse to the earthly, so must precisely the
content of the longing to grasp the sense world be deepened and
turned to the earthly. In the materialistic sense, to kill means to
end. In the spiritual sense, death means transformation. The naive
desires are killed and must now be transformed.

Next morning, when they all awoke, and went to the house-
door, there stood a strangely magnificent tree with leaves of silver,
and fruit of gold hanging among them, so that in all the wide world
there was nothing more beautiful or precious. They did not know
how the tree could have come there during the night, but Two-eye
saw that it had grown up out of the entrails of the goat, for it was
standing on the exact spot where she had buried them.

Through the transformation there now grows the silver tree with golden fruit. The German expression "trees itself up" (*bäumt sich auf* meaning "to rear up") uses the image of the tree. Our nervous system grows and branches and forks like a tree. The developed soul was, up to this point fully given over to the impressions of the sense world and took them in in such a way that it could satisfy and nourish itself from them. This simple relationship was destroyed by the retarding, backwards-directed forces. The soul recognizes that it must *deepen* everything. That means that to penetrate it though thinking and understanding. Now intellectual thinking can appear in the image of silver, for however beautiful and shiny it may be, yet is it not true wisdom but only its reflection. Just as the silver moon reflects the sun, so intellectual thinking mirrors true wisdom. In its coolness it is related to the moon while wisdom is warm and sun-related. Two-eye, living in the sense world, has through sensation and perception come to concepts and now grasps the world with her thinking. Her nervous system is like a silver tree, and this tree bears a glorious fruit, the golden apple.

Paradise was lost when Man ate the apple from the tree of the knowledge of good and evil. We have already noted (page 43) why the botany of the apple makes it the perfect fruit to represent the temptation. Man, the noblest fruit of the Garden of God, separated himself off from the "upper" spiritual world of his origin and "fell" with his consciousness into the lower sense world. From separation there originated sin. To the knowledge of Good there was added the knowledge of Evil. This apple has become in our tale a golden apple for it has transformed itself into wisdom. Two-eye has through thinking recognized the material sense world (the tree) as

made from the spirit (the entrails). Rightfully can the tale say, " in all the wide world there was nothing more beautiful or precious."

Then the mother said to One-eye, "Climb up, my child, and gather some of the fruit of the tree for us." One-eye climbed up, but when she was about to get hold of one of the golden apples, the branch escaped from her hands, and that happened each time, so that she could not pluck a single apple, let her do what she might. Then said the mother, "Three-eye, do you climb up; you with your three eyes can look about you better than One-eye." One-eye slipped down, and Three-eye climbed up. Three-eye was not more skillful, and might search as she liked, but the golden apples always escaped her. At length the mother grew impatient, and climbed up herself, but could get hold of the fruit no better than One-eye and Three-eye, for she always clutched empty air. Then said Two-eye, "I will just go up, perhaps I may succeed better." The sisters cried, "You indeed, with your two eyes, what can you do?" But Two-eye climbed up, and the golden apples did not get out of her way, but came into her hand of their own accord, so that she could pluck them one after the other, and brought a whole apronful down with her. The mother took them away from her, and instead of treating poor Two-eye any better for this, she and One-eye and Three-eye were only envious, because Two-eye alone had been able to get the fruit, and they treated her still more cruelly.

It so befell that once when they were all standing together by the tree, a young knight came up. "Quick, Two-eye," cried the two sisters, "creep under this, and don't disgrace us!" and with all speed they turned an empty barrel which was standing close by the tree over poor Two-eye, and they pushed the golden apples which she had been gathering, under it too. When the knight came nearer he was a handsome lord, who stopped and admired the magnificent

113

gold and silver tree, and said to the two sisters, "To whom does this fine tree belong? Any one who would bestow one branch of it on me might in return for it ask whatsoever he desired." Then One-eye and Three-eye replied that the tree belonged to them, and that they would give him a branch. They both took great trouble, but they were not able to do it, for the branches and fruit both moved away from them every time. Then said the knight, "It is very strange that the tree should belong to you, and that you should still not be able to break a piece off." They again asserted that the tree was their property. Whilst they were saying so, Two-eye rolled out a couple of golden apples from under the barrel to the feet of the knight, for she was vexed with One-eye and Three-eye, for not speaking the truth. When the knight saw the apples he was astonished, and asked where they came from. One-eye and Three-eye answered that they had another sister, who was not allowed to show herself, for she had only two eyes like any common person. The knight, however, desired to see her, and cried, "Two-eye, come forth." Then Two-eye, quite comforted, came from beneath the barrel, and the knight was surprised at her great beauty, and said, "Thou, Two-eye, canst certainly break off a branch from the tree for me." - "Yes," replied Two-eye, "that I certainly shall be able to do, for the tree belongs to me." And she climbed up, and with the greatest ease broke off a branch with beautiful silver leaves and golden fruit, and gave it to the knight. Then said the knight, "Two-eye, what shall I give thee for it?" - "Alas!" answered Two-eye, "I suffer from hunger and thirst, grief and want, from early morning till late night; if you would take me with you, and deliver me from these things, I should be happy." So the knight lifted Two-eye on to his horse, and took her home with him to his father's castle, and there he gave her beautiful clothes, and meat and drink to her heart's content, and as he loved her so much he married her, and the wedding was solemnized with great

rejoicing. When Two-eye was thus carried away by the handsome knight, her two sisters grudged her good fortune in downright earnest. The wonderful tree, however, still remains with us," thought they, "and even if we can gather no fruit from it, still every one will stand still and look at it, and come to us and admire it. Who knows what good things may be in store for us?" But next morning, the tree had vanished, and all their hopes were at an end. And when Two-eye looked out of the window of her own little room, to her great delight it was standing in front of it, and so it had followed her.

Two-eye lived a long time in happiness. Once two poor women came to her in her castle, and begged for alms. She looked in their faces, and recognized her sisters, One-eye, and Three-eye, who had fallen into such poverty that they had to wander about and beg their bread from door to door. Two-eye, however, made them welcome, and was kind to them, and took care of them, so that they both with all their hearts repented the evil that they had done their sister in their youth.

Atavistic forces may posses many riches, but the fruit of this tree they will never harvest. The Two-eye soul, the feminine in Man in his advanced aspect, has won this fruit. She must be united with the masculine of the I if the harmonious whole Man is to be achieved. The I appears in the image of the knight. The retarded sisters can prevent the advanced soul from being recognized at once – they throw a barrel over Two-eye. They would like to win the knight for themselves. But an I that is armored with an iron will is not deceived. As Two-eye offers him the golden apple, the paradise myth sounds in a higher octave.

The Frog King or Iron Henry

Original Version

In the old times, when it was still of some use to wish for the thing one wanted, there lived a King whose daughters were all handsome, but the youngest was so beautiful that the sun himself, who has seen so much, wondered each time he shone over her because of her beauty. Near the royal castle there was a great dark wood, and in the wood under an old linden-tree was a well; and when the day was hot, the King's daughter used to go forth into the wood and sit by the brink of the cool well, and if the time seemed long, she would take out a golden ball, and throw it up and catch it again, and this was her favorite pastime. Once when the ball had flown very high, she had stretched out her her hand and curved her fingers to catch it again, but it fell near by on the earth and rolled straight into the water.

Bottomless deep is the soul life of Man, especially where it is compared to a well, from which creative forces arise. The princess-soul is close to this arising force as long as she remains in childhood. There she plays with that cosmic wisdom (the golden ball) which lives unconsciously in the child. Of this wisdom Friedrich Rückert says

O du Kindermund,	O thou child's mouth,
o du Kindermund,	o thou child's mouth
Unbewußter Weisheit froh!	Happy in unconscious wisdom!
Vogelsprachekund,	Knowing bird speech,

Vogelsprachekund,   knowing bird speech
Wie Salomo;[27]   Like Solomon.

But then one day it sinks away and the soul can no longer grasp
and comprehend it.

*The king's daughter followed it with her eyes as it sank, but the
well was deep, so deep that the bottom could not be seen. Then she
began to weep, and she wept and wept as if she could never be
comforted. And in the midst of her weeping she heard a voice saying
to her: "What ails thee, king's daughter? Thy tears would melt a
heart of stone." And when she looked to see where the voice came
from, there was nothing but a frog stretching his thick ugly head out
of the water. "Oh, is it you, old waddler?" said she, "I weep because
my golden ball has fallen into the well." - "Never mind, do not
weep," answered the frog, "I can help you; but what will you give me
if I fetch up your ball again?" - "Whatever you like, dear frog," said
she, "any of my clothes, my pearls and jewels, or even the golden
crown that I wear." - "Thy clothes, thy pearls and jewels, and thy
golden crown are not for me," answered the frog, "but if thou
wouldst love me, and have me for thy companion and play-fellow,
and let me sit by thee at table, and eat from thy plate, and drink
from thy cup, and sleep in thy little bed, if thou wouldst promise all
this, then would I dive below the water and fetch thee thy golden
ball again." - "Oh yes," she answered, "I will promise it all, whatever
you want, if you will only get me my ball again." But she thought to
herself: What nonsense he talks! As if he could do anything but sit in*

---

27   And Sulaiman (Solomon) inherited (the knowledge of) Dawud (David). He
     said: "O mankind! We have been taught the language of birds, and on us
     have been bestowed all things. This, verily, is an evident grace (from
     Allah)." – *The Koran*, Surah 27, verse 16.

117

the water and croak with the other frogs, or could possibly be any one's companion.

But the frog, as soon as he heard her promise, drew his head under the water and sank down out of sight, but after a while he came to the surface again with the ball in his mouth, and he threw it on the grass. The King's daughter was overjoyed to see her pretty plaything again, and she caught it up and ran off with it to her house. The frog called after her, "Wait, Princess, and take me with you as you promised," but she did not listen.

The princess was distressed, but distress leads to change. Hidden deep within there rests another force. In childhood it does not yet manifest itself, though it may slip into this or that instinct; but the soul remains unaware of it. But when cosmic wisdom sinks into the depths and the soul experiences the pain of its loss, then this force rises up. In our tale, it appears as the frog. It is the I.

The frog lives in two worlds, in water and on land, and is quite sensitive to the atmosphere. It is a weather prophet. We call someone a dreamer whose life is not "grounded on facts," who easily "sinks" into himself, who often "has his head under water." But if the dreamer has a sense for the social or political atmosphere and knows what the time demands, he is like a frog.

The I wants to be the partner of the soul: the personal I development must begin. But here the crisis begins. The partner appears in frog form. Quite rightfully the princess feels aversion. She must refuse to live with a being which at first can manifest itself only as a sub-human beast. But the ruling power in the soul, the king, knows more. The soul must be ready for the awakening of the I, even if it leads to crises. The door must be opened to the frog.

118

The next day, when the King's daughter was sitting at table with the King and all the court, and eating from her golden plate, there came something up the marble stairs plitsh, platsch! plitsh, platsch!, and then there came a knocking at the door, and a voice crying: "Youngest King's daughter, let me in!" And she got up and ran to see who it could be, but when she opened the door, there was the frog sitting outside. Then she shut the door hastily and went back to her seat, feeling very uneasy. The King noticed how quickly her heart was beating, and said: "My child, what are you afraid of? Is there a giant standing at the door ready to carry you away?" - "Oh no," answered she, "no giant, but a horrid frog." - "And what does the frog want?" asked the King. "O dear father," answered she, "when I was sitting by the well yesterday, and playing with my golden ball, it fell into the water, and while I was crying for the loss of it, the frog came and got it again for me on condition I would let him be my companion, but I never thought that he could leave the water and come after me; but now there he is outside the door, and he wants to come in to me." And then they all heard him knocking the second time and crying:

"Youngest King's daughter,
Open to me!
By the well water
What promised you me?
Youngest King's daughter
Now open to me!"

"That which thou hast promised must thou perform," said the King, "so go now and let him in." So she went and opened the door, and the frog hopped in, following at her heels, till she reached her chair. Then he stopped and cried: "Pick me up and put me on a chair beside you." But she delayed doing so until the King ordered

119

her. When once the frog was on the chair, he wanted to get onto the table, and there he sat and said: "Now push your golden plate a little nearer, so that we may eat together." And so she did, but everybody might see how unwilling she was, and the frog feasted heartily, but every morsel seemed to stick in her throat. "I have had enough now," said the frog at last, "and as I am tired, you must bring me up to your little room, and make ready your silken bed, and we will lie down and go to sleep." Then the King's daughter began to weep, and was afraid of the cold frog, that nothing would satisfy him but he must sleep in her pretty clean bed. Now the King grew angry with her, saying: "That which thou hast promised in thy time of necessity, must thou now perform."

"Pick me up," says the frog, "and put me on a chair beside you." I will not live below hidden in dull instincts, I want to be on your level, on your plane; I want the soul to be aware of me – so speaks the I. "Now push your golden plate a little nearer, so that we may eat together." Gold as a metal is related to the sun, to the radiant, life-giving day star. Its stability, its noble radiance make it the symbol for all noble stability, for the soul's kinship with the sun. But that is true wisdom that warms and enlightens. It does not hide or reflect. What it radiates it makes from its own substance. Wisdom should should be the basis of what the I and the soul both embody. It is the golden plate which is appropriate for both.

"Bring me up to your little room, and make ready your silken bed, and we will lie down." The little room is the heart, where I and soul must meet to understand one another.

So she picked up the frog with two fingers, carried him upstairs to her room, got into bed, but instead of putting the frog next to her,

she threw him, bratsch! against the wall, crying: "Now you will leave me in peace, you horrid frog!"

But the frog did not fall dead to the floor, but fell upon the bed. And as he did so, he ceased to be a frog, and became a handsome young prince. He was now her beloved partner and she held him dear, as she had promised, and they went happily to sleep together.

In the morning there came to the door a carriage drawn by eight horses, with white plumes on their heads, and with golden harness, and behind the carriage was standing faithful Henry, the servant of the young prince. Now, faithful Henry had suffered such care and pain when his master was turned into a frog, that he had been obliged to wear three iron bands over his heart, to keep it from breaking with trouble and anxiety. When the carriage started to take the prince to his kingdom, and faithful Henry had helped them both in, he got up behind, and was full of joy at his master's deliverance.

And when they had gone a part of the way, the prince heard a sound at the back of the carriage, as if something had broken, and he turned round and cried:

"Henry, the wheel must be breaking!"
"The wheel does not break,
'Tis the band round my heart
That, to lessen its ache,
When I grieved for your sake,
I bound round my heart."

Again, and yet once again there was the same sound, and the prince thought it must be the wheel breaking, but it was the breaking of the other bands from faithful Henry's heart, because it was now so relieved and happy.

121

In order that the I and the soul should recognize one another, the ruler within the soul, the king, must once more intervene. To this recognition belongs the absolute transformation and uplifting of the I. From an instinctive inner experience in animal form it must rise to an insightful, reasoning, thinking I that is turned to the world. From there is takes fructifying thoughts for the soul, and the partner becomes the husband. The royal wedding can be celebrated.

The interpretation of "Iron Henry" will not be undertaken here, for it is not relevant to the rest of the tale.

Translator's comment: Note that this is the Grimms' original version. They later added some lines, which were in the translation of the tale used here. I have tried to remove them all but may have missed some.

The author does not comment on perhaps the most puzzling part of the story: Why did throwing the frog against the wall break the spell? Perhaps because as the frog landed on the bed, all the conditions had been met. What does it mean that the princess is so unappreciative of what the frog did for her?

The Seven Ravens

Grimm 25

There was once a man who had seven sons, and still he had no daughter, however much he wished for one. At length his wife again gave him hope of a child, and when it came into the world it was a girl. The joy was great, but the child was frail and small, and had to be privately baptized on account of its weakness. The father sent one of the boys in haste to the spring to fetch water for the baptism. The other six went with him, and as each of them wanted to be first to fill it, the jug fell into the well. There they stood and did not know what to do, and none of them dared to go home. As they still did not return, the father grew impatient, and said, "They have certainly forgotten it for some game, the wicked boys!" He became afraid that the girl would have to die without being baptized, and in his anger cried, "I wish the boys were all turned into ravens." Hardly was the word spoken before he heard a whirring of wings over his head in the air, looked up and saw seven coal-black ravens flying away.

Our tale is one of those based on the number seven. To understand it we must live into the thought world of the middle ages. In the conceptions of that time Man is a small world within a great world, a microcosmos in the macrocosmos. The twelve-foldness of the zodiac and the sevenfoldness of the planets is reflected in the picture language of many folktales. The relation of the human organs was so widely understood that Paracelsus, an outstanding medieval physician, could often used planet names in place of organ names. The brain is related to the moon; the lungs, to Mercury; the kidneys, to Venus; the heart, to the sun; the gall-bladder, to Mars; the liver, to Jupiter; and the spleen, to Saturn.

In "The Mother Goat and the Seven Kids" we learned to recognize instinctive nature that shows up as compulsive curiosity, and can appear sevenfold. Here we have to do with different forces, forces of a more spiritual sort. As spiritual offshoots of the all-encompassing spiritual-soul of Man (father and mother) they are the seven sons, the seven brothers. They work in every human and are connected with the seven organs just mentioned. Intellectual ability is related to the brain; Mars-like will forces, to the gall bladder; warm and loving sincerity, to the heart. Each contributes its part to the whole. The tale depicts them as boys – young, naive, enthusiastic forces, very much still being developed. So were they once in hamanity as it went through its childhood and youth. So are they still today in every individual, when in childhood and youth he or she repeats this stage of human evolution.

The father and mother want a daughter. A new soul consciousness should come to stand beside these youthful spiritual forces. The picture of the *one and only daughter* points to a future soul being which is beginning to recognize itself as an individuality. It took a long time before this individual soul could become reality. The individual was determined by family, clan and folk and remained inwardly unfree. The tale says, "And when the daughter was finally born, she was frail and small."

All seven of the spiritual brothers wanted to be creative (*schöpferish* – see note on page 87) for the newborn soul being and bring to her the life-giving water, the water of baptism. Here it is indicated that the soul seeks a connection to the Christ. The brothers have the capacity[28] – the jug – to creatively accompany

---

28 "Capacity" translates *Fassungvermögen,* ability to hold. The *fass* root appears also in the *Gefäß,* the pitcher in which the brothers were to fetch the water. *Capacity* derives from the Latin, *capere* "to hold" so the same root

this process, but they cannot work harmoniously together, "each wanted to be first," and so they loose the capacity to work creatively. The jug falls into the spring.

The acquisition of a new ability in someone often means a crisis for his other abilities. They cannot come along with the new one; they must remain behind. The birth of the new I-related soul brings a darkening of the older spiritual forces – they are turned into ravens. We speak of the flight of thought, for like a bird in the air our thoughts rise and fly. We say, thoughts have wings. There is a German expression, "He has a bird," meaning he is crazy, out of his mind. The eagle and the falcon symbolize soaring, uplifting thoughts. The raven is something else. His shiny black feathers, his grave, earnest appearance, his almost ghostly but powerful flight make him the symbol for thoughts and wisdom that have darkened. Such ravens fly back and forth like messengers between the over-world and the human-world, between the Beyond and the Here.[29] So Wotan had his ravens, Hugin and Mugin, understanding and memory. So now the seven brothers work only as ravens. In folktales, a transformation of a human into an animal always means that spiritual forces full of human insight and capacity for knowledge have sunken to a instinctive, animal like level.

The parents could not recall the curse, and however sad they were at the loss of their seven sons, they still to some extent comforted themselves with their dear little daughter, who soon grew strong and every day became more beautiful. For a long time she did not know that she had had brothers, for her parents were careful

---

relations hold in English but are less obvious.

29 It is surely just this quality that made the raven the perfect bird to perch upon the "pallid bust of Pallas" where in answer to all questions, "Quoth the Raven, 'Nevermore.'"

not to mention them before her, but one day she accidentally heard some people saying of herself, "that the girl was certainly beautiful, but that in reality she was to blame for the misfortune which had befallen her seven brothers." Then she was much troubled, and went to her father and mother and asked if it was true that she had had brothers, and what had become of them? The parents now dared keep the secret no longer, but said that what had befallen her brothers was the will of Heaven, and that her birth had only been the innocent cause. But the maiden took it to heart daily, and thought she must deliver her brothers. She had no rest or peace until she set out secretly, and went forth into the wide world to trace out her brothers and set them free, let it cost what it might. She took nothing with her but a little ring belonging to her parents as a keepsake, a loaf of bread against hunger, a little pitcher of water against thirst, and a little chair as a provision against weariness.

The "only daughter" grew stronger, and in time learned of the fate of the brothers. And indeed it was a fate foreordained by heaven, for the human soul should strengthen the I and that means in the beginning a diminution of its other forces. But the daughter is the loving soul, and so cannot rest until the brothers are restored. There is far to go before this restoration can happen.

She takes with her a ring. What kind of ring? It was a treasure of the parents, but she takes it and carries it into the world and then to the brothers. Just as the circle is the expression of the All-encompassing, so is the ring. Just as it seamlessly unites beginning and end, so the soul experiences itself as a being without beginning or end once it has become aware of its I as the divine spark. Until this I-consciousness has been won, one cannot grasp one's self as a complete, self-directed being. One remains dependent and unfree, and must be led. Western Man struggles to become a self-directed

126

personality, to find the force of self-mastery, and to bring Love to all others and to the world. (Richard Wagner's *Ring des Nibelungen* is about this development.) The possibility of this transformation was implanted long ago in the inherited forces within Man: the ring belonged to father and mother. But in the young soul it becomes fully effective: the girl carries the ring.

And now she went continually onwards, far, far to the very end of the world. Then she came to the sun, but it was too hot and terrible, and devoured little children. Hastily she ran away, and ran to the moon, but it was far too cold, and also awful and malicious, and when it saw the child, it said, "I smell, I smell the flesh of men." On this she ran swiftly away, and came to the stars, which were kind and good to her, and each of them sat on its own particular little chair. But the morning star arose, and gave her the drumstick of a chicken, and said, "If thou hast not that drumstick thou canst not open the Glass mountain, and in the Glass mountain are thy brothers."

Far must the maiden go to find where the brothers are, to the end of the world, that is, to where the sense world ends and the supersensible world begins. The great teachers who gave us the folktales were convinced that humans, already in this life, can have access to that other world. They knew that the soul must learn to lift itself up to the starry world if it is to recognize and master its own destiny. The microcosmic forces, the seven brothers, must be macrocosmically recognized. The soul takes with her on her way a loaf of bread – spiritual nourishment and knowledge such as the earth offers – and water, ensouled feeling, as far as the earth can grant it – and also the necessary conceptual capacity, the pitcher.

The sun and moon, as representatives of day and night, can give her no guidance. The sun – the wide- awake day consciousness is too strong and would destroy what is child-like (it eats little children), and the moon, the regent of the night, which dissolves the individual, is as such also averse to the development of the independent I. The soul must push on to the realm of the planets, for they are the regents of the seven forces of being that have been darkened.[30]

"Each (star) sat on its own particular little chair." Just as she had with her her little chair, so did each star. On a chair one sits alone; the chair is sign of the individual. The girl has therefore taken with her the "equipment" for being an individual when she awakens within herself the cosmic forces. She remains, the chair reminds us, even in this higher world, an individual as the macro-cosmic forces awaken in her. The intelligences of the planets each speak to her individually so that she can understand and follow their advice. Wisdom of the stars is thereby experienced individually. (Thomas Aquinas ascribes to each planet its own particular intelligence.) In olden times, plunging into the macrocosm meant giving up one's own personality. The soul in our story – the maiden – preserves her I as she converses with the stars; she sits on her own chair.

The seven brothers live in a sphere which the tale calls the *Glassberg* (Glass Mountain). This *Berg* (mountain) is *bergende* (sheltering) and *verbergende* (concealing). It is what must be climbed, (one must be *auf der Höhe* – up to (a task)) or something that must be overcome (*überm Berg sein* – to be over the

---

30 There is a little problem here, for the seven traditional planets include the sun and moon, corresponding to heart and brain. Did the tale anticipate the discovery of two more big planets?

mountain). Here it means something that is hidden and must be opened. Glass is the result of solidification; it has hardened from a molten mass. The glass mountain is a sphere of hardening forces. We say that someone has "glass eyes" when we speak of an unfeeling, cold person. Also the eyes of the dying become glassy. Into this realm of stiffening and rigidity must the loving soul now enter.

The maiden took the drumstick, wrapped it carefully in a cloth, and went onwards again until she came to the Glass mountain. The door was shut, and she thought she would take out the drumstick; but when she undid the cloth, it was empty, and she had lost the good star's present. What was she now to do? She wished to rescue her brothers, and had no key to the Glass mountain. The good sister took a knife, cut off one of her little fingers, put it in the door, and succeeded in opening it. When she had gone inside, a little dwarf came to meet her, who said, "My child, what are you looking for?" - "I am looking for my brothers, the seven ravens," she replied. The dwarf said, "The lord ravens are not at home, but if you will wait here until they come, step in." Thereupon the little dwarf carried the ravens' dinner in, on seven little plates, and in seven little glasses, and the little sister ate a morsel from each plate, and from each little glass she took a sip, but in the last little glass she dropped the ring which she had brought away with her.

Into the realm of stiffening and rigidity must the sister enter. She had had the key to it as the gift of the morning star, but she had lost it. Who bears the ring of the personality and has borne it through a higher world must find in himself alone the force to open this realm. The personal sacrifice is the key, a sacrifice which cost the sister her own blood.

A dwarf in a folktale points to a definite nature spirituality. We speak today abstractly of nature forces and natural laws. The clairvoyant Man saw more. He saw spiritual forces of being in inner pictures and called them nature spirits. The elementary spirits that which worked principally in the earth, in stone and metal, he saw in the image of the dwarf. Now we also carry the "earth" in us, for the human body is taken from the earth and will return to the earth. We have also the metallic in us, for example the iron in the blood. The seven ravens eat the food the dwarf brings them, that is to say, the sevenfold young human spirit that has darkened during the time of the developing I-consciousness experiences of the earthly only what is bodily perceptible. His knowing has become, we may also say, because it is limited to the earthly, small and dwarf-like. It is connected to the world of the elements, but with nothing higher. It swirls darkly around like a raven. He knows that his organs are part of nature and are subject to natural laws. He knows a lot about the gall bladder as a physical organ but little or nothing of how the planet Mars is active in his thinking, feeling and willing and how the function of the gall is the basis for soul and spiritual processes. His knowing is nourishment for him, but it is "dwarf" nourishment. The soul takes part in this nourishment. She eats from each plate a morsel and drinks from each cup a sip. She unites in herself what has been seven ways divided and dwarfed, and since in her it has been unified she can give the ring. With it the brothers also receive the force of the self-contained I consciousness. They can now work together harmoniously on a higher level. They now receive the gifts of the soul which has brought strength and knowledge from higher worlds.

Suddenly she heard a whirring of wings and a rushing through the air, and then the little dwarf said, "Now the lord ravens are

flying home." Then they came, and wanted to eat and drink, and looked for their little plates and glasses. Then said one after the other, "Who has eaten something from my plate? Who has drunk out of my little glass? It was a human mouth." And when the seventh came to the bottom of the glass, the ring rolled against his mouth. Then he looked at it, and saw that it was a ring belonging to his father and mother, and said, "God grant that our sister may be here, and then we shall be free." When the maiden, who was standing behind the door watching, heard that wish, she came forth, and at that all the ravens were restored to their human form again. And they embraced and kissed each other, and went joyfully home.

The tale describes a soul drama that took place in the development of humanity as it left a childhood-like stage and became self-aware. The same inner drama takes place in every human as he leaves childhood behind and awakens to his own personality. The tale should help ensure that this self awareness does not become egotistical, for otherwise the spiritual forces that work in the human soul remain stunted as compulsions. Man should become a being of fully self-aware spirit and loving and understanding soul.

The Poor Miller's Boy and the Cat

Grimm 106

In a certain mill lived an old miller who had neither wife nor child, and three apprentices served under him. As they had been with him several years, he one day said to them, "I am old, and want to sit in the chimney-corner, go out, and whichsoever of you brings me the best horse home, to him will I give the mill, and in return for it he shall take care of me till my death."

All the experience that one has in life is like a harvest that must be brought in. And just as the grain must be ground to make of it flour and later bread, so also the fruit of a lifetime must be worked over to make from it knowledge, spiritual nourishment. For this process there must an inner force which is always active. The picture language of the tale calls it the miller. And the three fundamental forces in humans – thinking, feeling, and willing – from this point of view are like three miller boys.

The third of the boys was, however, the drudge, who was looked on as foolish by the others; they begrudged the mill to him, and afterwards he would not have it. Then all three went out together, and when they came to the village, the two said to stupid Hans, "Thou mayst just as well stay here, as long as thou livest thou wilt never get a horse." Hans, however, went with them, and when it was night they came to a cave in which they lay down to sleep. The two sharp ones waited until Hans had fallen asleep, then they got up, and went away leaving him where he was. And they thought they had done a very clever thing, but it was certain to turn out ill for them. When the sun arose, and Hans woke up, he was lying in a

132

deep cavern. He looked around on every side and exclaimed, "Oh, heavens, where am I?" Then he got up and clambered out of the cave, went into the forest, and thought, "Here I am quite alone and deserted, how shall I obtain a horse now?"

When an old spiritual force – the old father, the old king, the old miller – draws back, there arises the question of what force will take over the leadership. In many tales, it proves to be the youngest of three. This youngest always has the property that he is ignorant or silly and dumb. That he is moreover often called Hans (John) is of deep significance, as we shall see.

The force of the Will is in fact the youngest in the human. We are just at the beginning of its formation. One must not confuse true Will with wishes or desires and also not with stubbornness and obstinacy. Many events of our time become understandable when they are seen as the birth pains of the free Will. But what should this free Will be? The wise tellers of the tales say it should be pure and devote itself wholeheartedly to purposes that the clever consider superfluous. As St. Paul says, "But God hath chosen the foolish things of the world to confound the wise. [31]

The German language has many expressions that make clear what the picture of the horse means. To have "horse sense" means (as in English) to have good common sense. To be "on his high horse" means (as in English) to be arrogant, and "the nag ran away with him"[32] means that faulty thinking (the nag) took control of him. The horse points to thinking. Plato compared the understanding with a horse that one holds with a bridle. Picture language uses expression like "bridle yourself," or "sit firmly in the

---

31 1. Corinthians 1:27. King James version.
32 "Der Gaul ist mit ihm durchgegangen."

saddle," "don't gallop off." Our tale tells how "Dumb Hans" wins his horse. Now there are various ways to develop a Will which will bear one "with understanding" through life so that one finally becomes a strong, understanding master of ones own will. This tale describes the transformation of the love drive as one such way. The two older boys – Feeling and Thinking – keep themselves far from the Will. The Will must "clamber out of the cave" by himself and set out on the way.

Whilst he was thus walking full of thought, he met a small calico[33]-cat which said quite kindly, "Hans, where are you going?" - "Alas, thou canst not help me." - "I well know your desire," said the cat. "You wish to have a beautiful horse. Come with me, and be my faithful servant for seven years long, and then I will give you one more beautiful than any you have ever seen in your whole life." - "Well, this is a wonderful cat!" thought Hans, "but I am determined to see if she is telling the truth."

In the folktales, animals are images of our drives and instincts. Hans knows that in the instincts there is a certain natural wisdom and that one can gain much if one deals with them in the right way. One cannot gain understanding without first consulting one's own instincts. But they must be the right instincts, and one must know clearly what one wants to learn – especially from cats.

If we will carefully observe a cat, how she slinks about on soft paws, lies still for a long time with sleepy eyes, then springs and pounces, and also observe how she becomes active and wide-awake at night, especially at full moon – then we know the calico cat Hans met. In ancient Egypt, Bastet, the goddess of love magic, was

---

33 The German is *bunte,* colorful. The calico cat has three colors, which is the most a cat can have. Such cats are always female.

depicted with a cat's head.[34] Hans now entrusts himself to his love instincts. The love-drive should bring him understanding; the cat helps him to get the horse.

So she took him with her into her enchanted castle, where there were nothing but cats who were her servants. They leapt nimbly upstairs and downstairs, and were merry and happy. In the evening when they sat down to dinner, three of them had to make music. One played the bass, another the fiddle, and the third put the trumpet to his lips, and blew out his cheeks as much as he possibly could.

More delightfully is this realm described in no other tale. In the evening, when the day's work is done, the longing for love awakens. It is important to live in harmony with this drive. Three parts of each human are clearly mentioned: the bass stands for lower part of the body, the fiddle for the middle, and the trumpet for the head.

When they had dined, the table was carried away, and the cat said, "Now, Hans, come and dance with me." - "No," said he, "I won't dance with a pussy cat. I have never done that." - "Then take him to bed," said she to the cats.

Now comes the crucial point of the story. The cat says, "Now, Hans, come and dance with me." - "No," said he, "I won't dance

---

34 Bastet does indeed have a cat's head, but her connection with love magic is not often mentioned. However, in *Ägyptische Magie im Wandel der Zeiten*, a document accompanying an exhibit of the Institute of Papyrology of the University of Heidelberg, 2011, in the article by Svenja Nagel und Fabian Wespi we read (in translation) "The Egyptian goddess Bastet, whose name means 'She of the ointment jar' was, like Isis and Hathor, responsible for, among other things, women's beauty and love in general." The ointment jar connection comes through the similarity of the words *Bastet* and ala*baster*.

with a pussy cat. I have never done that." That means: "I don't let myself spin round and round with cat-drives; I do not get drawn into that whirlpool." In other words, "I know how to master myself."

So one of them lighted him to his bed-room, one pulled his shoes off, one his stockings, and at last one of them blew out the candle. Next morning they returned and helped him out of bed, one put his stockings on for him, one tied his garters, one brought his shoes, one washed him, and one dried his face with her tail. "That feels very soft!" said Hans.

Tenderly but clearly the tale describes the relaxation of the whole being one may experience when, with inner self control one releases these caring forces and then, in the morning brings them back newly collected and ordered.

He, however, had to serve the cat, and chop fire wood every day, and to do that, he had an axe of silver, and the wedge and saw were of silver and the mallet of copper. So he chopped the wood small; stayed there in the house and had good meat and drink, but never saw anyone but the calico cat and her servants.

The human reproductive forces are related to the moon. To work with these in the right way is to use a silver tool. It serves to cut the wood into small pieces. Abstract, intellectual thinking is a sort of lignified thinking that is to its spiritual origin as harden wood is to a living tree. But this thinking is nevertheless important and must be practiced. To form concrete concepts, to take apart analytically is "to chop firewood" in picture language. Thinking is work; it warms and maintains the inner fire.

Since our hero is called Hans, it is not surprising that in addition to the silver ax, he gets a hammer of copper. For the wise alchemists of the Middle Ages, who in material processes meditatively experienced creative forces, copper was the symbol of piety. They called the condition of childlike piety the copper condition. With the driving force of the of active piety (the copper hammer) one can get to work with moon forces that have been lying fallow. So can one interpret the picture.

Once she said to him, "Go and mow my meadow, and dry the grass," and gave him a scythe of silver, and a whetstone of gold, but bade him deliver them up again carefully. So Hans went thither, and did what he was bidden, and when he had finished the work, he carried the scythe, whetstone, and hay to the house, and asked if it was not yet time for her to give him his reward.

Life, growth, and reproduction can lead to over-luxuriant proliferation. Analytical, abstract thinking has to be applied in diligent, woodchopper fashion to hold it in check – the meadow must be mowed. But the harvest – the gift of the youthful blooming forces – must be brought in. Much wisdom is hidden in the cat's love instinct. From it comes the golden whetstone with which the forces of judgment (the scythe) must be sharpened over and over, and good, well-sharpened power of judgment in necessary in this field. With it, Hans has come a step further in his development and can hope to soon have his horse.

"No," said the cat, "you must first do something more for me of the same kind. There is timber of silver, carpenter's axe, square, and everything that is needful, all of silver, with these build me a small house." Then Hans built the small house, and said that he had now

done everything, and still he had no horse. Nevertheless the seven years had gone by with him as if they were six months.

The totality of the inner moon forces must still be built and formed. When that is done, the love drive has received its desired housing, and everything that lives in this sphere is formed and firmed up. The process has required seven years. In each human this process generally occurs between the fourteenth and twenty-first years. During those years both abstract and concrete thinking must be developed and used, and the power of discretion and judgment gained. The "Moon-Man" must be completed.

The cat asked him if he would like to see her horses? "Yes," said Hans. Then she opened the door of the small house, and when she had opened it, there stood twelve horses, such horses, so bright and shining, that his heart rejoiced at the sight of them. And now she gave him to eat and drink, and said, "Go home, I will not give thee thy horse away with thee; but in three days' time I will follow thee and bring it."

The significance of twelve as a cosmic number has already been discussed (see page 20). The twelve constellations of the zodiac represent the totality of the macrocosmic forces that build the microsmic Man. Hans has continuously exercised his forces of understanding and formed and built out his inner moon sphere. Thereby has he attained an encompassing wisdom (twelve horses) and with it the *Understanding* which is to him as an I the most useful – his own horse.

So Hans set out, and she showed him the way to the mill. She had, however, never once given him a new coat, and he had been obliged to keep on his dirty old smock-frock, which he had brought with him, and which during the seven years had everywhere become

too small for him. When he reached home, the two other apprentices were there again as well, and each of them certainly had brought a horse with him, but one of them was a blind one, and the other lame. They asked Hans where his horse was. "It will follow me in three days' time." Then they laughed and said, "Indeed, stupid Hans, where wilt thou get a horse?" - "It will be a fine one!" Hans went into the parlour, but the miller said he should not sit down to table, for he was so ragged and torn, that they would all be ashamed of him if any one came in. So they gave him a mouthful of food outside, and at night, when they went to rest, the two others would not let him have a bed, and at last he was forced to creep into the goose-house, and lie down on a little hard straw.

Now when the two older miller's boys came home, it was revealed what each had won. The oldest – living only in feeling – had gotten an understanding that could see through nothing and had no insight – his horse is blind. The second boy, corresponding to thinking ability, has developed an understanding that can go no further in life: his horse limps. Hans in his development far surpassed the stage of a miller's boy, but that is revealed only when a transformation of the love-drive (the cat) has become visible. The tale continues:

In the morning when he awoke, the three days had passed, and a coach came with six horses and they shone so bright that it was delightful to see them! and a servant brought a seventh as well, which was for the poor miller's boy. And a magnificent princess alighted from the coach and went into the mill, and this princess was the little calico-cat whom poor Hans had served for seven years. She asked the miller where the miller's boy and drudge was? Then the miller said, "We cannot have him here in the mill, for he is so ragged; he is lying in the goose-house." Then the King's daughter

said that they were to bring him immediately. So they brought him out, and he had to hold his little smock-frock together to cover himself. The servants unpacked splendid garments, and washed him and dressed him, and when that was done, no King could have looked more handsome. Then the maiden desired to see the horses which the other apprentices had brought home with them, and one of them was blind and the other lame. So she ordered the servant to bring the seventh horse, and when the miller saw it, he said that such a horse as that had never yet entered his yard. "And that is for the third miller's boy," said she. "Then he must have the mill," said the miller, but the King's daughter said that the horse was there, and that he was to keep his mill as well, and took her faithful Hans and set him in the coach, and drove away with him. They first drove to the little house which he had built with the silver tools, and behold it was a great castle, and everything inside it was of silver and gold; and then she married him, and he was rich, so rich that he had enough for all the rest of his life. After this, let no one ever say that anyone who is silly can never become a person of importance.

The calico-cat has become a beautiful, royal young woman. That means: this unconscious, playful force of nature that had worked just instinctively, has become a soul force worthy of Man – it has become Love. And "dumb Hans" – the Will in Parzival-like purity – can unite with this force of Love.[35]

---

35 It seems fair to say that Hans's work transforms not only himself but also the cat. It is the house he has built – not the cat's house – which becomes the new palace. Hans never saw any horses until his work was completed. Did he perhaps create them also?

The Donkey

Grimm 144

The ass often seems to have a split personality. Anyone who gets well acquainted with one will notice this. He won't willingly take a bridle and bit and let himself be guided as does a horse. He is therefore not so much for riding as for carrying loads. If you need to reach a definite goal in a definite time, better not count on an ass to get you there. And in dealing with one, be prepared for surprises. If riding an ass in a group, best to have a driver, for the ass prefers to follow his own head and is willful and stubborn. He is sometimes therefore thought to be dumb, though he is a rather intelligent animal. Release him, for example in the mountains, and he will find his way with calm assurance; and when danger threatens, he knows what to do. In bearing of burdens he is exceptionally patient and has long been used for carrying sacks. Bad treatment and even blows with a stick he bears with stoic serenity. He is simultaneously unruly and dependable, stubborn and patient, dumb and wise.

Who bears us through life, without letting himself be much influenced, always goes his own way, does not gladly obey, follows obstinately and at his inherited tempo and must be constantly be urged on lest he sink into comfort and sloth? Who, however, serves us untiringly, bears for years the blows of an unwise life style, and often knows better than the one who presumes to direct him?

It is, of course, our bodily nature, our physical body itself, as bearer of soul and spirit. It is the "Brother Ass" as Francis of Assisi called it. "What an ass I am," we say when our spirit lets us down.

141

We scold others as a "dumb ass" or may say to them "Hold your ears up straight."[36]

The ass motif has a long history in literature. We first hear of it in ancient Egypt. Plutarch reports in his *Moralia,* in the section called "Isis and Osiris" [37] the following myth:

In most ancient times the god Osiris lived with his sister and wife Isis among a happy people. It was the golden age. Osiris had an envious brother, Typhon or Set, who secretly measured Osiris and made a beautiful casket in the form of the human body to exactly fit him. He then brought the casket to the court of Osiris and said that it should belong to whomever it best fit. One by one, everyone tried it, but there was no perfect fit until last of all Osiris got in. It fit perfectly, but Seth slammed the lid shut and Osiris suffocated. (Set-Typhon is depicted as a composite animal that is part ass, part aardvark, and part jackal. In late Egypt, he becomes either an ass or has the head of an ass.) Isis weeps and wails. Osiris, who is also called "the seeing eye" is no longer on earth. But the Egyptian myth says: In the life after death we find him again. There, in the other world the human soul, after purification, is received at heaven's gate by the gods with the words, "Thou, o Osiris, thou hast regained the solar-eye that was on earth taken from you by the evil forces."

From all this we see that Osiris once worked as a divine being not only *among* the people of the earth, but also as the higher self in each human being. But this age came to an end. Enclosed in a casket that has the form of the human body means: the human

---

36 "Haltet die Ohren steif" seems to have the idiomatic meaning of "Keep a stiff upper lip" or "Hold your chin up."

37 The passage begins at 356 B in the standard numbering. It is in volume 5, page 35 of the Loeb Classical Library edition of Plutarch's *Moralia.*

body so densified and hardened that the Osiris-self could no longer express and manifest itself in it. And therewith the all-seeing eye went out; clairvoyance died away.

But the initiate who has gone through certain purifications and transformations and knows a supersensible world from his own experience can, even in this life, come to inner vision and behold the living Osiris. Mozart's opera, *The Magic Flute* refers to this process.

To imaginative vision the love nature transformed by Seth appears in the image of the ass. For where the divine eye, supersensible perception, disappears, bodily sense perception becomes all the intensive. Where wisdom regarding the other world dies, knowledge of this world becomes more significant. Man becomes cosmically dumb and at the same time earthly clever. And the Will becomes split two ways – or more – and behavior is also split. Yet despite these contradictions, our body bears it all patiently like a good donkey.[38]

At the time of Joshua's conquest of Palestine there was a tribe called the Hivites living in the general area of Gilead that worshiped a god by the name of Thartak who had the form of an ass. Thartak made his way into Kabbalistic writings, and in *Les Mystères de la Kabbale* (1861), Eliphas Levi shows Thartak as a man with the head of an ass clutching a book to his chest and representing blind faith. The Roman writer Tertullian reports the

---

38 There follows here a paragraph about Thartuk which I believe to be inaccurate because based on a less than totally accurate source. I have replaced it with what I could learn about Thartuk from old, 19th century German scholarly tomes now found on the Internet. Simply searching for *Thartak* yielded nothing useful; searching instead for *Thartak Esel* brought up many relevant references in German.

appearance of this figure as a caricature. He relates that an apostate Jew one day appeared in the streets of Carthage carrying a figure robed in a toga, with the ears and hoofs of an ass, and labeled: *Deus Christianorum Onocoetes* (the God of the Christians begotten of an ass). "And the crowd believed this infamous Jew", adds Tertullian (*Ad nationes*, I, 14)[39] And yet there was a grain of truth in the accusation, for some Christians taught, "Learn to believe without seeing or understanding."

In the Bible we are told of a speaking ass, that of Bileam (Numbers 22:21-38) who sees the angel when his master does not. He saves his master but is beaten for it until "the Lord opened the mouth of the ass" and eventually the eyes of Bileam. Here the bodily nature works through inspiration; it knows instantly of deep connections which our consciousness recognizes more slowly.

Such knowledge is also the foundation for the *Golden Ass* of Apulius. This work coming from the second century is often viewed as just a picaresque novel, the adventures of a rogue. In reality, however, there is hidden in it a deep mystery wisdom which at that time could not be spoken of openly. A young man was turned externally into an ass, had many adventures, and only when the ass ate roses from the hand of a priestess of Isis was he changed back into his human form and was initiated into the mysteries of Isis. With his title of the *golden* ass, Apulius wished to say that the bodily nature is full of natural wisdom.

Later this bodily nature was impoverished; the ass was no longer golden, but he sometimes still spits gold, as the story "The Wishing-Table, the Gold-Ass, and the Cudgel in the Sack" (Grimm 36) tells us. However, one must have learned from the master for a

---

39 Again, more re-write than translation.

144

long time and must know the right word, then the ass gives gold (wisdom) from the front (consciously) and from the rear (unconsciously). Finally, we get a perfectly ordinary gray work donkey in Shakespeare's *Midsummer Night's Dream.* But Shakespeare knew what he was doing when he put the donkey's head on Bottom the *weaver,* who all day long works with threads-- and we recall the connection of thread and thought.

The question is now, How can we transform this gray ass, how can we make the body permeable by the spirit and submissive to it?

On a Sumerian vase there is a picture of an ass with a harp; on the south side of the Chartres cathedral stands carved in stone a rather large ass with a lyre – a symbol also on other French cathedrals. In the choir stalls of the St. Mary's Church in Lübeck we even see an ass playing the organ. Pursue music, say the pictures and sculptures, and you will transform your inherited bodily nature, you will release the ass from its enchantment. Our tale of the little donkey says the same.

Once on a time there lived a King and a Queen, who were rich, and had everything they wanted, but no children. The Queen lamented over this day and night, and said, "I am like a field on which nothing grows." At last God gave her her wish, but when the child came into the world, it did not look like a human child, but was a little donkey.

In the golden age of mankind, the human spirit was rich in manifestations of the spiritual world which were given by grace. Man was robed with the mantel of an encompassing dignity and wore the crown of wisdom. He was like a king; and his soul, like a queen. But they had no child. That means: the golden age long endured – Ovid and Hesiod say twenty thousand years – before the

transformation of consciousness and a new kind of human was born. The new kind had a physical body that was no longer in the same way permeable by the spirit and submissive to it. Man had put on a cloak of animality and no longer resembled his divine archetype.

When the mother saw that, her lamentations and outcries began in real earnest; she said she would far rather have had no child at all than have a donkey, and that they were to throw it into the water that the fishes might devour it. But the King said, "No, since God has sent him he shall be my son and heir, and after my death sit on the royal throne, and wear the kingly crown."

The soul despairs and won't recognize this fact. But the inner ruler says: Yes, God has allowed a transformation of consciousness of the human into the animal, and indeed given mankind animal skins to wear – just as the Bible says.[40] Moreover, this new man will someday inherit the kingdom, although it will be a very different kingdom. If the first was bestowed through grace, the second must be attained through hard work, pain and suffering. But Man attains through that process a higher goal; He achieves personality; He finds his I. Not the egotistical lower I – that is only one step of the way – but his higher, unselfish, love-filled true I.

The donkey, therefore, was brought up and grew bigger, and his ears grew up beautifully high and straight. He was, however, of a merry disposition, jumped about, played and had especial pleasure in music, so that he went to a celebrated musician and said, "Teach me thine art, that I may play the lute as well as thou dost." - "Ah, dear little master," answered the musician, "that would come very

---

40 "And the Lord God made for Adam and for his wife garments of skins, and clothed them." Genesis 3:21. RSV

146

*hard to you, your fingers are certainly not suited to it, and are far
too big. I am afraid the strings would not last." No excuses were of
any use. The donkey was determined to play the lute; he was
persevering and industrious, and at last learned to do it as well as
the master himself.*

To hold the ears up fine and straight means not to let oneself
be beaten down. That is the first strength the young I ripening into
personality must acquire. The main theme of the tale is then
sounded: the way that will lead to change and transformation is
music, music in both the narrow sense and in the broader sense of
harmony and consonance with the spiritual world. The ass becomes
both a listener and an artist. Should we not think of Socrates? At
the time when inner vision was coming to an end among the Greeks
and mankind was becoming insensitive to the cosmos but more and
more awake to the physical world, it was he who practiced and
taught intellectual thinking, like a true king's son in the skin of an
ass. His daimon told him, "Socrates, study music," but he did not
follow this advice.

One who can play the magic flute scares away the animal
forms of evil drives, goes unharmed through the fire of the lower
passions, does not sink helplessly into the waves of uncontrolled
feeling, and reaches finally the sun temple of initiation. One must,
however, find a master who can teach this art. And he must practice
diligently and patiently.

*The young lordling once went out walking full of thought and
came to a well, he looked into it and in the mirror-clear water saw
his donkey's form. He was so distressed about it, that he went out
into the wide world and only took with him one faithful companion.*

147

Now there must be an act of self-recognition, a realization that one is no longer like one's true cosmic archetype. This awareness does not much bother a superficial person, but to one who has studied with a master it is deeply disturbing. He knows that he cannot remain in the inherited realm of his father. He must seek another with his own forces.

They traveled up and down, and at last they came into a kingdom where an old King reigned who had an only but wonderfully beautiful daughter. The donkey said, "Here we will stay," knocked at the gate, and cried, "A guest is without; open that he may enter." As, however, the gate was not opened, he sat down, took his lute and played it in the most delightful manner with his two fore-feet. Then the door-keeper opened his eyes most wonderfully wide, and ran to the King and said, "Outside by the gate sits a young donkey which plays the lute as well as an experienced master!" - "Then let the musician come to me," said the King.

When, however, a donkey came in, every one began to laugh at the lute-player. And now the donkey was asked to sit down and eat with the servants. He, however, was unwilling, and said, "I am no common stable-ass, I am a noble one." Then they said, "If that is what thou art, seat thyself with the men of war." - "No," said he, "I will sit by the King." The King smiled, and said good-humouredly, "Yes, it shall be as thou wilt, little ass, come here to me."

Who is the king with an only but wonderfully beautiful daughter? This daughter is the soul and the father is the ruling power in the soul realm. The king's son has arrived from the realm of the fatherly Self into the realm of the soul. Music has given him access. Now follow the tests. First, is he aware of his own worth? He is seated among the servants, but he says "I am no common

148

stable-ass, I am a noble one." That means, the I is of a noble nature and as such is not related to the animals. One could also say, it should not make itself common. They say, "Then sit with the men of war." But the I is not of a waring nature. It desires the kingship of the soul, nothing less.

Then he asked, "Little ass, how does my daughter please thee?" The donkey turned his head towards her, looked at her, nodded and said, "I like her above measure, I have never yet seen anyone so beautiful as she is." - "Well, then, thou shalt sit next her too," said the King. "That is exactly what I wish," said the donkey, and he placed himself by her side, ate and drank, and knew how to behave himself daintily and cleanly.

Whoever strives for kingship approaches the I-bearing soul and begins to become acquainted. It is a fine touch of the tale that it mentions good and fine manners. What is good breeding other than mastery of forms? This also must one acquire precisely because the animal kinship of the body demands a constant moderation.

When the noble beast had stayed a long time at the King's court, he thought, "What good does all this do me, I shall still have to go home again?" let his head hang sadly, and went to the King and asked for his dismissal. But the King had grown fond of him, and said, "Little ass, what ails thee? Thou lookest as sour as a jug of vinegar, I will give thee what thou wantest. Dost thou want gold?" - "No," said the donkey, and shook his head. "Dost thou want jewels and rich dress?" - "No." - "Dost thou wish for half my kingdom?" - "Indeed, no." Then said the King, if I did but know what would make thee content. Wilt thou have my pretty daughter to wife?" - "Ah, yes," said the ass, "I should indeed like her," and all at once he

became quite merry and full of happiness, for that was exactly what he was wishing for.

When an I has reached the highest decision point, another trial must follow, and this trial is of a double nature. Love wants to become one, but may the I still afflicted with animal "hide" hope for this unification? Modesty dares not. Must not the ruler in the soul realm ask what is dearest to the I? Wisdom (gold)? Beauty (jewels)? Rulership (half the kingdom)? Or the eternal-feminine of the soul itself?

So a great and splendid wedding was held. In the evening, when the bride and bridegroom were led into their bed-room, the King wanted to know if the ass would behave well, and ordered a servant to hide himself there. When they were both within, the bridegroom bolted the door, looked around, and as he believed that they were quite alone, he suddenly threw off his ass's skin, and stood there in the form of a handsome royal youth. "Now," said he, "thou seest who I am, and seest also that I am not unworthy of thee." Then the bride was glad, and kissed him, and loved him dearly. When morning came, he jumped up, put his animal's skin on again, and no one could have guessed what kind of a form was hidden beneath it.

What now follows are pictures of the royal wedding, as this process is called. The spirit, the striving I, that through constant effort transforms itself, is accepted by the soul, who unites herself with him. This wedding takes place in two or three stages during the night. During the night, the I is not in the body (we are unconscious); it withdraws from the body and enters the world which is its true home. Sleep is holy, as was said in olden times. In this world the I can show itself in its true form. "Now thou seest

who I am, and seest also that I am not unworthy of thee." But in the morning, the animal skin must be put on again.

Soon came the old King, "Ah," cried he, "is the little ass merry? But surely thou art sad?" said he to his daughter, "that thou hast not got a proper man for thy husband?" - "Oh, no, dear father, I love him as well as if he were the handsomest in the world, and I will keep him as long as I live." The King was surprised, but the servant who had concealed himself came and revealed everything to him. The King said, "That cannot be true." - "Then watch yourself the next night, and you will see it with your own eyes; and hark you, lord King, if you were to take his skin away and throw it in the fire, he would be forced to show himself in his true shape." - "Thy advice is good," said the King, and at night when they were asleep, he stole in, and when he got to the bed he saw by the light of the moon a noble-looking youth lying there, and the skin lay stretched on the ground. So he took it away, and had a great fire lighted outside, and threw the skin into it, and remained by it himself until it was all burnt to ashes. As, however, he was anxious to know how the robbed man would behave himself, he stayed awake the whole night and watched. When the youth had slept his sleep out, he got up by the first light of morning, and wanted to put on the ass's skin, but it was not to be found. On this he was alarmed, and, full of grief and anxiety, said, "Now I shall have to contrive to escape." But when he went out, there stood the King, who said, "My son, whither away in such haste? what hast thou in mind? Stay here, thou art such a handsome man, thou shalt not go away from me. I will now give thee half my kingdom, and after my death thou shalt have the whole of it." - "Then I hope that what begins so well may end well, and I will stay with you," said the youth. And the old man gave him half the kingdom, and in a year's time, when he died, the youth had the

151

whole, and after the death of his father he had another kingdom as well, and lived in all magnificence.

One can both serve and rule, and often the servant in him knows more than the ruler, and the ruler should let himself be advised by the servant. And so here it is the servant who first recognizes the transformation. But only the ruler can burn the skin in the purifying fire of his spirit and declare the I free and recognize it with the words "Stay here, thou art such a handsome man." It is again a fine touch in the telling of the tale that the word "handsome" (in German, *schöne,* beautiful) is used. This word *schöne* is related to German *schein* (= English *shine*). "Through thee there shines thy genuine being; thou art again like thy true archetype (Urbild)."

With this recognition the prince wins a new realm which he, fully awake in spirit and richly endowed with soul, knows how to rule. He receives also his father's kingdom, from which he came.

No other of the Grimm tales is so full of humor. The teller must have been a master player of the lute, which was taught to the little donkey and which opened for him the way to his own self fulfillment. But the proverb says, "The ass that can't play the lute must carry sacks to the mill."

The Bremen City Musicians

Grimm 27

There was once an ass whose master had made him carry sacks to the mill for many a long year, but whose strength began at last to fail, so that each day as it came found him less capable of work. Then his master began to think of turning him out, but the ass, guessing that something was in the wind that boded him no good, ran away, taking the road to Bremen; for there he thought he might get an engagement as town musician. When he had gone a little way he found a hound lying by the side of the road panting, as if he had run a long way. "Now, Holdfast, what are you so out of breath about?" said the ass. "Oh dear!" said the dog, "now I am old, I get weaker every day, and can do no good in the hunt, so, as my master was going to have me killed, I have made my escape; but now, how am I to gain a living?" - "I will tell you what," said the ass, "I am going to Bremen to become town musician. You may as well go with me, and take up music too. I can play the lute, and you can beat the drum." And the dog consented, and they walked on together. It was not long before they came to a cat sitting in the road, looking as dismal as three wet days. "Now then, what is the matter with you, old shaver?" said the ass. "I should like to know who would be cheerful when his neck is in danger," answered the cat. "Now that I am old my teeth are getting blunt, and I would rather sit by the oven and purr than run about after mice, and my mistress wanted to drown me; so I took myself off; but good advice is scarce, and I do not know what is to become of me." - "Go with us to Bremen," said the ass, "and become town musician. You understand serenading." The cat thought well of the idea, and went with them accordingly. After that the three travellers passed by a yard, and a cock was

perched on the gate crowing with all his might. "Your cries are enough to pierce bone and marrow," said the ass; "what is the matter?" - "I have foretold good weather for Lady-day, so that all the shirts may be washed and dried; and now on Sunday morning company is coming, and the mistress has told the cook that I must be made into soup, and this evening my neck is to be wrung, so that I am crowing with all my might while I can." - "You had much better go with us, Chanticleer," said the ass. "We are going to Bremen. At any rate that will be better than dying. You have a powerful voice, and when we are all performing together it will have a very good effect." So the cock consented, and they went on all four together.

In all of the tales of the Brothers Grimm there are only two cities mentioned by name: Rome and Bremen. Rome is known as an old mystery center. But what does Bremen mean? In a true folktale, a place is not named without without deep reason. In the region around Bremen was a mystery center of large size. Stone circles, dolmens, initiation graves scattered for miles over the land are today still witness to its existence. So the question arises: Did this mystery center cultivate a wisdom to which the content of our tale might point? Look at the story. It is an animal tale, so it will deal with instinctual nature of humans as reflected in the symbols of the ass, the dog, the cat, and the cock.

We became acquainted with the symbol of the ass in the preceding tale, "The Donkey." Our physical body, no longer what the creator originally made it, but still capable of being made permeable by the spirit and submissive to the spirit, appears in the tales as the ass. This tale says that he is old and that death awaits him. He needs renewal and rejuvenation. Now he wants to do what that master wished to show who put on the outside of the Chartres cathedral a huge ass, carved in stone, standing on his hind legs like

a man and holding a lyre. He wants to be artistically active and resonate with the harmonies of the world.

That characteristic of a kind of animal that is most distinctive determines its use as a symbol. For the dog, this is his fine sense of smell. When we say, "I have a good nose for that," we are pointing to the dog in us. How this nose was developed we can't say, but we know very well when we are following it and when not. This instinct is not so easily recognized as some others; it is an subliminal instinct and sits deep in our nature below the level that consciousness reaches. The Greeks put it in the form of Cerberus, the hound of Hell, at the threshold between the Here and the Beyond. Herakles, the great Greek initiate, the first to withstand the tests of initiation on his own, had – as the twelfth and most difficult trial or labor – to bring Cerberus out of the underworld. The myth tells, in picture language, of a bringing to consciousness of this threshold guardian.

Just as there are many, many kinds of dogs, so the inner dogs are many and various. A whole pack of dogs can, speaking pictorially, be present in the instinctual life of a human being. And he may feel himself hounded by all of them. Like all drives, these can be both good and bad, so one needs wide-awake self knowledge to deal with them. A bad dog leads one into the world of the base and evil, into an inner hell. He is the snooper who lives in scents and spying. Etymologically, *cynicism* means thinking like a dog.[41] "Auf den Hund kommen" literally "come to the dog" is a German idiom meaning much the same as English "Gone to the dogs". Someone who has lost inner orientation and just follows the

---

41 This is folk etymology from the fact that κύων (cyon) means dog. There is, however, a more probable etymology not connected to dogs.

inclination to the common, who is no path seeker but just crowd-follower may be said to be an inner pig-dog.[42]

The good dog in us, on the other hand, helps us find the right way, leads us to the right people, and guides us to our proper destiny. He is our inner sense for life's direction. Thus he rightfully accompanies Dürer's knight who must face Death and the Devil.[43] How much Love needs a sure sense of direction is shown in the story of Tristan and Isolde. Love will show its manifold magic in thousands of ever new ways, but it always needs a good pathfinder.

The most noble of all dogs appears in the Grail epic *Titurel* by Wolfram von Eschenbach, author of *Parzifal*. As recounted by W. J. Stein in *The Ninth Century*,[44] a dog is caught bearing an elaborate collar and a long leash with an inscription beginning: 'The wild bearer of this letter is called Gardevias, Guard well the way. Let him remind thee above all to guard well the way that leads to the love of God."

If the natural tracking sense becomes diminished and threatens to die away, it needs renewal; it must recover its old striking power. The ass knows this and says to the dog, "You play the kettle drums."

More easily than the dog in us is the cat or kitten recognized. These drives are all above the threshold of perception. We are fully aware of our sensations, and therein they dwell. Whether they are

---

42 *Schweinehund* – pig-dog without the "inner" means "bastard" in its most pejorative sense.

43 There is a Wikipedia article on this engraving including an image. Search for Durer Knight Death Devil.

44 The full text of this book in English is now available on the Internet in Google Books. This paragraph is rewritten rather than translated.

white or multicolored – as they should be – or black as with those of witches, that is the question.

How daintily and ingratiatingly the kitten plays! This seemingly soft, fuzzy little ball can loll guilelessly and the floor for a long time and then suddenly wide awake pounce on its prey – simultaneously a dainty house pet and a lurking, springing beast of prey. Sleepy in the daytime, active at night, the cat is a picture of those drives that have less to do with the work of the daylight hours than with the pleasures of of the night. So the ass says to the cat: Come along and become a city musician; you understand night music so well. The physical bodily nature (the ass) knows that the love instincts also need harmonization; the cat must make music.

The fourth to join the team is the cock. To recognize this symbol just watch the rooster, how proudly he struts around the barnyard, thrust his chest out and his head up, always making himself important, parading before the hens, flapping his wings and blaring out his cocka-doodle-doo as if nothing in the world mattered except him and his voice. Notice also how quickly his comb swells and rises, a sign that blood easily rises to his head, and you will easily recognize this symbol. Also the cock has a special relation to the sun; he announces the coming of the day. Exactly so behaves the I of the human, while it is still experienced as an egotistical *drive* and gladly considers itself superior, indeed altogether too superior. It shouts its opinions to the world, is easily offended, and is always proclaiming its superiority. This is also the I that, every morning, gives the impulse to wake up. For it only counts for something when awake. The Germanic account of the gods, the Edda, says of the rooster, in the prophecy of the seeress, the Völuspa

42. On a hill there sat, and smote on his harp,
Eggther the joyous, the giants' warder;
Above him the cock in the bird-wood crowed.
Fair and red did Fjalar stand.

43. Then to the gods crowed Gollinkambi,
He wakes the heroes in Othin's hall;
And beneath the earth does another crow,
The rust-red bird at the bars of Hel. [45]

Fjalar, the bright red cock that sat in the birdwood (or by another translation, on the Tree of Cares) represents the drive-related I that lives and weaves in the blood and is dependent on the blood. Intoxicated with egoism, it mounts to self-importance. And the nervous system is indeed a Tree of Cares.

Besides this blood-related I, we have another, our timeless, eternal eye. Instinctively experienced, it is the cock with the golden comb; he calls to supersensible awakening. And a third I-consciousness joins in; Man wins it struggling and creating in the dark work of physical substance. With it, of course, he can grasp only the lifeless, the dead. His name is Rußkopf[46] (Soothead).

When all three cocks shrilly crow, then begins Ragnarök, the Twilight of the Gods. When Man experiences himself on all planes of being, and wills to master the dark material world, then the

---

45 . Quoted from *The Poetic Edda*, Translated from the Icelandic with an introduction and notes by Henry Adams Bellows, The American-Scandinavian Foundation, New York, 1923. Found on the Internet. The notes say that Fjalar wakes the giants for the final struggle, and Gollinkambi does the same for the gods.

46 I can find no reference to this Rußkopf bird in the Edda or elsewhere.

divine world grows dim; it must be found anew out of the freedom of the I personality.

"You, Redhead," says the ass in our tale, so Fjalar is meant, the Ego anchored in the Blood.

But Bremen was too far off to be reached in one day, and towards evening they came to a wood, where they determined to pass the night. The ass and the dog lay down under a large tree; the cat got up among the branches, and the cock flew up to the top, as that was the safest place for him.

The animals now put themselves in order in the "tree". We need but to recognize our nervous system as a "tree" to see here the ordering of the four instincts into a single unified instinctive nature.

The four-fold nature of Man as a being with physical body, etheric body, astral body and ego is presented to us symbolically in many ways in the folktales. This structure, first conceptually recognized by Aristotle, was familiar to the clairvoyant imagination of those teachers who, throughout the Middle Ages, created the folktales. To the physical body – pictured here as the ass – there is added the "vegetative soul" connected with life and reproduction. To it there belongs the formation of deep capacities and the innate temperament. Therein lives that special tracking sense that the picture language calls "dog". Above this is the sentient soul. Its love drive which appears, as we saw in the previous tale, as the cat. Above, in the Tree of Cares, Man becomes aware of his ego or experiences it as here as instinctive ability, as the cock.

The question may arise as to why the story describes each of the animals as near its end, and why do they have to find one another when, in the human being, they are all present? The tale

describes a crisis. In the childhood age of mankind, one could leave oneself to one's instinctive nature. Out of natural necessity the different drives worked together. In the course of time, this natural unity fell apart as that condition came to an end. A new order must come about, the I must take the lead. When the cock at the top of the tree "sees the light" this development can begin.

Before he went to sleep he looked all round him to the four points of the compass, and perceived in the distance a little light shining, and he called out to his companions that there must be a house not far off, as he could see a light, so the ass said, "We had better get up and go there, for these are uncomfortable quarters." The dog began to fancy a few bones, not quite bare, would do him good. And they all set off in the direction of the light, and it grew larger and brighter, until at last it led them to a robber's house, all lighted up. The ass, being the biggest, went up to the window, and looked in. "Well, what do you see?" asked the dog. "What do I see?" answered the ass; "here is a table set out with splendid eatables and drinkables, and robbers sitting at it and making themselves very comfortable."

When the physical body is experienced as the "housing" of our being, it is natural that it appears in picture language as a house. It is such a frequent and reliable image that depth psychology counts it as one the archetypes. The German expression "Er ist aus dem Häuschen" (literally, "He is out of the little house") means much the same as the English "He is out of his mind." He has lost connection with reality. People near death often dream that they must leave a house. Children, on the other hand, dream that they should find a house. "To move into the house" means to come to oneself, to wake up in one's physical body. To be sure, one always lives in the house of the body. But just as one can live in a house

but give it no thought or loving attention to make it one's own, so is it also with the house of the body.

- "That would just suit us," said the cock. "Yes, indeed, I wish we were there," said the ass. Then they consulted together how it should be managed so as to get the robbers out of the house, and at last they hit on a plan. The ass was to place his forefeet on the window-sill, the dog was to get on the ass's back, the cat on the top of the dog, and lastly the cock was to fly up and perch on the cat's head. When that was done, at a given signal they all began to perform their music. The ass brayed, the dog barked, the cat mewed, and the cock crowed; then they burst through into the room, breaking all the panes of glass. The robbers fled at the dreadful sound; they thought it was some goblin, and fled to the wood in the utmost terror. Then the four companions sat down to table, made free with the remains of the meal, and feasted as if they had been hungry for a month.

The united, advanced fourfold being now recognizes the "house" and sees that in it bad forces live, forces that, like robbers, thoughtlessly exploit external nature without recognizing it as God-created. They egotistically plunder the world without giving back the least little bit. Wherever the senses just want their own sensations, these "robbers" live.

To drive them out, the foursome must make a united attack. They had practiced in the "tree". Now each of them sounds forth his being in his own language, and thereby is the whole bodily house taken, and the fourfold Man becomes master in the house.

And when they had finished they put out the lights, and each sought out a sleeping-place to suit his nature and habits. The ass laid himself down outside on the dunghill, the dog behind the door, the

161

cat on the hearth by the warm ashes, and the cock settled himself in the cockloft, and as they were all tired with their long journey they soon fell fast asleep. When midnight drew near, and the robbers from afar saw that no light was burning, and that everything appeared quiet, their captain said to them that he thought that they had run away without reason, telling one of them to go and reconnoiter. So one of them went, and found everything quite quiet; he went into the kitchen to strike a light, and taking the glowing fiery eyes of the cat for burning coals, he held a match to them in order to kindle it. But the cat, not seeing the joke, flew into his face, spitting and scratching. Then he cried out in terror, and ran to get out at the back door, but the dog, who was lying there, ran at him and bit his leg; and as he was rushing through the yard by the dunghill the ass struck out and gave him a great kick with his hind foot; and the cock, who had been wakened with the noise, and felt quite brisk, cried out, "Cock-a-doodle-doo!" Then the robber got back as well as he could to his captain, and said, "Oh dear! in that house there is a gruesome witch, and I felt her breath and her long nails in my face; and by the door there stands a man who stabbed me in the leg with a knife; and in the yard there lies a black specter, who beat me with his wooden club; and above, upon the roof, there sits the justice, who cried, 'Bring that rogue here!' And so I ran away from the place as fast as I could." From that time forward the robbers never ventured to that house, and the four Bremen town musicians found themselves so well off where they were, that there they stayed. And the person who last related this tale is still living, as you see.

We experience in this tale how the instinctual nature of Man takes possession of the whole bodily nature. It must become a personality, so to speak, master in its own house. It falls therefore into the group of individualization tales. It was given as an impulse

towards development of the I. We can begin telling it to five-year olds.

We can assume that the mystery center near Bremen cultivated a wisdom which would help one gain self mastery. Traditions survive over long periods, even when only orally transmitted. Whenever our tale may have originated, it was out of this tradition that Bremen was named as the goal of the journey of our four musicians.

The Goose Girl

Grimm 89

The tale begins:

*There lived once an old Queen, whose husband had been dead
many years.*

As a widow remains alone in the earthly world when her
husband has died and, instead of a living relation with one another,
only memories live in her and she must turn to a higher world to
meet his spirit, so it now is with the human soul. The tale points to
the Silver Age. The silver moon receives its light from the golden
sun, and just as it reflects and throws back this light, so this age no
longer has the abundance of vision, of revelation, and of direct
certainty. It has only the reflection of remembering. The spiritual
world has withdrawn more and more, and the soul no longer has
direct access to it. The ancient Egyptian said: Osiris, the seeing eye,
the sun mankind is dead." Isis his sister and wife remains alone,
and her priests call themselves "Sons of the Widow." In the
Germanic myths it was expressed: Baldur, living in Breideblick
(Broad View) is dead; as a widow, Nanna weeps for him.

*She had a beautiful daughter who was promised in marriage to
a King's son living a great way off. When the time appointed for the
wedding drew near, and the old Queen had to send her daughter
into the foreign land, she got together many costly things, furniture
and cups and jewels and adornments, both of gold and silver,
everything proper for the dowry of a royal Princess, for she loved
her daughter dearly.*

As the daughter is born from the mother, so is the new soul nature born from the old. It is beautiful and destined to have a future kingdom, but it is a different kingdom. It the most ancient times it was not customary that a daughter should be married "over the fields and far away." Rather, endogamy, marriage within the clan or tribe, prevailed. Clairvoyant capacities, contact with the ancestral spirits, and continuous memory were dependent on the unmixed purity of the blood line. There are still today peoples among the so-called primitives where marriage outside the clan is punishable by death. And there is more to the story of the abduction of the Greek Helen by the Trojan Paris than just the theft of a woman, for as a consequence Troy falls, – Troy the city of seers, the center of clairvoyant priestly wisdom – and the rational culture of the Greeks triumphs – in the sign of the horse.

As the custom of exogamy began, Man was changed. The ancestor cult lost significance as the connection to the spirits of the the forebears weakened. Humans awoke to personality. No longer did the family make decisions, nor did the group ego of the clan and tribe, but the own individual I. "The highest happiness of the children of the earth is only the personality,"[47] said Goethe, thereby pointing to the development of our western consciousness. The I must be found, and when it appears in the form of the prince it is the I in full self-mastery, living in the full force of the spirit. Mankind required a long time on this road, and so does the individual who must perfect himself.

She gave her also a chambermaid to attend her and to give her into the bridegroom's hands.

---

47 In *West-Östliche Divan* (1818) Perhaps *Glück* should be translated "good fortune" rather than "happiness".

Where I development begins – and in the folktale that is where the journey to the bridegroom begins – the soul is a duality. The one side of our being strives for the spirituality of the I, becomes the "higher", the loving, selfless soul turned to the eternal. The other side remains bound to the earth, as the "lower" helping servant: princess and chambermaid.

But at this turning point of development, the crisis begins, as the tale wishes to show. The lower, necessarily earthly consciousness becomes self-seeking, proud and egotistical, and wants to take charge.

Goethe describes this crisis, in words put into the mouth of Faust,

> Zwei Seelen wohnen, ach! in meiner Brust,
> Die eine will sich von der andern trennen;
> Die eine hält, in derber Liebeslust,
> Sich an die Welt mit klammernden Organen;
> Die andere hebt gewaltsam sich vom Dust
> Zu den Gefilden hoher Ahnen.

> Two souls live, ah, within my breast;
> The one wants to separate from the other;
> The one clings in crude pleasure of love
> To the world, with clamoring organs;
> The other lifts itself powerfully from the dust
> To the realms of exalted ancestors.

And they were each to have a horse for the journey, and the Princess's horse was named Falada, and he could speak.

The duality in the soul corresponds to a duality of the instinctive understanding prevailing in Man. In ancient times, the understanding or reason was no independent force within Man, it

166

was much more bound to the body. The I-development in mankind's evolution goes along with the evolution of thinking. This development began around 2000 BC; one see its effects in Hammurabi around 1800 BC. At about the same time that it began, the horse, originally from the highlands east of Mesopotamia, first appears in civilized lands. It was first considered a form of wild ass; then when its intelligence and its adaptability to working with men was recognized, the domestication of the horse began and was to be one of the great human cultural accomplishments. Man could ride upon an animal that was more than a beast of burden. This animal would respond to his will; it could be bridled and directed and led destinations. What happened outwardly with the horse also happened inwardly with Man's own being; the I in the process of developing its independence learned how to bridle and direct the powers of reason and understanding to spiritual purposes. The horse therefore became symbol for the instinctive understanding. This understanding split as the I development began.

As Socrates says in Plato's *Phaedrus*, "As I said at the beginning of this tale, I divided each soul into three: two horses and a charioteer; and one of the horses was good and the other bad: the division may remain, but I have not yet explained in what the goodness or badness of either consists, and to that I will proceed. The right-hand horse is upright and cleanly made; he has a lofty neck and an aquiline nose; his color is white, and his eyes dark; he is a lover of honor and modesty and temperance, and the follower of true glory; he needs no touch of the whip, but is guided by word and admonition only. The other is a crooked lumbering animal, put together anyhow; he has a short thick neck; he is flat-faced and of a dark color, with grey eyes and blood-red complexion; the mate of

insolence and pride, shag-eared and deaf, hardly yielding to whip and spur.[48]

One may well picture the two horses of our tale in this way. One who would paint Falada must paint him white. Also, in the opening of the first seal in the Book of Revelation, the horse that comes forth is a white horse and the rider is a king; here is the rider a king's daughter. In the first intelligence age of humanity the instinctive understanding directed itself entirely to the supersensible – so the color is white – and has the force of inspiration and with it the force of expression – Falada can speak. The horse of the chambermaid must correspondingly be painted dark, even black, as in Plato, for the direction of the will of this other understanding ability is to what is dark and earthly, to matter.

When the time for parting came, the old Queen took her daughter to her chamber, and with a little knife she cut her own finger so that it bled; and she held beneath it a white napkin, and on it fell three drops of blood; and she gave it to her daughter and said, "Dear child, take good care of them, for you will need them on your way."

Here there is working the magic of the blood. It works in three ways: in feeling as pious devotion, in thinking as clairvoyant knowing, in willing in clan-conscious action. This power lives and *weaves* in it. The picture language calls this web of thought *linen*. A piece of it is given to the soul becoming free from its old bounds: the white napkin with the three drops of blood.

Then they took leave of each other; and the Princess put the napkin in her bosom, got on her horse, and set out to go to the bridegroom. After she had ridden an hour, she began to feel very

---

48 From near the middle of the dialogue. Translation of Benjamin Jowett.

thirsty, and she said to the chambermaid, "Get down, and fill my cup that you are carrying with water from the brook; I have great desire to drink." - "Get down yourself," said the chambermaid, "and if you are thirsty stoop down and drink; I will not be your slave." And as her thirst was so great, the Princess had to get down and to stoop and drink of the water of the brook, and could not have her gold cup to serve her.

The journey begins, and soon the princess experiences thirst. It is that desire that the Buddha called the thirst for experiences, for adventure, for quickening and filling of the soul. Through this desire, the lower part of the soul can get the upper hand: the chambermaid becomes haughty and refuses to obey. The golden cup from the dowry given by the mother, the gift of wisdom that can understand matters of the soul (can dip up water), is denied to the princess.

"Oh dear!" said the poor Princess. And the three drops of blood heard her, and said, "If your mother knew of this, it would break her heart." But the Princess answered nothing, and quietly mounted her horse again. So they rode on some miles farther; the day was warm, the sun shone hot, and the Princess grew thirsty once more. And when they came to a water-course she called again to the chambermaid and said, "Get down, and give me to drink out of my golden cup." For she had forgotten all that had gone before. But the chambermaid spoke still more scornfully and said, "If you want a drink, you may get it yourself; I am not going to be your slave." So, as her thirst was so great, the Princess had to get off her horse and to stoop towards the running water to drink, and as she stooped, she wept and said, "Oh dear!" And the three drops of blood heard her and answered, "If your mother knew of this, it would break her heart!" And as she drank and stooped over, the napkin on which

were the three drops of blood fell out of her bosom and floated down the stream, and in her distress she never noticed it; not so the chambermaid, who rejoiced because she should have power over the bride, who, now that she had lost the three drops of blood, had become weak, and unable to defend herself.

The day becomes hotter and stronger the burning thirst that demands to be quenched; and the further they get from the mother, the magical power of the blood recedes. Finally, it becomes completely washed away in the stream of onward flowing life. Inheritance from the tribe and folk-bound traditions henceforth count for nothing.

When she was going to mount her horse again the chambermaid cried, "Falada belongs to me, and this jade to you." And the Princess had to give way and let it be as she said. Then the chambermaid ordered the Princess with many hard words to take off her rich clothing and to put on her plain garments, and then she made her swear to say nothing of the matter when they came to the royal court; threatening to take her life if she refused. And all the while Falada noticed and remembered.

The chambermaid then mounting Falada, and the Princess the sorry nag, they journeyed on till they reached the royal castle. There was great joy at their coming, and the King's son hastened to meet them, and lifted the waiting woman from her horse, thinking she was his bride; and then he led her up the stairs, while the real Princess had to remain below.

The lower takes charge also of the inspired understanding: the chambermaid mounts Falada. She takes from the princess the regal clothes and replaces them with her own bad ones: the radiance (the clothes) of the soul is impoverished. Finally the false bride

succeeds in deceiving the prince, she captures him for herself; she will indeed become the bearer of an I but in the egotistical sense. The higher soul becomes literally unseated, disenthroned.

But the old King, who was looking out of the window, saw her standing in the yard, and noticed how delicate and gentle and beautiful she was, and then he went down and asked the seeming bride who it was that she had brought with her and that was now standing in the courtyard.

"Oh!" answered the bride, "I only brought her with me for company; give the maid something to do, that she may not be for ever standing idle."

Before the appearance of the I that becomes free in Man, there ruled the old self, the old king. This old self is no longer the inner regent, but he is awake and attentive, and follows what is happening.

But the old King had no work to give her; until he bethought him of a boy he had who took care of the geese, and that she might help him. And so the real Princess was sent to keep geese with the goose-boy, who was called Curty.

Soon after the false bride said to the Prince, "Dearest husband, I pray thee do me a pleasure." - "With all my heart," answered he. "Then," said she, "send for the knacker, that he may carry off the horse I came here upon, and make away with him; he was very troublesome to me on the journey." For she was afraid that the horse might tell how she had behaved to the Princess. And when the order had been given that Falada should die, it came to the Princess's ears, and she came to the knacker's man secretly, and promised him a piece of gold if he would do her a service. There was in the town a

great dark gate-way through which she had to pass morning and evening with her geese, and she asked the man to take Falada's head and to nail it on the gate, that she might always see it as she passed by. And the man promised, and he took Falada's head and nailed it fast in the dark gate-way.

Early next morning as she and Curty drove their geese through the gate, she said as she went by:

"O Falada, dost thou hang there?"

And the head answered:

"Princess, dost thou so meanly fare?
But if thy mother knew thy pain,
Her heart would surely break in twain."

But she went on through the town, driving her geese to the field.

The princess became a goose girl, but she is the one who, in Goethe's words, "lifts herself powerfully (*gewaltsam*) from the dust." "*Gewaltsam*" means "through the power of the will." The first deed of the Will is to be silently submissive to fate: to guard geese. Now geese are notoriously hard to herd and guard; they run hither and yon, and the flock breaks up. They are the very image of dispersion. "Guard thy senses" was an important motto in the age of the knights and troubadours. Our folktale says, "become a goose girl – hold your senses together – practice inner collectedness. To this practice belongs also the right sense of self-direction. It should be practiced especially in the morning and in the evening. In the morning, when we awaken and seemingly go out through a dark doorway into the bright light of day, we activate all our senses, and give ourselves over to all impressions. In the evening, when we come back into ourselves, then should the soul remember who she

really is, and that to her was once given an inspiration that could not be asserted, but which called forth memory of a lost kingdom. To win this kingdom back is the subject of this and many folktales.

Our tale shows up until now the development of the mind as a way and this way is necessarily bound up with thinking.

And when they came into the meadows, she sat down and undid her hair, which was all of gold, and when Curty saw how it glistened, he wanted to pull out a few hairs for himself. And she said:

> *"O wind, blow away Curty's hat;*
> *Make him run after as it flies,*
> *While I with my gold hair will plait,*
> *And put it up in seemly wise."*

Then there came a wind strong enough to blow Curty's hat far away over the fields, and he had to run after it; and by the time he came back she had put up her hair with combs and pins, and he could not get at any to pull it out; and he was sulky and would not speak to her; so they looked after the geese until the evening came, and then they went home.

The next morning, as they passed under the dark gate-way, the Princess said:

> *"O Falada, dost thou hang there?"*

And Falada answered:

> *"Princess, dost thou so meanly fare?*
> *But if thy mother knew thy pain,*
> *Her heart would surely break in twain."*

173

And when they reached the fields she sat down and began to comb out her hair; then Curty came up and wanted to seize two strands of it, and she cried:

"O wind, blow away Curty's hat,
Make him run after as it flies,
While I my golden hair will plait,
And set it up in seemly wise."

Then the wind came and blew Curty's hat very far away, so that he had to run after it, and when he came back again her hair was put up again, so that he could pull none of it out; and they tended the geese until the evening.

Just as hair grow on the head and through color and fineness reveal something of it bearer, so also the inner head – the one we should never "loose" – is not bald; it radiates outward. The hair should be radiant and add to the impression of an inner radiance. Thinking, like hair, must be ordered and cared for. In folktale, the motif of a comb or combing is always related to the inner world of the head. Wisdom (golden hair) is given to the king's daughter as her holy inheritance, but it must be cared for. The inherited possession does not alone lead to the goal. "To comb oneself" means "to think actively." In doing so, one must above all hold in check the naive will bent on self-satisfaction. It does, to be sure, guard the senses in traditional ways, but precisely out of its naiveté it can consider itself clever and superior and be proud of all it has in the head: Curty. The Grimm brothers add a note to Curty's name (which is Kürdchen in German); it is dialect for Konrädchen, little Conrad. Conrad is Germanic in origin and comes from *Kuonrad*, one who is "bold in counsel" (*kuhn in Rat* in modern German.) It is

174

that limited little Will that easily becomes cheeky and with a few borrowed thoughts – the golden hairs – wants to seem brilliant but only disturbs any serious concentration. Who does not know this joker, this disturber of the peace? We saw back on page 52 the vivid German expression "That makes my hat go high" meaning "That makes me really angry." Here the goose girl literally makes Curty's "hat go high," so of course he becomes angry with her, as happens when an earnest spiritual Will – that refuses to be disturbed by the cheeky joker – exerts itself.

In olden times there was a Magic of the Word which the sagas still report. Man could command the weather through incantation; the wind obeyed him. Marco Polo even experienced it on the court of Kubilai Kahn in the 13th century where the priests commanded wind and rain. Kings also often had magical powers. These abilities were lost in the course of development.

They work in our folktales in the picture of an inner event – as it says in the Bible, "The spirit bloweth where it listeth."[49] By thinking, the soul can ask of the spirit that it blow where the soul wishes, and it drives away the cheeky joker. She calmly puts her inner life in order in a three-fold way – thinking, feeling and willing – for plaiting always works with three strands. And then she "sets it up," that is, she preserves in inner composure what has been acquired.

And after they had got home, Curty went to the old King and said: "I will tend the geese no longer with that girl!" - "Why not?" asked the old King. "Because she vexes me the whole day long," answered Curty. Then the old King ordered him to tell how it was.

---

49 Gospel of John, 3:8. The Greek word *pneuma*, usually translated in this context as *wind* in both English and German, can also mean *spirit, Geist* in German, and is so rendered sometimes in German, especially in song.

"Every morning," said Curty, "as we pass under the dark gate-way with the geese, there is an old horse's head hanging on the wall, and she says to it:

'O Falada, dost thou hang there?'

And the head answers:

'Princess, dost thou so meanly fare?
But if thy mother knew thy pain,
Her heart would surely break in twain.'"

And besides this, Curty related all that happened in the fields, and how he was obliged to run after his hat.

The old King told him to go to drive the geese next morning as usual, and he himself went behind the gate and listened how the maiden spoke to Falada; and then he followed them into the fields, and hid himself behind a bush; and he watched the goose-boy and the goose-girl tend the geese; and after a while he saw the girl make her hair all loose, and how it gleamed and shone. Soon she said:

"O wind, blow away Curty's hat;
Make him run after as it flies,
While I my golden hair will plait,
And put it up in seemly wise."

Then there came a gust of wind and away went Curty's hat, and he after it, while the maiden combed and bound up her hair; and the old King saw all that went on. At last he went unnoticed away.

When now the soul (the princess) works so diligently upon itself, it becomes unbearable for the ordinary Will (Curty). He had, however, so far "herded the geese" alone, so the old king must be

the arbiter. The king's son, the I, had decided for the princess from "far across the fields" but had been deceived by the false bride. Only the old self remained awake and now stands helpfully beside the young king. He is attentive and tests the "maiden queen" at the gate and in the field.

And when the goose-girl came back in the evening he sent for her, and asked the reason of her doing all this. "That I dare not tell you," she answered, "nor can I tell any man of my woe, for when I was in danger of my life I swore an oath not to reveal it." And he pressed her sore, and left her no peace, but he could get nothing out of her. At last he said, "If you will not tell it me, tell it to the iron stove," and went away. Then she crept into the iron stove, and began to weep and to lament, and at last she opened her heart and said, "Here I sit forsaken of all the world, and I am a King's daughter, and a wicked chambermaid forced me to give up my royal garments and my place at the bridegroom's side, and I am made a goose-girl, and have to do mean service. And if my mother knew, it would break her heart." Now the old King was standing outside by the stove-door listening, and he heard all she said, and he called to her and told her to come out of the stove. And he caused royal clothing to be put upon her, and it was a marvel to see how beautiful she was.

To this day the stove plays the same role in dream life as in the folktale. Sick people who have heart trouble can sometimes speak of it, for the heart is the source of heat in the body just as the stove is in the house. And in a higher sense we speak of the warmth of love or of warmer or of chilled or extinguished love. (Iron underscores the picture, for the iron in the blood makes us awake and I-conscious. In the heart it becomes the basis for correct self-knowledge.) In the heart must the royal Soul of Man recognize who

she really is. That must the king demand of her. Only one who finds himself can attain personality. When that is done, the way is open to the I, the king's son. This whole process must take place in the heart for the development of understanding (the way on the horse) and the development of thinking (the care for the golden hair) can otherwise easily become one-sided. Here the heart must help as an organ for knowledge.

The maiden is again clothed with regal dignity and her rights restored to her.

The old King then called his son and proved to him that he had the wrong bride, for she was really only a chambermaid, and that the true bride was here at hand, she who had been the goose-girl. The Prince was glad at heart when he saw her beauty and gentleness; and a great feast was made ready, and all the court people and good friends were bidden to it. The bridegroom sat in the midst with the Princess on one side and the chambermaid on the other; and the false bride did not know the true one, because she was dazzled with her glittering braveries. When all the company had eaten and drunk and were merry, the old King gave the chambermaid a question to answer, as to what such an one deserved, who had deceived her masters in such and such a manner, telling the whole story, and ending by asking, "Now, what doom does such an one deserve?" - "No better than this," answered the false bride, "that she be put stark naked into a barrel studded inside with sharp nails, and be dragged along in it by two white horses up street, down streett to street, until she be dead."

The bridegroom between the true and the false bride stands as an essential picture before us. The decision must be made. Because the principle of freedom applies also to the haughty, self-seeking

being (the chambermaid) she is called up to speak the truth. But she is no longer able to recognize the true princess in her finery, and pronounces her own judgment.

"Stark naked" means to have lost all soul sheaths and radiance; put into a barrel studded inside with sharp nails means to have become very small, to have lost all possibility of action and to have to suffer all wounds on oneself. And two white horses must drag her "up street, down street" until she is dead: Falada has somehow newly arisen; and the horse of the chambermaid, which, up until now, has represented the drive to understand directed at what is dark and material, has been transformed and illumined into a spiritual force. This pair of new spiritual forces puts to death all baseness and selfseeking. The Soul is now filled with the thinking Spirit, the I is permeated by the soul, and the royal wedding can be celebrated.

"Thou hast spoken thy own doom," said the old King, "as thou hast said, so shall it be done." And when the sentence was fulfilled, the Prince married the true bride, and ever after they ruled over their kingdom in peace and blessedness.

On barns in Lower Saxony one can still see here and there[50] at the top of the roof gable two beams projecting above the ridge of the roof and with the upper ends carved into heads of horses and painted white. Why were they put there? The great love of our ancestors for horses is hardly a satisfying explanation. The house of the body stands in intimate relation to the house in which live. German has several picturesque expressions such as "He is out of his little house" meaning he is out of his mind, or "He has roof

---

50 For example, the Rischmannshof Heath Museum, a thatched house with a hipped gable roof and carved horse's heads on beams projecting above the gable. There are pictures on the Internet.

damage" with a similar meaning. The forehead corresponds to the gable of the house. Spiritual understanding should prevail there. Lower and higher understanding rise to that level and cross. Both are necessary to be "well housed"and to live and work in inner truthfulness. And there we have the symbol at the top of the gable of the old barn.

Cinderella (or Aschenputtel)

Grimm 21

There was once a rich man whose wife lay sick, and when she felt her end drawing near she called to her only daughter to come near her bed, and said, "Dear child, be pious and good, and God will always take care of you, and I will look down upon you from heaven, and will be with you." And then she closed her eyes and expired. The maiden went every day to her mother's grave and wept, and was always pious and good. When the winter came the snow covered the grave with a white covering, and when the sun came in the early spring and melted it away, the man took to himself another wife.

The new wife brought two daughters home with her, and they were beautiful and fair in appearance, but at heart were, black and ugly. And then began very evil times for the poor step-daughter. "Is the stupid creature to sit in the same room with us?" said they; "those who eat food must earn it. Out upon her for a kitchen-maid!" They took away her pretty dresses, and put on her an old gray smock, and gave her wooden shoes to wear. "Just look now at the proud princess, how she is decked out!" cried they laughing, and then they sent her into the kitchen. There she was obliged to do heavy work from morning to night, get up early in the morning, draw water, make the fires, cook, and wash. Besides that, the sisters did their utmost to torment her, mocking her, and strewing peas and lentils among the ashes, and setting her to pick them up. In the evenings, when she was quite tired out with her hard day's work, she had no bed to lie on, but was obliged to rest on the hearth among the cinders. And as she always looked dusty and dirty, they named her Cinderella.

Cinderella's father is a rich man, a merchant. A merchant is immersed in everyday affairs, He must manage and venture to preserve his property and acquire new. Today he is rich; tomorrow he may be bankrupt.

When a man no longer has direct experience of the spiritual world and no longer feels his inner kingly worth, when his only spiritual wealth is some traditions whose origins he may no longer know and who, to be sure, today has things of this world he cares about and manages – gold – but tomorrow may loose them all, then he is like a merchant. His soul is "a rich wife," but the rich wife dies – the best part of his soul withdraws into a higher world.

Out of old, rich depth of soul, out of unbroken unity of being, a new young force is born, a daughter. But she must mature and learn to overcome doubt and error. She must out of her own forces find that I which stands higher than the doubting, uncertain father-self. If this soul being, intrinsically capable of bearing an I, is to become more than "a rich wife", it has a rough road ahead. For when in the traditional human – the dealer in spirit – the spiritual soul – the true spouse – has died, the untrue one soon moves in. She becomes ruler in the house of the body and is for the child of the true spouse the wicked stepmother, for she is one-sided, turned only to the sense world of her own and those like her and persecutes the good always and everywhere.

Her two daughters are fair and beautiful in appearance but dark and horrid inside. With them come delusion and false piety. The sheath or aura that surrounds the core of being is dimmed under the influence of these evil forces. The manifold inner struggles and strivings ease off. The soul that had shone as if clad in colorful raiment turns dreary – they give her a gray smock. The

way she stands in life is hardened – she is given wooden shoes. From morn to even these adversarial forces oppress the soul, mock and scorn it, and make it into a scullery maid. We know this picture from countless folktales, for it describes the inner process that every soul in western civilization more or less goes through.

The fireplace, the hearth, as we have already seen, was once the most important place in the house. From there warmth streamed out; there was the center. In the house of the body this fireplace is the heart. Hearth and oven can symbolize in dreams the heart region or the heart is the center of the body's warmth system. One may dream of a glowing, warm oven if surrounded by warm friendship or glowing love, or of a cold oven if such feelings have been extinguished. Even though the genuine soul is given scarcely any interior space, it draws back into the deep recesses of the heart and there manages to keep the spark alive. One could also say that the adversarial forces drive it back. It can live only in the heart and work from there. In the picture language, she makes fires, cooks, carries water, sweeps ashes, in short, serves by the fire and with the ashes.

It happened one day that the father went to the fair, and he asked his two step-daughters what he should bring back for them. "Fine clothes!" said one. "Pearls and jewels!" said the other. "But what will you have, Cinderella?" said he. "The first twig, father, that strikes against your hat on the way home; that is what I should like you to bring me." So he bought for the two step-daughters fine clothes, pearls, and jewels, and on his way back, as he rode through a green lane, a hazel-twig struck against his hat; and he broke it off and carried it home with him. And when he reached home he gave to the step-daughters what they had wished for, and to Cinderella he gave the hazel-twig. She thanked him, and went to her mother's

183

grave, and planted this twig there, weeping so bitterly that the tears fell upon it and watered it, and it flourished and became a fine tree. Cinderella went under the tree three times a day, and wept and prayed, and each time a white bird rose up from the tree, and if she uttered any wish the bird brought her whatever she had wished for.

From the sun mysteries of Ancient Egypt stems the myth, already thousands of years old, of the Phoenix bird who sacrifices itself, is burned, and arises anew from its ashes. Fire and ash belong together, for ash is what remains from burning. Where the heart burns in the fire of a pure desire, of a noble resolution, where all that is lower is continuously burned away in a purifying fire, there remains that inner substance which, in the folktale pictures, is called ash. Purification implies transformation, a continual "die and become". [51] Would a human soul accomplish this "die and become," it must become Cinderella. The father, the human spirit become merchant, is not yet gripped by this "die and become." He has bound himself to the materialistically hardened soul. His insight is limited. He does not notice the suffering borne in the innermost kernel of the soul. Therefore Cinderella asks for a twig that on his way home strikes against his hat.

Hats and caps cover us above and close us off. They are pictures of our own thinking, brain thinking, our personal knowledge and responsibility. We have already noted the German expressions "I'll take that on my own cap" and "That makes my hat

---

51 A quote which most Germans would recognize from Goethe's poem "Selige Sehnsucht". The last verse is

Und so lang du das nicht hast,	And so long as you don't have
Dieses: Stirb und werde!	This: Die and become!
Bist du nur ein trüber Gast	You are but a murky guest
Auf der dunklen Erde.	On the dark earth.

go high." Something living – a sprouting twig – must shove the hat, and a hazel branch it is, that knocks his hat off.

Old peasant wisdom planted the hazel bush in the four corners of the garden and along the fences because they draw in cosmic forces the earth needs. Hazel nuts have a high nutritional value; they strengthen the nerves and give life force. There must also surely be good reasons that dowsers use precisely a hazel branch. The hazel tree, abounding with life and drawing in life forces, becomes the very image of the Tree of Life. Folksongs honor the hazel; a branch of it can protect against "the serpent." Celtic mythology tells us: the Salmon of Knowledge swims in the dark waters under the nine hazel nut trees. What must happen that this inner Tree of Life should grow and prosper?

Cinderella went under the tree three times a day, and wept and prayed.

If the soul preserves memories of the motherly world in which it originated and practices internalization in prayer, then life forces well up in her like a tree. There is here a quiet reference to an important principle: repetition and rhythm. Not just a single prayer gives the soul sufficient strength but repeated prayer. All repetition gives inner strength. If one prays regularly – three times a day – says the tale, then one builds into the body a spiritual force which, like a second, higher nature within us, sprouts and grows and becomes a tree of life. Then there descends upon the one who prays the grace of a pure spirituality, the white bird. This white bird is none other than the dove at the baptism of Jesus.

Now it came to pass that the king ordained a festival that should last for three days, and to which all the beautiful young women of that country were bidden, so that the king's son might

choose a bride from among them. When the two stepdaughters heard that they too were bidden to appear, they felt very pleased, and they called Cinderella, and said, "Comb our hair, brush our shoes, and make our buckles fast, we are going to the wedding feast at the king's castle." Cinderella, when she heard this, could not help crying, for she too would have liked to go to the dance, and she begged her step-mother to allow her. "What, you Cinderella!" said she, "in all your dust and dirt, you want to go to the festival! you that have no dress and no shoes! you want to dance!" But as she persisted in asking, at last the step-mother said, "I have strewed a dish-full of lentils in the ashes, and if you can pick them all up again in two hours you may go with us." Then the maiden went to the backdoor that led into the garden, and called out, "O gentle doves, O turtle-doves, And all the birds that be, The lentils that in ashes lie Come and pick up for me!

> The good must be put in the dish,
> The bad you may eat if you wish."

Then there came to the kitchen-window two white doves, and after them some turtle-doves, and at last a crowd of all the birds under heaven, chirping and fluttering, and they alighted among the ashes; and the doves nodded with their heads, and began to pick, peck, pick, peck, and then all the others began to pick, peck, pick, peck, and put all the good grains into the dish. Before an hour was over all was done, and they flew away. Then the maiden brought the dish to her step-mother, feeling joyful, and thinking that now she should go to the feast; but the step-mother said, "No, Cinderella, you have no proper clothes, and you do not know how to dance, and you would be laughed at!" And when Cinderella cried for disappointment, she added, "If you can pick two dishes full of lentils out of the ashes, nice and clean, you shall go with us," thinking to

herself, *"for that is not possible."* When she had strewn two dishes full of lentils among the ashes the maiden went through the backdoor into the garden, and cried,

> *"O gentle doves, O turtle-doves,*
> *And all the birds that be,*
> *The lentils that in ashes lie*
> *Come and pick up for me!*
> *The good must be put in the dish,*
> *The bad you may eat if you wish."*

So there came to the kitchen-window two white doves, and then some turtle-doves, and at last a crowd of all the other birds under heaven, chirping and fluttering, and they alighted among the ashes, and the doves nodded with their heads and began to pick, peck, pick, peck, and then all the others began to pick, peck, pick, peck, and put all the good grains into the dish. And before half-an-hour was over it was all done, and they flew away. Then the maiden took the dishes to the stepmother, feeling joyful, and thinking that now she should go with them to the feast; but she said "All this is of no good to you; you cannot come with us, for you have no proper clothes, and cannot dance; you would put us to shame." Then she turned her back on poor Cinderella, and made haste to set out with her two proud daughters.

As long as Cinderella had not yet planted the hazel bush she was helpless against the attacks of the bad stepsisters. She practiced patience in suffering. Now her forces "grow". She receives the call to the royal wedding and wants to follow it. Naturally, the restraining forces redouble their efforts. The lentils which the stepmother throws in the ashes are, to be sure, restraints; but at the same time they are seeds. The soul that has become active calls on new forces for help. Through overcoming the two opposing forces –

the two stepsisters – two special graces are attained, the two white doves. And where they alight there follow manifold other spiritual forces (the birds) and they accomplish what was set as a test. The lentils are not only picked out, they are separated into the good and the bad. A step forward has been made: the soul has learned to discriminate between what is genuine seed and can bare genuine fruit, and what is bad. It knows how to recognize what is fruitful and what is not. The grace of spirit takes away with itself the unfruitful – the birds take into their crops[52] the bad grains.

Now we must have a closer look at the two step sisters. Fundamentally we know them well, for everyone has them and must in some way deal with them. They have, as we learn below, "pretty feet." That means they live happily upon the earth and make themselves comfortable there, but for the golden shoe one has a toe that is too big and the other, a heel. They live "on the big foot" – a German expression meaning extravagantly.

In former times, one walked in a lighter, more lilting fashion than today, something towards tip-toeing, as one can see on some ancient Greek vases. Children often still have the toe-walk, as do people from East Asia. They tend to wear out the toe of a shoe rather than the heel. And as one thus gently touched the earth from above, one was less bound to it. Today the step is heavier, the foot clings more to the ground, even in dance. The modern man put his

---

52 There is a subtle irony in the German that gets lost in any rhyming translation I have been able to come up with. Of the lentils, the stepmother says

die guten ins Töpfchen,   The good into the little pot
die schlechten ins Kröpfchen.   The bad into the little crop.

The "crop" is a reference to the crop of birds. Unwittingly, the stepmother foretells the help from the birds. Our author refers here to this feature of bird anatomy.

weight more on his heels than on his toes. It is reported of Fichte, "the philosopher of the I" that he was always wearing out the heels of his shoes.

Foot and shoe represent our relation to the earth. If we grasp the earthly only superficially, we are earth-fleeing; if we grasp it too intensely, we are earth-clinging. The earth-fleeing soul happily withdraws itself from everyday duties. It happily floats in a higher world, not the genuine spiritual world, but in an imagined illusory world – it goes on tiptoe. It imagines itself to be "something better," is haughty, vain and proud. It soars into euphoria and plunges into illusion and and empty madness. Its commander-in-chief is that powerful opposing force, which already in paradise led Man to arrogantly set himself equal to God: Lucifer (the red devil).

The other sister, whose heel proves too big for the shoe, is the one too much clinging to matter. She cannot get interested in spiritual matters, lives in the lower aspects of life, and seeks material profit. She represents the forces that harden and ossify us and lame our ability to rise to higher goals. Only what the senses perceive does she consider real. Her commander-in-chief is a totally lying spirit called Satan in the Bible (the black devil). From the old Persian culture comes the name Ahriman for him. Where spiritual truths are not made precise, the two devils are merged into one. In reality, however, the world must deal with two opposed evil forces. In many soul properties this polarity can be recognized, and of course also the necessary good middle, for example:

ambitious – industrious – sluggish
oversensitive – balanced – dull
earth-fleeing – earth-diligent – earth-seeking
proud – modest – subservient
effusive – strong in feeling – cold in feeling

wasteful – moderate – stingy
fickle – persistent – stubborn.

Man must find his way between the two extremes. It is not so much a matter of fighting against the extremes as of working on and cleansing oneself through the force of the middle. He must create the best by harmonizing the drives. Cinderella has found the balanced middle in herself. The overcoming of the double Bad has brought to her double Grace – the two white doves. They come again when the true bride is made known.

As there was no one left in the house, Cinderella went to her mother's grave, under the hazel bush, and cried,

Rustle yourself, shake yourself, little tree,
Throw gold and silver over me.

Then the bird threw down a dress of gold and silver, and a pair of slippers embroidered with silk and silver. In all haste she put on the dress and went to the festival. But her step-mother and sisters did not recognize her, and thought she must be a foreign princess, she looked so beautiful in her golden dress. Of Cinderella they never thought at all, and supposed that she was sitting at home, arid picking the lentils out of the ashes. The King's son came to meet her, and took her by the hand and danced with her, and he refused to dance with any one else, so that he might not be obliged to let go her hand; and when any one came to ask it he answered, "She is my partner."

Resolution now grasps the soul; she will at all costs follow the call of the king. Our tale here reminds us of the Matthew Gospel, Ch. 22: "The kingdom of heaven is like unto a certain king, which

made a marriage for his son, ..." Both here and there, the wedding garment is important.

In the alchemy of the Middle Ages, gold and silver corresponded to the sun and moon, respectively. One knew, when the soul through inner activity became more and more permeated by the spirit, then the aura changed. The timeless Eternal shown around such as person like sun's radiance enlivened the visage of the seer.

Medieval painters and sculptors showed this golden aura, this circular or oval radiance around the head or figure of saints: the halo. The crown or headband was a picture of it. Just as gold is the symbol of sun-related wisdom, so is silver the symbol of moon-related devotion and sensitivity. Sol is masculine and Luna is feminine. "Throw gold and silver over me": "Grant me spiritual activity and soulful devotion!"

The wooden shoes are put aside, and the slipper of silk and silver ornaments the foot. Relative to the earthly, transformative power and devoted readiness have become active. Such characteristics lead to the king's son.

In the gospel, the world-father calls the human soul to the marriage with the world-son. The folktale describes the same thing in the human inner life. Man participates in the Father and in the Son. Where the soul can say, "Not I, but Christ in me" the higher, spiritual I replaces the lower I that works in the body. This selfless, loving, eternal I is the king's son, the bridegroom of the soul-bride. He is the Eternal Masculine that marries the Eternal Feminine. This meeting should take place in the daytime, that is, in the working of the day, so that the king's son can say, "She is my dance partner." In rhythm and harmony should the I grasp the earth and release the

earth in the heaviness and in the lightness of fate, that is, to master the royal art of the transformation of life.

They danced until the evening came to an end and she wanted to go home, but the prince said he would go with her to take care of her, for he wanted to see where the beautiful maiden lived. But she escaped him, and jumped up into the dovecote. Then the prince waited until the father came, and told him the strange maiden had jumped into the dovecote. The father thought to himself, "It cannot surely be Cinderella," and called for axes and hatchets, and had the dovecote cut down, but there was no one in it. And when they entered the house there sat Cinderella in her dirty clothes among the cinders, and a little oil-lamp burnt dimly in the chimney; for Cinderella had been very quick, and had jumped out of the dovecote again, and had run to the hazel bush; and there she had taken off her beautiful dress and had laid it on the grave, and the bird had carried it away again, and then she had put on her little gray kirtle again, and had sat down in. the kitchen among the cinders.

The next day, when the festival began anew, and the parents and step-sisters had gone to it, Cinderella went to the hazel bush and cried,

Rustle yourself, and shake yourself, little tree,
Throw gold and silver over me.

Then the bird cast down a still more splendid dress than on the day before. And when she appeared in it among the guests every one was astonished at her beauty. The prince had been waiting until she came, and he took her hand and danced with her alone. And when any one else came to invite her he said, "She is my partner." And when the evening came she wanted to go home, and the prince followed her, for he wanted to see to what house she belonged; but

192

she broke away from him, and ran into the garden at the back of the house. There stood a fine large tree, bearing splendid pears; she leaped as lightly as a squirrel among the branches, and the prince did not know what had become of her. So he waited until the father came, and then he told him that the strange maiden had rushed from him, and that he thought she had gone up into the pear-tree. The father thought to himself, "It cannot surely be Cinderella," and called for an axe, and felled the tree, but there was no one in it. And when they went into the kitchen there sat Cinderella among the cinders, as usual, for she had got down the other side of the tree, and had taken back her beautiful clothes to the bird on the hazel bush, and had put on her old gray smock again.

On the third day, when the parents and the step-children had set off, Cinderella went again to her mother's grave, and said to the tree,

> *Rustle yourself, and shake yourself, little tree,*
> *Throw gold and silver over me.*

Then the bird cast down a dress, the like of which had never been seen for splendor and brilliancy, and slippers that were of gold. And when she appeared in this dress at the feast nobody knew what to say for wonderment. The prince danced with her alone, and if any one else asked her he answered, "She is my partner."

And when it was evening Cinderella wanted to go home, and the prince was about to go with her, when she ran past him so quickly that he could not follow her. But he had laid a plan, and had caused all the steps to be spread with pitch, so that as she rushed down them her left shoe remained sticking in it. The prince picked it up, and saw that it was of gold, and very small and slender. The next morning he went to the father and told him that

none should be his bride save the one whose foot the golden shoe should fit.

The images of the dovecote and the pear tree are omitted in many children's editions, but they are the crowning touch of the whole story, for what would a golden shoe be without a dovecote and pear tree?

The dovecote represents the head realm, with the doves flying in and out, messengers – like the senses – from the outer world to the inner world. "With him it goes on like in a dovecote" we say of someone who has many, far too many, ever changing thoughts, perhaps some bright ideas, but no stability. While the image is not very complimentary, it clearly points to the head and therefore to thinking.

One who looks at a pear tree as did the man of the Middle Ages – to whom outer nature was the expression of something interior – will easily recognize the image of the pear tree as representing the middle realm of feeling. The pears have the forms of drops and melt and flow with ripe sweetness, so the whole tree seems to drop and flow like feelings. The tale says: it stands in the garden. Mittgart[53] our forefathers called this middle realm of feeling. The pear tree is a special picture of the "nerve-tree" for the realm of feeling.

But the middle realm, like the head realm is also only a passageway. The task of the soul for the moment is: back to the gray smock, back to the ashes, until the completion is achieved.

Now the old self, the merchant, begins to wake up. "Could that be Cinderella?" And he cuts down his dovecote and pear tree in

---

53 The German Wikipedia has an interesting article on *Midgard* but nothing to directly support this statement.

readiness for the prince. But thinking (the dovecote) and feeling (the pear tree) cannot alone long be the home of the soul. Therefore the prince cannot find Cinderella there. Had he found her in the dovecote, head-spirituality would have been achieved, but nothing more. Had he found her in the pear tree, only excessive feeling would have been attained, not full humanity. Only when one penetrates into the will and works out of the will is completeness achieved. This Will is the golden trace by which the prince finds the bride: the shoe is the measure! Where wisdom rules in life and destiny, where our earthly task is freely willed, there fits the golden shoe!

Then the two sisters were very glad, because they had pretty feet. The eldest went to her room to try on the shoe, and her mother stood by. But she could not get her big toe into it, for the shoe was too small; then her mother handed her a knife, and said, "Cut the toe off, for when you are queen you will never have to go on foot." So the girl cut her toe off, squeezed her foot into the shoe, concealed the pain, and went down to the prince. Then he took her with him on his horse as his bride, and rode off. They had to pass by the grave, and there sat the two doves on the hazel bush, and called,

"Rucke di goo, rucke di goo!
There is blood on her shoe;
The shoe is too small,
Not the right bride at all!"

Then the prince looked at her shoe, and saw the blood flowing. And he turned his horse round and took the false bride home again, saying she was not the right one, and that the other sister must try on the shoe. So she went into her room to do so, and got her toes comfortably in, but her heel was too large. Then her mother handed her the knife, saying, "Cut a piece off your heel; when you are queen

you will never have to go on foot." So the girl cut a piece off her heel, and thrust her foot into the shoe, concealed the pain, and went down to the prince, who took his bride before him on his horse and rode off. When they passed by the hazel bush the two doves sat there and called,

> *"Rucke di goo, rucke di goo!*
> *There is blood on her shoe;*
> *The shoe is too small,*
> *Not the right bride at all!"*

Then the prince looked at her foot, and saw how the blood was flowing from the shoe, and staining the white stocking. And he turned his horse round and brought the false bride home again.

Whoever, like the two sisters, believes that he can quickly completely change his life, overcome his earth-seeking or earth-fleeing nature only injures himself and is judged by the dove of the spirit. Blood is in the shoe. Force draws blood after it.

"This is not the right one," said he, "have you no other daughter?" - "No," said the man, "only my dead wife left behind her a little stunted Cinderella; it is impossible that she can be the bride." But the King's son ordered her to be sent for, but the mother said, "Oh no! she is much too dirty, I could not let her be seen." But he would have her fetched, and so Cinderella had to appear. First she washed her face and hands quite clean, and went in and curtseyed to the prince, who held out to her the golden shoe. Then she sat down on a stool, drew her foot out of the heavy wooden shoe, and slipped it into the golden one, which fitted it perfectly. And when she stood up, and the prince looked in her face, he knew again the beautiful maiden that had danced with him, and he cried, "This is the right bride!" The step-mother and the two sisters were

thunderstruck, and grew pale with anger; but he put Cinderella before him on his horse and rode off. And as they passed the hazel bush, the two white doves called,

"Rucke di goo, rucke di goo!
No blood on her shoe;
The shoe's not too small,
The right bride is she after all."

And when they had thus cried, they came flying after and perched on Cinderella's shoulders, one on the right, the other on the left, and so remained.

One who has overcome the two opposing forces by unceasing self-education comes to know continuous grace – the doves sit upon the shoulders.

And when her wedding with the prince was appointed to be held the false sisters came, hoping to curry favour, and to take part in the festivities. So as the bridal procession went to the church, the eldest walked on the right side and the younger on the left, and the doves picked out an eye of each of them. And as they returned the elder was on the left side and the younger on the right, and the doves picked out the other eye of each of them. And so they were condemned to go blind for the rest of their days because of their wickedness and falsehood.

Because the opposing forces make a final attempt, during the procession in church, they draw onto themselves the consequences of their own hypocrisy: they loose forever their sight, can no longer see through anything, and are "hit by blindness." The dove of the Spirit has judged them.

Allerleirauh

(All kinds of fur)

Grimm 65

There was once on a time a King who had a wife with golden hair, and she was so beautiful that her equal was not to be found on earth. It came to pass that she lay ill, and as she felt that she must soon die, she called the King and said, "If thou wishest to marry again after my death, take no one who is not quite as beautiful as I am, and who has not just such golden hair as I have: this thou must promise me." And after the King had promised her this she closed her eyes and died.

For a long time the King could not be comforted, and had no thought of taking another wife. At length his councillors said, "There is no help for it, the King must marry again, that we may have a Queen." And now messengers were sent about far and wide, to seek a bride who equalled the late Queen in beauty. In the whole world, however, none was to be found, and even if one had been found, still there would have been no one who had such golden hair. So the messengers came home as they went.

Now the King had a daughter, who was just as beautiful as her deceased mother, and had the same golden hair. When she was grown up the King looked at her one day, and saw that in every respect she was like his late wife, and suddenly felt a violent love for her. Then he spake to his councillors, "I will marry my daughter, for she is the counterpart of my late wife, otherwise I can find no bride who resembles her." When the councillors heard that, they were shocked, and said, "God has forbidden a father to marry his daughter, no good can come from such a crime, and the kingdom

will be involved in the ruin." The daughter was still more shocked when she became aware of her father's resolution, but hoped to turn him from his design.

The beginning of this folktale points, as in Briar Rose, to the Golden Age when Man still lived with his soul in unbroken unity, in that condition which the tale calls the Kingdom. The soul was still enlightened and made radiant by a wisdom that was given her by grace as a primal manifestation of the spiritual world – she had golden hair. But the primal manifestation must come to an end; the dreamy vision fades, (the queen dies and her like is no more to be found on earth). However, out of the old soul nature a new is born, like a daughter from a mother. It is like the mother in radiant spirituality, expressed in the folktale as beauty and also as innate wisdom, for the daughter also has golden hair. Should the father "marry" the daughter, there would be no development; mankind would remain stuck in its childhood stage. But the daughter knows that the home in paradise must be left behind. The way of mankind goes naturally downwards and must with one's own force be turned upwards again. This way leads through poverty and isolation, but by it Man can of his own free will become a child of the Father-spirit.

Then she said to him, "Before I fulfill your wish, I must have three dresses, one as golden as the sun, one as silvery as the moon, and one as bright as the stars; besides this, I wish for a mantle of a thousand different kinds of fur and hair joined together, and one of every kind of animal in your kingdom must give a piece of his skin for it." But she thought, "To get that will be quite impossible, and thus I shall divert my father from his wicked intentions." The King, however, did not give it up, and the cleverest maidens in his kingdom had to weave the three dresses, one as golden as the sun, one as silvery as the moon, and one as bright as the stars, and his huntsmen

199

had to catch one of every kind of animal in the whole of his kingdom, and take from it a piece of its skin, and out of these was made a mantle of a thousand different kinds of fur. At length, when all was ready, the King caused the mantle to be brought, spread it out before her, and said, "The wedding shall be to-morrow."

When, therefore, the King's daughter saw that there was no longer any hope of turning her father's heart, she resolved to run away from him. In the night whilst every one was asleep, she got up, and took three different things from her treasures, a golden ring, a tiny golden spinning-wheel[54], and a golden spool[55]. The three dresses of the sun, moon, and stars she put into a nutshell, put on her mantle of all kinds of fur, and blackened her face and hands with soot.

The king's daughter wishes for three dresses; they are so fine that they will fit within a nutshell, and she herself puts them in. Three sheaths of the soul, woven out of cosmic forces, the father-self is able to have made for her. The time will come for them to be unfolded, and she herself will take them from the nutshell. Though the pictures of the myths and folktales are often closed to the intellect they live on in our speech, and we speak more pictorially than we realize. In German, the skull is referred to as the "nut" colloquially. In English we say that someone is a nut-head or just a nut to convey a less than laudatory opinion of what goes on inside his skull. Paracelsus, a great medieval physician, was well versed in

---

54 I have inserted the word "tiny" before "spinning wheel" in the translation on grounds that the diminutive of "spinning wheel" is used in the German text. I think of it as something an inch of so high perhaps for a doll house. There is no indication that it is used to spin; rather it is put into a soup bowl. The author notes below that in other tales the golden spinning wheel is a golden spindle, which is still easier to picture. Substitution of spindle for spinning wheel in telling the tale would probably be quite permissible.

55 The German word *Haspel* is *spool* in American English but *reel* in British English.

200

speaking in picture language. According to old views, walnuts strengthen the brain; in its forms Nature gives us hints.

In the head – the nut, the thinking cerebrum – the abilities are enclosed – the three dresses – which will unfold when the time has come.

And besides that, there is a coat made out of all kinds of fur, out of thousands of pelts. In the folktales, animals represent our drives and instincts. And though Man is, as the crown of creation, related to the angels in his higher being, so is he also related to the beasts in his lower nature. Our language recognizes the animal similarities of our character traits. There is the instinctive slyness of the cunning fox, there is "horse sense" which must be bridled lest one "gallop off"; there is lion-hearted courage, asinine obstinacy and occasional stupidity, bull-headed determination, gentleness of the ox and the patience of the cow. Everything that has hair and is warm-blooded has in this coat a piece of skin – its corresponding trait. The soul puts on this coat, face and hands become covered with soot, the drive nature rules, and behavior darkens.

Then she commended herself to God, and went away, and walked the whole night until she reached a great forest. And as she was tired, she got into a hollow tree, and fell asleep.

The sun rose, and she slept on, and she was still sleeping when it was full day. Then it so happened that the King to whom this forest belonged, was hunting in it. When his dogs came to the tree, they sniffed, and ran barking round about it. The King said to the huntsmen, "Just see what kind of wild beast has hidden itself in there." The huntsmen obeyed his order, and when they came back they said, "A wondrous beast is lying in the hollow tree; we have never before seen one like it. Its skin is fur of a thousand different

kinds, but it is lying asleep." Said the King, "See if you can catch it alive, and then fasten it to the carriage, and we will take it with us." When the huntsmen laid hold of the maiden, she awoke full of terror, and cried to them, "I am a poor child, deserted by father and mother; have pity on me, and take me with you." Then said they, "Allerleirauh, thou wilt be useful in the kitchen; come with us, and thou canst sweep up the ashes."

Night and day represent two worlds. Night is dream time, the mythological age, the childhood of mankind. Day is thinking time, awakening and wide awake thinking with the intellect. The picture-forming soul-man goes to sleep in the nerve-tree; the sense-nerve-man awakens in it. All wealth is gone, and the soul hears, "Allerleirauh, thou wilt be useful in the kitchen; come with us, and thou canst sweep up the ashes." ("Allerleirauh" means "All kinds of fur".)

She now finds herself in the realm of the king who will someday be her spouse. The spouse of the soul is the I. Allerleirauh has left the soul world of the Father-self and entered the world of the I. She is still poor and must begin from the bottom. Knowledge-seeking forces, the king's huntsmen, have hunted Allerleirauh out and led her into that realm where purification and development begin.

So they put her in the carriage, and took her home to the royal palace. There they pointed out to her a closet under the stairs, where no daylight entered, and said, "Hairy animal, there canst thou live and sleep." Then she was sent into the kitchen, and there she carried wood and water, swept the hearth, plucked the fowls, picked the vegetables, raked the ashes, and did all the hard work.

We may recall the myth of the the Phoenix bird that sacrifices itself, is burned, and rises newborn from its ashes. This ancient image warns of long purification and transformation, of death and resurrection. Goethe puts it in these words:

Und so lang du das nicht hast,	And so long as you don't have
Dieses: Stirb und werde!	This: Die and become!
Bist du nur ein trüber Gast	You are but a murky guest
Auf der dunklen Erde.	On the dark earth.

Die and become must happen in the heart. "Swept the hearth, ... raked the ashes" says the tale. The hearth, the fireplace in the house becomes the symbol of the heat source in the body, the heart. "Serve out of the strength of the heart" the tale wants to teach us. Burn away all that is lower in the purifying flame, cleanse yourself in the fire of true spiritualization, and what remains, sweep away so that the flame is ever anew enkindled. Carry "wood": carry and bear everything dried-up, lignified, no longer living – including withered thinking – and stoke with it the flames that cleanse you. Carry "water": water-related expressions like "go to the source", be "dippery" (meaning "creative" – see page 87), "deepen yourself", "live a flowing, streaming life", "don't dry up" all tell us what is meant. Dip into the soul world; quench the thirst of the seeking heart through the good, the true and the beautiful.[56] There is an old Chinese expression:

Oh how wonderful, how full of mystery is this:
I draw water, I carry firewood.[57]

---

56 Footnote by the author: The other work mentioned – plucking fowl, washing vegetables – does not have symbolic meaning. They seem to be ornamental additions.

57 See footnote page 288.

Allerleirauh lived there for a long time in great wretchedness. Alas, fair princess, what is to become of thee now! It happened, however, that one day a feast was held in the palace, and she said to the cook, "May I go up-stairs for a while, and look on? I will place myself outside the door." The cook answered, "Yes, go, but you must be back here in half-an-hour to sweep the hearth." Then she took her oil-lamp, went into her den, put off her fur-dress, and washed the soot off her face and hands, so that her full beauty once more came to light. And she opened the nut, and took out her dress which shone like the sun, and when she had done that she went up to the festival, and every one made way for her, for no one knew her, and thought no otherwise than that she was a king's daughter. The King came to meet her, gave his hand to her, and danced with her, and thought in his heart, "My eyes have never yet seen any one so beautiful!" When the dance was over she curtsied, and when the King looked round again she had vanished, and none knew whither. The guards who stood outside the palace were called and questioned, but no one had seen her.

The development is at risk. Will the ascent succeed? The human soul has done what was within its powers. Its full commitment now calls another force into action; the I in the radiance of kingdom, the higher Man comes to meet her. While in the Cinderella tale, the soul responded to a call, here the soul out of its own force mounts up – the tale specifically says that she went **up** to the festival. And while Cinderella gets her festive dress from the dove by grace from above, Allerleirauh takes hers herself from the nut shell. The time has come when the cerebrum has become the organ for the development of wisdom. For thinking, Man needs the abilities which were implanted in the head but which only now can be unfolded by him: the golden dress. We have many

representations of this golden dress in medieval painting and sculpture. The radiance of the soul, well-known to the seer, is shown as an oval aura. While the Christ-being himself is shown with a rainbow-colored mandorla[58] – the sign of highest spiritual radiance – the golden aura indicates wisdom and activity in the *soul* realm. To present-day people this radiance is in general no longer visible but none the less noticeable. We say that someone is looking "radiant" or has a "shining" face.

She had, however, run into her little den, had quickly taken off her dress, made her face and hands sooty again, put on the fur-mantle, and again was Allerleirauh. And now when she went into the kitchen, and was about to get to her work and sweep up the ashes, the cook said, "Leave that alone till morning, and make me the soup for the King; I, too, will go upstairs awhile, and take a look; but let no hairs fall in, or in future thou shalt have nothing to eat." So the cook went away, and Allerleirauh made the soup for the king, and made bread soup and the best she could, and when it was ready she fetched her golden ring from her little den, and put it in the bowl in which the soup was served. When the dancing was over, the King had his soup brought and ate it, and he liked it so much that it seemed to him he had never tasted better. But when he came to the bottom of the bowl, he saw a golden ring lying, and could not conceive how it could have got there. Then he ordered the cook to appear before him. The cook was terrified when he heard the order, and said to Allerleirauh, "Thou hast certainly let a hair fall into the soup, and if thou hast, thou shalt be beaten for it." When he came before the King the latter asked who had made the soup? The cook replied, "I made it." But the King said, "That is not true, for it was

---

58 Mandorla is the Italian word for almond. In art, it is an almond-shaped form completely surrounding the holy figure.

much better than usual, and cooked differently." He answered, "I must acknowledge that I did not make it, it was made by the rough animal." The King said, "Go and bid it come up here."

When Allerleirauh came, the King said, "Who art thou?" - "I am a poor girl who no longer has any father or mother." He asked further, "Of what use art thou in my palace?" She answered, "I am good for nothing but to have boots thrown at my head." He continued, "Where didst thou get the ring which was in the soup?" She answered, "I know nothing about the ring." So the King could learn nothing, and had to send her away again.

From the height of her experience Allerleirauh returns to the everyday, but with a new ability: she cooks for the king. The cook prepares from the gifts of the earth the nourishment for our body and must know what is healthy and acceptable for it. We need an internal ability which processes the food for nourishment. That happens in everyone with a certain unconscious reliability. One can quickly determine whether one has been given bread of stones to eat, but also whether one spiritually hungers and thirsts. This primal action and distinguishing in the tale is called the old cook.

When the communication between the feminine of the soul and the masculine of the spirit is so well established as here, then can the soul itself prepare nourishment. She has gained knowledge in her learning and purification time and so can now offer it plentifully – a bowl full of bread soup. And more than that: through the poverty of her earthly life, that she has learned to bear and master – as poor child without father and mother – she can give what she had brought with her on the way as equipment: the closed-in-itself, timeless-rounded consciousness of the eternity of her I: the ring. She puts the ring in the bread soup: the self-enclosed I

consciousness rests in the knowledge won by the soul (in the bread). This knowledge has twice gone through the heart's warmth: the bread was first baked in the oven and then again cooked in the soup on the hearth. This process cannot be grasped by the intellect: "I know nothing about the ring." Such a high level of development can bring with it a certain danger. Therefore the probing question, "Who art thou?" gets only the modest answer "I am a poor girl who no longer has any father or mother." All inheritance has ended; the soul is totally on its own. Of the ring she knows nothing. Does modesty then know whether and how far the connection to the spiritual has already succeeded? Knowledge about that might already indicate pride.

After a while, there was another festival, and then, as before, Allerleirauh begged the cook for leave to go and look on. He answered, "Yes, but come back again in half-an-hour, and make the King the bread soup which he so much likes." Then she ran into her den, washed herself quickly, and took out of the nut the dress which was as silvery as the moon, and put it on. Then she went up and was like a princess, and the King stepped forward to meet her, and rejoiced to see her once more, and as the dance was just beginning they danced it together. But when it was ended, she again disappeared so quickly that the King could not observe where she went. She, however, sprang into her den, and once more made herself a hairy animal, and went into the kitchen to prepare the bread soup. When the cook had gone up-stairs, she fetched the little golden spinning-wheel, and put it in the bowl so that the soup covered it. Then it was taken to the King, who ate it, and liked it as much as before, and had the cook brought, who this time likewise was forced to confess that Allerleirauh had prepared the soup. Allerleirauh again came before the King, but she answered that she

was good for nothing else but to have boots thrown at her head, and that she knew nothing at all about the tiny golden spinning-wheel.

For the second time Allerleirauh goes to the feast and now unfolds the silver dress that had long lain in the nutshell. While the golden dress was like the sun and represented wisdom which warmed, enlivened, and awakened – and is therefore related to the sun – we would not be thinking beings without the sun – the silver dress indicates that in its depths the soul is also related to the moon.

The moon works into life rhythms; both seed and sprout, the unborn grow in moon rhythm The temperament with which we are born, the night-side of our being and the foundation of so much of our personality, is connected with moon rhythms. To master this foundation of being demands an even more intensive force than achieving wisdom through thinking, for it involves a change of character reaching into the inherited basis of our being. If a sanguine becomes thorough, or a phlegmatic quick, or choleric soft, or a melancholic happy, he has worked on the silver garment. Again it is taken from the nut, that is, it is won by head work, through thinking insight. When that has been done, a new mass of knowledge is possible – a new bowl of bread soup, and in it the golden spinning wheel (or spindle). The golden spinning wheel – the counter-symbol to the cursed spindle of Briar Rose – why can it only now be brought out? Because only now has one entered into the reproductive forces and into the hereditary basis of life. It is no longer just a question of thought content, and therefore of a wisdom that one can acquire by learning and practicing, but of one's *own activity* in thinking, of *how* one spins the threads of thought. Just think of how differently a choleric thinks from a phlegmatic! To completely master "spinning", to develop wisdom concerning the process of thinking, that is the golden spinning

wheel. Allerleirauh brings it to the king: up until now active thinking feminine and soul-related; now a subjective-soulful process has become an objective-spiritual process. Thinking becomes I-controlled. Thinking with soul forces becomes penetrated by the spirit. Again follows the questioning, and again modesty determines the answers.

When, for the third time, the King held a festival, all happened just as it had done before. The cook said, "Faith rough-skin, thou art a witch, and always puttest something in the soup which makes it so good that the King likes it better than that which I cook," but as she begged so hard, he let her go up at the appointed time. And now she put on the dress which shone like the stars, and thus entered the hall. Again the King danced with the beautiful maiden, and thought that she never yet had been so beautiful. And whilst she was dancing, he contrived, without her noticing it, to slip a golden ring on her finger, and he had given orders that the dance should last a very long time. When it was ended, he wanted to hold her fast by her hands, but she tore herself loose, and sprang away so quickly through the crowd that she vanished from his sight. She ran as fast as she could into her den beneath the stairs, but as she had been too long, and had stayed more than half-an-hour she could not take off her pretty dress, but only threw over it her fur-mantle, and in her haste she did not make herself quite black, but one finger remained white. Then Allerleirauh ran into the kitchen, and cooked the bread soup for the King, and as the cook was away, put her golden spool into it.

Now that the soul through continual communication with the higher I has bound itself with the spiritual world, it can know cosmic laws through thinking; it has become a microcosm in the macrocosm. She takes the starry garment out of the nut; it is the highest that Man can attain. With it, a new measure of knowledge

has become possible: a third bowl of bread soup. And the golden spool – brought along as equipment – can now be used and put in.

In making yarn for weaving, first fibers are twisted together to make a single, "simple" yarn. The "simple" wants to twist itself up, but when two simples with twists in opposite directions are spun together, the combined yarn does not curl. Yarn for weaving or knitting often has many simples spun together before being wound onto the spool or reel. Thus the spool represents combining of threads of thought into encompassing ideas.[59]

"Don't get all spooled up" we say in German meaning "Don't get confused by words" for the thoughts expressed in individual words are "wound up" in the spirit of the language, in the ideas of the language. This ability to wrap ideas in words was implanted into the soul. In his individual personality Man can now live in ideas – the king gets the spool.

When the King found the reel at the bottom of it, he caused Allerleirauh to be summoned, and then he espied the white finger, and saw the ring which he had put on it during the dance. Then he grasped her by the hand, and held her fast, and when she wanted to release herself and run away, her mantle of fur opened a little, and the star-dress shone forth. The King clutched the mantle and tore it off. Then her golden hair shone forth, and she stood there in full splendor, and could no longer hide herself. And when she had washed the soot and ashes from her face, she was more beautiful than anyone who had ever been seen on earth. But the King said, "Thou art my dear bride, and we will never more part from each other." Thereupon the marriage was solemnized, and they lived happily until their death.

---

59 This paragraph has been rewritten rather than translated to make it clearer.

The star garment has become a possession which cannot be lost. With it the soul is freed all domination by the drives of nature: the cloak of all kinds of furs falls away. The true being is revealed. The golden hair, formerly expression of an enlightenment granted by grace, becomes the manifestation of enlighten thinking attained by her own forces, her own purification and transformation. The dream vision of the past has been transformed into the thought vision of the future: "She was more beautiful than anyone who had ever been seen on earth." And as her appearance was ennobled, so also was her action: her hands were no longer covered with soot. The royal wedding is celebrated, and since the body and soul have been transformed we may call it a Chymical Wedding.

The Three Feathers

Grimm 63

There was once on a time a King who had three sons, of whom two were clever and wise, but the third did not speak much, and was simple, and was called the Simpleton. When the King had become old and weak, and was thinking of his end, he did not know which of his sons should inherit the kingdom after him.

One should strive for the wisdom of the "simpleton." And the great educators of the peoples wished to form the Will of Man so that he would become wise and have a genuine Spirit-Will. They therefore scattered around many tales of the simpleton. The simple fellow despised by the all-too-clever should serve as an example.

In our tale, the conduct of the genuine Spirit-Will – namely, that which always and everywhere counts as foolishness – in its relation to gender is depicted.

The King in Man – the fatherly self – (many call him the Old Adam) is old and weak. Up until now, he was the ruling power internally, but his life is coming to an end. The I must take hold of the rulership. It must prove itself out of its own forces, not out of tradition and inheritance as had the old king; it must win the kingdom for itself. The I of Man develops stepwise. Feeling, thinking, and willing are the fundamental forces of its development. One can experience them as active spiritual forces in the image of the three sons. One can also say: the I as feeling is the eldest, the I as thinking is the second, and the I as willing is the third. Which of the three sons will be most mature and capable of ruling the inner world, the kingdom, and therefore attain full self-mastery?

Then he said to them: "Go forth, and he who brings me the most beautiful carpet shall be King after my death." And that there should be no dispute amongst them, he took them outside his castle, blew three feathers in the air, and said: "You shall go as they fly." One feather flew to the east, the other to the west, but the third flew straight up and did not fly far, but soon fell to the ground. And now one brother went to the right, and the other to the left, and they mocked Simpleton, who was forced to stay where the third feather had fallen.

He sat down and was sad, then all at once he saw that there was a trap-door close by the feather. He raised it up, found some steps, and went down them, and then he came to another door, knocked at it, and heard somebody inside calling:

"Maiden green and small,
Hopping,
Hopping hither and thither;
Hop to the door,
And quickly see who is there."

The door opened, and he saw a great, fat toad sitting, and round about her a crowd of little toads. The fat toad asked what he wanted? He answered: "I should like to have the prettiest and finest carpet in the world." Then she called a young one and said:

"Maiden green and small,
Hopping,
Hopping hither and thither,
Hop quickly and bring me
The great box here."

The young toad brought the box, and the fat toad opened it, and gave Simpleton a carpet out of it, so beautiful and so fine, that

213

*on the earth above, none could have been woven like it. Then he
thanked her, and ascended again.*

*The two others had, however, looked on their youngest brother
as so silly that they believed he would find and bring nothing at all.
"Why should we give ourselves a great deal of trouble to search?"
said they, and got some coarse cloths from the first shepherds' wives
whom they met, and carried them home to the King. At the same
time Simpleton also came back, and brought his beautiful carpet,
and when the King saw it he was astonished, and said: "If justice be
done, the kingdom belongs to the youngest."*

The carpet, which covers the floor and beautifies it with
colorful figures and pictures is a symbol for colorful, happy, lively
warm Feeling that is rich in inner pictures, visualizations which
powerfully fill the soul, symbols and imaginations. One should
create this wealth of inner pictures as a result of feeling.

Through long ages there came from the East a great wealth of
spirituality. All of western humanity was influenced by it. And in
many people there is still a side which gladly turns in that direction
and seeks inner guidance in the the ancient, traditional ways
practiced there – *ex oriente lux*. Later the West became more and
more important, researched the physical world, strengthened
thinking and the I-personality, and thereby developed its own
Wisdom – *ex occidente lux*. Each of us also has both of these sides
within us, for what happens to all mankind is reflected in each
individual.

Towards the inner East the eldest brother, feeling, turns. One
can also call him sensation-man. To the west goes the second, the
thinking or understanding man. One could also say: the feeling is
eastern oriented; the thinking is western oriented. The the third, the

214

willing aspect, must seek and find where it already is. Every place is *the* place. He must grasp what is closest; he holds the middle ground. And there he must descend into the depths, into the depths of his own humanity. He goes down stepwise; the tale specifically mentions steps. And he knocks on the closed door of the toad.

The toad – formerly the symbol of spontaneous generation in moist, swampy mud – has today become the symbol of sexuality. The toad gives what the simpleton asks, for what is important is the manner of asking. The old toad calls the young one who should serve the simpleton "maiden green and small." Here "green" is used in the sense of "young and flourishing". The old toad[60] thus expresses what lives behind the toad instinct: a human virginal force still emerging is hidden in it.

Here, beneath the earth, the simpleton, the pure fool[61], wins that wealth of feeling, that beauty of transformation which covers the plain earth of outer reality and can make him king. Those who, like the older brothers take rough cloths from the first shepherds' wives they meet do not win the kingdom. Cloths are woven from spun threads. In picture language, thought threads are woven to thought cloth. So the older brothers bring back from the secular environment crude thoughts without pictures.

But the two others let their father have no peace, and said that it was impossible that Simpleton, who in everything lacked understanding, should be King, and entreated him to make a new

---

60 The author here uses the pronoun *sie* = *she* to refer to the old toad, but that does not mean that the old toad was female, only that the word for toad in German, *Krote*, is grammatically feminine. I have therefore repeated the noun to avoid a gender specific pronoun.

61 "Pure fool" = "reine Tor" is the characterization of Parzival at the outset of his adventures.

agreement with them. Then the father said: "He who brings me the most beautiful ring shall inherit the kingdom," and led the three brothers out, and blew into the air three feathers, which they were to follow. Those of the two eldest again went east and west, and Simpleton's feather flew straight up, and fell down near the door into the earth. Then he went down again to the fat toad, and told her that he wanted the most beautiful ring. She at once ordered her great box to be brought, and gave him a ring out of it, which sparkled with jewels, and was so beautiful that no goldsmith on earth would have been able to make it. The two eldest laughed at Simpleton for going to seek a golden ring. They gave themselves no trouble, but knocked the nails out of an old carriage-ring, and took it to the King; but when Simpleton produced his golden ring, his father again said, "The kingdom belongs to him."

The ring is closed in itself, without beginning and without end. Thus it becomes the picture of an encompassing consciousness where beginning and end are one. The end of our life in the spiritual world is the beginning of our life in the sense world, and the end of this life is there a new beginning. The I perceives itself no more as a time-limited being within an earthly life but as eternal. No goldsmith on earth can make this ring; each one of us must forge his own. And the precious stones with which it is ornamented point to the fact that all matter (stones) is ennobled and transformed through this experience. The material shines in the radiance of the spiritual. The Willing attains a universal consciousness when it strives for it. For in the ring the Will creates itself and heaves itself out of the temporal into the eternal. Fertilization and procreation draw cosmic forces into humans, and these forces bestow themselves upon those who ask and struggle to find their own eternal being. Our language uses both words for

processes that take place both bodily and spiritually. We speak of bodily *Zeugung* (fertililization) and of spiritual *Überzeugung* (conviction) and of physical and spiritual fructifying. To be truly Man means never to separate this duality of the physical and of the soul-spiritual in sexual life. (The maiden is in the toad.)

The two eldest did not cease from tormenting the King until he made a third condition, and declared that the one who brought the most beautiful woman home, should have the kingdom. He again blew the three feathers into the air, and they flew as before.

Then Simpleton without more ado went down to the fat toad, and said: "I am to take home the most beautiful woman!" - "Oh," answered the toad, "the most beautiful woman! She is not at hand at the moment, but still thou shalt have her." The toad then gave him a yellow turnip which had been hollowed out, to which six mice were harnessed. Then Simpleton said quite mournfully: "What am I to do with that?" The toad answered: "Just put one of my little toads into it." Then he seized one at random out of the circle, and put her into the yellow coach, but hardly was she seated inside it than she turned into a wonderfully beautiful maiden, and the turnip into a coach, and the six mice into horses. So he kissed her, and drove off quickly with the horses, and took her to the King. His brothers came afterwards; they had given themselves no trouble at all to seek beautiful girls, but had brought with them the first peasant women they chanced to meet. When the King saw them he said: "After my death the kingdom belongs to my youngest son." But the two eldest deafened the King's ears afresh with their clamor, "We cannot consent to Simpleton's being King," and demanded that the one whose wife could leap through a ring which hung in the centre of the hall should have the preference. They thought: "The peasant women can do that easily; they are strong enough, but the delicate

maiden will jump herself to death." The aged King agreed likewise to this. Then the two peasant women jumped, and jumped through the ring, but were so stout that they fell, and their coarse arms and legs broke in two. And then the pretty maiden whom Simpleton had brought with him, sprang, and sprang through as lightly as a deer, and all opposition had to cease. So he received the crown, and has ruled wisely for a long time.

The third task for the three brothers, to find the most beautiful woman, means to find the soul itself. Just as the two older brothers brought only rings from peasant wagons – that is, they brought only an I-consciousness directed towards the earthly – they now bring the first peasant women they meet. That is, they win souls that are turned only to the earthly, for the peasant works the earth, and since they are stout and heavy they cleave all too much to the earth and cannot lift themselves to something higher.

The simpleton again goes into the depths. The turnip hitched to six mice and the young toad inside is a grotesque image. Did the teacher who created this tale wish to indicate that the world of the toad appears grotesque if experienced without soul?

The turnip is a plant that grows mostly underground. Its edible "fruit" grows downward into the dark earth. The realm of the toad is the realm of *Fortpflanzung* (reproduction), and this is – as the name itself says – related plant kingdom (***Pflanzen****reich*). It can take place, as happens in the plant kingdom, free from self-seeking desires. The simpleton grasps the toad and puts her in the hollowed out turnip: sexual forces are surrounded and borne by what is natural and therefore experienced in plant-like innocence.

Mice live and dig in the earth. In folk traditions they are, out of old clairvoyance, connected with the the devil. In his *Mythology*,

Jakob Grimm gives many examples. And also in Goethe's *Faust*, Mephistopheles is the Lord of the Mice. He is the spirit of lies, and reveals himself to Faust more and more as the dark spirit of hardening, of the materialistic lie, which turns everything spiritual into the unspiritual, everything supersensible into the sensible. How has this realm of sexuality become Satanized! From the bright light of plantlike innocence, it has been shifted deceitfully into the darkness of passion-driven guilt. Virginal soul forces have been made into toads. Even the forces that lead upward to the "King" have been reinterpreted and "Satanized." They have become mice. But in truth there prevails in the bodily nature of Man the Wisdom of Nature, the divine Intelligence. One who knows this cannot fall for the Mephistophelean Lie. This Wisdom of Nature rules six-fold; six horses draw the coach upward.

The mineral body is built up out of the substances of the earth according to high natural laws. It is given human form and brought to life, capable of reproduction and therefore related to the plants. In being sensitive to pleasure and pain and having drives and instincts, humans are related to the animals. We thus have Form, Life and Sensitivity. Who cannot perceive an Intelligence that works in this threefold way? And then further experience how this bodily nature is expands and rises to the soul nature? Sensing becomes feeling; feeling becomes penetrated with thinking, and both are the lifted up to willing. Whoever fails to recognize this Intelligence of our deeply ensouled body, and not even at least sense it – must he not forever remain in the uncertain darkness of Mephistophelean untruth?

To transform the mice to horses and to drive upward to the king means to transform the whole process: the toad becomes

virginal soul force, the most beautiful woman is found, the animal has become Man.

The one so freed from enchantment can spring through the ring before the king. She has been lifted up out of the earthly-instinctive force of the toad to the cosmic-ensouled virgin. For the animal is more strongly turned toward the earth; but Man, through his spirit, more strongly to the cosmos.

The all-too-earthly souls of the brothers cannot do that. They must break up on this trial. The self in Man – the old king – can now pass on the crown. For the third son, the one
who has mastered Will,
who treads the realm of the toad with pure heart,
has now
through the wealth of Feeling (the carpet),
through an I-consciousness that is eternal (the ring)
and through the courage for transformation and knowledge attained the kingdom of the true I.

The Clever Little Tailor

Grimm 114

"But not true," said the little Wolfgang Goethe to his mother when she had just told him the beginning of "The Clever Little Tailor" ending with a graceful phrase and promised him the rest for the next day. "Not true, the damned tailor doesn't get the princess, does he?" And with those words this spiritually confident lad without realizing it expressed his life problem. Throughout his life, Goethe fought for the "princess" and against the "tailor".

What happens during the handwork of a tailor? The tailor must first cut the fabric according to a pattern and measure and then put it back together into a whole, always working with scissors and needle and taking the utmost care to get the right fit. The new whole that is created is totally different from the old whole and is completely his own work. No wonder that one must keep a watchful eye on the tailor, so much depends on him.

And how much depends on the inner tailor who constantly goes after a whole and cuts it to pieces with sharpened mind and and fine wits and then puts the pieces together again into a new whole according to his own discretion! It is the intellect that the picture language calls the "tailor." It is that cleverness that seeks less to grasp a comprehensive whole than to boldly "trim" the matter to "fit" his understanding and then to deal with details. Where it gets the upper hand, there is the danger that one becomes a meager, hair-splitting, conceited fellow. To cut something big into pieces and to put it back together according to one's own discretion can easily lead to pride. For example, that other folktale-tailor

221

claims "Seven at one blow" even if they were only flies.[62] Goethe could never stand this tailor. But where the tailor takes his proper place in our inner workforce he is welcome, and we can use him well. But his wife, the little tailor soul, must not get too curious, as happened once in Cologne.[63] If the little tailors think they can make visible those elementary forces that work secretly in the realm of nature, then they are wrong. With the light or the intellect one only drives away the Heinzelmännchen.

Our tale begins:

There was once upon a time a princess who was extremely proud. If a wooer came she gave him some riddle to guess, and if he could not find it out, he was sent contemptuously away. She let it be made known also that whosoever solved her riddle should marry her, let him be who he might. At length, therefore, three tailors fell in with each other, the two eldest of whom thought they had done so many dexterous bits of work successfully that they could not fail to succeed in this also; the third was a little useless vagabond, who did not even know his trade, but thought he must have some luck in this venture, for where else was it to come from? Then the two others said to him, "Just stay at home; thou canst not do much with thy little bit of understanding." The little tailor, however, did not let himself be discouraged, and said he had set his head to work about this for

---

62 A reference to "The Valiant Little Tailor", Grimm 20.

63 The Heinzelmännchen of Cologne were elves that finished at night all the work people had left undone during the day. This was very nice indeed for the people. But the tailor's wife became curious. She scattered dried peas on the floor. The Heinzelmännchen slipped and fell. She heard them fall and came with a light, but the Heinzelmännchen vanished from sight and never came back. The author quotes in a footnote a brief verse by August Kopish about the tailor's wife's curiosity and its consequence.

once, and he would manage well enough, and he went forth as if the whole world were his.

They all three announced themselves to the princess, and said she was to propound her riddle to them, and that the right persons were now come, who had understandings so fine that they could be threaded in a needle. Then said the princess, "I have two kinds of hair on my head, of what color is it?" - "If that be all," said the first, "it must be black and white, like the cloth which is called pepper and salt." The princess said, "Wrongly guessed; let the second answer." Then said the second, "If it be not black and white, then it is brown and red, like my father's company coat." - "Wrongly guessed," said the princess, "let the third give the answer, for I see very well he knows it for certain." Then the little tailor stepped boldly forth and said, "The princess has a silver and a golden hair on her head, and those are the two different colors." When the princess heard that, she turned pale and nearly fell down with terror, for the little tailor had guessed her riddle, and she had firmly believed that no man on earth could discover it.

In our tale, the tailor is confronted with the princess, and he is certainly not shy. He knows perfectly well that the riddle does not have to do with anything everyday, but that something from two different worlds is shining in, from two worlds that correspond to one another like sun and moon, like gold and silver. But there is a hair from each on the head of our princess who with proud questions tests any suitor. She must contend with the tailor and in the end be his.

When her courage returned she said, "Thou hast not won me yet by that; there is still something else that thou must do. Below, in the cellar is a bear with which thou shalt pass the night, and when I

get up in the morning if thou art still alive, thou shalt marry me."
She expected, however, she should thus get rid of the tailor, for the
bear had never yet left any one alive who had fallen into his
clutches. The little tailor did not let himself be frightened away, but
was quite delighted, and said, "Boldly ventured is half won."

The tailor's second task, to deal with the bear below in the
cellar, is weightier. The bear plods along as an ungainly four-footed
beast, but can stand up on his hind legs, look strikingly human and
even dance. It is a picture of that dullness and weight that indeed
strives to be upright, lighter and more mobile but ever and again
draws the human down. It is extraordinarily strong, this earth-heavy
giant, ofter paired with a certain good humor and can represent
earthly stability. In this sense, the bear often appears in a coat of
arms. But if this strength and stability is stirred to action with
smoldering passion, then the bear becomes dangerous.

When therefore the evening came, our little tailor was taken
down to the bear. The bear was about to set at the little fellow at
once, and give him a hearty welcome with his paws: "Softly, softly,"
said the little tailor, "I will soon make thee quiet." Then quite
composedly, and as if he had not an anxiety in the world, he took
some nuts out of his pocket, cracked them, and ate the kernels.
When the bear saw that, he was seized with a desire to have some
nuts too. The tailor felt in his pockets, and reached him a handful;
they were, however, not nuts, but pebbles. The bear put them in his
mouth, but could get nothing out of them, let him bite as he would.
"Eh!" thought he, "what a stupid blockhead I am! I cannot even
crack a nut!" and then he said to the tailor, "Here, crack me the
nuts." - "There, see what a stupid fellow thou art!" said the little
tailor, "to have such a great mouth, and not be able to crack a small
nut!" Then he took the pebble and nimbly put a nut in his mouth in

the place of it, and crack, it was in two! "I must try the thing again," said the bear; "when I watch you, I then think I ought to be able to do it too." So the tailor once more gave him a pebble, and the bear tried and tried to bite into it with all the strength of his body. But no one will imagine that he accomplished it.

The question is: Which is stronger, the intellect or weight and dullness? How can the tailor master the bear? We know what "cracking a nut" means. In German, the expression *Kopfnuss,* literally "headnut" has the meaning of *clout.* The walnut gives the picture. The skull, in which the brain is embedded like the kernel in the nutshell, is the hard nut. That the tailor "cracks nuts" means that the intellect solves thought tasks. The dull bearer that lives below must learn how to do it. The tailor shows the bear that he cannot distinguish nuts from stones, that is, good, genuine thoughts from unfruitful, materialistic ones, and occupies the dim-witted beast with getting the nut kernels from the stones. But this exercise stimulated mobility.

When that was over, the tailor took out a violin from beneath his coat, and played a piece on it to himself. When the bear heard the music, he could not help beginning to dance, and when he had danced a while, the thing pleased him so well that he said to the little tailor, "Hark you, is the fiddle heavy?" - "Light enough for a child. Look, with the left hand I lay my fingers on it, and with the right I stroke it with the bow, and then it goes merrily, hop sa sa vivallalera!" - "So," said the bear; "fiddling is a thing I should like to understand too, that I might dance whenever I had a fancy. What dost thou think of that? "Wilt thou give me lessons?" - "With all my heart," said the tailor, "if thou hast a talent for it. But just let me see thy claws, they are terribly long, I must cut thy nails a little." Then a vise was brought, and the bear put his claws in it, and the little tailor

screwed it tight, and said, "Now wait until I come with the scissors,"
and he let the bear growl as he liked, and lay down in the corner on
a bundle of straw, and fell asleep.

If the intellect becomes musical – if the tailor plays the violin – and works artistically harmonizing, then is heaviness finally overcome – the bear dances and wants to make music himself. In any event, he is mastered by the tailor.

When the princess heard the bear growling so fiercely during
the night, she believed nothing else but that he was growling for joy,
and had made an end of the tailor. In the morning she arose
careless and happy, but when she peeped into the stable, the tailor
stood gaily before her, and was as healthy as a fish in water. Now
she could not say another word against the wedding because she
had given a promise before every one, and the King ordered a
carriage to be brought in which she was to drive to church with the
tailor, and there she was to be married. When they had got into the
carriage, the two other tailors, who had false hearts and envied him
his good fortune, went into the stable and unscrewed the bear again.
The bear in great fury ran after the carriage. The princess heard
him snorting and growling; she was terrified, and she cried, "Ah, the
bear is behind us and wants to get thee!" The tailor was quick and
stood on his head, stuck his legs out of the window, and cried, "Dost
thou see the vise? If thou dost not be off thou shalt be put into it
again." When the bear saw that, he turned round and ran away. The
tailor drove quietly to church, and the princess was married to him
at once, and he lived with her as happy as a woodlark. Whosoever
does not believe this, must pay a thaler.

No matter how much the proud princess wanted to get out of her promise, she must now recognize the tailor. The intellect has

proven itself; she can now ensoul it. In picture language, the princess can marry the tailor. But in the background are the two other tailors, who envy the third his abilities. (We recognize the three fellows or brothers from various tales and know how often the other two block the one who has made progress.) Here they are guilty of wanting to make the bear-dullness once more powerful. But the tailor knows how to take care of himself: he stands on his head. Hieronymus Herzogenbusch, called Bosch, the great symbol painter, often shows a head stand in his pictures.[64] It indicates a complete turn around. Not only to be securely anchored on the firm ground of facts in the earthly realm but also on occasion to stand in a higher world – that is what is important. When the intellect has become so adroit that it has mastered this "below and above" then all bear-like dullness and weight is for ever overcome, and nothing more stands in the way of the marriage.

---

64 There is one in the central panel of "The Garden of Earthly Delights".

Mother Holle

Grimm 24

A widow had two daughters; one was pretty and industrious, the other was ugly and lazy. And as the ugly one was her own daughter, she loved her much the best, and the pretty one was made to do all the work, and be the drudge of the house.

Feminine figures are the picture for the soul and soul forces. When the living connection to the spiritual-masculine is no more present and the soul is on its own, then it is like the widow. If she is also a stepmother – a stiff mother – the she is in herself no longer spiritually alive but has become materialistic and committed herself solely to the sense world.

But every soul is many sided. Youthful forces of being arise out of the old and have their evolution and their goal: the "daughter". The one, more oriented to the spiritual father is active and creative; the other, oriented to the stepmother, is passive and lazy. The first is translucent for the noble and beautiful; the second, for the forces of hatred and the ugly.

Every day the poor girl had to sit by a spring on the high road and spin until her fingers bled. Now it happened once that as the spool was bloody, she dipped it into the spring to wash it; but it slipped out of her hand and fell in. Then she began to cry, and ran to her step-mother, and told her of her misfortune; and her stepmother scolded her without mercy, and said in her rage: "As you have let the spool fall in, you must go and fetch it out again!" Then the girl went back again to the spring, not knowing what to do, and in the despair of her heart she jumped down into the spring to get the spool.

Spinning is an age-old picture word for thinking. In German, we say, slightly disparagingly, of a one-sided thinker, "he spins." But we also speak of the "threads of logic." To sit on the high road and spin means that this thinking is no longer a quietly harbored practice occupied with the secrets of the spirit, but is open and general, turned toward the manifestations of the sense world. But even there, it is creatively deep, mysteriously giving rise to soul experiences: the spring.

German has an expression "*aufs Blut*" – literally "onto the blood" – meaning to the utmost extreme. When thinking has been so intense that it goes even "onto the blood", then the result of the thinking, the thread wound on the spool, must be dipped into the cleansing spring. But ultimately we are not masters of our thoughts; they escape us. The thinking and the thought content of the diligent daughter are of a spiritual nature, and the spiritual goes into the "depths." The spool sinks into the spring. The stepmother, the representative of the material sense world, cannot help there. On the contrary, her hardness gives the impetus to even greater deepening. One must dare to jump into the depths for one's self. What has been thought up until then no longer matters: the spool has disappeared. What follows is a new awakening on different plane.

After that she knew nothing; and when she came to herself she was in a beautiful meadow, and the sun was shining on the flowers that grew round her. And she walked on through the meadow until she came to a baker's oven that was full of bread; and the bread called out to her: "Oh, take me out, take me out, or I shall burn; I am baked enough already!" Then she drew near, and with the baker's peel she took out all the loaves one after the other.

229

This other plane appears as a green, blossoming plain before the inner vision. The maiden has stepped out of the object world of the senses and into the sphere of continual growth bursting with life. Immediately demands and tests meet her. In the sense world, bread is the most important nourishment for the body; in the world where she now finds herself the most important nourishment for the soul is spiritual knowledge. "We are on earth to know God" says Christian doctrine. Knowledge of the spirit is the "bread" of the soul.

The hearth, the fireplace, and the oven give heat to the house. The warmth center of the house of the body is the heart. In dreams and in folktales it often appears in the picture of the heart. There, the tale wants to say, in the center of inner heart warmth, thou hast won this spiritual knowledge because on the other side of thy being thou hast thought, thou hast spun. But now thou must be active and use thy will to bring it to light. And the soul accustomed to diligence brings the bread to light.

And she went farther on till she came to a tree weighed down with apples, and it called out to her: "Oh, shake me, shake me, we apples are all of us ripe!" Then she shook the tree until the apples fell like rain, and she shook until there were no more to fall; and when she had gathered them together in a heap, she went on farther.

The old clairvoyance from which the folktales stem sees the upward-reaching spinal nervous system, that somewhat resembles a tree, in this image. Also there is knowledge attained, but it is a different knowledge from that of the heart. The fruit of the tree, the apple, becomes the symbol of the Fall as the fruit of the tree of knowledge of good and evil. This fruit must now be harvested.

At last she came to a little house, and an old woman was peeping out of it, but she had such great teeth that the girl was terrified and about to run away, only the old woman called her back. "What are you afraid of, my dear child? Come and live with me, and if you do the house-work well and orderly, things shall go well with you. You must take great pains to make my bed well, and shake it up thoroughly, so that the feathers fly about, and then in the world it snows, for I am Mother Holle."

Mother Holle was doubtless once one of the three great mother goddesses, who since earliest times were revered in the Celtic world. Perhaps she corresponds to the earth mother. In many regions she is regarded as the last memory of the lovely Freia, the most beautiful daughter goddess of the race of the Vanir, the shining divinities of earliest times. As Mother Hulda, Freia watched over the blessing of the fields. In her realm was a tree which threw down gold and silver when shaken. Later she was seen as the originator of spinning. As we have seen, early mankind associated this activity of the hand with the thinking of the brain. Mother Hulda was the protector of spinning; she praised the diligent and reproached the lazy. And when one no longer could see her striding over the land spreading blessings, one could still see her in her realm that had grown dark like an mysterious cave, and one called her Mother Holle. Whoever crossed the border between this world and the other world – and of old that happened constantly – encountered this fate-ruling power.

As the old woman spoke so kindly, the girl took courage, consented, and went to her work. She did everything to the old woman's satisfaction, and shook the bed with such a will that the feathers flew about like snow-flakes: and so she led a good life, had never a cross word, but boiled and roast meat every day. When she

had lived a long time with Mother Holle, she began to feel sad, not knowing herself what ailed her; at last she began to think she must be home-sick; and although she was a thousand times better off than at home where she was, yet she had a great longing to go home. At last she said to her mistress: "I am homesick, and although I am very well off here, I cannot stay any longer; I must go back to my own home." Mother Holle answered: "It pleases me well that you should wish to go home, and, as you have served me faithfully, I will undertake to send you there!" She took her by the hand and led her to a large door standing open, and as she was passing through it there fell upon her a heavy shower of gold, and the gold hung all about her, so that she was covered with it. "All this is yours, because you have been so industrious," said Mother Holle; and, besides that, she returned to her her spindle, the very same that she had dropped in the well. And then the door was shut again, and the girl found herself back again in the world, not far from her mother's house; and as she passed through the yard the cock stood on the top of the well and cried:

> *"Cock-a-doodle doo!*
> *Our golden girl has come home too!"*

Then she went in to her mother, and as she had returned covered with gold she was well received.

"The weather is like people," one can still hear today. According to old views, there is a direct connection between the soul world of people and the elementary processes of nature. Souls who accomplish their fated tasks pass their destiny-assigned tests, like our diligent daughter, do not disturb the harmony of nature but fit in and work with nature.

But one can look at the image of snowing also in another way. The pure snow crystals in their innumerable star forms coming down from the heavens and covering the earth with bright white, can they not also be a picture for the noble, pure forces of a higher world? Certainly the tale indicates that a soul that always properly spins and does its share of good thinking, participates in such creativity. Mother Holle's words, "It pleases me well that you should wish to go home," show us that she belongs to the progressive good powers. For life in the earthly world is schooling for a higher life, and what is accomplished in the higher worlds works into this one. In the transition from the spiritual to the sense world, the maiden stands beneath the gate – and a wealth of spiritual experience and transformation is showered upon her, wisdom that cannot be lost. Mother Holle gives her back the spool that had fallen, bloody, into the well. A purified new thinking can now begin. With the gold that has been won, the returning girl is well received, for the wealth benefits also those who have not been transformed.

The lazy daughter wants what the one diligent in thinking has attained. She can, however, win no spiritual knowledge (no bread) either out of the heart forces (which were never active in her) nor by a distinguishing between good and evil, for the good was foreign to her. She cannot fit into the extra-sensory world and its order and into order of the sensory world she has through her sloth also failed to fit. The ruler of the extrasensory world must throw her out. Her reward is the bucket of pitch. She does not get back the spool. One who tries without purification and transformation to get Wisdom's gold darkens his being and becomes poorer than before. And this darkening remains with him.

So the girl related all her history, and what had happened to her, and when the mother heard how she came to have such great riches she began to wish that her ugly and idle daughter might have the same good fortune. So she sent her to sit by the well and spin; and in order to make her spindle bloody she put her hand into the thorn hedge. Then she threw the spindle into the well, and jumped in herself. She found herself, like her sister, in the beautiful meadow, and followed the same path, and when she came to the baker's oven, the bread cried out: "Oh, take me out, take me out, or I shall burn; I am quite done already!" But the lazy-bones answered: "I have no desire to dirty my hands," and went on farther. Soon she came to the apple-tree, who called out: "Oh, shake me, shake me, we apples are all of us ripe!" But she answered: "That is all very fine; suppose one of you should fall on my head," and went on farther. When she came to Mother Holle's house she did not feel afraid, as she knew beforehand of her great teeth, and entered into her service at once. The first day she put her hand well to the work, and was industrious, and did everything Mother Holle bade her, because of the gold she expected; but the second day she began to be idle, and the third day still more so, so that she would not get up in the morning. Neither did she make Mother Holle's bed as it ought to have been made, and did not shake it for the feathers to fly about. So that Mother Holle soon grew tired of her, and gave her warning, at which the lazy thing was well pleased, and thought that now the shower of gold was coming; so Mother Holle led her to the door, and as she stood in the doorway, instead of the shower of gold a great kettle full of pitch was emptied over her. "That is the reward for your service," said Mother Holle, and shut the door. So the lazy girl came home all covered with pitch, and the cock on the top of the well seeing her, cried:

"Cock-a-doodle doo!
Our dirty girl has come home too!"

And the pitch remained sticking to her fast, and never, as long
as she lived, could it be got off.

The cock, the herald of the day, greets both of the girls on
their return. Was the time with Mother Holle a night experience?
This world in which under is like over knows neither space nor
time. We experience it in dreams. Traditions tell of countless
experiences in which humans were transported into the elementary
world. To them it seems that they have been long years in the
service of dwarfs or with elves in blessed joy, or with wonderful
forest women or with Mother Holle. But the experience actually
lasted only a few minutes or hours, or a day or so at most. The
folktale also allows this possibility.

But every man or woman is at the same time a member of
mankind and of the world and so much deeper karmic connections
can be at work, connections that go beyond the limits of one earthly
life.

The entry into the spiritual world in which the experiences of
earthly life approach the soul as from outside and a kind of
judgment takes place and finally a return to the sense world, blessed
or burdened with the consequences of this judgment – all this
points to the reincarnation of the human spirit. Reincarnation was
known to the Celtic and Germanic peoples. Julius Ceasar and
Diodorus Siculus report it. The Edda, the Germanic story of the
gods, mentions it in the Song of Kara. Here the knowledge had not
fallen into decadence as in the Far East where reincarnation was
reduced to mere soul wandering. But in the West, this knowledge
was taken away. Man should turn all his forces to the material sense

235

world. But in some folktales there are reverberations of this ancient knowledge.

If we look at our Mother Holle folktale in this way, then the cock appears not just as the announcer of the day, he becomes much more the symbol for the instinctive ego. For the I awakening in a new incarnation the call of the cock summons to the crucial decision: to be Man endowed with wisdom or to be a pitchpot.[65]

---

65 The word translated as "pitchpot" is "*Pechvogel*", literally "pitch bird" but with the meaning of "unlucky person" or "walking disaster". The word translated as "crucial decision" is "*Weichenstellen*" literally "soft spots" but with the idea of places where small changes can make a big difference.

Fitcher's Bird

Grimm 46

*There was once a sorcerer who used to take the form of a poor
man, and went to houses and begged, and caught pretty girls. No
one knew whither he carried them, for they were never seen again.
One day he appeared before the door of a man who had three pretty
daughters; he looked like a poor weak beggar, and carried a basket
on his back, as if he meant to collect charitable gifts in it. He begged
for a little food, and when the eldest daughter came out and was
just reaching him a piece of bread, he did but touch her, and she
was forced to jump into his basket. Thereupon he hurried away with
long strides, and carried her away into a dark forest to his house,
which stood in the midst of it. Everything in the house was
magnificent; he gave her whatsoever she could possibly desire, and
said: "My darling, thou wilt certainly be happy with me, for thou
hast everything thy heart can wish for."*

What does a magician do? He throws two worlds through one
another; he stands the natural laws of our normal world on their
head. Reality becomes appearance, and appearance becomes
reality. The sorcerer in the folktale does the same on a higher
plane. He represents the sense man in us, for this sense man is a
great magician. For him there matters only the colorful world of the
senses, therefore everything that the senses perceive. And because
he knows how to make this world perceived by the senses *appear to
be* the only valid one, the hidden spiritual world becomes enchanted
within it. Where does this magician hide within the human being?
There are many realms within the human totality, so exactly where
does he hide? The tale says he resides deep in the forest, that is
where plant life grows and abounds, where man has his vegetative

life, or – as modern speech puts it – vegetates away. From there he grabs after soul forces (beautiful maidens) and brings them under his power.

For the soul to be the bride of the sense-bound, vegetative part of the human being is the exact opposite of its being the bride of the spirit-king, celebrated in countless folktales. The sorcerer's brides are unwilling and must be numbed and carried off in the dark sack on his back.

This lasted a few days, and then he said: "I must journey forth, and leave thee alone for a short time; there are the keys of the house; thou mayst go everywhere and look at everything except into one room, which this little key here opens, and there I forbid thee to go on pain of death." He likewise gave her an egg and said: "Preserve the egg carefully for me, and carry it continually about with thee, for a great misfortune would arise from the loss of it." She took the keys and the egg, and promised to obey him in everything. When he was gone, she went all round the house from the bottom to the top, and examined everything. The rooms shone with silver and gold, and she thought she had never seen such great splendour. At length she came to the forbidden door; she wished to pass it by, but curiosity let her have no rest. She examined the key, it looked just like any other; she put it in the keyhole and turned it a little, and the door sprang open. But what did she see when she went in? A great bloody basin stood in the middle of the room, and therein lay human beings, dead and hewn to pieces, and hard by was a block of wood, and a gleaming axe lay upon it. She was so terribly alarmed that the egg which she held in her hand fell into the basin. She got it out and washed the blood off, but in vain, it appeared again in a moment. She washed and scrubbed, but she could not get it out.

238

It was not long before the man came back from his journey, and the first things which he asked for were the key and the egg. She gave them to him, but she trembled as she did so, and he saw at once by the red spots that she had been in the bloody chamber. "Since thou hast gone into the room against my will," said he, "thou shalt go back into it against thine own. Thy life is ended." He threw her down, dragged her thither by her hair, cut her head off on the block, and hewed her in pieces so that her blood ran on the ground. Then he threw her into the basin with the rest.

The world of the senses can shine before the soul with imposing splendor: the house of the sorcerer gleams with silver and gold; the soul may – and should – enjoy it. There are ever new aspects to discover and unknown spaces to explore. The task and test imposed by the sorcerer is to preserve the egg. The egg is a germ of life. Out of it arises new life. In antiquity, it was often found on grave stones. There it appears as the symbol of that inner germ of life which Man, as he passes through death, should become. It represents the eternal and everlasting in Man, the consciousness of his true I. Whether here or there, whether in the sense world or in the spiritual world, the eternal core of the I is the central germinating force of life.

The sorcerer takes first the eldest daughter. The firstborn is the first-developed soul member in Man, his sentient, feeling soul. It emerges early in childhood. Here it must be forced to be a bride, to become a *sensuous soul*. Whether she will enter the blood chamber or not, she is free to decide; but she is given the key. A spiritual place is meant, the place of blood fallen to sensuality that can take the soul prisoner. There the lower passions rule. The test is to win this knowledge and nevertheless to preserve the purity of the eternal I consciousness. But she lets the egg fall into the blood. The

eternal as an inner sublime experience is subordinated to the lower passion nature of the blood. The soul falls to the sorcerer. She can no longer assert[66] herself and preserve her unity. She becomes headless, torn apart and cut to pieces.

"Now I will fetch myself the second," said the sorcerer, and again he went to the house in the shape of a poor man, and begged. Then the second daughter brought him a piece of bread; he caught her like the first, by simply touching her, and carried her away. She did not fare better than her sister. She allowed herself to be led away by her curiosity, opened the door of the bloody chamber, looked in, and had to atone for it with her life on the sorcerer's return.

The second daughter – we know her from the ancient order as the soul turned toward thinking – suffers the same fate. To open the world of the sense-bound sorcerer through thinking is her task. But she also "lets the egg fall into the blood." So she looses her unity, becomes headless, and the force of the sense-man fells her.

Then he went and brought the third sister, but she was clever and crafty. When he had given her the keys and the egg, and had left her, she first put the egg away with great care, and then she examined the house, and at last went into the forbidden room. Alas, what did she behold! Both her sisters lay there in the basin, cruelly murdered, and cut in pieces. But she began to gather their limbs together and put them in order, head, body, arms and legs. And when nothing further was wanting the limbs began to move and unite themselves together, and both the maidens opened their eyes

---

66 The word here conventionally translated as "assert" in "she cannot assert herself" is *behaupten* with the root *haupt*, meaning "head". To be sure that the reader does not miss the morbid pun, the author writes it as *be-haupt-en.*

and were once more alive. Then they rejoiced and kissed and caressed each other.

On his arrival, the man at once demanded the keys and the egg, and as he could perceive no trace of any blood on it, he said: "Thou hast stood the test, thou shalt be my bride." He now had no longer any power over her, and was forced to do whatsoever she desired. "Oh, very well," said she, "thou shalt first take a basketful of gold to my father and mother, and carry it thyself on thy back; in the meantime I will prepare for the wedding."

Then she ran to her sisters, whom she had hidden in a little chamber, and said: "The moment has come when I can save you. The wretch shall himself carry you home again, but as soon as you are at home send help to me." She put both of them in a basket and covered them quite over with gold, so that nothing of them was to be seen, then she called in the sorcerer and said to him: "Now carry the basket away, but I shall look through my little window and watch to see if thou stoppest on the way to stand or to rest."

The sorcerer raised the basket on his back and went away with it, but it weighed him down so heavily that the perspiration streamed from his face. Then he sat down and wanted to rest awhile, but immediately one of the girls in the basket cried: "I am looking through my little window, and I see that thou art resting. Wilt thou go on at once?" He thought it was his bride who was calling that to him; and got up on his legs again. Once more he was going to sit down, but instantly she cried: "I am looking through my little window, and I see that thou art resting. Wilt thou go on directly?" And whenever he stood still, she cried this, and then he was forced to go onwards, until at last, groaning and out of breath, he took the basket with the gold and the two maidens into their parents' house.

241

At home, however, the bride prepared the marriage-feast, and sent invitations to the friends of the sorcerer. Then she took a skull with grinning teeth, put some ornaments on it and a wreath of flowers, carried it upstairs to the garret-window, and let it look out from thence. When all was ready, she got into a barrel of honey, and then cut the feather-bed open and rolled herself in it, until she looked like a wondrous bird, and no one could recognize her. Then she went out of the house, and on her way she met some of the wedding-guests, who asked:

> *"O, Fitcher's bird, whence com'st thou here?"*
> *"I come from Fitze Fitcher's house quite near."*
> *"And what may the young bride be doing?"*
> *"From cellar to garret she's swept all clean,*
> *And now from the window she's peeping, I ween."*

At last she met the bridegroom, who was coming slowly back. He, like the others, asked:

> *"O, Fitcher's bird, whence com'st thou here?"*
> *"I come from Fitze Fitcher's house quite near."*
> *"And what may the young bride be doing?*
> *"From cellar to garret she's swept all clean,*
> *And now from the window she's peeping, I ween."*

The bridegroom looked up, saw the decked-out skull, thought it was his bride, and nodded to her, greeting her kindly. But when he and his guests had all gone into the house, the brothers and kinsmen of the bride, who had been sent to rescue her, arrived. They locked all the doors of the house, that no one might escape, set fire to it, and the sorcerer and all his crew had to burn.

The third daughter is the first to take control of the situation. We recognize her as Will force of the soul. The Will is the last

developed and highest of the soul forces. It must not be confused with wishes or desires, nor with one-sided stubbornness. It must have insight and cleverness in action. She was clever and crafty says the tale. She opens the whole of the sorcerer's house, but she had first laid the egg carefully aside. She determines her own actions. She knows that the gleaming world of sense experience must be tred wide awake. And so she learns how the clout of evil had cut apart and killed her two soul sisters. But because she has preserved the egg, she can heal the feeling and thinking souls and restore their unity. (Do we not say: "I am totally torn apart," and then again "I've gotten myself back together."?)

Because she has overcome the magician, she can restore the original unity of the whole soul being. She sends the two sisters back to the house of the parents; that is, she attaches herself again to the old Self, to the primal soul. And since Knowledge and Overcoming-of-Evil *carry* Wisdom in themselves, the sisters are covered with gold and *carried* back.

Because the third daughter has withstood the trial and gained complete self-knowledge of herself as Will-Soul, she can now undertake the redemption of the man-of-the-senses, the sorcerer. First she will show him what he has become and then bring about his purification, for he also had once known the lofty flight of the spirit. In those long-ago times, the sense world was not yet reduced to the bare material world. In it there wove and flowed a spiritual world which was still visible to Man. The white soul-bird with uplifting wings represented him. He was a Fitcher.[67]

---

67 In all of German literature, this story and references to it are the occurrences of the word *Fitcher*. The Grimms thought it might be related to Icelandic *fitfugal* which they believed to have been a swan-like bird, but now seems to be any web-footed bird, possibly but not necessarily white. Other writers think the word *Fitcher* it is related to German *Feder* "feather" or *Fittich*

But now in the sorcerer's house, in the body of one turned only to the sense world, there is no more life. For he experiences only death processes, for matter passes away and only spirit remains.

The highest possible insight and outlook (the window in the gable) shows him the bride he has won by killing the living. Moreover, the spirit-filled Will forces of the soul show the sorcerer what has become of his once-lofty soul bird. Indeed, she says "I come from Fitze Fitcher's house to here." Running on the ground, without wings to bear her upward, covered with plucked feathers, spreading lies and deception, and in the background the grinning skull – she shows to the sorcerer what he has become, a soul separated from the spirit. All the forces from which the soul arises – the parents and relatives – must stand together and ignite the spiritual fire that puts to death this sorcerer and his riffraff.

Translator's note: I feel the author has come close but missed an important point at the end. For is there not something of the sorcerer in all of us? Was he perhaps hoping to find the bride that would not drop the egg? And does he not prove a pretty decent fellow to the sister who does not let the egg fall into the blood? She does not have him hacked apart, as might seem appropriate. Rather, after showing him the grotesque image of his fallen nature – an experience designed to lead to repentance – she has him die by fire. And fire is purifying.

"wings". In any event, the sorcerer and his friends immediately recognize the relation of the bizarre creature made by the third sister to the sorcerer. Indeed, it appears that the sorcerer's name was Fitze Fitcher.

Jorinde and Joringel

Grimm 69

There was once an old castle in the midst of a large and thick forest.

When the inner picture world in us begins to paint, every situation presents itself pictorially to the soul – a waking, true-to-life dream begins. Folktales are these true-to-life dreams of a people. Into what depths is the picturing process within us reaching when it paints an old castle deep in a thick forest? The house of the body, the castle of our being, stands before us as it once appeared in grandeur and richness, with many ways to enter or leave, gates and towers, and even more possibilities to look out or look in – windows without number. But it is far away, old and forgotten behind luxuriant plant life. To be sure, the abundance of life forces can be enlivening as is the vegetation of the forest in the outer world. But here there is only trackless wilderness and confusion; a darkening twilight and uncertainty surround us. To enter it and enlighten it is a kind of testing, of withstanding forces that lurk therein and press upon the seeking soul with tasks and testing.

In it lived all alone an old woman who was an arch-magician.

Not in that brightly-lighted, heavenly theater of the soul where a throng of colorful characters play for us do we meet this one. She was somehow left out, left behind as a foreboding memory: magical knowledge out of a time long-past that still spooks around and attacks souls. Let no one suppose that there is not in his own being a hidden province where this witch lurks. All of us carry the past in us, and how can we hope to turn the present into a better future if we do not master the past.

245

In the day-time she changed herself into a cat or a screech-owl, but in the evening she took her proper shape again as a human being. She could lure wild beasts and birds to her, and then she killed and boiled and roasted them. If any one came within one hundred paces of the castle he was obliged to stand still, and could not stir from the place until she bade him be free. But whenever an innocent maiden came within this circle, she changed her into a bird, and shut her up in a wicker-work cage, and carried the cage into a room in the castle. She had about seven thousand cages of rare birds in the castle.

The arch-magician had her day side and her night side. The owl that sleeps by day and is awake at night is a symbol of a wisdom that is blind in wide-awake, daytime thinking but opens its eyes in the realm of dreams. The owl was used as the soul-expression bird of Pallas Athena who brought open-eyed knowledge to the dream picture world of the night.

The cat – a soft plaything animal and a little beast of prey all in one – is sleepy during the day and wide awake at night. In ancient Egypt, the goddess of love magic was the cat-headed Bastet (see page 134). Is love not always an enchantment, and does it not always have its day and night sides? Here is depicted how the night side awakes during the day. In the love drive, the cat prowls about; and in the knowledge drive, the owl flits past. And as in the night the human is to be sure awake but also the fires of desire are ignited and to them fall prey innocent natural drives (wild animals and birds are slaughtered and roasted.)

Magic lames the Will and holds fast. Virginal soul forces (pure maidens) are spellbound in this region. From knowing, reason-

endowed, human forces they are reduced to an instinctive, animal-like level: they become birds.

Now, there was once a maiden who was called Jorinde, who was fairer than all other girls. She and a handsome youth named Joringel had promised to marry each other. They were still in the days of betrothal, and their greatest happiness was being together.

More beautiful than all the properties of the soul (the other girls) is the soul itself. When she has matured and become aware of the spiritual nature of the I and is prepared for devotion and dedication, then she can become a bride. The individual human spirit which has won from all areas the convincing[68] thoughts to fructify the soul is the bridegroom.

One day in order that they might be able to talk together in quiet they went for a walk in the forest. "Take care," said Joringel, "that you do not go too near the castle." It was a beautiful evening; the sun shone brightly between the trunks of the trees into the dark green of the forest, and the turtle-doves sang mournfully upon the young boughs of the birch-trees.

Jorinde wept now and then: she sat down in the sunshine and was sorrowful. Joringel was sorrowful too; they were as sad as if they were about to die. Then they looked around them, and were quite at a loss, for they did not know by which way they should go home. The sun was still half above the mountain and half set.

Joringel looked through the bushes, and saw the old walls of the castle close at hand. He was horror-stricken and filled with deadly fear. Jorinde was singing,

---

68 Untranslatable German word fun. *Überzeugend* means *convincing,* but *zeugen* means "to beget". To be sure we don't miss the play, the author writes *überzeugend* as *über-zeugend.*

"My little bird, with the necklace red,
Sings sorrow, sorrow, sorrow,
He sings that the dove must soon be dead,
Sings sorrow, sor -- jug, jug, jug."

Joringel looked for Jorinde. She was changed into a nightingale, and
sang, "jug, jug, jug."

When day fades and evening begins, one easily falls into that in-between mood that the tale so charmingly describes of Jorinde. One sinks into dreams, and these dreams can become so strong that the soul can no longer shake free. It sinks into itself, is completely absorbed into an unconscious element. Enchantment takes hold of it. Young women are especially at risk for this situation.

When developing personality and individuality, soul and spirit converse with one another about their eternal destiny, the spiritual octave of this mood can take possession of the inner Man. Soul and spirit stand between two worlds. These worlds are called in the picture language night and day. Night and day are the picture for two aspects of the inner world. The moon was in olden times the regent of time keeping; time was reckoned in moon-periods, months, and approximate subdivisions of the month, weeks (or sennights) and fortnights (14 nights – note the counting of nights rather than days). These were the times when the gift of natural clairvoyance, truth dreams and prophetic revelation was decisive. It was the age of original matriarchy, the feminine age of mankind. The picture language says: Mankind was Nightman and calls this age "night." In the masculine age, the sun became the regent of time, thinking was developed, nature clairvoyance and dream-picture wisdom faded. Mankind became Day Man. The picture language calls this age "Day". Wakefulness in the sense world, active thinking is called "Day". Wakefulness in the dream world,

passivity in thinking is called "Night". Night and Day are both present in Man, night as past, day as bright present. But former, ancient conditions can – dissolving the present day consciousness – rise to the surface. This folktale describes such a crisis. The soul, Jorinde, senses it in advance, sings of it in advance.

Were the soul once elated and gifted with soaring forces and closed within itself like the ring and filled with full-blooded activity (My little bird with necklace red), so must it experience that the original spirituality must perish, a spirituality which had been received as a gift, an inheritance by grace (the dove). The soul can no longer be a bride, ready for devotion and unification. Ancient magic spooks about; she sinks down into the purely instinctive. Her voice now sounds only at night; she becomes a nightingale. People who fall into such medial or somnambulist states resemble such birds of the night. But it does not have to always be an illness. In any human, the inner feminine of the soul may fall into such a condition. Then, in the picture language, the bridegroom must protect the bride. The I must remain awake; but here the I has also fallen under the influence of the enchantment.

A screech-owl with glowing eyes flew three times round about her, and three times cried, "to-whoo, to-whoo, to-whoo!"

Joringel could not move: he stood there like a stone, and could neither weep nor speak, nor move hand or foot.

The sun had now set. The owl flew into the thicket, and directly afterwards there came out of it a crooked old woman, yellow and lean, with large red eyes and a hooked nose, the point of which reached to her chin. She muttered to herself, caught the nightingale, and took it away in her hand.

Joringel could neither speak nor move from the spot; the nightingale was gone. At last the woman came back, and said in a hollow voice, "Greet thee, Zachiel. If the moon shines on the cage, Zachiel, let him loose at once." Then Joringel was freed. He fell on his knees before the woman and begged that she would give him back his Jorinde, but she said that he should never have her again, and went away. He called, he wept, he lamented, but all in vain, "Ah, what is to become of me?"

In the Eleusinian mysteries an offering was brought by moonlight in a basket. We no longer know what was in the basket, but it was important that the moon should shine upon it. In Hebrew, the syllable *el* means a divine being, and Zachariel is the name of an archangel. But what does Zachiel mean? The name is sometimes applied to the devil. Does the silencing of Joringel mean that this nocturnal enchantment was the distorted remains of a once holy mystery wisdom? We have an example of this sort of thing in etymology of *Hexe,* the German word for *witch.* Originally the *hagazussa* was the seeress living in an enclosed space (the *hag*) who protected the tribe's spiritual identity. But *hagazussa* degenerated into *Hexe*, witch, in German and into *hag* in English. If the soul is torn away by such atavistic powers, then the I needs new development. Protecting, caring forces must be developed.

Joringel went away, and at last came to a strange village; there he kept sheep for a long time. He often walked round and round the castle, but not too near to it.

As the shepherd helps his flock to multiply and nurtures naturally given life that he has not created but caringly preserves, so there is a stage of inner development in which the same happens in a spiritual sense. Man learns to protect and care for what has been

given from above as living revelation. Also here he does not beget life but preserves and cares for it, and what streams into him multiplies and multiplies. Sheep herding people lived in this awareness. They accepted what was given as dream revelation. The Bible refers to this condition with the words "To his own the Lord gives in sleep."[69] Their outer actions correspond to their inner experience. (The Able myth speaks of this.) The I must now experience this night consciousness in its positive effects and in a new sense relive it. Otherwise the I cannot do right by the soul which has fallen prey in unhealthy ways to the night influences. The tale says: Joringel became a shepherd and for a long time herded sheep.

At last he dreamt one night that he found a blood-red flower, in the middle of which was a beautiful large pearl; that he picked the flower and went with it to the castle, and that everything he touched with the flower was freed from enchantment; he also dreamt that by means of it he recovered his Jorinde.

In the morning, when he awoke, he began to seek over hill and dale if he could find such a flower. He sought until the ninth day, and then, early in the morning, he found the blood-red flower. In the middle of it there was a large dew-drop, as big as the finest pearl. Day and night he journeyed with this flower to the castle.

The blood-red blossom with the pearl in it is the picture of active love, as our blood carries it, but it carries it in plant-like innocence. This love must enclose what has condensed as precious reward from the depths of the soul like the pearl born of water. Is not water in all folktales the picture of that bottomless, surging soul world in which thoughts come to the surface but may swim away, in

_____

69 Psalm 127, verse 2. English translations generally omit the "in".

which a picture world arises and fades away? What has been won as a precious extract from the water-soul-depths must be surrounded and borne by I-aware love which is truly earthly like the red flower that grows from the earth.

Nine days must Joringel seek the flower; nine members has Man: body in its mineral, plant, and animal related nature; soul in its feeling, thinking and willing functions; and spirit that unifies body and soul and lifts to an overall unity in three steps – that is the nine-fold Man referred to in many folktales.[70] Man must make progress to explore consciously this nine-fold structure of his being. On the morning of the ninth day is the blood-red flower found. The pearl has become a drop of dew – a gift of the night to the beginning day. To carry the blossom through day and night means: forward-striding to know both with wide-awake consciousness and reality-grasping thinking and also to see in night-waking pictures, in imaginations.

When he was within a hundred paces of it he was not held fast, but walked on to the door. Joringel was full of joy; he touched the door with the flower, and it sprang open. He walked in through the courtyard, and listened for the sound of the birds. At last he heard it. He went on and found the room from whence it came, and there the witch was feeding the birds in the seven thousand cages.

When she saw Joringel she was angry, very angry, and scolded and spat poison and gall at him, but she could not come within two paces of him. He did not take any notice of her, but went and looked at the cages with the birds; but there were many hundred nightingales, how was he to find his Jorinde again?

---

70 The nine-fold structure of Man is described in detail in Rudolf Steiner's *Theosophy* and *Esoteric Science.*

Just then he saw the old woman quietly take away a cage with a bird in it, and go towards the door. Swiftly he sprang towards her, touched the cage with the flower, and also the old woman. She could now no longer bewitch any one; and Jorinde was standing there, clasping him round the neck, and she was as beautiful as ever! Then he made all the other birds maidens again and went home with his Jorinde, and they lived long and happily together.

Love is the greatest force for knowing of which Man is capable, for it demands of us to penetrate into another being as if we were that other being. Such activity, which is total unselfishness, allows one to cross the line that magical enchantment has drawn and to advance opening doors.

To touch the enchantress with the blossom means to make harmless through knowledge old, decadent magic. To touch the cage with the nightingale means to know what encloses and isolates the soul and to redeem what has been reduced to what is kin to the animal. From being bound to what is related to animals, the soul is becomes free and I-connected. It is essentially unselfish love that blesses all whom it touches. Thus other souls that have fallen captive and lost their freedom are restored by Joringel's act of love.

(This story was transcribed by Jung-Stilling, a friend of Goethe in college days in Strassburg. It had been told to him by an older woman cousin.)

The Three Little Men in the Forest
Grimm13

There was once a man, whose wife was dead, and a woman, whose husband was dead; and the man had a daughter, and the woman had also a daughter.

There was once an I whose soul had died, and there was a soul which had become without an I, without spirit. This soul lacking spirit wants to attach itself to the I. If this happens, an inner drama will unfold, for the young soul forces, the two daughters, will suffer. They are as absolutely different in their nature as are their parents whom they bring together in marriage.

The girls were acquainted with each other, and used to play together sometimes in the woman's house. So the woman said to the man's daughter, "Listen to me, tell your father that I will marry him, and then you shall have milk to wash in every morning and wine to drink, and my daughter shall have water to wash in and water to drink." The girl went home and told her father what the woman had said.

Milk is made in a living being in connection with reproduction and thus under the influence of moon forces. It is therefore no direct product of the earth. But it makes the child earthly strong. In folktales, milk always points to health-giving cosmic forces. Wine is quite different. It is a noble product of the earth; it prospers under the influence of the sun. In cultural history, it has had an individualizing effect because it increases I-consciousness. This effect was celebrated in antiquity in the Dionysian festivals. The

254

promise of the woman is therefore: thou shalt enrich thy being through cosmic forces and help it develop earth-conscious individuality. Progress is yours, and all will go well with you.

Water for washing and water to drink for her own daughter point to the opposite. We have learned to recognize water as a creative and life-giving element. Here a negative aspect is no doubt intended. Water existed before milk and wine. Evolution goes into reverse. We use the expression that something has been "watered down". To have to do only with water means to make no progress in the unstable, back-and- forth flow of the feeling life.

The man said, "What shall I do! Marriage is a joy, and also a torment." At last, as he could come to no conclusion, he took off his boot, and said to his daughter, "Take this boot, it has a hole in the sole; go up with it into the loft, hang it on the big nail and pour water in it. If it holds water, I will once more take to me a wife; if it lets out the water, so will I not. "The girl did as she was told, but the water held the hole together, and the boot was full up to the top. So she went and told her father how it was. And he went up to see with his own eyes, and as there was no mistake about it, he went to the widow and courted her, and then they had the wedding.

How uncertain the I has become since the death of his wife, the soul bound to him, is shown by his question to fate. His possibility and ability to go through life confidently is used up – the boots are worn out. As has been already mentioned, in folktale language the roof in a house corresponds to the head in the body. We Germans say, "You have roof damage" to mean "Your thinking is confused." The man in our tale shows himself aware of the damage to his thinking. Connection to the materialistic soul falls to him by fate when he leaves the decision to chance.

The next morning, when the two girls awoke, there stood by the bedside of the man's daughter milk to wash in and wine to drink, and by the bedside of the woman's daughter there stood water to wash in and water to drink. On the second morning there stood water to wash in and water to drink for both of them alike. On the third morning there stood water to wash in and water to drink for the man's daughter, and milk to wash in and wine to drink for the woman's daughter; and so it remained ever after. The woman hated her stepdaughter, and never knew how to treat her badly enough from one day to another. And she was jealous because her stepdaughter was pleasant and pretty, and her real daughter was ugly and hateful.

The new wife becomes a harsh, pseudo-mother to the daughter of the man. She is averse to all inner feeling; for her only the material world is important. She loves only what the senses can grasp and is averse to everything supersensible. The folktales describe her again and again, for as confidence of soul and spiritual insight have faded, she has become the fate of everyone of our stage of cultural development.

Once in winter, when it was freezing hard, and snow lay deep on hill and valley, the woman made a frock out of paper, called her stepdaughter, and said, "Here, put on this frock, go out into the wood and fetch me a basket of strawberries; I have a great wish for some."

Norse mythology says: When the time of Fenris-Wolf has come, the time of swords, distress, and adultery, then comes the Fimbul-Winter, the Great Winter. Our forefathers foresaw a time in which souls would fall into rigidity and coldness and the icy breath of the intellect would kill warm, life-filled feeling so that it

would be difficult for people to find the way to one another. This Fimbul-Winter is indeed the landscape of the bad stepmother. She is cold in feeling, calculating, and she hates the Good. In the middle of winter she fains a desire for strawberries, and the noble daughter must get them.

Let us observe the strawberry[71], how under the foliage of its tripartite leaves there ripens on the earth sweet, red fruit with marvelous aroma. When we note its great healing properties, we understand why the Medieval painters gave strawberries to the divine child, putting a strawberry plant beside the crib or even putting the crib on a bed of strawberries. The great symbol painter Hieronymus Bosch put into his "Garden of Delights" several people finding or carrying huge strawberries in their hands, or on their back or head.[72] For the life-awakening, healing, blossom-renewing strawberry represents that force which becomes active in us when embraced by all-healing love. This healing love came to earth with the divine child. Therefore the strawberry stands near the mother with the child. The hardened soul longs for this love, for she needs it but cannot find it herself; she needs it as a healing force when Fimbul-Winter rules.

"Oh dear God," said the girl, "there are no strawberries to be found in winter; the ground is frozen, and the snow covers

---

71 The strawberry fruit drops down to the earth and ripens lying on the ground. That is why it is called *Erdbeer "earth berry"* in German. To better preserve the fruit during the ripening process, straw is often placed on the ground for the fruit to rest on. That is why it is called "strawberry" in English.

72 The picture is in El Prado in Madrid where it is called "El Jardin de las Delicias". The strawberries, several of them bigger than a man's head, are mostly in the lower part of the central panel. The picture is often called the "Garden of Earthly Delights" but here our author called it "The Garden of Heavenly Delights." The official title in the Prado is just "The Garden of Delights" which I have used in the translation.

everything. And why should I go in the paper frock? it is so cold out of doors that one's breath is frozen; the wind will blow through it, and the thorns will tear it off my back!" "How dare you contradict me!" cried the stepmother, "be off, and don't let me see you again till you bring me a basket of strawberries." Then she gave her a little piece of hard bread, and said, "That will do for you to eat during the day," and she thought to herself, "She is sure to be frozen or starved to death out of doors, and I shall never set eyes on her again."

So the girl went obediently, put on the paper frock, and started out with the basket. The snow was lying everywhere, far and wide, and there was not a blade of green to be seen.

Poorer and needier can the bodily bearer of a human soul not be than when it must wear a paper dress. The wicked stepmother has given it to her, that is to say, she has robbed her of her original radiance of soul force.

The maiden is obedient; she takes on the cold and is ready in her scant garment to undertake the search for strawberries.

When she entered the wood she saw a little house with three little men peeping out of it. She wished them good day, and knocked modestly at the door.

Up to the beginning of the 16th century many people could still experience the elementary beings such as dwarfs. They saw not only the external, object world that we see but also experienced the elemental world. That was possible only because the soul-spiritual nature of man that today is so tightly bound to the physical was more mobile. It could partially loosen itself from the bodily and dip into the elementary world. It that way, it received images of these

258

forces, imaginations. There are countless nature spirit stories, reports of supersensible experiences that describe them so visually that one can recognize in them real experiences. These more or less conscious crossing of the threshold to a different kind of perception came upon people not only outside but also indoors. Indeed, many people could not separate the inner and the outer experiences. Man lived in a single, unified world: the outer, sensory world and the inner extra-sensory sensory world were all one world. There is in German an expression, "Gibt acht wie ein Wichtelman!" – Pay attention like a wichtelman! Wichtelmen are described as extraordinarily clever beings that quickly observe everything. They appear as little old men with big heads and caps for they are images of ancient nature wisdom. Our tales presumes the reality of these beings.

Where technology – the product of the human spirit – sets in, Nature can no longer create just as it wishes; Nature spirituality draws back. The picture language says: the dwarfs and gnomes have moved out. For the sight of modern Man, they are no longer perceptible; but we still experience the difference of landscapes – their abundance or their poverty. In a time of cold calculation and egotistical exploitation of nature there is scant place for these little beings.

They called her in, and she came into the room and sat down by the side of the oven to warm herself and eat her breakfast. The little men said, "Give us some of it." "Willingly," answered she, breaking her little piece of bread in two, and giving them half. They then said, "What are you doing here in the wood this winter time in your little thin frock?" "Oh," answered she, "I have to get a basket of strawberries, and I must not go home without them." When she had eaten her bread they gave her a broom, and told her to go and

259

sweep the snow away from the back door. When she had gone outside to do it the little men talked among themselves about what they should do for her, as she was so good and pretty, and had shared her bread with them. Then the first one said, "She shall grow prettier every day." The second said, "Each time she speaks a piece of gold shall fall from her mouth." The third said, "A king shall come and take her for his wife."

The genuine daughter enters modestly into this sphere; she brings the dwarfs compassion and love, for the nature spirits also hunger and starve when Fimbul-Winter rules. It is very important for nature with what attitude Man meets her, whether he exploits and destroys her with a cold heart or recognizes and cooperates with the forces naturally working in her. Even when in general cold, rigidifying soul forces prevail, healing, loving soul forces are present though hidden. – Forces of love that brought the divine child into the world, they have grown beneath the snow and have borne fruit. One must be but able to sweep the snow away. One who does not fall for the temptation to fight Evil with its own weapons but is ready to suffer need and cold wins the capacity to sweep away snow. He finds the strawberries and helps nature and serves mankind at the same time. But nature rewards him also for his service.

In one in whom compassion and love prevail, the true creative image of Man shines from his features – the maiden becomes more and more beautiful every day. The words which come from her mouth gain content and significance. They are full of wisdom so that they enrich those around them like minted gold. And the soul will mature towards its higher, true I (the king) and finally become one with him.

260

In the meanwhile the girl was doing as the little men had told her, and had cleared the snow from the back of the little house, and what do you suppose she found? fine ripe strawberries, showing dark red against the snow! Then she joyfully filled her little basket full, thanked the little men, shook hands with them all, and ran home in haste to bring her stepmother the thing she longed for. As she went in and said, "Good evening," a piece of gold fell from her mouth at once. Then she related all that had happened to her in the wood, and at each word that she spoke gold pieces fell out of her mouth, so that soon they were scattered all over the room. "Just look at her pride and conceit!" cried the stepsister, "throwing money about in this way!" but in her heart she was jealous because of it, and wanted to go too into the wood to fetch strawberries. But the mother said, "No, my dear little daughter, it is too cold, you will be frozen to death." But she left her no peace, so at last the mother gave in, got her a splendid fur coat to put on, and gave her bread and butter and cakes to eat on the way.

The step-mother soul, bound to matter, takes care of her own and does not let her experience hunger or cold. Her daughter wears a warm fur coat: she is warmed by what comes from the animal and instinctual.

The girl went into the wood and walked straight up to the little house. The three little men peeped out again, but she gave them no greeting, and without looking round or taking any notice of them she came stumping into the room, sat herself down by the oven, and began to eat her bread and butter and cakes. "Give us some of that," cried the little men, but she answered, "I've not enough for myself; how can I give away any?" Now when she had done with her eating, they said, "Here is a broom, go and sweep all clean by the back

door." "Oh, go and do it yourselves," answered she; "I am not your housemaid."

To the elemental forces of nature she has no connection; she shares nothing with them, is egotistical and entirely self-centered. She cannot contribute to them even a sweeping away of the all-covering cold. She must become active in order for love to grow and bear fruit.

But when she saw that they were not going to give her anything, she went out of the door. Then the three little men said among themselves, "What shall we do to her, because she is so unpleasant, and has such a wicked jealous heart, grudging everybody everything?" The first said, "She shall grow uglier every day." The second said, "Each time she speaks a toad shall jump out of her mouth at every word." The third said, "She shall die a miserable death." The girl was looking outside for strawberries, but as she found none, she went sulkily home. And directly she opened her mouth to tell her mother what had happened to her in the wood a toad sprang out of her mouth at each word, so that every one who came near her was quite disgusted.

Ugliness is the opposite of beauty. The soul bound to the lower sense nature can ever less and less bring the Good to expression. And with that degeneration another process goes hand-in-hand: speech changes. With every word, a toad springs from the mouth.

Formerly the toad was a symbol of the dark, upward-swelling fertility of the earth. It lives in swamp and mud, and swamp and mud were regarded as the place of spontaneous generation. Later the toad became the symbol for the sexual. Medieval painters, many of whom created from the same sources as did our folktale teachers, used the toad in this sense. We may note also the toad-

shaped gargoyles on our cathedrals that strive outwards away from the building. In people without love, who have turned away from genuine Nature spirituality, the sexual forces become estranged from their higher sense, are narrowed to mere sexuality – and slump to toads. Their speech becomes lewd and poisonous, and what they say becomes repulsive and loathsome.

The stepmother became more and more set against the man's daughter, whose beauty increased day by day, and her only thought was how to do her some injury. So at last she took a kettle, set it on the fire, and scalded some yarn in it. When it was ready she hung it over the poor girl's shoulder, and gave her an axe, and she was to go to the frozen river and break a hole in the ice, and there to rinse the yarn. She obeyed, and went and hewed a hole in the ice, and as she was in the midst of chopping there came by a splendid coach, in which the King sat.

The unselfishness, goodness and patience of upright people stimulate imitation ever and again. But in the soul realm there is a spiritual law: the greater the good that one has achieved, the greater the evil temptations. The stepmother demands more and more. She has boiled thick yarn and the diligent girl must rinse it clean. In German we have the picture word *Hirngespinste,* roughly "a fixed idea having little relation to reality" in English; the roots are *Hirn* (brain) and *Gespinste* (something spun). When such a *Hirngespinste* is over and over insistently pushed with hot passion, then is truly "yarn boiled." The one who "bears" the pain (carries the yarn) is the maiden obedient to destiny and striving for the Good. On her is the burden of this *Hirngespinste* laid. (The stepmother hangs the yarn on her shoulder.) Finally she is sent out to wash the yarn.

Again it is the one obedient to fate who must pay[73] for what the others have "cooked up."

The rigidifying and hardening has become even more impenetrable. Chopping through ice with an ax is even more demanding that sweeping snow with a broom. Only the strongest action succeeds in reaching the living and flowing. The maiden must indeed use the ax with mighty clout to break through the hard and rigid ice. But by so doing she gains access to that purifying element which alone can wash clean the *Hirngespinste* the materialistic soul has thought up. That is the same in the outer as in the inner world. "And as she was in the midst of chopping there came by a splendid coach, in which the King sat."

The coach stood still, and the King said, "My child, who art thou, and what art thou doing there?" She answered, "I am a poor girl, and am rinsing yarn." Then the King felt pity for her, and as he saw that she was very beautiful, he said, "Will you go with me?"

"Oh yes, with all my heart," answered she; and she felt very glad to be out of the way of her mother and sister.

So she stepped into the coach and went off with the King; and when they reached his castle the wedding was celebrated with great splendour, as the little men in the wood had foretold. At the end of a year the young Queen had a son.

When the soul is active in good work, it calls spiritual activity into play. We have in German for the ensuing process the picture word *sich ermannen,* literally "to make oneself manly" but with the idiomatic meaning "to pluck up courage." The inner masculine, the I, is called up, and it is the "can do" force, the spiritually rich inner

---

73 The author uses the German idiom *ausbaden* with the literal meaning of "wash out" but the idiomatic meaning of "pay for".

I – the kingly I that calls the soul to marriage. The becoming one with the confidence-giving, fructifying force of the spirit was called in the speech of Middle Ages the Mystical Wedding. The fruit of this wedding the mystics called the spiritual child in the bosom of the soul. This new beginning in one, this subtle happening requires careful wakefulness, for just as the body of a woman is in the highest sense creative when it brings a child into the world, so is the soul in the highest sense creative when the fruit of the spirit becomes manifest in her. Anyone who has done something creative must exercise the watchfulness. Never is one more vulnerable than when he has put something of himself into his work and brought it out into the world. So when the child is born, the adversarial forces will seek to claim it.

And as the stepmother had heard of her great good fortune she came with her daughter to the castle, as if merely to pay the King and Queen a visit. One day, when the King had gone out, and when nobody was about, the bad woman took the Queen by the head, and her daughter took her by the heels, and dragged her out of bed, and threw her out of the window into a stream that flowed beneath it. Then the old woman put her ugly daughter in the bed, and covered her up to her chin.

When the King came back, and wanted to talk to his wife a little, the old woman cried, "Stop, stop! she is sleeping nicely; she must be kept quiet today." The King dreamt of nothing wrong, and came again the next morning; and as he spoke to his wife, and she answered him, there jumped each time out of her mouth a toad instead of the piece of gold as heretofore. Then he asked why that should be, and the old woman said it was because of her great weakness, and that it would pass away.

265

But in the night, the boy who slept in the kitchen saw how something in the likeness of a duck swam up the gutter, and said,

> *"My King, what mak'st thou?*
> *Sleepest thou, or wak'st thou?"*

But there was no answer. Then it said,

> *"What cheer my two guests keep they?"*

So the kitchen-boy answered,

> *"In bed all soundly sleep they."*

It asked again,

> *"And my little baby, how does he?"*

And he answered,

> *"He sleeps in his cradle quietly."*

Then the duck took the shape of the Queen and went to the child, and gave him to drink, smoothed his little bed, covered him up again, and then, in the likeness of a duck, swam back down the gutter. In this way she came two nights, and on the third she said to the kitchen-boy, "Go and tell the King to brandish his sword three times over me on the threshold!" Then the kitchen-boy ran and told the King, and he came with his sword and brandished it three times over the duck, and at the third time his wife stood before him living, and hearty, and sound, as she had been before.

It belongs to the nature of compassion and love that it is open and understanding to all, without suspicion, even to those with evil intent. For it always believes in the power of transformation. But when the new germ, the fruit of the spirit, is born, compassion and love must be paired with vigilance. Evil must be recognized, not

266

just tolerated. This watchfulness was still lacking in the young pair. The tale says: the king has gone out and left the queen alone. We would say: the spirit is absent just when its presence is most necessary.

The queen is thrown into the stream and becomes a duck. The soul must submit to the will of the evil one. One whose "head swims" is clearly incapable of action. Only in the dream realm of the night does the true being of the young mother appear. The I, however, has completely fallen prey to illusion. The unspiritual ugliness that shows itself in base, toad-like speech has moved in. But a naive, fresh young force, the kitchen boy, is receptive to the warning call. Three times should the king brandish his sword over his rightful wife, the spirit-soul – for she is spirit-soul since she was wed to the spirit.

The sword can help and protect but also wound and kill. It is truly double-edged. The Word is also double-edged; it can help and save but also wound and kill. To ask for the blessing of the sword means to ask for help through the spiritual force of speech. The one who had sunken is pulled up into full life. The Word has been sinned against in that it has become lewd, sexual. Word power can heal and atone.

The King was greatly rejoiced, but he hid the Queen in a chamber until the Sunday came when the child was to be baptized. And after the baptism he said, "What does that person deserve who drags another out of; bed and throws him in the water?"

And the old woman answered, "No better than to be put into a cask with iron nails in it, and to be rolled in it down the hill into the water." Then said the King, "You have spoken your own sentence;"and he ordered a cask to be fetched, and the old woman

and her daughter were put into it, and the top hammered down, and the cask was rolled down the hill into the river.

What manifests and completes itself at night still needs protection. Again this folktale shows how profoundly Christian it is without, however, saying so in so many words. In baptism the one being baptized receives his name and is bound to Christ through the words of the ceremony. Only then does the confrontation with evil begin. Before the judging might of the completed Man – of the king *and* of his wife – evil pronounces its own judgment. As experience shows: injury that one has done to another returns sooner or later upon doer. As the saying goes: "Who digs a pit for another falls into it himself." The picture word "pit" in the saying, like the "cask" in the folktale, points to evil being driven into a narrow space, to its being confined. That the cask has nails sticking into it says: All wounding speech or action that one directed at others is now directed at one's self. The cask is nailed shut: Evil is enclosed and handed over to the river of life and destiny. Slanderous evil intentions and hateful evil actions have judged themselves.

The King's Son Who Feared Nothing

Grimm 121

There was once a King's son, who was no longer content to stay at home in his father's house, and as he had no fear of anything, he thought, "I will go forth into the wide world, there the time will not seem long to me, and I shall see wonders enough." So he took leave of his parents, and went forth, and on and on from morning till night, and whichever way his path led it was the same to him. It came to pass that he got to the house of a giant, and as he was so tired he sat down by the door and rested. And as he let his eyes roam here and there, he saw the giant's playthings lying in the yard. These were a couple of enormous balls, and nine-pins as tall as a man. After a while he had a fancy to set the nine-pins up and then rolled the balls at them, and screamed and cried out when the nine-pins fell, and had a merry time of it. The giant heard the noise, stretched his head out of the window, and saw a man who was not taller than other men, and yet played with his nine-pins. "Little worm," cried he, "why art thou playing with my balls? Who gave thee strength to do it?" The King's son looked up, saw the giant, and said, "Oh, thou blockhead, thou thinkest indeed that thou only hast strong arms, I can do everything I want to do."

When a son has grown up, he must leave his father's house to look around in the world and to test himself. It is exactly the same in the inner world. The young, strong maturing I wants to become a free, independent individuality. The old self (the father) and the soul being from whom he was born (the mother) can no longer give him what he needs. He needs a *Welt-Anschauung*, a world view, and must mature to full self mastery. In folktale language, he must "find his kingdom." Along the way there are many tasks, many

dangers threaten. The first danger is the giant, and he is obviously the mightier the stronger the I is.

Giants are imaginations of gross, uncouth, untamed nature forces. As frost- and ice-storm giants they were long seen by clairvoyants. They throw their weight around mightily but senselessly and rate as big but dumb. Also in humans, "giant" forces work, untamed and intemperate. Indeed, the whole of the Nature-Man in us is such a giant. Everyone must wrestle this giant, especially one who would attain to kingly dignity.

Giants like to play with balls, especially balls as big as a man. The ball, like the ring, represents in its spherical form the cosmos. The Nature-Man in us manages such forces, deals with them unconsciously; he plays. The I of Man must learn to manage these forces and effects but from a free and conscious position. It must indeed be able to confront this inner giant and say: You have nothing more than your blockheaded wildness, your physical strength; I, however, can consciously control these forces.

The giant came down and watched the bowling with great admiration, and said, "Child of man, if thou art one of that kind, go and bring me an apple of the tree of life." - "What dost thou want with it?" said the King's son. "I do not want the apple for myself," answered the giant, "but I have a betrothed bride who wishes for it. I have traveled far about the world and cannot find the tree." - "I will soon find it," said the King's son, "and I do not know what is to prevent me from getting the apple down." The giant said, "Thou really believest it to be so easy! The garden in which the tree stands is surrounded by an iron lattice, and in front of the lattice lie wild beasts, each close to the other, and they keep watch and let no man go in." - "They will be sure to let me in," said the King's son. "Yes,

but even if thou dost get into the garden, and seest the apple hanging to the tree, it is still not thine; a ring hangs in front of it, through which any one who wants to reach the apple and break it off, must put his hand, and no one has yet had the luck to do it." - "That luck will be mine," said the King's son.

In the West, the fruit of the Tree of Knowledge is the apple. It is the symbol of that process by which Man "fell" from a higher consciousness to a lower and exchanged "paradise" for the sense world that surrounds us. But through the "fall" he gained knowledge of good and evil. Representing all of us, our ancestors of long ago ate this "apple". But what is the apple of life? The garden image points to region where in luxuriant abundance plants grow and fruits and seeds ripen. It is a world of the forces of life and growth that permeate us and bring about life everywhere. But it is also the special region of those forces in humans that Aristotle calls the "vegetative soul". This region is protected – there is an iron lattice around it. One needs an iron-breaking will to enter it. This will must be under the full control of the I. (The blood, the organ of the I, requires iron.)

In front of the lattice lie wild beasts, one next to another, and they keep watch and let no humans in. Our sentient world is full of drives and desires. These wild drives are the beasts that deny us entry into the Garden of Eden in which the best fruit grows. It takes invincible trust in the divinity of the human soul to believe in this image of paradise and to find it within oneself. One must know that one can deal with all wildness, with all drives and desires when the goal is firm before one. "They will be sure to let me in," said the king's son. "That luck will be mine," answered king's son about the ring. When one recognizes that the I-consciousness that forms in the course of ordinary life is not his whole I but only that part

271

which belongs to the sense world, not a true fruit but only a semblance.[74] But if he bestirs himself to live, not just out of this lower I but also out of a higher one, then he overcomes this "Fall" into separation or sin. The descent into the sense world has brought knowledge not just of good but also of evil. But if one becomes aware that with this knowledge the choice between good and evil is bound up, and that this choice makes him free, then the fall into sin is for him canceled. He can in freedom transform the lower I into a higher I in that he no longer acts out of egotism but out of love. While in this world he comes to know death forces and must take death into himself, in the other world there is no death, only life. In place of the apple, the fruit of the Tree of Knowledge of Good and Evil, there is the fruit of the Tree of Life.

The tale says: Whoever would pluck this fruit must reach through the ring. The ring, the circle closed in itself, makes the picture clearer. When does one act out of the whole that rests complete in itself? When for him beginning and end, birth and death are one, when his consciousness has become rounded to a continuous, unbroken whole that grasps itself as a eternal being. Richard Wagner's *Ring of the Niebelungen* is about this consciousness of the personality. And there also is the ring the symbol. Only one who reaches through this ring can pluck the fruit of the Tree of Life.

Then he took leave of the giant, and went forth over mountain and valley, and through plains and forests, until at length he came to the wondrous garden.

---

74 The author uses the word *Scheinfrucht.* Elsewhere she uses it in its precise botanical sense of "accessory fruit" but I do not believe that is the case here.

The beasts lay round about it, but they had put their heads down and were asleep. Moreover, they did not awake when he went up to them, so he stepped over them, climbed the fence, and got safely into the garden. There, in the very middle of it, stood the tree of life, and the red apples were shining upon the branches. He climbed up the trunk to the top, and as he was about to reach out for an apple, he saw a ring hanging before it; but he thrust his hand through that without any difficulty, and gathered the apple. The ring closed tightly on his arm, and all at once he felt a prodigious strength flowing through his veins. When he had come down again from the tree with the apple, he would not climb over the fence, but grasped the great gate, and had no need to shake it more than once before it sprang open with a loud crash. Then he went out, and the lion which had been lying down before, was awake and sprang after him, not in rage and fierceness, but following him humbly as its master.

The King's son took the giant the apple he had promised him, and said, "Seest thou, I have brought it without difficulty." The giant was glad that his desire had been so soon satisfied, hastened to his bride, and gave her the apple for which she had wished. She was a beautiful and wise maiden, and as she did not see the ring on his arm, she said, "I shall never believe that thou hast brought the apple, until I see the ring on thine arm." The giant said, "I have nothing to do but go home and fetch it," and thought it would be easy to take away by force from the weak man, what he would not give of his own free will. He therefore demanded the ring from him, but the King's son refused it. "Where the apple is, the ring must be also," said the giant; "if thou wilt not give it of thine own accord, thou must fight with me for it."

273

He who has won the fruit of the Tree of Life can open the door to this Garden of Eden. The wild animals (the drives) sleep. They are tamed. "Wild drives have now gone to sleep" says Faust.[75] Audacious daring has been transformed to steadfast courage: the lion follows the king's son and serves him.

The beautiful and clever bride of the giant is the innocent human nature-soul. The apple is fetched for her. The picture says: Life's fruit is naturally incorporated into the depths of the human soul. But the consciousness that Man has thereby won (the ring) he can never relinquish; he must fight for it and never let the giant tear it away for his own.

They wrestled with each other for a long time, but the giant could not get the better of the King's son, who was strengthened by the magical power of the ring. Then the giant thought of a stratagem, and said, "I have gotten warm with fighting, and so hast thou. We will bathe in the river, and cool ourselves before we begin again." The King's son, who knew nothing of falsehood, went with him to the water, and pulled off with his clothes the ring also from his arm, and sprang into the river. The giant instantly snatched the ring, and ran away with it, but the lion, which had observed the theft, pursued the giant, tore the ring out of his hand, and brought it back to its master. Then the giant placed himself behind an oak-tree, and while the King's son was busy putting on his clothes again, surprised him, and put both his eyes out.

A strong I is often paired with being unsuspecting, with too much trust. One filled with world-conquering strength may lack caution against the forces of evil, and the folktales show over and

---

75 *Entschlafen sind nun wilde triebe,* in *Faust I*, scene in Faust's study with the poodle.

over how evil is not sufficiently recognized and how the forces that drag down and limit are not penetrated. In this case, the dull, giant nature forces were indeed the stimulus to win the rounded personality consciousness (the ring) but in the water it was put aside. Water represents the enlivened soul world, (in the sense of Goethe's poem "The human soul is like water"[76]) where our feelings, moods and passions well up and pass over us in waves, where dreams and unconscious thoughts "surface". We have picture words like "sunken into himself". How often does the giant not tempt us to dip into this world of dreamy feelings and endanger our I-consciousness! But there courage that has been won – the lion – helps.

When the deception of the giant fails, he makes a different attack. He hides behind an oak tree, then jumps out and puts out both eyes of the king's son. In ordinary life any thick tree would do for the robber, but for expressing the inner life the oak tree is the best hiding place and of special meaning. The wild man with the oak tree – often holding in his hand an oak tree pulled up by the roots – is one of the most frequent symbols of the Middle Ages. It appeared in the coat of arms of families and of cities and in the shields of inns (such as *Gasthaus zum Wilden Man* – "Wild Man Inn") and was a constant admonition to be aware of this force in us and to control it. The oak tree is the picture of the upward-rising will forces with roots deep within the human being. A fearless Man

---

76

Des Menschen Seele	The soul of man
Gleicht dem Wasser:	Is like water:
Vom Himmel kommt es,	It comes from heaven,
Zum Himmel steigt es,	It rises back to heaven,
Und wieder nieder	And again down
Zur Erde muß es	To earth it must,
Ewig wechselnd.	Ever alternating.

has, so to speak, a mighty oak tree within himself. Behind it the giant likes to hide and put out our eyes, that is, he takes from us the ability to see through things, to get a right view of things. One who looses himself in the life of feeling (in water) can easily let his will get out of control. He becomes blind to every reasonable insight.

And now the unhappy King's son stood there, and was blind and knew not how to help himself. Then the giant came back to him, took him by the hand as if he were someone who wanted to guide him, and led him to the top of a high rock. There he left him standing, and thought, "Just two steps more, and he will fall down and kill himself, and I can take the ring from him." But the faithful lion had not deserted its master; it held him fast by the clothes, and drew him gradually back again. When the giant came and wanted to rob the dead man, he saw that his cunning had been in vain. "Is there no way, then, of destroying a weak child of man like that?" said he angrily to himself, and seized the King's son and led him back again to the precipice by another way, but the lion which saw his evil design, helped its master out of danger here also. When they had got close to the edge, the giant let the blind man's hand drop, and was going to leave him behind alone, but the lion pushed the giant so that he was thrown down and fell, dashed to pieces, on the ground.

Many a climb to a peak, many a high point in our lives we owe to the giant in us, if we let him have his way. But if he has taken away one's sight, one can no longer see through anything and stands on the edge of the abyss. Courage of heart, the lion, must be the true guide and put an end to the rule of untamed nature.

The faithful animal again drew its master back from the precipice, and guided him to a tree by which flowed a clear brook.

The King's son sat down there, but the lion lay down, and sprinkled the water in his face with its paws. Scarcely had a couple of drops wetted the sockets of his eyes, than he was once more able to see something, and remarked a little bird flying quite close by, which wounded itself against the trunk of a tree. On this it went down to the water and bathed itself therein, and then it soared upwards and swept between the trees without touching them, as if it had recovered its sight again. Then the King's son recognized a sign from God and stooped down to the water, and washed and bathed his face in it. And when he arose he had his eyes once more, brighter and clearer than they had ever been.

Here is shown how the same element – in this case, water – that can be a danger to one who dips into it without being careful to preserve the integrity of his personality can also conversely help heal if one pays attention to potent hints from the heart. A new sight is won. He becomes clairvoyant in the sense of Richard Wagner's world clairvoyance.[77] It is now not long until the way to knowledge of the I leads into the realm of the higher soul itself.

The King's son thanked God for his great mercy, and traveled with his lion onwards through the world. And it came to pass that he arrived before a castle which was enchanted. In the gateway stood a maiden of beautiful form and fine face, but she was quite black. She spoke to him and said, "Ah, if thou couldest but deliver me from the evil spell which is thrown over me." - "What shall I do?" said the King's son. The maiden answered, "Thou must pass three nights in the great hall of this enchanted castle, but thou must let no fear enter thy heart. When they are doing their worst to torment thee, if thou

---

77 In *Parsifal*, Act 2, Scene 2, Kundry says to Parsifal:
  So war es mein Kuss,   So was it my kiss
  der welt-hellsichtig dich machte?   That made you world-clairvoyant?

bearest it without letting a sound escape thee, I shall be free. Thy life they dare not take." Then said the King's son, "I have no fear; with God's help I will try it." So he went gaily into the castle, and when it grew dark he seated himself in the large hall and waited. Everything was quiet, however, till midnight, when all at once a great tumult began, and out of every hole and corner came little devils. They behaved as if they did not see him, seated themselves in the middle of the room, lighted a fire, and began to gamble. When one of them lost, he said, "It is not right; some one is here who does not belong to us; it is his fault that I am losing." - "Wait, you fellow behind the stove, I am coming," said another. The screaming became still louder, so that no one could have heard it without terror. The King's son stayed sitting quite quietly, and was not afraid; but at last the devils jumped up from the ground, and fell on him, and there were so many of them that he could not defend himself from them. They dragged him about on the floor, pinched him, pricked him, beat him, and tormented him, but no sound escaped from him. Towards morning they disappeared, and he was so exhausted that he could scarcely move his limbs, but when day dawned the black maiden came to him. She bore in her hand a little bottle wherein was the water of life wherewith she washed him, and he at once felt all pain depart and new strength flow through his veins. She said, "Thou hast held out successfully for one night, but two more lie before thee." Then she went away again, and as she was going, he observed that her feet had become white. The next night the devils came and began their gambols anew. They fell on the King's son, and beat him much more severely than the night before, until his body was covered with wounds. But as he bore all quietly, they were forced to leave him, and when dawn appeared, the maiden came and healed him with the water of life. And when she went away, he saw with joy that she had already become white to the tips of her fingers. And

278

now he had only one night more to go through, but it was the worst. The hob-goblins came again: "Art thou there still?" cried they, "thou shalt be tormented till thy breath stops." They pricked him and beat him, and threw him here and there, and pulled him by the arms and legs as if they wanted to tear him to pieces, but he bore everything, and never uttered a cry. At last the devils vanished, but he lay fainting there, and did not stir, nor could he raise his eyes to look at the maiden who came in, and sprinkled and bathed him with the water of life. But suddenly he was freed from all pain, and felt fresh and healthy as if he had awakened from sleep, and when he opened his eyes he saw the maiden standing by him, snow-white, and fair as day.

The eternal feminine, the highest aim of soul development, has become darkened. Man is detained from meeting this archetype of his soul. Evil forces allow no suitors of the royal maiden. One must meet her without fear. The evil spirits that according to oldest traditions come out especially around midnight are the Ahrimanic-Mephistophelian. They inspire materialism. They lie to humans, telling them that the earthly, material world is the only true one. They win access to the soul through cowardice. The coward fears for his earthly possessions and falls to the devil. The materialist knows only the life of the body and will not risk losing it. The materialistic person also has a deep fear of everything supersensible. Anxiety and fear are his tormentors. The genuine spiritual seeker learns, however, that despite self discipline and fearlessness, illusion, error and falsehood work in him, for they are deeply implanted in Man and darken his soul.

This last test of knowledge must be withstood in three stages, just as, according to ancient mystery traditions, there were three nights of initiation. Then the soul being begins to shine forth, first

in the way of life (in the feet), then in action (in the hands), and then in thoughtful knowing (in the head). She then dips (see note page 87) into the well of primal wisdom, and that is Water of Life for one who has come to the very gate of death.

"Rise," said she, "and swing thy sword three times over the stairs, and then all will be delivered." And when he had done that, the whole castle was released from enchantment, and the maiden was a rich King's daughter. The servants came and said that the table was already set in the great hall, and dinner served up. Then they sat down and ate and drank together, and in the evening the wedding was solemnized with great rejoicings.

The stairs are the steps that lead to the Eternal Feminine. Even these steps have fallen to evil magic. As the steps are the last thing that needs redemption, we may suppose that they were the first to fall into error. Only the two-edged sword in the hand of the new king can help: spirit-filled speech. One who has gone through the mystic death opens the way for courageous seekers to follow.

Iron John

Grimm 136

There was once on a time a King who had a great forest near his palace, full of all kinds of wild animals. One day he sent out a huntsman to shoot him a roe, but he did not come back. "Perhaps some accident has befallen him," said the King, and the next day he sent out two more huntsmen who were to search for him, but they too stayed away. Then on the third day, he sent for all his huntsmen, and said, "Scour the whole forest through, and do not give up until ye have found all three." But of these also, none came home again, and of the pack of hounds which they had taken with them, none were seen again. From that time forth, no one would any longer venture into the forest, and it lay there in deep stillness and solitude, and nothing was seen of it, but sometimes an eagle or a hawk flying over it.

The Man of olden times was like a king, and there was in his inner world (in his kingdom) a region that was still but little open. It was an area of vegetative life, of luxuriant growth of forces in oppressive abundance that could not yet be explored and mastered. The picture language calls this region the great forest. Hunters, royal hunters, had indeed gone into this forest hoping to deal with "the wild one" – the drive nature – who naturally ruled in this realm. But in it they all perished.

This lasted for many years, when a strange huntsman announced himself to the King as seeking a situation, and offered to go into the dangerous forest. The King, however, would not give his consent, and said, "It is not safe in there; I fear it would fare with thee no better than with the others, and thou wouldst never come out

again." The huntsman replied, "Lord, I will venture it at my own risk, of fear I know nothing." The huntsman therefore betook himself with his dog to the forest. It was not long before the dog fell in with some game on the way, and wanted to pursue it; but hardly had the dog run two steps when it stood before a deep pool, could go no farther, and a naked arm stretched itself out of the water, seized it, and drew it under, When the huntsman saw that, he went back and fetched three men to come with buckets and bale out the water. When they could see to the bottom there lay a wild man whose body was brown like rusty iron, and whose hair hung over his face down to his knees.

Only when the time is fulfilled can one who fearlessly and of his own free will penetrates this forest learn what lives and breathes here. His tracking sense (the dog) is active and hurries ahead. He is, to be sure, drawn into an unknown deep pool, but thereby the hunter sees what must be done. Every "deep pool" must be encountered "creatively" (see note page 87). So the unerring and fearless seeker puts to work the three equally active soul forces (feeling, thinking, and willing) – here represented as three men – to "get to the bottom" of the "deep pool". The combined action accomplishes what was previously not possible, namely to "discover" what lay at the bottom of the deep pool, namely, a powerful nature force which previously dragged down everything, but never came into the daylight, the wild man, the Iron John.

The Wild Man was, as previously mentioned (page 275), one of the most common emblems of the Middle Ages and early Renaissance. In museums, house walls, and inn signs we still meet him. He is always shown naked. "Naked" means "in essence" – not in the sheath of the body. Often he has a club or uprooted tree in his hand. Often there is foliage around his head or hips. It should

be brought to Man's attention how strong and unrestrained his nature forces are and how, as spiritual Man, he must deal with this Nature-Man. In our tale he is "brown like rusty iron". He represents that natural force that lives in the iron in our blood. "Rusty iron" is iron that has been left to the elements. It has not yet been used and cared for by the transformative force of the human I.

They bound him with cords, and led him away to the castle. There was great astonishment over the wild man; the King, however, had him put in an iron cage in his court-yard, and forbade the door to be opened on pain of death, and the Queen herself was to take the key into her keeping. And from this time forth every one could again go into the forest with safety.

The old self in Man (the king) tries to restrain this alien to him natural force and to maintain order. Historically, iron was long not known as a material to be worked with, but the development that began with the discovery of how to work with it, once underway, was not to be halted.

The King had a son of eight years, who was once playing in the court-yard, and while he was playing, his golden ball fell into the cage. The boy ran thither and said, "Give me my ball out." - "Not till thou hast opened the door for me," answered the man. "No," said the boy, "I will not do that; the King has forbidden it," and ran away. The next day he again went and asked for his ball; the wild man said, "Open my door," but the boy would not. On the third day the King had ridden out hunting, and the boy went once more and said, "I cannot open the door even if I wished, for I have not the key." Then the wild man said, "It lies under thy mother's pillow, thou canst get it there." The boy, who wanted to have his ball back, cast all thought to the winds, and brought the key. The door opened with

difficulty, and the boy pinched his fingers. When it was open the wild man stepped out, gave him the golden ball, and hurried away. The boy had become afraid; he called and cried after him, "Oh, wild man, do not go away, or I shall be beaten!" The wild man turned back, took him up, set him on his shoulder, and went with hasty steps into the forest. When the King came home, he observed the empty cage, and asked the Queen how that had happened? She knew nothing about it, and sought the key, but it was gone. She called the boy, but no one answered. The King sent out people to seek for him in the fields, but they did not find him. Then he could easily guess what had happened, and much grief reigned in the royal court.

In our tale the prince is eight years old as the drama begins. Although the ancestral self (the father) could hold in check this scary nature force, at this age the naive force of the developing I (the son) unavoidably collides with it: the prince looses his golden ball to Iron John. Up to eight years old there lives in all actions of a child an unconscious, dreaming something. It is not his free I that acts but child-related life forces play with "*ball*ed together" Wisdom, with the golden ball. This instinctive gift now falls to that iron force that wants to be free. Iron is necessary to anchor our consciousness in our body. It is the physical basis of our I-con- sciousness. We become limp and weak-willed when the blood is lacking in iron. Iron John becomes free and immediately frees the boy, whom he carries away. This freeing of a nature force does not happen without pain. The boy's finger gets pinched. His actions[78], up until now unselfconscious play, become suddenly restricted, "pinched". He becomes painfully aware of his own actions. The

---

78 German word play: the word translated as "actions" is *Handeln*, which the author writes as *"Hand"-eln* to be sure we get the connection to the boy's *hand* injury. (The German word for hand is also *Hand*.)

young I shakes free of the ancestral inheritance, the fatherly spiritual and the motherly soulful, and now stands under the might of iron.

When the wild man had once more reached the dark forest, he took the boy down from his shoulder, and said to him, "Thou wilt never see thy father and mother again, but I will keep thee with me, for thou hast set me free, and I have compassion on thee. If thou dost all I bid thee, thou shalt fare well. Of treasure and gold have I enough, and more than anyone in the world." He made a bed of moss for the boy on which he slept, and the next morning the man took him to a spring, and said, "Behold, the gold spring is as bright and clear as crystal, thou shalt sit beside it, and take care that nothing falls into it, or it will be polluted. I will come every evening to see if thou hast obeyed my order." The boy placed himself by the margin of the well, and often saw a golden fish or a golden snake show itself therein, and took care that nothing fell in. As he was thus sitting, his finger hurt him so violently that he involuntarily put it in the water. He drew it quickly out again, but saw that it was quite gilded, and whatsoever pains he took to wash the gold off again, all was to no purpose. In the evening Iron John came back, looked at the boy, and said, "What has happened to the spring?" - "Nothing, nothing," he answered, and held his finger behind his back, that the man might not see it. But he said, "Thou hast dipped thy finger into the water, this time it may pass, but take care thou dost not again let anything go in." By daybreak the boy was already sitting by the spring and watching it. His finger hurt him again and he passed it over his head, and then unhappily a hair fell down into the spring. He took it quickly out, but it was already quite gilded. Iron John came, and already knew what had happened. "Thou hast let a hair fall into the spring," said he. "I will allow thee to watch by it once

more, but if this happens for the third time then the spring is polluted, and thou canst no longer remain with me."

On the third day, the boy sat by the spring, and did not stir his finger, however much it hurt him. But the time was long to him, and he looked at the reflection of his face on the surface of the water. And as he still bent down more and more while he was doing so, and trying to look straight into the eyes, his long hair fell down from his shoulders into the water. He raised himself up quickly, but the whole of the hair of his head was already golden and shone like the sun. You may imagine how terrified the poor boy was! He took his pocket-handkerchief and tied it round his head, in order that the man might not see it. When he came he already knew everything, and said, "Take the handkerchief off." Then the golden hair streamed forth, and let the boy excuse himself as he might, it was of no use. "Thou hast not stood the trial, and canst stay here no longer. Go forth into the world, there thou wilt learn what poverty is. But as thou hast not a bad heart, and as I mean well by thee, there is one thing I will grant thee; if thou fallest into any difficulty, come to the forest and cry, "Iron John," and then I will come and help thee. My power is great, greater than thou thinkest, and I have gold and silver in abundance."

From now on, the Iron leads and teaches the boy. The first lesson is: Wisdom's golden spring – the existence of which the naive I only now becomes clearly aware – must be guarded. In it still shine "golden fish" – thoughts that are not laboriously worked out but just arise spontaneously, full of wisdom, to the surface – and the golden snake that has not yet become the seducer of the intellect. It is "iron" necessity that the golden spring be guarded. Filled with pain, the prince falls in conflict and cannot keep the gold spring pure. The same thing that happens in action (*Handeln*)

happens in the thinking realm (the hair). There the conflict becomes conscious, and because the youth – now free from father and mother – wants to see and know himself indeed catches a perception of himself, but what looks back at him is the golden-spring self of childhood. The dip into this creative spring fills with wisdom – his hair falls in and becomes golden. But self observation and self knowledge are not yet ripe. One can never be content with the gold won in this way. Childish wisdom – though it rise to the level of genius – cannot guide life if exact individual thinking is not also developed. Without head work – without that brain work that first cuts us off from the cosmos but then lets us become independent personalities – we get no where. For this head-thinking, caps and hats are the picture in folktales. "Thou art an I" says the iron in the blood, "thou must take responsibility for everything, " – or as we say in German, "Take it on thy cap." And the hair is first covered with the handkerchief and later with a cap.

Iron further instructs the prince: Go into the world and learn to know poverty; what you posses you must attain through your own work. You must begin your development and attain a worldwide consciousness, a view of the whole world. For some this way has been opened by other seekers; others must find it themselves.

Then the King's son left the forest, and walked by beaten and unbeaten paths ever onwards until at length he reached a great city. There he looked for work, but could find none, and he had learnt nothing by which he could help himself. At length he went to the palace, and asked if they would take him in. The people about court did not at all know what use they could make of him, but they liked him, and told him to stay. At length the cook took him into his service, and said he might carry wood and water, and rake the cinders together. Once when it so happened that no one else was at

hand, the cook ordered him to carry the food to the royal table, but
as he did not like to let his golden hair be seen, he kept his little cap
on. Such a thing as that had never yet come under the King's notice,
and he said, "When thou comest to the royal table thou must take thy
hat off." He answered, "Ah, Lord, I cannot; I have a bad sore place
on my head." Then the King had the cook called before him and
scolded him, and asked how he could take such a boy as that into
his service; and that he was to turn him off at once. The cook,
however, had pity on him, and exchanged him for the gardener's
boy.

The prince comes to a different, a new king. He enters a new
realm, the realm of the soul. First he must serve in the kitchen,
carry wood, draw water and rake ashes. To "carry wood" always
means to take on and carry away what has become hardened and
dried, for example, abstract, non-living thought. "Water" is, on the
contrary, the moving, flowing element of the soul. One must learn
to penetrate to "the sources" and to grasp what is flowing and
creative. There is an old Chinese saying[79]

How miraculous and wondrous,
Hauling water and carrying firewood!

And he sweeps ashes. Ash in alchemy is what has been purified.
The fire of the will, that blazes within, leads to inner transformation.

---

79 The originator of the saying is known as Layman Pang (740 -808) 龐蘊居士
Páng Yùn Jūshì. Páng is his family name, Yùn is his given name, and Jūshì is
his title, meaning a lay follower of Buddha. There is a Wikipedia article on
Layman Pang. The original of the quoted passage is:

神通並妙用
運水及槃柴

To serve the king's cook means to experience what is genuine nourishment for the soul and spirit. And so he is finally able to meet the ruler of this realm. Many who have reached this stage decide to remain here and renounce further progress. They would take off the cap. Not so our hero who detects in himself the calling to higher development. The time has not yet come to reveal the treasure of the golden hair. A new step of self-education begins.

And now the boy had to plant and water the garden, hoe and dig, and bear the wind and bad weather. Once in summer when he was working alone in the garden, the day was so warm he took his little cap off that the air might cool him. As the sun shone on his hair it glittered and flashed so that the rays fell into the bed-room of the King's daughter, and up she sprang to see what that could be. Then she saw the boy, and cried to him, "Boy, bring me a wreath of flowers." He put his cap on with all haste, and gathered wild field-flowers and bound them together. When he was ascending the stairs with them, the gardener met him, and said, "How canst thou take the King's daughter a garland of such common flowers? Go quickly, and get another, and seek out the prettiest and rarest." - "Oh, no," replied the boy, "the wild ones have more scent, and will please her better." When he got into the room, the King's daughter said, "Take thy cap off, it is not seemly to keep it on in my presence." He again said, "I may not, I have a sore head." She, however, caught at his cap and pulled it off, and then his golden hair rolled down on his shoulders, and it was splendid to behold. He wanted to run out, but she held him by the arm, and gave him a handful of ducats. With these he departed, but he cared nothing for the gold pieces. He took them to the gardener, and said, "I present them to thy children, they can play with them." The following day the King's daughter again called to him that he was to bring her a wreath of field-flowers, and

289

when he went in with it, she instantly snatched at his cap, and wanted to take it away from him, but he held it fast with both hands. She again gave him a handful of ducats, but he would not keep them, and gave them to the gardener for playthings for his children. On the third day things went just the same; she could not get his cap away from him, and he would not have her money.

The prince becomes a gardener; our language has many pictures for this stage. One who can plant the seed of the word into the earthly realm, one who can cultivate and care for shoots, support the weak and with patience wait for the fruit to ripen, he is like the gardener who cares for living things and brings all that is noble to fruition. It is a stage which every educator should reach, especially kindergarten and elementary teachers. Of course, the higher soul (the king's daughter) notices the youth. She detects the wealth that from childhood has been his and which he, by constant development of logical thinking, has made into a treasure that watches over him. It is characteristic for the I that is becoming free that in the presence of the king's daughter, and of the king himself, he keeps his hat on. He will decide for himself, when the time comes, whether to let go of this personal, thinking-for-himself. Also, he sets no great store by the golden ducats the princess gives him, knowing well that the seeker of wisdom will never be content with such "coined" wisdom.

Not long afterwards, the country was overrun by war. The King gathered together his people, and did not know whether or not he could offer any opposition to the enemy, who was superior in strength and had a mighty army. Then said the gardener's boy, "I am grown up, and will go to the wars also, only give me a horse." The others laughed, and said, "Seek one for thyself when we are gone, we will leave one behind us in the stable for thee." When they

had gone forth, he went into the stable, and got the horse out; it was lame of one foot, and limped hobblety jig, hobblety jig; nevertheless he mounted it, and rode away to the dark forest. When he came to the outskirts, he called "Iron John," three times so loudly that it echoed through the trees. Thereupon the wild man appeared immediately, and said, "What dost thou desire?" - "I want a strong steed, for I am going to the wars." - "That thou shalt have, and still more than thou askest for." Then the wild man went back into the forest, and it was not long before a stable-boy came out of it, who led a horse that snorted with its nostrils, and could hardly be restrained, and behind them followed a great troop of soldiers entirely equipped in iron, and their swords flashed in the sun. The youth made over his three-legged horse to the stable-boy, mounted the other, and rode at the head of the soldiers. When he got near the battle-field a great part of the King's men had already fallen, and little was wanting to make the rest give way. Then the youth galloped thither with his iron soldiers, broke like a hurricane over the enemy, and beat down all who opposed him. They began to fly, but the youth pursued, and never stopped, until there was not a single man left. Instead, however, of returning to the King, he conducted his troop by bye-ways back to the forest, and called forth Iron John. "What dost thou desire?" asked the wild man. "Take back thy horse and thy troops, and give me my three-legged horse again." All that he asked was done, and soon he was riding on his three-legged horse.

When the realm of the soul is in danger and his kingdom threatened, then must the I be ready to make the greatest commitment. All valiant forces are called upon. They are always available to one of earnest will who uses the iron forces of the blood. For fighting the hero needs a strong horse. This horse is the

symbol of instinctive understanding, of that force which, tamed and bridled, can actively lead to spiritual goals. Plato compares a man's reason with a horse which he holds by a bridle. Our language has a number of horse-related expressions: "He is on his high horse", "he has horse sense," "he sits tight in the saddle." The prince is given a horse that is lame in one foot and limps. He does not turn it down. We find the motif of the pathetic, mangy, limping horse in many I-related folktales. The image points to the fact that only through his own work does Man transform his reason into the best possible motive force. All of the forces that have been summoned up have been "armed in iron" and therefore the intervention of the I does what the soul-king alone could not do: drive back the adversarial forces. The true spiritual warrior returns modestly to his everyday life.

When the King returned to his palace, his daughter went to meet him, and wished him joy of his victory. "I am not the one who carried away the victory," said he, "but a stranger knight who came to my assistance with his soldiers." The daughter wanted to hear who the strange knight was, but the King did not know, and said, "He followed the enemy, and I did not see him again." She inquired of the gardener where his boy was, but he smiled, and said, "He has just come home on his three-legged horse, and the others have been mocking him, and crying, "Here comes our hobblety jig back again!" They asked, too, "Under what hedge hast thou been lying sleeping all the time?" He, however, said, "I did the best of all, and it would have gone badly without me." And then he was still more ridiculed.

The King said to his daughter, "I will proclaim a great feast that shall last for three days, and thou shalt throw a golden apple. Perhaps the unknown will come to it." When the feast was announced, the youth went out to the forest, and called Iron John.

292

"What dost thou desire?" asked he. "That I may catch the King's daughter's golden apple." - "It is as safe as if thou hadst it already," said Iron John. "Thou shalt likewise have a suit of red armour for the occasion, and ride on a spirited chestnut-horse." When the day came, the youth galloped to the spot, took his place amongst the knights, and was recognized by no one. The King's daughter came forward, and threw a golden apple to the knights, but none of them caught it but he, only as soon as he had it he galloped away.

On the second day Iron John equipped him as a white knight, and gave him a white horse. Again he was the only one who caught the apple, and he did not linger an instant, but galloped off with it. The King grew angry, and said, "That is not allowed; he must appear before me and tell his name." He gave the order that if the knight who caught the apple, should go away again they should pursue him, and if he would not come back willingly, they were to cut him down and stab him.

On the third day, he received from Iron John a suit of black armour and a black horse, and again he caught the apple. But when he was riding off with it, the King's attendants pursued him, and one of them got so near him that he wounded the youth's leg with the point of his sword. The youth nevertheless escaped from them, but his horse leapt so violently that the helmet fell from the youth's head, and they could see that he had golden hair. They rode back and announced this to the King.

The apple is the fruit of the Tree of the Knowledge of Good and Evil. It becomes a golden apple when this knowledge is transformed to wisdom. The kingly soul would give this fruit to the one who can catch it. The I wants to catch it, and it is again the natural might of iron that helps him do so, for he receives the red

armor and the red horse. Our blood is foundation for the I in the body. Healthy red blood is necessary for us to confront the world wide awake, perceive our environment correctly, commit ourselves to improve it. We are armed with this iron force. It works also in our understanding, of which the red horse is the expression. When we think of Parzival, who becomes the red knight and rides the red horse, we have the same image before us.

To this insight won out of the blood there must be added knowledge of the spirit. Where the understanding concerns itself with the supersensible (becomes a white horse) there appears in Man the purity of an immaterial world (white armor is put on) and this leads to a further encounter with the king's daughter, who also on this plane can throw forth the fruit.

On the third day, the hero wears black armor and rides a black horse. Black is the color of the earthly-material. The turning towards material sense world has long been practiced as the helper in the kitchen and garden. "Go into the world and learn to know poverty" was the order from Iron John. The earthly world is poverty so long as one regards it as only material. But when a high degree of spiritual knowledge has been attained – as indicated by the red and white armor – then the divine creative powers which lie at the base of the material world and sustain it become known. The prince wins the black armor and masters the black steed. Since the spiritualized reason has now seen through and mastered this dark sense world, the curse is lifted: the golden apple is won also on this plane.

The following day the King's daughter asked the gardener about his boy. "He is at work in the garden; the queer creature has been at the festival too, and only came home yesterday evening; he

294

*has likewise shown my children three golden apples which he has
won."*

*The King had him summoned into his presence, and he came
and again had his little cap on his head. But the King's daughter
went up to him and took it off, and then his golden hair fell down
over his shoulders, and he was so handsome that all were amazed.
"Art thou the knight who came every day to the festival, always in
different colours, and who caught the three golden apples?" asked
the King. "Yes," answered he, "and here the apples are," and he took
them out of his pocket, and returned them to the King. "If you desire
further proof, you may see the wound which your people gave me
when they followed me. But I am likewise the knight who helped you
to your victory over your enemies." - "If thou canst perform such
deeds as that, thou art no gardener's boy; tell me, who is thy father?"
- "My father is a mighty King, and gold have I in plenty as great as I
require." - "I well see," said the King, "that I owe thanks to thee; can
I do anything to please thee?" - "Yes," answered he, "that indeed you
can. Give me your daughter to wife." The maiden laughed, and
said, "He does not stand much on ceremony, but I have already seen
by his golden hair that he was no gardener's boy," and then she went
and kissed him. His father and mother came to the wedding, and
were in great delight, for they had given up all hope of ever seeing
their dear son again. And as they were sitting at the marriage-feast,
the music suddenly stopped, the doors opened, and a stately King
came in with a great retinue. He went up to the youth, embraced him
and said, "I am Iron John, and was by enchantment a wild man, but
thou hast set me free; all the treasures which I possess, shall be thy
property."*

Now the cap – in the form of a helmet – can fly from his head
revealing the golden hair. Its significance has been changed by the

independent thinking won by so many sacrifices. Now it is highest wisdom in the life of thought that shines out. What was attained in the golden spring (of childhood) has through purification become his inalienable own possession.

In no other folktale do we find such a brief – almost cheeky – courtship. The I-Man expresses himselff even in his style. Now the royal wedding can be celebrated. As the I ripens to the Eternal Masculine it unites with the Eternal Feminine of the soul. The hidden natural force of iron lets itself be recognized in its true significance and richness. It has been ennobled to a regal spiritual being by the man who has transformed himself.

The Star Money

Grimm 153

There was once on a time a little girl whose father and mother were dead, and she was so poor that she no longer had any little room to live in, or bed to sleep in, and at last she had nothing else but the clothes she was wearing and a little bit of bread in her hand which some charitable soul had given her. She was, however, good and pious. And as she was thus forsaken by all the world, she went forth into the open country, trusting in the good God.

Then a poor man met her, who said: "Ah, give me something to eat, I am so hungry!" She reached him the whole of her piece of bread, and said: "May God bless it to thy use," and went onwards. Then came a child who moaned and said: "My head is so cold, give me something to cover it with." So she took off her cap and gave it to him; and when she had walked a little farther, she met another child who had no jacket and was frozen with cold. Then she gave it her own; and a little farther on one begged for a skirt, and she gave away that also. At length she got into a forest and it had already become dark, and there came yet another child, and asked for an undershirt, and the good little girl thought to herself: "It is a dark night and no one sees thee, thou canst very well give thy long undershirt," and took it off, and gave away that also.

And as she so stood, and had not one single thing left, suddenly stars began to fall from heaven, and they were pure, hard, shiny golden coins, and although she had just given her little undershirt away, she had a new one which was of the very finest linen. Then she gathered together the coins into this, and was rich all the days of her life.

When is the human soul like a poor orphan child? When motherly soul forces and fatherly spiritual forces, from which it is descended, no longer stand behind it but have died, when its inherited spiritual wealth has been exhausted, and homelessness has become its daily feeling. Then the soul is completely on its own and living in a world in which it is helpless and inexperienced. Out of its own forces it must find a home, a purpose, and inner wealth.

This child had nothing but the clothes on her back and a small piece of bread in her hand which a good-hearted soul had given her. What soul nourishment she had was not inherited, nor had she earned it; it was a gift. But – and here appears the fundamental theme of the whole tale – full of compassion, she gives it to those that hunger. Unselfishness is the Leitmotiv.

The only thing the girl still has left are the clothes on her back. For one who has absolutely nothing else, the clothes on the body become very important. One's self respect depends on them. Also for the soul is its clothing, its aura, of great importance. The more the soul has given up in the general descent of mankind, the more it has won in other ways, for its aura has become totally personal. Everyone has his own individual soul garment. It can be a blessing for the whole surrounding world when piety and goodness fill it and compassion, the fundamental force of love, moves the heart.

Here again we have the cap that we have seen repeatedly. We Germans say, as has been mentioned, "I take it on my cap" when we mean "I take full responsibility." The expression makes clear that the responsibility is experienced where we think: in the head. The personal life of thoughts and concepts that separates each of us from the general spiritual world and makes possible our own individual inner world, our brain thinking, is like an individual cap

that each of us has made. This inner cap is highly valuable to the modern Man and conditions his whole picture of the world. In the age of I-development, it creates a very personal life of thought and outlook on the world. One who has developed this inner "cap" can assist others whose "heads are cold" – that is, who need help in their thought life. That gift is a step on an inner path.

And with feeling and the gift of the jacket, it is the same. The feeling life of modern Man has also become personal, individual. It is woven through with his opinions, drenched with his heart's blood. No two humans have the same life of feeling. It has its seat in the region of the heart and lungs, in the middle of our being, the area covered by a jacket. We Germans say "The jacket it too small for him" when someone feels a loss. Likewise, we say "He has a white vest" when we want to point to the innocence and purity of someone's life of feeling. This meeting with the freezing child shows empathy, the capacity to truly participate in the feeling of another and to give without expecting anything in return.

Thirdly, the little skirt is given away. The skirt covers the lower torso and limbs. In those parts works the third aspect of the soul, the Will. It largely escapes notice. We know only that we will to do something and what that something is, but the process between the concept of what we want to do and the doing of it eludes our consciousness. Just think of walking. One foot goes in front of the other with scarcely any thought on our part, but with much action of muscle and nerve. That is Will at work. See how a child stomps about when seized by a Will attack! But a strong Will is necessary to actually get things done. Moreover, to inspire others to action is to give Will power to them. That is another step on the inner way. It is the gift of the skirt.

Only one thing remains to be given, the long undershirt. In the picture language of the folktales, we hear over and over of this shirt. In the head thoughts are formed – threads are spun. But they live and weave further in the unconscious and form a spiritual sheath. The picture of this sheath is the shirt. This shirt the girl gives away out of compassion. Even the last possession the soul gives away, everything right down to the life forces. But after this complete renunciation, a new consciousness is given her, a new shirt of finest linen. The picture says to us that the thinking of the soul is no longer merely natural and without rules. Now a clear, ordered, carefully logical but imaginative thinking is woven into the soul. Finest linen points to highest perfection in thinking.

The gold of wisdom comes to her from a higher world. One who unselfishly works thinking, feeling and willing right down into the subconscious does not become poorer thereby, for compassion and love are the highest forces for the attainment of knowledge and lead to inner wealth. This wealth come out of the world of the Moral, from the starry world. And the childlike soul can grasp and preserve this treasure of wisdom because it was minted in heaven for the tasks it will face on earth.

Our tale may stem from the circles of medieval mystics such as Meister Eckehart or Johannes Tauler in the 13th and 14th centuries, for they had the teaching: "O Man, divest thyself, for the more you give of yourself, the richer you become."

Contents

PART 1

the **CORE**

CHAPTER 1

Don't Ignore Your Core!

Physical training is good, but training for godliness is much better,
promising benefits in this life and in the life to come.
—1 Timothy 4:8 NLT

When I worked as a personal trainer, I had a client named Lynne. Despite her many attempts to get in shape, Lynne had been unable to achieve long-term success. She had tried various programs and diet plans on her own but couldn't make progress in controlling her weight. Lynne hired me because she was desperate for change. She recognized that without accountability in this area of her life, she would never reach her goals.

I still remember the day we met. The scowl on her face said it all: the gym was the last place in the world she wanted to be.

During our first workout, Lynne informed me, "I hate to exercise." I thought, *This should be interesting.* However, I knew she had potential. As the owner of a thriving human resources firm, Lynne had already demonstrated self-discipline in building her company. She just needed to learn how to apply that determination to her health.

I began meeting with Lynne three times per week, instructing her in various cardiovascular and weight training exercises. Mostly, though, we focused on strengthening her core, the group of muscles in the center of the body that work together to produce movement.

The transformation that occurred in Lynne in the first few months was incredible. As she performed the exercises I prescribed, her energy level soared and her body size got smaller. Her attitude toward the gym also changed. She no longer despised her workouts. Instead she looked forward to them! Once Lynne experienced the benefits of a well-balanced core, she was all in. There was no way she was going to quit.

Nearly fifteen years later Lynne is still going strong. Even though she admits to seasons of inactivity, she hasn't given up. In July 2012, she completed two half marathons, and she plans to finish her first marathon in 2014 at age fifty-four. What began as a dreaded duty for Lynne has become a lifelong habit, one that has reaped huge rewards in every area of her life.

At this point, you may be thinking, *Well, that's a nice story. I'm happy for Lynne, but what does that have to do with my relationship with God?*

Everything.

You see, just as you have a physical core, you also possess a spiritual core. The Bible tells us about it in Mark 12:30: "You must love the LORD your God with all your heart, all your soul, all your mind, and all your strength" (NLT).

Your spiritual core consists of four "muscles" — your heart, soul, mind, and strength. When you're healthy in all of these areas, you're free to move as God leads. However, if you allow your spiritual muscles to atrophy, you prevent yourself from attaining your full potential in Christ. Instead of having joy and peace, you become weighed down by depression and anxiety. You're vulnerable to attacks from the Enemy and powerless to resist temptation.

What is the condition of *your* spiritual core? Could your muscles use some fine-tuning, or do they need an overhaul?

No matter what your fitness level is, the program provided in this book can help you achieve greater health. Think of me as your personal trainer. I'll show you what it takes to get in better spiritual shape. I promise to push you to do more than you would do on your own. You and I will work together to reach your goals, so you can be spiritually strong. In this training program, you will learn to

- study the Bible and understand what God is saying to you,
- pray with power,
- incorporate periodic fasting into your life,
- honor God with your body through nutritious eating and exercise,
- practice good stewardship of the resources God has given you,
- serve others in humility as a demonstration of God's love,
- experience the joy that accompanies self-discipline.

God's Promise to You

In case you feel overwhelmed, let me remind you of something: you aren't doing this program on your own, because "the LORD is with you when you are with him" (2 Chron. 15:2). Not only is God right by your side; he has already provided for your success! His divine power has given you everything you need for life and godliness (2 Peter 1:3), including the self-control and motivation to complete this core conditioning program.

How This Book Will Help You

Spiritually Strong provides the information, instruction, encouragement, and accountability you need to strengthen your spiritual core muscles. The book is divided into three main parts:

> PART 1: "The Core"
> PART 2: "The Exercises"
> PART 3: "The Program"

Part 1 presents the muscles of the physical and spiritual core, with an introduction to the exercises that strengthen them and a discussion about the importance of self-discipline in training.

Part 2 explains the six essential exercises for training the core: Bible study, prayer, fasting, healthy living, financial stewardship, and serving others.

Part 3 helps you name goals for your core conditioning program, establish a training schedule, and set the stage for your success. In this section, you'll implement the spiritual and physical exercises during a six-week Bible study.

I'm thankful the Lord led you to this book. I believe he's going to use it to bless your life in many ways. May God fill you with his power as you train yourself in godliness!

CHAPTER 2

Training Your Core

A few years ago, I struggled with constant throbbing in my lower legs. Assuming it was shin splints, I did everything I could to reduce the inflammation. I applied ice, rested, and took ibuprofen. However, the aching persisted. After dealing with this issue for several months, I finally went to the doctor. He ordered an X-ray and an MRI, thinking I might have stress fractures. Surprisingly, both tests were clear of any abnormalities. Although I was thankful nothing was seriously damaged, I was frustrated.

My husband, who works as a physical therapist, was equally discouraged. His job is to repair broken people, and it bothered him that he couldn't help me. However, one day God gave my husband insight into my situation. Justin told me, "We've been treating the wrong part of your body. I think the pain in your legs is actually coming from your lower back."

Turns out, he was right. What I felt is known as referred pain, which is pain perceived at a location other than the site of the pathology. Instead of feeling pain where the problem is, I felt it in a different part of my body.

In my case, I had a severe imbalance in my abdominal muscles. Even though my *rectus abdominis* (the "six-pack" muscle) was strong, my *transverse abdominis* (the deepest abdominal muscle) was extremely weak. (See page 16 for illustration.) To build strength in that area, I needed to focus on developing my core muscles.

When I was instructed on the exercises I should do, I thought, *That's it?* The movements were subtle, and I doubted they would work. But I did them faithfully, and my perseverance paid off. After a few weeks, the throbbing in my shins became less intense. Within three to four months, my leg pain disappeared. Those basic core exercises, performed day after day, eventually brought healing to my body.

Core Muscles

The "core" refers to the group of muscles which provide stabilization to the body. These muscles work as a team to produce efficient movement for the extremities. A person with a well-developed physical core has good balance and is flexible, while someone with a weak core is more prone to injury. Following are the muscles of your physical core.

1. Abdominal Muscles *(Fig. 1)*

Transverse abdominis. This muscle is the deepest of the abdominal muscles and acts as a natural weight-lifting belt for the body. It lies underneath the obliques (the muscles of the waist), runs horizontally underneath the belly button, and wraps around the spine to provide protection and stability.

Rectus abdominis. This muscle stretches vertically along the front of the abdomen.

Internal and external obliques. These two groups of muscles make up the intermediate layer of the abdominals and aid in trunk rotation. The external obliques are located on the side and front of the abdomen around your waist. The internal obliques lie under the external obliques but run in the opposite direction.

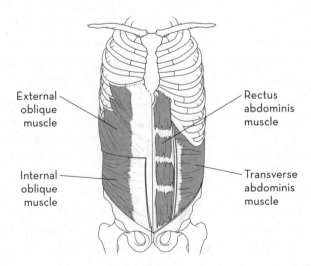

External oblique muscle

Rectus abdominis muscle

Internal oblique muscle

Transverse abdominis muscle

Figure 1. Abdominal Muscles

2. Back Muscles *(Fig. 2)*

Erector spinae. This collection of three muscles extends along your neck down to your lower back.

Multifidus. This muscle runs between the vertebrae in the spine, providing extension and rotation to each spinal segment.

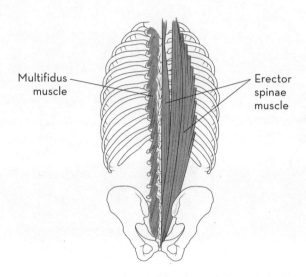

Multifidus
muscle

Erector
spinae
muscle

Figure 2. Back Muscles

3. Chest Muscles *(Fig. 3)*

Pectorals. The pectorals are the large, highly visible muscles located on each side of the chest. The *pectoralis major* is the thick, fan-shaped muscle which makes up the bulk of the chest muscles in the male and lies under the breast in the female. Underneath the *pectoralis major* is the *pectoralis minor*, a thin, triangular muscle.

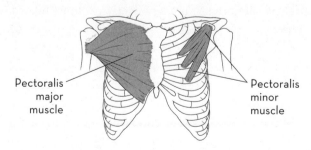

Pectoralis
major
muscle

Pectoralis
minor
muscle

Figure 3. Chest Muscles

4. Pelvic Muscles *(Fig. 4)*

Pelvic floor. The muscles which extend from the pubic bone in the front to the tailbone in the back are known as the pelvic floor. Their primary functions include providing support for the organs in the pelvis and stopping the flow of urination.

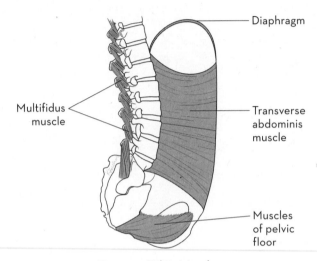

Figure 4. Pelvic Muscles

When it comes to strengthening the core, most people think the answer is performing crunches. However, as we have just learned, the abdominals are only part of the equation. Many people suffer from lower back pain because their abs have been overworked while surrounding muscles have been neglected. Core strength exercises ensure that equal power is distributed throughout the muscles of the core, which helps to reduce muscle imbalances.

For a core training program to be effective, it must take an integrated approach. The focus should not be on working the muscles in isolation, such as doing hundreds of sit-ups or crunches; it should be on moving the body as a unit. The best exercises are ones which recruit many muscles at the same time. Such exercises create stability, which increases the amount of power available for activity and reduces the likelihood of injury.

Everything you do involves your core, whether it's swinging a golf club, lifting a large bag of dog food, or sitting in a chair. Following are five reasons why a core conditioning program is beneficial to your body.

1. It builds balance.

2. It develops proper posture.

3. It enables you to perform tasks with ease.

4. It protects you from pain and injuries.

5. It increases energy.

The importance of having a strong physical core cannot be over-emphasized. Later, in the "Healthy Living" chapter, we'll take a closer look at exercises for training your physical core. For now, though, let's turn our attention to the components of your spiritual core and consider why these muscles are even *more* crucial to the quality of your life.

Your Spiritual Core

Your spiritual core consists of your heart, soul, mind, and strength. By examining the Greek definitions of each of these words in Mark 12:30, we can gain deeper insight into their meanings.

Heart: Kardia *(Kar-DEE-ah)*

The Greek word *kardia* refers to the "inner life or inner self; the place of thoughts and feelings." It's often considered to be the center of our emotions and will.

- "The LORD is my strength and my shield; my heart trusts in him, and he helps me. My heart leaps for joy, and with my song I praise him" (Ps. 28:7).

- "For it is with your heart that you believe and are justified, and it is with your mouth that you profess your faith and are saved" (Rom. 10:10).

Soul: Psuche *(Psoo-KHAY)*

Soul is defined as "the vital breath; the breath of life." When God made the sun, moon, stars, plants, and animals, he spoke them into existence. However, God formed man from the dust of the ground. He "breathed into his nostrils the breath of life, and the man became a living being" (Gen. 2:7). The soul is what sets human beings apart from the rest of creation and gives us a unique capacity to live in relationship with God.

- "Now devote your heart and soul to seeking the LORD your God" (1 Chron. 22:19).
- "Yes, my soul, find rest in God; my hope comes from him" (Ps. 62:5).

Mind: Dianoia *(Dee-AN-oy-ah)*

The mind includes understanding, intellect, and insight. It contains the capacity for critical thinking and reasoning, which is unique to human beings.

- "You will keep in perfect peace those whose minds are steadfast, because they trust in you" (Isa. 26:3).
- "Those who live according to the flesh have their minds set on what the flesh desires; but those who live in accordance with the Spirit have their minds set on what the Spirit desires" (Rom. 8:5).

Strength: Ischus *(Is-KHOOS)*

Your strength refers to your ability, power, and might. Two types of strength are needed in a believer's life — spiritual and physical. Unfortunately, many Christians emphasize the spiritual but fail to recognize the significance of the physical. For example, you can't serve the Lord with all your strength if you disregard his command to take care of your body. To maximize your spiritual strength, you need to build your physical health and rely on the Lord's power to help you.

- "Be strong in the Lord and in his mighty power" (Eph. 6:10).
- "Do you have the gift of speaking? Then speak as though God himself were speaking through you. Do you have the gift of helping others? Do it with all the strength and energy that God supplies. Then everything you do will bring glory to God through Jesus Christ" (1 Peter 4:11 NLT).

Your heart, soul, mind, and strength work together to produce spiritual growth, much like your physical muscles depend on each other to perform body movement. Next, let's look at specific exercises which target your spiritual core. All of these exercises will be discussed in greater detail in part 2 of this book.

Spiritual Core Exercises

You build strength and stability in your spiritual core by doing targeted exercises. These exercises are not difficult. But they do require your time, energy, and focus. The six spiritual core exercises are:

1. *Bible study.* There's a big difference between merely reading Scripture and doing an in-depth study of it. Both are beneficial, of course, but the latter will result in far greater knowledge and understanding of God's Word. Studying the Bible requires focus as you consider the context of the passage, examine Hebrew and Greek definitions, and find ways to apply God's Word to your life.

2. *Prayer.* Prayer is often defined as "talking to God." However, prayer is actually a dialogue. Even though you don't hear the Lord's audible voice, you can learn to "listen" to him as he speaks to you through his Word.

3. *Fasting.* Although fasting is taught repeatedly in Scripture, many Christians have yet to embrace this powerful spiritual discipline. However, we must not rely on our opinions on this matter but pay close attention to what the Bible says. When Jesus was preaching the Sermon on the Mount, he gave instructions on how to fast. His first three words, "*When* you fast" (Matt. 6:16, emphasis added), make it obvious that fasting should be practiced by every believer.

4. *Healthy living.* The Bible says our bodies are temples of the Holy Spirit. If you're a believer in the Lord Jesus Christ, his Spirit lives in you. When it comes to taking care of yourself, the command in 1 Corinthians 6:20 is pretty straightforward: "Honor God with your body" (NLT). Two ways you can obey this verse are through healthy eating and regular exercise. By making wise choices and submitting to the Lord in these areas, you demonstrate respect for the earthly house in which the Spirit of God dwells.

5. *Financial stewardship.* Everything we have belongs to the Lord. God has entrusted his resources to us, and our responsibility is to practice good stewardship with our money and possessions.

6. *Serving others.* Jesus taught the disciples an important lesson when he washed their feet. He said, "I have set you an example that you should do as I have done for you" (John 13:15). Jesus wasn't suggesting the disciples hold regular foot baths; he wanted them to serve others.

We can know the Bible forward and backward, attend church every Sunday, and even give half our income to the Lord, but if we're not reaching out to people in the name of Jesus, our sacrifices are worthless. However, when we obey the command in Galatians 5:13, which says, "Serve one another humbly in love," we reap a harvest of blessing.

The Benefits of Core Training

For the first few months of life, babies are sustained by milk alone. Milk provides the complete range of nutrients their bodies need. However, there comes a time when infants are ready for solid food, usually around six months of age.

A new believer is like a newborn child. Just as an infant must have milk to survive and thrive, a baby Christian must have *spiritual* food to develop. Peter, one of Jesus' disciples, encouraged believers to hunger for this type of nourishment. He said, "Like newborn babies, crave pure spiritual milk, so that by it you may grow up in your salvation" (1 Peter 2:2). The milk in this verse is the Word of God, specifically the basic truths of the gospel — humankind's sinful state, God's mercy and grace, repentance, and faith in Jesus Christ.[1] Once you've learned the foundational doctrines of Scripture, you'll have an increased appetite for deeper spiritual truth. The core exercises in this book will equip you to "move beyond the elementary teachings about Christ and be taken forward to maturity" (Heb. 6:1). The self-discipline you gain will lay the groundwork for the solid food God has for you. Following are five ways in which spiritual core training benefits your life.

1. *It builds balance.* Balance is "the ability to move or to remain in a position without losing control or falling."[2] A person who has a good sense of balance can stay upright and steady, even when walking on rough terrain. Spiritually, your balance improves as you grow in the Lord and in the knowledge of his Word. When trials and temptations come, your faith is not shaken. "The LORD makes firm the steps of the one who delights in him; though he may stumble, he will not fall, for the LORD upholds him with his hand" (Ps. 37:23 – 24). This core conditioning program recognizes that you are a multifaceted creation. The six spiritual core exercises don't operate independently but work together to create a solid "fitness" base for life.

2. *It develops proper posture.* Correct physical posture occurs when your body is in alignment with itself. Your spine is straight, shoulders back, chest out, and stomach pulled in. Proper *spiritual* posture is a deep, abiding trust in the Lord and a life that lines up with the truth of God's Word. Such a position of faith enables you to stand firm in Christ (2 Cor. 1:21), knowing that "the word of the LORD is right and true; he is faithful in all he does" (Ps. 33:4).

3. *It enables you to perform tasks with ease.* Everyday movements — bending, twisting, and lifting — are significantly easier when your body is healthy and strong. Navigating the challenges and pressures of life is also smoother when your spiritual core is finely tuned. Instead of being overwhelmed by daily struggles, you'll rely on God's power and rest in his perfect peace. Your mind will be set on things in heaven (eternal matters) rather than things on earth (temporary concerns). The Lord's favor will be upon you, and he will bless the work of your hands (Ps. 90:17).

4. *It protects you from pain and injury.* A weak physical core can cause all kinds of problems, the most common of which is lower back pain. When muscles that support the spine are underdeveloped because of inactivity or atrophy, the whole body's health is compromised. By strengthening the deep core muscles, you can prevent falls and injuries. Likewise, you can protect yourself spiritually through core conditioning. For example, knowing God's Word will guard you from dangerous situations. The writer of Psalm 119 recognized the value of memorizing Scripture. He said, "I have hidden your word in my heart that I might not sin against you" (v. 11) and "I will never forget your precepts, for by them you have preserved my life" (v. 93). Much of the suffering in our lives — emotional, financial, and moral — can be avoided if we simply read and heed the Bible.

5. *It increases energy.* One common excuse for a lack of regular physical activity is, "I'm too tired." Samantha Heller, a nutritional advisor for the Journey for Control diabetes program, says of exercise, "It literally creates energy in your body. Your body rises up to meet the challenge for more energy by becoming stronger."[3] As I used to tell my clients, "You have to expend energy to get energy." Exercise delivers blood, oxygen, and nutrients to your muscles and tissues, which helps your body to operate more efficiently. Your spiritual life is no different. Living by faith requires strength, endurance, and perseverance. No

one knew this truth better than the apostle Paul. In his letter to the Colossians, Paul wrote about his driving passion to help believers mature in Christ. He said, "That's why I work and struggle so hard, depending on Christ's mighty power that works within me" (1:29 NLT). Paul relied on God to supply the power he needed to build up the church. When you make time for spiritual exercise, you will reap the energy required to complete the work God has for *you*.

Before you begin this training program, tell yourself you're going to stay with it, no matter what. Even if you feel you're not making progress, keep going. Remember, every day you exercise your muscles, you get stronger. Each completed workout brings you one step closer to your goal of becoming more like Jesus.

CHAPTER 3

Discipline Is Not a Dirty Word!

For every disciplined effort
there is a multiple reward.
— Jim Rohn

It's early in the morning, still dark outside. You lie in bed, comfortably nestled under your covers. All is well until an annoying, high-pitched sound interrupts your sleep. You wince and let out a frustrated groan. Eyes still closed and brain only half awake, you wonder, *Is it a phone? A car alarm? A siren?*

After a minute or so, you realize that the awful noise isn't going away. In fact, it seems to be getting louder. Even with the pillow over your head, you can still hear it. When you realize the source of the disturbance, your right arm shoots out from under the covers to put an end to this nonsense. Sweet silence fills the room as your hand meets the small device on your nightstand. You roll over and resume your restful state. The exercise program you planned to start can wait. *I'll begin tomorrow,* you think. *Today I want to rest.*

Every believer has a built-in alarm clock, known as the Holy Spirit. Each morning, he beckons, "Spend time with me! Talk to me!" When God speaks, you have a choice to make. You'll either jump (or crawl) out of bed, or you'll tune out his voice and continue your spiritual slumber. What makes you put one foot in front of the other instead of staying where you are?

It's *discipline.*

Discipline is mental toughness. It's choosing to act on what you *should* do rather than what you *feel* like doing. It's saying, "No!" to your flesh and, "Yes!" to the Spirit. Discipline takes the desires of your heart and puts them

25

into motion, enabling you to reach your goals. You can have the most comprehensive exercise program in the world, but if you lack the discipline to implement it, your efforts will be sabotaged from the start.

Without self-discipline, your goals will always remain just that — *goals*. However, when you train your heart, soul, mind, and body to adhere to a set of rules which are beneficial to your life, you'll experience the joy of seeing your dreams become reality.

Training in Discipline

Training yourself to be more disciplined is like training your muscles. In order to get stronger physically, you have to challenge your muscles to work harder. If you consistently lift weights that are too light, you won't get stronger. A similar type of progressive overload is required to improve your level of discipline.

You develop more self-control by *practicing* self-control. To build discipline, you have to learn not to cater to your emotions, which is something that's clearly outside of your comfort zone. However, if you don't challenge yourself, you can't grow. If you don't grow, you stay the same. If you stay the same, you won't reach your goals.

When our daughters were toddlers, we gave them two rules about playing in the front yard. First, they couldn't be out there by themselves. Second, they weren't allowed to go past the sidewalk. We live on a very busy street, and cars frequently speed by our house in excess of forty-five miles per hour. At first, my husband and I had to watch the girls like hawks. They took turns at testing us to see if we would enforce the sidewalk rule. Whenever they got too close to the concrete, Justin or I used a firm voice to remind them of the boundary. Had the girls refused to submit to our authority, they would have been confined to the back yard. However, since they chose to exercise self-control, they were given freedom to play in the front. Eventually Isabelle and Jocelyn chose to follow the second rule on their own and didn't go near the sidewalk. Now that the girls are older (Isabelle is eleven years old, and Jocelyn is nine), they can be in the front yard without much supervision.

When it comes to training in discipline, you need to take three action steps. I'll use the example with our daughters to demonstrate how this process works.

1. *Identify your goals.* Our goal with Isabelle and Jocelyn was simple: we wanted them to play safely in the front yard. Think about the physical and spiritual goals *you* have. What would you like to achieve by the end of this six-week program? If you want to prosper — spiritually, physically, financially, or relationally — determine the specific action steps needed to get you where you want to be. Be sure to state long-term *and* short-term goals. Your short-term goals pave the way for your success. As you meet your short-term goals one by one, you gain confidence and motivation to keep working toward your larger goal. You'll have the opportunity to write down your goals in chapter 10, "Plan for Success."

2. *Define your boundaries.* When our daughters were young, they were incapable of understanding the danger of playing in the road. We had to teach them self-control by establishing and enforcing physical boundaries. Self-control, or the ability to keep one's emotions, desires, and/or actions in check, is a virtue that's highly valued in children *and* adults. "Better a patient person than a warrior, one with self-control than one who takes a city" (Prov. 16:32). Clearly defined boundaries keep you from making unwise decisions and falling into sinful behavior. Give careful thought to what "rules" need to be put in place for your success in this program. You might need to rearrange your schedule or cut out a few things. For example, if your plan is to exercise at 5:30 a.m., your boundary might be a 10:00 p.m. bedtime. Such parameters will help you remain focused and keep you moving forward toward your goals.

3. *Recognize rewards.* In the situation with our daughters and their play area, we reaped several rewards for their obedience. First, Isabelle and Jocelyn enjoyed the freedom and fun of being in the front yard with us. Second, they learned self-discipline. Third, Justin and I were able to trust the girls because we saw that they respected our rules. Finally, all four of us were able to make memories together in the front yard as a family. When it comes to setting goals, this third action step is often overlooked. Many people begin strong. They jump off the starting block with a sprint but then fizzle out after a few hundred meters. The problem is, they fail to keep their eyes on the finish line. They forget the power of the reward. That's what happens when you don't recognize the motivation behind your goals. Be sure to list specific rewards that will accompany your success. The rewards will keep you in the race when your energy level is low. If you

can't pinpoint at least one reward for reaching your goal, you should probably choose a different goal. If you're not excited about the prize you'll receive, you most likely won't push very hard to obtain it.

Perhaps you don't see yourself as a disciplined person. Don't worry! Self-control is not something you produce by your own strength. Just as our daughters trusted us to keep them from harm, you also must rely on your heavenly Father to teach you the way of discipline. God, through the Holy Spirit, will supply you with *his* wisdom and power. He will guide you into all truth (John 16:13) and supply you with the self-control you need (2 Tim. 1:7). You can be confident the Lord will lead you in the path of righteousness and give you success.

The Benefits of Discipline

During Bible times, a city was often surrounded by impenetrable walls to keep its inhabitants safe from their enemies. Without such barriers, the people were vulnerable to attack. The Bible says, "A person without self-control is like a city with broken-down walls" (Prov. 25:28 NLT). Self-discipline is like a wall around your life. It protects you from Satan's evil schemes and prevents you from succumbing to various temptations that will destroy you. The boundaries that accompany discipline keep you from venturing out into the Enemy's territory, where sin seeks to overtake you. Unfortunately, though, many people view discipline as torture and avoid it at all costs. They believe self-denial takes the fun out of life and limits their freedom. However, the opposite is true. When you choose the way of discipline, you're not held back in any way. Discipline isn't bondage. It's *freedom*. God wants to protect you from the heartache that lies outside his plan for your life. So don't fear discipline. *Embrace it.* Following are a few ways in which discipline is beneficial to your life.

1. *It helps you establish order.* Discipline keeps your schedule under control so you can be more effective for the kingdom. "God is not a God of disorder but of peace" (1 Cor. 14:33). The Lord has plans for your life, plans that are meant to prosper you (Jer. 29:11). However, if your days are filled with chaos, you won't be prepared to carry out God's purposes.

2. *It allows you to hear from God.* Discipline adds structure to your life, freeing you to respond to the Lord when he speaks and prompts

you to act. By regularly spending time in God's Word, you'll learn more about him and how he works. Your mind and heart will be sensitive to the Lord's voice, and you'll recognize his hand in your circumstances.

3. *It keeps you accountable.* Discipline guards you from patterns of laziness and procrastination. For example, if my aim is to exercise three to four times a week, I'm much more likely to stick to it if I have a plan. Commitment to a course of action is always easier when you have a system in place.

4. *It positions you for success.* Success doesn't just happen. It's preceded by months and sometimes years of hard work. Motivational speaker and author Brian Tracy says, "Most people think success comes from good luck or enormous talent, but many successful people achieve their accomplishments in a simpler way: through self-discipline."[1] Success is the result of making plans and sticking to them. Therefore, learning self-control is truly the key to reaching your goals.

5. *It teaches you perseverance.* I'm not going to lie: discipline isn't easy. It can be downright grueling when your inner desires are fighting hard for control. But when your self-discipline partners with the power of the Holy Spirit to override your emotions, it's a beautiful thing. You keep going toward your goal, even though in the moment you want to do the opposite.

6. *It builds confidence.* If your goal is to cut out added sugar for six weeks, you'll gain momentum every time you resist the temptation to have "just a little." Your confidence moves up another rung on the ladder to your success. Your attitude becomes, "I can do everything through Christ, who gives me strength" (Phil. 4:13 NLT) instead of "I'll never make it."

7. *It produces more discipline.* When you practice self-control in one part of your life, the positive changes carry over into other areas as well. For example, when you begin an exercise program, you'll be more motivated to make healthier food choices. As you study the Bible and pray for others, you'll be more sensitive to the Spirit's leading in other disciplines, such as fasting and serving.

8. *It leads to satisfaction in the Lord.* When you submit to God in every area of your life, you'll discover peace and joy in your obedience. You won't be tempted to look to other things to fulfill you — work, relationships, money, food, or life-controlling substances. Your

greatest desire will be to know God and follow in his ways. You'll be fully satisfied as with the richest of foods, and your mouth will be filled with continual praise (Ps. 63:5).

The hardest part of any training program is getting started. It takes courage to force yourself into a different way of living. However, once you get going and settle into a new rhythm, the struggle won't seem as intense.

Anytime you disrupt your status quo to make positive changes, you're in for a battle. Your mind and body are comfortable with the old patterns and won't adapt without a fight. Before you begin working toward a goal, determine to be 100 percent committed to the task from the outset. A half-hearted attempt won't be enough to take you to success. If you feel overwhelmed, remember Joshua's words to the Israelites when they were facing a fearful situation: "Be strong and courageous. Do not be afraid; do not be discouraged, for the LORD your God will be with you wherever you go" (Josh. 1:9). God's presence will give you peace and power.

Discipline takes *time.* When teaching children the importance of dental hygiene, you don't show them once how to brush their teeth and expect them to remember to do it every day from then on. You have to remind them frequently until they practice this good habit on their own. Give yourself grace as you adjust to new patterns of living. Some days you might walk right past your boundaries. Your heart may gravitate toward rebellion rather than obedience. Remember, God understands your struggle. He doesn't condemn you when you make mistakes. "The LORD is gracious and compassionate, slow to anger and rich in love" (Ps. 145:8).

Your goal in self-discipline is not perfection but *direction.* So don't get frustrated if you miss a few days of exercise or don't pray as often as you'd like. Continue to press on and press in with the Lord. Failure in a race doesn't occur when you trip and fall; it happens when you give up and stop running.

How Discipline Leads to Delight

The Olympics have fascinated me since I was a little girl. I used to think the life of an Olympic athlete was exciting and glamorous. I was oblivious to the years of rigorous training required to compete at such an elite level — intense workouts (sometimes twice a day), structured eating plans, time away from family and friends, frequent travel, and nagging physical injuries. Now that I'm older, I know better. The road to the games is paved with difficulty. Preparing for the world's greatest sporting event takes years of sacrifice. Only the most committed, determined athletes will have the chance to compete for a gold medal.

In 2002, I went to the Winter Olympics in Salt Lake City, Utah. My husband and I were on a mission trip, and we were able to attend two medal ceremonies. As I watched several American athletes receive their medals, I could only imagine the joy and satisfaction they felt in reaching the pinnacle of their sport.

What does it take for an Olympic athlete to be successful?

Discipline.

If you're a believer, you're also an athlete in strict training. You must be committed to intense spiritual exercise. Your reward doesn't even *compare* with an Olympic gold medal. Your prize — the reason why you keep working, keep pushing, and keep serving — is the Lord Jesus Christ. He's the one you want to please. You long to see his smiling face when he awards you with a crown of righteousness (2 Tim. 4:8) for your devotion to him.

Your journey toward greater discipline begins with *desire*. If you have the desire to change — and you do, or you wouldn't be reading this book — you're well on your way to achieving your goals. However, the anticipation you feel right now may not always be there. In a few weeks, you may experience a different kind of desire — the desire to quit! If you find yourself struggling, simply ask God to renew a right spirit in you and restore your motivation. He is faithful, and he will help you.

Next, *decide* you're going to make the necessary changes to your schedule in order to put your plans into motion. Make the commitment to *devote* yourself to the spiritual exercises in this book. As you *depend* on the Lord, you'll find *delight* in growing closer to him and following his Word. This is what the process looks like:

Desire → Decide → Devote → Depend → Delight

One of my favorite promises in the Bible is, "Take delight in the LORD, and he will give you the desires of your heart" (Ps. 37:4). If you truly want to grow in this area of discipline, you will not come away empty. God promises, "Those who hope in me will not be disappointed" (Isa. 49:23). Trust the Lord to provide the motivation, strength, and perseverance required for increased physical and spiritual self-control. This book can help you develop positive habits that will benefit every aspect of your life. As we conclude this chapter on discipline, I'd like to share *my* goals for you as you complete this six-week program. I want you to

- find joy in studying God's Word on a regular basis,
- pray for yourself and others with persistence and power,
- commit to periodic fasting throughout the year,
- make healthy choices with your body that honor God,
- take steps to establish good financial stewardship,
- look for opportunities to serve others.

I spent so much time on this topic of discipline because it's impossible for a believer to reach maturity in Christ without self-control. In her book *Discipline: The Glad Surrender*, Elisabeth Elliot says, "*Discipline* is the disciple's career. It defines the very shape of the disciple's life."[2] In other words, you cannot be a disciple without discipline.

Now that you've learned how discipline lays the foundation for your conditioning program, you may be wondering, *Where do I begin?* I'm glad you asked! In part 2, we'll take an in-depth look at each of the exercises for your spiritual core.

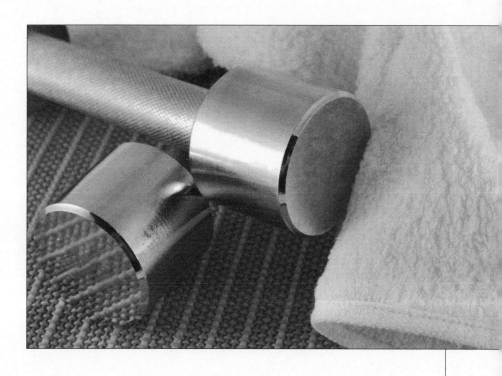

PART 2

the **EXERCISES**

CHAPTER 4

Bible Study

These instructions are not empty words—
they are your life!
—Deuteronomy 32:47 NLT

When I was younger, I saw the Bible as a book of rules, a long list of dos and don'ts. Although I was saved at a young age, my view on God's love was severely skewed. I thought I was a "good" Christian if I did what God said, and "bad" when I failed.

During my first year in college, I was introduced to the concept of having a quiet time, a daily "appointment" with the Lord. I started reading Scripture, praying, and journaling regularly. As I did, the Bible became alive to me! No longer did I see it merely as a set of instructions; I began to view God's Word as a powerful, life-changing letter of his love for me.

Now, more than twenty years later, I still start my day with the Lord. When I sit down to study the Bible and pray each morning, I know God is waiting. Words cannot express how special that time is. It truly is the best part of my day.

Do you want to know God in a deeper way and hear his voice more clearly? If so, make the commitment to become a student of his Word. Read the Bible every day, and let the Lord speak to your heart. Your joy will overflow as you think about God's goodness. You'll say along with the psalmist, "Oh, how I love your law! I meditate on it all day long" (Ps. 119:97).

Why Should I Read the Bible?

The Bible is a sacred writing, a gift given to us by our Creator so we can know him in a personal way. In his bestselling book *Experiencing God:*

Knowing and Doing the Will of God, Henry Blackaby says, "God speaks through a variety of means. In the present God primarily speaks by the Holy Spirit through the Bible, prayer, circumstances, and the church."[1] Although we can hear from God in a number of ways, we most clearly discern his voice through reading his Word. Tragically, though, this priceless treasure is often overlooked and undervalued. Instead of being opened with enthusiasm, the Bible often sits untouched on a shelf, collecting dust. Its pages remain in pristine condition, rather than worn and torn from frequent use.

If the Bible is supposed to be our handbook for holy living, why do so many believers neglect it? Following are five of the most common reasons people give for not reading God's Word on a regular basis.

- *Excuse 1: "I don't have time."* Truth: We're all given twenty-four hours in each day. You *do* have time.

- *Excuse 2: "It's boring."* Truth: The Bible is anything but boring! It contains stories of miraculous healings, supernatural events, and people being raised from the dead. Pretty exciting stuff, if you ask me!

- *Excuse 3: "I can't understand it."* Truth: The Bible can be intimidating at times. It speaks of events that are unexplainable, in language that isn't always easy to decipher. However, when you approach the study of God's Word with a true desire to learn, the Lord will give you insight and understanding.

- *Excuse 4: "It's not relevant to my life."* Truth: Even though the Bible was written thousands of years ago, it still speaks to our circumstances today. Its truth is unchanging and eternal.

- *Excuse 5: "I don't get anything out of it."* Truth: To get something out of the Bible, you have to read it with an open mind and heart. You have to be willing to listen to what God is saying, then learn to apply his truth to the specific situations in your life.

If your relationship with the Lord seems stagnant, it's probably because you aren't increasing your knowledge of the Bible. You can't grow closer to the Lord apart from his Word. Wayne Cordeiro, author of *The Divine Mentor*, makes this observation: "Neglecting devotions will cause you more problems, more quickly, than just about anything you can name."[2] He also says, "Spending unrushed time alone with God in His Word releases a fountain of refreshment from the very core of your being."[3]

It's time to stop making excuses and start studying the Bible. The pages of Scripture have the power to transform your life. This is what God's Word can do:

- *Save you.* "Get rid of all the filth and evil in your lives, and humbly accept the word God has planted in your hearts, for it has the power to save your souls" (James 1:21 NLT).

- *Help you grow in wisdom.* "Fear of the LORD is the foundation of true wisdom. All who obey his commandments will grow in wisdom. Praise him forever!" (Ps. 111:10 NLT).

- *Teach you how to live.* "All Scripture is God-breathed and is useful for teaching, rebuking, correcting and training in righteousness, so that the servant of God may be thoroughly equipped for every good work" (2 Tim. 3:16 – 17).

- *Protect you from being deceived.* "See to it that no one takes you captive through hollow and deceptive philosophy, which depends on human tradition and the elemental spiritual forces of this world rather than on Christ" (Col. 2:8).

- *Develop your faith.* "Faith comes from hearing the message, and the message is heard through the word about Christ" (Rom. 10:17).

- *Keep you from sin.* "I have hidden your word in my heart that I might not sin against you" (Ps. 119:11).

- *Fill you with hope.* "Everything that was written in the past was written to teach us, so that through the endurance taught in the Scriptures and the encouragement they provide we might have hope" (Rom. 15:4).

- *Bring you joy.* "How I delight in your commands! How I love them!" (Ps. 119:47 NLT).

- *Give you peace.* "Great peace have those who love your law, and nothing can make them stumble" (Ps. 119:165).

- *Prosper your life.* "Keep this Book of the Law always on your lips; meditate on it day and night, so that you may be careful to do everything written in it. Then you will be prosperous and successful" (Josh. 1:8).

Moses was a man who revered the Word of God. As leader of the Israelites, Moses devoted his life to instructing people in the Lord's ways. When Moses was an old man and about to die, he gathered the Israelites together for his farewell address. He said, "Take to heart all the words of warning

I have given you today. Pass them on as a command to your children so they will obey every word of these instructions. These instructions are not empty words — they are your life! By obeying them you will enjoy a long life in the land you will occupy when you cross the Jordan River" (Deut. 32:46 – 47 NLT).

A person who is near death usually shifts his or her focus to what really matters. That's exactly what Moses is doing here. He's saying, "If you don't remember anything I've taught you all these years, remember this." He wants the Israelites to understand that nothing is more important than knowing God's Word and living according to his commands. He also assures the people their obedience will result in God's blessing. What was true then is still true today. Give yourself to diligent study of the Bible, and you'll experience the victorious life God has for you and know his favor in a special way.

To love God is to love his Word. You can't do one without the other.

How to Study the Bible: Practical Tools

We've already looked at why we should study the Bible, but how do we move beyond simply reading Scripture to *studying* it? In this next section, I'll give you information that will teach you how to dig deeper into God's Word.

What Do I Study?

Sometimes people have the desire to read the Bible but just don't know where to begin. Following are a few suggestions to give you direction.

- *Start with the six-week Bible study on pages 134 – 87,* which will help you jump-start the good habit of daily Bible reading. During those six weeks, be sure to give some thought to how you'll continue studying the Bible once that time is finished.

- *Read the whole Bible through in a year.* Studies show it takes an individual of average reading ability about ninety hours to read the entire Bible. That's one hour a day for three months, half an hour a day for six months, or fifteen minutes a day for twelve months. When you break it down like that, going through the Bible doesn't seem like an impossible task. You can buy a one-year Bible or find a reading plan online. I use *ewordtoday.com*, which allows you to choose your preferred version of the Bible (NIV, NLT, ESV, and so on) and how you want the passages listed (chronologically, beginning to end, and so on). Another benefit of an online plan is a calendar that lists the verses to read for every day of the year.

- *Use a specialized Bible.* Your local Christian bookstore has Bibles that target every conceivable interest or need. If you want hard-core study aids, look for a study Bible. If you want help in applying the Bible to your life, look for the *Life Application Study Bible.* If you're a mother, father, student, or child, there are a number of devotional Bibles designed to appeal to you. Spend some time browsing the Bibles to find one that meets your needs.

- *Try a daily devotional.* Devotional books are a good option, especially if you're just getting started. They're usually fairly concise and don't require a huge time commitment.

- *Join a Bible study group or purchase a Bible study workbook.* Your church likely offers weekly Bible studies. In addition, there are nationally known programs, such as Bible Study Fellowship, which are open to the wider community. Bible study groups offer accountability and often require a certain amount of homework (such as daily Bible reading!). If you don't have time to join a group study, you can find numerous Bible study workbooks at your local Christian bookstore. Browse the Bible study area and choose a topic that will hold your interest.

Where Do I Study?

Where you study is almost as important as what you study. Find a place that's quiet and free from distraction. I like to sit at my kitchen table early in the morning before anyone else wakes up. Wherever you choose, make sure it's somewhere you can relax in God's presence and focus your attention on him.

When Do I Study?

Everyone has a different schedule when it comes to Bible study. Some people do their devotions in the morning. Others have their quiet time at night. The most important thing is that you *do it.* When you look at Scripture, though, you find many verses that speak of seeking God during the first part of the day. King David was one who sought God early. He writes, "Listen to my voice in the morning, LORD. Each morning I bring my requests to you and wait expectantly" (Ps. 5:3 NLT). In another psalm, David says, "Let the morning bring me word of your unfailing love, for I have put my trust in you. Show me the way I should go, for to you I entrust my life" (Ps. 143:8). Jesus also modeled this type of self-discipline. On at least one occasion while preaching throughout Galilee, he got alone with the Father even before sunrise: "Very early in the morning, while it was still dark, Jesus got up, left the house and went off to a solitary place, where he prayed" (Mark 1:35).

If you have trouble getting motivated in the morning, try going to bed earlier. Ask God to help you. If you truly desire to start your day with the Lord, you can be sure he will answer your prayer. Believe me, you won't regret sacrificing a few minutes of shut-eye for precious moments with your Savior.

How Do I Study?

When you sit down with God's Word, your first order of business should be to pray. This may seem obvious, but it needs to be mentioned. I know from experience how easy it is to rush into reading without taking a few moments to prepare.

Before I begin, I often pray, "Open my eyes that I may see wonderful things in your law" (Ps. 119:18). I come expectantly, knowing that God has something specific to show me. I listen to what he is saying and look for ways he wants me to obey. For example, one January I was feeling anxious about several speaking engagements scheduled for the following month. On January 31, part of my daily Bible reading was from Exodus 4, where God told Moses to appear before Pharaoh. When Moses doubted his competence for the job, God said, "Now go! I will be with you as you speak, and I will instruct you in what to say" (Ex. 4:12 NLT). I knew it was no coincidence I was reading this passage on that particular day. I sensed God telling me, "Kristen, I will be with you. I have provided these opportunities, and I will show you what to say." God gave me encouragement from his Word when I needed it.

The system I use for Bible study is simple: I read God's Word, record what he shows me, and then respond in obedience. The three Rs make it easy to remember.

1. *Read*
    • Read the passage slowly.

2. *Record*
- Underline or highlight any words, phrases, or verses that jump out at you.
- Write down insights, such as seeing something new in a familiar story.

3. *Respond*
- Thank God for speaking to you.
- Tell God your desire to align your life with his Word.
- List an action step you can take.

Part of responding to the Lord should include journaling. Writing down insights from God's Word keeps his truth in the forefront of your mind. If you don't already have a journal, I highly recommend getting one to use during this program.

The apostle James says, "If you look carefully into the perfect law that sets you free, and if you do what it says and don't forget what you heard, then God will bless you for doing it" (James 1:25 NLT). Did you catch that order? First *look*, then *do*, then *remember* to do it again! My prayer for you is this: As you *look* into God's holy Word, may he fill you with the knowledge of his will and with all wisdom and understanding. May you *do* as he asks, living a life worthy of the Lord and pleasing him in every way. May you *remember* to do what is right so that you bear fruit in every good work and are strengthened by the power of the Holy Spirit. I pray your life overflows with blessings because of your faithfulness to God and his Word.

CHAPTER 5

Prayer

Time spent in prayer is never wasted.
— François Fénelon

One of my favorite authors is Edward McKendree (E. M.) Bounds. Each morning Bounds got up at 4:00 a.m. to pray for three hours. No doubt there were times when he would have preferred staying under his covers instead of rising in the dark. However, Bounds faithfully sought God through persistent prayer. The introduction to the book *E. M. Bounds on Prayer* says this about Bounds: "Prayer was as natural to him as breathing the air. He made prayer first and foremost in his life because he knew it as the strongest link between man and God."[1] Bounds understood prayer to be the lifeline to his heavenly Father.

To be effective in prayer, you must have an understanding of what it involves. In this chapter, you will learn (1) the definition of prayer, (2) how God speaks, (3) the four parts of prayer, (4) principles of prayer, (5) postures in prayer, and (6) how to pray with power.

What Is Prayer?

If you've been born again, think back to the day you were saved. What did you do to receive God's gift of eternal life? You *prayed.* Prayer began your relationship with the Lord, and it continues to be one of the primary ways God converses with you.

Wikipedia defines prayer as "an invocation or act that seeks to activate a rapport with a deity, an object of worship, or a spiritual entity through deliberate communication." Wow. That definition makes prayer sound as exciting as watching grass grow! Prayer is not meant to be an empty ritual.

On the contrary, it's an awesome opportunity to dialogue with Almighty God! Just think about it for a moment: through prayer, you can participate in a divine exchange with the Creator of all living things. The very thought is mind-boggling. Yet God *does* choose to speak with us on a personal basis, and he promises to respond when we cry out to him.

Prayer is communion with God. Another word for communion is *fellowship*, which comes from the Greek word *koinonia.* Fellowship implies a sharing of common interests, motivations, and desires and is usually accompanied by emotional transparency. Prayer is intimate conversation between you and the Lord, characterized by moments of talking and listening.

When You Talk, God Listens

Have you ever wondered whether God really hears from heaven? Most people have asked this question at one time or another. The Bible answers with a resounding, "Yes!" "The Lord hears his people when they call to him for help" (Ps. 34:17 NLT).

God's ears are inclined in your direction when you talk to him. In fact, the Lord doesn't just hear your prayers; he knows exactly what you need before you ask him (Matt. 6:8). However, even though God is fully aware of your situation, he wants you to learn to depend on him and not on your own strength. By bringing your needs to God in prayer, you demonstrate faith in his ability to provide.

When You Listen, God Speaks

Frank Laubach, an evangelical Christian missionary, said, "The trouble with nearly everybody who prays is that he says 'Amen' and runs away before God has a chance to reply. Listening to God is far more important than giving Him our ideas."

If you want to hear God's voice, you have to learn to *wait*.

Merriam-Webster Dictionary defines *wait* as "to stay in a place of expectation." I believe prayer involves two types of waiting. The first is being still before the Lord and letting him speak to your heart. We see a beautiful portrayal of this when Mary sat at the feet of Jesus to hear him teach (Luke 10:39). The second type of waiting involves the gap in time between presenting your request to God and seeing evidence of his answer. During this longer season, you continue to place your hope in the Lord and hold fast to his promises: "Be still in the presence of the LORD, and wait patiently for him to act" (Ps. 37:7 NLT).

Waiting on the Lord in prayer takes patience and perseverance. One of the reasons people don't linger in prayer is because they get frustrated. They'd like to hear from God but don't know how to recognize his voice.

How God Speaks

Nearly every believer has struggled with an inability to hear God. It's not that the Lord *can't* communicate audibly, as he did in the Old Testament. It's just that now he chooses a different way to talk to us. He speaks through the Holy Spirit.

After Jesus rose from the dead, he appeared to the disciples to give them an important assignment. He told them to continue his mission on earth after he returned to the Father in heaven. Jesus breathed on the disciples and said to them, "Receive the Holy Spirit" (John 20:22). This act was symbolic of the impartation of spiritual life, much like the giving of physical life at the creation: "The LORD God formed a man from the dust of the ground and breathed into his nostrils the breath of life, and the man became a living being" (Gen. 2:7). According to Clarke's Commentary on the Bible, Jesus wanted the disciples to understand that "they were to be made new men, in order to be properly qualified for the work to which he had called them."[2] Later, during Pentecost, the disciples experienced the fulfillment of God's promise to send them a Helper, whom Jesus promised would empower them for ministry (Acts 2:1 – 4; John 16:7).

Jesus said anyone who follows him will also be filled with the Holy Spirit. If you have been born again, God's Spirit lives in you (John 14:16 – 17; Acts 2:38; Eph. 1:13), which means you have the ability to hear his voice.

One way God communicates through prayer is by bringing specific Bible verses to your mind. For example, one day a friend asked me to intercede for her spiritual and physical protection. As I was praying, I recalled this psalm: "The LORD is my rock, my fortress and my deliverer; my God is my rock, in whom I take refuge, my shield and the horn of my salvation, my stronghold" (18:2). I was able to pray God's Word over her, which was far more effective than my feeble words would have been. This is one reason why Scripture memorization is crucial in prayer. The Holy Spirit cannot remind you of truth that hasn't already been hidden in your heart

(Ps. 119:11). E. M. Bounds said, "He who wants to learn to pray well, must first study God's Word and store it in his memory and thought."[3]

The Lord also speaks when you read Scripture aloud (more on this topic later in the chapter). As you proclaim God's promises with *your* voice, you also hear *his* voice. Declaring truth builds your faith and gives you strength.

Finally, God often guides you in prayer through your thoughts. I experience this situation all the time with my writing. I can definitely tell when I'm working in my own strength versus when God is helping me. If I trust in the Lord and lean on his wisdom, words and illustrations flow from my fingertips. If I try to force it, the result is disastrous.

One morning while working on this chapter, I sat at my computer, feeling overwhelmed. I'd just learned from my publisher that I had three months to finish the book. I didn't see how it could be done. I was *trying* to trust God but failing miserably in the process. Feeling discouraged, I opened up the Bible to get my mind centered on truth. My Scripture reading for the day was 1 Chronicles 28, where King David summoned all his officials to assemble at Jerusalem for a special announcement. David said, "Listen to me, my fellow Israelites, my people. I had it in my heart to build a house as a place of rest for the ark of the covenant of the LORD, for the footstool of our God, and I made plans to build it. But God said to me, 'You are not to build a house for my Name, because you are a warrior and have shed blood.… Solomon your son is the one who will build my house and my courts, for I have chosen him to be my son, and I will be his father'" (vv. 2 – 3, 6).

David then presented Solomon with detailed instructions on the project. "Every part of this plan," he said, "was given to me in writing from the hand of the LORD" (v. 19 NLT). David told his son, "Be strong and courageous, and do the work. Don't be afraid or discouraged, for the LORD God, my God, is with you. He will not fail you or forsake you. He will see to it that all the work related to the Temple of the LORD is finished correctly" (v. 20 NLT).

As soon as I read that last verse, I heard the Lord's voice speak gently to my heart. He said, "Kristen, be strong and courageous. I am with you. Do the work, and I'll take care of the rest. I have chosen you to write this book, just as I chose David to be king and Solomon to build the temple. You can trust me to provide everything you need. I will see to it that the book is written correctly." God spoke directly to my fears. I was able to hear him because I sought comfort and direction in his Word.

If you desire a deeper prayer life, my friend, you can have it. However, in order to enjoy sweet communion with the Lord, you have to *trust* him. "All he does is just and good, and all his commandments are trustworthy" (Ps. 111:7 NLT). When you place your confidence in the Lord, prayer becomes a natural outpouring of your devotion to him.

Now that we've seen how important prayer is in the life of a believer, let's dive into the Word to see what God says about this powerful spiritual discipline.

The Parts of Prayer

Effective prayer contains four essential elements: adoration, confession, thanksgiving, and supplication. An easy way to remember them is the acronym ACTS. The ACTS model is merely a tool to guide your prayer time, not a legalistic formula to follow. This method keeps your prayers balanced, so you don't focus only on your needs. Following is a description of each type of prayer.

Adoration

Adoration, or praise, is one of the most important components of prayer, but it's also probably the most neglected. Many people think they're praising God when they're actually giving thanks to him. Although both parts are necessary in prayer, they're not the same. Praise is acknowledging God for *who he is*, while thanksgiving is offering words of gratitude for *what he has done*. When you praise God, you tell him how awesome he is!

Jesus modeled adoration in the Sermon on the Mount. He instructed the disciples, "This, then, is how you should pray: 'Our Father in heaven, hallowed be your name'" (Matt. 6:9). Jesus began the Lord's Prayer by declaring God's name as holy. We should follow his example and begin our prayers with praise. One idea is to open your prayer with a verse, such as Psalm 145:8. Your prayer could be, "God, you are 'merciful and compassionate, slow to get angry and filled with unfailing love'" (NLT).

One creative way to express your adoration for the Lord is to declare his attributes by going through each letter of the alphabet. I call it the ABC exercise. Simply say, "God, you're ..."

A — amazing, the Alpha and Omega

B — beautiful, the Bread of Life
C — compassionate, the God of all comfort, caring
D — my deliverer
E — eternal, excellent in all your ways
F — faithful, Father, friend, forgiving
(And so on, all the way to Z)

In his book *With Christ in the School of Prayer*, Andrew Murray says, "It is in the adoring worship of God — the waiting on and for Him, the deep silence of soul that yields itself for God to reveal Himself — that the capacity for knowing and trusting God will be developed."[4] Too often we rush past this important aspect of prayer. We go right into our long list of personal requests and forget to contemplate God's goodness. To counteract this tendency, we should take time to focus on the Lord and praise him before praying about our needs or interceding for others.

Confession

After adoration, you should move to confession. Usually this transition is a natural progression. Once you have focused on God's goodness, you are very much aware of how you fall short of his glory.

Confession is acknowledging your specific sins to the Lord. You agree that your behavior has violated God's holy standard. This step in prayer is essential because of what the Bible says: "If I had not confessed the sin in my heart, the Lord would not have listened" (Ps. 66:18 NLT); "If anyone turns a deaf ear to my instruction, even their prayers are detestable" (Prov. 28:9). These verses indicate that sin in our lives can block our prayers. But when we admit our transgressions to the Lord, we can find comfort in this truth: "If we confess our sins, he is faithful and just and will forgive us our sins and purify us from all unrighteousness" (1 John 1:9).

During your confession time, ask the Lord to reveal where you have been wrong. Not only will he help you see your sin, but also he will cleanse your heart and renew a right attitude within you (Ps. 51:10). God says, "If my people, who are called by my name, will humble themselves and pray and seek my face and turn from their wicked ways, then I will hear from heaven, and I will forgive their sin and will heal their land" (2 Chron. 7:14). Confession brings restoration and healing. Praise the Lord!

Thanksgiving

Thanksgiving is offering words of gratitude to God for his wonderful deeds. The Bible repeatedly admonishes us to give thanks: "Give thanks to the Lord and proclaim his greatness. Let the whole world know what he has done" (1 Chron. 16:8 NLT).

When I was in college at Southwest Baptist University, one of my favorite professors was Dr. Bernard Holmes. He loved to praise the Lord and always opened his class with a song.

Shortly before I graduated, Dr. Holmes became critically ill. He was hospitalized several times, which kept him from teaching for months. When he finally returned to SBU, he spoke in our chapel service. I'll never forget it. Dr. Holmes's body seemed to have aged twenty years, and one of his hands was paralyzed. Tears poured down my face as I listened to him speak. What made me cry, though, was not pity. It was seeing that, despite the afflictions Dr. Holmes had endured, his zeal for the Lord was as strong as ever.

Not long after that time, Dr. Holmes retired from teaching, but he didn't retire from ministry. He and his wife, Joyce, traveled around the world to far-off places, such as India, Africa, and Russia, to teach Christians about prayer and discipleship. Dr. Holmes continued to serve the Lord with the energy of a thirty-year-old man until his death in 2008.

While writing this book, I came across an old cassette tape of one of his sermons. Dr. Holmes shared with his audience the importance of ongoing thanksgiving in our lives. He asked, "When was the last time you thanked God for your kidneys?" When the audience laughed, he replied, "I'm serious! How would you be without them? Have you ever thanked him for your eyes and your legs and your feet? Have you thanked him for your parents and your country?"

Dr. Holmes said, "Whatever your circumstances are, give God thanks for them. It is his will for you today. You may have problems, but God uses problems to bring you to full maturity in faith. Give him thanks."

I believe one reason why the command "Give thanks" appears so often in Scripture is because God knows our tendency to complain. When things don't go the way we want, we get upset. We moan and grumble, just like the Israelites did after God delivered them from bondage in Egypt (Ex. 16).

God has called us to be thankful. As author John MacArthur says, "A thankful heart is one of the primary identifying characteristics of a believer. It stands in stark contrast to pride, selfishness, and worry. And it helps fortify the believer's trust in the Lord and reliance on His provision, even in the toughest times. No matter how choppy the seas become, a believer's heart is buoyed by constant praise and gratefulness to the Lord."[5] When your heart is full of gratitude for God's abundant blessings, your joy will be evident to others and have a positive impact on their lives.

Supplication

Supplication can be subdivided into petition and intercession. Petition involves a personal request, while intercession asks God to work in the life of someone else. Both types of prayers are found in the Bible. David prayed a prayer of petition in Psalm 5:8: "Lead me, LORD, in your righteousness because of my enemies — make your way straight before me." Isaac interceded for his wife, Rebekah, who was childless. After Isaac prayed for her, she became pregnant (Gen. 25:21). Whenever you face a tough situation, what do you do? Call or text a friend? Get worried and stressed? Notice this counsel: "Do not be anxious about anything, but in every situation, by prayer and petition, with thanksgiving, present your requests to God" (Phil. 4:6). The Lord *wants* you to bring your concerns to him. He cares about every detail of your life. However, God also wants you to pray for others.

Austin Phelps, a nineteenth-century minister and educator, said, "We are never more like Christ than in prayers of intercession."[6] Jesus prayed continually for people, and if we want to imitate him, we must follow in his footsteps. The apostle Paul, in his letter to young Timothy, wrote, "I urge you, first of all, to pray for all people. Ask God to help them; intercede on their behalf, and give thanks for them" (1 Tim. 2:1 NLT). Paul *urged* Timothy to lift up others in prayer, which shows just how vital intercession is.

Not every prayer you utter will contain all four components. However, you should try to include them as often as possible to keep your prayers God-centered rather than self-centered.

Principles of Prayer

Reading Scriptures on prayer helps us understand what God expects from us in this spiritual discipline. Following are four basic principles we need to remember.

1. Prayer Is Commanded by God

"Pray without ceasing" (1 Thess. 5:17 ESV). The New Living Translation puts it this way: "Never stop praying." Scripture is clear: for believers, prayer is not optional.

2. Prayerlessness Is a Sin

If God commands you to pray — and he does — but you refuse to obey him, you're guilty of sin. That sounds harsh, but it's true.

In 1 Samuel 12, the prophet Samuel gives his farewell address to the Israelites after serving as their judge for several years. Even though God has done many wonderful things through Samuel's leadership, the people demand to be ruled by a king. Such a request could have offended Samuel and made him angry. Instead of reacting in bitterness, Samuel shows humility and love. He promises to continue teaching and guiding the Israelites, despite their decision. Because he's concerned about how this change will affect their future, Samuel makes the following statement: "Far be it from me that I should sin against the LORD by failing to pray for you" (1 Sam. 12:23).

Even though Samuel was certain the people were making a mistake, he knew it would be a sin to stop interceding for them. We must take this truth to heart and make the same commitment to pray for others.

3. Prayer Is Something You Learn

Early in our marriage, my husband, Justin, and I attended Second Baptist Church in Springfield, Missouri. We have many good memories from our years at Second, including our wedding ceremony! I recall one event in particular which had a significant impact on my view of prayer.

Our pastor, Dr. John Marshall, stood at the front of the church. Next to him was an elderly man, whom our pastor introduced as Ed. Dr. Marshall explained to the congregation that Ed, who was his longtime friend, would be assisting him with pastoral duties. He then asked Ed to pray. When Ed opened his mouth and began to talk to God, my jaw dropped. I felt as if I'd been ushered into the throne room of heaven. His voice wasn't loud, but he spoke with authority, boldness, and deep reverence. It was obvious the Lord was most precious to Ed. I'd never heard anyone pray with such faith. As I listened, I thought, *I want to learn to pray like that.*

I believe that's how the disciples felt in Luke 11. After hearing Jesus cry out to the Father, one disciple said, "Lord, teach us to pray" (v. 1). This story proves prayer can be developed through observation and practice. No matter what kind of prayer life you have (or don't have), you can learn. You can grow. You can experience the fullness of joy that comes from being in God's presence. William Law, a British theological writer, said, "He who has learned to pray has learned the greatest secret of a holy and happy life."[7] Prayer skills can be developed and improved in three ways: (1) by reading prayers in the Bible, (2) by listening to other people pray, and (3) by praying.

Reading Prayers in the Bible

The writers of Scripture teach us how to pray. I love Hannah's prayer when she enthusiastically praises God for giving her a son (1 Sam. 2:1 – 10). After Jeremiah buys a field, he questions the wisdom of his purchase, but instead of allowing anxiety to set in, Jeremiah prays, focusing on God's greatness. As he meditates on the Lord's attributes, his fears are put to rest (Jer. 32:17 – 25). Finally, we see David's brokenness over his adulterous affair with Bathsheba (Ps. 51). Our hearts go out to David as he pleads for God's mercy and restoration. His humility shows us how we should respond when *we're* in need of forgiveness.

Listening to Others Pray

God has used several people in my life to teach me about prayer. I think of my good friend Linda, who is now with the Lord. When she prayed, nearly every sentence out of her mouth was a Bible verse. Linda's example continues to challenge me to intercede using God's Word and not just my own words.

My children teach me about prayer. They bring every request, big or small, to God. No matter what the need is, their first response is to pray. I often see giant-size faith in my little girls, and it inspires me.

My in-laws have taught me boldness and urgency in prayer. Since Justin's parents live in New York, we don't see them as often as we'd like. We keep in touch through phone calls and Skype sessions. Anytime I share a prayer request with either of them, the response is the same: "Let's pray right now." Jerry and Arlene have taught me a valuable lesson, one I try to practice when someone comes to me with a need: Don't just say, "I'll pray for you." Pray with that person immediately.

Praying

Prayer is a skill, and like any skill, it takes practice. For example, if you want to be a better sprinter, you have to sprint. The more you work at it, the faster you'll get. The same principle applies to prayer. You get better at praying by *praying*. The more time you spend talking and listening to the Lord, the more comfortable you'll be in his presence.

When you talk to God, you don't need to be formal. In fact, you don't have to sound spiritual at all! Author Max Lucado says, "Our prayers may be awkward. Our attempts may be feeble. But since the power of prayer is in the one who hears it and not the one who says it, our prayers do make a difference."[8] However, you should always keep one thing in mind: You're speaking with the great "I AM," the one who is worthy of all glory, honor, and praise! Your heart should be humble and reverent when you pray. But don't worry about how you sound. Just let your heart do the talking. Imagine you're having a chat with a good friend, because you are.

4. Prayers Are Potential Miracles

Our God can do anything. Nothing is too difficult for him! Job says, "He does great things too marvelous to understand. He performs countless miracles" (Job 5:9 NLT). Prayer provides opportunities to partner with the Lord and participate in displays of his supernatural power: "Then Abraham prayed to God, and God healed Abimelech, his wife, and his female servants, so they could have children" (Gen. 20:17 NLT). Your prayers carry unlimited potential, not because *your* words are powerful but because *God* is powerful.

Postures in Prayer

I grew up in a small church where the main prayer position was head bowed, eyes closed, and no one looking around. Occasionally I might have seen people on their knees at the altar, but that was about it. Now, before you think I'm bashing my roots, please don't misunderstand what I'm saying. I'm incredibly thankful for my Christian heritage. However, I wish I would have known then what I know now: there is more than one way to position our bodies when we pray. I believe God calls us to worship him with all that we are, so I want to throw not only my heart, soul, and mind into my prayers but my body as well! Various postures of prayer are recorded in Scripture, which gives us the freedom to choose the form we desire. Depending on your background, this information may be new to you. Read this section with an open mind and heart. God may want to stretch you! Following are postures of prayer seen in the Bible.

Sitting

Most of us are well acquainted with this position. When you sit before the Lord, your posture indicates a desire to wait upon God. You show him you have a teachable spirit and are ready to listen.

- "King David went in and sat before the LORD and prayed, 'Who am I, O Sovereign LORD, and what is my family, that you have brought me this far?'" (2 Sam. 7:18 NLT).

Standing

When someone important enters the room, people typically stand to show their respect. If we're willing to get on our feet for another human being, we should definitely stand to honor the Lord.

- "Solomon stood before the altar of the LORD in front of the entire community of Israel, and he lifted his hands in prayer" (2 Chron. 6:12 NLT).

Kneeling/Bowing

James 4:10 says, "Humble yourselves before the Lord." When we pray, we show humility by getting low. Personally, I'm more comfortable with my face to the ground in prayer than with any other position. It has not always been this way, but the more I grow in Christ, the more I'm in awe of his majesty. I cannot help but bow in his presence.

- "Jehoshaphat bowed down with his face to the ground, and all the people of Judah and Jerusalem fell down in worship before the LORD" (2 Chron. 20:18).

Raising Hands

Raising our hands is a natural expression of excitement and joy. Just watch the crowd at any sporting event or concert. The people in the stadium are usually on their feet, yelling, with their hands waving wildly in the air.

Raising your hands expresses adoration. It's also a sign of surrender. When you extend your arms toward heaven, your body language says, "I'm yours, Lord. Take all of me. I hold nothing back."

My pastor frequently encourages our church to lift hands in worship. Sometimes he says, "If you're not comfortable raising your hands, just lift a finger!" It's all said in fun, but his perspective is accurate. You have to start somewhere. If you're afraid, trust God to guide you and give you strength.

When you talk to God, offer your whole body in prayer. It doesn't matter whether you're "charismatic" or not! Praise the Lord with uplifted arms. Don't let fear keep you from freely worshiping the Lord.

- "I will praise you as long as I live, lifting up my hands to you in prayer" (Ps. 63:4 NLT).

Laying Hands on People

In the early church, a person laid hands on someone to confer a blessing, commission the other person for ministry, heal sickness, and impart the power of the Holy Spirit. This position demonstrates an act of spiritual leadership and should not be taken lightly: "Do not be hasty in the laying on of hands" (1 Tim. 5:22). So we should heed the warning of Scripture and be wise in practicing it.

- "One day some parents brought their children to Jesus so he could lay his hands on them and pray for them" (Matt. 19:13 NLT).

Lying Prostrate

A person who is prostrate before God is lying facedown before him. This position displays humility and complete submission.

- "Moses and Aaron fell facedown and cried out, 'O God, the God who gives breath to all living things, will you be angry with the entire assembly when only one man sins?'" (Num. 16:22).

Prayer does not *require* a specific body position, but your posture is important. When you lift your hands in worship or get on your knees to pray, you communicate with your body what you feel in your heart. True prayer involves not just your lips but your whole self. "Praise the LORD, my soul; all my inmost being, praise his holy name" (Ps. 103:1). Explore new ways to worship. Let your love for the Lord lead you in the outward expression of your inward devotion to him.

How to Pray with Power

The Bible says, "The earnest prayer of a righteous person has great power and produces wonderful results" (James 5:16 NLT). If you and I want to see this promise unfold in our lives, we must rely not on our own words in prayer but on God's.

Praying Scripture is the secret to successful prayer. It's what makes our intercession powerful and effective. God says, "As the rain and the snow come down from heaven, and do not return to it without watering the earth and making it bud and flourish, so that it yields seed for the sower and bread for the eater, so is my word that goes out from my mouth: It will not return to me empty, but will accomplish what I desire and achieve the purpose for which I sent it" (Isa. 55:10 – 11). The Lord responds to the truth of his Word. When you claim Scripture over people and situations, you invite God's purposes to be fulfilled. You play a part in bringing his will to pass. However, it's not enough just to quote a Bible verse during prayer. You must also *believe* it.

One day when Jesus was teaching, a ruler named Jairus came and knelt before him. Jairus's daughter had just died, and he said to Jesus, "Come and put your hand on her, and she will live" (Matt. 9:18). Jesus got up from what he was doing and went to the girl.

While they were on the way, a woman came up behind Jesus and placed her hand on his cloak. She was desperate, for she had suffered from a bleeding disorder for twelve years. She thought, "If I can just touch his robe, I will be healed" (v. 21 NLT). The Bible says Jesus turned to the woman and *saw* her. He noticed her physically standing there, yes. But it was more than that. Jesus looked with compassion right into her heart. He saw her physical pain, her shame, and her longing to be free from affliction.

Jesus saw something else as well. He said to her, "Take heart, daughter … your faith has healed you" (v. 22). The woman's health was restored at that very moment.

After leaving the woman, Jesus walked to Jairus's house. When he arrived, Jesus told the crowd gathered there, "Go away. The girl is not dead but asleep" (v. 24). The people laughed at him, for they knew she had died. What they didn't realize was that Jesus was speaking life into the situation, foreshadowing what was about to happen. Jesus ordered the people to go outside. He went to the girl, took her by the hand, and helped her stand up. When the crowd saw her, they were amazed and told everyone in the region.

As Jesus continued down the road, he was followed by two blind men. They called out, "Have mercy on us, Son of David!" Jesus knew the men wanted not just mercy but also healing. He asked them, "Do you believe that I am able to do this?" They replied, "Yes, Lord." Then Jesus touched their eyes and said, "According to your faith let it be done to you." Immediately they could see (vv. 27 – 30).

What Jesus saw in the woman, he also saw in Jairus and the blind men. He saw faith.

In each situation, faith opened the door to release God's power. In each situation, God performed a miracle.

The woman believed and received what she wanted. So did Jairus. So did the blind men.

R. C. Sproul said, "I think the whole concept of faith is one of the most misunderstood ideas that we have, misunderstood not only by the world but by the church itself. The very basis for our redemption, the way in which we are justified before God, is through faith. The Bible is constantly talking to us about faith, and if we misunderstand that, we're in deep trouble."[9]

The Christian definition for faith is given in the book of Hebrews: "Faith is confidence in what we hope for and assurance about what we do not see" (11:1). A person who has faith possesses solid belief in God's promises, even when there isn't any proof or evidence to support such belief. "Without faith it is impossible to please God, because anyone who comes to him must believe that he exists and that he rewards those who earnestly seek him" (v. 6).

Faith is essential in prayer. It's the catalyst that invites God's power into the circumstances of our lives. Without faith, our prayers are empty wishes.

George Müller, a nineteenth-century evangelist, was a mighty prayer warrior who saw the Lord provide in miraculous ways. In 1877, when Müller was traveling to Quebec on the *SS Sardinian*, the ship ran into a thick fog. When the captain slowed the ship for safety reasons, Müller explained to the captain that he needed to be in Quebec by the following afternoon. When Müller realized he was going to miss his appointment, he went to the chart room to pray. The captain followed him. Müller asked God to lift the fog, and then the captain started to pray. Müller stopped him because he doubted the captain had faith that God would do it. Müller also believed his request had already been answered, so he didn't see the need to keep praying about it. When the two returned to the bridge of the ship, they saw the fog had lifted. The ship resumed normal speed, and Müller made his appointment on time. The captain became a Christian shortly after that experience.[10]

My friend, this type of experience is not limited to men like George Müller. God wants to do the miraculous in your life as well! When you have a need, take it to the Lord and expect him to answer. The answer might not come in the way you expect, though. God's ways are beyond our understanding, and his thoughts are far above our thoughts (Isa. 55:8 – 9). However, he promises to work everything out for good for people who love him (Rom. 8:28).

Sometimes we believe in God but we're still unsure whether he will answer our prayers. Mark 9 tells the story of a man who brought his demon-possessed son to Jesus. "When the spirit saw Jesus, it immediately threw the boy into a convulsion. He fell to the ground and rolled around, foaming at the mouth." The father said to Jesus, "If you can do anything, take pity on us and help us" (vv. 20 – 22).

Jesus answered, "'If you can'?... Everything is possible for one who believes." The boy's father cried, "I do believe; help me overcome my unbelief!" (vv. 23 – 24).

I love the Lord's response to the man's honesty. He doesn't condemn the man for his lack of faith. Instead, Jesus lovingly reminds him of the Lord's omnipotence!

God can do big things with little faith. Jesus said, "If you have faith as small as a mustard seed, you can say to this mountain, 'Move from here to there,' and it will move. Nothing will be impossible for you" (Matt. 17:20).

If you struggle with doubt, like the father in this story, simply confess it to the Lord. Acknowledge your sin, and he will help you overcome your lack of trust. As you meditate on God's promises, your tiny mustard seed of belief will grow into an enormous tree of faith! Your prayers will be full of God's power and produce wonderful results for his kingdom.

CHAPTER 6

Fasting

Our greatest victories are won on our knees
and with empty stomachs.
— *Julio C. Ruibal*

It was Sunday morning, day one of my January 2013 Daniel Fast. I woke up, filled with anticipation about what God was going to do. While worshiping the Lord at church, I could sense his nearness. By the time I got home, though, I didn't feel well at all. My body ached, and my head was pounding. Within a few hours, I was in bed with a high fever and chills. The first day of my fast was also the beginning of a five-week battle with the flu.

The fast was not the spiritual high I'd expected. Most days I spent sleeping. Nausea kept me from going outside the house except to take my daughters to and from school. A couple of times, I couldn't even do that and had to rely on the help of a friend. I tried to talk to God, but all I heard was silence. I felt abandoned and alone.

At one of my lowest points, I remembered Paul's story in 2 Corinthians 12:7 – 10. God allowed an affliction in Paul's life, and three times Paul pleaded with him to remove it. The Lord replied, "My grace is sufficient for you, for my power is made perfect in weakness" (v. 9). Instead of healing Paul, God gave him strength to endure the trial. Paul's response was to write to the Christians in Corinth, "I will boast all the more gladly about my weaknesses, so that Christ's power may rest on me. That is why, for Christ's sake, I delight in weaknesses, in insults, in hardships, in persecutions, in difficulties. For when I am weak, then I am strong" (vv. 9 – 10). Those verses kept me going when I thought I couldn't make it another day.

Even though I couldn't "feel" the Lord with me, I believed Deuteronomy 31:6, which says, "He will never leave you nor forsake you." God was faithful. Every day, he supplied his power when I didn't have the strength to continue. Every day, he provided time for my body to rest. Every day, he held me, just like a shepherd carries a frightened lamb close to his heart. Even though it was one of the darkest valleys of my life, I can honestly say I'm thankful for the suffering I endured. God used that experience to deepen my faith in him and in his promises.

François Fénelon, who was the archbishop of Cambrai, France, in the seventeenth century, frequently wrote to various believers to counsel them. In one letter, Fénelon said to someone who was ill, "In this time of physical weakness, I pray you may become more and more aware of your spiritual weakness. Not that I want you to remain weak. For while the Lord ministers healing and strength to your body, I pray that he will also minister strength to your soul, and that weakness will finally be conquered. But you need to understand that you cannot become strong until first you are aware of your weakness."[1]

When it comes to the spiritual exercises mentioned in this book, no other exercise makes you more painfully aware of your weakness than the discipline of fasting.

What Is Fasting?

When you fast, you willingly afflict your body to pursue the nourishment of your soul. You choose to abstain from food, or certain foods, for a period of time as an act of surrender and worship to God. Someone who undergoes a fast is saying, "Lord, I'm desperate for you. I'm willing to sacrifice my time, my physical comfort, and my desires so I can hear from you."

Through fasting, you participate in the sufferings of Christ. You learn submission, humility, and brokenness. At the same time, you develop perseverance, character, and hope. Arthur Wallis, author of *God's Chosen Fast*, says, "Fasting *is* important, more important perhaps, than many of us have supposed.... When exercised with a pure heart and a right motive, fasting may provide us with a key to unlock doors where other keys have failed."[2]

In this chapter, we'll discuss the different types of fasts, why you should fast, when you should fast, how you should fast, how long you should fast, and the physical and spiritual benefits of fasting.

Types of Fasts

When most people think of a fast, they imagine going without food for several days and drinking only water, broth, and/or juice. Although that is one way to fast, there are others. Following are the three main types of fasts.

1. *Absolute.* No liquids or food. Usually this type of fast is three days or less, simply because it becomes dangerous to go without water for a longer amount of time. An example of this fast is seen in Esther 4:16, where Queen Esther asks the people of Susa to fast and pray with her for three days before she approaches the king.

2. *Liquid.* No food. Only liquids, such as water, fruit and vegetable juices, and/or broth, may be consumed.

3. *Partial.* Certain foods are allowed, while others are restricted. The most popular type of partial fast is the Daniel Fast. The food guidelines for the Daniel Fast are based on accounts of Daniel's experiences as recorded in the Bible. Daniel received a vision from God that disturbed him so much he entered into a state of mourning, or fasting. Daniel 10:2 – 3 says he abstained from "choice food" and didn't have meat or wine for three weeks. The English Standard Version of Daniel 10:3 says, "I ate no delicacies." Another translation puts it this way: "I did not eat any tasty food" (NASB). Most commentaries agree choice food would have probably included bread and sweets. Daniel ate only what was necessary for physical sustenance. Foods allowed on the Daniel Fast are fruits, vegetables, whole grains, beans, legumes, nuts, seeds, and oils. Restricted foods include meat, dairy, sugar, all forms of sweeteners, caffeine, yeast, refined and processed foods, deep-fried foods, and solid fats. The goal of the Daniel Fast is not to duplicate Daniel's menu but to imitate the spirit in which he sought the Lord. His passion for God caused him to long for spiritual food more than physical food, which should be the ultimate desire of anyone choosing to participate in a fast. (If you're interested in more information on the Daniel Fast, be sure to get my book *The Ultimate Guide to the Daniel Fast*, which is available in bookstores and online.)

A popular Christian practice in our culture is to pull away from electronic distractions — such as the computer, television, or Facebook — and call it a fast. Although these self-denials certainly have benefits, they are not true fasts according to biblical examples. In every instance of fasting in the Bible, people either went without food (or certain types of food) or went without food and water. To fast means to reduce food intake as you spend time in prayer.

Why Should I Fast?

Although the Bible doesn't give a direct command on this issue, examples of fasting appear in both the Old and the New Testaments. One of the most telling passages in which fasting is mentioned is Matthew 6:16, where Jesus is teaching his disciples basic principles of godly living. When speaking on fasting, he begins with, "When you fast," not "*If* you fast." Jesus' words imply that fasting will be a regular practice in his followers' lives. Dietrich Bonhoeffer, in his book *The Cost of Discipleship*, said, "Jesus takes it for granted that his disciples will observe the pious custom of fasting. Strict exercise of self-control is an essential feature of the Christian life. Such customs have only one purpose — to make the disciples more ready and cheerful to accomplish those things which God would have done."[3]

Fasting prepares you for the works God has ordained for you to do. Wesley Duewel, a twentieth-century writer, said, "You and I have no more right to omit fasting because we feel no special emotional prompting than we have a right to omit prayer, Bible reading, or assembling with God's children for lack of some special emotional prompting. Fasting is just as biblical and normal a part of a spiritual walk of obedience with God as are these others."[4]

People fast for a number of reasons. Following are seven circumstances in the Bible in which believers sought God through this discipline.

1. *To prepare for ministry.* Jesus spent forty days and nights in the wilderness fasting and praying before he began God's work on this earth. He needed time alone to prepare for what his Father had called him to do (Matt. 4:1 – 17; Mark 1:12 – 13; Luke 4:1 – 14).

2. *To seek God's wisdom.* Paul and Barnabas prayed and fasted for the elders of the churches before committing them to the Lord for his service (Acts 14:23).

3. *To show grief.* Nehemiah mourned, fasted, and prayed when he learned Jerusalem's walls had been broken down, leaving the Israelites vulnerable and disgraced (Neh. 1:1 – 4).

4. *To seek deliverance or protection.* Ezra declared a corporate fast and prayed for a safe journey for the Israelites as they made the nine-hundred-mile trek to Jerusalem from Babylon (Ezra 8:21 – 23).

5. *To repent.* After Jonah pronounced judgment against the city of Nineveh, the king covered himself with sackcloth and sat in the dust. He then ordered the people to fast and pray. Jonah 3:10 says, "When God saw what they did and how they turned from their evil ways, he relented and did not bring on them the destruction he had threatened."

6. *To gain victory.* After losing forty thousand men in battle in two days, the Israelites cried out to God for help. Judges 20:26 says all the people went up to Bethel and "sat weeping before the Lord." They also "fasted that day until evening." The next day the Lord gave them victory over the Benjamites.

7. *To worship God.* Luke 2 tells the story of an eighty-four-year-old prophetess named Anna. Verse 37 says, "She never left the temple but worshiped night and day, fasting and praying." Anna was devoted to God, and fasting was one expression of her love for him.

Despite biblical examples throughout Scripture, many Christians are slow to fast. I believe there are three main factors that cause believers to be hesitant — fear, ignorance, or rebellion.

1. *Fear.* They're afraid. Afraid of the unknown. Afraid of feeling hunger pangs. Afraid of starting and not finishing. Afraid of fasting alone. The Enemy has them convinced they could never do it. Instead of looking to the Lord's strength for help, they become consumed with their own weaknesses and paralyzed by fear.

2. *Ignorance.* Many Christians simply have not been taught about the importance of seeking God in this way. Churches often do not encourage fasting, and in many cases never even mention it from the pulpit. For example, I grew up in a Bible-believing church, but I don't recall hearing a message on fasting until I was an adult.

3. *Rebellion.* A large segment of the Christian population is aware of the benefits of fasting, yet they're unwilling to do it. Their hearts are hardened when it comes to the idea of fasting. When God invites them to draw near, they dig their heels into the ground and refuse to obey.

Dr. Bill Bright, founder of Campus Crusade for Christ, was a firm believer in the power of prayer and fasting. In his guide *Why You Should Fast*, he listed the following reasons for seeking God through self-denial.

- Fasting was an expected discipline in both the Old and New Testament eras.
- Fasting and prayer can restore the loss of the "first love" for your Lord and result in a more intimate relationship with Christ.
- Fasting is a biblical way to truly humble yourself in the sight of God.
- Fasting enables the Holy Spirit to reveal your true spiritual condition, resulting in brokenness, repentance, and a transformed life.
- Fasting will encourage the Holy Spirit to quicken the Word of God in your heart and His truth will become more meaningful to you.
- Fasting can transform your prayer life into a richer and more personal experience.
- Fasting can result in a dynamic personal revival in your own life and make you a channel of revival to others.[5]

Many times we don't fast because we've lost our spiritual appetite. John Piper says, "The absence of fasting is the measure of our contentment with the absence of Christ."[6] Piper adds, "If we don't feel strong desires for the manifestation of the glory of God, it is not because we have drunk deeply and are satisfied. It is because we have nibbled so long at the table of the world. Our soul is stuffed with small things, and there is no room for the great."[7]

Fasting is a much-needed discipline in the life of a believer. It truly is the "path of pleasant pain," as John Piper calls it.[8] As you empty yourself physically and spiritually, you open the door for God to step in and do the miraculous. Your relationship with the Lord is taken to a whole new level. You also become more sensitive to the work of the Holy Spirit, which enables you to hear God's voice more clearly.

Anyone who has done a fast — whether absolute, liquid, or partial — would agree fasting is difficult. Physically, you may suffer from unpleasant side effects, such as headaches, fatigue, and intestinal discomfort, as your body attempts to adjust to the reduced caloric intake. Spiritually, attacks from the Enemy increase in frequency and intensity, resulting in a barrage of frustrations that can seem overwhelming. However, the same people who would be honest about the challenges of fasting would also concur that the sacrifices are well worth the rewards. So don't resist the suffering that accompanies fasting. Rejoice in it! Fasting is a spiritual exercise which God honors. He promises to heap blessings on people who are hungry for him (Matt. 5:6).

When Should I Fast?

A common question I get from readers is, "When should I fast?" In the past, I advised people to fast if the Lord had laid it on their heart. The more I've studied the Bible, however, the more I've realized that my counsel wasn't biblical. It's not that it was wrong; it just wasn't complete.

When you consider the various passages on fasting, you can assume God expects it to be a regular practice in our lives, just as it was in Bible times. So I think it's safe to say God has *already* led you to fast! You don't need to wait until you *feel* like doing it. Now when people ask when they should fast, my answer is, "Anytime!"

Fasting can be scheduled or spontaneous. An example of a scheduled fast is one you plan to do months or weeks ahead of time. For example, I like to begin the New Year in prayer and fasting. In January 2012, I held my first online Daniel Fast through my website (*www.ultimatedanielfast.com*). People who signed up received a daily email from me, which contained a short devotion, new recipes, and other helpful information. I anticipated many people would respond, since January is an ideal time for fasting. However, I was blown away when more than 2,000 people participated! The following year, nearly 2,700 people signed up. I challenge you to commit to the Daniel Fast this January. You can sign up on my website for encouragement and support.

John Wesley, the founder of the Methodist Church, fasted two days a week — on Wednesdays and Fridays in his younger years, and on Fridays when he was older. He would fast from after his evening meal up until (but not including) the evening meal of the following day. During his fast, he focused on prayer. Wesley's example prompted me to launch the "STOP to Pray" campaign, a weekly fast featured on my website. In August 2012, I invited parents and grandparents to commit to fast and pray for their children and/or grandchildren every Thursday during the school year. This idea was born out of my own need for accountability in praying for my daughters. I wanted my intercession to be more than, "God, protect them. God, help them. God, bless them." If you're a parent and/or grandparent, make time to intercede for your little ones (even if they're not so little any longer). Your prayers make an eternal difference! Abraham Lincoln is purported to have said, "I remember my mother's prayers and they have always followed me. They have clung to me all my life."

Another kind of fast is one that's spontaneous, or unplanned. You might choose to seek God's guidance for an important job decision. Another example is to pray for the physical healing of a family member who has a severe illness. Whatever the occasion is, you fast because you need God's immediate intervention, and time is of the essence.

How Should I Fast?

Fasting is a sacred experience between you and the Lord. It's also acceptable as a means of locking arms with other believers to advance the kingdom of God. The Bible makes it clear that both styles are appropriate when your heart is centered on glorifying God. Let's examine the two ways you can fast — individually and corporately.

1. Individual, or Private, Fasts

Jennifer was twenty-three and newly married to a wonderful Christian man. She and her husband, Walter, were attending a dynamic church, and she was growing in her relationship with the Lord. However, Jennifer began to feel increasingly convicted about her nicotine habit. "I had been smoking off and on for a couple of years," she says. "It was becoming more and more of an internal conflict for me. I obviously knew it was unhealthy for me physically, not to mention a poor example for my son."

One morning, Jennifer woke up and felt "a gentle nudging from God." She knew it was time to give up cigarettes for good. "I knew the Lord wanted to do a work in my life. I also believed he was calling me to a three-day fast." Jennifer had done shorter fasts, such as skipping a meal or fasting for twenty-four hours, but she had never gone three full days without food.

The following day Jennifer began her fast in faith, and she experienced God's grace in a way that amazed her. Three days later, on November 18, 1993, she knew her smoking days were finished forever. "I believe that three-day fast was the key to my deliverance," Jennifer says.

Here are some examples of individual fasts in the Bible.

- Daniel fasted and prayed for the Israelites after God revealed their future destruction (Dan. 9:1 – 3).

- David fasted and prayed for his son, who was sick (2 Sam. 12:15 – 23).

- Jesus fasted for forty days and nights in the wilderness before beginning his public ministry (Matt. 4:1 – 11).

Many Christians argue fasting *always* has to be private. Their logic is usually based on a misinterpretation of the following passage in the Bible: "When you fast, don't make it obvious, as the hypocrites do, for they try to look miserable and disheveled so people will admire them for their fasting. I tell you the truth, that is the only reward they will ever get. But when you fast, comb your hair and wash your face. Then no one will notice that you are fasting, except your Father, who knows what you do in private. And your Father, who sees everything, will reward you" (Matt. 6:16 – 18 NLT).

What Jesus is saying is, "When you fast, don't be showy about it. Don't try to convince others how holy you are by making it obvious that you're fasting. Put a smile on your face, wear nice clothes, and show the joy of the Lord!"

Unless you live alone, it's nearly impossible to keep your fast confidential. Family members in your household will know of your sacrifice. Sometimes you might want to confide in one or two close friends and ask them to pray for you. I recommend telling as few people as possible, though, to protect yourself from prideful thoughts.

2. Public, or Corporate, Fasts

A corporate fast can be a unifying time for a group of believers to come together in prayer. Bob Rodgers, pastor of Evangel Christian Life Center, in Louisville, Kentucky, has witnessed the power of this type of fast.

When Bob's father died suddenly of a heart attack in 1988, the church voted for Bob to succeed him as pastor. The church had just come through a massive building program and was carrying a huge debt. Bob, not knowing what to do, decided to fast and pray. He invited his congregation to join him in abstaining from one meal a day for twenty-one days. Bob says, "Immediately I noticed a change in my life. I preached with greater power and authority. Our church began to grow, and finances began to increase. Then the Lord impressed upon me to have our church fast three days every month — we took the first Monday, Tuesday, and Wednesday each month."[9]

The people started strong, but it didn't take long for their motivation to wane. "It was easy to get several thousand people to begin fasting on Monday, but when Wednesday came I was fortunate to have a handful still fasting," Bob says. "After several months I initiated a miracle service on the third day — intending to have a goal for the people to reach so they could complete the three days."[10]

When Pastor Rodgers arrived for that first miracle service, he was shocked to find the chapel packed with people. Some couldn't even get in the door. After preaching a simple message, Rodgers prayed. Two people with terminal cancer were healed. Another woman, who had a growth the size of a grapefruit on her leg, saw her tumor disappear when she got home.

Evangel Christian Life Center has since instituted regular times of seeking the Lord together through corporate fasts. Pastor Rodgers says, "The results in our church have been startling. Our income has multiplied over threefold. We have restructured our finances and are paying our bills. In the past months we baptized seventy-three, and eighty-seven joined the church. All these are the result of fasting and prayer."[11]

Here are three biblical examples of corporate fasts.

1. The prophet Joel called for a nationwide fast because of the famine in the land (Joel 2:15).

2. Esther, her maidens, and the Jews of Susa fasted from food and drink for three days before she went to the king (Est. 4:16).

3. The church at Antioch fasted and prayed together before sending out Paul and Barnabas (Acts 13:1–3).

How Long Should I Fast?

People in the Bible who sought the Lord did so for varying lengths of time. For example, the Israelites fasted at Mizpah for one day (1 Sam. 7:6), Esther and her people fasted three days (Est. 4:16), the people of Jabesh Gilead fasted seven days (1 Sam. 31:13), Daniel fasted twenty-one days (Dan. 10:3), and both Jesus and Moses fasted forty days (Deut. 9:9; Matt. 4:2). So you have options as to the length of your fast. Pray and ask God what *he* would have you do.

Physical Benefits of Fasting

Fasting has been recognized as an effective therapy and observed as a religious practice for thousands of years. Hippocrates, the father of Western medicine, believed fasting enabled the body to heal itself. Paracelsus, another medical pioneer, wrote five hundred years ago that "fasting is the greatest remedy, the physician within."

What occurs during a liquid fast is not starvation but rather the body's burning of stored energy. Starvation occurs when the body no longer has any reserves and begins using essential tissues as an energy source. A therapeutic fast ends long before such a process occurs. The principle of fasting is simple: when food intake is temporarily ceased, the body is provided a much-needed break from the constant demands of digestion, which gives it a chance to repair tissue. Following are a few ways in which the body benefits from fasting.

1. *Rest.* Your body undergoes a cleansing process when you fast. Harmful ingredients, such as chemicals, additives, and preservatives, are filtered and removed. Energy that would normally be spent breaking down and transporting food is diverted to other areas of your body. Your metabolism slows. You feel less stressed and more at peace. Even when on a Daniel Fast, you're still allowing your body a chance to rest from foods that are difficult to digest, such as meat. As a result, your body is able to operate more efficiently.

2. *Repair.* Your body has an amazing ability to heal itself. During a fast, the amount of repair that occurs depends on three factors: (1) the length of your fast, (2) the current condition of your body, and (3) your food choices leading up to your fast. First, the longer you go on a fast, the more healing that can take place. Second, if you've abused your body for years by overeating and not exercising, you will not experience major transformation unless you participate in an extended fast (seven days or more). A short-term fast, while beneficial, is not sufficient to effect significant changes in cholesterol levels, heart rate, or any other tangible marker of health. Third, your food choices leading up to your fast play an important role in your healing. For example, if you are a heavy meat eater, drink alcohol, smoke, and are addicted to sugar, your body will need more time to reverse your condition.

3. *Reduction in the risk of illness and disease.* Studies have shown that regular and/or long-term fasts can result in a decreased risk of a variety of physical conditions, including cancer and autoimmune disorders. In an April 2011 report, cardiac researchers at the Intermountain Medical Center Heart Institute concluded that routine periodic fasting is good for your health and your heart. Their research showed that fasting not only lowers the risk of coronary artery disease and diabetes but also causes significant changes in blood cholesterol levels.[12]

4. *Retraining.* Fasting helps you gain self-control over your body's physical cravings. It can also be an effective tool to help break destructive eating habits, such as emotional eating or bingeing. If you have an unhealthy relationship with food, admit it. Own up to the fact that you've sought escape from your emotional pain through eating instead of working through it in a productive way. Then begin to change the way you think about food. Refuse to believe food is the answer to your problems. For example, when you're depressed and want to devour a whole bag of chips, tell yourself, "No!" Over time, such self-denial will train your mind to see food for what it is — fuel for your body and not your comforter in crisis.

Spiritual Benefits of Fasting

When accompanied by passionate prayer, fasting will help you develop intimacy with the Savior like nothing else can. God promises when we seek him wholeheartedly, we'll be richly rewarded: "Blessed are those who hunger and thirst for righteousness, for they will be filled" (Matt. 5:6). Following are additional reasons why you should include periodic fasts in your relationship with the Lord.

1. *Fasting is the example set by Jesus.* We should fast because Jesus did. Our Savior spent forty days and nights in the wilderness fasting before he began his public ministry (Matt. 4:1 – 11). During that time, the Lord was able to defeat Satan's attacks because he was prayed up and armed with the Word of God. Jesus' example shows us how fasting equips and empowers us for victory over sin.

2. *Fasting helps you grow in faith.* Self-denial doesn't come naturally or easily, because the flesh is wired for indulgence. When you commit

to a fast, you understand and acknowledge that you can't do it on your own. You realize how completely dependent you are on the Lord's strength. You learn to lean on him for the perseverance to finish strong.

3. *Fasting changes you.* There's something about fasting that causes you to be more sensitive to what God is doing around you. It's as if the hunger in your body is replaced by a unique filling of the Holy Spirit. You can hear the Lord's voice more clearly and sense his nearness in a special way. You pray with greater intensity and urgency. During a fast, your mind and heart are transformed as you meditate on the truth of God's Word and apply his promises to your life.

When Jesus was traveling through Caesarea Philippi with his disciples, he summoned the crowd who had gathered around them, and he said, "If any of you wants to be my follower, you must turn from your selfish ways, take up your cross, and follow me" (Mark 8:34 NLT).

What did Jesus mean when he said, "Take up your cross"? Author Wesley Duewel suggests, "To take up a cross is not to have someone place the cross upon you. Sickness, persecution, and antagonism of other people are not your real cross. To take up a cross is a deliberate choice. We must purposely ... pick up the cross for Jesus. Fasting is one of the most biblical ways to do so."[13]

I pray you discover the indescribable joy that comes when you deny yourself and seek God wholeheartedly. May the Lord fill you with his power as you humble yourself before him through prayer and fasting.

CHAPTER 7

Healthy Living

The greatest wealth is health.
— Virgil

When John and Christy started dating, he was twenty-six years old. She was eighteen. He weighed 150 pounds, and she was barely 110 pounds. Christy exercised like crazy. John didn't work out at all. Shortly after getting married, the couple moved to Dallas. Christy says, "We went to restaurants all the time — breakfast, lunch, and dinner. None of our friends cooked, so we got into the habit of eating out. We had the money, so it wasn't a problem." However, after eleven years of marriage, two children, and a combined weight gain of 238 pounds, their unhealthy lifestyle had become a problem. *A big one.*

John's wake-up call came when he discovered he had bicuspid aortic valve disease, a condition in which the valve that controls blood flow from the heart is defective. The diagnosis was the shock he needed to force him out of his complacency.

"I remember sitting at my desk one day at work," John said. "It was during my break time, so I took a few moments to watch a sermon online. At the end of the message, the congregation was singing praise to God. As I watched the people worship, I sensed the Lord saying, 'John, this joy is what I have for you. Now lose weight.' I knew my ability to fulfill what God had called me to do was dependent on my being healthy."

When John and Christy came to me for help, we sat down and talked through some of the issues that led to their destructive eating habits. I gave them ideas on steps they could take to make better choices. The first change they made was to replace their highly processed snacks with fruit smoothies. They also began walking and biking three to four times each week. Within a few months, John and Christy lost more than thirty pounds total, and they have continued to make positive changes with their eating and exercise habits. Though the weight loss has been encouraging, they're even more excited about continuing to improve their *spiritual* health. After years of desecrating God's temple, John and Christy are committed to building their bodies in a way that honors the Lord.

Your Body Is a Temple

The temple of the Old Testament was primarily a house of worship and a monument to God's greatness. It was a holy, sacred site, a special place in which God's presence dwelled. Today God still lives among his people, only in a more personal way.

When Jesus died on the cross, his victory over death changed how we relate to our heavenly Father. Jesus' sacrifice made a way for us to have peace with God (Rom. 5:1). Instead of having to communicate through a priest, we now have direct access to God and can boldly approach his throne of grace (Heb. 4:16). Animal sacrifices are no longer required for the forgiveness of sin. Jesus' shed blood cleanses us from all unrighteousness. Finally, the presence of the Lord isn't limited to a special building; his Spirit lives in us. *We* are God's temple (2 Cor. 6:16).

The apostle Paul was passionate about helping believers understand these truths. He wrote to the church at Corinth, "Do you not know that your bodies are temples of the Holy Spirit, who is in you, whom you have received from God? You are not your own; you were bought at a price. Therefore honor God with your bodies" (1 Cor. 6:19 – 20). If Paul were alive today, I believe he would be appalled at the condition of God's temple. Nearly 70 percent of people over twenty years of age in the United States are overweight or obese. This means that more than *150 million* adults are carrying around excess body weight.[1] What makes the problem worse is that our children are following in our footsteps. The American Heart Association estimates that approximately 23.9 million children in America ages two to nineteen are overweight or obese — 33 percent of boys and 30.4 percent of girls. In the last thirty years, childhood obesity has *tripled*.

Unfortunately, Christians aren't doing any better than the rest of the country. A 2011 Northwestern University study, which tracked 3,433 men and women for eighteen years, found that young adults who attend church or a Bible study once a week are 50 percent *more* likely to be obese.[2] Matthew J. Feinstein, who conducted the study, believes one explanation could be that religious gatherings are often centered on unhealthy or high-calorie meals. "It's possible that getting together once a week and associating good works and happiness with eating unhealthy foods could lead to the development of habits that are associated with greater body weight and obesity," Feinstein said.[3] Kenneth Ferraro of Purdue University conducted a similar study in 2006. His research showed that among religious groups, the Baptists had a 30 percent obesity rate, compared with Jews at 1 percent and Buddhists and Hindus at 0.7 percent.[4] When asked to comment on the reason for such high rates among Christians, Ferraro said, "American churches are virtually silent on excess body weight."[5] Sadly, many Christians either ignore God's command in 1 Corinthians 6:20 or are simply unaware of what God expects of them. Instead of honoring God with their bodies, they dishonor him.

In 2008, Pastor Steve Willis of First Baptist Church, in Kenova, West Virginia, lost a friend because of complications from heart surgery. His friend had been 150 pounds overweight and might not have even needed the surgery if he had been healthier. That's when Steve decided to address the issue of obesity with his congregation.

One week before he was scheduled to preach his sermon, the Centers for Disease Control and Prevention released a report that named the Huntington area — including Kenova — as the most obese and unhealthiest region in America. Pastor Steve's community had been declared America's Fattest City, ranking first in the nation in adults who didn't exercise, first in heart disease, and first in diabetes. Their community was also first in high blood pressure, circulation problems, kidney disease, vision problems, and sleeping disorders. Willis saw the report as an affirmation from God that he was on the correct path. He said, "My personal experience bore out those statistics. People were dying, and many were members of my church."[6]

Pastor Steve's message inspired many people at First Baptist to make healthy changes to their lifestyles. Within a year, about sixty people each had an average weight loss of thirty to forty pounds, and together they lost more than two thousand pounds.[7]

When Pastor Steve shared his story in 2011 with students at East Texas Baptist University, he challenged them with this question: "Why can we talk about all matters of sin in the church, but we don't talk about the sin of not taking care of the temples that God has given us?" He then encouraged his listeners to consider exercise and eating healthy as an act of worship. "It matters what Christians do to their bodies," he said. "Our bodies belong to God."[8]

Pastor Steve is right. It *does* matter how you treat your body. That's what Paul was trying to tell the Corinthians. Your body is a holy vessel, created to bring honor, glory, and praise to God. The Lord has entrusted this amazing creation to you, and your job is to take care of it as best you can.

Slaves No More!

In 1863, President Abraham Lincoln issued an executive order which called for the release of American slaves. This order, known as the Emancipation Proclamation, granted freedom to millions of people. Yet despite Lincoln's attempt, slavery still exists in our country today. However, the difference is that people are *choosing* to forfeit their freedom instead of having it taken from them.

The Bible says people who live in spiritual darkness are slaves to sin. They're described as hostile to God, governed by selfishness, unable to submit to God's law, and unable to please him (Rom. 8:1 – 17). Their lives are controlled by the power of the Enemy. The good news is, that's exactly why Jesus came! His sacrifice on the cross made an eternal declaration of our release from captivity. "He gave his life to purchase freedom for everyone" (1 Tim. 2:6 NLT). Jesus abolished spiritual slavery forever! So if you're a believer in the Lord Jesus Christ, you have been set free from sin to live a righteous life.

Charles Kingsley, a nineteenth-century clergyman, professor, historian, and novelist, said, "There are two freedoms — the false, where a man is free to do what he likes; the true, where he is free to do what he ought." People who think they have the right to do whatever they want with their bodies are living under a false freedom. They don't understand the significance of the body and why it was created. They're blind to how destructive their behavior is. Their lack of discipline keeps them in bondage.

First Lady Eleanor Roosevelt said, "With freedom comes responsibility." If you're guilty of neglecting to care for your body as you should, let God's truth rescue you. Make wise choices which build up your body, not foolish ones which tear it down. Demonstrate your love for the Lord by obeying his command. Remember, God paid a high price to bring you out of captivity

(1 Cor. 7:23). You're no longer a slave to sin; you're now a slave to righteousness (Rom. 6:18). Accept the responsibility of caring for God's temple so you can experience the freedom that's already yours.

In the next two sections, we will examine two areas of healthy living in relation to caring for your body — eating and exercise. In "Honoring God through Eating," you will learn (1) the definition of healthy eating, (2) the most common unhealthy eating habits, (3) the trap of emotional eating, and (4) tips to improve your eating. In "Honoring God through Exercise," you will discover (1) the benefits of physical exercise, (2) the three main forms of exercise, and (3) how to stay committed to your exercise program.

Honoring God through Eating

> Whether you eat or drink, or whatever you do,
> do it all for the glory of God.
> — *1 Corinthians 10:31 NLT*

Raynald (Reginald) III was a fourteenth-century French duke of modern-day Belgium. When his father died unexpectedly, Raynald, at ten years old, was next in line for succession. Because of his age, Raynald's mother held the regency until he was old enough to take office. When Raynald assumed leadership, he became known for his turbulent disposition. His younger brother, Edward, was equally volatile, and the two quarreled continually in their struggle for power. Not only was Raynald a hothead; he was also quite large. He was often called by his nickname, Crassus, which means "The Fat."

In 1350, with pressure from his mother, Edward sought control of the Duchy of Guelders, which resulted in a fierce battle for power between the brothers.[9] Edward eventually captured Raynald and imprisoned him. He placed Raynald in a cell in which the doors and windows were always open. Because of his size, though, Raynald couldn't squeeze through any of them. To be free, Raynald needed to lose weight.

When Duke Edward was accused by a palace worker of being unnecessarily cruel, he said, "My brother is not a prisoner. He may leave when he so wills," to which the palace worker replied, "But, Your Grace, he is too broad to get through the doors!" Edward responded, "Am I to blame, then, that my brother is a gormandizer [glutton]?"

Raynald remained in the castle for ten years while his brother ruled. He was finally released in 1371, after Edward was killed in battle. By that time, though, Raynald's health was so ruined that he died within a few months, a prisoner of his own appetite.[10]

Food has been a struggle for us since the beginning. God commanded Adam and Eve not to eat of the Tree of the Knowledge of Good and Evil, yet they chose to taste its luscious fruit. Even though Adam and Eve had a home in paradise, they still weren't satisfied. They longed for *more*. Their discontent resulted in broken fellowship with God, their banishment from the Garden of Eden, and the introduction of sin into the world.

Although food was a factor in the first transgression, it's not inherently evil. The Bible says, "Everything God created is good" (1 Tim. 4:4). The Lord has given us a vast array of flavors, colors, and textures to enjoy. Food is the fuel that provides energy for our bodies so we can carry out God's purposes. Our responsibility as caretakers of the Lord's temple is to be wise about the kind of fuel we consume.

What Is Healthy Eating, Anyway?

Healthy eating is balanced eating. It involves feeding your body a variety of nutritious foods so it can function properly. Your body requires six basic nutrients to maintain optimal health — carbohydrates, protein, fat, vitamins, minerals, and water. Following is a brief description of each nutrient.

1. *Carbohydrates.* Carbohydrates are the primary energy source for your body, particularly your muscles and brain. They can be grouped into two categories: simple and complex. Simple carbohydrates are sugars; complex carbohydrates consist of starch and dietary fiber. Grain products, such as breads, cereals, pasta, and rice, as well as fruits and vegetables, are all sources of carbohydrates.

2. *Protein.* Protein is essential for building and repairing muscles, red blood cells, hair, and other tissues. It's also needed for the manufacture of hormone enzymes and for antibody function. Adequate protein intake is also important for a healthy immune system. Main sources of protein are animal products (meat, fish, poultry, milk, cheese, and eggs), beans, legumes, nuts, and seeds.

3. *Fat.* Dietary fat maintains skin and hair, cushions vital organs, provides insulation, and is necessary for the production and absorption of certain vitamins and hormones. Sources include avocados, nuts, olives, and oils.

4. *Vitamins.* Vitamins help to regulate chemical reactions in the body. There are thirteen vitamins, including vitamins A, B complex, C, D, E, and K. Since most vitamins cannot be manufactured in the body, they must be obtained through food. Supplements may be used, but it's always best to obtain your vitamins through a varied diet.

5. *Minerals.* Minerals are components of foods that are involved in many bodily functions. For example, calcium and magnesium are important for bone structure, and iron is needed for red blood cells to transport oxygen. Like vitamins, minerals are not a source of energy and should be obtained through a nutritious diet rather than through supplements.

6. *Water.* Water is vital for good health. It provides structure and form to the body, suppresses the appetite, helps metabolize stored body fat, regulates body temperature, carries nutrients to and waste products from our cells, and lubricates joints.

The food choices you make the majority of the time determine the condition of your body. So you can have occasional treats without sabotaging your health. In fact, I used to allow my clients to have a "free day" on which they were permitted flexibility with their food plan. It proved to be very effective in keeping them on track. Most were ready to resume their regular eating by the end of the day because they felt bloated and lethargic after indulging themselves.

Unhealthy Eating Habits

Even the most disciplined eater can slip into patterns of imbalance when it comes to food. Following are five of the most common unhealthy eating habits.

1. *Skipping breakfast.* Breakfast really is the most important meal of the day. When you wake up in the morning, your body has been at rest for several hours, and it's ready for fuel. To break your nighttime fast and have energy for the day, you should consume a well-balanced meal. Going without breakfast is not a wise choice. It not only disrupts your metabolism but also causes you to burn fewer calories.

2. *Not having enough fruits and vegetables.* When I taught health classes at a local university, I had the students keep a three-day food log. Talk about an eye-opener! I was shocked to see that many of them

didn't eat one fruit or vegetable in that time frame. Unfortunately, this trend is reflective of our society in general. A large number of Americans don't get an adequate supply of fruits and vegetables. The value of these foods cannot be overemphasized. They provide vitamins, minerals, fiber, and antioxidants, which have been shown to protect against chronic diseases, such as heart disease and cancer. The number of servings you need depends on your age, weight, gender, and activity level. For example, the USDA chart recommends that I have a minimum of two cups of fruit and two and a half cups of vegetables each day.

3. *Eating while doing other activities.* If you eat while watching television, while working, while reading, or even while cooking, you're probably consuming more calories than you realize. Food psychologist Brian Wansink says, "Folks who eat while watching the tube take in 20 to 60 percent more than if they are focused on their food."[11]

4. *Finishing off other people's plates.* Parents, I know how painful it is to throw part of your child's meal away. However, it's better for a little food to go to waste than for ten extra pounds to go to *your* waist! To avoid this scenario, try serving your children smaller portions. They'll be more likely to clean their plates, and you won't feel the need to do it for them.

5. *Eating too much fast food.* After a long day of work, the last thing you want to do is cook. If you're like many Americans, you don't. Instead you drive to your favorite fast-food joint. Yes, fast food is convenient. Yes, it tastes good. But it's extremely high in fat and calories. It's also loaded with salt and provides little nutrition. A number of studies have linked fast food to increased risk of obesity, diabetes, heart disease, and stroke. So it's wise to limit consumption of fast food in order to preserve your health.

Emotional Eating

Sometimes unhealthy eating habits can become chronic. People who continue in these patterns for a long time often form an emotional attachment with food. It becomes much more than just fuel for their bodies. Food becomes their friend.

Nearly all of us battle emotional eating to some degree. God designed us to have strong feelings, so it's natural to seek an outlet for them. However, when we look for fulfillment in the things of the world — such as money, power, sex, or food — we're deceived and start to worship those things, making us guilty of idolatry (Rom. 1:25). Idolatry isn't just bowing down to a statue, carving, or painting. It's looking to something or someone other than the Lord to satisfy us.

When you're tempted to find comfort in food, ask yourself, "What is my need right now? What am I really seeking?" To change your eating habits, you have to change the way you think. Behavior begins with thoughts. For example, when you're depressed, do you head to the refrigerator or pantry? Do you treat yourself with dessert to take the sadness away? Read the following five statements to see if any of them sound familiar.

- "This cake will make me feel better."
- "If I keep eating, I can stop the pain."
- "I don't want to feel empty. Eating makes me feel full and less lonely."
- "Food makes me happy."
- "I need something sweet."

Guilty, right? Yeah, me too (especially that last one).

When you experience an intense emotion — whether it's frustration, sadness, anger, or anxiety — don't head to the refrigerator and stuff your face. Go to God and release your cares to him in prayer. Focus on what the Bible says instead of letting your emotions lead you. Following are two verses that speak of the power of God's love to fulfill you like nothing else can.

- "Satisfy us in the morning with your unfailing love, that we may sing for joy and be glad all our days" (Ps. 90:14).
- "I will praise you as long as I live, and in your name I will lift up my hands. I will be fully satisfied as with the richest of foods; with singing lips my mouth will praise you" (Ps. 63:4 – 5).

Each time you overcome a temptation, you'll find that saying no gets easier. You'll build strength as you stand on God's Word. You'll also grow in self-control. Eventually you'll have a new attitude toward food, one that's healthy and honoring to God. You'll be filled with the measure of all the fullness of God instead of trying to fill yourself with food.

Tips to Improve Your Eating Habits

You develop a healthy lifestyle by making one positive choice after another. Read this list for ideas on how to improve your current habits.

1. *Start your day with breakfast.* Breakfast jump-starts your metabolism and gives you energy. You don't have to eat as soon as you wake up, but do eat something before lunchtime.

2. *Drink water as your main beverage.* Your daily intake of water has a huge effect on your overall health. The body needs water to function properly.

3. *Eat foods as close to their natural state as possible.* Foods God created are designed to satiate your appetite, so when you eat them, your body is satisfied. Fresh is best. Shop at the farmer's market. Cut down on processed items. (If food is in a box or is packaged, it's processed.) Avoid preservatives, chemicals, additives, and anything artificial, including sweeteners.

4. *Limit your intake of added sugars.* Sugar and highly processed foods have little nutritional value and only exacerbate a food addiction. Instead use natural sugars in recipes, such as applesauce, fruit (fresh or dried), 100 percent fruit juices, honey, or unsweetened shredded coconut flakes.

5. *Eat regular meals with snacks in between.* Healthy snacks are good and keep your energy levels high. Skipping meals is counterproductive and leads to overeating, especially at night.

6. *Avoid trigger foods.* Get rid of anything in your house that tempts you. Don't buy a half gallon of ice cream and tell yourself it's for your husband or kids! If the food is in your refrigerator or pantry, you'll probably eat it eventually. If you don't want to throw tempting food away, give it to a neighbor or donate it to a food bank.

7. *Cut up a variety of fresh vegetables and store them in the refrigerator.* Use them as snacks between meals or as appetizers.

8. *Have plenty of fresh fruit on hand.* When you experience a strong craving for something sweet, choose fruit rather than candy, cookies, or ice cream.

9. *Ask a friend to keep you accountable.* Make a commitment to call one another when you're tempted to make an unhealthy choice.

10. *Eat out less frequently.* You'll save calories *and* money. When you do eat out, check the menu ahead of time. (Many restaurants post detailed nutrition facts online.) Decide on a healthy choice before you go.

11. *Visit my Ultimate Daniel Fast website* (www.ultimatedanielfast.com). Find recipes, tips, and cooking videos that will inspire you to eat healthier.

12. *Develop a simple meal plan.* Lack of proper planning often results in poor food choices. One way to counteract this problem is to plan your meals in advance. One system that has worked well for me is to have a theme for each day of the week. For example, the following meal plan is one my family used for a few months.

> Sunday: crockpot meal/soup/chili
> Monday: chicken
> Tuesday: vegetarian
> Wednesday: Mexican
> Thursday: fish
> Friday: homemade pizza
> Saturday: Italian

> I posted the schedule on the front of the refrigerator, so everyone in the family could see it. My daughters could look at the menu instead of asking, "Mom, what's for dinner?" Also, this system resulted in much less stress for me. I wasn't standing in front of the pantry at 5:00 p.m. in a panic, trying to decide what to cook. I highly recommend coming up with a similar plan for your family.

Don't try to implement all twelve of these suggestions at once. Take one or two at a time and commit to working on them. Then, as you make progress, add a couple more. In part 3, "The Program," I'll remind you of some of these tips so you can implement them. Remember, any change you make is moving you in the right direction. Healthy eating is not beyond your reach. *You can do it.* You just need to make up your mind to start.

Honoring God through Exercise

> Lack of activity destroys the good condition
> of every human being, while movement
> and methodical physical exercise save it and preserve it.
>
> — *Plato*

As a young girl, I never thought I was pretty. I remember crying in bed when I was about ten years old because I felt so ugly. My mother tried to comfort me, telling me I *was* pretty, but I didn't believe a word of it. Through angry tears, I said, "You *have* to say that, because you're my mom!" I continued to feel insecure about my looks throughout high school and college, but I never let anyone know it. Instead I found my identity in activities such as academics and sports.

When I was in my mid-twenties, I joined a gym with a friend and started an exercise program. Within a few months, I noticed significant changes in my physical appearance. My muscles became more defined, and I lost inches of fat. I liked the way my body looked, so I poured my time and energy into perfecting it.

Shortly after Justin and I were married, I left my job at an advertising agency to work as a personal fitness trainer. I wanted to take my passion for health to a whole new level. Every day, I spent hours at the gym. If I wasn't training a client or teaching a class, I was going through my own workout. Slowly my desire to be fit became a serious obsession. I pushed myself to be leaner and stronger. I kept trying to lose more weight, even though my body fat level hovered around 12 percent. I counted calories and weighed myself constantly. I worked out religiously because I was afraid of getting fat. My thoughts were consumed by anything and everything related to my body.

If anyone suggested I slow down or take a break, I got defensive. *They don't understand*, I reasoned. People assumed I was anorexic, and I was, only not in a physical sense. I consumed plenty of food, I assure you (sadly, I even have detailed food logs on my computer to verify this fact). However, my spirit was starving.

During this season of my life, my time with the Lord was sporadic at best. Oh, I'd skim a few Scripture verses every day, just to ease my conscience, but my heart was not in it. Bible reading was merely a task to be checked off my mental to-do list. Because I put more energy into my physical core than into my spiritual core, my life became increasingly self-absorbed.

This unhealthy pattern continued for several years. However, in 2009, I was forced to take a six-week hiatus from my exercise regimen because of chronic inflammation in my shins. At first, I welcomed the break. However, after a couple weeks of doing nothing, I started getting restless. And angry. And afraid.

I felt as if God had taken everything from me. The activities I enjoyed — biking, running, lifting weights — all of them were out of the question. I tried brisk walking, but even that was too painful. Since I couldn't exercise, I started to write. It was during this time that God led me to participate in my first Daniel Fast, which led to the publication of my book *The Ultimate Guide to the Daniel Fast*. If I hadn't been forced to rest, the book never would have happened.

I also read the Bible more frequently. God's Word was a soothing balm to the wounds of my heart. Instead of staying bitter, I let go of my frustration. I also came face-to-face with my sin. The following journal entries reveal how the Lord was working in my heart and mind as I meditated on his truth.

August 12, 2009. Exercise has always been a high priority for me, but God is showing me that it is *too* high. I'm trying to rest in him and not seek security in fitness. My identity is not in how I look or what I do. I believe God is allowing me to stay injured to teach me something.

August 13, 2009. I have developed an unhealthy relationship with food and exercise. I'm slowly learning to loosen my grip on these things and let go. I've allowed myself to be bound to them instead of to the Lord, which has resulted in a major stronghold. God has been working on me for a long time, and I'm finally surrendering! He has used my persistent shin splints to get my attention.

August 17, 2009. Physically, I'm resting. I believe God is breaking my addictions one by one. He is helping me find my worth and identity in him alone, not in how I look. My body is his temple, so I need to take care of it, except I don't need to worship it or obsess about how it looks. Scripture memory is becoming a bigger part of my life. God is using his Word to give me strength and victory. I'm so thankful for all that the Lord is teaching me. He is good, and what he is doing is good. I pray that as he continues to transform me, I will be obedient in all he wants me to do.

God's Word exposed the lies I'd believed for years. Psalm 107:13 – 14 says, "They cried to the LORD in their trouble, and he saved them from their distress. He brought them out of darkness, the utter darkness, and broke away their chains." That verse describes what God did for me. When I called out to him for help, he was faithful to rescue me. Even though there are still moments when I struggle with body image (I am a woman, after all), my identity is no longer determined by how much I exercise or what I look like. It's found in Christ alone. My security rests in his unfailing love for me.

The Bible says, "Physical training is good, but training for godliness is much better, promising benefits in this life and in the life to come" (1 Tim. 4:8 NLT). Yes, physical exercise is beneficial, and God is certainly pleased with your efforts to be healthy and strong. However, your goal should not be to sculpt your body or compete in races so other people will admire you. Rather you should exercise to improve your health so you can maintain God's temple and have more energy to serve the Lord and others.

Benefits of Physical Exercise

Americans love fitness, or at least we love the *idea* of it. Every year, we invest billions of dollars in gym memberships, fitness equipment, exercise attire, and workout DVDs. However, you'd never know it by looking at our waistlines. The United States currently ranks as the most obese nation in the world (30.6 percent of population). Although we know exercise is important, many of us don't live like we do. Recent statistics provide evidence of that fact.

- Sixty percent of Americans don't get the recommended amount of physical activity[12] — two hours and thirty minutes of moderate-intensity aerobic activity per week, and muscle-strengthening activities on at least two days each week.[13]

- Approximately 25 percent of people aren't active at all (beyond regular activities of daily living, like cooking, cleaning, and doing household projects and chores).[14]

- The average person spends nearly three hours per day watching television, compared with less than twenty minutes of physical activity.[15]

- More than forty-five million people in the United States have a gym membership, yet only about 33 percent of those people ever use it. The other 67 percent pay an average of fifty-five dollars per month *for nothing*.[16]

Not too many years ago, exercise was built into life. Our ancestors didn't need to go to a gym, because their whole day was a workout. Instead of sitting at a desk, they labored in the fields for eight or more hours every day. Although some people still have physically demanding jobs, the majority of professions today are sedentary. That means we have to be intentional with exercise. Even if you don't like physical activity, your body does. God created your body to *move*. When you exercise on a regular basis, your heart works more efficiently. That's not the only benefit, though. Following are a few ways in which physical activity enhances your health.

1. *It strengthens your bones and muscles.* Julius Wolff, a nineteenth-century German anatomist and surgeon, stated, "Bone in a healthy person will adapt to the loads under which it is placed."[17] This theory, known as Wolff's Law, also applies to your muscles. Because muscles are living tissues, they respond to the stresses and strains placed on them. For example, when you push your body through physical exercise, your muscle mass increases, which results in greater overall strength for your body.

2. *It controls your weight.* Regular exercise enables your body to use excess calories for energy. Cardiovascular activities, such as swimming, running, and biking, increase your rate of breathing, which causes your body to begin burning stored fat as fuel. However, in order to dip into your body's fat stores, you need to perform an aerobic exercise for twenty minutes or more. For less than twenty minutes, your body uses energy from food you ate during the day.

3. *It helps prevent health conditions and diseases.* On the American Heart Association website, you can find a list of more than twenty benefits of exercise.[18] Many are directly related to the prevention of illness. Regular physical activity has been shown to lower blood pressure, improve blood circulation and cholesterol levels, prevent or reverse type 2 diabetes, reduce the risk of stroke, decrease the risk of heart disease and cancer, and enhance your immune system. If more people would engage in moderate cardiovascular activity just three times a week, our nation would see a dramatic drop in these health issues. Type 2 diabetes might even disappear.

4. *It lifts depression.* Research suggests that burning 350 calories three times a week through sustained physical activity can reduce symptoms of depression almost as effectively as antidepressants. Going for a bike ride or walking on the treadmill for thirty minutes also increases levels of soothing brain chemicals that leave you feeling happy and relaxed.[19]

5. *It improves learning.* Exercise increases the level of brain chemicals called growth factors. These chemicals help make new brain cells and establish additional brain-cell connections that enable us to learn. Complicated physical activities, like playing tennis, provide the biggest brain boost. John Ratey, a Harvard Medical School psychiatrist, says, "Exercise is the single best thing you can do for your brain in terms of mood, memory, and learning. Like muscles, you have to stress your brain cells to get them to grow."[20]

6. *It promotes better sleep.* If you have trouble sleeping at night, try exercising regularly. Exercise can help you experience more restful slumber. However, make sure your workout isn't too close to bedtime, or you could have trouble falling asleep because of the increase in your metabolism.

7. *It boosts your energy.* When you feel tired after a long day of work, the last thing you probably want to do is exercise. However, that's the very thing your body needs to recharge! Physical activity delivers oxygen and nutrients to your tissues, which makes your cardiovascular system work more efficiently. The result is energy for your body. Sitting on the sofa won't cut it. Get up and get moving! You'll feel better, physically and emotionally, if you do.

Forms of Exercise

A comprehensive fitness program should include the following three components: cardiovascular exercise, strength training, and core conditioning.

Cardiovascular Exercise

Cardiovascular, or aerobic, exercise is any physical activity that uses large muscle groups and increases your heart rate for a minimum of ten consecutive minutes. The Centers for Disease Control and Prevention recommend at least two and a half hours (150 minutes) of moderate-intensity aerobic activity (for example, brisk walking) or one and a quarter hours (75 minutes) of vigorous-intensity aerobic activity (for example, jogging or running) every week. To prepare yourself for part 3, "The Program," spend some time thinking about the type of aerobic exercises you most enjoy and will fit into your schedule. Do you like to exercise in a group setting? Join a class at a local gym, YMCA, or community center. Do you love the outdoors? Try running, biking, tennis, or hiking. Do you have injuries that make exercise painful? Consider swimming. Think you're too busy to exercise? Put on some comfortable shoes and do the easiest, most convenient exercise of all — walking!

Strength Training

Strength training, also known as weight training or resistance training, is aimed at improving the strength and function of muscles. This form of exercise involves free weights (dumbbells), resistance bands, weight machines, and body-weight exercises, such as push-ups and pull-ups. Dr. Edward R. Laskowski, a physical medicine and rehabilitation specialist at Mayo Clinic, advises, "Two to three strength-training sessions a week lasting just twenty to thirty minutes are sufficient for most people."[21] Since muscle mass naturally decreases with age, strength training should be used to counteract this decline. Dr. Laskowski says, "Strength training can help you preserve and enhance your muscle mass — at any age."[22]

Core Conditioning

Core strength is a key element to any well-rounded fitness program. As we've already seen, the core is the foundation for the body's overall strength. Having well-developed core muscles can improve your power, agility, and balance. To target your core, you need to perform exercises that don't rely on external support (such as lying on a bench or sitting on a weight machine) and that target your abdominals, back, chest, and pelvic muscles. A Pilates exercise class can give you excellent training in this area. If you're not able to attend a class, you can practice the following exercises at home. Your goal should be to complete a core conditioning workout at least two to three times per week. For some examples, see page 90.

In addition to building strength, core conditioning also helps your body become more flexible. Flexibility refers to the total range of motion around a joint. Several factors determine a person's flexibility, including age, gender, activity level, and amount of adipose tissue (fat).[23] Flexibility can be improved through exercise.

Many fitness professionals are big supporters of stretching exercises to increase flexibility. I'm not one of them. Although static stretching can

Core Conditioning

Hip Raises, or Bridges. Lie on your back on the floor with your knees bent. Keep your feet flat on the floor. Focus on using your glutes (butt muscles) to raise your hips, being careful not to activate your lower back to push your hips up. Your body should form a straight line from your shoulders to your knees. Hold the position at the top for three to five seconds, and then slowly lower your hips to the ground.

Planks. Start in a push-up position, with your chest raised off the floor. Slowly lower your body until your forearms are flat on the floor. Curl your toes, and engage your abdominals by tilting your pelvis and pulling your belly button toward your spine. Your body should make a straight line from your heels to the back of your head. Keep your back straight and your hips from sagging. Hold the position for ten to fifteen seconds, and repeat.

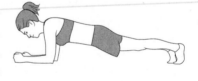

Roll-ups. Lie on your back on the floor. (A) Stretch your arms above your head and extend your legs. Inhale, bring your arms forward, and begin to curl your upper body off the floor. (B) Exhale when halfway up and continue rolling forward to reach your toes. Inhale. Reverse the movement, and exhale as you curl down one vertebra at a time. Return to starting position.

be helpful in some cases, the exercises are often performed incorrectly, causing damage to tissue. According to a study published by the *Journal of Athletic Training*, static stretching before a resistance training workout can result in muscular weakness and should be avoided. Research also shows that it results in decreased athletic performance.[24]

That's why you won't find specific stretching exercises in this program. I believe that the most effective (and safest) way to improve your flexibility is through smooth, controlled movements, such as the core exercises I recommend in this book.

How to Stay Committed to Exercise

When January 1 rolls around each year, gyms all across the country are bursting at the seams. Exercisers come out in droves to get started on their New Year's resolutions. However, by mid February, most of those well-intentioned individuals are nowhere to be found. Their fitness frenzy has fizzled.

One of my favorite quotations is, "If you fail to plan, then you plan to fail." This statement applies to many different areas of life, and it's certainly true with exercise. When you start a program, you're highly motivated, but over time those feelings fade. To stay committed, you should implement the following strategies.

1. *Make an appointment with yourself.* Block out time for exercise. Write it on your calendar, or put it in your phone. You may be tempted to squeeze in an appointment or run errands during that scheduled workout, but don't. That is your time, and you need it. You shouldn't feel guilty for guarding your health.

2. *Develop an exercise regime you can maintain and enjoy.* You'll be much more likely to stick to your program if you like doing it. This may take some trial and error as you experiment with a variety of exercises, classes, fitness centers, workout DVDs, and exercise equipment. If you find that something isn't working, don't give up. Just try a different activity. Sometimes it helps to look up ideas online or find examples in magazines. Keep in mind, though, that another person's plan may not be right for you. As long as you make a concerted effort to tailor your regime to your personality, schedule, interests, and abilities, you'll be more successful than the person who merely forks over a monthly membership fee at a gym.

3. *Start slowly.* Don't try to do too much too quickly. This is especially directed toward men, who often return to the weight room after years of inactivity and expect to pick up where they left off in high school! That's just an injury waiting to happen. Start with light to moderate activity. Then, as you build strength and endurance, you can increase the intensity and frequency of your exercise.

4. *Create a balanced workout schedule.* Some people naturally gravitate toward aerobic exercise, while others enjoy the muscle-building effects of strength training. However, I encourage you to find ways to incorporate *all three* elements of exercise — aerobic activity, strength training, and core conditioning — over the course of a week. To help you achieve this balance, the program in part 3 asks you to focus on aerobic training on Monday, Wednesday, and Friday, strength training on Tuesday and Thursday, and core conditioning on Tuesday and Saturday, with Sunday as a day of rest. Scheduling your exercise this way will have you doing aerobic exercise at least three times a week and strength training at least two times a week, as recommended. In addition, it will help you get accustomed to a routine. When it's Thursday, you can easily remind yourself, "I need to lift weights today!"

5. *Make exercise a habit.* The goal in setting up a weekly plan is to help you make exercise automatic. Do you debate with yourself every morning about whether to shower or brush your teeth? No, of course not. *You just do it.* Years of habit have made the decision for you. Make exercise as natural for you as daily hygiene, so it becomes another important part of your day. Keeping a consistent schedule of exercise also eliminates indecision and even guards against laziness. The six-week program in part 3 will help you develop daily exercise habits you can continue for the rest of your life.

According to the American Heart Association, "For each hour of regular exercise you get, you'll gain about two hours of additional life expectancy, even if you don't start until middle age."[25] Regular exercise is something you can't afford to dismiss. Your life depends on it!

I pray the Lord strengthens you with his mighty power as you care for his temple. May he reward you with long life and excellent health for your obedience to his commands.

CHAPTER 8

Financial Stewardship

In all of my years of service to my Lord, I have discovered
a truth that has never failed and has never been compromised.
That truth is that it is beyond the realm of possibilities
that one has the ability to out give God. Even if I give the whole
of my worth to Him, He will find a way to give back
to me much more than I gave.
— *Charles Spurgeon*

When Mark and Joy first married, their large house contained more than enough room for their small family. Joy had been raised by hospitable parents, so she saw the extra space as an opportunity for guests. Mark, on the other hand, hadn't grown up with frequent visitors in his home. Even though Mark wasn't used to having company, he was open to the idea of it.

After hosting several people in their home, Mark decided to add a guesthouse for missionaries passing through the area. Joy was surprised and thrilled. "I never dreamed Mark would want to build bigger. It had to be God working in his heart."

Mark did most of the work himself, with the help of a few friends. The result was a relaxing place for families on furlough to stay for a night or a few weeks at a time. The Lord began sending people to Mark and Joy right away, and their ministry was established. "It was our way of being involved in missions, keeping in touch with missionaries, and saving them money they would normally spend on hotel and food costs," Joy says.

Although this type of arrangement might seem like a major inconvenience, Mark and Joy consider it a blessing. "It has been fun to see how God has used our home over the last eleven years," Joy says. "We've had missionaries and pastors quite regularly. Churches have held teen retreats and youth overnight events here. One time, God made the house available to a family in need."

It has also been a wonderful opportunity to teach their four children about giving. "God has been so good to allow us the privilege of being able to host so many people," Joy says. "We're thankful for the ability to bless him with our home." Mark and Joy are an example of wise stewardship, and God is being glorified by their commitment to unselfish living and giving.

Stewardship is a term not commonly used in our language today. However, it's important that we understand it. If you're a child of God, you are also a steward of his resources. The Merriam-Webster online dictionary defines *steward* as a "manager" or a "fiscal agent."[1] Another description is, "One who manages another's property, finances, or other affairs."[2] God is the rightful owner of everything, yet he entrusts you and me with the responsibility of looking after his assets. Author Randy Alcorn says, "Stewardship isn't a narrow subcategory of the Christian life. On the contrary, it *is* the Christian life. When we come to Christ, God puts all his resources at our disposal. He also expects us to put all our resources at *his* disposal. That is what stewardship is all about."[3]

Psalm 24:1 says, "The earth is the LORD's, and everything in it, the world, and all who live in it." Nothing you have is truly yours. You may hold a title to a car or a deed to a house, but you don't actually *own* those items. You're merely a manager of them and the other resources God has given you. Your job, then, is to be a wise steward of the Lord's possessions.

Money Matters

More than two thousand verses in the Bible speak about finances, and nearly half of Jesus' parables have to do with possessions. Money matters to God. That means it should matter to us.

People tend to think in extremes when it comes to finances. Some view money as evil and the cause of many of our world's problems. However, money is not the culprit. It's the *love* of money that's destructive. First Timothy 6:10 says, "The love of money is a root of all kinds of evil." Randy Alcorn, author of *Managing God's Money: A Biblical Guide*, says, "The evil doesn't reside in the money. It resides in the men."[4]

Others believe money is the answer for everything. The Bible has strong words for people who put their hope in wealth: "No one can serve two masters. Either you will hate the one and love the other, or you will be devoted to the one and despise the other. You cannot serve both God and money" (Matt. 6:24).

The Bible speaks directly to this issue because our attitude toward finances reflects the condition of our hearts. How we choose to spend money reveals what's most important to us. Colossians 3:2 admonishes, "Set your minds on things above, not on earthly things." In other words, we should invest our affection and energy in people, who are eternal, rather than in accumulating stuff, which is temporal.

God doesn't bless us financially so we can have everything we desire. The Lord filters his assets through our hands so we can make long-term investments for his kingdom. Following are specific ways in which God uses money in your life.

1. *To demonstrate his faithfulness.* In his Sermon on the Mount, Jesus told the disciples not to worry about anything, such as what they would eat, what they would drink, or what they would wear. He said, "Look at the birds of the air; they do not sow or reap or store away in barns, and yet your heavenly Father feeds them. Are you not much more valuable than they?" (Matt. 6:26). Through the money God sends your way, he is proving his love to you, and at the same time assuring you of his provision in your life.

2. *To develop your self-control.* God uses money to teach you to say no when tempted to make unnecessary purchases or unwise investments. He helps you grow in self-control, which is one of the fruits of the Spirit (Gal. 5:22 – 23).

3. *To direct your steps.* Many times, God will lead you in the direction he wants you to go through your finances. Proverbs 20:24 says, "A person's steps are directed by the LORD." Sometimes his guidance is in the form of an unexpected monetary gift. Other times, though, the Lord might use a financial setback to put you on a different path, just like he did for Jackie and Kay.

   Jackie had a high-paying job with Coca-Cola as one of their top route salesmen. After working with the company for seven years, Jackie lost his route to someone with more seniority, and his salary was cut in half. However, Jackie and his wife, Kay, continued to trust God. They also continued to tithe regularly. Soon they began to realize that his new position was actually a huge blessing! With his old route, Jackie was required to put in twelve to fifteen hours a day. With his new route, he got off early enough to pick up their children from school. Kay says, "The best part, though, was that my husband surrendered to preach. Looking back, it would have been so hard to give up that big salary to go into the ministry. However, when we made the choice to trust God, he blessed our family beyond measure!"

4. *To bless you.* One way in which God shows favor to his people is by meeting our monetary needs. Proverbs 10:22 says, "The blessing of the LORD brings wealth." Everything we have comes from God, so our hearts should be filled with gratitude for the Lord's generous supply. Whether you make $30,000 or $300,000, you should thank God for his provision.

5. *To bless others.* You and I are conduits of God's blessings. The gifts we receive from the Lord are not just for our enjoyment. They're also given to us to benefit others. God wants us to be generous with what we have. In his book *The Treasure Principle*, Randy Alcorn states, "God prospers me not to raise my standard of living, but to raise my standard of giving."[5] We are blessed to be a blessing to the people around us. Besides, "giving gifts is more satisfying than receiving them" (Acts 20:35 GW).

During his third missionary journey, Paul visited a number of Gentile churches. His purpose was to collect money for the impoverished believers in Jerusalem, who were struggling financially because of a recent famine.[6] In 2 Corinthians 8:1 – 7, Paul shares how the Macedonian churches overwhelmed him with their giving. He writes, "In the midst of a very severe trial, their overflowing joy and their extreme poverty welled up in rich generosity" (v. 2). The Bible says the Macedonians gave as much as they were able, and even beyond their ability. They were eager to help and even begged Paul for the privilege of "sharing in this service to the saints" (v. 4). What would cause people in such poor conditions to give so much? Paul explains the reason in verse 5: "They gave themselves first of all to the Lord, and then by the will of God also to us."

They gave themselves first of all to the Lord. The Macedonians were extravagant with their financial gifts because they were extravagant in their devotion to God.

Giving is a natural response of love. When you love the Lord, you consider it a joy to give yourself, your time, your possessions, and your finances toward his work. Rather than being bound up in selfishness and greed, you hold everything loosely. You're free to give as God leads.

Later in his letter, Paul commends the Corinthians for their service to the Lord. He says, "Since you excel in everything — in faith, in speech, in knowledge, in complete earnestness and in the love we have kindled in you — see that you also excel in this grace of giving" (2 Cor. 8:7). If you want to excel as the Corinthians did, then you need to understand how God's grace enables you to give.

Principles of Giving

The summer after I graduated from college, I went to New Zealand on a mission trip. Before we left the country to serve overseas, our team met periodically to prepare. During one of our meetings, Todd, our leader, handed each of us a piece of paper. At the top of the paper was a word, followed by a few Bible study questions. Every person received a different word. My word was *grace*. I thought, *I know what grace is. I've got this one covered.* However, when I looked up *grace* in the dictionary, I learned something new.

The definition of grace is "undeserved or unmerited favor." It was the "undeserved" part that jumped out at me. Although I was confident in God's love for me, in the back of my mind, I believed the Lord's affection was dependent on my performance.

Grace isn't something you can earn. The Bible says, "God saved you by his grace when you believed. And you can't take credit for this; it is a gift from God" (Eph. 2:8 NLT). When you put your trust in Jesus as Lord and Savior, his grace is transferred to you. Second Corinthians 8:9 says, "You know the grace of our Lord Jesus Christ, that though he was rich, yet for your sake he became poor, so that you through his poverty might become rich." Jesus gave up everything for us so we could inherit eternal life.

Grace is a gift we receive, but it's also a gift we give. John 1:16 says that we have received "grace upon grace" (ESV) from the Lord. God has poured countless blessings into our lives, and those blessings are meant to be shared with other people. So if you and I want to imitate Christ's example, we must practice giving in God's grace. Following are six Bible verses which give us direction in how we should handle our money and possessions.

1. *Give generously.* "Give generously to the poor, not grudgingly, for the LORD your God will bless you in everything you do" (Deut. 15:10 NLT).

2. *Give secretly.* "When you give to the poor, do not let your left hand know what your right hand is doing, so that your giving will be in secret; and your Father who sees what is done in secret will reward you" (Matt. 6:3 – 4 NASB).

3. *Give regularly.* "On the first day of every week, each one of you should set aside a sum of money in keeping with your income, saving it up, so that when I come no collections will have to be made" (1 Cor. 16:2).

4. *Give joyfully.* "God loves a cheerful giver" (2 Cor. 9:7).

5. *Give voluntarily.* "Each of you should give what you have decided in your heart to give, not reluctantly or under compulsion" (2 Cor. 9:7).

6. *Give sacrificially.* "[Jesus] sat down opposite the treasury, and began observing how the people were putting money into the treasury; and many rich people were putting in large sums. A poor widow came and put in two small copper coins, which amount to a cent. Calling His disciples to Him, He said to them, 'Truly I say to you, this poor widow put in more than all the contributors to the treasury; for they all put in out of their surplus, but she, out of her poverty, put in all she owned, all she had to live on'" (Mark 12:41 – 44 NASB).

People who follow these giving principles make an impact on others around them. People like my husband's friend Mike.

Justin and Mike got to know each other through our Life Group at church. Justin used to tease Mike, who is a professional fisherman, about fishing not being a real sport. Mike was determined to change his mind. He invited my husband to go fishing with him on several occasions, but Justin never went. Finally, Justin gave in. After cruising around the lake in Mike's 250-horsepower bass boat, Justin decided maybe fishing had some merit after all!

Mike took Justin under his wing and taught him the basics: how to read the water and weather; how to use a baitcaster; lure choice and presentation; and, most important, to never give up, even when the fish aren't biting. The more Justin learned, the more he developed a love for fishing. He even competed in a few tournaments. From time to time Justin would say to me, "I'd really like to have my own boat someday."

Not long after Justin met Mike, he learned Mike owned another boat, a much smaller, flat-bottomed one with a six-horsepower engine. When Justin saw the boat sitting in Mike's driveway, he thought, *That's exactly what I want. Not too big. It's the perfect size.* Justin even took pictures with his phone to show me. Even though I tried to sound open to the idea, I knew getting a boat was out of the question. We didn't have anywhere to store it, except for beside the house, which I was *not* in favor of doing.

About two years after the guys started fishing together, I received a phone call from Mike. He said, "As I was praying this morning, I felt like the Lord wanted me to give the little boat to Justin. What are your thoughts on that?" I was taken aback by Mike's offer. Mike had blessed Justin in the past with free poles, lures, and other fishing gear. But his *boat*? "Wow, Mike. That's very generous of you," I said. "I don't know what to say. If God told you to give the boat to Justin, then you should. I certainly don't want to get in the way of what the Lord wants to do." That afternoon, Mike brought the boat over to our house while Justin was at work. He parked it on Justin's side of the garage. I couldn't wait to see the look on Justin's face when he opened the garage door.

When I heard Justin's truck pull in the driveway, I went outside to meet him. As the garage door went up, I could tell by the look on his face he was trying to process the scene before him. "At first, I thought Kristen got the boat for my birthday," he says. "But when I asked her about it, she said, 'It's not from me.'" Justin walked up to the boat with a confused smile. He saw a card on the seat and opened it. Inside was a handwritten message: "God is faithful. Justin, keep moving forward in your walk with the Lord. I am certain he is well pleased with you. Take me fishing in *your* boat sometime. Your brother in Christ, Mike."

Just a few days prior to my conversation with Mike, Justin had expressed his frustration to me about our financial situation. He had recently gotten back into currency trading, hoping to make more money to give to missions. However, nearly every transaction ended up as a loss. "I felt like such a failure," Justin says. "Here I was, trying to do a good thing, a God-honoring thing, and I just didn't understand why I kept losing money. I was using the same system I'd used in the past, only it wasn't working." I could tell he was depressed. That night I began praying for God to do something big in Justin's life.

Justin finally reached his breaking point one day at work. "I was at my desk. No one else was in the office. I felt beaten down, but I sensed God saying, 'Your relationship with me is more important than what you can do for me. I don't need your help.'" Justin lifted his hands in surrender and said out loud, "Okay! I give up!" Immediately he felt a wave of relief wash over him.

A few days later Justin received the boat, an unexpected gift from a good friend. A demonstration of love from his Lord.

"God gave me that boat," Justin says. "The Lord wanted me to know that he can supply *more* than just my needs. He can give me the deepest desires of my heart if I'll just trust him."

One little boat. Three big blessings. Mike experienced the joy of sacrificial giving. Justin was encouraged, his strength renewed. My heart overflowed with praise because of answered prayer. When God prompted Mike to give, he didn't argue. He simply obeyed. Mike told me later, "After I bought the boat, I spent hours getting it back to brand-new condition. I thought it was for me. However, God was using me to prepare the gift for Justin."

The Bible says in Proverbs 11:25, "A generous person will prosper; whoever refreshes others will be refreshed." When you give freely to others, your kindness will be rewarded. Don't give with the motivation to get something in return. Give because Christ gave everything for you.

Principles of Stewardship

Financial managers are responsible for the financial health of an organization. They produce reports, direct investment activities, and develop strategies for the long-term financial goals of their organization. Most managers work full-time and are paid well for their services, on average more than one hundred thousand dollars a year.

God has appointed *you* as financial manager over a portion of his resources. In a sense, he has hired you for this job, and he fully expects you to carry out the responsibilities of your position with due diligence. Your workload, while consistent, isn't too demanding. God promises to guide you by his Spirit and give you wisdom for your work. The best part about being employed by God is the benefits package. His rewards far outweigh any earthly compensation.

Good stewardship begins with a wise financial plan. Such a plan should include the following: (1) creating a budget, (2) reducing your debt, (3) planning for the future, and (4) tithing and giving.

1. Creating a Budget

The word *budget* is scary for some people. Instead of thinking "plan," they envision "pain." They imagine being surrounded by steel bars, not frolicking in a peaceful meadow. I used to view budgeting as a torturous device designed to steal all the fun in life. For years, I refused to live according to a budget. I wanted to be free to purchase items without restriction, but God kept speaking to me about my rebellion in this area. Finally I submitted to him. Since creating a financial plan several years ago, I haven't felt limited at all. In fact, I've experienced more joy and peace in following a budget than I ever did without one! I don't feel like I'm missing out on anything, nor do I feel cheated in any way. Once I tasted the freedom of living within financial boundaries, I was amazed at how palatable it is! Our family has been greatly blessed for making the decision to discipline ourselves in how we spend the Lord's money.

A budget isn't designed to make your life miserable; it is simply a guide to help you manage your money, which is really God's money. Think about it this way: the laws in our country aren't meant to take away our freedom; they're written to *define* our freedom. The same idea applies to sex before marriage. God doesn't forbid it because he wants to rob us of the pleasure of intimacy. Instead he wants us to experience the abundant joy that comes when we save our bodies for our spouses. Boundaries don't limit our freedom; they protect it.

Having a financial plan allows you to save more money for your short- or long-term goals. It can also help you pay off existing debt and reduce wasteful and impulsive purchases. When you create a budget, you take control of your money so it doesn't take control of you.

Before you work on your budget, gather as much of your financial information as you can. Collect records that show income and expenses, such as bank statements, paycheck stubs, utility bills, and credit card bills. Block out at least an hour or two to create your budget. Don't try to throw everything together in fifteen minutes. If you're married, sit down with your spouse and work on it together. It's important that you're both involved in the process. Also, you have a few options when it comes to keeping a record of your budget. You can write it all out by hand in a ledger notebook (you go, Dad!), use personal finance software (such as Quicken), or create your own spreadsheet (such as in Excel). Choose a system that will work for you. When you have your financial information in front of you, then you're ready to begin.

- *Write down all sources of net income.* Your net income is your take-home pay, which is gross income minus deductions, such as taxes. It's best to use net income when creating a financial plan, because that is the money you have available for expenses and investments. Examples of net-income sources are salaries, child support checks, work bonuses, and real estate profits (such as rent paid to you).

- *Make a list of monthly expenses.* Start with the main categories, such as tithe, groceries, utilities, and mortgage payment. Then add smaller categories, such as entertainment, clothing, and gifts. Be sure to include a personal spending category for yourself (and your spouse, if applicable). Justin and I call this expense our "fun money." If he wants to buy fishing lures with that money, he can. Personally, I'm getting a massage or a pedicure! To estimate your expenses, track them for two to three months. This step will give you a more accurate picture of your spending habits over time, so you can make better decisions about how to allocate your resources.

- *Total your monthly income and expenses.* Once you've calculated everything, and your income is more than your expenses, you're off to a good start. If you're spending more money than you're making, then you need to make changes to your budget.

- *Make adjustments to your expenses.* If your expenses are greater than your income, find categories that can be cut completely or at least reduced. For example, if you're in the habit of buying coffee and a bagel every morning before work, resolve to make your own coffee and eat breakfast at home. Go through your budget line by line, and ask yourself the following three questions about each item.
    1. Do I need this item?
    2. Can I substitute a similar item that costs less money?
    3. Will this expense hinder me from achieving my financial goals?

- *Review your budget each month.* Once you've implemented your budget, you'll need to give it a few months to see how it works and whether changes are needed. For example, when Justin and I started our budget, we estimated we'd spend a certain amount on gasoline.

After only a couple of months, though, the price per gallon increased significantly. We exceeded the total we'd allocated, so we needed to adjust our budget for that category. We simply added another fifty dollars for gasoline and decreased our spending in another category.

2. Reducing Your Debt

When it comes to debt, Americans are in sad shape. Look at these statistics from 2012.

- We owe $8.15 trillion in mortgages.
- We have $914 billion in outstanding student loans.
- We are $852 billion in the hole with credit card debt.
- The average student loan debt is $34,703.
- The average credit card debt is $15,328.[7]

Being in debt is like trying to exercise with a 350-pound weight strapped to your chest. It doesn't work, and you *will* get hurt. The Bible makes it clear that debt is damaging, not only to your finances but also to your spiritual growth. When you choose to be in debt, you choose to limit your freedom. According to the Bible, you are "a slave to the lender" (Prov. 22:7).

One of the main disadvantages of being strapped financially is it limits God's work in your life. Indebtedness keeps you from being free to serve others and hinders the effectiveness of your witness for Christ. For example, what if the Lord has plans for you to travel on mission trips with your family, but you can't afford it because of your foolish spending habits? Your debt can cause you to miss out on God's best for your life. If you're in that situation right now, don't despair! God wants to help you. However, you have to accept his assistance and make changes in the way you spend his money.

Your first step toward financial freedom is to make at least the minimum payments on all outstanding bills. That will keep you from digging yourself into a deeper financial hole. Next, you need to begin accumulating an emergency fund of one thousand dollars.[8] The money in this fund should be set aside for unforeseen events, such as a job loss, medical expenses, or major repairs on your car. It's for *emergencies*, not for new clothes or a vacation. The purpose of the emergency fund is to have money available when you need it, so you don't have to use your credit card. After your fund reaches one thousand dollars, then you're ready to focus on removing your debt.

Financial counselor Dave Ramsey suggests using his debt snowball plan to get your finances in order. He explains, "When you were a kid rolling a snowball in the back yard, the best way to do it was to pack some snow into a tight ball, then start rolling it through the yard. Your snowball would become a snow boulder much quicker than it would if you just built it up by hand."[9] The idea behind Ramsey's plan is to build momentum by paying as much as possible on one bill at a time, while paying the minimum amount on the rest. Following is how the debt snowball works, according to Ramsey in his bestselling book *The Total Money Makeover*.[10]

1. *List your debts in order from the smallest to the largest according to the amount owed.* Write down everything — school loans, credit card bills, small business loans, home equity loans, mortgage payments, and/or car payments — in order from the smallest to the largest.

2. *Pay off your smallest debt first.* Even though it may seem counterintuitive to pay the smallest debt before the larger ones, especially if the smaller debt is at a lower interest rate, Ramsey says, "You need some quick wins in order to stay pumped enough to get out of debt completely. Paying off debt is not always about math. It's about motivation. Personal finance is 20 percent head knowledge and 80 percent behavior. When you start knocking off the easier debts, you will see results and you will stay motivated to dump your debt."[11] Make the minimum payments on all of the debts except the smallest one, and attack that with a vengeance. Once that debt is paid, focus on doing the same with the next bill. Continue this pattern until all your debts are paid.

Debt may seem unavoidable in our society, but it's not. The Bible advises, "Owe nothing to anyone — except for your obligation to love one another" (Rom. 13:8 NLT). God does not command you to do something that's impossible. You can become debt free, if you're not already, and you can *continue* that lifestyle. God's plan is not for you to be a slave to your debtors. He wants you to enjoy freedom in Christ, which includes freedom in your finances.

3. *Planning for the Future*

The third step in tackling your finances is to plan for the future. Once your emergency fund is in place and your debts are gone, follow these additional steps recommended by Dave Ramsey.

1. *Save three to six months' worth of expenses.* While having a thousand dollars in an emergency fund is a good start, that account can be depleted quickly through unexpected expenses. What if you get injured and can't work for six months? Your goal in this step is to set aside enough money in savings to carry you through a period of unemployment or some other major financial crisis.

2. *Save 10 to 15 percent of income toward retirement.* Ramsey recommends investing 15 percent of your household income into Roth IRAs and pre-tax retirement plans. Prepare now for the years ahead when you're no longer employed.

3. *Save toward college.* Education is expensive, and it's not getting any cheaper. When I attended college, I went to a private Christian school. Although my parents helped me pay for tuition, they weren't able to cover all my expenses. I worked to make up the difference, but it still wasn't enough. I had to take out a student loan. Thankfully, my loan was manageable. However, many students graduate with a shockingly high amount of debt, especially those who go on to postgraduate work. Don't wait until your children are in high school to start saving for their college years. Begin when they're born. Have a separate fund designated for their education. The best way to save, according to Dave Ramsey, is through Education Savings Accounts (ESAs) and 529 plans.[12]

4. *Pay off your mortgage early.* Justin and I both had school loans when we got married. For the first few years, we paid only the minimum amounts each month. As soon as our income allowed, we put extra money toward our loans to pay them off as quickly as possible. When we bought our first house in 2002, our school debt was gone. To buy our home, we borrowed $75,000, which made our mortgage payment around $475. We paid as much as we could each month, sometimes doubling or tripling the amount. With God's help, Justin and I paid off our mortgage in eight years. When we made that final payment, I felt like dancing! It was as if a large boulder had been taken off my shoulders. Our family still lives in the same home, and even though there are times when I entertain the idea of a larger house, I don't want to make that move until we can pay cash for it. There's no way I'd choose to be enslaved again. Financial freedom is much too sweet. If you have a mortgage, do what you can to pay it off early.

4. Tithing and Giving

The practice of tithing goes back to ancient times. In the Bible, Mosaic law required the Israelites to give a tithe, or one-tenth, of the produce of their land and livestock to support the priesthood. According to the Bible, "A tithe of everything from the land, whether grain from the soil or fruit from the trees, belongs to the LORD; it is holy to the LORD" (Lev. 27:30). The money was to be given to the priests for their service in God's temple (Num. 18:21).

We see the command to tithe repeated in Deuteronomy 12:11, where God instructs the Israelites, "You must bring everything I command you — your burnt offerings, your sacrifices, your tithes, your sacred offerings, and your offerings to fulfill a vow — to the designated place of worship, the place the LORD your God chooses for his name to be honored" (NLT). Once they reached the Promised Land, the people were to worship God in various ways, and tithing was one of them.

The Bible provides many examples of this practice and frequently encourages us to give to the Lord. Yet many Christians *don't* tithe. Some may not be aware of God's instructions on this matter. Most, though, know what the Bible says about tithing; they just choose not to do it. Malachi was a prophet whom God called to confront the people of Judah with their sins, specifically the sin of not tithing. Look at what God says in Malachi 3:7 – 9:

> "Ever since the time of your ancestors you have turned away from my decrees and have not kept them. Return to me, and I will return to you," says the LORD Almighty.
> "But you ask, 'How are we to return?'
> "Will a mere mortal rob God? Yet you rob me.
> "But you ask, 'How are we robbing you?'
> "In tithes and offerings. You are under a curse — your whole nation — because you are robbing me."

God called the people to stop ignoring his command to tithe and to repent of their sin. He assured them their obedience would be rewarded: "Bring the whole tithe into the storehouse, that there may be food in my house. Test me in this," says the LORD Almighty, "and see if I will not throw open the floodgates of heaven and pour out so much blessing that there will not be room enough to store it" (Mal. 3:10).

When Jason and Gretchen were married, their goal was to be debt free.

"We both wanted to be good stewards of God's blessings," Gretchen says. They worked part-time jobs while in college to avoid school loans. They saved what money they could and paid for their cars in cash. They also tithed regularly. The only money Jason and Gretchen owed was the mortgage on their house.

After Gretchen graduated from college, she started teaching. She and Jason committed to applying 50 percent of her income toward their debt. "I thought we were doing a great job," Gretchen says. However, when she got pregnant with their first child, it put a dent in their financial plan.

Gretchen expressed to Jason her desire to be a stay-at-home mom, but he didn't think they could afford to lose her income. Gretchen says, "So I followed my husband's leadership and continued working and praying about it."

Within six months, Jason knew he'd made the wrong decision. Gretchen immediately gave notice at work, but she still had five months of teaching to finish out her contract. "We knew it would affect our ability to pay off the house, but we believed God would help us," Gretchen says.

A few weeks later Gretchen received an unexpected check in the mail for ten thousand dollars. Her uncle had recently passed away and left her the money in his will. Jason and Gretchen tithed on the full amount, giving one thousand dollars to the Lord. A few months later they received another ten thousand dollars from her uncle's estate, and they tithed again. "We knew the Lord was confirming our decision for me to stay home," says Gretchen.

Just as Gretchen's five-month teaching stint was coming to an end, Jason lost his job. "We both struggled with feeling overwhelmed," Jason says. "However, we prayed and sought the Lord." In less than a month, Jason found work. Also, the house that Gretchen's uncle had lived in sold, which meant they inherited another forty thousand dollars! After receiving that check, they were able to pay off their house. Jason says, "The money we entrusted to the Lord was given back to us many times over. Our God is a God of supply, and he faithfully gives to those who trust him with their finances."

One of my favorite tithing stories in the Bible occurs in 2 Chronicles 29 – 31:5, when Hezekiah was king of Judah. Just to give you some background on Hezekiah's character, read what 2 Kings 18:5 – 6 says about him: "Hezekiah trusted in the LORD, the God of Israel. There was no one like him among all the kings of Judah, either before him or after him. He held fast to the LORD and did not stop following him; he kept the commands the LORD had given Moses." Hezekiah was a man who was serious about following God.

During the first month of his reign, Hezekiah gave the order to open the doors of the temple, which had been nailed shut by Hezekiah's father, Ahaz. The people were instructed to purify themselves from their idolatrous ways and to serve the Lord wholeheartedly. Hezekiah also reinstated the practice of tithing: "He required the people in Jerusalem to bring a portion of their goods to the priests and Levites, so they could devote themselves fully to the Law of the LORD. When the people of Israel heard these requirements, they responded generously by bringing the first share of their grain, new wine, olive oil, honey, and all the produce of their fields. They brought a large quantity — a tithe of all they produced" (2 Chron. 31:4 – 5 NLT).

I want you to notice three important points in this passage.

1. Being fully devoted to the Lord included the practice of tithing.
2. When the people became aware of what God expected, they responded immediately.
3. They gave generously to the Lord — a tithe of all they produced.

Tithing is a necessary discipline for good biblical stewardship. Everything we have belongs to the Lord. Psalm 50:10 says, "Every animal of the forest is mine, and the cattle on a thousand hills." God wants us to tithe, not because he needs our money but because tithing teaches us to seek him first in our lives. When we refuse to obey God's command, we rob him, making us guilty of the grandest larceny of all.

Even if money is tight, honor your commitment. As my pastor always says, "God can do more with 90 percent than you can do with 100 percent." Also, don't wait until all your bills are paid to give. Return God's money to him *first*. Proverbs 3:9 says, "Honor the LORD with your wealth and with the firstfruits of all your produce" (ESV). Where should you give your tithes? In Malachi 3:10, God told the people to bring the tithe into the storehouse, meaning the temple. I believe the Lord intends your tithe to be given to the church where you attend. Many Christians disagree on this issue, just as they debate about whether the tithe should be based on their gross or net income. Personally, I think the tithe amount should be calculated on the total amount you bring home. Every cent you make is God's, so it just wouldn't be right to short-change him by tithing off the net.

If you have trouble releasing control in this area, Isaiah 49:23 has a promise for you: "I am the LORD; those who hope in me will not be disappointed." God is faithful. When you return to God what is rightfully his, you won't be left high and dry. You'll experience wonderful downpours of blessing!

The Joy of Giving

God wants you to enjoy the resources he has given you. His desire for you is abundant life in him, but he doesn't want your stuff to get in the way. His instruction is, "Keep your lives free from the love of money and be content with what you have" (Heb. 13:5).

Contentment is the key to being an effective steward of God's property. The apostle Paul spoke about how he learned true satisfaction in life. He wrote, "I know what it is to be in need, and I know what it is to have plenty. I have learned the secret of being content in any and every situation, whether well fed or hungry, whether living in plenty or in want" (Phil. 4:12). What was the secret Paul discovered? "I can do all this through him who gives me strength" (v. 13). You gain contentment by placing your confidence in the Lord. When you look to God to guide your steps and direct your giving, you will find strength in him.

Paul also wrote to Timothy, "Godliness with contentment is great gain. For we brought nothing into the world, and we can take nothing out of it. But if we have food and clothing, we will be content with that" (1 Tim. 6:6 – 8). How would Paul advise Christians today to be content with simple living, especially considering our materialistic, self-indulgent culture? The IVP New Testament Commentary gives this answer: "Certainly not by accepting the standards set by this world. Paul suggests that an eternal perspective and an attitude of detachment toward things are prerequisites. As an eternal perspective develops, dependence on things material will decline."[13]

Wise stewards of God's assets find joy in distributing resources to people in need. Such people are rich in good deeds, and they're always willing to share. They lay up for themselves treasures in heaven and take hold of the life that is *truly* life (1 Tim. 6:17 – 19).

Barry still remembers the shame he felt as a young boy when bill collectors knocked at their door. He vowed never to be like his parents with his own finances.

As a young man, Barry worked hard and quickly climbed the corporate ladder. His job in the sales industry required frequent travel, so Barry was often separated from his wife, Judy, and their three children for long stretches of time. However, Barry was determined to keep his promise to himself. He poured all his energy into stockpiling for the future. "Accumulating money was my focus," he says.

When Barry was in his forties, he, Judy, and the kids moved to Buffalo, New York. They began attending a local church, and Barry joined a men's Bible study group. One evening as the men were meeting, they each shared their salvation experiences. When it was Barry's turn, he admitted he wasn't 100 percent committed to the Lord. "I knew *about* God, but I didn't *know* him. I was afraid of not having any fun if I gave my life completely to him," he says. That night Barry became a follower of Jesus Christ. "I'd been sitting on the banks of the Jordan River too long," he says. "It was time to cross over to the Promised Land."

Everything about Barry changed when he became a Christian, including his attitude toward finances. "I realized my money was really *God's* money," Barry says. Instead of continuing to hoard, Barry learned to give. "I became much more generous to people's needs," he says. Barry recalls one incident in which the Lord prompted him to help a stranger at a gas station who asked him for money. Barry could tell he was desperate. He filled up the man's car and gave him a few dollars so his family could get something to eat.

Since Barry's retirement, God has opened up many opportunities for him to serve in the community. Every Tuesday, he drives a van to shuttle volunteers around town. Because of Barry's commitment, many senior citizens who don't have transportation are able to help in local hospitals and senior centers. On Thursdays, Barry also gives his time to deliver food for the local Meals on Wheels program. "Every time I give — whether it's my time, talents, or treasure — it's always replenished to me in some way," he says.

For many years, Barry worshiped the almighty dollar. Today he worships Almighty God. "Money has lost its importance to me. It has become more of a hobby instead of a driving force in my life," he says. "I used to put all my security in money. Now I put it in the Lord." What advice would Barry give to someone reluctant to trust God with their finances? "Don't be afraid. What you give will be returned to you. God will reward you for your obedience."

Barry has learned that joy in life is found in giving yourself to God's work, not in amassing large amounts of money. He now realizes that people who are truly wealthy in this world find their contentment in Christ. My prayer is that you too will experience the satisfaction that comes when you trust God completely with all you have. May you be filled with much joy as you give faithfully to his work!

CHAPTER 9

Serving Others

Living as a servant is everyone's calling.
Service to God and other people yields
the highest rewards that heaven holds.
— *Ron Marinari*

It was a bitter cold day in December. The temperature was below freezing, and the windchill was dangerously low. I had just picked up my daughter, Jocelyn, from preschool when I spotted an elderly lady walking along the sidewalk. All bundled up in a parka, she was doing her best to shield herself from a fierce headwind. She was tiny and couldn't have weighed more than one hundred pounds.

As I drove past her, I sensed the Lord saying, "You should stop." I kept driving. *I'm too busy,* I thought. *It's inconvenient. I just want to get home for lunch.* After about thirty seconds, though, my desire to obey the prompting of the Holy Spirit was greater than the selfishness of my flesh. I turned the car around. I headed toward the woman and pulled up beside her.

"It's too cold for anyone to be out in this weather. Can I give you a ride?" I asked.

"Yes, that would be nice," she said quietly. Her nose was dripping, so I quickly handed her a tissue and helped her into the front seat. Once she got settled, I introduced myself and my daughter. When I asked her name, she said, "Georgia."

Georgia was on her way to the bank, which was more than a mile away. As I drove in that direction, I learned a little about my new friend. She was from California. She'd never married or had children but had worked for many years as a kindergarten teacher. Judging by her kind disposition and warm personality, I was sure she was an excellent one.

After we left the bank, I took Georgia home. I was surprised to learn she lived in our neighborhood. Georgia invited us to come inside her house.

What I saw when she opened the front door caused a deep ache in my heart. In the middle of Georgia's living room were at least fifty stuffed animals, all placed neatly in rows, facing a small television — much like a classroom setting. Georgia introduced me to her "babies" and took great pride in showing them off. Most of the animals were battery-powered, and they would sing or talk at the push of a button. It made me sad to think the voices of those animals were probably the only sounds that broke the silence in Georgia's world.

Next, she led us into her kitchen. The first thing I noticed was a small baker's rack, which displayed a gorgeous set of dark-red dishes. Since I love to cook, I was fascinated by her collection. The second detail that caught my eye wasn't something she had but rather something she didn't have — a refrigerator. Tears flooded my eyes, and a lump formed in my throat.

"Georgia, what do you do for food? You do eat, don't you?" I asked.

"Yes, when I'm out walking," she answered. Georgia told me that she would grab something at a restaurant or grocery store if she got hungry.

If, I thought.

Georgia then showed us her sunroom. Thick black plastic covered the windows. She pulled aside one "curtain" to reveal what was behind it. Two cans of fruit cocktail and one can of mandarin oranges sat on the window-sill. It was her pantry.

As Georgia wrapped up the tour of her house, I told her I'd come to see her again. After giving Georgia a hug, I said goodbye, and Jocelyn and I left. On our way home, I called my husband at work to tell him what had happened. "Justin, we have to do something," I said. God had put this precious lady in my path for a reason, and I knew it wasn't just to give her a ride.

That night, the Feola family had a very special guest for dinner.

In this chapter, we'll explore how love is essential in service, how we should serve, the servant's wardrobe, and why we need to serve.

Labor Prompted by Love

At another special meal more than two thousand years ago, Jesus sat down with twelve of his closest friends for their last supper together. However, the purpose was more than fellowship. Jesus wanted to teach his disciples an important lesson in leadership.

John 13:4 says Jesus did something highly unusual that night. "He got up from the meal, took off his outer clothing, and wrapped a towel around his waist." He then poured water into a basin and began washing the disciples' feet.

Peter was shocked and offended. He couldn't stand the sight of his Master acting like a servant! One commentary notes, "It would have been appropriate for one of the disciples to have washed Jesus' feet, but the reverse is intolerable."[1]

"Lord, are you going to wash my feet?" Peter asked.

Jesus, realizing how scandalous his act seemed to the disciples, said, "You do not realize now what I am doing, but later you will understand."

"No," Peter objected, "you shall never wash my feet."

Jesus answered, "Unless I wash you, you have no part with me."

After Jesus finished cleaning the disciples' feet, "he put on his clothes and returned to his place." He said, "Now that I, your Lord and Teacher, have washed your feet, you also should wash one another's feet. I have set you an example that you should do as I have done for you" (John 13:14 – 15). Jesus wasn't encouraging his friends to open a foot-washing clinic. He was showing them how they would be most effective in sharing the gospel.

Serving others is a spiritual discipline which can be defined as action motivated by love. First John 3:18 says, "Let's not merely say that we love each other; let us show the truth by our actions" (NLT). Sincere affection is shown, not through what we say, but through what we do. It's true: actions speak louder than words.

The ultimate expression of love was shown when God sent his Son, Jesus, to die on the cross. The Bible says, "Very rarely will anyone die for a righteous person, though for a good person someone might possibly dare to die. But God demonstrates his own love for us in this: While we were still sinners, Christ died for us" (Rom. 5:7 – 8). Although we didn't deserve salvation, Jesus took the punishment for all of our wrongdoing — past, present, and future — so we could escape eternity in hell and live with him forever.

Jesus showed us by his example that a life of service is a life of sacrifice: "The Son of Man did not come to be served, but to serve, and to give his life as a ransom for many" (Matt. 20:28). Being a servant requires laying down your pride and taking up humility. It demands your time and frequently involves your money or possessions. However, these things amount to nothing when you consider what Jesus did. John 15:13 says, "Greater love has no one than this: to lay down one's life for one's friends." You and

I may not be called to give our lives for someone, but we *are* called to give ourselves to serving them. Our job is to love with the love God has given us. Jesus said in John 13:34 – 35, "Love one another. As I have loved you, so you must love one another. By this everyone will know that you are my disciples, if you love one another." Your acts of service provide outward evidence of your inward love for God.

When Jesus was asked, "What is the greatest commandment in the Law?" he answered, " 'Love the Lord your God with all your heart and with all your soul and with all your mind.' This is the first and greatest commandment. And the second is like it: 'Love your neighbor as yourself' " (Matt. 22:37 – 39). In other words, you love others best when you love God most.

Love prompted the King of Kings to humble himself and wash the disciples' dirty feet. Love led our Lord to the cross. Love is what we need to serve others.

How to Serve Others

When you accept Jesus' payment for your sin, the Bible says, you're born again. You become a new creation in Christ (2 Cor. 5:17), and God's love is poured into your heart through the Holy Spirit (Rom. 5:5). One transformation that occurs upon salvation is a deeper spiritual sensitivity. You learn to respond as Christ would to someone in need. Instead of making excuses, you get involved. You do what you can to help. You reach out because God's love compels you to act (2 Cor. 5:14).

When it comes to loving others, though, you can't do it in your own power. Following are three truths to keep in mind. You serve people (1) in God's strength, (2) with the gifts God has given you, and (3) for God's glory. Let's take a quick look at each of these points.

1. *Serving in God's strength.* The desire to help people is not natural. It's *super*natural, which means you must have God's help. The Bible says, "If anyone serves, they should do so with the strength God provides" (1 Peter 4:11).

2. *Serving with the gifts God has given you.* God has equipped you with certain gifts he intends for you to use for his glory. His instruction is, "Each of you should use whatever gift you have received to serve others, as faithful stewards of God's grace in its various forms"

(1 Peter 4:10). If you're in Christ, the Holy Spirit empowers you to serve.

3. *Serving for God's glory.* Our acts of service should be prompted by a sincere desire to help people, not to gain recognition or applause. We should serve because we love God and want him to be glorified. First Peter 4:11 says, "If anyone speaks, they should do so as one who speaks the very words of God. If anyone serves, they should do so with the strength God provides, so that in all things God may be praised through Jesus Christ. To him be the glory and the power for ever and ever. Amen."

If you want to serve others in Jesus' name, you have to be willing to roll up your sleeves and get dirty. Be prepared to encounter situations that are unpleasant and uncomfortable. Be willing to extend a helping hand to someone who doesn't deserve it. But when God brings needy people your way, don't complain. Instead offer hospitality to them without grumbling (1 Peter 4:9). Maintain an attitude of gratitude as you serve.

Dressed and Ready for Service

When it comes to physical exercise, comfortable clothing is best. The wrong outfit can hinder your movement and slow you down. For example, running is more difficult if you're wearing jeans instead of sweatpants or shorts. Spiritual exercise is no different. You're most effective when fitted with the appropriate attire, when you're clothed with the Lord Jesus Christ (Rom. 13:14). Clothing yourself with Christ means putting on his character, acting like he would act, and serving as he would serve. Colossians 3:12 lists five garments in a servant's wardrobe.

1. *Compassion.* "Jesus went through all the towns and villages, teaching in their synagogues, proclaiming the good news of the kingdom, and healing every disease and sickness." Matthew 9:36 says when "he saw the crowds, he had compassion on them." Jesus loved people, so he was deeply affected by their pain. We should follow Jesus' example of comforting and caring for those who are hurting.

2. *Kindness.* The Bible says, "Love is kind" (1 Cor. 13:4). We show God's love to others when we are kind to them. In a letter to the church at Thessalonica, the apostle Paul said, "Always strive to do what is good

for each other and for everyone else" (1 Thess. 5:15). When you're kind to people, you esteem them and build them up. Kindness is also important because it honors God and draws people to him.

3. *Humility.* Jesus Christ is the ultimate example of humility. He took the very nature of a servant by submitting to the worst form of punishment—death by crucifixion. Jesus made himself nothing to give us everything, even eternal life. We should have the same attitude as Christ (Phil. 2:5). Does that mean we have to die for people? Probably not. However, we are to imitate Christ's humble spirit and his willingness to sacrifice. Paul gives us three specific instructions in Philippians 2:3–4.

   • "Do nothing out of selfish ambition or vain conceit" (v. 3).

   • "Value others above yourselves" (v. 3).

   • "Don't look out only for your own interests, but take an interest in others, too" (v. 4 NLT).

   In his book *Celebration of Discipline*, Richard Foster says, "Of all the Spiritual Disciplines, service is the most conducive to the growth of humility."[2] Helping others forces us to lay down our pride so we can lift others up. God commands us to love others humbly, as Jesus did. "Even the Son of Man did not come to be served, but to serve, and to give his life as a ransom for many" (Mark 10:45).

4. *Gentleness.* As followers of Christ, we should "pursue righteous-ness, godliness, faith, love, endurance and gentleness" (1 Tim. 6:11). In this verse, the Greek word for "gentleness" is *prautes*, which is translated as "mildness or meekness." Meekness is not weakness, as is commonly believed. A person who is meek possesses a gentle strength—power with reserve and control. Jesus was the epitome of this character trait. He said, "Take my yoke upon you and learn from me, for I am gentle and humble in heart, and you will find rest for your souls" (Matt. 11:29). The best way to develop gentleness in your life is to learn from the Master.

5. *Patience.* The Bible commands, "Be patient with everyone" (1 Thess. 5:14). That's right. You read that correctly—*everyone*. No exceptions. I must admit, this particular character trait is a constant challenge for me. When I feel stressed, I have a tendency to get snippy with others, forgetting that "whoever is patient has great understanding, but one who is quick-tempered displays folly" (Prov. 14:29). The only way to grow in this area is to face situations that test you! You learn

to overcome the temptation to lose control by trusting in the Lord and leaning on his unlimited patience.

Why We Need to Serve

One day when Jesus was walking, he came across a blind man, who sat by the roadside begging. The man had lived in darkness since birth. He hadn't ever seen the sun; he had only felt its warmth on his face. He had never looked into the eyes of another person; he had only heard people's voices in his ears. When Jesus saw the blind man, he was filled with compassion and was moved to action. John 9:6 says, "[H]e spit on the ground, made some mud with the saliva, and put it on the man's eyes." Then Jesus told him to go wash in the Pool of Siloam. The man did as Jesus said and was miraculously healed.

The people in the town were astounded, but many of the Pharisees remained skeptical. They questioned the man and were ruthless in their accusations of deception. They even called for the man's parents to find out if he truly had been born blind! Eventually the Pharisees became so incensed that they threw the man out of the temple.

"Jesus heard that they had thrown him out, and when he found him, he said, 'Do you believe in the Son of Man?'

" 'Who is he, sir?' the man asked. 'Tell me so that I may believe in him.'

"Jesus said, 'You have now seen him; in fact, he is the one speaking with you.'

"Then the man said, 'Lord, I believe,' and he worshiped him" (John 9:1 – 41).

Who in your life has a need God wants you to meet? Maybe it's your neighbor — a single mom with three kids. Or perhaps it's a coworker with a car in the shop who could use a ride home. When you reach out to someone in love, you open the door for the Holy Spirit to work in that person's life. Don't view any opportunity to serve as trivial or unimportant. You never know what God is doing behind the scenes to soften someone's heart toward him.

When Jesus was in Capernaum, a large crowd gathered in the house where he was to hear him teach. Four men came carrying a paralyzed man on a mat. They had hoped to lay him before Jesus, but there was no room. However, these men wanted desperately to help their friend. They climbed onto the roof and lowered him through the tiles, right in front of the crowd. Right in front of Jesus.

Jesus, seeing their faith, said to the paralyzed man, "Son, your sins are forgiven.... I tell you, get up, take your mat and go home" (Mark 2:5, 11). The man stood up, gathered his mat, and walked out in full view of everyone. The crowd was amazed and gave praise to God. They said, "We have never seen anything like this!" (Mark 2:12).

I love the determination of the four men in this story. They wouldn't let anything stop them from bringing their friend to Jesus.

I also love how Jesus responded to their disruption. Instead of being offended, Jesus stopped what he was doing and immediately addressed the man's needs. He healed him physically and spiritually.

Go and Do Likewise

The day Georgia climbed into my car, she also made her way into my heart. She's a sweet lady who is also extremely witty. She likes stuffed animals, fancy clothes and hats, and VHS movies. Her favorite pastime is shopping at the Goodwill store. She adores my daughters and reminds me often that Justin is the greatest husband in the world. (She's right!) Georgia, once a stranger, is now my friend.

Drive down any street, and you'll see a Georgia. In fact, you'll see hundreds and thousands of them in any given day. People who are cold, not physically but spiritually. People wandering alone in the world and fighting with all their strength against the harsh realities of life. God wants to rescue them, and he invites *you* to get involved. He says, "Make the most of every opportunity" (Eph. 5:16 NLT). So prepare your heart for action by beginning each day in the Word. Keep your eyes and ears open, and pray for God's wisdom to recognize his hand at work. Also, don't be upset when your schedule gets interrupted. Often what appears to be an inconvenience is actually a divine appointment. If the Holy Spirit prompts you to help someone, do it. Your simple act of kindness could yield eternal rewards.

As a servant of the Most High God, you should be on the alert for spontaneous opportunities to help others. That's part of what it means to be "led by the Spirit" (Rom. 8:14). When your heart is sensitive to what God is doing, you're more aware of people's needs. In addition to watching for chances to perform random acts of kindness, look for ways to exercise your serving muscles on a regular basis. Teach a Sunday school class, tutor a child, volunteer at a food bank, serve on a board, lead a Bible study, visit prisoners or shut-ins, raise money for charity — there are a number of ways to get involved in your church, school, or community. In part 3, "The Program," I'll give you a practical idea each Saturday on how you can serve.

God is pleased when you show love to people. Even if no one says thank you for what you've done, your Father in heaven sees. As Ron Marinari wrote, "To be a servant does involve sacrifice. And those who benefit from our service may not always offer thanks. But when God examines the works of our hands, His reward will encompass eternity."[3]

Galatians 6:9 says, "Let us not become weary in doing good, for at the proper time we will reap a harvest if we do not give up." May your heart always be ready and willing to serve in God's strength. I pray you'll keep in step with the Spirit so you can receive the wonderful harvest that awaits!

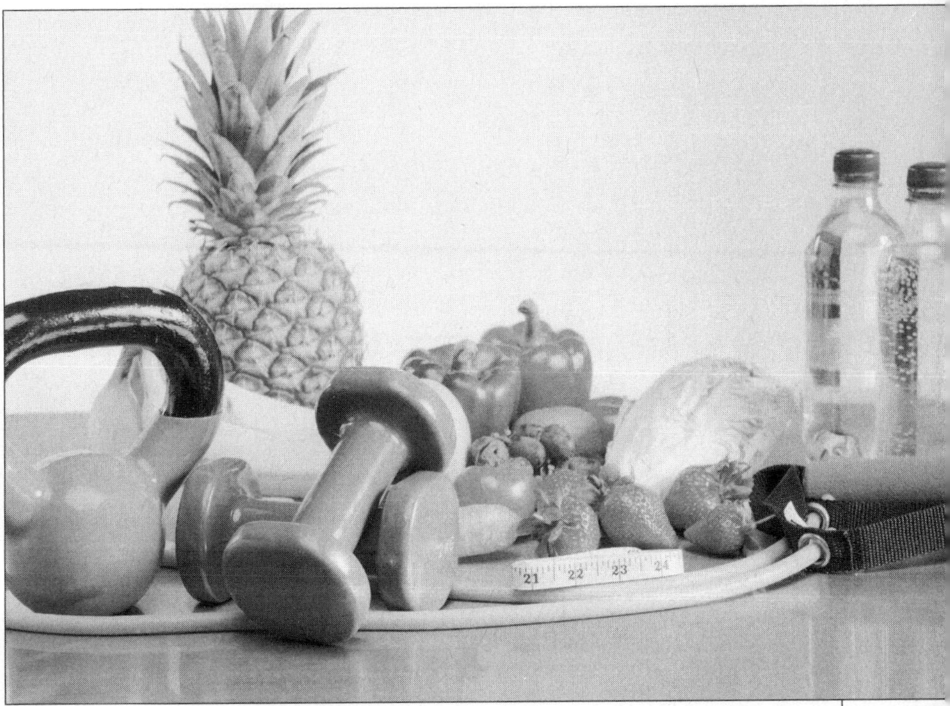
21
22
23
24

PART 3

the PROGRAM

Plan for Success

*Always bear in mind that your own resolution to succeed
is more important than any other one thing.*
—Abraham Lincoln

George Washington is often hailed as one of our nation's most successful military leaders. However, did you know that Washington *lost* more battles than he *won*? "Despite this roster of tactical defeats, Washington brought many important characteristics to his military command. His ability to rally men under fire, his ability to sustain the Continental Army's morale, his administrative talents, and his grasp of the larger strategic imperatives all made Washington the great general that history remembers and celebrates."[1]

Throughout his life, Washington exuded discipline, and he began practicing it at a young age. When he was only twelve years old, he copied the "110 Rules of Civility and Decent Behavior in Company and Conversation," in the hope of one day becoming a Virginian gentleman. Years later, when Washington served as general of the Continental Army, he gave his soldiers six rules for sound military strategy. Some of the guidelines apply directly to military combat, but two apply to any situation requiring courage, such as embarking on this six-week program.

1. Nothing is so important in war as an undivided command.
2. Never do what the enemy wishes you to do.[2]

Great advice, don't you think? Your success in this program will be determined by your level of obedience to God's Word and how well you implement the tools in this book. In addition, you need to apply the wisdom Washington instilled in his men: Don't listen to the voice of the Enemy.

Tune your ears to the voice of your Holy Commander. He will lead you to victory.

You may be a novice when it comes to biblical knowledge and/or regular exercise. Or you might be a veteran of both. Wherever you are on the spiritual and physical spectrum, this chapter will help you understand what you need to do to achieve success. If you're a novice, it will introduce you to the basics and help you lay a solid foundation of fitness. If you're an expert, you'll receive fresh motivation and new ideas to challenge you.

Your conditioning program will include three elements: (1) establishing a core training schedule, (2) setting goals, and (3) putting the plan to work.

1. Establish Your Training Schedule

One pitfall of exercise is doing the same routine month after month. People who make this mistake often get frustrated when they don't see the results they want. To keep making progress with physical training, you have to challenge your body continually. You need to shock it from time to time by adding variety and intensity to your workouts. If you don't, you'll remain stuck in a rut. To prevent this plateau effect, you need a periodized training program.

Periodization is a systematic plan for physical training. Although commonly geared toward athletes, periodized training can benefit anyone who wants to improve overall fitness. Periodization helps you continue to make measurable progress, which keeps you motivated in reaching your goals. It also maximizes physical results in a minimal amount of time.

Exercises in a periodized program are changed frequently to prevent your muscles from adapting to your routine. If you want to improve performance, your workouts must progress to a higher level of difficulty. Many training variables can be manipulated to keep your body challenged, such as types of exercises and number of sessions per day and per week. Marisa Carter, owner and head coach of Evolve Multisport, explains why this type of training is effective: "If you were to focus on developing all aspects of fitness all at once, you may end up injured, ill, or completely burned out. By drawing out a map of the year ahead or developing an annual training outlook, you can designate blocks of time to focus on each aspect of fitness."[3]

Three cycles make up a periodized program: *macrocycle*, *mesocycle*, and *microcycle*. The macrocycle is the entire training period, which is typically a year. The goal of the macrocycle is to achieve peak conditioning by the end of the program by implementing short-term cycles along the way. A mesocycle focuses on a particular goal, such as endurance or power, and can be one or more weeks in length. A microcycle is a shorter period, made up of specific training sessions to implement the goals of the mesocycle.[4]

To make this concept clear, let's use the example of a runner training for a marathon. The months of preparation are made up of mesocycles, and each mesocycle will have a different goal. The first mesocycle might focus on building endurance by gradually increasing mileage each week through longer, easier-paced runs. The second mesocycle could work on improving speed through hill repeats. Finally, the last cycle, the microcycle, occurs in the final weeks leading up to the marathon. It's designed to sharpen the speed and efficiency of the runner by melding the longer, easier-paced runs with the shorter, faster efforts. Following is a sample microcycle for a long-distance runner.

> Monday: hill repeats
> Tuesday: medium/long run
> Wednesday: rest
> Thursday: shorter, fast-paced intervals
> Friday: short, easy-paced run
> Saturday: longer, steady run
> Sunday: rest

Now, let's apply this idea of periodization to your spiritual core training program. Following is what your training plan looks like.

- *Macrocycle:* Six-week program.

- *Mesocycle:* Six weeks of Bible study, with each week having a different theme.

   Week 1: Commitment
   Week 2: Power
   Week 3: Perseverance
   Week 4: Joy
   Week 5: Peace
   Week 6: Victory

- *Microcycle:* Six days of Bible study, with each day focusing on a particular spiritual discipline. The seventh day is an active rest day, which means you're still in the Word. However, your "workout" for that day is less intense than those for the other days.

Monday: Bible study
Tuesday: prayer
Wednesday: fasting
Thursday: healthy living
Friday: stewardship
Saturday: serving
Sunday: rest

Your six-week training plan will help you do the following:

1. Establish a daily habit of studying God's Word.

2. Grow in the art of prayer by practicing adoration, confession, thanksgiving, and supplication.

3. Participate in periodic fasting (in this case, every Wednesday).

4. Improve your health by increasing your amount of exercise and making more nutritious food choices.

5. Organize your finances so you can be a faithful steward of God's resources.

6. Seek ways to serve others in your family, your church, and your community.

This schedule is designed to push you toward your overall goal of getting in peak condition for the Lord. Remember, spiritual conditioning doesn't occur overnight, just as you don't whip your body into shape in one workout session. Your spiritual transformation will take time. Allow yourself several weeks to settle into your schedule. As you work hard on your exercises every day, you'll bulk up spiritually. God's power will be evident in your life in mighty ways!

2. Set Your Goals

Stating your goals up front is crucial to the success of your program. It's not enough to think about what you want to accomplish. *You need to write it down.* As Zig Ziglar said, "A goal properly set is halfway reached." Don't begin your program until you've completed this important step. The process of putting your goals on paper brings them to life and makes them more real. Also, make your goals as specific and measurable as possible. For example, instead of, "I want to read my Bible more often," a more defined goal is, "I will read my Bible every day for six weeks." Do you see the difference? The first statement merely expresses a desire; the second is a well-defined plan. Brian Tracy, motivational speaker and author, says, "People with clear, written goals accomplish far more in a shorter period of time than people without them could ever imagine."[5]

Below I've provided a sample of specific goals this program will target during the next six weeks. But you need to ask yourself, "What do *I* want to achieve?" Let's say your goal is to lose weight. If that's the case, specify how much weight you want to lose and in what time frame. Also, figure out *how* you will do it. To make this goal measurable, your long-term plan could be to lose twenty pounds in three months. Your short-term plan might consist of walking for thirty minutes four times per week. Breaking a big goal into smaller, realistic goals can help you both mentally and physically. This method can also help you improve your fitness level gradually and safely, which helps to build confidence.

Once your goals are in place, be sure to add specific rewards for each of them. The best rewards are ones which motivate *you*. Every person is unique, so we're not all excited about the same things. For example, if you like to travel, you could schedule a weekend trip after completing this program. Other reward ideas include a massage (one of my favorites), fishing equipment (that would be my husband's), jewelry, or movie passes. Be sure to avoid food-related items as rewards. Treating yourself to a double-dip ice cream when you reach a goal is *not* a good idea!

Finally, record the benefits you'll receive when you reach your goals. For example, when you read the Bible every day, you will develop a deeper understanding of who God is. After you become debt free, you'll have more money to give to missions. It's important to remind yourself of the gratification your success will bring, especially if your motivation level starts to decline.

Another thing: be prepared for resistance during this program. Challenges may come in the form of people or circumstances. When you face opposition, be like Nehemiah, who continued the work of rebuilding the wall of Jerusalem despite mockery and persecution. Even when his enemies sent persistent requests for him to cease his efforts and meet with them, Nehemiah refused to be distracted. He replied, "I am engaged in a great work, so I can't come" (Neh. 6:3 NLT). Nehemiah was determined to stay focused on the task before him.

God has called you to this work, and he is with you. Just keep your eyes on the Lord and don't let the Enemy intimidate you. You can be sure the good work God has begun in you *will* be completed (Phil. 1:6). Our God is faithful, and he will guide your steps as you strengthen your spiritual core.

Sample Goals

Bible Study

My Goals for Bible Study:

1. Read the Bible daily.

2.

Benefits I Will Receive:

_____

Prayer

My Goals for Prayer:

1. Incorporate adoration, confession, thanksgiving, and supplication into my prayers.

2. Practice new prayer postures.

3.

Benefits I Will Receive:

_____

Fasting

My Goals for Fasting:

1. Fast from one meal every Wednesday.

2.

Benefits I Will Receive:

_____

Healthy Living

My Goals for Healthy Living:

1. Do aerobic exercise three times per week.

2. Do strength training twice a week.

3. Do core training twice per week.

4. Plan healthy meals.

5.

Benefits I Will Receive:

_____

Financial Stewardship

My Goals for Financial Stewardship:

1. Create a budget.

2. Begin tithing regularly.

3. Choose a financial step to work on.

4.

Benefits I Will Receive:

_____

Serving Others

My Goals for Serving Others:

1. Pay for a stranger's groceries at the store.

2.

Benefits I Will Receive:

_____

---

3. Put Your Plan to Work!

A physical workout typically consists of three phases: (1) the warmup, (2) the exercises, and (3) the cooldown. The purpose of the first phase, the warmup, is to give your body time to adjust to the increase in the demands placed on it. For example, if you plan to run five miles, you should start by jogging at a slow to moderate pace. If you go too hard too quickly, you'll most likely either have a cramp, fatigue your muscles, or get injured. You might even have a heart attack! The second phase is the exercise portion of the workout, which requires you to exert energy and push yourself so your muscles can grow. If you have concerns about performing any of the physical exercises, consult your physician. Also, you can always modify an exercise if needed. For example, if you're unable to complete regular pushups, you can do them with your knees on the floor. (But only until you get strong enough to do them the other way!) The final phase is the cooldown, the time when you gradually decrease the intensity of your activity. The same three elements are also the basic structure for your daily spiritual workouts.

---

1. *Warmup.* Read the assigned Scripture passage.

2. *Exercises.* Answer the study questions, which are designed to teach you how to dig deeper into God's Word. Record your answers in a journal or in the space provided.

3. *Cooldown.* Reflect on what God has shown you, and pray.

Each workout also contains an additional component — the daily challenge. This part of the study is your action step, a practical way to implement the focus of the day. If the suggested step does not apply to you, choose your own action step based on the goals you established for yourself in the previous section.

As a reminder: On Mondays, you'll focus on Bible study. Tuesdays will highlight prayer. Wednesdays will stress fasting. Thursdays will emphasize healthy living. On Fridays, you'll invest in financial stewardship. The focus on Saturdays will be serving others. My aim is to train you to raise your awareness and increase your strength in each of these six disciplines. By taking a day to look at each one, you'll recognize areas of weakness and continue to strengthen those areas once this program is over. You'll find that as you build one spiritual muscle, you'll also see improvement in the others. For example, focusing on financial stewardship may inspire you to plan healthier, low-cost meals. Meanwhile Bible study and prayer provide the truth and the power required to make needed changes in your life. These disciplines are all tied together, so if you seek the Lord first, he will provide both motivation and materials to help you grow.

Now that you have a good idea of where we're headed over the next six weeks, let's get started!

WEEK 1

Commitment

It is the LORD your God you must follow, and him you must revere.
Keep his commands and obey him; serve him and hold fast to him.
— *Deuteronomy 13:4*

When you commit to someone or something, you make a promise. As you begin this six-week training program, make a pledge to God and yourself to put your heart, soul, mind, and strength into it. Decide now to stay focused and to finish strong. With the Lord's help, you *will* make progress. You *will* grow. You *will* reach your goals!

MONDAY: Bible Study

Commit yourselves wholeheartedly
to these words of mine.
— *Deuteronomy 11:18 NLT*

WARMUP

Read Psalm 119:1 – 8.

EXERCISES

1. Underline or highlight the word *blessed* in verses 1 – 2.

2. The Hebrew word for "blessed" in this passage is *esher* (EH-sher), which denotes happiness or contentment. What are the requirements for receiving God's blessing as mentioned in verses 1 – 2?

3. What does verse 4 say about God's precepts (laws)?

4. The psalmist expresses a desire, in verse 5, to be steadfast in obeying God's decrees. *Steadfast* means "to be firmly established." Other definitions are "steady and immovable." Why is it important to be rooted in God's Word?

5. In verses 7 – 8, we see a commitment to praise God, learn his Word, and obey his commands. Underline or highlight the words *I will obey*

in verse 8. How will you make studying the Bible a priority over the next six weeks?

6. What is God saying to you in this passage? Write any insights or ways in which God wants you to respond.

COOLDOWN

Thank you, Lord, for hearing my prayer and for speaking to me through your Word. You are worthy of all praise, for you alone are God.

CHALLENGE

Write the first half of Deuteronomy 11:18 ("Fix these words of mine in your hearts and minds") on an index card or small piece of paper. Use it in your Bible as a bookmark to remind you to be a diligent student of God's Word.

Cardio: Complete a thirty-minute workout today (walk, run, bike, or hike).

TUESDAY: Prayer (Adoration)

O God, we give glory to you all day long
and constantly praise your name.
— *Psalm 44:8 NLT*

WARMUP

Read 1 Chronicles 29:1 – 20.

EXERCISES

1. Why were David and the people filled with such joy?

2. What did David do in response to God's abundant provision?

3. Write down the words in verses 10 – 13 which David used to describe the Lord.

4. What evidences of David's humility do you see in this passage?

5. Read verse 20 again. What postures did the people use to worship the Lord?

6. David led the Israelites in praising the Lord. How can your adoration of God influence the people in *your* life?

COOLDOWN

Lord, you are awesome in power! There's no one like you. You alone are the one true God, worthy of all worship and praise. I give you glory, Lord, and exalt your holy name.

CHALLENGE

Prayer: Practice praising God by using the "ABC" exercise on pages 47 – 48.

Strength: Perform one set of four upper body exercises (1 – 4; see "Key to Exercises" on p. 199) and one set of four lower body exercises (1 – 4). Do ten repetitions for each set. Add resistance (dumbbells or a band) where you can. Use a weight that's challenging but doesn't cause you to use incorrect form. Keep in mind the amount of resistance may be different for each exercise. See *www.kristenfeola.com* for video instruction on proper form and for ideas on exercise modifications.

Core: Perform one set of exercises 1 – 3 (ten repetitions for hip bridges, and hold both types of planks for fifteen seconds).

WEDNESDAY: Fasting

> She never left the temple but worshiped night and day,
> fasting and praying.
> *– Luke 2:37*

WARMUP

Read Luke 2:1 – 38.

EXERCISES

1. In verse 36, Anna is called a "prophet," or in some translations a "prophetess." The main role of a prophet or prophetess was to speak for

God and proclaim his truth. What habit did Anna have in her life that demonstrated her devotion to the Lord?

2. Even though Anna was eighty-four years old, she still practiced regular fasting. How does her example challenge you in this area?

3. Why do you think God allowed Anna to be among the first people to see Jesus?

4. When Anna saw the baby Jesus, what did she do?

5. Anna was filled with joy in the presence of the Lord, and she told everyone about seeing the Messiah. How does fasting fill our hearts with joy and help us to "see" God more clearly?

6. Why should you fast? Write down specific reasons why this exercise is beneficial for you.

COOLDOWN

I trust you, Lord, for the strength I need to fast. Even though fasting isn't easy, I'm not afraid. I know you will help me. Thank you for this unique spiritual discipline which teaches me how to be more like Jesus.

CHALLENGE

Fasting: Fast from at least one meal today, and spend that time in prayer.

Cardio: Try a different exercise than you did on Monday. Your goal is thirty minutes of sustained activity. If you're fasting from more than one meal today, you might need to decrease the intensity of your workout. Also, make sure you drink plenty of water before and after you exercise.

THURSDAY: Healthy Living

I urge you, brothers and sisters, in view of God's mercy,
to offer your bodies as a living sacrifice, holy and pleasing
to God — this is your true and proper worship.
— Romans 12:1

WARMUP

Read Romans 12:1 – 2.

EXERCISES

1. In this passage, the apostle Paul is addressing the Christians in Rome, but his message is for all believers. What does his use of the word *urge* in his instruction tell us?

2. Underline or highlight how you are to offer your body. What does it mean to present your body to God in this way?

3. When we make wise choices regarding eating and exercise, our sacrifice is acceptable to the Lord. What will God do in response to your commitment to follow his ways, according to verse 2?

4. How is healthy living an act of worship?

5. What behaviors are characteristic of the "pattern of this world" in relation to the body?

6. Where does transformation begin?

7. How is your mind being renewed in this study?

COOLDOWN

Lord, I offer myself as a living sacrifice to you. I will worship you by obeying your command to take care of my body. Instead of following the ways of this world, I choose to set my mind on your truth.

CHALLENGE

Invest in exercise equipment that will help you meet your physical goals. For example: good walking shoes, dumbbells, workout DVDs, or workout clothes.

Strength: Perform one set of four upper body exercises (5 – 8) and one set of four lower body exercises (5 – 8). Do ten repetitions for each set. Add resistance (dumbbells or a band) where you can. Use a weight that's challenging but doesn't cause you to use incorrect form. Keep in mind the amount of resistance may be different for each exercise. See *www .kristenfeola.com* for video instruction on proper form and for ideas on exercise modifications.

FRIDAY: Financial Stewardship

Store up for yourselves treasures in heaven.
— *Matthew 6:20*

WARMUP

Read Matthew 6:19 – 21.

EXERCISES

1. What are examples of storing up treasures on earth?

2. The Greek word for "treasure" in this passage is *thesauros* (thay-sow-ROS), which means "deposit."[6] How does your financial giving make deposits for eternity?

3. Read Colossians 3:2. This verse supports the idea that our primary focus in this life should be on eternal matters. Gill's Exposition of the Bible explains, "If your treasure is on earth, and lies in earthly things, your hearts will be set upon them.... But if your treasure is put into the hands of God, your hearts will be with him, and be settled on him; your desires will be after heavenly things; your affections will be set on things above."[7] How does tithing provide evidence that your heart is set upon the things of the Lord?

4. Although tithing and giving are examples of storing up treasures in heaven, the scope of Matthew 6:20 includes *all* aspects of obedience to the Lord. What are other, nonmonetary ways to invest in God's kingdom?

5. What is the reward for putting all your treasures in the hands of God?

COOLDOWN

Even though I live in the world, my heart is with you and settled on you, Lord. Keep me from becoming attached to temporal things. My desire is to store up treasures in heaven, for true riches are found in you alone.

CHALLENGE

Your tithe should be at least 10 percent of everything you make (gross income). Based on that figure, what should your weekly tithe be? Write a check for that amount and send it to your church.

Cardio: Exercise for at least thirty minutes with a friend or attend a fitness class.

SATURDAY: Serving Others

> Serve one another humbly in love.
>
> —*Galatians 5:13*

WARMUP

Read Galatians 5:13 – 14.

EXERCISES

1. Verse 13 says that God has called us to be free. How would you define freedom in Christ?

2. The apostle Paul warns against using our liberty to indulge selfish desires. What, then, is the purpose of the freedom we've been given?

3. How are we to serve one another?

4. What happens when acts of service aren't motivated by love?

5. In verse 14, it says, "Love your neighbor as yourself." Who is your neighbor? How do you love others "as yourself"?

6. Write about a time when someone did something unexpected that blessed you.

COOLDOWN

Father, thank you for setting me free from sin and calling me to a life of service. Help me to take action when I see a need, instead of finding excuses not to get involved.

CHALLENGE

Do something kind for a friend or neighbor (mow the lawn, shovel snow, rake leaves, or cook a meal).

Core: Perform one set of exercises 4 – 6 (five roll-ups, ten side bends on each side, and one set of the hundred exercise).

Meal plan: Plan out your meals for next week. Post the schedule on your refrigerator.

SUNDAY: Rest Day

Lord God, I trust you with all my heart. I don't lean on my own understanding but rely on your omniscience to guide me. I acknowledge and submit to you in all my ways, for you will make my paths straight. You watch over me and will establish your plans for my life.

I will not neglect your Word but will make it a priority. I'm committed to seeking your kingdom above all else. May your favor rest upon me and make my efforts successful. My desire is to live righteously so I can bring honor and glory to you!

- "Trust in the LORD with all your heart and lean not on your own understanding; in all your ways submit to him, and he will make your paths straight" (Prov. 3:5 – 6).

- "Commit to the LORD whatever you do, and he will establish your plans" (Prov. 16:3).

- "I will not neglect your word" (Ps. 119:16).

- "Seek the Kingdom of God above all else, and live righteously, and he will give you everything you need" (Matt. 6:33 NLT).

- "May the Lord our God show us his approval and make our efforts successful. Yes, make our efforts successful!" (Ps. 90:17 NLT).

Power

My grace is sufficient for you,
for my power is made perfect in weakness.
—*2 Corinthians 12:9*

Progress is not possible without power. However, the ability to continue moving forward in this program does not depend on your strength. Your strength is not enough. You must rely on the Holy Spirit in you. The Lord is able to accomplish far more than you could ever ask or even imagine (Eph. 3:20–21). Now, my friend, go forth in *his* power, and be amazed at what God does!

MONDAY: Bible Study

Man does not live on bread alone
but on every word that comes from the mouth of the LORD.
—*Deuteronomy 8:3*

WARMUP

Read Matthew 4:1–11.

EXERCISES

1. What was God's purpose in sending Jesus into the desert?

2. Jesus had already fasted forty days and nights when Satan came to him. Jesus was hungry, physically weak, and alone, which made him especially vulnerable to temptation. The Devil often tempts us when we're in a similar situation. When do you feel most vulnerable to the Enemy's schemes?

3. Three times Satan tried to get Jesus to sin, and three times Jesus resisted him. What weapon did Jesus use to overcome his attacks?

4. Read Hebrews 4:15. How does Jesus' firsthand knowledge of what it's like to be tempted give you comfort and strength?

5. How did Satan respond when Jesus quoted God's Word?

6. James 4:7 says, "Humble yourselves before God. Resist the devil, and he will flee from you" (NLT). What is one way you can resist the Enemy?

COOLDOWN

I love your Word, O Lord! It gives me strength to overcome temptation and teaches me how to live a godly life. Increase my desire to study the Bible, so I can learn more about you and your ways.

CHALLENGE

Identify three areas of temptation in your life. Then search the Scriptures for a verse that applies to each temptation. Use those three truths from God's Word to defeat the Enemy when he attacks.

Cardio: Mix up your thirty-minute workout today. Do fifteen minutes of one cardiovascular exercise, and then do fifteen minutes of something different.

TUESDAY: Prayer (Confession)

> People who conceal their sins will not prosper,
> but if they confess and turn from them,
> they will receive mercy.
> — *Proverbs 28:13 NLT*

WARMUP

Read Psalm 51.

EXERCISES

1. Why is David pleading to God for mercy? (See 2 Sam. 11.)

2. In Psalm 51:1, David acknowledges two of God's attributes. What are they?

3. David lusted after Bathsheba, had her husband killed, and then took her as his wife. To make matters worse, he tried to cover it up! Yet when David was confronted by Nathan the prophet (2 Sam. 12:1 – 13),

he was broken over his sin. Can you think of a time when you experienced deep sorrow over something you did? Describe how you felt.

4. Proverbs 28:13 offers hope when we fail to live within the boundaries God has given us. What can you expect to receive from the Lord when you repent?

5. Read Psalm 51:7. Hyssop was a plant used in Jewish purification rituals, usually to signify a cleansing or purging. David is expressing a longing for an internal cleansing of his desires. What is the "hyssop" that makes us whiter than snow?

6. Verses 10 – 12 indicate that David's impure thoughts and actions caused him to lose his zeal for the Lord. How does sin result in apathy toward God and his Word?

7. Toward the end of David's prayer, he turns his thoughts away from his wrongdoing and toward God's goodness. He asks God to open his lips so he can praise him (v. 15). What happens in our hearts when we receive mercy?

COOLDOWN

Holy God, you do not treat me as my sins deserve. Instead you show kindness, love, and mercy when I fail. Thank you for removing my sin as far as the east is from the west. I praise you, Lord, my Redeemer and the Lover of my Soul.

CHALLENGE

Ask God to search your heart and reveal any sin that needs to be confessed. He will bring to mind anything blocking your communion with him. When the Holy Spirit shows you something, confess it and receive God's forgiveness. Then remember to thank and praise him!

Strength: Perform one set of four upper body exercises (1 – 4) and one set of four lower body exercises (1 – 4). Do fifteen repetitions for each set.

Core: Perform one set of exercises 1 – 3 (fifteen repetitions for hip bridges, and hold planks for thirty seconds).

WEDNESDAY: Fasting

> We have no power to face this vast army that is attacking us.
> We do not know what to do, but our eyes are on you.
>
> *— 2 Chronicles 20:12*

WARMUP

Read 2 Chronicles 20:1 – 30.

EXERCISES

1. When King Jehoshaphat learned of the enemy's plans, he sought the Lord in prayer. What did he do next (v. 3)?

2. Instead of focusing on the looming disaster, Jehoshaphat praised God and focused on the Lord's power. How should you react when facing difficult circumstances?

3. God told the people not to be afraid or discouraged. He promised he would be with them and fight for them. How did the people respond to his words?

4. When the people went out to face their enemies, Jehoshaphat gave the men at the front of the army two special jobs. What were they appointed to do?

5. The people of Judah fasted and prayed for God's help, and the Lord answered with an awesome display of his power. However, notice the timing in verse 22. When did God set ambushes against the enemies who were invading Judah? Underline or highlight the phrase in your Bible, and write it here.

6. The story in 2 Chronicles 20 begins with the people of Judah calling on God and ends with the sound defeat of their enemies. How can prayer and fasting help bring about victory in your life?

COOLDOWN

Father, you are the God in heaven, and you rule over the nations of this world. Power and might are in your hand, and no one can withstand you. I worship you, Lord, for you are worthy of all glory, honor, and praise!

CHALLENGE

Consider doing a smoothie or juice fast today.

Cardio: Walk, run, bike, or hike for thirty minutes.

THURSDAY: Healthy Living

> Do not worry about your life, what you will eat or drink; or about
> your body, what you will wear. Is not life more than food, and the
> body more than clothes? Look at the birds of the air; they do not sow
> or reap or store away in barns, and yet your heavenly Father feeds
> them. Are you not much more valuable than they?
>
> *— Matthew 6:25 - 26*

WARMUP

Read 1 Kings 17:1 – 16.

EXERCISES

1. Because of the idolatry of King Ahab and his people, Elijah prophesied a drought in the land. After Elijah confronted Ahab about it, God told Elijah to go hide in the Kerith Ravine. What did God do for Elijah while he was there?

2. When the water in the brook dried up, God told Elijah to go to Zarephath to find a certain widow, who would supply him with food. However, when Elijah found her, he discovered she was desperately poor, with just enough oil and flour for one more meal for her family. What was the first thing Elijah told her, in verse 13?

3. God provided for the widow, her son, and Elijah in a miraculous way when the woman exercised faith in the Lord. How does her example encourage you during times when you feel afraid?

4. What was the purpose of Elijah's time near the brook in the Kerith Ravine? What role do you think it played in the miracle that followed?

5. Obedience results in God's blessing. It also opens the door to displaying God's power in your life. When you follow God's

instructions in taking care of your body, what is the result of your obedience?

6. Do you struggle with doubt or fear when it comes to eating and/or exercise? If so, list the specific areas in which you struggle. Then write a prayer of commitment to the Lord, stating how you will lean on his strength instead of your willpower.

COOLDOWN

God, when I am afraid, I will trust in you. I don't have to worry, because you are faithful in all your ways. Thank you for helping me when I call out to you.

CHALLENGE

Focus on your water intake today. Set a goal for how many glasses you want to drink, and then chug away!

Strength: Perform one set of four upper body exercises (5 – 8) and one set of four lower body exercises (5 – 8). Do fifteen repetitions for each set.

FRIDAY: Financial Stewardship

The plans of the diligent lead to profit
as surely as haste leads to poverty.
— *Proverbs 21:5*

WARMUP

Read 2 Kings 4:1 – 7.

EXERCISES

1. According to Mosaic law, a creditor could claim the children of a debtor and force them to be his hired workers until the Year of Jubilee (Lev. 25:39 – 40). The widow in this story couldn't pay her husband's debts, so her sons were going to be taken away from her. When the woman asked Elisha for help, what did he tell her to do?

2. Why do you think Elisha said to ask for *several* jars?

3. God honored the widow's obedience by providing resources for her family in a supernatural way. How has the Lord met your financial needs?

4. The widow started with only a little oil, but when she trusted the Lord with what she had, he multiplied it. Verse 6 indicates that there weren't enough jars for the amount of oil God provided. How can creating a budget result in multiplication of your resources?

5. Read Proverbs 21:20. How does this verse relate to living within a budget?

6. What is the Lord saying to you through the widow's example?

COOLDOWN

Lord, I want my life to be pleasing to you in every way. Fill any empty spaces in my heart with your love, and help me to grow in faith.

CHALLENGE

Begin to create a budget by writing down your expenses (see page 101 for help).

Cardio: If you have a gym membership, get on a different machine today. If you exercise at home, try using a DVD. Or, better yet, go outside for your thirty-minute workout!

SATURDAY: Serving Others

This is my commandment:
Love each other in the same way I have loved you.
—*John 15:12 NLT*

WARMUP

Read John 21:1 – 14.

EXERCISES

1. In the first part of this passage, we learn that Peter and some of the other disciples returned to fishing after Jesus' resurrection. What does this decision indicate about their level of faith?

2. Luke 5:1 – 6 tells of another time when Jesus told Simon Peter to cast his net into a certain part of the lake. Even though Peter had been fishing all night without success, he did what Jesus said. Peter's obedience resulted in a miraculous catch! What should *your* response be when Jesus asks you to do something, even though it doesn't make sense?

3. Read John 21:7. What did Peter do when he realized it was the Lord speaking to them? Why do you think he reacted this way?

4. When the disciples made it to shore, what did they see waiting for them (besides Jesus)? Not long before this event, the disciples had all betrayed Jesus. One by one each of them fell away, at a time when he needed their support the most. Yet Jesus isn't at all bitter about his friends' betrayal. Instead, he makes them breakfast. What does this act of service tell you about the Lord? How does Jesus respond when *you* fail him?

COOLDOWN

Lord, I want to obey your command to love others, but sometimes I'm selfish. I get focused on myself and fail to respond when I see a person in need. Teach me how to serve people in your power and with your joy.

CHALLENGE

Serve your spouse or another family member today by doing something that speaks directly to his or her love language. For example, if your wife or husband feels most loved through words of affirmation, write a letter that lists ten things you appreciate about him or her. (Dr. Gary Chapman, author of *The 5 Love Languages*, identifies the languages as words of affirmation, acts of service, gifts, quality time, and physical touch.)

Core: Perform two sets of exercises 4 – 6 (total of ten roll-ups, twenty side bends). Do only one set of the hundred exercise.

Meal plan: Check to make sure your breakfast recipes are a good mix of protein, carbohydrates, and healthy fat. Begin your day by fueling your body with the nutrients it needs. Replace any processed or high-sugar foods with healthier choices.

SUNDAY: Rest Day

*God, there's no one like you! You are great, and your name is mighty
in power. I praise you for your wonderful works! I praise you for your
unequaled greatness! You made the earth by your power and founded the
world by your wisdom. You laid out the heavens by your understanding.*

   *Your Word says you give power to the weak and strength to the
powerless. Lord, I'm weak! I'm powerless! I can't do anything without you.
But with you I can do all things through Christ who strengthens me.*

- "No one is like you, LORD; you are great, and your name is mighty in power" (Jer. 10:6).

- "Praise him for his mighty works; praise his unequaled greatness!" (Ps. 150:2 NLT).

- "God made the earth by his power; he founded the world by his wisdom and stretched out the heavens by his understanding" (Jer. 10:12).

- "He gives power to the weak and strength to the powerless" (Isa. 40:29 NLT).

- "Apart from me you can do nothing" (John 15:5).

- "I can do everything through Christ, who gives me strength" (Phil. 4:13 NLT).

WEEK 3

Perseverance

Suffering produces perseverance;
perseverance, character; and character, hope.
— Romans 5:3 - 4

This training program is like a steep mountain hike. Two weeks ago, you took the first step, excited about the journey ahead. You've worked hard and done well. As you reach the midway point, though, your legs may start to feel tired. However, now is not the time to rest. You have to keep going! Ask God to provide what you need. He will give you the persistence, tenacity, and mental strength to persevere. Climb on!

MONDAY: Bible Study

I have chosen the way of faithfulness;
I have set my heart on your laws.
— Psalm 119:30

WARMUP

Read Psalm 119:9 – 11.

EXERCISES

1. The psalmist says the only way to remain pure in this fallen world is to live under the authority of Scripture. How does living according to God's Word keep you from falling into sin?

2. What does it mean to seek God with all your heart?

3. When are you most likely to stray from God's commands?

4. Two other translations of Psalm 119:11 are, "I have stored up your word in my heart" (ESV) and "I have treasured your promise in my heart" (GW). The idea is to possess a sincere, unwavering devotion to the Bible. How has your love for God's Word grown in the first two weeks of this study?

5. When you study the Bible, you store truth in the secret places of your heart. Then when your faith is tested, the Holy Spirit can bring those verses to your mind. What happens, though, if you haven't taken the time to deposit those Scriptures into your memory bank?

6. Scripture memorization can help you during times of weakness. However, it's not enough to know the promises in the Bible; you also have to apply them. Give one example of a time when God's Word gave you strength to endure temptation.

COOLDOWN

Lord, the Bible is a treasure to me. Thank you for speaking so clearly through the pages of Scripture. Give me strength and motivation to be more diligent with memorizing your Word.

CHALLENGE

Memorize Psalm 119:30. Write it on a note card and place it on your refrigerator, bathroom mirror, or anywhere else that's highly visible.

Cardio: Increase your level of intensity today. Also, try to exercise for more than thirty minutes. If you're walking or running, pick up the pace. Go faster on the bike. If using an elliptical machine, set it to a higher resistance. Push yourself! Work harder than you did last week. Your goal is at least 70 percent of your maximum effort (slightly short of breath, but still able to carry on a conversation).

TUESDAY: Prayer (Thanksgiving)

> I will give thanks to you, LORD, with all my heart;
> I will tell of all your wonderful deeds.
> —Psalm 9:1

WARMUP

Read Psalm 136.

EXERCISES

1. The Hebrew word for "give thanks" is *yadah*, which can be translated

as "to throw."[8] In this psalm, the writer is literally casting out God's glory among the people. How does remembering God's faithfulness result in a heart of thanksgiving?

2. What are the two phrases repeated throughout this psalm?

3. When you see phrases repeated in the Bible, stop and pay attention. God is emphasizing a concept he wants you to understand and accept. Why do you think "his love endures forever" appears twenty-six times in twenty-six verses? What does God want you to understand?

4. The format of this psalm indicates it might have been a responsive reading, with the congregation saying the words in unison after each phrase. How do our prayers sometimes become similar, spoken more out of habit than genuine gratitude?

5. Read Matthew 6:7. How can we guard against praying empty words that aren't heartfelt?

6. The psalmist says in Psalm 136:4 to give thanks "to him who alone does great wonders." Then in the following verses, he lists specific ways in which God has worked. Write down five great things that God has done in your life.

COOLDOWN

God, you have blessed my life in more ways than I can count. Thank you for creating me. Thank you for saving me. Thank you for this study, which is helping me grow closer to you. Thank you for my family and friends. Thank you for the promise that nothing can separate me from your love. You are good, and your love endures forever!

CHALLENGE

Write down three ways God has blessed you this week. Then spend time in prayer, thanking God for his goodness to you.

Strength: Perform two sets of four upper body exercises (1 – 4) and two sets of four lower body exercises (1 – 4). You're ready to increase your level of resistance, so use the next-heaviest dumbbell (where applicable). Do ten repetitions for each set.

Core: Perform two sets of exercises 1, 3, and 5. Do two sets of ten advanced hip bridges and side bends (each side) with resistance. Hold side planks for thirty seconds.

WEDNESDAY: Fasting

> Persevere in prayer.
> — *Colossians 4:2 DARBY*

WARMUP

Read Daniel 10:1 – 14.

EXERCISES

1. God gave Daniel a vision that allowed him to foresee the future of the Jewish people. Daniel was so upset by this vision that he entered into a state of mourning. How long did he seek the Lord in prayer and fasting?

2. The Bible says Daniel refrained from eating "choice food" and meat during his fast. Most commentaries agree that "choice food" would have included breads and sweets. Why do you think he eliminated these particular foods?

3. Three days after Daniel completed his fast, he received another vision. Even though Daniel was accompanied by other men, he was the only one who could see it. How did the heavenly being in the vision refer to Daniel?

4. The words in the angel's greeting are also translated as "greatly loved; very precious to God; highly respected; of great value; treasured by God." Do you believe God sees you this way? Why or why not?

5. The angel said he had been sent by God to assure Daniel that his prayers had been heard. Why wasn't the angel able to appear to Daniel until after his fast?

6. Daniel continued to seek the Lord through fasting, even though nothing seemed to be happening in response to his prayers. In reality, though, an intense spiritual battle was delaying God's answer. How does this story inspire you to persevere in prayer?

COOLDOWN

Lord God, help me not to grow weary in prayer. Thank you for the reminder that you hear my prayers and are working, even if my eyes don't see it. I trust you, Lord, to bring about the answers in your way and in your timing.

CHALLENGE

Participate in a Daniel Fast for today, and consider doing it for the full three weeks at a later time. Ask God to show you when you should do it. My book *The Ultimate Guide to the Daniel Fast* is a helpful resource that provides the tools you need. Also, check my website (*www.ultimatedaniel fast.com*) for information on upcoming online fasts.

Cardio: Go for a walk or run at a nearby park, trail, or nature center. If the weather is too cold, walk or run on a treadmill. Do something to get your body moving for at least thirty minutes today!

THURSDAY: Healthy Living

> I discipline my body like an athlete,
> training it to do what it should.
> —*1 Corinthians 9:27 NLT*

WARMUP

Read 1 Corinthians 9:24–27.

EXERCISES

1. Paul compares the Christian life to a race. How do we run "in such a way as to get the prize" (v. 24)?

2. Who (or what) is our prize?

3. What kind of spiritual training is necessary in order for believers to finish strong?

4. What is the "crown that will last forever" (v. 25)? Who will receive it? (See James 1:12.)

5. In 1 Cor. 9:27, Paul says, "I strike a blow to my body and make it my slave." How do you beat your body into submission when you practice the disciplines of regular exercise and nutritious eating?

6. How does having a healthy body keep you from becoming disqualified in your spiritual training?

7. What physical successes have you experienced in the first half of this session? What improvements do you still need to make?

COOLDOWN

Dear Lord, I'm running this race of life with my gaze fixed directly on you. I will do my best to train my body so I'm physically fit for spiritual service.

CHALLENGE

Remove any trigger foods in your kitchen cabinets or refrigerator (or anywhere else they might be stashed). Throw tempting foods away or donate them.

Strength: Perform two sets of four upper body exercises (5 – 8) and two sets of four lower body exercises (5 – 8). Do ten repetitions for each set. (Use the same amount of resistance for each exercise that you used on Tuesday.)

FRIDAY: Financial Stewardship

> My God will meet all your needs according
> to the riches of his glory in Christ Jesus.
> —*Philippians 4:19*

WARMUP

Read Matthew 6:24 – 34.

EXERCISES

1. What two basic principles does Jesus teach his disciples in verse 24?

2. Why do you think Jesus addresses the issue of worry when speaking about money?

3. What causes people to become fearful in regard to their finances?

4. Do you have worries about your current financial situation? If so, list them here. (Be honest!)

5. What does verse 33 say you should do instead of worry?

6. List two reasons why you shouldn't worry (vv. 27 – 34).

7. Read Philippians 4:12 – 13, 19. Paul says he has learned to be content whether living in poverty or in abundance. What is the secret to his peace?

COOLDOWN

Lord, you are a God of unlimited supply. When I start to get anxious about my financial situation, remind me to focus on your promises. You are the Master of my life. I trust you to care for all my needs.

CHALLENGE

Take another look at the expenses in your budget. Identify an area or two where you can trim. See page 102 for help.

Cardio: Try an exercise class you've never taken or a new DVD workout. Many fitness centers will allow you to try a class for free, even if you aren't a member. Take advantage of that and sample one or two classes, such as spinning, Zumba, cardio kickboxing, step aerobics, or Jazzercise. Exercise for thirty minutes.

SATURDAY: Serving Others

> Never walk away from someone who deserves help;
> your hand is **God's** hand for that person.
> *— Proverbs 3:27 MSG*

WARMUP

Read Matthew 25:31 – 46.

EXERCISES

1. This passage describes the future judgment of all humanity, when people will be separated before the Lord into two groups — believers and unbelievers. Jesus says one group will be on his right and the other on his left. How does Jesus address the group on his right, and what does he tell them to do?

2. When Jesus commends believers for their acts of mercy toward him, why are they confused?

3. Why was the group on Jesus' left banished from his presence?

4. Isaiah 58 promises abundant blessings for people who spend their energy helping the hungry and satisfying the needs of the oppressed. Who are the "least of these" (Matt. 25:40) whom God wants *you* to reach?

5. What is the inheritance that all believers will receive?

6. What is one way you can resist the temptation to do nothing when the needs around you seem overwhelming?

COOLDOWN

Lord, you are the Good Shepherd. Thank you for taking care of me. I want to show my love for you by serving others. Help me not to turn my back when I see someone in need but to be your hand extended in love.

CHALLENGE

Bless a single mom in your church or neighborhood by buying groceries for her, paying her electric bill, watching her children one evening, or giving her a gift card to a spa.

Core: Perform two sets of exercises 2 and 6 and one set of exercise 4. Hold planks for forty-five seconds, do fifteen roll-ups, and go through the hundred exercise twice.

Meal plan: Be sure to stock your refrigerator and pantry with healthy snacks. That way, you won't resort to convenience foods between meals when you need an energy boost.

SUNDAY: Rest Day

Lord, I choose to be joyful whenever I face trials of many kinds, because I know that the testing of my faith produces perseverance. Such perseverance is necessary to build my faith so I can be mature and complete in you. I gladly endure hardship for the sake of your name. I will not grow weary, because my hope is in you.

God, direct my heart in your love and in Christ's perseverance. Help me to run with perseverance the race you have marked out for me. I throw off everything that will slow down my pace or trip me up as I pursue righteousness.

Your Word promises blessing to people who pass the test of perseverance. Thank you for blessing me now and for the blessings to come! One day, I will stand in your presence, and you will award me with the crown of righteousness. How I long for that day!

- "Consider it pure joy, my brothers and sisters, whenever you face trials of many kinds, because you know that the testing of your faith produces perseverance. Let perseverance finish its work so that you may be mature and complete, not lacking anything" (James 1:2 – 4).

- "You have persevered and have endured hardships for my name, and have not grown weary" (Rev. 2:3).

- "My hope is in you all day long" (Ps. 25:5).

- "May the Lord direct your hearts into God's love and Christ's perseverance" (2 Thess. 3:5).

- "Since we are surrounded by such a great cloud of witnesses, let us throw off everything that hinders and the sin that so easily entangles. And let us run with perseverance the race marked out for us" (Heb. 12:1).

- "Blessed is the one who perseveres under trial because, having stood the test, that person will receive the crown of life that the Lord has promised to those who love him" (James 1:12).

WEEK 4

Joy

You make known to me the path of life;
you will fill me with joy in your presence,
with eternal pleasures at your right hand.
— Psalm 16:11

You've come so far in just three weeks! I'm proud of all your hard work. As you begin the second half of your program, remember God's faithfulness and be encouraged by it. He has helped you forge new pathways of living through daily discipline, and he has given you success. Don't wait until week 6 to celebrate. Find joy in your journey *now*.

MONDAY: Bible Study

The commandments of the LORD are right,
bringing joy to the heart.
— Psalm 19:8 NLT

WARMUP

Read Psalm 119:14, 24, 97, 111, 143, 167.

EXERCISES

1. Bible scholars aren't sure who wrote Psalm 119, but whoever it was obviously had a deep reverence for God's commands. In verse 14, the psalmist says he gets as excited about the Lord's statutes as someone who rejoices in great riches. What does it take to reach that level of devotion to God's Word?

2. In verse 24, the psalmist calls God's statutes his counselors. He would literally sit down with God's law and receive wisdom for life, and it filled his heart with joy. How is God's Word like a counselor to you?

3. Can you sense the intense emotion and passion in verse 97? The psalmist loves God's law so much that he thinks about it all the time! Matthew's Concise Commentary says, "A good man carries his Bible with him, if not in his hands, yet in his head and in his heart."[9] How are you doing with carrying God's Word in your heart and meditating on it throughout the day? What can you do to improve?

4. What does the psalmist mean in verse 111 when he says God's statutes are his heritage forever?

5. In verse 143, the psalmist says he continues to delight in God's commands even during hard times. Have you found this to be true in your own life? Give an example.

6. In verse 167, the psalmist shows his great love for God's statutes by obeying them. How does obedience lead to joy?

COOLDOWN

Oh, Lord, I love your commands more than gold, more than pure gold! Your Word is precious to me, and I treasure it more than my daily bread. Increase my desire to study your truth and apply it to my life.

CHALLENGE

Read through Psalm 119 this week. It will take you an average of twenty-five verses each day to complete it. You'll find it impossible to study this wonderful chapter and *not* grow in your love for God's Word.

Cardio: Engage in at least thirty minutes of cardiovascular activity. At the end of your workout, add five minutes of additional exercise by doing a circuit of jumping rope (or jumping in place), squats, jumping jacks, crunches, and push-ups. Perform ten repetitions of each exercise, and repeat until the five minutes is completed.

TUESDAY: Prayer (Supplication)

Hear my cry for help, my King and my God,
for to you I pray.
— Psalm 5:2

WARMUP

Read 1 Sam. 1 – 2:2.

EXERCISES

1. In Old Testament times, a woman who was childless was disgraced and considered a failure. When Hannah couldn't conceive, her husband remained devoted to her, despite the social stigma of their situation. How do you know Elkanah's heart was tender toward her?

2. What reason does this passage give for why Hannah was unable to have children?

3. Year after year, Hannah was provoked by Elkanah's other wife, Peninnah, who had many sons and daughters. Year after year, Elkanah and his family went to Shiloh to worship and sacrifice. Year after year, Hannah prayed. What promise did Hannah make during one particular trip to Shiloh?

4. Eli the priest saw Hannah at the tabernacle and thought she was drunk. What was it about her appearance and behavior that led him to this conclusion?

5. God answered Hannah's prayer, and she gave birth to a son, Samuel. What is the meaning of his name?

6. After Samuel was weaned, Hannah took him to the tabernacle, just as she had promised she would. Even though it must have been heartwrenching for Hannah to let her son go, she fulfilled her vow to the Lord with a thankful spirit. How do you know she maintained a joyful attitude?

7. Hannah's perseverance in prayer resulted in God's granting her request at just the right time. Is there something you have been bringing to the Lord in prayer for years? How can Hannah's story encourage you to press on and not give up?

COOLDOWN

Father God, I will continue to pray, even when it seems nothing is happening. The answer will come in your perfect timing. I choose to wait on you, Lord, and not to worry.

CHALLENGE

Find a Bible verse to attach to a request you've been praying about for years. As you speak truth over a person or situation, let your heart be filled with joy in anticipation of God's answer.

Strength: Perform two sets of four upper body exercises (1 – 4) and two sets of four lower body exercises (1 – 4). Do fifteen repetitions for each set, and increase resistance where you can.

Core: Perform three sets of exercise 2 and two sets of exercise 6. Hold planks for one minute, and rest one minute (one set). Go through the hundred exercise twice.

WEDNESDAY: Fasting

You satisfy me more than the richest feast.
I will praise you with songs of joy.
— *Psalm 63:5 NLT*

WARMUP

Read Isaiah 55:1 – 3.

EXERCISES

1. What word occurs five times in these three verses? What does this repetition tell you?

2. Who does God invite to come to him?

3. People "who are thirsty" and those "who have no money" (v. 1) can be either the unsaved or God followers who are hungry for more of him. In verse 1, what does God offer people who listen to him and accept his invitation?

4. How does fasting demonstrate your hunger and thirst for the Lord?

5. What does it mean to "eat what is good" (v. 2)?

6. How can fasting help you hear God's voice more clearly?

7. In verses 2 and 3, how will people who listen to God and seek him be rewarded?

COOLDOWN

Dear God, nothing in this world can satisfy the hunger and thirst in my soul. I'm listening to you, Lord. My ears are inclined in your direction. Speak to my heart, and fill me up with your wonderful words of life. My heart overflows with joy because of your unfailing love for me!

CHALLENGE

As you fast today, ask God to reveal ways in which you attempt to satisfy your deep longings apart from him. Confess areas of idolatry, and rejoice in his promise to bring fulfillment to your life.

Cardio: Engage in thirty to forty-five minutes of aerobic activity (moderate intensity, which is about 60 to 70 percent of your maximum effort).

THURSDAY: Healthy Living

> The kingdom of God is not a matter of eating and drinking,
> but of righteousness, peace and joy in the Holy Spirit.
> — *Romans 14:17*

WARMUP

Read John 15:5 – 11.

EXERCISES

1. In this passage, Jesus compares himself to a vine. What must his branches do to bear fruit?

2. What happens to branches that become detached?

3. The word *remain* means "to abide, to dwell, or to wait." What does it mean to remain in Christ?

4. John 15:16 says Jesus has chosen you and appointed you to "go and bear fruit — fruit that will last." What fruit does Jesus want you to bear?

5. What does God give us when we remain in Christ and in his love?

6. Jesus not only promises to give us joy but also says our joy will be *complete.* What do you think that means?

7. How does taking care of your body result in joy?

COOLDOWN

Lord, I can't do anything without you, but I can do all things in and through you! Bless my efforts to get healthy, so I can be a fruitful branch in every part of my life.

CHALLENGE

Try a new fruit or vegetable today.

Strength: Perform two sets of four upper body exercises (5 – 8) and two sets of four lower body exercises (5 – 8). Do fifteen repetitions for each set. (Use the same amount of resistance for each exercise that you used on Tuesday.)

FRIDAY: Financial Stewardship

Each of you should give
what you have decided in your heart to give,
not reluctantly or under compulsion,
for God loves a cheerful giver.
— *2 Corinthians 9:7*

WARMUP

Read 1 Chronicles 29:1 – 22.

EXERCISES

1. King David led the people in giving money for the construction of the temple. He donated from his personal treasures of gold and silver. What does the Bible say was his motivation?

2. David gave the people an opportunity to join him in supporting the work of the temple. Notice the question he asked them in verse 5. What is the meaning of the word *consecrate*?

3. The Hebrew word for "consecrate" is *male* or *mala* (maw-LAY), which means "to fill or to be full." David invited the people to fill their hands with offerings to the Lord. Why do you think he made the opportunity to give voluntary rather than mandatory?

4. In verses 1 – 17, the word *willing* appears twice, the word *willingly* three times, and the phrase *gave freely* once. This repetition indicates voluntary giving is a theme of the chapter. How did the people respond when they saw the generosity of their leaders? How did David respond?

5. David's generosity inspired others to give to the Lord. When has someone else's generosity motivated you to give?

6. Read verses 12 – 14 again. What attitude toward money is necessary in order to be a cheerful giver?

COOLDOWN

God, everything I have is yours. I give cheerfully and willingly to your work. Help me to grow in generosity and to be devoted to your commands.

CHALLENGE

One benefit of not having debt is that it frees you up to give generously. Make a list of your debts and begin the debt snowball (see page 104). If you don't have any debt, turn to pages 104 – 5 and begin planning your future.

Cardio: Exercise for at least thirty minutes. At the end of your workout, go through the circuit you did on Monday. Perform ten repetitions of the following exercises, and repeat until five minutes is completed: jumping rope (or jumping in place), squats, jumping jacks, crunches, and push-ups.

SATURDAY: Serving Others

Serve wholeheartedly,
as if you were serving the Lord, not people.

—*Ephesians 6:7*

WARMUP

Read Colossians 3:22–24.

EXERCISES

1. What does it mean to work at something with all your heart?

2. Ephesians 6:7 says, "Serve wholeheartedly." The word *wholeheartedly* can be translated as "good will, benevolence, and kindness." It also implies being enthusiastic in your service. Why does Paul say we should be joyful in our work?

3. Work is an opportunity to worship the Lord. How does having this perspective change your attitude about whatever you're doing, whether it's closing an important sale or folding a basket of laundry?

4. Read Ephesians 2:10. What has God created us to do?

5. Who are we serving when we serve others?

6. How does God promise to reward our faithfulness?

COOLDOWN

God, I want to serve you wholeheartedly. Help me to remember that when I show love to other people, I show my love for you. May I be enthusiastic in the tasks you give me to do.

CHALLENGE

Perform an act of kindness for a stranger today. Ask God to show you the person he wants you to bless.

Core: Perform three sets of exercise 3 and two sets of exercises 1, 4, and 5. Complete ten advanced hip bridges, roll-ups, and side bends for each set. Hold side planks for thirty seconds and rest thirty seconds (1 set).

Meal plan: Find two new recipes you've never cooked to incorporate into next week's meal plan. Get ideas from a cookbook, search online, or visit my Daniel Fast website, *www.ultimatedanielfast.com.*

SUNDAY: Rest Day

Lord, you are my strength and my shield. Thank you for protecting me and surrounding me with your favor. My heart trusts in you, and I am helped. My heart leaps for joy when I think of you. I praise your holy name!

You restore my soul and guide me in the paths of righteousness. Your commands are my joy and my heart's delight. I feast on your truth every day. I love your commands because they teach me how to live.

Though I have never seen you, God, I love you. I believe in you and am filled with an inexpressible and glorious joy in your presence. You make me glad by your deeds, and I sing for joy when I think about all you have done!

- "The LORD is my strength and my shield; my heart trusts in him, and he helps me. My heart leaps for joy, and with my song I praise him" (Ps. 28:7).

- "Surely, LORD, you bless the righteous; you surround them with your favor as with a shield" (Ps. 5:12).

- "[The LORD] restores my soul; He guides me in the paths of righteousness for His name's sake" (Ps. 23:3 NASB).

- "When your words came, I ate them; they were my joy and my heart's delight, for I bear your name, LORD God Almighty" (Jer. 15:16).

- "Though you have not seen [Jesus], you love him; and even though you do not see him now, you believe in him and are filled with an inexpressible and glorious joy" (1 Peter 1:8).

- "You make me glad by your deeds, LORD; I sing for joy at what your hands have done" (Ps. 92:4).

WEEK 5

Peace

Now may the Lord of peace himself
give you peace at all times and in every way.
— 2 Thessalonians 3:16

You can experience God's perfect peace in any and every situation. That's because peace has very little to do with your surroundings and everything to do with what's going on inside your heart. The key to resting in the Lord is trusting in him. This week, when the challenges of this program come at you full force, choose the way of peace. Refuse to let anxiety get a foothold in your life. Instead of being worried, trust in the Prince of Peace to help you remain calm at all times and in every way.

MONDAY: Bible Study

Great peace have those who love your law,
and nothing can make them stumble.
— Psalm 119:165

WARMUP
Read John 20:19 – 20.

EXERCISES

1. The events in this passage take place three days after Jesus was crucified, and the disciples were assembled behind locked doors. When Jesus came and stood among them, he declared, "Peace be with you!" (v. 19). What was he saying?

2. The Greek word for "peace" in this verse is *eirene* (i-RAY-nay), which means "peace of mind; quietness." Why did the disciples need God's peace?

3. Notice that when the disciples were full of fear, Jesus came to them and set their hearts at rest. How has God's presence given you peace when you were afraid?

4. During Paul's ministry in Jerusalem, he experienced violent opposition. Acts 23:1 – 15 gives the account of the accusations against Paul and the plot to kill him. What does Acts 23:11 say the Lord did to strengthen Paul and encourage him?

5. Peace is not only something God gives; it's also *who he is.* One of the names of God is Jehovah-Shalom, the Lord our Peace (Judg. 6:24). So when God gives us his peace, he is giving us himself. Think of a difficult time in your life when you knew the God of peace was near. How did his presence strengthen you?

6. Ephesians 6:15 refers to the Word of God as the "gospel of peace." How can regular Bible study keep you from being overcome by fear?

COOLDOWN

Lord God, you are my peace. I find rest in you today as I meditate on your great and precious promises.

CHALLENGE

Write down on a piece of paper all the things that cause you to worry. Confess each one to the Lord, and then thank God for giving you his peace. Finally, as a statement of your freedom from those burdens, tear up the paper and throw it in the trash!

Cardio: Today you'll focus on interval training during your thirty-minute workout. Warm up for ten minutes. Then increase your intensity to about 80 percent of your maximum effort for one minute (breathing very hard and heart beating rapidly). After you push it for one minute, slow down for two minutes for an easy recovery. Repeat sequence five times, and cool down the last five minutes.

TUESDAY: Prayer (Posture)

Come, let us bow down in worship,
let us kneel before the LORD our Maker.
—*Psalm 95:6*

WARMUP

Read Daniel 6:1 – 23.

EXERCISES

1. Daniel's enemies knew he was a man of prayer, so they convinced King Darius to issue an edict saying anyone who prayed to a god or man other than the king would be thrown into the lions' den. How did Daniel react when he heard the news?

2. Where did Daniel pray?

3. Why do you think the Bible includes the detail that he prayed near open windows?

4. What was Daniel's posture of prayer?

5. Daniel's commitment to prayer resulted in his being thrown into the lions' den. But God miraculously intervened and spared his life. What reason does verse 23 give for why Daniel was saved?

6. How has God shown his power in response to your prayers? Write down one or two ways.

COOLDOWN

Practice Daniel's prayer posture today. Call out to God on your knees. You can even open your windows if you like!

CHALLENGE

Strength: Perform three sets of four upper body exercises (1, 3, 5, and 7) and two sets of four lower body exercises (1, 3, 5, and 7). Do ten repetitions for each set.

Core: Perform three sets of exercise 2 and two sets of exercise 4. Hold planks for one minute, and rest one minute (one set). Complete ten roll-ups for each set.

WEDNESDAY: Fasting

> Is not this the kind of fasting I have chosen:
> to loose the chains of injustice and untie the cords of the yoke,
> to set the oppressed free and break every yoke?
>
> — Isaiah 58:6

WARMUP

Read Isaiah 58:1 – 12.

EXERCISES

1. In this passage, the Lord responded to the people's complaints about his apparent indifference to their times of fasting. Why were their sacrifices unacceptable to God?

2. The Israelites were going through all the motions of fasting, but their hearts were not in it. Although the people seemed eager to seek the Lord, they were guilty of hypocrisy. What were they doing?

3. What kind of a fast pleases the Lord?

4. How can we prevent our fasts from being offensive to God?

5. God promises to reward people who fast and pray according to his Word. What are some of the blessings outlined in verses 8 – 12?

6. This passage shows us that fasting involves more than private prayer. It also includes public action. Our prayers are incomplete if we don't show compassion and love toward people around us. What can you do today to "spend yourself" on behalf of someone else? Write down at least one way in which you will satisfy someone else's need.

COOLDOWN

Lord God, I don't want my fasts to be repulsive to you. Show me any specific sins which need to be confessed, and cleanse my heart of any impurity. May your grace and peace cover me as I devote myself to sharing your love with others.

CHALLENGE

As you fast today, follow through with the commitment you made on question 6 in the exercise section above. If you're not sure what to do, ask God for wisdom and then wait for direction. Remember the promise in Isaiah 58:11: "The LORD will guide you always."

Cardio: Engage in thirty to forty-five minutes of aerobic activity (moderate intensity, which is about 60 to 70 percent of your maximum effort).

THURSDAY: Healthy Living

> The mind governed by the Spirit
> is life and peace.
> — *Romans 8:6*

WARMUP

Read Romans 8:5 – 11.

EXERCISES

1. This passage describes two categories of people — those who chase after selfish desires and those who pursue God. How does a person move from living according to the sinful nature to living according to the Spirit?

2. Paul makes the connection between thought patterns and behavior. What does he say is the product of having a mindset geared toward the things of this world?

3. Paul mentions two characteristics of a Spirit-governed mind. What are they?

4. The only way we can keep our thoughts holy and pure is by depending on the Holy Spirit's help. Read Philippians 4:8. What kinds of thoughts should fill our minds?

5. When it comes to how you think about your body, is your mind governed more by your flesh or by the Spirit? Give examples to back up your answer.

6. Read Romans 8:11 again. While this verse refers to the promise of eternal life, how does it apply to your body now? In other words, how do you experience life and peace when you care for God's temple?

COOLDOWN

Lord God, your Word says I have the mind of Christ. Thank you for giving me the power to cast aside selfish thinking and be led by your Spirit. May my thoughts honor you today.

CHALLENGE

Make your workout a time of worship. Listen to praise music while you exercise.

Strength: Perform two sets of four upper body exercises (2, 4, 6, and 8) and three sets of four lower body exercises (2, 4, 6, and 8). Do ten repetitions for each set.

FRIDAY: Financial Stewardship

The prudent give thought to their steps.
— *Proverbs 14:15*

WARMUP

Read Proverbs 6:6 – 8.

EXERCISES

1. This passage describes the ant as a wise creature. What does the ant do that we should imitate?

2. Saving and investing money is one way of storing provisions. However, it's important to have a plan in place. How are you setting aside money for the future?

3. Read Luke 14:28 – 30. What are some "towers" in your life that require (or will require) proper financial planning?

4. What will happen if you don't estimate the cost?

5. Proverbs 6:8 says the ant is rewarded for its preparation during summer by being able to gather food at harvest time for the winter months. What are some benefits of making wise financial investments?

COOLDOWN

Father God, teach me how to use wisdom when making investment decisions. I look to you, O Lord, to guide me and show me the way to go.

CHALLENGE

Choose one of these steps to begin planning for the future: (1) save three to six months' worth of expenses; (2) save 10 – 15 percent of your income for retirement; (3) save toward college; (4) pay off your house early. See page 105 for help.

Cardio: Complete thirty minutes of interval training. Warm up for ten minutes. Then increase your intensity to about 80 percent of your maximum effort for one minute (breathing very hard and heart beating rapidly). After you push it for one minute, slow down for two minutes for an easy recovery. Repeat sequence five times, and cool down the last five minutes.

SATURDAY: Serving Others

> As the body without the spirit is dead,
> so faith without deeds is dead.
> — James 2:26

WARMUP

Read Romans 2:6 – 11.

EXERCISES

1. God promises to reward our good deeds. What does he say he will give people who persist in doing his will?

2. What awaits people who reject God's truth and follow evil?

3. Which people are declared righteous in God's sight?

4. At first glance, it might appear the apostle Paul is implying we gain eternal life through good works. But that's not what he's saying at all. In Romans 1:16, Paul is very clear about who does the saving, and it's not us. He also says our righteousness, from first to last, is by faith alone (Rom. 1:17). What role, then, do deeds play in our salvation experience?

5. Read James 2:14 – 19. While acts of service do not save us, our faith is dead if we refuse to take action when we see people in need. How does reaching out with God's love to other people result in peace?

6. Why are good deeds evidence of true faith in the Lord?

COOLDOWN

Lord, you have called me to reach out and help people. That is my duty. Thank you for equipping me with everything I need and for the peace you promise as I fulfill this responsibility.

CHALLENGE

If you have children, teach them how to serve by having them help set the table for dinner. Then have them clean it up. If you're single or don't have children, send a card to a child in your life. Children love to get mail, and your thoughtfulness will be much appreciated.

Core: Perform three sets of exercise 3 and three sets of exercise 6. Hold side planks for thirty seconds, and rest thirty seconds (one set). Finish with three sets of hundreds.

Meal plan: Dedicate an hour to prepping meals for next week.

SUNDAY: Rest Day

Lord, you are Jehovah-Shalom, the God of Peace. Thank you for the perfect peace you give me through Jesus Christ. When troubles come, I can rest in you and in your promise of victory instead of getting anxious.

The desire of my heart is to be a peacemaker. Your Word says you bless people who work for peace. I trust you to equip me with everything I need to produce a harvest of righteousness. May your abundant grace and peace be upon my life as I grow in my knowledge of your Word.

- "Gideon built an altar to the LORD there and called it The LORD Is Peace" (Judg. 6:24).

- "I have told you these things, so that in me you may have peace. In this world you will have trouble. But take heart! I have overcome the world" (John 16:33).

- "God blesses those who work for peace, for they will be called the children of God" (Matt. 5:9 NLT).

- "May the God of peace ... equip you with everything good for doing his will" (Heb. 13:20 – 21).

- "Peacemakers who sow in peace reap a harvest of righteousness" (James 3:18).

- "Grace and peace be yours in abundance through the knowledge of God and of Jesus our Lord" (2 Peter 1:2).

Victory

Thanks be to God! He gives us the victory
through our Lord Jesus Christ.
—1 Corinthians 15:57

This final week is all about celebrating your successes in this program. Your work isn't finished yet, though. Keep your gaze fixed firmly on the Lord and his provision. After all, you're in the home stretch now. The finish line is in sight. I can almost hear your shout of joy as you reflect on God's faithfulness: "The LORD's right hand has done mighty things!" (Ps. 118:15). Praise God for the victory he has given you in Christ!

MONDAY: Bible Study

Be strong in the Lord
and in his mighty power.
—Ephesians 6:10

WARMUP

Read 2 Corinthians 10:3 – 5.

EXERCISES

1. How is the Christian life described in verse 3?

2. In these verses, Paul uses military terminology to describe spiritual warfare. What weapons do we fight with? See Ephesians 6:12 – 18.

3. Verse 4 says our weapons "have divine power to demolish strongholds." What is a stronghold?

4. Paul says we fight not only against external attacks but also against internal attacks. What are some ways you experience battles within yourself?

5. How do we bring our emotions into captivity so they line up with God's Word?

6. Read Romans 8:11 and Ephesians 1:18–20. The same power that raised Christ from the dead lives in people who know him as Lord and Savior. How does knowing this truth give you confidence when you face trials and temptations?

7. Read Psalm 18:2. Make this verse a personal prayer by declaring God's attributes.

COOLDOWN

Lord, you're the God of my salvation. You're my rock, my fortress, and my deliverer. You're my place of safety, my stronghold. Thank you for being my shield and protecting me from the Enemy.

CHALLENGE

Speak the truths of Ephesians 6:10–18 out loud, and personalize them. For example, say, "I am strong in the Lord and in his mighty power. I put on the full armor of God so I can stand against the Devil's schemes." Say these words with conviction, as a mighty soldier in God's army!

Cardio: Engage in forty minutes of aerobic activity. At the end of your workout, add five minutes of additional exercise by doing a circuit of burpees, crunches, chair dips, lunges, and mountain climbers. Perform ten repetitions of each exercise until the five minutes is completed.

TUESDAY: Prayer (Power)

> You will receive power
> when the Holy Spirit comes on you.
> *— Acts 1:8*

WARMUP

Read Acts 1:1–14.

EXERCISES

1. What did Jesus tell the disciples to wait for in verse 4?

2. What was "the gift"?

3. Jesus said the Holy Spirit would come upon the disciples to empower them for ministry. In what two ways would the disciples be affected by this gift?

4. The disciples were commissioned by the Lord to share the gospel with the world. However, they first needed to be filled with power from on high. How did the disciples wait for the promised Holy Spirit? Write your answer, and then underline the phrase in your Bible.

5. God has called you to a special work, just as he called the disciples. How does prayer equip you to be an effective witness for Christ?

6. What is God saying to you about prayer? Write how you will make it more of a priority in your life.

COOLDOWN

Lord God, thank you for the gift of the Holy Spirit, who provides the power I need for a supernatural life.

CHALLENGE

Claim Colossians 1:13 over someone in your life who doesn't know the Lord. Have faith in God's power to rescue. He is mighty to save!

Strength: Perform three sets of four upper body exercises (1, 3, 5, and 7) and two sets of four lower body exercises (1, 3, 5, and 7). Do ten repetitions for each set. Increase resistance if you can. (And I *know* you can!)

Core: This week you'll focus on planks and hundreds. Today, perform four sets of exercise 2 and three sets of exercise 6. Hold planks for one minute, and rest one minute (one set). Go through the hundred exercise three times. *You can do it!*

WEDNESDAY: Fasting

> If my people, who are called by my name,
> will humble themselves and pray and seek my face
> and turn from their wicked ways, then I will hear from heaven,
> and I will forgive their sin and will heal their land.
>
> *— 2 Chronicles 7:14*

WARMUP

Read Esther 3 – 4; 5:1 – 2.

EXERCISES

1. When Mordecai learned of Haman's plot and the king's edict, he urged Queen Esther to intervene. At first, Esther was reluctant to get involved. Why?

2. Mordecai sent word back to Esther, trying to persuade her to take action. He basically said, "You're our only hope." He also reminded Esther that her royal position would not save her from annihilation. Mordecai's words were convincing, so Esther finally agreed. What do you think changed her mind?

3. Esther realized the safety of the Jewish race was more important than her life. What did she instruct Mordecai to do?

4. How did Esther prepare her heart before going to the king?

5. Why do you think Esther sought the prayer support of other believers?

6. The king showed mercy to Esther, and the Jewish people were saved. How is this an illustration of what happens when we humble ourselves before God through prayer and fasting?

7. Have you experienced the unity of a corporate fast? Write about what you learned as you joined with other believers to seek the Lord. If you haven't fasted with a group, write about a time when you witnessed the unity of the Spirit among Christians.

COOLDOWN

Lord God, my desire is to be bold like Esther. You have placed me in a position of influence with family and friends who don't know you. Help me to fast and pray regularly for their salvation.

CHALLENGE

Ask a Christian family member or friend to fast with you today. Remember, there is power when God's people pray!

Cardio: Engage in forty-five minutes of aerobic activity (moderate intensity, which is about 60 to 70 percent of your maximum effort).

THURSDAY: Healthy Living

I can do everything through Christ,
who gives me strength.
—*Philippians 4:13 NLT*

WARMUP

Read Nehemiah 1 – 2:18; 4:1 – 9; 6:1 – 9, 15 – 16.

EXERCISES

1. When Nehemiah shared his plan to repair the city wall in Jerusalem, nearby government officials ridiculed him. What did Nehemiah say in response to their mockery?

2. The residents of Jerusalem caught Nehemiah's vision and worked with all their heart to repair the wall. What does the first part of Nehemiah 4:9 say the Jews did when Sanballat continually harassed them?

3. As you've worked to build your body by improving your eating and exercise habits, what forms of opposition have you faced (or are you facing)?

4. When Sanballat, Tobiah, and other enemies of the Israelites saw the progress the people were making, they became more aggressive. They hurled insults at the Israelites and made fun of them. Nehemiah,

sensing the people's discouragement, said to the workers, "Don't be afraid of them. Remember the Lord, who is great and awesome, and fight" (Neh. 4:14). When you grow weary in trying to make positive changes with your health, how can Nehemiah's words give you strength?

5. Just before the wall was completed, Sanballat and his crew made one final attempt to stop the construction. They tried to convince Nehemiah to take a break and meet with them. Nehemiah, knowing their intentions were evil, refused to be distracted. What does Nehemiah's response tell you about his commitment level?

6. Nehemiah was determined not to let anyone or anything stop him from reaching the goal God had placed on his heart. As a result, the wall of Jerusalem was completed in fifty-two days — a true miracle. When surrounding enemies heard about it, they realized the work had been done with the help of God. When you're dedicated to healthy living, how does God receive the glory?

COOLDOWN

Lord, help me to be as resolved as Nehemiah when it comes to doing your work. Give me motivation, courage, determination, and wisdom through your Word so when the Enemy attacks, I am armed and ready.

CHALLENGE

Identify an obstacle that hinders your effort to achieve a healthier lifestyle. Then pray for a plan or the motivation to have victory over that obstacle.

Strength: Perform two sets of four upper body exercises (2, 4, 6, and 8) and three sets of four lower body exercises (2, 4, 6, and 8). Do ten repetitions for each set, and use resistance where you can. Today is your last strength workout of this program. *Give it all you've got!*

FRIDAY: Financial Stewardship

Whoever is generous will be blessed.

—*Proverbs 22:9 GW*

WARMUP

Read Mark 12:41 – 44.

EXERCISES

1. As Jesus watched the crowd put their offerings into the temple treasury, he noticed that the rich gave large amounts of money. But what captured his heart was a gift of two small copper coins, given by a poor widow. Why?

2. Why was it significant that the woman was a widow?

3. What did the widow's offering indicate about her faith in God's provision?

4. The woman was giving faithfully to the Lord, even though she lived in poverty. How does her example challenge you in regard to your giving?

5. What keeps you from giving to the Lord? List forms of resistance you encounter or excuses you make.

6. God cares more about *how* you give than about *how much* you give. Jesus observed the woman's heart and saw her gratitude and trust. What does God see in *your* heart when it comes to giving? Write your answer in the form of a prayer, asking God to help you be generous in your giving.

COOLDOWN

Lord, you've blessed me with so much! I don't ever want to be selfish with what you've given me. Help me to have the heart of the widow in this story.

CHALLENGE

Give your tithe if you haven't already this week (or month). If you've already given to the Lord, make an additional eternal investment by donating to a ministry or mission project.

Cardio: Engage in forty minutes of aerobic activity. At the end of your workout, add five minutes of additional exercise by doing a circuit of burpees, crunches, chair dips, lunges, and mountain climbers. Perform ten repetitions of each exercise until the five minutes is completed. Make this workout count. *Go hard!*

SATURDAY: Serving Others

God is not unjust;
he will not forget your work
and the love you have shown him
as you have helped his people
and continue to help them.

— Hebrews 6:10

WARMUP

Read Exodus 17:8 – 13.

EXERCISES

1. The Amalekites were descendants of Amalek, a grandson of Esau. They were a fierce, nomadic tribe who killed for pleasure and made part of their livelihood by raiding nearby settlements. When the Amalekites attacked God's people, Moses formulated a plan. What did he command his assistant, Joshua, to do?

2. Moses didn't go out with the other men. Instead he fought the battle on a different front. Why do you think Moses stood on top of a hill?

3. What was the significance of Moses' hands raised toward heaven?

4. What did Aaron and Hur do when Moses' arms grew tired?

5. Moses received strength from Aaron and Hur. Because of their service, God's people defeated the Amalekites. How important is it to have support from other believers when we're in the throes of battle?

6. Write a prayer of thanksgiving to the Lord for a time when your hands were lifted by another believer.

COOLDOWN

Lord God, you are my shield. Many times, you have given me strength through the encouragement of family and friends. Thank you for giving me what I need at just the right time. You always provide when I trust in you.

CHALLENGE

Who is someone you know whose arms are growing weary? Think of a practical way in which you can help ease his or her burden, and do it.

Core: Perform three sets of exercises 3 and 6. Hold side planks for forty-five seconds, and rest thirty seconds (one set). Finish with four sets of hundreds.

Meal plan: Even though your six-week program is nearly completed, continue the discipline of planning your meals each week. Not only will you stay on track physically, but also you'll save money in the long run by being more organized and not eating out as frequently.

SUNDAY: Rest Day

Lord, you are a mighty warrior. You are the God who saves. Your awesome power defeats my enemies and gives me victory. Thank you for answering from heaven when I cry out for help, and thank you for reaching down for me with your righteous right hand.

When the Enemy attacks, you are with me, fighting the battle for me. All I have to do is remain calm and not give way to fear. You surround me with your protection because you love me. You take delight in every detail of my life and rejoice over me with singing. I rejoice in your strength, O God. My heart is thankful and joyful when I think about the victories you give!

- "The LORD your God is the one who goes with you to fight for you against your enemies to give you victory" (Deut. 20:4).

- "The LORD gives victory to his anointed. He answers him from his heavenly sanctuary with the victorious power of his right hand" (Ps. 20:6).

- "The LORD himself will fight for you. Just stay calm" (Ex. 14:14 NLT).

- "The LORD your God is with you, the Mighty Warrior who saves. He will take great delight in you; in his love he will no longer rebuke you, but will rejoice over you with singing" (Zeph. 3:17).

- "The king rejoices in your strength, LORD. How great is his joy in the victories you give!" (Ps. 21:1).

Acknowledgments

Justin: Thank you for loving me so much and always encouraging me in whatever I'm doing. You're a wonderful husband and father. I still can't believe I get to be your wife! I love you. "Every time I think of you, I give thanks to my God" (Phil. 1:3 NLT).

Isabelle and Jocelyn: Thank you for being patient and understanding when I had to work on this book and couldn't play with you. I love you and am extremely proud of the young ladies you are. I pray you'll always "love the LORD your God, listen to his voice, and hold fast to him" (Deut. 30:20).

Family and friends: Thank you for your faithful prayers and support. I especially want to thank friends who watched Isabelle and Jocelyn when I needed uninterrupted writing time. I couldn't have met my deadlines without your help. "May the Lord reward you well for the kindness you have shown me" (1 Sam. 24:19 NLT).

Friends who contributed testimonies: Thank you for sharing what God has done in your lives. Thousands of people will be positively impacted by your stories of his faithfulness. May the Lord bless you and refresh you as you have refreshed others (Prov. 11:25).

Sandra Vander Zicht, Executive Editor: Thank you for believing in me and going to bat for this book. What an honor to be able to partner with you a second time! And now, "may the Lord our God show us his approval and make our efforts successful. Yes, make our efforts successful!" (Ps. 90:17 NLT).

Brian Phipps, Senior Editor: Thank you for helping me put the finishing touches on this manuscript. It was truly a pleasure to work with you again. I pray "the LORD your God will bless you in all your work and in all that you undertake" (Deut. 15:10 ESV).

Tom Dean, Senior Director of Marketing: Thank you for your enthusiasm for this book and for being available whenever I had questions or concerns. May God continue to give you wisdom, knowledge, and joy in abundance as you serve him (Ecc. 2:26a).

Les Stobbe, Literary Agent: Thank you for your wisdom and guidance. Your years of experience in the publishing industry often provided me with much-needed insight. "May you be blessed by the LORD, the Maker of heaven and earth" (Ps. 115:15).

Exercise Plan

Week 1

Monday — *Cardio:* Complete a thirty-minute workout today (walk, run, bike, or hike).

Tuesday — *Strength:* Perform one set of four upper body exercises (1 – 4; see "Key to Exercises" on p. 199) and one set of four lower body exercises (1 – 4). Do ten repetitions for each set. Add resistance (dumbbells or a band) where you can. Use a weight that's challenging but doesn't cause you to use incorrect form. Keep in mind the amount of resistance may be different for each exercise. See *www.kristenfeola.com* for video instruction on proper form and for ideas on exercise modifications.

Tuesday — *Core:* Perform one set of exercises 1 – 3 (ten repetitions for hip bridges, and hold both types of planks for fifteen seconds).

Wednesday — *Cardio:* Try a different exercise than you did on Monday. Your goal is thirty minutes of sustained activity. If you're fasting from more than one meal today, you might need to decrease the intensity of your workout. Also, make sure you drink plenty of water before and after you exercise.

Thursday — *Strength:* Perform one set of four upper body exercises (5 – 8) and one set of four lower body exercises (5 – 8). Do ten repetitions for each set. Add resistance (dumbbells or a band) where you can. Use a weight that's challenging but doesn't cause you to use incorrect form. Keep in mind the amount of resistance may be different for each exercise. See *www.kristenfeola.com* for video instruction on proper form and for ideas on exercise modifications.

Friday — *Cardio:* Exercise for at least thirty minutes with a friend or attend a fitness class.

Saturday — *Core:* Perform one set of exercises 4 – 6 (five roll-ups, ten side bends on each side, and one set of the hundred exercise).

Sunday — *Rest.*

Week 2

Monday — *Cardio:* Mix up your thirty-minute workout today. Do fifteen minutes of one cardiovascular exercise, and then do fifteen minutes of something different.

Tuesday — *Strength:* Perform one set of four upper body exercises (1 – 4) and one set of four lower body exercises (1 – 4). Do fifteen repetitions for each set.

Tuesday — *Core:* Perform one set of exercises 1 – 3 (fifteen repetitions for hip bridges, and hold planks for thirty seconds).

Wednesday — *Cardio:* Walk, run, bike, or hike for thirty minutes.

Thursday — *Strength:* Perform one set of four upper body exercises (5 – 8) and one set of four lower body exercises (5 – 8). Do fifteen repetitions for each set.

Friday — *Cardio:* If you have a gym membership, get on a different machine today. If you exercise at home, try using a DVD. Or better yet, go outside for your thirty-minute workout!

Saturday — *Core:* Perform two sets of exercises 4 – 6 (total of ten roll-ups, twenty side bends). Do only one set of the hundred exercise.

Sunday — *Rest.*

Week 3

Monday — *Cardio:* Increase your level of intensity today. Also, try to exercise for more than thirty minutes. If you're walking or running, pick up the pace. Go faster on the bike. If using an elliptical machine, set it to a higher resistance. Push yourself! Work harder than you did last week. Your goal is at least 70 percent of your maximum effort (slightly short of breath, but still able to carry on a conversation).

Tuesday — *Strength:* Perform two sets of four upper body exercises (1 – 4) and two sets of four lower body exercises (1 – 4). You're ready to increase your level of resistance, so use the next-heaviest dumbbell (where applicable). Do ten repetitions for each set.

Tuesday — *Core:* Perform two sets of exercises 1, 3, and 5. Do two sets of ten advanced hip bridges and side bends (each side) with resistance, and hold side planks for thirty seconds.

Wednesday — *Cardio:* Go for a walk or run at a nearby park, trail, or nature center. If the weather is too cold, walk or run on a treadmill. Do something to get your body moving for at least thirty minutes today!

Thursday — *Strength:* Perform two sets of four upper body exercises (5 – 8) and two sets of four lower body exercises (5 – 8). Use same weight as Tuesday. Do ten repetitions for each set.

Friday — *Cardio:* Try an exercise class you've never taken or a new DVD workout (at least thirty minutes or longer). Many fitness centers will allow you to try a class for free, even if you aren't a member. Take advantage and sample one or two classes, such as spinning, Zumba, cardio kickboxing, step aerobics, or Jazzercise.

Saturday — *Core:* Perform two sets of exercises 2 and 6 and one set of exercise 4. Hold planks for forty-five seconds, do fifteen roll-ups, and go through the hundred exercise twice.

Sunday — *Rest.*

Week 4

Monday — *Cardio:* Engage in at least thirty minutes of cardiovascular activity. At the end of your workout, add five minutes of additional exercise by doing a circuit of jumping rope (or jumping in place), squats, jumping jacks, crunches, and push-ups. Perform ten repetitions of each exercise, and repeat until the five minutes is completed.

Tuesday — *Strength:* Perform two sets of four upper body exercises (1 – 4) and two sets of four lower body exercises (1 – 4). Do fifteen repetitions for each set (use the same weight you used last week or a heavier weight).

Tuesday — *Core:* Perform three sets of exercise 2 and two sets of exercise 6. Hold planks for one minute, and rest one minute (one set). Go through the hundred exercise twice.

Wednesday — *Cardio:* Engage in thirty to forty-five minutes of aerobic activity (moderate intensity, which is about 60 to 70 percent of your maximum effort).

Thursday — *Strength:* Perform two sets of four upper body exercises (5 – 8) and two sets of four lower body exercises (5 – 8). Do fifteen repetitions for each set. (Use the same weight you used Tuesday.)

Friday — *Cardio:* Exercise for at least thirty minutes. At the end of your workout, go through the circuit you did on Monday. Perform ten repetitions of the following exercises, and repeat until five minutes is completed: jumping rope (or jumping in place), squats, jumping jacks, crunches, and push-ups.

Saturday — *Core:* Perform three sets of exercise 3 and two sets of exercises 1, 4, and 5. Complete ten advanced hip bridges, roll-ups, and side bends for each set. Hold side planks for thirty seconds, and rest thirty seconds (one set).

Sunday — *Rest.*

Week 5

Monday — *Cardio:* Today you'll focus on interval training during your thirty-minute workout. Warm up for ten minutes. Then increase your intensity to about 80 percent of your maximum effort for one minute (breathing very hard and heart beating rapidly). After you push it for one minute, slow down for two minutes for an easy recovery. Repeat this sequence five times, and cool down the last five minutes.

Tuesday — *Strength:* Perform three sets of four upper body exercises (1, 3, 5, and 7) and two sets of four lower body exercises (1, 3, 5, and 7). Do ten repetitions for each set.

Tuesday — *Core:* Perform three sets of exercise 2 and two sets of exercise 4. Hold planks for one minute, and rest one minute (one set). Complete ten roll-ups for each set.

Wednesday — *Cardio:* Engage in thirty to forty-five minutes of aerobic activity (moderate intensity, which is about 60 to 70 percent of your maximum effort).

Thursday — *Strength:* Perform two sets of four upper body exercises (2, 4, 6, and 8) and three sets of four lower body exercises (2, 4, 6, and 8). Do ten repetitions for each set.

Friday — *Cardio:* Complete thirty minutes of interval training. Warm up for ten minutes. Then increase your intensity to about 80 percent of your maximum effort for one minute (breathing very hard and heart beating rapidly). After you push it for one minute, slow down for two minutes for an easy recovery. Repeat this sequence five times, and cool down the last five minutes.

Saturday — *Core:* Perform three sets of exercise 3 and three sets of exercise 6. Hold side planks for thirty seconds, and rest thirty seconds (one set). Finish with three sets of hundreds.

Sunday — *Rest.*

Week 6

Monday — *Cardio:* Engage in forty minutes of aerobic activity. At the end of your workout, add five minutes of additional exercise by doing a circuit of burpees, crunches, chair dips, lunges, and mountain climbers. Perform ten repetitions of each exercise until the five minutes is completed.

Tuesday — *Strength:* Perform three sets of four upper body exercises (1, 3, 5, and 7) and two sets of four lower body exercises (1, 3, 5, and 7). Do ten repetitions for each set. Increase resistance if you can. (And I *know* you can!)

Tuesday — *Core:* This week you'll focus on planks and hundreds. Today, perform four sets of exercise 2 and three sets of exercise 6. Hold planks for one minute, and rest one minute (one set). Go through the hundred exercise three times. *You can do it!*

Wednesday — *Cardio:* Engage in forty-five minutes of aerobic activity (moderate intensity, which is about 60 to 70 percent of your maximum effort).

Thursday — *Strength:* Perform two sets of four upper body exercises (2, 4, 6, and 8) and three sets of four lower body exercises (2, 4, 6, and 8). Do ten repetitions for each set, and use resistance where you can. Today is your last strength workout of this program. *Give it all you've got!*

Friday — *Cardio:* Engage in forty minutes of aerobic activity. At the end of your workout, add five minutes of additional exercise by doing a circuit of burpees, crunches, chair dips, lunges, and mountain climbers. Perform ten repetitions of each exercise until the five minutes is completed. Make this workout count. *Go hard!*

Saturday — *Core:* Perform three sets of exercises 3 and 6. Hold side planks for forty-five seconds, and rest thirty seconds (one set). Finish with four sets of hundreds.

Sunday — *Rest.*

Exercise Plan

	Mon	Tues	Wed	Thurs	Fri	Sat	Sun
Week 1	**Cardio:** 30 min • Walk, run, bike, or hike	**Strength:** Ex 1 – 4 • 1 set of 10 reps **Core:** Ex 1 – 3 • 1 set of 10 hip bridges • 1 set of both planks (15 sec)	**Cardio:** 30 min • Different exercise than Mon	**Strength:** Ex 5 – 8 • 1 set of 10 reps	**Cardio:** 30 min • Exercise with a friend or attend a fitness class	**Core:** Ex 4 – 6 • 1 set of 5 roll-ups • 1 set of 10 side bends • 1 set of 100s	Rest
Week 2	**Cardio:** 30 min • Two different exercises, 15 min each	**Strength:** Ex 1 – 4 • 1 set of 15 reps **Core:** Ex 1 – 3 • 1 set of 15 hip bridges • 1 set of both planks (30 sec)	**Cardio:** 30 min • Walk, run, bike, or hike	**Strength:** Ex 5 – 8 • 1 set of 15 reps	**Cardio:** 30 min • Different machine at gym, or exercise outdoors	**Core:** Ex 4 – 6 • 2 sets of 5 roll-ups • 2 sets of 10 side bends • 1 set of 100s	Rest
Week 3	**Cardio:** 30+ min • Increase intensity to at least 70% of max effort	**Strength:** Ex 1 – 4 • 2 sets of 10 reps • Increase resistance **Core:** Ex 1, 3, 5 • 2 sets of 10 adv bridges and side bends (db or band) • 2 sets of side planks (30 sec)	**Cardio:** 30+ min • Walk or run outside (inside if too cold)	**Strength:** Ex 5 – 8 • 2 sets of 10 reps • Use same weight as Tues	**Cardio:** 30+ min • New fitness class or DVD workout	**Core:** Ex 2, 4, 6 • 2 sets of planks (45 sec) • 15 roll-ups • 2 sets of 100s	Rest

Exercise Plan *continued*

	Mon	Tues	Wed	Thurs	Fri	Sat	Sun
Week 4	**Cardio:** 30 min +5 min circuit (jump rope, squats, jacks, crunches, push-ups; 10 reps each, then repeat)	**Strength:** Ex 1 - 4 • 2 sets of 15 reps • Increase resistance **Core:** Ex 2,6 • 3 sets planks (1 min, rest 1 min) • 2 sets 100s	**Cardio:** 30 – 45 min • Moderate intensity (60 – 70% of max effort)	**Strength:** Ex 5 - 8 • 2 sets of 15 reps • Use same weight as Tues	**Cardio:** 30 min +5 min circuit (jump rope, squats, jacks, crunches, push-ups; 10 reps each, then repeat)	**Core:** Ex 1, 3, 4, 5 • 3 sets of side planks (30 sec, rest 30 sec) • 2 sets 10 adv hip bridges, roll-ups, side bends	Rest
Week 5	**Cardio:** 30 min interval training • 10 min warmup • 15 min intervals • 5 min cooldown	**Strength:** Ex 1, 3, 5, 7 Upper: 3 sets of 10 reps; Lower: 2 sets of 10 reps; increase resistance **Core:** Ex 2, 4 • 3 sets planks (1 min, rest 1 min) • 2 sets 10 roll-ups	**Cardio:** 30 – 45 min • Moderate intensity (60 – 70% of max effort)	**Strength:** Ex 2, 4, 6, 8 Upper: 2 sets of 10 reps Lower: 3 sets of 10 reps	**Cardio:** 30 min interval training • 10 min warmup • 15 min intervals • 5 min cooldown	**Core:** Ex 3, 6 • 3 sets of side planks (30 sec, rest 30 sec) • 3 sets 100s	Rest
Week 6	**Cardio:** 40 min +5 min circuit (burpees, crunches, chair dips, lunges, mountain climbers; 10 reps each, then repeat)	**Strength:** Ex 1, 3, 5, 7 Upper: 3 sets of 10 reps; Lower: 2 sets of 10 reps; increase resistance **Core:** Ex 2,6 • 4 sets planks (1 min, rest 1 min) • 3 sets 100s	**Cardio:** 45 min • Moderate intensity (60 – 70% of max effort)	**Strength:** Ex 2, 4, 6, 8 Upper: 2 sets of 10 reps Lower: 3 sets of 10 reps	**Cardio:** 40 min +5 min circuit (burpees, crunches, chair dips, lunges, mountain climbers; 10 reps each, then repeat)	**Core:** Ex 3,6 • 3 sets of side planks (45 sec, rest 30 sec) • 4 sets of 100s	

Key to Exercises

Upper Body Exercises

1. Push-ups
2. Dumbbell Rows
3. Biceps Curls
4. Triceps Kickbacks
5. Chair Dips
6. Dumbbell Shoulder Presses
7. Lateral Arm Raises
8. Front Arm Raises

Lower Body Exercises

1. Squats
2. Lunges
3. Step-ups
4. Calf Raises
5. Jumping Jacks
6. Burpees
7. Jumping Squats
8. Mountain Climbers

Core Exercises

1. Hip Bridges
2. Planks
3. Side Planks
4. Roll-ups
5. Side Bends
6. Hundreds

Notes

CHAPTER 2: Training Your Core

1. Matthew Henry, *Matthew Henry's Concise Commentary on the Whole Bible* (Nashville: Nelson, 1997), 1098.

2. "Balance," Merriam-Webster.com, *www.merriam-webster.com/dictionary/balance*.

3. Colette Bouchez, "Exercise for Energy: Workouts That Work," *www.webmd.com/fitness-exercise/features/exercise-for-energy-workouts-that-work*.

CHAPTER 3: Discipline Is Not a Dirty Word!

1. Brian Tracy, *No Excuses! The Power of Self-Discipline* (New York: Vanguard Press, 2010), intro.

2. Elisabeth Elliot, *Discipline: The Glad Surrender* (Old Tappan, N.J.: Revell, 1982), 17.

CHAPTER 4: Bible Study

1. Henry Blackaby, Richard Blackaby, and Claude King, *Experiencing God: Knowing and Doing the Will of God* (Nashville: B&H, 2008), 83.

2. Wayne Cordeiro, *The Divine Mentor: Growing Your Faith as You Sit at the Feet of the Savior* (Bloomington, Minn.: Bethany House, 2007), 52.

3. Ibid.

CHAPTER 5: Prayer

1. Introduction to E. M. Bounds, *E. M. Bounds on Prayer* (New Kensington, Penn.: Whitaker House, 1997), 8.

2. Clarke's Commentary on the Bible (Nelson Reference, 1997), *http://biblehub.com/commentaries/john/20-22.htm*.

3. Bounds, *E. M. Bounds on Prayer*, 175.

4. Andrew Murray, *With Christ in the School of Prayer* (Springdale, Penn.: Whitaker House, 1981), 99.

5. John MacArthur, *"Grace to You" Newsletter* (March 16, 2009).

6. Austin Phelps, *The Still Hour: Communion with God in Prayer* (Pelham, Ala.: Solid Ground Christian Books, 2005), 117.

7. William Law, *The Works of the Reverend William Law, M.A., Sometime Fellow of Emmanuel College, Cambridge, England: A Practical Treatise upon Christian Perfection* (London, 1726), 214.

8. Max Lucado, *He Still Moves Stones* (Nashville: Nelson, 1993), 92.

9. R. C. Sproul, *Now, That's a Good Question!* (Wheaton, Ill.: Tyndale, 1996), 309.

10. Roger Steer, *George Müller: Delighted in God* (Ross-shire, Scotland: Christian Focus Publications, 1997), 177.

CHAPTER 6: Fasting

1. François Fénelon, *Let Go* (New Kensington, Penn.: Whitaker House, 1973), 59.

2. Arthur Wallis, *God's Chosen Fast* (Fort Washington, Penn.: CLC, 1980), 9.

3. Dietrich Bonhoeffer, *The Cost of Discipleship* (New York: Touchstone, 1959), 169.

4. Wesley Duewel, *Mighty Prevailing Prayer* (Grand Rapids, Mich.: Zondervan, 1990), 184.

5. Bill Bright, *Why You Should Fast*, www.cru.org/training-and-growth/devotional -life/personal-guide-to-fasting/02-why-you-should-fast.htm.

6. John Piper, *A Hunger for God* (Wheaton, Ill.: Crossway, 1997), 93.

7. Ibid., 23.

8. Ibid., 10.

9. Bob Rodgers, "Why Every Church Must Fast," *http://ag.org/top/church_workers/ pergrw_sptlf_fasting.cfm.*

10. Ibid.

11. Ibid.

12. Science Daily, "Routine Periodic Fasting Is Good for Your Health, and Your Heart, Study Suggests" (May 20, 2011), *www.sciencedaily.com/releases/2011/04/ 110403090259.htm.*

13. Wesley Duewel, *Mighty Prevailing Prayer* (Grand Rapids, Mich.: Zondervan, 1990), 184.

CHAPTER 7: Healthy Living

1. National Health and Nutrition Examination Survey (NHANES), 2009 – 10, *www.cdc.gov/nchs/data/factsheets/factsheet_nhanes.htm.*

2. Scott Stoll, "Fat in Church" (January 4, 2013), *www.foxnews.com/opinion/ 2012/06/03/obesity-epidemic-in-america-churches/#ixzz2X9iaqmqF.*

3. Eryn Sun, "Firm Faith, Fat Body? Study Finds High Rate of Obesity among Religious," *www.christianpost.com/news/firm-faith-fat-body-study-finds-high-rate -of-obesity-among-religious-49568/.*

4. Stoll, "Fat in Church."

5. Sun, "Firm Faith, Fat Body?"

6. The 700 Club, "Steve Willis: Winning the Food Fight," *www.cbn.com/700club/ guests/bios/Steve_Willis_011112.aspx?option=print.*

7. Ibid.

8. The Baptist Standard, "Pastor Sees Healthy Lifestyle As Act of Worship," *www.baptiststandard.com/news/texas/12319-pastor-sees-healthy-lifestyle-as-act -of-worship.*

9. Wikipedia, "Reginald III, Duke of Guelders," *http://en.wikipedia.org/wiki/Reginald_III,_Duke_of_Guelders.*

10. Thomas Costain, *The Three Edwards: The Pageant of England* (Garden City, N.Y.: Doubleday, 1958), 166–67.

11. Sally Wadyka, "How to Break Bad Eating Habits," *www.realsimple.com/health/nutrition-diet/healthy-eating/break-bad-eating-habits-10000001667118/index.html.*

12. Centers for Disease Control and Prevention, "Exercise Statistics" (July 27, 2013), *www.statisticbrain.com/exercise-statistics/.*

13. Centers for Disease Control and Prevention, "How Much Physical Activity Do Adults Need?" (December 1, 2011), *www.cdc.gov/physicalactivity/everyone/guidelines/adults.html.*

14. Centers for Disease Control and Prevention, "Exercise Statistics."

15. U.S. Department of Labor, "Daily Activity Statistics" (February 6, 2012), *www.statisticbrain.com/average-daily-activities/.*

16. "Gym Membership Statistics" (April 18, 2012), *www.statisticbrain.com/gym-membership-statistics/.*

17. "Julius Wolff," Wikipedia, *http://en.wikipedia.org/wiki/Wolff's_law.*

18. American Heart Association, "Physical Activity Improves Quality of Life" (July 24, 2013), *www.heart.org/HEARTORG/GettingHealthy/PhysicalActivity/StartWalking/Physical-activity-improves-quality-of-life_UCM_307977_Article.jsp.*

19. Deborah Kotz and Angela Haupt, "7 Mind-Blowing Benefits of Exercise," *http://health.usnews.com/health-news/diet-fitness/slideshows/7-mind-blowing-benefits-of-exercise.*

20. Ibid.

21. Mayo Clinic Staff, "Strength Training: Get Stronger, Leaner, Healthier," *www.mayoclinic.com/health/strength-training/HQ01710.*

22. Ibid.

23. Wikipedia, "Flexibility (anatomy)," *http://en.wikipedia.org/wiki/Flexibility_(anatomy).*

24. Sarah M. Marek, Joel T. Cramer, and Julie Y. Culbertson, "Acute Effects of Static and Proprioceptive Neuromuscular Facilitation Stretching on Muscle Strength and Power Output," *Journal of Athletic Training* (Apr–Jun 2005), 94–103.

25. American Heart Association, "Physical Activity Improves Quality of Life," *www.heart.org/HEARTORG/GettingHealthy/PhysicalActivity/StartWalking/Physical-activity-improves-quality-of-life_UCM_307977_Article.jsp.*

CHAPTER 8: Financial Stewardship

1. "Steward," Merriam-Webster.com, *www.merriam-webster.com/dictionary/steward.*

2. "Steward," The Free Dictionary, *http://www.thefreedictionary.com/steward.*

3. Randy Alcorn, *Managing God's Money: A Biblical Guide* (Carol Stream, Ill.: Tyndale, 2011), 19–20.

4. Ibid., 36.

5. Randy Alcorn, *The Treasure Principle* (Colorado Springs: Multnomah, 2005), 75.

6. IVP New Testament Commentary, *http://www.biblegateway.com/resources/commentaries/IVP-NT/2Cor/Paul-Sets-Forth-Guidelines.*

7. *http://visual.ly/us-consumer-debt-statistics-and-trends-2012.*

8. Dave Ramsey, "Baby Step 1: $1,000 Emergency Fund," *http://www.daveramsey.com/new/baby-step-1/.*

9. Dave Ramsey, "Debt Snowball Breakdown," *http://www.daveramsey.com/article/debt-snowball-breakdown/lifeandmoney_debt/.*

10. Dave Ramsey, *The Total Money Makeover: A Proven Plan for Financial Fitness*, classic ed. (Nashville: Nelson, 2013), 106–7.

11. Dave Ramsey, "Baby Step 2: Pay Off All Debt Using the Debt Snowball," *www.daveramsey.com/new/baby-step-2/.*

12. Dave Ramsey, "Baby Step 5," *www.daveramsey.com/new/baby-step-5/.*

13. IVP New Testament Commentary, *www.biblegateway.com/resources/commentaries/IVP-NT/1Tim/Christian-View-Money.*

CHAPTER 9: Serving Others

1. IVP New Testament Commentary, "Jesus Washes His Disciples' Feet," *www.biblegateway.com/resources/commentaries/IVP-NT/John/Jesus-Washes-Disciples-Feet.*

2. Richard Foster, *Celebration of Discipline* (San Francisco: HarperSanFrancisco, 1978), 130.

3. Ron Marinari, "The Calling of a Servant," *Pentecostal Evangel* (March 10, 2013): 12.

CHAPTER 10: Plan for Success

1. "Key Facts about George Washington," *www.mountvernon.org/georgewashington/facts.*

2. Mrs. Franklin B. Wildman, "George Washington: The Commander in Chief," *www.ushistory.org/valleyforge/washington/george2.html.*

3. Marisa Carter, "How to Periodize Your Training," *www.active.com/triathlon/Articles/How-to-Periodize-Your-Training.htm.*

4. Ken Johnson, "Periodization," *http://www.3-fitness.com/tarticles/periodization.htm.*

5. Brian Tracy, "The Law of Clarity," *www.briantracy.com/blog/leadership-success/the-law-of-clarity/.*

6. Strong's Concordance, *http://biblesuite.com/strongs/greek/2344.htm.*

7. John Gill's Exposition of the Entire Bible, *http://biblecommenter.com/matthew/6-21.htm.*

8. Strong's Concordance, *http://biblesuite.com/strongs/hebrew/3034.htm.*

9. Henry, *Matthew Henry's Concise Commentary*, 556.

The Ultimate Guide to the Daniel Fast

100+ Recipes plus 21 Daily Devotionals

Kristen Feola

The Ultimate Guide to the Daniel Fast is an inspiring resource for Christians who want to pursue a more intimate relationship with God through the twenty-one-day commitment to prayer and fasting known as the Daniel Fast. As you deny yourself certain foods — such as sugars, processed ingredients, and solid fats — you will not only embrace healthier eating habits, you'll also discover a greater awareness of God's presence.

Author Kristen Feola explains the Daniel Fast in easy-to-understand language, provides twenty-one thought-provoking devotionals for each day of the fast, and shares more than one hundred tasty, easy-to-make recipes that follow fasting guidelines. In a conversational style, Feola helps you structure the fast so you can spend less time thinking about what to eat and more time focusing on God. You will also discover that "to fast" means "to feast" on the only thing that truly nourishes — God's powerful Word. For more info, please visit *www.ultimatedanielfast.com*.

Available in stores and online!